THE OXFORD HANDBOOK OF

SOCIAL JUSTICE
IN MUSIC
EDUCATION

THE OXFORD HANDBOOK OF

SOCIAL JUSTICE IN MUSIC EDUCATION

Edited by

CATHY BENEDICT,
PATRICK SCHMIDT,
GARY SPRUCE,

and

PAUL WOODFORD

OXFORD
UNIVERSITY PRESS

OXFORD
UNIVERSITY PRESS

Oxford University Press is a department of the University of Oxford. It furthers
the University's objective of excellence in research, scholarship, and education
by publishing worldwide. Oxford is a registered trade mark of Oxford University
Press in the UK and certain other countries.

Published in the United States of America by Oxford University Press
198 Madison Avenue, New York, NY 10016, United States of America.

Library of Congress Cataloging-in-Publication Data
The Oxford handbook of social justice in music education / edited by Cathy Benedict, Patrick Schmidt,
Gary Spruce, and Paul Woodford.
pages cm
Includes bibliographical references and index.
ISBN 978-0-19-935615-7 (hardcover : paper); 978-0-19-088663-9 (paperback : paper)
1. Music—Instruction and study—Social aspects.   2. Social justice.   I. Benedict, Cathy.
II. Schmidt, Patrick K.   III. Spruce, Gary.   IV. Woodford, Paul, 1955–
MT1.O96 2016
780.71—dc23
2015010695

Contents

SECTION IV TOWARD SOCIAL JUSTICE PEDAGOGY: PROBLEMS AND OPPORTUNITIES

SECTION V SOCIAL JUSTICE IN PRACTICE: EXAMPLES OF EDUCATIONAL PROJECTS FROM BEYOND THE SCHOOLS AND AROUND THE WORLD

Preface

Why Social Justice and Music Education?

CATHY BENEDICT, PATRICK SCHMIDT, GARY SPRUCE, AND PAUL WOODFORD

Social justice remains a critical challenge for any democratic space. It is a term that is often employed in the educational literature as a catch-all expression and a political call to action for those seeking the amelioration of any number of social problems relating to, for example, class, ethnicity, gender, sexuality, disability, and cultural identity. The alleviation of inequity, powerlessness, and discrimination has long been the goal, although, as will become evident to readers of this Handbook, the pursuit of social justice in music education implies more than just recognition of difference and allowing for greater diversity and inclusivity in the classroom and other educational spaces. Social justice is a complicated endeavor involving, among other things, adjudication of conflicting values and interests, political action, and a concern for the welfare of the public, but especially of those who have been marginalized or oppressed.

If self-righteousness and oversimplification are to be avoided, speaking about and working toward social justice must start from the recognition of the complexity of lived and shared experience, coupled with a concern for humanity as a whole, and not just this or that group. Ultimately, as philosopher John Dewey (1921) expressed it, the goal should be the creation of more equitable environments where growth is feasible and the capacity for communicative acts can revitalize democratic communities; otherwise the pursuit of social justice might only benefit a fortunate few, possibly at the expense of others suffering equally compelling claims to injustices. One need only look around the world today to realize that justice for some can all too easily result in, or be perceived as, injustice for others.

Among the many problems with which researchers, teachers, and community practitioners must grapple if they are to be successful in creating more equitable educational environments is that the term "social justice" (as well as social *injustice*) is itself vague and conceptually fleeting. Its practical dynamics can also make effective implementation and sustainability remarkably challenging. Social justice can be pursued and experienced in many different ways and settings, and can be triggered by a range of factors. Nor for many of the same reasons is there much in the way of common understanding of the concept of social justice—it is often defined differently by particular individuals, groups, policies, and laws. Moreover, the social justice ideal is itself sometimes appropriated by hegemonic groups as a rhetorical device (including governments and religious factions), and unfortunately can be used to mask the perpetuation of social injustice and inequality. Such tensions, then, place a premium on defining social justice as a form of moral and ethical agency while locating it—as an ideal, a set of dispositions, and tangible practices—at the center of any educational endeavor. As the authors in this Handbook help to explain and illustrate, only through an understanding of social justice in all of its conceptual, political, ethical, practical, and pedagogical complexity can there be much hope of ensuring that educative action (be it scientific, vocational, or artistic) contributes to a more just and humane society.

This point bears some elaboration as it goes to the crux of *why* and *how* the pursuit of socially just musical and educational practices should matter to those engaged in educational enterprises. The fundamental issue is one of equity, particularly in this age of neoliberal globalization, when the gap between the rich and the poor continues to widen. A concern with and practices aimed at achieving social justice can help to mitigate some of the worst effects of social and educational Darwinism by taking student differences into account while ensuring what philosopher John Rawls (1999) calls "fair equality of opportunity." Implied here is the framing of a more equitable and just distribution of educational resources according to students' needs. We place this in contradistinction to the rather simplistic, and often pernicious, notion of equality of opportunity in order to draw attention to a process that tends to favor the talented and culturally privileged, who are thought to be most able to benefit from access to scarce educational resources. Thinking through issues of equity, rather than equality of opportunity, can potentially better help to dismantle the long dominant and persistent economic argument for the status quo that is premised on a deficit model of education, where resources are assumed to be permanently insufficient and certain individuals and communities are perceived as constantly lacking.

Indeed, as education philosopher Jane Roland Martin (1998) remonstrates, "The world has grown so accustomed to adopting a framework of thought whose fundamental premise is scarcity, we forget that in the case of culture the issue is one of superabundance" (p. 24). In formal music education, this deficit model of education is often epitomized by an overly narrow definition of what counts as legitimate musical knowledge, which intimidates children who lack the appropriate cultural capital while allowing teachers to ignore much of the wealth of music that exists in the world. As Roland Martin continues,

> Were cultural wealth a concept devoid of practical import this might be of little consequence. However, the wealth of cultures constitutes the material out of which curricula are constructed: it is the source not only of curricular content and subject matter, but also of education's goals and its methods of instruction. (p. 25)

The focus here is not so much on the importance of inclusivity and diversity per se—although it is of course on that, too—as it is on critical engagement, empowerment, and creativity.

Central to this Handbook is the notion that diverse and inclusive curricula and educational practices that facilitate the critical examination of any musics and music education methods, and thereby also wider participation and communication, are more likely to enhance personal and collective agency and satisfaction, while also contributing to a more creative, equitable, and productive society (Freeland, 2012).

At the same time, and because the world is a complex place that is often characterized by conflict and ignorance, proponents of social justice need to be careful not to patronize or rush to judgment of cultural and educational workers who have successfully utilized traditional music or methods to address serious social problems in sometimes challenging circumstances and sociopolitical contexts. There are many encouraging pathways for music education action taking place both inside and outside the "normal" and traditional institutional parameters of schooling that can help us to make tangible Dewey's notion of participatory democracy as an ethical ideal and communal way of life resulting in a releasing of human capacity. Alternative programs and instructional models can potentially challenge teachers and others to rethink their understandings of the democratic purposes and responsibilities of educational institutions and programs to contribute to a more equitable and just society.

Dewey, however, also warned that the kinds of authoritarian, hegemonic, and hierarchical educational practices implicit or embedded in, for example, Western classical music and its pedagogical traditions could potentially discourage creativity and growth by limiting opportunities for exploration and by discouraging individual interest and responsibility. This should give pause to teachers or social activists wishing to adopt pro grams, models, or "brands"—such as Venezuela's renowned El Sistema program—for their own regional and national contexts without first taking into account important political and cultural differences and also determining whether their proposed programs are actually consistent in purpose, ideology, and pedagogical approach with the parent program and thus warrant the name.

This Handbook therefore underscores the fact that there are no facile answers to the complex enterprise of music and education. Put plainly, context and professional intent matter, and practices that are deemed to be hierarchical and hegemonic in one social context may in certain locations and situations be successfully employed as means of ameliorating social problems. Alternatively, some musics, programs, and methods may not travel well and might only exacerbate problems by, for example, diverting scarce government funding from existing social programs. Then, too, there is always the possibility of abuse or ethical lapse. As already suggested, governments or other organizations might use music programs or methods for their own ends and in ways their creators would never have condoned (e.g., as propaganda), just as individual instructors, owing to insufficient pedagogical knowledge or inattention to children's needs, might fail to achieve or maintain equitable educational spaces. There are no panaceas or easy and formulaic programs and pedagogies for teachers or others seeking to identify appropriate educational practices that can work safely and reliably within and across different social or cultural contexts to guarantee success in alleviating inequity, powerlessness, and discrimination for all. For all of these and other reasons, teachers wishing to promote social justice in and through their own programs and practices will need to exercise careful thought and professional self-reflection.

This recognition of the complexity and difficulty involved in pursuing a social justice agenda for music education brings us to another of the central themes of the Handbook, which is the importance of fostering critical awareness of music and pedagogy among researchers, teachers, and students alike. The call for a renewed educational emphasis on the development of critical thought and awareness of music among pre-service teachers and children is especially important in this age of casino-capitalism and hyper-commercialism. As corporate marketers seek to go beyond the schools and universities to "infiltrate the most intimate spaces of children and family life" and create "consuming subjects rather than civic minded and critical citizens" (Giroux, 2010, p. 415), vigilance, recognition, and responsibility must be part and parcel of the educative space. When lacking awareness of how major corporations seek to monopolize virtually all forms of communication, and the ways in which popular music and media "hold sway over the stories and narratives that shape children's lives" (p. 415), the latter might not realize the processes of indoctrination to consumer culture and thus may be rendered silent "before the spectacle of commodities" (Attali, 1985, p. 112). And when that happens, and because music is "absorbed by children as entertainment and often escapes any critical or self-reflection," they may have no authentic voices of their own, thereby failing to realize their creative potential (p. 415).

For many of the same concerns raised in the foregoing discussion, the pursuit of social justice as a political call to action should itself be critically examined, lest it exacerbate existing problems or result in other unintended negative social consequences. Music education has had a historically tense relationship with social justice. Educators concerned with music practices have long preoccupied themselves with ideas of open participation and the potentially transformative capacity that can be fostered within musical interaction. On the other hand—as already suggested, but which needs to be said more explicitly—they have often done so while privileging particular musical practices, traditions, forms of musical knowledge, or ideologies, resulting in the alienation or exclusion of many children, youth, and adults from music education opportunities. Multicultural practices, for example, have historically provided potentially useful pathways for music practices that are thought to be socially just. However, the intent behind these practices has sometimes been negated through the mapping of alien musical values onto other music(s) and has been grounded in simplistic politics of difference, wherein "recognition of our differences" limits the push that might take us from mere tolerance to respect and to renewed understanding and interaction.

Regardless of the historical challenges, music education as a field of inquiry, as a global community, and as a set of practices—within schools, in communities, and as part of nongovernmental organizations—is experiencing an awakening. Discussions linking music education to the challenges of urban education, gender and sexual inequality, class difference, cultural identity, racial segregation, and corporate intrusion into and control over music education have grown exponentially and are now widely seen in both scholarly work and as part of teacher education and professional development. At the levels of curriculum, pedagogy, and content development, many educators concerned with musical practices have focused more attention on the formation of democratic classroom environments, the development of agency-driven student participation, the support of critical pedagogies, and the expansion of interactive forms of multiculturalism, and less attention on "sampling exotic" musical cultures. But it remains unclear the extent to which the pursuit of social justice and socially just practices has moved beyond the rhetoric of, for instance, inclusion, literacy, creativity, educational access, and market equality in ways that would help us better envision and enact music as a formative element in how we see ourselves as "global citizens." Discovering ways to engage in socially just music educational practices is a process deeply linked to discoveries of who we are and how we can better relate to and interact with others within and outside our communities and one that underscores the purpose of this Handbook.

WHY THIS BOOK?

Regardless of the extraordinary importance of social justice as an educational outcome today, and despite the pervasive manner in which related issues are discussed among some quarters of the music teaching profession, no significant effort has been expended thus far to frame this theme as a widespread, artistically and educationally vital aim or goal within music education practices both *within* and *beyond* the school and university. This book is intended to meet this need by serving as a diverse and authoritative source for conceptual, research-based, and practically oriented guidance for how music educators can further define social justice's purposes and forms, its goals and aims, and for revealing some of the many guises under which socially just musical and educational practices can be made manifest and explored in the home, school, and community. As we continue to consider social justice in our society and in music education, in our practices and in our daily lives, this book will serve as a source of insight and guidance for the field of music education as a whole.

This book, however—for the reasons identified earlier as to the importance of contextualizing social problems—is not intended as a prescriptive guide to *daily* teaching practice. Rather, its purpose is to facilitate the development of a complex but accessible understanding of social justice for the field of music education by addressing key themes that frame social justice action within music teaching and learning globally. It is intended as an idea book that will hopefully provoke and inspire teachers and scholars to rethink their understandings of their own practice and whether, to what extent, and in what ways it contributes to the creation of a better world.

Each section is prefaced with a brief introduction to the major themes addressed in the various chapters therein. The invited authors from around the world, many of whom are the foremost experts in each of the areas selected, and themselves scholars and practitioners with national and international reputations, present a collection of ideas, models, concepts, and strategies for how best to solidify and expand our understanding of the relationship between music education and social justice as global concerns. Further, because the pursuit of social justice often implies recognition of common purposes and, if it is to succeed, collaboration, the editors have sought to go beyond merely aligning and coordinating themes to establish linkages with allied disciplines and fields of inquiry. To that end, several authors from outside the immediate field of music education were invited to write commentary chapters for the larger thematic sections of the book, helping to locate music education research and practice within broader social, educational, and political contexts and developments. A concluding synthetic chapter draws out and emphasizes shared strands of thought, common problems, and recommends potentially fruitful new directions for future research and practice. We hope that, by virtue of its scope, diversity of foci, and balanced approach, the book will be helpful to the uninitiated and inviting to experts.

REFERENCES

Attali, J. (1985). *Noise: The political economy of music* (B. Massumi, Trans.). Minneapolis: University of Minnesota Press.

Dewey, J. (1921). *Democracy and education: An introduction to the philosophy of education*. New York: MacMillan.

Freeland, C. (2012, May 19). Equality fosters strong economy. *The London Free Press*, p. E8.

Giroux, H. A. (2010). Stealing of childhood innocence—Disney and the politics of casino-capitalism. *Cultural Studies—Critical Methodologies, 10*(5), 413–416.

Rawls, J. (1999). *A theory of social justice*, rev. ed. Cambridge, MA: The Belknap Press.

Roland Martin, J. (1998). The wealth of cultures and problems of generations. In S. Tozer (Ed.), *Philosophy of Education Society yearbook* (pp. 23–38). Urbana, IL: Philosophy of Education Society.

Contributors

Joseph Abramo is an Assistant Clinical Professor of Music Education in the Neag School of Education at the University of Connecticut, where he teaches undergraduate and graduate courses. He has publications in journals including the *Music Educators Journal*, *The Journal of Research in Music Education*, *The Bulletin of the Council for Research in Music Education*, and *The Philosophy of Music Education Review*, among others. He also regularly presents at national and international conferences. He serves on the advisory committee of the *Music Educators Journal* and is Chair of the Philosophy Special Research Interest Group of the National Association for Music Education.

Carlos Abril is Associate Professor and Director of Undergraduate Music Education at the Frost School of Music at the University of Miami, where he teaches courses in cultural diversity, music in childhood, and philosophy of music education. Abril's research focuses on sociocultural issues in music education, music education policy, curriculum, and music perception. His work has been published in books, research journals, and professional journals. He serves on many editorial boards, including the *Journal of Research in Music Education*. Abril received a Ph.D. in music education at The Ohio State University, M.M. in performance at the University of Cincinnati College-Conservatory of Music, and a B.M. in music education at the University of Miami.

José Luis Aróstegui is Professor in the Department of Music Education at the University of Granada, Spain. He has presented papers at many international conferences and has published papers in international journals and books. Appointed by the European Commission to coordinate a major evaluation of music teacher education programs in Europe and Latin America, he has served as a commissioner of the Music in Schools and Teacher Education Commission (MISTEC) from 2004 to 2010, and was Chair from 2008 to 2010. He is a member of the ISME Board and editor of the *Revista Internacional de Educación Musical* journal.

Julie Ballantyne is known for her work in the areas of music teacher identities, social justice, music teacher education, and the social and psychological impacts of musical engagement. Her latest research project, www.musicteachersproject.net, aims to investigate developing teacher identities while supporting those at the beginnings of their careers as music teachers. A Senior Lecturer in the School of Music at The University of Queensland, Julie has published work in key music journals, has published a book *Navigating Music and Sound Education*, and teaches preservice and in-service teachers at the Bachelor and Master's Level, as well as supervising several Ph.D. students.

Janet R. Barrett is the Marilyn Pflederer Zimmerman Endowed Scholar in Music Education at the University of Illinois at Urbana-Champaign. Her research interests include the re-conceptualization of the music curriculum, secondary general music, interdisciplinary approaches in music, qualitative research pedagogy, and music teacher education. Barrett has published widely in music education and is an author or editor of five books, including the 2014 *The Musical Experience: Rethinking Music Teaching and Learning* (with P. Webster, Oxford University Press). She serves as editor for the *Bulletin for the Council of Research in Music Education.*

Cathy Benedict joined the Music Education faculty at Western University, Ontario, Canada in July 2015. She has taught at New York University and served as Undergraduate Coordinator for Music Education at Florida International University. She has taught classes such as elementary pedagogy, Orff, curriculum design, music psychology, critical readings, and music and special needs students. Her scholarly interests lay in facilitating environments in which students take on the perspective of a justice-oriented citizen. To this end, her research focuses on the processes of education and the ways in which teachers and students interrogate taken-for-granted, normative practices. She has published in such journals as *Philosophy of Music Education Review, Music Education Research*, and *Research Studies in Music Education*, and the Brazilian journal *ABEM.*

Louis S. Bergonzi is the Daniel J. Perrino Chair in Music Education, and Professor of Orchestral Conducting at the University of Illinois, where he teaches courses in the sociology of music education, orchestral conducting, and string education. He is Music Director of the Philharmonia Orchestra. He was co-director of *Establishing Identity: LGBT Studies and Music Education I and II (2010/2012)*, symposia designed to provide energy to the discussion of how LGBT issues operate within music education in terms of research, curriculum, teacher preparation, and the musical lives and careers of LGBT music students and teachers.

Deborah Bradley was Assistant Professor in Music Education at the University of Wisconsin-Madison from 2006 to 2010. Since retiring, she has taught at the University of Toronto Faculty of Music and Emmanuel College. She is a leading scholar in anti-racism and critical multiculturalism in music education; her work is published in such journals as *Philosophy of Music Education Review, Journal of Aesthetic Education, Music Education Research*, and *Action, Criticism, and Theory for Music Education*. She has also published several book chapters, including a chapter in the 2012 *Oxford Handbook of Philosophy of Music Education.*

Pamela Burnard is Reader in Education at the University of Cambridge in the United Kingdom. Her research interests include diverse creativities, digital technologies, intercultural arts-based practices and knowledge building in education, industry, and community. Her books include *Musical Creativities in Practice* (Oxford University Press), *Creativities in Higher Music Education* (Routledge), *Activating Diverse Musical Creativities* (Bloomsbury), *Bourdieu and the Sociology of Music, Music Education and*

Research (Ashgate), *Music Education with Digital Technologies* (Continuum), and *Teaching Music Creatively* (Routledge). She is Co-convenor of the British Educational Research Association (BERA) *Creativity in Education* SIG and Convenor of the *Creativities in Intercultural Arts Network,* http://www.educ.cam.ac.uk/centres/cce/initiatives/projects/cian.

Patricia Shehan Campbell is Donald E. Peterson Professor of Music at the University of Washington, where she teaches courses at the interface of education and ethnomusicology. She is the author of *Music in Cultural Context* (1996), *Songs in Their Heads* (1998, 2010), *Teaching Music Globally* (2004), *Music and Teacher* (2008), co-author of *Music in Childhood* (2013, fourth edition), co-editor of the Global Music Series and *The Oxford Handbook of Children's Musical Cultures* (2013). Campbell was designated the MENC Senior Researcher in Music Education in 2002, and in 2012 received the Taiji Prize for the preservation of traditional music. She is Chair of the Advisory Board of Smithsonian Folkways and President of the College Music Society.

Mary L. Cohen is Associate Professor, Area Head of Music Education, and Dean's Scholar at the University of Iowa. She researches wellness through music making in prison contexts, writing and songwriting, and collaborative communities. In 2009, she founded the Oakdale Community Choir, a joint inmate-volunteer choir that performs original songs inside the prison. Her research is published in the *International Journal of Research in Choral Singing, Journal of Research in Music Education, Australian Journal of Music Education, Journal of Historical Research in Music Education, Journal of Correctional Education,* the *International Journal of Community Music,* and the *International Journal of Music Education.*

Carolyn Cooke is currently completing a PhD at the University of Aberdeen focusing on music student teachers' perspectives on music pedagogy. Previously, she studied at Durham, Bristol, and The Open University. She has worked as a music teacher and Head of Department in a large secondary school, as a national curriculum regional advisor, and as a Lecturer in Music with particularly responsibility for initial teacher education. In addition she has taken an active role as a Regional Representative and Vice Chair of the music subject association (NAME), has written for a variety of music education publications both in print and online, and is currently working as a consultant writer and editor for online educational materials. Her publications and research interests include music teacher development, critical pedagogy, metacognition, and inclusion in music education.

Alice-Ann Darrow is Irvin Cooper Professor of Music in the College of Music at Florida State University. Her areas of research and clinical specialization include nonverbal communication in the classroom, and disability in music education. She is co-author of *Music+ in Special Education (2005), Music Therapy and Geriatric Populations* (2005), and editor of *Introduction to Approaches in Music Therapy* (2008). She has served on the editorials boards of *JRME, Update: Applications of Research in Music Education,*

General Music Today, Bulletin for the Council on Research in Music Education, Reviews of Research in Human Learning and Music, and *Florida Music Director.*

Niyati Dhokai received a Ph.D. in Music (Ethnomusicology) from the University of Alberta in 2012. Her research has focused on the institutionalization of diasporic music practices and urban music cultures in Gujarat, India, from the time of Indian Independence to the present. During her graduate studies and research in India as a Fulbright Scholar, she developed a strong interest in applied ethnomusicology, specifically community integration through music. She currently works with participants who are recovering from traumatic brain injury in a community-based rehabilitation program as a music instructor and ethnomusicologist in the metropolitan Washington, D.C., area.

Stuart Paul Duncan received a D.M.A. in composition from Cornell University in 2010 and is currently finishing his Ph.D. at Yale University in Music Theory, which explores issues surrounding meter and hypermeter in Benjamin Britten's early vocal music. Duncan is currently a Yale Teaching Center Fellow, where he helps design and lead workshops on various areas of pedagogy. In addition to his research in education and prisons, other interests include the music of twentieth-century British composers and rhythmic and metric theory. Stuart is also the music director and organist at St. Peter's Episcopal Church in Cheshire, CT.

Martin Fautley is Professor of Education at Birmingham City University, United Kingdom, where he is Director of the Centre for Research in Education. He teaches widely across a range of programs, including undergraduate and postgraduate teacher education courses, and supervises research and doctoral students. For many years he was a secondary school music teacher, subsequently undertaking his Doctoral research at Cambridge University, investigating the teaching, learning, and assessment of composing in the classroom. He is currently researching assessment in music education, and the teaching and learning of composing in secondary schools. He is the author of eight books, including *Assessment in Music Education*, published by Oxford University Press, and has written numerous journal papers and book chapters on aspects of music education, creativity, and assessment.

Rubén Gaztambide-Fernández is an Associate Professor at the Ontario Institute for Studies in Education of the University of Toronto. He teaches courses in curriculum theory, cultural studies, and the arts in education. His current research focuses on the experiences of young artists attending urban arts high schools in Canada and the United States. He is also the Principal Investigator of *Proyecto Latin@,* a participatory action research project with Latin@ youth in Toronto. His theoretical work focuses on the relationship between creativity, decolonization, and solidarity. He is particularly interested in the pedagogical and creative possibilities that arise from the social and cultural dynamics of urban centers.

Elizabeth Gould joined the University of Toronto faculty in 2005, and teaches philosophically based courses in music education. Her research interests include gender and sexuality in the context of feminisms and queer theory. In addition to serving as lead editor for the book *Exploring Social Justice: How Music Education Might Matter* (2009), Gould has published articles in a variety of journals, including *Philosophy of Music Education Review, Music Education Research, Women and Music: A Journal of Gender and Culture, College Music Symposium, Educational Philosophy and Theory*, and the Brazilian journal, *labrys: études féministes estudos feministas*. She has served in leadership roles with professional organizations such as Gender Research in Music Education-International and the International Society for Philosophy of Music Education, and organized the conferences, musica ficta: A Conference on Engagements and Exclusions in Music, Education, and the Arts (2008), and Feminist Theory and Music 6: Confluence and Divide (2001).

Lucy Green is Professor of Music Education at the London University Institute of Education. Her research is in the sociology of music education, specializing in meaning, ideology, gender, popular music, informal learning, and the development of new pedagogies. She created the informal learning pathway of Musical Futures, and then took the work into the instrumental tuition context. She is the author of five books and scores of articles, the editor of two anthologies, and sits on the boards of 13 journals. She was a private piano teacher, then a secondary Head of Music, before joining the Institute of Education in 1990.

Laura Hassler was born and raised in New York. From an early age, she was active in US civil rights and peace movements. She studied cultural anthropology and music, then worked for social change organizations in the United States and Europe. After moving to the Netherlands in 1977, she built a career in music. In 1999, Laura mobilized her large network of socially conscious musicians to found Musicians without Borders. Today, still drawing on this ever-broadening network, Musicians without Borders is one of the world's pioneers in using music to bridge divides, build community, and heal the wounds of war.

Maud Hickey is Associate Professor and Coordinator of Music Education at the Bienen School of Music, Northwestern University, in Evanston, Illinois. Her research interests revolve around creative thinking through improvisation and composition. Hickey has recently been focusing on youth in detention and the potential for music creativity in their lives. She has published articles in several music education research journals and recently published a book titled *Music Outside the Lines: Ideas for Composing in K–12 Music Classrooms* (2012).

Lee Higgins is the Director of an Associate Professor of Music Education at the Boston University School of Music, USA and Director of the International Centre of Community Music based at York St. John University, UK. Committed to people, places, participation, inclusivity, and diversity, he is a community musician who has worked across the education sector as well as within health settings, prison and probation service, youth and community, and orchestra outreach. As a presenter and guest speaker, Professor Higgins has worked on four continents in university, school, and NGO settings. He is the senior editor for the *International Journal of Community Music* and was author of *Community Music: In Theory and in Practice* (2012, Oxford University Press).

Wai-Chung Ho is Professor in the Department of Music, Hong Kong Baptist University. She received her Ph.D. from the University of London, Institute of Education. Her main research areas are the sociology of music, music education curriculum, values education, and the comparative study of East Asian music education. Her articles have been published in top-ranking journals such as the *British Journal of Music Education, Bulletin of the Council for Research in Music Education, International Journal of Music Education, Music Education Research, Popular Music, Popular Music and Society*, and *Comparative Education*.

Stephanie Horsley is Adjunct Assistant Professor in the Department of Music Education at Western University, London, Ontario, Canada. Her research interests include global economic systems and their effects on music education reform at the state and local pluralize—levels. Her recent work examines the development of neoliberal education policy and the ways in which it has shaped and been shaped by sociohistorical events at the state level and the subsequent development of music education policies and programs. She is particularly interested in the field of comparative education. Her work has been published in *Arts Education Policy Review* and has been presented at numerous international symposia.

Otto de Jong is a choir and orchestra conductor specialized in working with large groups of children. Since 1999, he has been working as a trainer for Musicians without Borders, training others to work with children. His music workshops, lessons, and rehearsals demonstrate and teach trainers to use the power of nonverbal communication and team building. For de Jong, music is a means for children to receive attention, to learn to concentrate, to be in a safe environment in a group setting and, last but not least, is a source of joy.

Estelle R. Jorgensen is Professor Emerita of Music (Music Education), Indiana University Jacobs School of Music and Contributing Faculty Member, Richard W. Riley College of Education and Leadership at Walden University. She is the author of *In Search of Music Education* (1997), *Transforming Music Education* (2003), *The Art of Teaching Music* (2008), and *Pictures of Music Education* (2011), and her articles have appeared in leading journals and essay collections in music education. She is the editor of the *Philosophy of Music Education Review* and of the *Counterpoints: Music and Education* book series published by Indiana University Press.

Panagiotis A. Kanellopoulos is Associate Professor of Music Education at the University of Thessaly, Greece. His interests include sociocultural perspectives on musical creativity, ethnographic approaches to musical improvisation, as well as possible conjunctures between philosophy of music education and political philosophy. Panagiotis has co-edited the volume *Arts in Education-Education in the Arts* (Athens, Nissos, 2010);

his work has been published in international edited volumes and major research journals (including *Psychology of Music, Philosophy of Music Education Review, Action Criticism & Theory for Music Education, British Journal of Music Education, Educational Philosophy & Theory*). He is active as a mandolinist, performing and recording in a variety of contexts.

Sidsel Karlsen is Professor of Music Education at Hedmark University College in Norway as well as docent at the Sibelius Academy, University of the Arts, Helsinki, Finland. She has published widely in international research journals and is a contributor to anthologies such as *Sociology and Music Education* (2010) and *Collaborative Learning in Higher Music Education* (2013). Her research interests cover, among other things, multicultural music education, the interplay between formal and informal arenas for learning, and the social and cultural significance of music festivals. Currently, she is also involved in a research project investigating musical gentrification and sociocultural diversities from a Norwegian perspective.

Jacqueline Kelly-McHale is Associate Professor and Coordinator of Music Education at DePaul University in Chicago, Illinois. Kelly-McHale's research focuses on culturally responsive teaching in K–12 music classrooms, issues of social justice, and composition in K–12 classrooms. She has published articles in *Journal of Research in Music Education* and *Mountain Lake Reader*. Kelly-McHale is an active presenter, having presented sessions at state, national, and international conferences. Kelly-McHale earned her doctorate at Northwestern University, an MAME degree from The University of St. Thomas in St. Paul, Minnesota, and a BSME from Duquesne University in Pittsburgh, Pennsylvania.

Jason Kubilius is Head of Creative Arts at George Green's school in Tower Hamlets, and previous to that he spent most of his career at Forest Hill School in Lewisham as Head of Music and Director of the Performing Arts Specialism. He has taught for 18 years and has tried to make the music department accessible and inclusive for all. Forest Hill School has been a Musical Futures Champion School and has been involved in leading INSETs for teachers and PGCE students interested in making a music department successful and inclusive.

Gloria Ladson-Billings is the Kellner Family Chair in Urban Education in the Department of Curriculum and Instruction and Faculty Affiliate in the Departments of Educational Policy Studies, Educational Leadership and Policy Analysis, and Afro-American Studies at the University of Wisconsin-Madison.

Roberta Lamb is Associate Professor in Music and Music Education at the School of Music, Queen's University. She is cross-appointed to the Faculty of Education and Department of Gender Studies. She is a docent in Music Education at the Sibelius Academy, Helsinki University of the Arts, Finland, where she advises graduate students in music education. Lamb was a founding member of Gender Research in Music Education, and, according to one of her high school teachers, was a feminist before the word existed. In addition to academic writing, she is proudest of her work to establish the Symphony Education Partnership (since 1993) in Kingston, Ontario, and her project for teaching university students how to teach ukulele to grade 6 and 7 students in the Limestone School Board.

Wing-Wah Law is Professor in the Faculty of Education, The University of Hong Kong. He received his Ph.D. from the University of London, Institute of Education. His research interests and publications cover the areas of education and development, globalization and citizenship education, education policy and legislation, education reform and Chinese societies, music education and social change, and culture and school leadership. His publications have appeared in international journals in education, including *Cambridge Journal of Education, Compare, Comparative Education, Comparative Education Review, International Journal of Educational Development, Journal of Curriculum Studies, Music Education Research*, and *Teachers College Record*.

Paul Louth works at Youngstown State University in Youngstown, Ohio, where he teaches graduate and undergraduate courses in music education methods, philosophy, technology, and research. He holds Ph.D. and Master's degrees in Music Education from the University of Western Ontario, as well a Bachelor of Education and a Bachelor of Music (performance) degree from the University of Toronto. He is particularly interested in philosophical and sociological issues in music education. His research involves applications of critical pedagogy to music education, music, and lifelong learning, and issues surrounding the use of technology in music education.

Kathryn Marsh is Associate Professor of Music Education at the University of Sydney. She has undertaken large-scale cross-cultural collaborative research into children's musical play in Australia, Europe, the United Kingdom, the United States, and Korea. Her research interests also include children's creativity and cultural diversity in music education, most recently exploring the role of music in the lives of refugee children. She is editor of *Research Studies in Music Education* and has written numerous scholarly publications, including *The Musical Playground: Global Tradition and Change in Children's Songs and Games*, published by Oxford University Press and winner of two international awards.

Richard Matthews is a political philosopher and peace scholar with specific interests in violence, evil, and the nature of oppression. In particular he is an expert on the nature and ethics of torture. His main publication is *The Absolute Violation: Why Torture Must Be Prohibited* (Montreal & Kingston: MQUP, 2008). In addition he has published a variety of essays on torture, as well as articles on ethics and metaphysics. He teaches philosophy at Huron University College at the University of Western Ontario.

Marie McCarthy is Professor of Music Education at the University of Michigan, and prior to this position she was on the faculty of the University of Maryland from 1990 to 2006. Her research studies address the historical, social, and cultural foundations of music education, the transmission of music in cultural context, and spiritual dimensions of music teaching and learning. Her publications include two books, *Passing It On: The Transmission of Music in Irish Culture* (1999), and *Toward a Global Community: A History of the International Society for Music Education, 1953–2003* (2004).

Carmen Mills is Lecturer in the School of Education at The University of Queensland, Australia. Her research interests are informed broadly by the sociology of education and specifically by issues of social justice in education, schooling in disadvantaged communities, and teacher education for the development of socially just dispositions. Her current research as a chief investigator on an Australian Research Council project explores social justice dispositions informing teachers' pedagogy in advantaged and disadvantaged secondary schools.

Lis Murphy is the UK Founder and UK Director of Musicians without Borders. She has pioneered the use of singing and songwriting workshops, to find a way of enabling refugees and torture survivors to find peace through expression and collective experience. Lis is also a professional performing musician, who previously supported New Order, Billy Bragg, and Balkan Beatbox. Lis has also performed with Mali superstars Amadou and Mariam and a world premiere by William Orbit.

Flávia M. Narita is Lecturer at Universidade de Brasília (UnB/Brazil) and, from 2007 to 2010, she coordinated the Music Teacher Education course offered by that university through the Distance Education program of the Open University of Brazil. She is currently finishing her Ph.D. studies at the Institute of Education, University of London, under the supervision of Professor Lucy Green. She completed her first degree in Music Education at the Universidade de São Paulo (USP/Brazil).

Susan A. O'Neill has an interdisciplinary background with graduate degrees in three disciplines (music performance, psychology, education). She is Associate Professor in Music Education at Simon Fraser University in Vancouver, Canada. She is Director of MODAL Research Group (Multimodal Opportunities, Diversity and Artistic Learning) and Research for Youth, Music and Education (RYME). She has held Visiting Fellowships at Trinity College Dublin, University of Melbourne, and University of Michigan, United States. Her international projects explore young people's music engagement in ways that contribute to expansive learning opportunities, positive values, self-identities, motivation, resiliency, learning relationships, and cultural understandings. She is has published widely in the fields of music psychology and music education.

Chris Philpott is Deputy Pro Vice-Chancellor and Reader in Music Education in the Faculty of Education and Health at the University of Greenwich, United Kingdom. He became a teacher-educator after working for 16 years as a secondary school music teacher. He has research interests in the pedagogy of teacher education, the body and musical learning, and music as language. He has written and edited books, online texts, and resources widely used in initial teacher education programs.

André de Quadros is a professor of music and chair of the Music Education Department at Boston University, where he also holds positions in African, Asian, and Muslim studies and in prison education. He directs several international ventures, including a new socially responsible conducting course in Sweden. He conducts the Manado State University Choir, Indonesia, and partners with several community projects in Mexico, Israel, and the Arab world.

J. Christopher Roberts teaches K–5 music in Seattle, Washington, and is an Affiliate Assistant Professor of Music Education at the University of Washington. He holds degrees from the University of Washington (Ph.D., M.A.) and Swarthmore College (B.A.), with research and clinical interests in children's musical cultures, cultural diversity in music education, and the nature of children's interest in music. Recent articles have appeared in publications including *Oxford Handbook of Children's Musical Cultures* (2013), *Journal of Research in Music Education* (2013), *Multicultural Perspectives in Music Education* (2011), and *Alternative Approaches in Music Education* (2011).

Leslie Stewart Rose is faculty member in the Department of Curriculum, Teaching and Learning at the Ontario Institute for Studies in Education (OISE) at the University of Toronto. She brings her experiences as a classroom teacher to her work at OISE, which has included teaching music education courses, serving as Director of the elementary teacher education program, and leading research and teacher inquiry in partnership with Toronto District School Board's inclusive education initiatives. Related major publications include *Exploring Social Justice: How Music Education Might Matter* (2009) and *Deepening Inclusive And Community-Engaged Education in Three Schools: A Teachers' Resource* (2014).

Gabriel Rusinek is Associate Professor at the Faculty of Education, Complutense University of Madrid. He edits the peer-reviewed open access research journal *Revista Electrónica Complutense de Investigación en Educación Musical* (http://revistas.ucm.es/index.php/RECI/). He is a member of the editorial boards of ISME's *International Journal of Music Education-Practice* and *Revista Internacional de Educación Musical*, and of the advisory boards of the *International Journal of Education & the Arts* and *Music Education Research,* and a commissioner at ISME Music in Schools and Teacher Education Commission, His research interests include collaborative composition, inclusive teaching practices, school failure, and audience experience.

Jonathan Savage is Reader in Education at the Faculty of Education, Manchester Metropolitan University, United Kingdom. He has a number of research interests, including implementing new technologies in education, cross-curricular approaches to teaching and learning, creativity and assessment. He is Managing Director of UCan.tv (www.ucanplay.tv), a not-for-profit company that provides support and advice for educators using music, audio, and video technologies. He is a widely published author, having written and edited for Routledge, Oxford University Press, Open University Press, SAGE, and Learning Matters. Jonathan runs an active blog at www.jsavage.org.uk and can be followed on Twitter @jpjsavage.

Patrick Schmidt is Chair and Associate Professor of Music Education at Western University in London, Ontario, Canada. He also served as the Associate Director of Florida International University's School of Music in Miami, and taught at the Westminster Choir College. His innovative work in critical pedagogy, urban music education, and policy studies is recognized nationally and internationally. His most recent publications can be found in the *International Journal of Music Education; Arts Education Policy Review; Journal of Curriculum Theorizing; Philosophy of Music Education Review; Action, Criticism, and Theory for Music Education; ABEM Journal* in Brazil; and the Finnish *Journal of Music Education*. He has co-edited the 2012 NSSE book with Teachers College Press and a special issue of the education journal *Theory into Practice*. Schmidt is currently working on a single-authored book on policy for Oxford.

Eric Shieh is a founding teacher at the Metropolitan Expeditionary Learning School in New York City and author of numerous articles and chapters on progressive music pedagogies and curriculum reform. He is a former policy strategist for the New York City Department of Education and has founded music programs in prisons across the United States. In 2012, he was awarded a Fund For Teachers Fellowship to research educational responses to poverty and youth violence in Caracas, Venezuela. Eric holds degrees in music education, multicultural theory, and curriculum policy from the University of Michigan, Ann Arbor, and Teachers College, Columbia University.

John Sloboda is Research Professor at the Guildhall School of Music, in London, and Emeritus Professor at Keele University. He was a staff member of the School of Psychology at Keele from 1974 to 2008, where he was Director of its Unit for the Study of Musical Skill and Development. Sloboda is internationally known for his work on the psychology of music. He is a committee member of the Society for Education and Music Psychology Research, and was Editor-in-Chief of its journal *Psychology of Music* from 1985 to 1989. He was the recipient of the 1998 British Psychological Society's Presidents Award for Distinguished Contributions to Psychological Knowledge, and in 2004 was elected to Fellowship of the British Academy. John is also co-director of Every Casualty Worldwide (www.everycasualty.org) and co-founder of the Iraq Body Count Project (www.iraqbodycount.org).

Amanda Soto is Assistant Professor of Music Education at Texas State University. She co-teaches the Smithsonian Folkways Certification Course in World Music Pedagogy. After earning her teaching certification at the University of North Texas, she taught middle school band in South Texas, where she was born and raised. She also taught general music to children within the Seattle Public Schools. She completed an M.A. in Ethnomusicology and a Ph.D. in Music Education from the University of Washington. She has undertaken certification studies in Orff and Kodály pedagogical approaches and holds a certification in world music pedagogy from the Smithsonian Institute.

Gary Spruce is Senior Lecturer in education at The Open University and subject leader for the university's music teacher training course. Before coming to the university he was a head of music in two comprehensive schools in Birmingham, United Kingdom.

He has published widely, including co-editing a number of key texts on music teacher education as well as presenting papers at national and international conferences. From 2007 to 2012 he was co-editor of the *British Journal of Music Education* and from 2007 to 2010 was involved in developing a national CPD program for primary music teachers, which was used by over 4,000 teachers. Gary is a practicing musician with a particular interest in music for the theater.

Heidi Westerlund is Professor at the Sibelius Academy, University of the Arts Helsinki, Finland, as well as the Administrative Chair of the Center for Educational Research and Academic Development in the Arts (CERADA). She has published widely in international journals and books, and she is the co-editor of *Collaborative Learning in Higher Music Education*. She has served as an Associate Editor or reviewer in several international journals and she is the Editor-in-chief of the *Finnish Journal of Music Education*. Her current research interests cover teacher education, higher music education, collaborative learning, cultural diversity, and democracy in music education.

Joel Westheimer is University Research Chair in Democracy and Education at the University of Ottawa and education columnist for CBC Radio's *Ottawa Morning Show*. He began his career teaching in the New York City Public School system before obtaining a Ph.D. from Stanford University. He has published more than 50 scholarly and professional articles and book chapters and frequently addresses radio and television audiences nationally and internationally. His award-winning books include *Among Schoolteachers: Community, Autonomy and Ideology in Teachers' Work* (1998) and the edited collection *Pledging Allegiance: The Politics of Patriotism in America's Schools* (foreword by the late Howard Zinn, 2007). His third book—*What Kind of Citizen?*—was published in 2015 by Teachers College Press.

Paul Woodford is Professor of Music Education at Western University in London, Ontario, Canada. He is past Co-Chair of the executive committee of the International Society for the Philosophy of Music Education (2005–2007) and is a member of the International Advisory Boards of the *British Journal of Music Education*, the *Philosophy of Music Education Review*, and the *Bulletin of the Council for Research in Music Education*. His interests in philosophical and historical issues affecting the profession have led to many publications, including his 2005 book, *Democracy and Music Education*, and many chapters and articles in leading books and journals.

Sheila C. Woodward is Chair of Music and Associate Professor of Music at Eastern Washington University, United States. She is a native of South Africa and earned her Ph.D. from the University of Cape Town and a Performer's Licentiate in Organ from the Associated Board of the Royal Schools of Music. Dr. Woodward is President of the International Society for Music Education. She previously served two terms as an ISME Board member and as Chair of the Early Childhood Music Education Commission (ISME). Dr. Woodward's research focus is music and well-being, exploring this from before birth to adulthood.

Ruth Wright is Associate Professor in the Don Wright Faculty of Music at Western University, London, Ontario, Canada. Wright's earlier career included teaching high school music, maintaining a large private piano studio, and lecturing in music education at the University of Wales Institute, Cardiff (now Cardiff Metropolitan University). She received her PhD in Education from this institution in 2006. She is the co-founder of Musical Futures Canada, an informal learning music program, and publishes regularly in books and refereed journals on the subjects of sociology, social justice, and music education. Her edited book *Sociology and Music Education* was published by Ashgate Press in September 2010.

THE OXFORD HANDBOOK OF

SOCIAL JUSTICE IN MUSIC EDUCATION

UNDERSTANDING SOCIAL JUSTICE IN MUSIC EDUCATION CONCEPTUALLY, HISTORICALLY, AND POLITICALLY

INTRODUCTION

From Pioneers to New Frameworks

PAUL WOODFORD, SECTION EDITOR

WHAT is social justice, and how might it apply to music education? These are the primary questions explored in this first section of this Handbook in which the authors work to explain and illustrate what social justice means and what it might imply for professional practice, while also contextualizing its pursuit in and through the field of music education with reference to history and contemporary politics. As historian Marie McCarthy explains in Chapter 2, the study of music education's history can help us to better understand some of the roots and causes of social *in*justice in our own field, while also realizing why and how music education has always been inextricably linked with politics. Such study might expose long-term patterns of oppression that have gone unnoticed, and thus unchallenged, while revealing gaps in the historical record with respect to the untold stories of marginalized or persecuted groups. In short, historical research and study can inform our understanding of present circumstances by revealing how our beliefs, practices, and ways of thinking have to a significant extent been shaped by the past. It can also, of course, help individuals to realize that history is itself a politically charged and contested subject, the study of which involves—or should involve—adjudication of often conflicting interpretations of the historical record, because this record is inevitably incomplete and therefore only partial.

The pursuit of social justice, however, whether through historical or other research and study, presupposes an interest in creating or fostering a more humane society. This involves questioning or otherwise challenging the authority of the status quo; otherwise individuals, especially children, are not likely to notice or recognize oppression, let alone develop a sense of moral agency and social responsibility. Estelle Jorgensen, in Chapter 1, explains why music educators of all kinds should be interested in this task, while also warning against overly simplistic understandings both as to why social justice should matter to them and of the concept itself, which is in reality complex and difficult. Jorgensen carefully teases out a "multifaceted view of social justice" involving various overlapping, and sometimes conflicting, conceptions of social justice that provides a conceptual framework for virtually all that follows in these pages. For this reason, her chapter has accordingly been placed at the beginning of this Handbook and section, followed by McCarthy's chapter on the need for historical perspective.

The next three chapters in this section are more directly concerned with issues relating to policy. Patrick Schmidt in Chapter 3 makes an ethical call to music teachers at all levels to attend to, and become more involved in, policymaking, lest they continue to be marginalized in policy discourses affecting them, their students, and society as a whole. If policy provides the political means for enacting some collective vision, policymaking is the realm wherein that vision is created and honed through discourse. Policy discourse, though, is inevitably biased because it is influenced by politics and power and thus is selective, privileging some people and their ideas and values, while excluding or devaluing others. Thus, if music teachers committed to fostering social justice in and through their own teaching and programs are to be realistic and effective in striving to accomplish their goals, they need to become more aware of, and savvy about, policy, while finding ways to lend their voices to that discourse so that they can be heard by government and others.

Whereas the chapters thus far in this section are relatively general in nature insomuch as they involve concerns about the concept(s) of social justice, the need for historical perspective, and greater and critical involvement in educational policymaking, the next two chapters are more specific in nature, albeit still related to policy issues. Stephanie Horsley in Chapter 4 summarizes and critiques the essential elements of the neoliberal ideology that is now so pervasive in our world, including policy discourse, while explaining that it is based in significant part on a conception of negative rights (e.g., equality of opportunity) that favors capitalist over democratic interests and that may in certain respects be inimical to the pursuit of social justice. She proffers several recommendations for how music teachers might work to counter some of the more Darwinian aspects of the neoliberal social and educational agenda so that they can better contribute to a more inclusive and humane society.

Gabriel Rusinek and José Luis Aróstegui, however, writing from a European perspective in Chapter 5, take a somewhat different tack in observing that some transnational institutions associated with neoliberal education reform contend that an "economy-based curriculum" can work to promote social justice by improving academic achievement among disadvantaged children, thereby reducing income inequality in the future. This might seem a contentious claim to some readers since, as just suggested, neoliberal education reform tends to favor the already privileged while reducing education for the masses of children to technocratic or vocational training. Rusinek and Aróstegui, however, argue that if music is to remain a part of the school curriculum, and thereby accessible to the majority of children, then teachers must be able to convince government of the relevance and efficacy of those programs in meeting the goals of compulsory education. As in other subject areas, music teachers will have to rely to a greater extent than before on standards and quantitative measures for purposes of accountability, but there is also a need for the development of evidence-based qualitative assessment tools that more accurately represent the kinds of knowledge, skills, and dispositions that children have traditionally learned in music classes that are important to their future economic success *and* personal fulfillment. The profession has not done an adequate job of explaining and demonstrating to government and the public how, in what ways, and to what extent the study of music and the arts exercises critical thinking, creativity, and imagination—qualities and habits of mind that are, or should be, of value as much to business elites as to the arts community (Winner, Goldstein, & Vincent-Lancrin, 2013). Hence there is a need for alternative forms of assessment that can show politicians what music teachers have always known: that music matters profoundly to society in ways that cannot be assessed by quantitative measures alone. Viewed thusly, the development of more and better qualitative assessment tools of the sort described by Rusinek and Aróstegui might arguably be seen as a form of political resistance, as a bulwark against those who would eliminate school music programs because they are perceived as educational frills and therefore are expendable.

The last two chapters in this section help to place the ideas presented in the foregoing chapters into broader context by linking music education more explicitly to citizenship education. In Chapter 6, Wai-Chung Ho and Wing-Wah Law explore how the Chinese government uses music and music education to help shape the public's ideas of citizenship and national, regional, and ethnic identity in this age of globalization and free trade. There is a tension in Chinese education policy affecting music education as the government attempts to acknowledge, while tempering, the growing materialism and individualism among youth that are associated with globalization by also recognizing music education's potential contribution to social stability, nation building, and the "Chinese Dream." Thus far, the Chinese government has had little to say about democracy and social justice as they relate to education, but some music educators are attempting to engage the state in a broader conversation about social justice and the role of music education in an increasingly complex world.

It is fitting that we conclude this section of the Handbook with a commentary by Joel Westheimer, University Research Chair in Democracy and Education at the University of Ottawa and author of the book *What Kind of Citizen?* (Teachers College Press, 2015). His Chapter 7, entitled "What Did You Learn Today? Music Education, Democracy, and Social Justice," engages with and builds on ideas presented by other authors in this section, with a view to relating music education to wider developments in education and other disciplines and fields. Clearly, as Westheimer realizes, music education is subject to the same social, political, and cultural forces that would reduce all education to technical or vocational training. Far from defeatist, however, he believes that music and arts teachers can inspire other educators who are opposed to what he describes as "myopic education reform goals." Among the themes raised in the preface to this Handbook was that the pursuit of social justice, if it is to succeed, may require recognition of common purposes, leading to collaboration with individuals from allied fields and disciplines. As Westheimer notes, were music educators to form partnerships with other educators who conceive of education as a "profoundly human and liberatory endeavor," then music education might be "as threatening as some neoliberal reformers perceive it to be." John Dewey said almost the same thing eight decades ago when he enjoined teachers to ally themselves with "social forces which promote educational aims" (1933, p. 48). This was to better defend public educational institutions from those who would undermine their democratic purpose of creating a critically informed and engaged citizenry that could protect the public interest from domination by economic elites. We ignore Dewey's and Westheimer's calls to action at our peril!

References

Dewey, J., & Childs, J. L. (1933). The social and economic situation and education. In W. H. Kilpatrick (Ed.), *The educational frontier* (pp. 32–72). New York and London: Century Co. Re-printed in Dewey, J. (1989). *The later works*, Vol. 8: *1933, Essays and How we think* (Rev. ed.), Jo Ann Boydston (Ed.) (pp. 43–76). Carbondale and Edwardsville: Southern Illinois University Press.

Winner, E., Goldstein, T. R., & Vincent-Lancrin, S. (2013). *Art for art's sake? The impact of arts education*. Paris: Educational Research and Innovation, OECD Publishing.

CHAPTER 1

....

INTERSECTING SOCIAL JUSTICES AND MUSIC EDUCATION

....

ESTELLE R. JORGENSEN

THREE interrelated philosophical questions lie at the heart of this chapter: Why should music educators be interested in justice? What is meant by social justice and what are the types of social justice? How should music educators act on behalf of justice? Throughout this chapter, I make the case for a multifaceted view of social justice. I also meld theoretical and practical facets of social justice and sketch some implications for music education theory and practice. Thinking of justice in the plural complicates the analysis; outlining the practical implications of these ideas moves ideas closer to the phenomenal world in which music education transpires. Although I deal with each of these questions in conceptually independent ways, practically speaking, it becomes clear that they intersect.

WHY SHOULD MUSIC EDUCATORS BE INTERESTED IN JUSTICE?

....

Matters of justice constitute an imperative for music educators for at least four principal reasons. There may be other and more pressing considerations, and I do not claim that my list is exhaustive. Still, these reasons seem to be resilient in various communities and cultures and throughout history. Writing against the backdrop of a North American reality, in which music education has been a part of publicly supported education for the greater part of two centuries, it is natural to construe this problem in political and secular terms. In North America, at least, music education is conducted particularly within the aegis of the state and is manifested in its various political institutions. Viewed within a pervasively secular framework, music education has also taken on a humanistic cast (e.g., Mursell, 1934). In the West, it has adopted a democratic and communitarian stance influenced by the ideas of such writers as John Dewey ([1916]1944). In parts of the world, religious, familial, commercial, and artistic institutions are some of the principal means for musical education writ large (Jorgensen, 1997). Even within North America, the private studio, conservatory, and church, as well as informal family and peer instruction in music, remain important ways through which people come to know music. Each of these institutions (and the musical communities that comprise and represent them) has its own value sets, some of which run counter to those of state-supported music education. Among state music educators, different values also obtain, exemplified in various curricula, instructional methods, administrative approaches, and means of teaching and learning. These realities complicate what might otherwise be a too simplistic or facile response to the question of why justice matters to and for music education. As the interests of state-supported music education remain paramount in the profession's consciousness, I begin by addressing the reasons that have the widest currency for music education. Some of the complications and dissonances—when the interests of other societal institutions in matters of justice and music education are taken into account—also become apparent.

First, from antiquity, justice underlies conceptions of humane and civil society. Its reference to conduct that is just, noble, and righteous is premised on particular conduct that is normative and prescribed by systems of rules that govern it. Rooted in mythic and theological ideas, justice is also spelled out in secular notions of how society should be organized and governed (e.g., Plato, 1993). The ancient Greek notion of *paideia* (Jaeger, 1943–1945), the ideal of an educated and cultured citizen, has been rearticulated and defended in our time by writers such as Martha Nussbaum (1997) and applied to educational thought and practice by Mortimer Adler (1982, 1983, 1984), among others. Justice is premised on the reality of pervasive evil-doing, inhumanity, and incivility, and the imperative to delimit and redress them insofar as possible. It both prompts right-doing and punishes evil-doing.

Practically speaking, what is considered to be "right" conduct is framed by those with the power to create and enforce the rules that define it. Societal institutions, whether political, religious, commercial, artistic, or familial, are characterized by different rule sets and power brokers from place to place and time to time. For music educators located within a pervasively political milieu, these rule sets are inscribed in laws and regulations that are enforced by courts (Heimonen, 2002). Each institution has rule sets that possibly conflict with those of other institutions, and these rule sets are contested in the public arena. Conduct valued as "just" or "right" by one institution may not be accepted as "just" or "right" by another. For example, justice conceived in terms of providing a gender-blind musical education in state-supported schools may not be acceptable in conservative Islamic, Jewish, or Christian-supported schools. Although they represent Abrahamic faiths, committed alike to broad principles of humanity and civility, their particular theologies give rise to differing conceptions of justice in taking into account gender in music education. All may seek to redress differing evils and point toward various conceptions of righteousness, articulated by the governors of these faith communities and schools. Nevertheless, what one institution may view as just and right may represent for others what is unjust and wrong—this, notwithstanding that all may ascribe to the value of justice in the educational community or society. Music teachers may agree in general terms about the importance of justice as a value underlying humane and civil society, but the particular circumstances in which they do their work are likely to shape the specific ways in which their notions of justice are framed and realized in their musical instruction. While there may be widespread general agreement about the proposition of justice as a basis for humane and civil society, the closer one comes to the ground of music educational practice, the more fraught the problem of what is meant by justice and how it can be achieved practically.

Second, music education is centrally concerned with matters of justice because music education is a facet of cultural and public policy. It constitutes a means of developing dispositions of citizens within a particular society (Arnstine, 1995), recognizing and rectifying evil and wrongdoing and transforming society toward greater civility, humanity, and artistic expression (Jorgensen, 2003). Dewey ([1927]1954) makes the case that communities, institutions, and societies are predicated on the idea that the people who comprise them delegate authority (or it is delegated on their behalf) to those who perform tasks that cannot easily be accomplished by individuals acting alone. Such public actions especially benefit the very young and old, those who are vulnerable in society and may be physically or mentally unable to act on their own behalf, and those who do not possess the education, money, and power to act on their own behalf. This is especially the case in educational and artistic endeavors that often require decision-making on behalf of the collective good (Gingell, 2014). Whether under the aegis of the state, religion, commerce, family, or the music profession, music education lies within the realm of policies or general principles that guide action in regard to which particular musical beliefs and actions are valued as contributors to the well-being of the sponsoring group, community, institution, or society. Music education's value to a particular group is also adjudicated on the basis of its contribution not only to music but to the other beliefs, values, and mores by which this group lives. From the beginning of state-supported music education in the nineteenth century (Woodbridge, 1831), music education has been expected to develop the propensities to act in ways expected of citizens. This expectation has continued as a compelling argument during the twentieth (Mursell, 1934) and into the twenty-first centuries (Jorgensen, 2002, 2003). The same is true of religiously supported music education in the ancient world (Wellesz, 1969), and within the education of Cathedral choristers in the Christian church (Rainbow & Cox, 2006).

The notion of cultivating dispositions as the end of education admits that education cannot be wholly successful, and that some students may not develop the desirable character traits or ways of living for which educators might hope (Highet, [1950]1955). Being disposed to think and act in particular ways does not mean that one will always do what one wishes one might do or knows one should do. Kant's recognition of human frailty and imperfection aptly suits the human predicament (Berlin, 1990, foreword; Kant, [1784]1923, p. 23). Recognizing and rectifying evil and transforming education and society toward more civility and humanity are contingent and problematic. Practically speaking, much depends on how evil and wrongdoing are defined within the sponsoring groups, communities, institutions, or societies, and the degree to which educators are empowered to solve often intractable problems. The notion of transforming music education is a complex one, depending on what one means by transformation and how it can take place (Jorgensen, 2003). Societally based notions of the particular good and right-doing toward which music education aspires are contested within and outside music education. Even if music educators agree on the particular ends they seek, there is the ever-present problem that they will not do what they believe they should. The notion that one could train music educators to act in particular ways is ultimately fraught and unsuccessful. Donald Arnstine's (1995) more modest project of seeking to develop dispositions to act in ways that improve the situation in education, as well as more broadly in society, is a more realistic plan. This approach admits that one might hope for music educators, as cultural workers (Giroux, [1992]1993), to seek justice. Ultimately, one cannot be assured of success in the project. Transformation from evil-doing to right-action, toward that which is just, is not only relative and contingent but far from assured, even if there is agreement and collective effort in the direction of the particular justice that is sought. My response to this dilemma is that even though this is the case, education remains a hopeful enterprise (Freire, 1994). Albeit an idealistic hope—hope in the face of the prospect of defeat—educational hope still represents a powerful incentive to improve the situation.

Third, justice emphasizes the worth, dignity, and preciousness of individual human beings (Gaita, 2000) and reinforces a sense of self-respect and self-worth in those who pursue and receive it. Thinking of justice in these humane and personal terms brings notions of justice closer to the beliefs and practices of music educators. Music teachers typically think of their work as having to do with valuing all of their students and developing their personal confidence, self-worth, and self-respect. Notwithstanding the different genders, ethnicities, colors, languages, ages, religious affiliations, social classes, and musical proclivities of their students, doing justice necessitates a commitment to all one's students, irrespective of their particular characteristics. Doing justice requires that one regards all people of worth with the same claims to honor, courtesy, and care.

This is more easily said than done because differences between people often prompt bias, suspicion, and hostility. When empathy falters, these biases are caricatured as stereotypes that harden into habits and mores. It then becomes easy to act dismissively, disrespectfully, critically, and thoughtlessly against different others. Carried to an extreme, this behavior may incite injustice and violence. Paulo Freire (1990) points to the tendency for those who once were oppressed, disempowered, and alienated but now come into power to act just as those who oppressed them, so ingrained is the "image of the oppressor" in their consciousness and unconsciousness. When people throw off the yoke of oppression, they may act like others did to them; they, in turn, can become oppressors of others who do not agree with them and are reluctant to give up the perquisites of power. Although overcoming these tendencies is a principal educational task, it may not suffice. As Seyla Benhabib (2002) notes, laws may also be needed to settle disputes and enforce a measure of civility and humane conduct. One hopes, like Raymond Gaita (2000), to create the circumstances in which all people will be regarded as precious. Nevertheless, there is the ever present possibility that ingrained cultural and societal habits and norms, and an inability to empathize with different others and to imagine how things might be more humane and civil, stand in the way of realizing this principle.

Fourth, justice assists in negotiating the different perspectives, worldviews, and mindsets that compete for ascendancy, and it seeks to adjudicate conflicts and settle disputes through the exercise of reason, dialogue, and legal intervention (Benhabib, 2002; Morgan & Guilherme, 2014). Music education is centrally concerned with transmitting and transforming a plethora of musical traditions from one generation to the next. Negotiating today's globally interconnected world of musics poses significant challenges for music teachers and their students. The farther from the students' musical lives in time and space—the more disparate the musics studied from those they have experienced at home, in their place of worship, on the Internet, or in the live musical performances in which they have participated—the more difficult it is for them to grasp the claims of musics with which they are, as yet, unfamiliar. Musical values sometimes clash or rub up against each other, and each tradition is interested in its own survival. For this reason, the supporters of local musical traditions in the service of nationalistic movements may also resist efforts to introduce students to the musics of other cultures.

Justice, by its appeal to reason, hopes to negotiate the sometimes conflicting claims of this plethora of musical traditions. Paul Woodford (2005) posits that a reasoned approach to music education requires the exercise of critical thinking on the part of music educators and their students in unmasking taken-for-granted assumptions and practices and forging more humane and civil approaches. Such thoughtful approaches may fly in the face of educational and more broadly cultural realities. For example, a backlash against multiculturalism is already evident in some educational circles in the United States. As I write, the "Common Core" movement attempts to standardize certain elite knowledge as normative (Cardany, 2013; Porter, McMaken, Hwang, & Yang, 2011). This approach represents a return to the thinking of writers such as E. D. Hirsch (1987), who sought to define what every American ought to know. Hirsch privileged certain masculine, esoteric, establishment, and Eurocentric knowledge over that which was feminine, popular, accessible, and emanated from the lower social classes and other parts of the world. Educators in some quarters are now lining up uncritically behind notions of the Common Core and are applying it to all aspects of the school curriculum. For music educators desirous of introducing their students to a world of diverse musical traditions, it is now necessary to critique notions of the Common Core while going beyond it. To do this effectively requires a reasoned approach to problems that may be difficult to surmount. Although thinking of music education in terms of justice offers an important means of carefully evaluating authorized knowledge (Apple, 2000), it cannot hope to be successful within the public sphere in circumstances where music educators are disempowered. In order to effect change, it is necessary for music educators to win wide public support for their positions and act cohesively to insist that their views are heard and valued. Sometimes, it is necessary to ensure change through legal means.

WHAT IS MEANT BY SOCIAL JUSTICE AND WHAT ARE THE TYPES OF SOCIAL JUSTICE?

During the past decade, music educators have theorized aspects of social justice (Allsup, 2007, introducing a special issue of *Music Education Research*; Bowman, 2007, introducing an issue of *Action, Criticism, and Theory for Music Education*). Cathy Benedict and Patrick Schmidt (2007) are among those to grasp the problematic ways in which the claims of justice have been articulated and applied in the past. My own tack in this present writing is to unpack some of the lenses through which justice has been viewed in order to construe social justice conceptually and to reflect on implications for music education thought and practice.

Among these lenses, social justice can be thought of as a form of what is generally referred to as distributive justice (Allingham, 2014a, 2014b). That is, its focus is upon ensuring the "common good," or fairly sharing the wealth and benefits of society among all its members. This view of justice has a decidedly economic ring, articulated especially in welfare economics, a field of economic theory concerned with taking account of and attending to the well-being of members of society. John Rawls (1999a) interprets distributive justice broadly to include educational, cultural, political, and legal benefits to which people in democratic societies are entitled. Distributive justice seeks reciprocity between individual and societal rights because of the tensions and conflicts between specific individual needs, wants, and interests and those of the communities of which they are a part. It also concerns matters of access to justice in every area of life. In education, distributive justice has been thought of in terms of rights to schooling (Levine & Bane, 1975). For example, in music education, distributive justice refers to the imperative of ensuring that music education is available equitably and that particular individuals or minorities are not disadvantaged or excluded from instruction. Such a position would require working with students who differ, often markedly, in language, ethnicity, family background, social class, musicality, and musical experience and forging music programs that ensure the benefits of music education irrespective of these differences.

The communitarian purpose of the "common good," as "justice of the community" or "justice of common welfare," is emphasized by educational writers such as Dewey ([1916]1944), Maxine Greene (1988), and Parker Palmer (1998). These writers embrace a democratic view of the community as a group of people united around particular beliefs and practices, responsible for their own governance, holding each other in esteem, and acting humanely toward one another. The community is more than the sum of the individuals who comprise it. Individuals act not only in their own hedonistic interests but for the benefit of the good to the entire community. Welfare is understood not only to be individual, but collective or common to all those who comprise the community. Justice applies not only to individuals but also to their collective well-being and to the community as a whole. Viewed within this prism, as a music teacher, one would need to think not only of one's self or of each of the individuals who comprise one's class or ensemble, but of the well-being of the entire class or ensemble as a community. Social justice focuses on this collective, communitarian, or common welfare.

Commutative justice may also intersect with social justice. Thomas Aquinas (2013–2014) distinguished distributive and commutative justice in his *Summa theologica* (question 61). By commutative, I mean contractual obligations that exist between individuals, groups, and the societies of which they are a part. For Dewey ([1927]1954), the public has entrusted the work of teaching the young to educational policymakers, administrators, and teachers. By virtue of accepting employment in school districts, teachers are contractually responsible to teach in ways that follow certain rules and regulations. Likewise, the public, politicians, and educational policymakers are responsible for fulfilling their contractual obligations by providing the conditions under which this educational work can be carried on successfully. Too often, these obligations are unmet. When this occurs, social justice insists on their being met. In the United States, for example, the conditions described by Jonathan Kozol (2005) of crumbling schools, unsanitary conditions, inadequate supplies, and unqualified teachers in some schools represent a failure of commutative justice on the part of the public and the school boards that represent them. Social justice can be understood in terms of these contractual matters and the need to ensure that contracts are honored by all the parties to them. Where public commitments are made to music education in schools, it is just as incumbent on the public and its policymakers to provide the resources to accomplish agreed-upon ends and means as it is for music teachers to offer programs that address the means and ends of music instruction for which they have been hired.

Social justice can also be viewed in terms of contributive justice. Contributive justice concerns what people are able to contribute to society, that is, their rights to give to others and the societies of which they are a part. Race remains an important factor in contributive justice in the workplace (Gomberg, 2007; Sayer, 2009). Whereas distributive justice concerns what is given to people, contributive justice focuses on what people give to each other and to their communities. For example, in economic terms, it concerns the rights of people to work; in artistic terms, it relates to the rights of people to create artistic products and engage in artistic activities; in social terms, it concerns the rights of people to marry and raise families. Social justice concerns the rights of women to vote and to contribute economically in ways that, in the past, may have been more stereotypically male. In music education, these gender roles may play out, among other ways, in the rights of females to play musical instruments or assume musical roles typically and historically played by males.

In terms of procedural justice, social justice focuses on the notion of the process and a sense of fair play whereby individuals and groups interact with each other, according each other rights and responsibilities (Rawls, 1971, 1999b). It concerns the means whereby justice is seen to be done in every aspect of life in ways that are transparent to all, and the procedures that are conducted in individual and collective life are understood by all in sharing the goods that society provides. This notion of justice emphasizes process rather than product and means rather than ends. For example, the process whereby music teachers select members of their ensembles is crucial in determining whether or not the teachers' conduct is perceived or understood to be just. Biases have historically been evident to people of differing cultural heritage in race-based admission to educational opportunities. Social justice may involve the effort to clarify the procedures whereby such admission decisions are made. When this is the case, social justice encompasses procedural justice that focuses on the means whereby particular educational ends are reached.

Social justice may sometimes include retributive justice. This view of justice has ancient roots in the Babylonian Code of Hammurabi (ca. 1750 BCE) and Jewish Mosaic Law. In the Law of Moses, for example, punishment is rendered to evil-doers so that they also suffer in an "eye for an eye" and "a tooth for a tooth" (Exodus 21:23; Deuteronomy 19:17–21). Notwithstanding Immanuel Kant's (1972) link between punishment and moral wrongdoing and his argument that those who have done evil to others deserve punishment that is measured and appropriate to the evil they have done, retributive justice may be harsh and vengeful. Penalties are exacted from evil-doers for the purpose of punishing them and causing them sorrow, suffering, and even death. Wishing to see people suffer in return for the evil that they have or are supposed to have done is a common human response. For those who have suffered persecution and oppression, it is difficult to see beyond a desire for their persecutors and oppressors to suffer as they have suffered. Their anger and outrage are understandable. Still, retaliating with hatred can consolidate and perpetuate an inhumane situation; instances of punishment and revenge can spiral, moving outward as they, in turn, consolidate and perpetuate themselves. Throughout history, religious dogma has often not only tolerated but encouraged this view of justice. Too often, education (and music education) has been conducted within an ethic of suffering and retribution. Some administrators, teachers, and students are mean and cruel; they delight in the suffering of others in the misguided belief that this is a necessary part of the educational process. In these and other ways, social justice may be retributive in its desire to punish evil-doers and see them suffer.

Restorative justice as a frame in which to construe social justice focuses on correcting past iniquities and inequities and, insofar as possible, putting right the evil that has been done. In recent decades, this notion has been explored in a variety of contexts, including criminal law, philosophy, and theology (Braithwaite, 1989; Gilligan, 1982; Noddings, 1982; De Gruchy, 2002; and Govier, 2006). This transformational and redemptive notion of justice assumes that traditional thought and practice concerning individuals and groups may need to be rethought and reworked in order to restore what has been lost to those who have been wronged. For example, Gaita (2000) writes of the need to restore to Aboriginal peoples of Australia the land, livelihood, and dignity that have been stolen or seized from them. Correcting past abuse, neglect, and ostracism seeks to create a more just reality in which those who have been marginalized or excluded from society are welcomed into it as fully participating and respected citizens. In education, such a view of justice requires the special effort of atonement in order to put things right. Here, since some individuals and groups have suffered injustice in the past, it is necessary to go beyond simply ensuring that all have a fair share of the benefits of society to give special attention to their needs and wants. One is not simply creating "a level playing field," where all play by the same rules. Rather, realizing the burden of the sins of the past and the vulnerability of those who have not had the same access to education, wealth, security, respect, and love as their more privileged fellows requires "affirmative action." Here, an effort is made to ensure that minorities and the more vulnerable in society have the support they need to succeed in a world where long-standing biases and stereotypes may make it difficult for them to succeed. For example, music teachers who, in the past, may have been biased toward their white middle-class students would need to reach out to meet the needs and interests of their minority, differently abled, and lower- and under-class students. These efforts may be perceived as privileging their minority students. Still, this is how it will likely be when restorative justice takes hold. Social justice can involve corrective justice when it seeks to put right the evils perpetrated by one group on another. From this perspective, social justice is transformational in seeking to right past wrongs and creating or restoring a more humane and civil society.

Social justice may also be seen as a form of poetic justice (Nussbaum, 1995). Such justice recognizes that doing evil causes harm to the evil-doer. Oppression harms the oppressor as much as the oppressed. Cruelty, violence, incivility, and lack of empathy for those less fortunate than oneself render people less moral, just, and good. In so doing, they are soul-destroying, isolating one from human friendship and love and even psychologically and physically debilitating. In myth and poem, such evil people often come to a bad end. Seen in this way, social justice recognizes the harm done to the perpetrators of evils such as slavery, patriarchy, xenophobia, racism, homophobia, cruelty to animals, and raping the earth. Within the realm of education, bullying and mean-spiritedness do harm to the bullies and the mean people as well as those whom they hurt. For this reason, social justice necessitates making the point that all will be better off in a civil and humane society in which everyone is regarded as precious, worthy of respect, and treated with dignity. When minorities are valued as part of the school community, all its members grow physically and spiritually, and the educational process is enhanced for teachers and students alike.

Instrumental justice as a way of construing social justice views justice as a means to other ends (Mill, [1863]2001; Plato, 1993). Among its purposes, it can promote happiness, facilitate democratic governance, foster peace and tranquility, and ensure the maintenance of societal structures that particularly benefit the society's establishment and powerful elites. This view of justice is parasitic on the notion of justice as a human creation that, as Plato (1994, book I) has Thasymachus say, can also imply trickery. As such, justice is not always agreed upon by the powerful and powerless alike. It may appear to be done, without being actually done to all the people. For example, teachers may invoke justice as a tool to create the appearance of beneficence and care for their students, meanwhile conducting programs that are unjust in the treatment of those who are disadvantaged by this system. Social justice, viewed within this instrumental lens, can serve to create a more humane and collegial educational environment, as it may also perpetuate commitments to justice that are more apparent than real and that benefit some people more than, or to the detriment of, others.

Social justice construed as legal justice concerns the systems of laws, rules, and regulations that protect the individual and the collective rights of members of a society in which a particular legal system prevails. Aristotle (1994–2009, book 5) distinguishes this type of justice from natural justice that he regards as universal. Overlaying the differing legal systems in nation-states is a body of international law that governs relationships among nation-states. Nation-states may or may not agree to be bound by particular principles, treaties, and obligations articulated internationally. For example, the United States is not a signatory to the United Nations Convention on the Rights of the Child (United Nations General Assembly, 1989), and does not regard itself legally bound by this Convention. Aside from precedent, professional and public pressure, or legal protections in the US Constitution, American children do not necessarily have the same legal right to know their own culture (including its music) as children living in other countries covered by this international Convention. If it is the right of every child to know the music of her or his own culture, social justice concerns contesting and possibly reworking the laws, regulations, and conventions that apply to music education in particular states and countries. Such a notion is inevitably fraught with legal and constitutional issues.

Thinking of divine justice in the Abrahamic faiths as a lens through which to view social justice envisages justice as vested ultimately in a deity who commands humans to think and act in particular ways that are considered to be just. In polytheistic religions, the gods share and sometimes contest responsibilities for justice, which is meted out to humans. Plato (1994) saw the gods as possessing the clearest and highest notion of the virtues, and human beings as grasping them less directly, less completely, and more imperfectly. Animistic religions ascribe power to particular beings with supernatural abilities that possess forces of retribution if not appeased. All these religions share the presumption that the divine beings that are worshipped will reward or punish those who follow or depart from particular religious prescriptions and proscriptions. Social justice, in these terms, is addressed within theologies of major faith traditions such as Islam, Hinduism, Christianity, Judaism, and Buddhism and in assumptions concerning the presence or otherwise of supernatural powers or deities in animistic, humanistic, and atheistic traditions. Systems of belief and practice that have built up around deities that are worshiped or repudiated are also interpreted differently, even within the faiths themselves. This ambiguity gives rise to factions, sects, and denominations that may be hostile to each other. Present denominational conflicts within Islam evoke similar and often violent conflicts within Christianity. For example, in multicultural societies, questions relating to the musical education of Muslim boys and girls who constitute a minority in countries in which Christianity is established, or that of Christian boys and girls who constitute a minority in countries in which Islam is established, are matters that concern social justice. How social justice should be defined in theological terms, and the extent to which religious accommodations in education need to be made and how, are matters that go to the heart of music education. Believers in the various faith traditions begin their understanding of these matters within the frame of the divine commands or theological beliefs to which they assent.

Social justice is also interpreted in the frame of natural law, the assumption that the right to justice is a human right that is self-evident, and that all people ought to agree with this presumption (Aristotle, 1994–2009, book 5). The Enlightenment writers of the US Constitution could write in sweeping terms: "We hold these truths to be self-evident, that all men are created equal, that they are endowed by their Creator with certain unalienable Rights, that among these are Life, Liberty and the pursuit of Happiness" (US Congress, 1776). In this view, human rights are universal, trump particular cultural rights, and arbitrate other rights. Where religious and other cultural rights run counter to natural law, they must accommodate to natural law. Viewed within the lens of natural law, music educators interpret social justice as applying universally, equally to musical and educational opportunities for females and males in spite of religious proscriptions and cultural stereotypes. For such music educators, the claims of natural law, envisaged in terms of human rights, transcend all other religious and cultural claims.

Seeing social justice through these various overlapping lenses provides a way of understanding a plethora of intersecting visions of social justice that relate to music education. The difficulties in describing social justice result from the ambiguity of these and other ways in which it can be construed. These types overlap, resonate with, and conflict with others. If one accepts that each frame contributes to the richness and ambiguity of the notion of social justice as it applies to music education, it becomes necessary to adjudicate the claims of these various perspectives. All have to do with aspects of human rights. The claim that human rights trump other cultural rights is a false dichotomy. One's imagination is shot through with socially and culturally ingrained understandings that shape one's perceptions of the possibilities of human rights. Just as the architects of the US Constitution could not see the injustice of slavery and the inferior treatment of women in the natural law they espoused in their own time, other blind spots may prevent us from seeing the injustice in ours. This fallibility suggests a more modest position of seeking to do the best one can in the particular situations in which one finds oneself. Such an approach necessitates considering which of these particular approaches to social justice most meet the claims of one's particular situation and how they should be navigated. This is a situational approach to one's ethical predicament, but I cannot see a humane way out of it that takes into account all of these nuances (and others besides) and the practical realities in which music teachers work. I caution that these differing perspectives on social justice suggest that one may talk past others without hearing them. These differences may be the source of disagreements about what should be done about social justice in music education. So it is important to inquire how music educators should act on behalf of justice.

How Should Music Educators Act on Behalf of Justice?

Thus far, I have unpacked some of the lenses through which social justice should be viewed. This analysis complicates the situation that music educators may face, but it may still not be a sufficiently broad view (Jorgensen, 2007). New frontiers of justice concerning such matters as disability, nationality, and species membership (Nussbaum, 2006) problematize our human and social relationships and advance the claims of the natural world and the plethora of other living things that share our planet. These complications lead me to prefer to think about justice more broadly, notwithstanding the importance of the social considerations to which social justice relates. I would prefer to focus, therefore, on the ways in which music educators may act on behalf of justice. Moving beyond my earlier writing (Jorgensen, 2007), I sketch implications of the various sorts of social justice for music education thought and practice.

Over the years, I have been concerned with the importance of dialogue within a fallibilist perspective as a means of articulating and negotiating differing perspectives (Jorgensen, 2003). When participants remain open to the possibility that they may be wrong, and they regard others' divergent and sometimes conflicting ideas with respect and empathy, it is possible to find common ground in which all may act together in the interest of certain shared interests and values and a humane and civil society. Drawing on Buber's ideas of human interrelationships, Morgan and Guilherme (2014) suggest that dialogue can serve as an important means of conflict resolution. This proposition assumes, like Greene (1995), that mutual respect and civility undergird social interaction, as one would hope they do in decent societies. Although this may be a somewhat idealistic and "improbable" hope (Benedict & Schmidt, 2007), dialogue may fail as a means of adjudicating different perspectives, and legal intervention may be needed (Benhabib, 2002), it can be a useful way in which music educators can think about and through the claims of justice in their particular situations in democratic societies.

In this present writing, I reflect on the implications of the various views on social justice and justice more generally for ways in which music educators ought to act. Among these perspectives, aspects of the distribution of music education across the population are a crucial consideration. Within the United States, for example, it is incumbent upon researchers to ascertain the state of this distribution. In recent decades, notwithstanding the importance for policy decision-making of understanding the specific situations in which music education is conducted, descriptive status studies have been eclipsed by scientific research in music education. The claims of distributive justice would necessitate ascertaining the precise state of the distribution of all aspects of music education, not only within particular schools, local areas, regions, and nation-states, but comparatively and internationally. One would expect such data to include musical, teaching, learning, instruction, curricular, and administrative aspects (Jorgensen, 2011a). With the availability of such comprehensive and systematic data, it should be possible to identify and defend those particular areas and people most in need of various sorts of music education and devise, implement, and evaluate plans to remedy shortfalls, wherever they may be. Rescuing status studies from the margins of music education research is an important initiative in thinking distributively about justice for the field's research and practice.

Communitarian notions of social justice focus centrally on ways in which music education serves the common good. The preservation of democratic ideals, while not a perfect political solution, provides one of the most humane approaches to governance of which I am aware. Even totalitarian states understand the power, or even the illusion of power, to shape one's own society. Since democracies are vulnerable to the influence of money and the exercise of power by a few, Dewey ([1916]1944) and R. S. Peters (1966) are among those to emphasize the crucial role of education as a means of cultivating civility, powers of critical thought, and a populace with the capacities and skills to participate fully in their societies. In the United States, at least from the early nineteenth century, publicly supported schools have sought to fill this role. One of the principal aims of music education in this context must be a social one of preparing citizens of a democracy. To this end, David Elliott (2012), Woodford (2005, 2014) and Richard Colwell (2014) variously consider the importance of artistic citizenship as an end of music education. Focusing on citizenship as a music educational aim necessitates planning particular ways in which music education is conducted in order to express this objective. Randall Allsup, Heidi Westerlund, and Lauri Väkevä (Allsup & Westerlund, 2012; Väkevä & Westerlund, 2007; Westerlund, 2002) are among those to reflect critically on the implications of this aim for the practice of music education in publicly supported schools.

Commutative justice in music education concerns at least two different responsibilities: that of music teachers to fulfill their contractual obligations in serving their students and the wider public to which they are responsible; that of the public in providing the resources for teachers to be able to conduct their programs effectively. In the past, music educators have been more inclined to think in terms of their own obligations to their students and to the music profession and less apt to focus on the wider public policy questions concerning the context in which music education is conducted. Professional organizations in the United States such as the National Association for Music Education (along with its predecessors, the Music Supervisors National Conference and the Music Educators National Conference), informal think tanks such as the Mayday Group, and writers such as Charles Fowler (1996) have sought to articulate the responsibilities of public education to cultivate the arts. American music education professional organizations have engaged in political and policy action nationally, have published reports such as *Growing Up Complete: The Imperative for Music Education* (National Commission on Music Education, 1991) and the *National Standards for Arts Education* (Blakeslee, 1994), and have lobbied for educational reforms (Aguilar, 2011). As Aguilar demonstrates, however, in notable instances, this policy decision-making has been uninformed by the extant educational policy decision-making literature. Music teachers in some states have successfully impacted policy changes by virtue of the personal connections established by music and art education leaders with policymakers and the public at large. For example, in Indiana, the Indiana Arts Coalition of stakeholders in the arts and general education (www.inartscoalition.org) is an important advocate for the arts and arts education. My sense is that these efforts are crucially important for commutative justice in music education, and policymaking research projects that document successful endeavors need to be emphasized. Research and policy action need to contribute to and reflect the educational policymaking literature, and strong links need to be forged between policymaking research and practice in music education. To some degree, doing this requires subverting the present scientific bias in what is considered "respectable" research in some quarters in music education and plowing the middle ground between research and practice.

Contributive aspects of social justice require that all men and women, boys and girls, of whatever ethnicity, color, language, religious affiliation, sexual orientation, and social class, among the many barriers that separate people, are able to contribute musically in the many ways in which they are interested and capable. Too often, music education has privileged males over females at all levels, from elementary to advanced instruction. Stereotypically gendered musical instruments often contribute to difficulties experienced by females who desire to be conductors, composers, and performers of instruments that are considered "masculine." Throughout history, religious affiliation has prescribed and proscribed particular musical roles for the various genders and has limited the means by which females, those who are differently gendered, and various minority populations can participate musically. In our own time, the provision of gender-restricted musical education in some Cathedral choirs in Church of England, Roman Catholic, and Orthodox Christian traditions and the proscription of mixed-gender music education by some strains of Islam narrow the opportunities for all children to receive musical education. Notwithstanding the contributions of composers such as Hildegard of Bingen (belatedly, a Doctor of the Church) in women's religious communities, the Western classical tradition still traces a largely masculine history throughout the Middle Ages, when religious music education was in the ascendancy (e.g., Burkholder, Grout, & Palisca, 2010). Papal restrictions on the musical education of girls by men other than immediate family members long limited the opportunities for girls to become professional musicians, and castrati were preferred to women as singers in the Baroque Italian opera. In our own time, the long-standing discomfort and silence of the music education profession on matters concerning differently gendered people and the important barriers in their way was only lately broken at a conference entitled "Establishing Identity: GLBT Studies and Music Education" (2010). Despite the presence of many teachers and students involved in music education who are gender-identified in other ways than heterosexuality, open discussions of these sometimes vexed issues have come only recently to music education. Rather than being marginalized in the profession, as feminism too often has been (Gould, 2011), these and other frontiers of justice need to be at the core of the music education research enterprise and its policymaking practice.

The claims of procedural justice in music education require a careful and critical rethinking of the means and ends of music education. The various means of education, while well-intentioned, may in fact patronize, diminish, and dehumanize people. Carried out under the guise of other social ends, the procedures employed in the selection of musical repertoire, students for particular musical ensembles, instructional methods, and assessment methods may not be as procedurally transparent and even-handed as they need to be. I worry, particularly, about the appearance rather than the reality of democratic governance. Invoking allegiance to democratic principles without a corresponding spirit of inclusiveness, mutual respect, and civility can be an evil because it disguises a lack of democracy under the mantle of humane principles. Recent philosophical conversations concerning the operation of instrumental music education have focused on the evils that may be in evidence and the possible goods to which such ensembles may be put (e.g., Allsup & Benedict, 2008; Gould, 2005; Koza, 2005; Tan, 2012). This conversation is important in reminding music educators of the need to critically examine the methods and ends of instrumental music education as it is typically practiced. For me, the truth lies somewhere in the messy ground between the good that can be accomplished through the conduct of instrumental ensembles and the evil that may also lurk. The continuing challenge for instrumental music educators, as all music teachers, is to attempt to rescue the good while also avoiding the evil. It is incumbent on music teachers to decide for themselves where the truth lies in their particular situations. Glossing over the potential problems or viewing the possibilities with rose-tinted glasses are mistaken and simplistic positions. Instead, music education policymakers and teachers need to be comfortable with the problem of a two-edged sword that potentially benefits and harms the work of music education if procedural justice is to be served.

Retributive justice demands a response to evil-doing. It seeks punishment of the evil-doer as a curb on evil. In noting the vexed nature of this view of justice, I have suggested that vengeance is often counterproductive. Punishment may be defensible in some respects and indefensible in others (Jorgensen, 2003). It may be a deterrent to further evil, and it may also contribute to further evil. Music teachers need to weigh their actions in order to determine in their best light what should be the correct course of conduct in a particular situation. It is important for the young to learn the value of discipline and for those who are older to practice it. Still, my sense is that one's conduct needs to be humane and helpful to the student's subsequent growth insofar as possible. As a teacher, I confess to sometimes being at a loss as to what to do. My fallibility means that I do not understand all of the relevant aspects of the situation. I am cognizant of the fact that the aspects that I do not know may be the very ones that may make all of the difference in my interpretation of events. The times when one errs in retributive justice can stick like burrs. They are reminders of the wisdom of a restrained, thoughtful, and careful view of the situations in which one may be tempted to seek retribution as a means of justice. For this reason alone, it is imperative to prepare music teachers as critical and constructive thinkers and doers.

Restorative justice is likewise problematic because of the unintended consequences of actions and changes in the distribution of power. In seeking to restore or ensure justice for those who have been beyond it or on its margins, it is possible to act in ways that have unforeseen effects. This is particularly the case for policymaking that seeks action on behalf of groups and populations. Such actions may also remove advantages from one group in order to bequeath them to another, resulting in shifts in the distribution of power among people. Losing one's privileged status can be painful, just as altering power relations can place unexpected burdens on those who have not been privileged in the past. School desegregation during the Civil Rights movement in the United States was intended to help people of color but, instead, placed the greater part of the burden on them. It not only resulted in eventual school re-segregation, but it also impacted the wider society geographically in ways that still disadvantage people of color. Affirmative action measures in university and college admissions became equally vexed as white people resisted real and apparent efforts to privilege people of color. Efforts to restore or ensure justice for all people by privileging those who have been disempowered and treated as of lesser worth need to be thoughtfully and critically undertaken. Importantly, policymakers need to understand that policies are inevitably shortsighted and inadequate; they will need to be revisited critically from time to time and reformulated when change is necessary. Although these decisions are fraught, I see no other alternative than that music educators act hopefully and humanely to improve their situations where they can. When unexpected consequences undoubtedly occur, they require the humility and courage to make the changes deemed necessary according to their best understanding of the circumstances.

Poetic justice relies on the imaginative powers of music teachers and their students. In other writing, I have urged the importance of developing imaginative thought and practice in music education (Jorgensen, 2008). As Greene (1988, 1995) observes, thinking imaginatively is a communal as well as an individual activity. So important is the artistic community to this enterprise that without being present to and within it, one may not imagine how things might be different. Seeing beyond the literal, prosaic, and ordinary to the figurative, artistic, and extraordinary are qualities that need to be emphasized in music education. Simply meeting or even surpassing literal standards, notwithstanding their value, cannot suffice. Rather, music teachers and their students need to experience those consummatory moments that Dewey ([1934]1979) describes as intensely satisfying and gripping, when one is caught up in undergoing the arts while at the same time actively creating them. Such experiences have a quality of what Abraham Maslow (1943, 1968) terms "peak experiences" and "self-actualization," or Mihaly Czikszentmihalyi (1990) describes as "flow," "optimal experience," and the sense of effortlessness and fluid and dynamic movement. Whether through literature, visual arts, music, drama, or other fine arts and crafts, as imagination grows, one is better able to imagine difference and divergence and embrace ambiguity. This reality may help to explain why Western philosophers since Plato (1993) have posited that the arts may constitute a means toward moral development. If those involved in music education possess this capacity, even though flawed and certainly not sufficient when taken alone, they may play a role in expressing justice and may be helping others to move toward it.

Construed instrumentally, music teachers may think of social justice as parasitic on other aims. Viewed in this way, social justice does not constitute an end in itself so much as a means to other ends. This notion fits well within the raison d'être that music teachers often see for themselves as musicians and educators. As with notions of procedural justice, such a view focuses especially on ensuring congruence between one's beliefs and practices and embodying and living one's convictions about justice in all of one's dealings with others. One not only ascribes to justice, but one loves to live its principles. Although one's primary objective is helping others to come to know music, and through these experiences, helping them to better understand themselves and their responsibilities to others around them, thinking about social justice instrumentally becomes the "hidden curriculum" of music education, the substrata of all that is done, said, and not done or said. In teacher education, students may come to understand that their work is not only and primarily with the students for whom they have responsibility, or on behalf of musical knowledge as a part of culture, but that the wider impact of their actions is felt throughout the wider society and beyond. As in education more generally, living justice in all of one's life is far more important than mere assent to its principles. Practically speaking, this is problematic. For example, auditioning students for a jazz combo may seem to be a just way to select students for particular musical and educational experiences. Still, girls and women or those with little previous exposure to jazz may lack the confidence to improvise and can be disadvantaged by the audition process. On the other hand, creating opportunities for auditioned and open entry music ensembles may serve as a just means to accomplish high student morale and a range of educational experiences tailored to needs of a diverse student body.

Legal notions of social justice require music teachers to think of their work and the claims of the laws and regulations that guide their work as crucially important (Heimonen, 2002, 2006). For example, in the United States, the rights of children to know the music of their culture are delimited by a constitutional prohibition on the establishment of religion and legal interpretations of this prohibition. Even the performance of instrumental music with religious title but without religious text is subject to significant restriction in American state-supported schools (Perrine, 2013). The claims of social justice would suggest including and valuing minority religious perspectives in music education within the particular legal frameworks that obtain and seeking to change the laws in these countries where deemed necessary. Should these laws and regulations need to be altered in pursuit of justice, teachers require the skills to effectively forge better laws and regulations. The music profession is fortunate to have in its midst those with legal knowledge and skill. Still, it is tempting for music teachers to rely on others to do this work. Excusing one's avoidance of such necessarily legal and political policymaking on the grounds that one is primarily an artist and musician cannot suffice. Rather, music teachers are duty-bound to learn how to navigate this territory successfully and to participate actively in the life of the profession in order to help create the kinds of laws and regulations that will best serve the interest of justice. Often, local school authorities and regional, national, and international bodies are reluctant to provide sufficient support for the arts in general education, and it is necessary to mount legal pressure on them to do what they should do or say they believe in doing. Thinking of justice in legal terms requires music teachers to be professionally committed to articulating and defending justice and helping to frame the policies that can best serve their particular situations.

Thinking of the divine role in justice inevitably requires reflecting critically on the role of the religions in music education. In other writing, and drawing on the work of Paul Tillich (1986) especially in regard to the visual arts, I have traced several types of religious experiences in music education, each of which is parasitic on particular theological notions (Jorgensen, 1993, 2011b). Contemporary secularized notions of music education largely bypass addressing the theological implications of justice. While music educators have recently explored aspects of spirituality and music education, the international and interdisciplinary conference entitled "Critical Perspectives on Music, Education, and Religion," sponsored by the University of the Arts, Helsinki, Sibelius Academy Faculty of Music, in August 2014 was a welcome departure. Unpacking these issues as they apply particularly to justice in music education, undertaking research in these areas, and developing practical ways in which to address the religions and music education in the contemporary world lie ahead. This particular view of justice would insist on the importance of such initiatives for music education writ large.

The universal claims of natural law as they apply to music education have prompted music educators to espouse notions that everyone is musical and is entitled to participate actively in music education (Jorgensen, 2004). In recent decades, some philosophers of music education have been inclined to critique claims that music is a universal language and that its values are universal, preferring instead to emphasize the differing and specific practices that may be construed to be music (e.g., Elliott, 1995, 2013). Leonard Tan (2012) has argued, however, for a transnational approach to instrumental music education that grasps the commonalities in different musical traditions between East and West. I am attracted to this view because it explores the middle ground between the extremes of universalism, on the one hand, and extreme relativism, on the other. It suggests that while music teachers need to emphasize the particular and distinctive musics and musical practices, it is also important to mine some of the important commonalities and values that unite them. Recognizing the claims of justice as both universal in certain respects and relative in others puts music education thought and practice near the messy, sensual, and phenomenal world that it concerns while also pointing to widespread human aspirations to create with instruments, dance, song, visual arts, and drama, among a host of other ways, that have to do with the spiritual aspects of experience.

In sum, I have sketched four compelling reasons that music educators need to be concerned about social justice, or justice generally, have outlined various perspectives on or types of social justice as they might apply educationally, and have sketched some implications for music education thought and practice. It is evident that these differing types of, or perspectives on, social justice potentially enrich music education while also challenging its thought and practice. None suffices when taken alone. These ambiguities, tensions, and dissonances complicate and trouble taken-for-granted assumptions of music education. It remains to music education policymakers and those committed to its work to navigate this terrain in ways that make sense in their particular situations. Together, these theoretical and practical initiatives can help secure more just practices of music education.

References

Adler, M. J. (1982). *The paideia proposal: An educational manifesto.* New York: Collier Books, Macmillan.

Adler, M. J. (1983). *Paideia problems and possibilities: A consideration of questions raised by* The paideia proposal. New York: Collier Books, Macmillan.

Adler, M. J. (1984). *The paideia program: An educational syllabus. Essays by the Paideia Group.* New York: Collier Books, Macmillan.

Aguilar, C. (2011, April). *The development and application of a conceptual model for the analysis of policy recommendations for music education in the United States* (Unpublished doctoral dissertation, Indiana University, Bloomington).

Allingham, M. (2014a). *Distributive justice.* London: Routledge.

Allingham, M. (2014b). Distributive justice. *The internet encyclopedia of philosophy,* ISSN: 2161-0002. Retrieved from http://www.iep.utm.edu/.

Allsup, R. E. (2007). Editorial. *Music Education Research, 9*(2), 167–168.

Allsup, R. E., & Benedict, C. (2008). The problems of band: An inquiry into the future of instrumental music education. *Philosophy of Music Education Review, 16*(2), 156–173.

Allsup, R. E., & Westerlund, H. (2012). Methods and situational ethics in music education. *Action, Criticism, and Theory for Music Education, 11*(1), 124–148.

Apple, M. W. (2000). *Official knowledge: Democratic education in a conservative age* (2nd ed.). New York: Routledge.

Aquinas, T. (2013–2014). *Summa theologica: Selected questions on law and justice.* Lonang Institute. Retrieved from http://www.lonang.com/exlibris/aquinas/sum22061.htm.

Aristotle. (2014). *Nicomachean ethics* (W. D. Ross, Trans.). The internet classics archive. Retrieved from http://classics.mit.edu/Aristotle/nicomachaen.5.v.html.

Arnstine, D. (1995). *Democracy and the arts of schooling.* Albany: State University of New York.

Benedict, C., & Schmidt, P. K. (2007). From whence justice? Interrogating the improbable in music education. *Action, Criticism, and Theory for Music Education, 6*(4), 21–42.

Benhabib, S. (2002). *The claims of culture: Equality and diversity in the global era.* Princeton, NJ: Princeton University Press.

Berlin, I. (1990). *The crooked timber of humanity: Chapters in the history of ideas.* (H. Hardy, Ed.). Princeton, NJ: Princeton University Press.

Blakeslee, M. (Ed.). (1994). *National standards for arts education: What every young American should know and be able to do in the arts.* Reston, VA: Music Educators National Conference.

Bowman, W. D. (2007). Who's asking? (Who's answering?): Theorizing social justice in music education. *Action, Criticism, and Theory for Music Education, 6*(4), 1–20.

Braithwaite, J. (1989). *Crime, shame and reintegration.* Cambridge: Cambridge University Press.

Burkholder, J. P., Grout, D. J., & Palisca, C. V. (2010). *A history of Western music* (8th ed.). New York: W. W. Norton.

Cardany, A. B. (2013). General music and the common core: A brief discussion. *General Music Today, 27*(1), 35–39.

Colwell, Richard. (2014). Response to David Elliott's "Music education as/for artistic citizenship." *Philosophy of Music Education Review, 22*(1), 105–108.

Czikszentmihalyi, M. (1990). *Flow: The psychology of optimal experience.* New York: Harper and Row.

De Gruchy, J. W. (2002). *Reconciliation: Restoring justice.* Minneapolis, MN: Fortress, 2002.

Dewey, J. ([1916]1944). *Democracy and education: An introduction to the philosophy of education.* New York: Macmillan.

Dewey, J. ([1934]1979). *Art as experience.* Reprinted, New York: Paragon Books.

Dewey, J. ([1927]1954). *The public and its problems.* Reprinted, Denver, CO: Alan Swallow.

Elliott, D. J. (1995). *Music matters: A new philosophy of music education.* New York: Oxford University Press.

Elliott, D. J. (2012). Another perspective: Music education as/for artistic citizenship. *Music Educators Journal, 99*(1), 21–27.

Elliott, David J. (2013). *Music matters: A praxial philosophy of music education* (2nd ed.). New York: Oxford University Press.

Establishing identity: LGBT studies and music education. (2010, May). University of Illinois, School of Music, Urbana, IL. Electronic conference proceedings. *Bulletin of the Council for Research in Music Education.* Retrieved from http://bcrme.press.illinois.edu/proceedings/Establishing_Identity/.

Fowler, C. (1996). *Strong arts, strong schools: The promising potential and shortsighted disregard of the arts in American schooling.* New York: Oxford University Press.

Freire, P. (1990). *Pedagogy of the oppressed* (M. B. Ramos, Trans.). New York: Continuum.

Freire, P. (1994). *Pedagogy of hope: Reliving* Pedagogy of the oppressed (R. R. Barr, Trans.). New York: Continuum.

Gaita, R. (2000). *A common humanity: Thinking about love and truth and justice* (2nd ed.). London: Routledge.

Gilligan, C. (1982). *In a different voice.* Cambridge, MA: Harvard University Press.

Gingell, J. (2014). *Education and the common good: Essays in honor of Robin Barrow.* New York: Routledge.

Giroux, H. A. ([1992]1993). *Border crossings: Cultural workers and the politics of education.* Reprinted, New York: Routledge.

Gomberg, P. (2007). *How to make opportunity equal: Race and contributive justice.* New York: Wiley.

Gould, E. (2005). Nomadic turns: Epistemology, experience, and women university band directors. *Philosophy of Music Education Review, 13*(2), 147–164.

Gould, E. (2011). Feminist imperative(s) in music and education: Philosophy, theory, or what matters most. *Educational Philosophy and Theory, 43*(2): 130–147. doi: 10.1111/j.1469-5812.2008.00424.x.

Govier, T. (2006). *Taking wrongs seriously.* Amherst, MA: Humanity Books.

Greene, M. (1988). *The dialectic of freedom.* New York: Teachers College Press.

Greene, M. (1995). *Releasing the imagination: Essays on education, the arts, and social change.* San Francisco, CA: Jossey-Bass.

Heimonen, M. (2002). *Music education and law: Regulation as an instrument.* Helsinki, Finland: Sibelius Academy, *Studia Musica, 17.*

Heimonen, M. (2006). Justifying the right to music education. *Philosophy of Music Education Review, 14*(2), 119–141.

Highet, G. ([1950]1955). *The art of teaching.* Reprinted, New York: Vintage Books.

Hirsch, E. D., Jr. (1987). *Cultural literacy: What every American needs to know.* Boston, MA: Houghton Mifflin.

Jaeger, W. (1943–1945). *Paideia: The ideals of Greek culture* (G. Highet, Trans.). 3 vols. (2nd ed.). New York: Oxford University Press.

Jorgensen, E. R. (1993). Religious music in education. *Philosophy of Music Education Review, 1*(2), 103–114.

Jorgensen, E. R. (1997). *In search of music education.* Urbana: University of Illinois Press.

Jorgensen, E. R. (2002). The aims of music education: A preliminary excursion. *Journal of Aesthetic Education, 36*(1), 31–49.

Jorgensen, E. R. (2003). *Transforming music education.* Bloomington: Indiana University Press.

Jorgensen, E. R. (2004). *Pax Americana* and the world of music education. *Journal of Aesthetic Education, 3* (3), 1–18.

Jorgensen, E. R. (2007). Concerning justice and music education. *Music Education Research, 9*(2), 169–189. doi: 10.1080/14613800701411731.

Jorgensen, E. R. (2008). *The art of teaching music.* Bloomington: Indiana University Press.

Jorgensen, E. R. (2011a). *Pictures of music education.* Bloomington: Indiana University Press.

Jorgensen, E. R. (2011b). How can music education be religious? *Philosophy of Music Education Review, 19*(2), 155–163.

Kant, I. ([1784]1923). Idee zu einer allgemeinem geschichte in weltbügerlicher absicht (1784). In *Kant's gesammelte schriften,* vol. 8. Berlin: Walter de Gruyter.

Kant, I. (1971). Justice and punishment (W. Hastie, Trans.). In G. Ezorsky (Ed.), *Philosophical perspectives on punishment* (pp. 102–106). Albany: State University of New York Press.

Koza, J. E. (2005). A response to Elizabeth Gould, Nomadic turns: Epistemology, experience, and women university band directors. *Philosophy of Music Education Review, 13*(2): 147–164.

Kozol, J. (2005). *The shame of the nation: The restoration of apartheid schooling in America.* New York: Crown Publishers.

Levine, D. M., & Bane, M. J. (1975). *The "inequality" controversy: Schooling and distributive justice.* New York: Basic Books.

Mill, J. S. ([1863]2001). *Utilitarianism.* Reprinted, London: Electric Book Co. Retrieved from www.elecbook.com.

Maslow, A. H. (1943). A theory of human motivation. *Psychological Review, 50*(4), 370–396. doi: 10.1037/h0054346.

Maslow, A. H. (1968). Music, education, and peak experiences. In R. A. Choate (Ed.), *Documentary report of the Tanglewood Symposium* (pp. 70–73). Washington, DC: Music Educators National Conference.

Morgan, W. J., & Guilherme, A. (2014). *Buber and education: Dialogue as conflict resolution.* New York: Routledge.

Mursell, J. L. (1934). *Human values in music education.* New York: Silver Burdett.

National Commission on Music Education. (1991). *Growing up complete: The imperative for music education: The report of the National Commission on Music Education.* Reston, VA: Music Educators National Conference.

Noddings, N. (1982). *Caring: A feminine approach to ethics and moral education.* Berkeley: University of California Press.

Nussbaum, M. C. (1995). *Poetic justice: The literary imagination and public life.* Boston: Beacon Press.

Nussbaum, M. C. (1997). *Cultivating humanity: A classical defense of reform in liberal education.* Cambridge, MA: Harvard University Press.

Palmer, P. J. (1998). *Courage to teach: Exploring the inner landscape of a teacher's life.* San Francisco, CA: Jossey-Bass.

Perrine, W. (2013). Religious music and free speech: Philosophical issues in Nurre v. Whitehead. *Philosophy of Music Education Review, 21*(2), 178–196.

Peters, R. S. (1966). *Ethics and education.* London: George Allen and Unwin.

Plato. (1993). *Republic* (R. Waterfield, Trans.). Oxford: Oxford University Press.

Porter, A., McMaken, J., Hwang, J., & Yang, R. (2011). Common core standards: The new U.S. intended curriculum. *Educational Researcher, 40*(3), 103–116.

Rainbow, B., & Cox, G. (2006). *Music in educational thought and practice: A survey from 800 BC.* Woodbridge, UK: Boydell Press.

Rawls, J. (1971). *A theory of justice.* Cambridge, MA: Belknap Press of Harvard University Press.

Rawls, J. (1999a). *A theory of justice* (rev. ed.). Cambridge, MA: Belknap Press of Harvard University Press.

Rawls, J. (1999b). *The law of peoples with "The idea of public reason revisited."* Cambridge, MA: Harvard University Press.

Sayer, A. (2009, January). Contributive justice and meaningful work. *Res Publica, 15,* 1–16. doi: 10.1007/s11158-008-9077.

Tan, L. (2012). *Towards a transcultural philosophy of instrumental music education* (Unpublished doctoral dissertation). Indiana University, Bloomington.

Tillich P. (1986). Art and ultimate reality. In D. Apostolos-Cappadona (Ed.) *Art, creativity, and the sacred* (pp. 219–235). New York: Crossroad.

United Nations General Assembly. (1989, 12 December). *Convention on the rights of the child.* Document A/RES/44/25. Retrieved from http://www.cirp.org/library/ethics/UN-convention/.

US Congress. (1776, July 4). *Declaration of independence.* Retrieved from http://www.archives.gov/exhibits/charters/declaration_transcript.html.

Väkevä, L., & Westerlund, H. (2007). The method of democracy in music education. *Action, Criticism, and Theory for Music Education, 6*(4), 96–108.

Wellesz, E. (Ed.). (1969). *Ancient and oriental music. New Oxford history of music,* vol. 1. London: Oxford University Press.

Westerlund, H. (2002). *Bridging experience, action, and culture in music education.* Helsinki, Finland: Sibelius Academy, *Studia Musica, 16.*

Woodbridge, W. C. (1831). *A lecture on vocal music as a branch of common education. Delivered in the Representatives' Hall, Boston, August 24, 1830.* Boston: Hilliard, Gray, Little, and Wilkins.

Woodford, P. (2005) *Democracy and music education: Liberalism, ethics, and the politics of practice.* Bloomington: Indiana University Press.

Woodford, P. (2014). The eclipse of the public: A response to David Elliott's "Music education as/for artistic citizenship." *Philosophy of Music Education Review, 22*(1), 22–37.

CHAPTER 2

UNDERSTANDING SOCIAL JUSTICE FROM THE PERSPECTIVE OF MUSIC EDUCATION HISTORY

MARIE MCCARTHY

ISSUES of social justice in contemporary music education can be informed in important ways when examined from a historical perspective. Conversely, historians of music education can benefit from looking at the past, using social justice as a vantage point. A survey of the documented history of music in public education reveals who authored historical narratives and who is represented in such works. It also brings into relief those individuals and groups whose stories remain untold. Saltman (2008) points out that people have struggled over the representation and retelling of history, and these contests over the meanings of the past are inextricably tied to broader material and symbolic struggles, forces, and structures of power (p. 1). Insights gained from historical knowledge can contribute to ongoing discussions about professional history and can create more democratic, equitable, and emancipatory practices in music education, reflecting core values of social justice.

Music education history is created at the confluence of music, a sociocultural phenomenon, and public education, a foundational social institution. As a subject in the school curriculum, music education is powerfully positioned to reproduce values that seek to promote justice in the community and in society at large. Thus, music education history provides a particularly rich site for examining issues of social justice. If one of the tasks of music educators is to educate ourselves and to be concerned about matters of justice (Jorgensen, 2007, p. 173; Vaugeois, 2009, p. 3), then history has an important place in that process, exposing the roots of social injustice and highlighting patterns of oppression over time.

Historical perspectives can provide new vantage points for looking differently at music education legacies, can give voice to people through oral history, and can disrupt canonical narratives of the past. Thus, a more nuanced and complicated story of the past can be developed to expose the existence of multiple and often contradictory interpretations of historical data (Williamson, Rhodes, & Dunson, 2007). Woodford (2012) calls for more overtly political histories of music education that seek to tell us

> not just the "who, what, and when" of educational reforms but also the "why" by identifying and critiquing the ideologies and social agendas of vested interests who would place their own needs above those of children, teachers and the public, or who would assume that they have a monopoly on truth. (p. 97)

Examining the past from such perspectives, and more broadly all perspectives that address issues of social justice, is facilitated by new approaches to historiography. The mainstream historical narrative is challenged by the possibility of multiple narratives created around the stories of those whose voices were not deemed important or worthy enough to be included in the grand narrative. At the same time, there is increased interest in revisiting and revisioning the past, using social and cultural perspectives to infer meaning and draw together threads of cause and effect. There is also a focus on the lives of ordinary citizens and their contributions to social and cultural development. In a sense, historiography is experiencing its own renewal that is in large part located in the realm of social justice.

Using new approaches to history can open up spaces of inquiry heretofore unexamined and can reveal roots of injustice and practices that were oppressive. At the same time, one must be cautious when using present values to critique actions of the past. The great advocate of emancipatory justice, Maxine Greene, expressed such caution about revisionist educational history, seeing "a doubleness" in it (1973, p. 5). On the one hand, she writes, without the new history "we might not have begun looking at the connections between schools and politics, education and social stratification, endemic racism" (p. 6). At the same time, she found questionable the oversimplification of social control where all individuals are perceived as malleable and passive, with little said about the different ways they internalize control, experience the influences of community, or order their life worlds.

Care must be taken when critiquing the past through the lens of social justice, taking into consideration Greene's observations, among others. It is important to critique past events and actions in the context of what constituted public good at that time, and to avoid interpreting human motivation and actions in the name of labeling actions and events to fit contemporary discourse in social justice. For example, examining the content and viewpoint of E. B. Birge's (1928) first history of public school music must be done considering the context of the 1920s. Rather than critiquing Birge for the many omissions—women in music education, music education in segregated schools, music education for the disabled—it is more instructive to ask: Who or what inspired him to document the history of public school music? What social and political ideologies and values framed his outlook? What sources did he access? The goal is to bring a sensitive ear and empathetic eye to the words and actions of past generations of music educators and those who penned the story of music education through the decades.

The overall purpose of this chapter is twofold: first, to examine historical narratives of American music education from the perspective of social justice in its changing meanings and manifestations since music entered public education in the United States in the 1830s; and second, to offer recommendations for researching music education history and for teaching music and music education history. The chapter originates in these questions: How is social justice reflected in narratives of American music education history? What was the language used to advocate social justice in each era? In what ways did music educators respond to policies that sought to achieve equality and social justice in education? Did the profession offer an alternative narrative to contest injustice of any form? What journey has the profession taken to arrive at a lively discourse in social justice in contemporary times? How can historical research and the teaching of history advance the cause and nurture the practice of social justice in music education? The chapter is developed as follows: a conceptual framing of social justice is presented, followed by a narrative of American music education history through the lens of social justice. Implications for researching and teaching music education history from a social justice perspective are identified. The chapter closes with reflections on social justice from a historical perspective.

Conceptual Framing

The topic of social justice has a history within education. Ayers, Quinn, and Stovall (2008b) state that "education for social justice is the root of teaching and schooling in a democratic society, the rock upon which we build Democracy" (p. xiv). Classical ideals of social justice can be traced back to Plato's *Republic*, the first in-depth treatment of justice and education (Boyles, Carusi, & Attick, 2008, p. 31). However, theorizing about justice is a distinctively modern enterprise (Miller, 1999) that emerged in the late eighteenth century as the child of the industrial and French revolutions (Jackson, 2005). The phrase "social justice" itself was introduced into political discourse from the late nineteenth century onward. As framed in contemporary discourse, the concept implies that schools and society are, and always have been, replete with injustice. Thus, public education is seen as a critical site for changing that reality and for engaging individuals as "agents for social change in a participatory democracy" (Boyles, Carusi, & Attick, 2008, p. 30).

Serving the good of the individual and the common good of society simultaneously creates a tension that is central to understanding social justice in public education. Greene (1973) saw this tension as irreducible since education takes place "at the intersection where the demands for social order and the demands for autonomy conflict," and thus it must proceed through and by means of the tension (p. 9). Ayers, Quinn, and Stovall (2008a) describe the contradictory nature of this tension:

> The ideal of education as humanization—an enterprise in which opportunities and resources are organized to overcome embedded and historical injustices and to allow everyone to realize herself or himself in the full participation in political, social, cultural, and economic life—stands in direct contradiction to the demands of a system that objectifies everyone and enforces the acquiescence of each to the demands of the corporate body. (p. 727)

Historical narratives of music in public education shed light on the interaction between the needs of the individual and those of the common good. Schools, as state-sponsored institutions, are expected to inculcate and model the citizenship values of the state (Mantie, 2009, p. 97). Educational agendas focused on promoting national identity and citizenship are often couched in the language of social justice. Vaugeois (2009) states that looking critically at stories of nationhood is important for developing an understanding of social justice. Mantie (2009) goes so far as to suggest that how we evaluate justice in the sense of social justice is "a direct reflection of how we conceive of our political associations as a nation state" (p. 96).

Citizenship and nationhood are recurring themes in the history of music education internationally. Their meanings differ from one era to another, at times rationalized on the basis of social cohesion and social equilibrium, or patriotism in wartime, or national identity, or artistic citizenship as a right for all students (Elliott, 2012; McCarthy, 2011, 2014).

The ways in which social justice is framed theoretically can form the basis for examining it historically. For the purpose of this chapter, I draw on three contemporary approaches to explaining social justice in education contexts: distributive, cultural, and emancipatory justice. Distributive justice refers to the morally equitable distribution of goods in education, cultural justice to the absence of both cultural domination and marginalization of cultural groups, and emancipatory justice to that which seeks to free people from oppression and grant them the full participation in decisions that affect their lives (Boyles, Carusi, & Attick, 2008; Furman, 2012; Rizvi, 2008).

Distributive justice is fundamental to social justice because of the importance of the equitable distribution of resources and material goods in education. However, scholars have noted that, as a singular paradigm, it has limitations. Rizvi (2008) argues that it is inadequate in fully accounting for nonmaterial resources such as respect, recognition, rights, opportunities, and power, because injustice can also be rooted in social patterns of representations, interpretation, and communication (p. 92). When cultural and emancipatory forms of justice are implemented, they can account for these nonmaterial resources.

Similarly, Boyles, Carusi, and Attick (2008) note that distributive justice can emphasize the allocation of goods at the expense of less quantifiable qualities such as virtues, actions, and ideas, "each of which comprise in part the very 'good' social justice seeks to attain" (p. 38). Furthermore, the authors argue, the emancipatory emphasis found in social justice that seeks to free people from oppression can be absent from the egalitarian concept of distributive justice (p. 38). Rizvi (2008) also notes that the distributive paradigm is no longer sufficient to capture the complexities of global interconnectivity and interdependence, on the one hand, and of contemporary identity politics, on the other. Thus, all forms of justice—distributive, cultural, and emancipatory—must operate in tandem when attempting to bring about social change by addressing social injustice in schools and the greater community (Boyles, Carusi, & Attick, 2008, p. 40).

The three forms of justice described above, aimed at nurturing practices of social justice, can be related to sociological theories of education, specifically functionalism and critical theory. Functionalist approaches operate using top-down approaches to education with a macro perspective in which social justice is explained using principles of equity involving access, equal outcomes, social cohesion, or citizenship. Approaches to social justice that draw on critical theories focus on challenging the effects of injustice and promoting emancipation in education. They are viewed from a more bottom-up micro perspective of actions that impact individuals' lives in time and place. The goal is to undo structures that "produce raced and gendered oppressions and systematic poverty" (Vaugeois, 2009, p. 3). For example, Ayers, Quinn, and Stovall (2008b) identify an aspect of social justice that is particularly relevant to historical study, that is, social literacy, where individuals become aware of their identities and how history is implicated in the ways those identities are formed and lives are negotiated (p. xiv).

While historical research cannot undo structures that produced raced and gendered oppressions and systematic poverty, it can expose the roots and impact of such structures in education, and explain how efforts to address injustice were framed and implemented in different eras. Historical work brings to the surface the sheer complexity of social justice in the context of music education. For example, one group can advocate a program of social justice that another group may experience as oppressive. In the nineteenth century, the white middle class who guided the course of music in Western and colonial education advocated music for its civilizing influence on all races and social classes; in retrospect, that same motivation can be interpreted as imperialist for the majority who were seen to benefit from it. Using principles of social justice in conjunction with social theories, I examine music education history developmentally from the following perspectives—music education as a sociocultural good, a national asset, a human right, a sociopolitical good, and a social responsibility.

A Narrative of American Music Education History Through the Lens of Social Justice

Music Education as a Sociocultural Good

Music entered a system of public education in the United States that was flawed in terms of its assumptions of social justice. Horace Mann (1848) marketed the common school by focusing on education as "the great equalizer of the conditions of men—the great balance wheel of the social machinery" (p. 87, cited in Williamson, Rhodes, & Dunson, 2007, p. 215). Even in the mid-1800s, the idea of a "public" education system for all young people meant specifically all white young people, and the curriculum was rooted in the common experiences and values of nineteenth-century life (Boyles, Carusi, & Attick, 2008). These experiences and values were seen as an avenue toward social justice, as they would eventually eliminate inequity among socioeconomic classes.

When music was placed within this system, it was advocated as a subject that had physical, intellectual, and moral benefits. The rationale was based on a philosophy of social equality. All students would participate in singing, which would instill values for participation in a civilized society and elevate the tastes of working-class people. Music education, then, would contribute to the development of better citizens. There were at least two narratives of social justice at work in this philosophy—a salvationist narrative, and one of cultural imperialism.

A salvationist narrative, Vaugeois (2009) argues, is built on the notion of rescuing Others, in this case the poor and the illiterate who would be rescued by schooling to follow the pathway of upward social mobility. The narrative of cultural imperialism is related to the salvationist view of education in that the culture of the dominant group is established as the norm, and often without noticing it, the dominant group projects its culture as representative of humanity. In the process, the perspectives of other groups are rendered invisible and their identity perceived as the Other (Young, 2013). In the context of American music education in the nineteenth century, the salvationist narrative was visible in bringing music to the masses of white people, regardless of social class. The cultural imperialist approach was evident in the exclusive emphasis on European music and its pedagogical practices in the curriculum. The ways of music making popular among the poor or marginalized groups were not deemed as appropriate for inclusion in the school curriculum—for example, shape notes as a form of music literacy or the music that students learned informally as part of their everyday lives.

The nationalization of music education took root in an experiment at the Hawes School in Boston when Lowell Mason offered free vocal music instruction during the 1837–1838 school year. Its success led to the spread of school music programs. Such programs were documented in the official records of white schools, and the news media of their communities, facilitating the later writing of a historical narrative of music education for the period. By 1900, most black children continued to be educated in segregated schools that received little support from the education establishment (Boyles, Carusi, & Attick, 2008, p. 36). Stories of the transmission of music in black and other minority communities in that period are yet to find their place in the landscapes of music education history and to transform its canons.

Music Education as a National Asset

In the new twentieth century, progressive educators were vocal in their critique of the role of education in maintaining social injustices and the system's lack of attention to social justice (Boyles, Carusi, & Attick, 2008, pp. 34–35). The focus in some educational discourse shifted from top-down ideals of equity to a belief that "the creation of a just society requires the active participation of all society's members in the democratic process" (Boyles, Carusi, & Attick, 2008, p. 35). According to John Dewey (1923), schools should be living, active communities that deliberated over issues relating to social inequality. They should serve as a means of developing a social consciousness and social ideals in children. The Music Supervisors National Conference (MSNC), founded in 1907, made valiant efforts between 1914 and the end of the 1920s to reach out to school communities to develop a culture of singing and to foster school-community relationships. Such activity was aligned with Dewey's philosophy of schooling and contained the seeds of cultural and emancipatory social justice. However, it was also connected with other prevailing narratives of social development and nationality, which came to dominate education.

In the same time period, the influx of new immigrants demanded that the school system accommodate ethnically diverse students in unprecedented ways. The assimilation of immigrants into mainstream culture, often articulated as the melting pot theory, emerged as a primary goal of schooling. Émile Durkheim, a founding figure in the field of sociology, wrote: "Society can survive only if there exists among its members a sufficient degree of homogeneity; education perpetuates and reinforces this homogeneity by fixing in the child, from the beginning, the essential similarities that social life demands (Durkheim, 1972, p. 203). Durkheim's functionalist view of education was aligned with the social ideal of Americanization, in which all immigrants became nationalized through learning the language, participating in national holidays and celebrations, attending public schools, and learning the values of citizenship.

In public-school music education, as Volk (1998) points out, music was seen as an activity that could unite people of different ethnic backgrounds, social classes, and religious beliefs through singing and playing instruments together, thus instilling ideals of American nationality. Music teachers did their part to assimilate immigrants through singing patriotic songs and folk songs of various western European countries beyond the German canon, which had dominated school music up to that point (pp. 40–44). The use of international folk songs to achieve nationalist goals was well intentioned. However, it begs the question: Whose histories were represented in the folk songs transmitted? How were folk songs appropriated for use in public school? What connections were made between "music of foreign lands" and the realities of cultural pluralism in school communities? The focus was less on the identity of individual students in their communities and more on the achievement of cultural homogeneity and national citizenship through music education.

The underlying principles of functionalist social theory were evident in the way education was structured and implemented. This was not limited to the goals of American nationalism that focused on homogeneity and distributive justice alone. Other educational practices of the time were also questionable when set in the context of social justice. The science of individual and group differences in intelligence and ability that emerged in the early twentieth century bolstered racial rankings and provided "scientific proof" of intellectual and moral variance between racial and ethnic groups (Williamson, Rhodes, & Dunson, 2007). The educational norms of intelligence testing and ranking and profiling influenced thinking in music education, evident in the publication of tests of music talent and ability.

In sum, the direction of music in education aligned with the dominant functionalist social theory. Two world wars intensified the functionalist approach to education and the need to unite peoples in time of war (McCarthy, 1993, 1995). The powerful metaphor of music as an international language served as a way to justify music in education, particularly in the early and middle decades of the twentieth century. The universal values of music were seen to unite peoples and nations in the name of international harmony, justice, and peace (McCarthy, 2004).

The climate of war and the educational goals of nationality and citizenship in the first four decades of the century influenced the direction of music and maintained the narrative of music education as a national asset.

Music Education as a Human Right

The goal of "Music for Every Child, Every Child for Music," presented by MSNC in 1923, reflected the educational philosophy of child-centered education of the early twentieth century and the principles of democratic education. Thus, it can be interpreted as an effort to include all children in music instruction while advocating the value of music in education. The further development of a democratic approach to music in public education became visible again in post–World War II America when the rhetoric of war and nationalism shifted to one of freedom, justice, and peace. These principles were set forth in the Universal Declaration of Human Rights, which was adopted by the General Assembly of the United Nations in December 1948. In response, MENC (formerly MSNC) applied certain aspects of the Declaration to music education and issued a six-article document, "The Child's Bill of Rights in Music," in March 1950 (Morgan, 1955, pp. 298–299).

A focus on the individual's right to a music education was also evident in other documents of the 1950s. When Lilla Belle Pitts wrote an open letter to music educators in 1957, she focused on the profession's responsibility to individuals: "*We believe* that we can make *Music in American Life* a living reality of the great American dream—the inalienable right of every human being to the pursuit of happiness" (Pitts, 1957, p. 7). Again, in 1958, the report of the MENC Study Committee on Purposes and Goals of Music Education focused on the individual: "everyone is accorded the right and the obligation to improve American culture by improving himself or herself" (Pitts, 1958, p. 19). If the intention was to develop "American culture" in all its manifestations and contexts, however, then the curriculum did not reflect such intention. Whose cultures were represented? Whose cultures were to be developed through music education? The divisions between school music and music in the culture at large were clear, thus limiting the ways in which students could develop skills in school that would carry over into the diverse musical practices that were alive in their communities and in popular culture. In sum, while the ideal of music as a human right entered the narrative of music education between the 1920s and 1960s, its implementation was limited to distributive justice. The right to a music education in public education was but a first step in developing each child's musical potential, framed in the context of personal and family history, identity, and values.

Music Education as a Sociopolitical Good

Metaphors that projected music as transcending cultural differences and as building international harmony began to fall out of favor with the rise of multiculturalism in the transformative and tumultuous decade of the 1960s. The notion that universal meanings were somehow embedded in music was rejected, and the cultural significances and contextual meanings of music took center stage. New metaphors such as mosaic, patchwork quilt, or kaleidoscope took the place of the "melting pot" to visualize the complex makeup of cultural groups and the dynamic nature of music cultures. Such metaphors captured the ever-evolving relationships between the identities of individuals, social and cultural groups, and nations in a globalized world.

The relationship between school, music, and society was to be reimagined in the 1960s, a time of profound social change. As the dominant social theory in education, functionalism was no longer adequate to accommodate the principles of a democratic system of education. Social conflict theory and critical theory provided alternatives to address the inequalities underpinning educational practices. Their introduction into the discourse of music education was gradual in the later decades of the century, reflecting a move from distributive and representative justice to cultural and, more recently, emancipatory justice. Efforts to expand curricular choices and repertoire selections to include diverse peoples and cultures were evident from the 1970s forward, framed in the context of multiculturalism.

A more lateral definition of music as a system of different but equally worthwhile traditions and practices began to transform views of and approaches to curricular music. However, the equal representation of peoples through their music was but a first step in understanding the meanings of music in the lives of diverse peoples. Moving from distributive justice to cultural justice demanded changes to pedagogy as well—finding ways to integrate voices of the Other into the curricular canon already in place, preparing teachers to teach from a place of cultural and musical diversity, and honoring the musical and social preferences of students through curricular experiences.

Some scholars question the limits of multiculturalism as an educational philosophy, and return to a more functionalist approach to education. Reports from European countries, Canada, and Australia indicate that educators are revisiting multiculturalism in the context of nationality and national identity. James Banks (2009b), the great proponent of multiculturalism, reported that citizenship education is being used in nations such as Australia, Canada, and the United Kingdom to promote a new form of assimilation called "social cohesion," originating in concerns about the fracturing of national identity and the maintenance of national unity (p. 3). These concerns are in part a reaction to increasing diversity in nation-states, which is forcing nations to rethink how they can develop civic communities that incorporate the diversity of people and yet have an overarching set of values, ideas, and goals (Banks, 2009a, pp. 306–308). Entwistle ([1999]2000) argues that we should engage in "a detailed discussion of what a healthy, multicultural society needs in order to ensure both justice for the individual immigrant and the necessary social cohesion for citizens to feel connected to each other as contributors to the common good" (p. 14). Jacoby (2004) goes further when he writes that we may need a new understanding of assimilation:

> . . . a definition that makes sense today, in an era of globalization, the internet, identity politics. . . . Just what kind of assimilation is taking place today? What is possible? What is desirable? And how can we reframe the melting-pot vision to make it work for a cosmopolitan, twenty-first century America? (pp. 4–5)

In this century, awareness of the social responsibility of educators to the individual has competed for attention with the need to find a larger, shared narrative focused on social cohesion and the common good.

Music Education as a Social Responsibility

The period of representative justice in the late twentieth century was dominated by a politics of identity in education. The content of educational textbooks and repertoire lists changed to include the stories and music of marginalized groups; musical diversity was highlighted as a performance goal in school programs; and research publications reflected a new focus on the experiences and contributions of individuals from underrepresented groups. However, representation alone is not sufficient in achieving the vision of emancipatory social justice in which individuals have "a sense of their own agency as well as a sense of social responsibility toward and with others, their society, and the broader world in which we live" (Bell, 2013, p. 21).

Issues of social justice must also be embraced in pedagogical practices and the value systems that underlie such practices (Allsup & Shieh, 2012). Discourses in music education are beginning to approach deeper spaces of social justice beyond representation. A more humanistic view of music teaching and learning that emphasizes the experiences of individual students within groups is evident in both research and practice-based literature. For example, the June 2012 issue of the *Music Educators Journal* posed the question: "Music for All . . .?" on its front cover. Authors responded with several articles on music and justice viewed through the lens of social class, culturally responsive pedagogy, access, and music in prisons. Related articles in other recent issues of the journal on gender and sexual orientation (Bergonzi, 2009; Taylor, 2011) and social class (Hoffman, 2013), as well as the September 2012 issue devoted to disability, attest to a strong focus on the social and ethical responsibility of music educators to all students.

The MayDay Group, an international think tank in music education founded in 1993, has addressed issues of social justice in several forums, and specifically in the December 2007 issue of its online journal, *Action, Criticism and Theory*. Two organizations, Gender Research in Music Education and the Gender and Sexuality Special Research Interest Group of the National Association for Music Education, have served in notable ways to advocate for and to study issues related to gender and sexuality in music teaching and learning.

Embedded in efforts to advance the vision of emancipatory justice is a renewed focus on distributive justice aimed at underserved populations. Efforts to ameliorate the lives of socially disadvantaged students and to provide an opportunity for upward social mobility and cultural enrichment have been a hallmark of public education since its roots in the early nineteenth century. In Chapter 36 of this Handbook, Eric Shieh presents the reader with a critique of El Sistema, the Venezuelan youth orchestra program, as a social program. He exposes the various social agendas propelling the evolution of the program—social, economic, political, and cultural—and ends on a note of hope regarding its potential growth "as a force for valuable social, and simultaneously, musical transformation." This case study illustrates how a social program focused on music must be rooted in a broad social policy, and how it must constantly re-evaluate the direction and impact of the program on its participants, their communities, and society at large.

Unlike the national political agenda underpinning El Sistema, there is a marked absence of reference to the nation and nationalism in contemporary music education discourse in the United States. Recent documents such as the *Strategic Plan 2011–2016* of the National Association for Music Education reflect values that emphasize well-being, both personal and collective. This is expressed in a focus on "the joy and power that music education brings in uplifting the human spirit and fostering the well-being of society," and the strength that comes from "working together with stakeholders . . . to promote music, music education, and policies that build a better society for all" (National Association for Music Education, 2012, p. 4).

Music Education History and Social Justice

I have examined music education history since the introduction of music into US public education from the perspectives of music education as a sociocultural good, a national asset, a human right, a sociopolitical good, and a social responsibility. If issues of justice can be captured along the continuum from the good of the individual to the good of society or the common good, the music education profession has responded primarily to the call of the common good, evident in responses to sociopolitical ideologies such as assimilation, social cohesion, patriotism, and nationalism. As such, music was viewed as a national asset, and a sociocultural and sociopolitical good. The very nature of its underlying pedagogical structures, focused primarily on ensemble culture at the secondary level, aligned well with the ideals of social ordering and social cohesion. Narratives of individual rights to a music education and the need to acknowledge the diversity of individuals' musical needs and interests were slowly integrated into the discourse of education in the latter half of the twentieth century. This movement coincided with the incorporation of critical theory into expanding paradigms of music education. And with this expansion of consciousness came an ethical and moral sense of responsibility to all students, regardless of social class, age, race, ability, or sexual orientation.

The historical evolution of music education viewed through the lens of social justice sheds light on the ways that music was advocated in the name of justice—from its power to provide a sociocultural good to maintain social control, to contribute to sociopolitical ordering, to build international harmony among nations, to represent the interests of marginalized groups, and to enrich the lives of youth from lower socioeconomic or underserved populations.

Researching and Teaching Music and Music Education History from a Social Justice Perspective

An examination of the history of music education in the public schools reveals a dominant narrative around the development of public school music as represented in the interests and values of the dominant social group. Several narratives of music education are not yet told, and others are constructed from narrow ideological foundations. In other words, a study of music education historiography problematizes professional history itself. Hegemonies are perpetuated through the appropriation of historical narratives. Thus, historians assume a critical role in opening a dialogue that challenges past practices and ultimately changes music educators' relationship to their past and, thus, their view of the present and hope for the future.

As early as 1980, Finkelstein (1980) addressed the need for a richer, more comprehensive, and sophisticated history of education, one that is

> ... attentive to the aspirations of all groups in American society. ... a history that is also sensitive to public action when it undermines the capacity of individuals and groups to transmit their own values, create their own meanings, and define their own communities. (p. 122)

Hebert (2009) critiques historical research from the vantage point of documented musical traditions and practices. He argues that what is "sorely needed is an actual book-length history of American music education that is truly inclusive in terms of both culture and genre, especially popular music traditions associated with African-American heritage" (p. 177). Likewise, Woodford (2012) calls for "alternative and radical histories" that challenge the roots of conventional music education policies and practices while presenting perspectives that cause teachers and students to examine their own assumptions. Only then can the profession confront and address issues of social justice.

In music education history, scholars have been slow to assume leadership in revisiting the past to uncover new meanings around issues of social justice, to examine canons and "truths" from multiple vantage points, to question whose voices have been included and whose remain silent, to evaluate what is remembered and how and why, and to complicate historical interpretations with competing and even contradictory narratives. Cox (2002) and McCarthy (2012, 2013) have identified an agenda to expand the scope and methodology of historical research. In relation to social justice, it includes histories of the transmission of music in the schools and communities of African Americans and other minority populations, histories of disability and gender in music education, critiques of the impact of colonialism on music pedagogy, exposition of the life histories of music teachers, and comparison of social justice issues in music education in different countries during the same historical period.

As stated earlier, the methods of the new history, as well as contemporary technologies used in oral history, contribute in significant ways to approaching historical topics from the perspective of social justice. For example, Vaugeois (2009) suggests that educators explore, together with their students, the life histories of different musical practices. By life histories, she means "the conditions of production of different musics such as available instruments, technologies, legal and institutional structures, as well as physical, social, and economic conditions." In life histories, the researcher also asks "who is and is not present in different forms of music-making, where race, gender and class reside within musical expressions, how different musics are situated in relation to discourses of respectability, degeneracy, emancipation, and virtuosity" (pp. 3–4).[1] Approaching history in this way is not limited to scholars of music education history. It ought to permeate all instances of examining and teaching music and music education history, from elementary to higher education levels.

Findings from historical research need to be presented to the profession at large through teachers' journals and included in textbooks and media produced for music education purposes. As the K–12 music curriculum expands to embrace a more comprehensive range of music-making practices across time and cultures, it behooves the profession to create sensitive and provocative curriculum materials that reflect a socially and morally conscious narrative of music history. Critical classroom discussions based on such materials contain the seeds of action for a socially just school and community, with carryover into lifelong engagement with issues of social justice through and with music.

Students can engage in oral history to gather personally the stories of musical lives. Furman and Gruenewald (2004) describe projects of cultural journalism that engage students in interviewing community members, gathering stories about local traditions, and producing knowledge about local cultural life by publishing articles, journals, and books. The authors continue to say that a critical pedagogy of place demands that local cultural study engage in questions of social and ecological justice (p. 60). What would a critical pedagogy of place look like in a music classroom? How might local narratives of music be studied in a way that exposes possible roots of injustice and hegemony? How might students better understand the various political and social roles of music in their time? What actions might they take to inform the community about a particular practice? How would such work at the local level assist students in approaching music and musical narratives from other times and places?

Junda (2013) provides an exemplary model for approaching the study of history and culture through song. In her curricular approach developed in the course "Sing and Shout! A History of America in Song," she combines the study of American history with the singing of songs that represent critical times, significant events, and unique cultures in our shared past. A primary goal is for students to understand the use of folk songs as a force for social change, as an expression of spirituality, and as a means to build community in the lives of underrepresented populations, thus broadening and enriching their understanding of American history and culture. In a sense, she uses song lyrics as primary source material, a text for examining issues of social justice in historical context.

Similar pathways can be created between "texts" of music history and the experiences of K–12 and college students. Students can re-enact historical musical events and practices to get inside the lived experiences of musicians. They can also be asked to imagine the life of a music teacher in a particular era or in the context of a particular historical event that influenced music education. For example, a preservice or inservice music teacher is asked to create a life history for a music teacher who taught in the 1920s. What was her musical and cultural background? What was the background of her students? How did she interact with them? What music did she bring to them? What assumptions were embedded in that pedagogical practice? Who determined the practice? What evidence of justice and injustice issues can be gleaned from primary sources?

The landscapes of historical knowledge can serve as a foundation for deepening students' knowledge of music as social text, and it can stimulate and provoke questions that highlight issues of injustice. When we argue for the enduring values of a music education, music history approached through the lens of social justice is important work. Such work, in turn, can develop in students a lifelong connection among the ways of music making, the conduct of a humane society, and the vital role of music in creating and sustaining democratic ideals.

CLOSING REFLECTION

I brought a number of questions to this chapter regarding the presence of social justice in narratives of music education history. I presented a perspective that is based on documented professional history, which provides a comprehensive view of certain dominant aspects of the landscape. By examining social justice within the canon of music education history, it becomes clear that there is an acute need to engage with alternative and radical views of music education history. As more of the canvas is studied and revealed in high relief, the images that dominate current historical knowledge will shift in relation to one another. Such work will not only complicate and disrupt established histories but will also provide an invaluable perspective for examining the roots of social justice and injustice in current practices. The past is in the present, and permeates the philosophies and practices of music education.

Greene (1973) argued that education takes place "at the intersection where the demands for social order and the demands for autonomy conflict" and must proceed through and by means of this tension (p. 9). Nasaw (1979) described another tension that is played out in the social arena of public education between "the promise of democracy and the reality of class division" (p. 243). School music education is practiced in contested spaces that embody complex tensions and multiple agendas. In the end, the profession has no choice but to follow its social consciousness and seek to keep open the doors that lead to spaces of democracy and social justice. American poet Walt Whitman reminds us at the conclusion of the poem "Song of the Broad-Axe," from *Leaves of Grass* ([1900]1986, p. 225), to have faith and patience along this most challenging of human journeys, that toward a world of justice and peace for all. He challenges us to keep the ideal before us as we proceed.

> The main shapes arise!
> Shapes of Democracy total, result of centuries
> Shapes ever projecting other shapes,
> Shapes of turbulent manly cities,
> Shapes of the friends and home-givers of the whole earth,
> Shapes bracing the earth and braced with the whole earth.

NOTE

1. Vaugeois (2009) provides a valuable series of questions that can be used to guide the study of musical histories. They are intended to disrupt taken-for-granted versions of social histories (see pp. 9–10).

REFERENCES

Allsup, R., & Shieh, E. (2012). Social justice and music education: The call for a public pedagogy. *Music Educators Journal, 98*, 47–51.

Ayers, W. C., Quinn, T., & Stovall, D. (2008a). Editor's conclusion. In W. C. Ayers, T. Quinn, & D. Stovall (Eds.), *Handbook of social justice in education* (pp. 725–728). New York: Routledge.

Ayers, W. C., Quinn, T., & Stovall, D. (2008b). Preface. In W. C. Ayers, T. Quinn, & D. Stovall (Eds.), *Handbook of social justice in education* (pp. xiii–xv). New York: Routledge.

Banks, J. A. (2009a). Diversity, group identity, and citizenship education in a global age. In J. S. Banks (Ed.), *The Routledge international companion to multicultural education* (pp. 303–322). New York: Routledge.

Banks, J. A. (2009b). Introduction. In J. A. Banks (Ed.), *The Routledge international companion to multicultural education* (pp. 1–5). New York: Routledge.

Bell, L. A. (2013). Theoretical foundations. In M. Adams et al. (Eds.), *Readings for diversity and social justice*, 3rd ed. (pp. 21–26). New York & London: Routledge.

Bergonzi, L. (2009). Sexual orientation and music education: Continuing a tradition. *Music Educators Journal, 96*, 21–25.

Birge, E. B. ([1928]1966). *History of public school music in the United States.* (New and augmented edition). Reston, VA: Music Educators National Conference.

Boyles, D., Carusi, T., & Attick, D. (2008). Historical and critical interpretations of social justice. In W. Ayers, T. Quinn, & D. Stovall (Eds.), *Handbook of social justice in education* (pp. 30–42). New York: Routledge.

Cox, G. (2002). Transforming research in music education history. In R. Colwell & C. Richardson (Eds.), *The new handbook of research on music teaching and learning* (pp. 695–706). New York: Oxford University Press and Music Educators National Conference.

Dewey, J. (1923). The school as a means of developing a social consciousness and social ideals in children. *Journal of Social Forces, 1*(5), 513–517.

Durkheim, E. (1972). *Emile Durkheim: Selected writings* (A. Giddens, Trans.). Cambridge, UK: Cambridge University Press.

Elliott, D. J. (2012). Music education as/for artistic citizenship. *Music Educators Journal, 99*, 21–27.

Entwistle, H. (1999/2000). Educating multicultural citizens: Melting pot or mosaic? *International Journal of Social Education, 14*(2), 1–15.

Finkelstein, B. (1980). Educational history in the pursuit of justice. *Reviews in American History, 8*(1), 122–128.

Furman, G. (2012). Social justice leadership as praxis: Developing capacities through preparation programs. *Educational Administration Quarterly, 48*(2), 191–229.

Furman G. C., & Gruenewald, D. A. (2004). Expanding the landscape of social justice: A critical ecological analysis. *Educational Administration Quarterly, 40*(1), 47–76.

Greene, M. (1973). Identities and contours: An approach to educational history. *Educational Researcher, 2*(4), 5–10.

Hebert, D. G. (2009). Rethinking the historiography of hybrid genres in music education. In V. Kurkela & L. Väkevä (Eds.), *De-canonizing music history* (pp. 163–184). Newcastle upon Tyne, UK: Cambridge Scholars Publishing.

Hoffman, A. R. (2013). Compelling questions about music, education, and socioeconomic status. *Music Educators Journal, 100*, 63–68.

Jackson, B. (2005). The conceptual history of social justice. *Political Studies Review, 3*, 356–373.

Jacoby, T. (2004). Defining assimilation for the 21st century. In T. Jacoby (Ed.), *Reinventing the melting pot: The new immigrants and what it means to be American* (pp. 3–16). New York: Basic Books.

Jorgensen, E. R. (2007). Concerning justice and music education. *Music Education Research, 9*(2), 169–189.

Junda, M. E. (2013). *Sing and Shout!* The study of history and culture through song. Retrieved from   http://symposium.music.org/index.php?option=com_k2&view=item&id=10387:is ing-and-shout-i-the-study-of-history-and-culture-through-song&Itemid=124.

Mantie, R. (2009). Take two aspirins and don't call me in the morning: Why easy prescriptions won't work for social justice. In E. Gould, J. Countryman, C. Morton, & L. Stewart Rose (Eds.), *Exploring social justice: How music education might matter* (pp. 90–104). Waterloo,

ON: Canadian Music Educators' Association/Association Canadienne des musiciens éducateurs.

McCarthy, M. (1993). The birth of internationalism in music education, 1899–1938. *International Journal of Music Education, 21*, 3–15.

McCarthy, M. (1995). *Canticle to Hope*: Widening horizons in international music education, 1939–1953. *International Journal of Music Education, 25*, 38–49.

McCarthy, M. (2004). *Toward a global community: The International Society for Music Education, 1953–2003*. Nedlands, Western Australia: International Society for Music Education.

McCarthy, M. (2011). Music education and narratives of social cohesion: From national melting pot to global community. In J. O'Flynn (Ed.), *Proceedings of the 6th International Symposium on the Sociology of Music Education*, Dublin: St. Patrick's College.

McCarthy, M. (2012). Developments and trends in historical research as reflected in the *Journal of Historical Research in Music Education*, Volumes 21–30 (1999–2009). *Journal of Historical Research in Music Education. 33*(2), 152–171.

McCarthy, M. (2013). Historical inquiry: Getting inside the process. In H. Froehlich & C. Frierson-Campbell (Eds.), *Inquiry in music education: Concepts and methods for the beginning researcher* (pp. 120–143). New York: Routledge.

McCarthy, M. (2014). "We who have the destiny of musical America in our hands": History speaks to us through 100 years of *MEJ. Music Educators Journal, 100*(4), 29–38.

Miller, D. (1999). *Principles of social justice*. Cambridge, MA, & London: Harvard University Press.

Morgan, H. N. (Ed.). (1955). *Music in American education*. Washington, DC: Music Educators National Conference.

Nasaw. D. (1979). *Schooled to order: A social history of public schooling in the United States*. New York: Oxford University Press.

National Association for Music Education. (2012). *Strategic Plan 2011–2016*: National Association for Music Education. *Music Educators Journal, 98*, 4.

Pitts, L. A. (1957). Open letter to music educators from the Chairman of the Golden Anniversary Commission. *Music Educators Journal, 43*, 7.

Pitts, L. A. (1958). Purposes and goals of music education in 1958. *Music Educators Journal, 44*, 19–21.

Rizvi, F. (2008). International perspectives on social justice and education. In W. Ayers, T. Quinn, & D. Stovall (Eds.), *Handbook of social justice in education* (pp. 91–94). New York: Routledge.

Saltman, K. J. (2008). Historical and theoretical perspectives. In W. Ayers, T. Quinn, & D. Stovall (Eds.), *Handbook of social justice in education* (pp. 1–3). New York: Routledge.

Taylor, D. M. (2011). Bullying: What can music teachers do? *Music Educators Journal, 98*(1), 41–44.

Vaugeois, L. C. (2009). Music education as a *practice* of social justice. In E. Gould, J. Countryman, C. Morton, & S. Rose, S. (Eds.), *Exploring social justice: How music education might matter* (pp. 2–22). Waterloo, ON: Canadian Music Educators Association/Association Canadienne des musiciens éducateurs.

Volk, T. M. (1998). *Music, education and multiculturalism: Foundations and principles*. New York; Oxford: Oxford University Press.

Whitman, W. ([1900] 1986). Song of the broad-axe, from *Leaves of Grass* (1900). In F. Murphy (Ed.), *Walt Whitman: The complete poems*. (p. 225). London: Penguin Books.

Williamson, J. A., Rhodes, L., & Dunson, M. (2007). A selected history of social justice in education. *Review of Research in Education, 31,* 195–224.

Woodford, P. (2012). Music education and social justice: Towards a radical political history and vision. In C. Philpott & G. Spruce (Eds.), *Debates in music teaching* (pp. 85–101). London & New York: Routledge.

Young, I. M. (2013). Five faces of oppression. In M. Adams et al. (Eds.), *Readings for diversity and social justice,* 3rd ed. (pp. 35–45). London & New York: Routledge.

CHAPTER 3

....

THE ETHICS OF POLICY

Why a Social Justice Vision of Music Education
Requires a Commitment to Policy Thought

....

PATRICK SCHMIDT

As a concept and in practice, policy has permeated the deepest recesses of civil society. Policy has played an increasingly significant role in the lives of those who are engaged in education. Yet, regardless of its growing reach and marked presence, policy continues to evoke images of a forbidden or alien environment for music teachers. The policy realm is commonly seen as *above our pay grade*, beyond our duties and responsibilities, and outside the reach of our capacities. But nothing could be further from the truth.

The aim of this chapter is to delineate the need for *policy thought* as a key element of the education and professional life of any teacher, and in particular those charged to educate in and through music. This argument is built upon the ethical imperative of bringing music educators and policy together, in an approximation of sorts that can be attained and sustained by the understanding that policy discourses often organize their own specific rationalities in problematic ways, making particular sets of ideas seem obvious, commonsensical, and "true." Awareness of policy as a field of action and of policy discourses as working "to privilege certain ideas and topics and speakers and exclude others" (Ball, 2009, p. 5) is essential. The bias in this chapter is obvious in two ways: first, it sees policy as a realm of possibilities for educators; second, it sees policy as a complex and adaptable environ, one that needs shedding of traditional strictures. Finally, this chapter offers a framework and rationale to approximate social justice and policy, establishing both as integral parts of the political lives of teachers.

As this Handbook compellingly argues, social justice is a multifaceted endeavor, with complex reach and varied definition. Its purposes are manifold and its practices are deeply contextual, though ethically far-reaching. Social justice's face, while not amorphous, is certainly multiple and ever changing. These are, I will argue, also exacting descriptors of policy, making the link between social justice and policy not only clear but also necessary. The premise is simple: Education is a deeply political process and policy is a critical pathway through which varied and often divergent political discourses are made manifest in practice. Policy is the realm in which vision is constructed and actualized. Therefore, understanding the complexities of policy, becoming skilled in how to think, speak, and act in policy terms is both a necessity in the professional lives of educators and essential to any music educator who considers herself ethically bound to a democratic, critical, and socially just education. Failing to engage with such considerations is to be at the margins of the political process shaping all education.

DEMYSTIFYING POLICY AND RELATING IT TO SOCIAL JUSTICE

While social justice as a construct and ideal has many origins and tributaries—from Aristotelian ethics, to Augustinian morals, to Hobbesian social contract, to Rawlsian legalism, to civil rights activism, and beyond—a modern understanding of social justice is strongly marked by a preoccupation with identity delineations and democratic engagements with equity and access. While in the United States identity politics and democratic practices are deeply ensconced as significant representations of social justice within and outside education, I would like to bring to the reader's attention the fact that contemporary social justice discourse is—directly or indirectly, knowingly or not—enmeshed in both governmentality and power.

It is important to note, then, that policy and social justice are both constantly permeated by questions of authority, deference, and legitimacy. Indeed, said questions often actively play a role in prescribing the normative boundaries of official forms of knowledge, which in turn qualify what is deemed appropriate, deviant, able, immoral, feasible, or utopian. Thus, at the individual and the community levels, policy and social justice thinking are constantly ensnarled in the question of who has voice and who has permission to speak—both in the sense of who is visible and privileged, as well as in the sense of who is allowed to lead, to construct ideas, to institute directives.

This all means that a near radical structural and organizational change of the life of our disciplines within schools would need to be presupposed if establishing music education for social justice is to be required, particularly if we were to focus on significantly unaddressed curricular and pedagogical responses to learner diversity (Booth & Ainscow, 2000). This chapter argues that this radicality requires a pragmatic but conceptually robust and imaginative discourse. In simple (perhaps simplistic) terms, social justice and policy require both structural considerations (with a focus on institutions, economics, and labor, among others) as well as conceptual considerations (with a focus on subjectivity, adaptability, and variegation). This means that the policy-minded educator who also actively pursues a socially just agenda is not, and can no longer be seen, as a contradiction in terms. Consequently, just as social justice must go beyond the classroom, policy thought developed by educators for education must permeate our classrooms. This is a sensible notion with important implications, particularly when balancing the conservative tendencies of institutions and the ever-expanding diversity of the individuals we encounter within our schools.

A key challenge for a more socially just education, then, is the current absence of a policy vernacular built into teachers' formative experiences, and the resulting gap in their understanding of and preparation for policy (Darling-Hammond & Bransford, 2005). Of course, these programmatic problems are met by and amplify numerous external issues, resulting in a state of affairs in which "very often education policy and practice concentrate on the products of learning rather than process of learning" (Liasidou, 2012, p. 19). My response is that an apt and proactive social justice commitment to education must associate itself with policy thinking. Perhaps as significant, teachers must be invested in such a vision and must embody that disposition.

Following Dyson (1999), this chapter suggests such a vision can be approached by marrying two discourses: the discourse of rights, which develops language facilitating an ethical and pedagogical commitment to socially just educational practices and environs, and the discourse of efficacy (not to be misunderstood as mere efficiency), which is concerned with the pragmatics of how mindful and participative policy can change schooling structures in order to facilitate diversity, inclusion, and ultimately social justice. The pathway forward, I suggest, is also twofold: to foster the notion of policy thought in teachers young and old; and to more clearly articulate policy beyond the mystique of legislation and "data crunching," placing it as a constructive, malleable, and even subjective aspect of educational life.

ESTABLISHING POLICY THINKING
AND DISPOSITIONS

The first step in developing policy thought (which here I intend to mean the capacity to understand, speak, and act with a policy frame of mind) relevant to teachers is to demystify the idea that policy is a rarefied arena, equated simply with legislative action, legal jargon, and the realm of "those in power." Policy is embedded in our day-to-day work, is ensconced in the language we use, and is present in the simple enactments we construct in our classrooms. Tangible products such as state standards, legislation such as No Child Left Behind, a US federal mandate placing heavy emphasis on testing, and the rule lists that populate thousands of classrooms are all policy. But policy must also be understood as a process, established in and by, for example, the (mis)communication between teachers and principals, the tensions in curricular or professional development, or the political apportioning and tension when vision meets economic restrictions. Policy breathes with us, and is indeed constituted by us, requiring—in fact ethically demanding—our attention, our analysis, and most important, our contribution.

To abnegate participation in what I call *policy thought*—understood as a discourse (encompassing concept and practice) that involves multiple processes, including policy deliberation, development, enactment, and critique—is thus to hand over significant power to others who might not share our ideals, intentions, and vision. Further, failing to be actively involved in developing our own—or our field's—policy discourses has ethical consequences, and it might suggest that one is relinquishing one's responsibility as a member of a professional class and a civic society. Particularly in times of economic encroachment, to abnegate policy thought is to abandon the pursuit of a vision for critical, democratic, and socially just education.

A second step in developing policy thought is to rupture the often undisputed link between policy and authority. We can approach this by repositioning policy as a practice that requires active participation, disavowing the notion that teachers must stand permanently at the receiving end of policy dictums (see Schmidt, 2009). To do so, we must replace the Hobbesian vision in which power is always limited, always a zero-sum game, and always determined by enforcing hierarchical structures. To redesign the relationship between policy and authority, we must first understand that power can be productive, fluid, and located in multiple places—just as Michel Foucault (1980) has argued. Teachers must experience the fact that power can be generated in and by the constructions of their own discourses; Bullough (1998) has shown that we teachers can and continuously do this.

The examples are many. In the United States, educators working with national associations eased the draconian evaluation structures initially suggested by states committed to President Obama's Race to the Top funding; community-oriented schools such as the Success Academy in Harlem and the Paulo Freire Charter School[1] in Philadelphia develop collective ways of looking at school policy in which teachers, administration, and community meet regularly. Teachers' networks find ways to impact district policies on allocated time for curricular meetings, independent peer observation, and evaluations, such as those outlined by Coburn and Russell (2008). At the international level, we see examples as well. Consider the linkage between social justice and policy in the "Rights Education" initiative promoted globally by UNESCO. The language of the 2006 Human Rights Action Plan is one of the aspects of a larger discourse committed to ensuring that "all the components and processes of education—including curricula, materials, methods and training—are conducive to the learning of human rights and of 'human rights in education'" (UNESCO, 2006, p. 8). Key policy mandates established in Finland claim that "equal opportunity in education is realized when all, whatever their background, have the opportunity to pursue education without their background predetermining participation or learning outcome" (Ministry of Education and Culture, 2012, p. 10). In Brazil, cultural policy directives request that cultural actors and teachers carefully consider the interaction among symbolic, economic, and citizenship dimensions when developing curriculum (Ministry of Culture, 2010).

All these examples exemplify how power can and is used in a fluid, less hierarchical way, but such actions also require that we educators be "prepared to enact and assert [these ideals] plainly and publicly" aiding pragmatically the "genuine progress toward equality for all children and their families" (Kenworth & Whittaker, 2000, p. 223). This can only materialize gradually, and indeed must start early on, in teacher education. Teacher education is the ideal place where policy can become active in our own discourse, helping young educators to become aware of the full weight of policy and the tangible consequences it has for both our professional lives and the learning experiences of those under our tutelage.

Some may argue that there is an incompatibility between policy and teachers, suggesting that teacher impact can only be felt at the individual level—the small number of students with whom he or she interacts daily. Such discourse reads to me as either defeatist or repressive. I find it difficult to deny that, today, the teacher who buys into these ideas and "closes her door," hoping that the macro pressures of the education business will go away, is contributing to the de-skilling of her profession and the narrowing of the curricula that her students will ultimately experience. The major challenges, however, do not spring from a disconnected teaching labor force, but from educational politics that all but exclude the teaching force as a significant locus for educational change (Bullough Jr., 2008, p. 352). When that happens, teachers are responsible providers who contradictorily have little impact on decision-making; that is, they are accountable, but have few avenues to construct accountability.

I argue, alongside Wilson (2006), that the mystique, fear of, and disconnect with policy are significant elements in this state of affairs. The aim, then, must be to help music teachers realize that "policy making and day-to-day operations are not separate spheres of influence but inextricably linked" (Wilson, 2006, p. 153). This involves linking a commitment to classrooms to a new commitment to the political life of the school community and the professional community. The "trick" is to join the long history of curricular and pedagogical activism to a burgeoning policy activism. The policy thought "turn" I am proposing requires epistemic habits, ethical habits, and collaborative habits. And while that is a lot to ask, my own research with teachers working with nongovernmental organizations (NGOs) in Brazil (Schmidt, 2014) or special education in Finland (Laes & Schmidt, forthcoming) shows the myriad ways in which policy thought is key to music teacher activism. My research, as that of many others, demonstrates that neither ideology nor strongly held beliefs are central to this activist stance. What is key is how these educators become cognizant of a nuanced view of policy and how they learn to be adaptable analysts while holding on to strong visions. What they show us is that music educators not only can engage with policy, they already do!

Toward a More Complex and Subjective Understanding of Policy

We can start to rethink our understandings of policy by considering that policy is pursued from someone's vantage point and is contingent on interpretation (Gale, 2001,

p. 134). This means that policy is complex and contested, as is any educational endeavor. In fact, educative environments are substantial representations of policy environments; that is, they are "multidimensional and interactive networks made of structures and actors" (Liasidou, 2012, p. 74). Thus, both education and policy must contend with "hierarchies that overlook the powerful interactive force of networks and/or other structures and actors in a world of pluralistic [endeavors]" (Raab, 1994, p. 14) and, therefore, they are prone to failure and in need of constant adjustment and redesign.

Understanding its complexity and difficulty is important because of the mystique of policy. Part of the reason it has remained detached from teachers—and from teaching and learning—is that policy is often presented as a self-standing structure, established via "formulation" and "implementation" patterns that are detached from contextual insight and constituency contact, that is, from those "on the ground." Traditional stances on policy at times become anathema to an encompassing *civic culture*, with systems and protocols "responsive" only to a very few (Lowi, 1979). The lack of trust we see created in such instances can easily "recast the role of policy in society from the 'pursuit of the public welfare' to the weighing and balancing of competing interests," generating disillusion and lack of participation (Schneider & Ingram, 1997, p. 20).

A preponderance of what is seen today as *policy science* has distanced policy from context and constituency, through an overemphasis on cycles of data-driven decision-making. While reliable data and decision-making should be essentially linked, *policy science* has often displaced concerns with process, constituencies, contextual-needs, and contestation as secondary or merely auxiliary. The misguided establishment of efficiency and what Ball (2003) has called "performativity" as the bona fide outcomes of policy practice has implications not simply for policy thinking itself (in terms of design, implementation, and analysis), but is easily traced to school reform paradigms based on input-output formats focused on streamlining instruction and standardizing assessment. Not unlike conservative views of planning and curriculum writing—where one is to simply produce a lesson and then "teach" it, ignoring context, student input, improvisation, generative questions that arise during the lesson, learning styles, or knowledge disputes over divergent points of view—*carelessly technical* views of policy tend to reduce and/or dismiss difficult and contentious questions of social justice and equitable learning.

What is key, then, is to see policy as we have come to perceive research, that is, as a malleable endeavor that is shaped by "social constructions of knowledge and the identities of participant populations" and influenced by "power relationships and institutions" (Schneider & Ingram, 1997, p. 5). This means that *policy on the ground* really matters (particularly given that certain contexts or views facilitate undemocratic policy outcomes)! As Schneider and Ingram (1997) argue, "policy designs can enable citizens to participate, learn, and create new, different institutions, and that breakdown of divisive and negative social constructions of social groups lays the foundations for self-correcting policy dynamics and a more genuine democratic society" (p. 6). The aim, then, is to create participation patterns that approximate policy to the daily realities of teaching and what educators consider the purview of their work.

According to this view, music teachers are bona fide actors in the policy realm who can establish ourselves as capable of what Grace (1991) calls "policy scholarship," that is, generating "a tool box of diverse concepts and theories" and consequently decentering a now old-fashioned notion of "policy science" that is "seductive in its distance, concreteness, and apparent value free stance" (p. 7). Policy, in this view, requires our participation in order to be a more adaptive, co-constructed, debated, and democratic space.

An Eye on Design and Process: Conceptualizing Socially Just Policy Thinking

What the reader has certainly noticed is that we are moving toward a renewed image of policy. As proposed here and by policy scholars in many arenas (e.g., Moran, Rein, & Goodin, 2006), policy is a human construction, both communal and individual. As such, policy is fallible: at times myopic or permeated by ideology, but at times also complex and representative of careful and varied standpoints. This view offers a compelling reason for the valuation of *policy as science* to be constantly matched by a democratic disposition toward policy thought.

Like any kind of structured endeavor, policy depends on design. And design is essential to sustainable social justice projects. Design on its own is limiting, however, as policy is also *process centered*. Process is as significant as design, for it can generate or deflect participation, can be tension filled or normative, can claim fairness and openness, or can prove to be inefficient and insufficient. It is thus vital that policy be seen as in constant need of evaluation and reconstruction. This is key in policy as well as in social justice thinking, as it helps us to invoke the notion of *governance*, that is, the constant interaction with deliberation, critique, development, and (re)enactment.

Governance that is participative presupposes a better relationship with an understanding of *contestation*. Contrary to traditional views of limited and hierarchical power, contestation—as I argue here—is not based on impediment or diatribe, but as a key pathway toward strengthening the dialogical nature of policy work. Placed in different terms, contestation is central to a social justice view of policy, as it asserts that participative *governance* is both a means and a central aim and outcome of policy thought. All this is significant for us given that a serious commitment to design and process—linking social justice and policy—might help us to constitute a professional frame of mind that sees social justice and policy practices as convergent, which may in turn help us articulate the role of music education in the lives of individuals as both plausible, in curricular and educative terms, and meaningful, in cultural and social terms. It is essential, however, that teachers and other *on-the-ground* policymakers see the contested terrains of educational policy (designs and processes) as part of the political work of schooling—not always easy, often frustrating, but continuously requiring short- and long-term review and action.

Seeing policy and education as contested terrains might lead teachers to look at them not as pointless, convoluted, arcane, or outside their professional responsibility. The contested nature of policy and of education is not the result of a "faulty" system, but a representation of the democratic potential in both. The task at hand, then, is quite simple and at the same time extremely challenging: to establish that doing educational work committed to social justice is to accept tensions between standpoints while also understanding how they may impact resources and their allocation, and consequently shape possible action (Fulcher, 1999). We do this by becoming part of the conversation and "committing to a critical analysis of the values in current policies" (Berkhout & Wielemans, 1999, p. 407). Our action plan, then, is to find formal and informal ways to shape the policy discourses of our workplaces and within our professional fields, as teachers' voices are crucial to "bring together structural, macro level analyses of education systems and educational policies and micro level investigation, especially that which takes account of people's perceptions and experiences" (Ozga, 1990, p. 359).

For me, as for Bowe et al. (1992), "schools are sites of contestation and politics and hence *policy recontextualization*, whereby policy is not only implemented but also is *recreated*, not so much *reproduced* as *produced*" (p. 56, italics added). In music education, we must come to embrace what others have already articulated, namely, that educational practitioners are "important policymakers within the contexts of practice whereby they have the discretionary power to translate official policy into practice according to their beliefs, expectations and contextual realities" (Fulcher, 1999, cited in Liasidou, 2012, pp. 83–84). The daily work that such vision implies creates the need for a professional formation that goes beyond the immediacy of skills training, calling rather for *professionalism* as a form of discretionary capacity that all teachers must have in order to engage as active members of civic society, and that might be a most significant step toward social justice in music education.

FRAMING POLICY: FROM PERMANENT RECEIVERSHIP TO SOCIALLY JUST EDUCATION

What we need to discuss next are the consequences of the absence of action, both in terms of becoming more engaged with policy information, and working to develop a capacity to *frame policy action*. As we promote action based on awareness, it is crucial to understand and challenge policy discourses that are distant from the daily realities of teaching and learning. Teachers can and must amplify a critique of policies that generate misguided authority or power, particularly as they may "mark out children as different, as deficit, as objects of the official knowledge, and human silences of policing and wel-fare" (Luke, 1996, p. 36). Engaging with policy is thus not only a professional right for us teachers, but also an ethical necessity and responsibility.

It is difficult to deny that a portion of current teaching practice demonstrates how policy designs can be harmful, naming and establishing patterns of worth, while estab-lishing who is and is not "deserving." There is no doubt also that it is difficult to challenge local school policy that establishes decision-making as "off-limits" to teachers, creating hierarchical and authoritarian educative environs that name teachers as "undeserving" of the political process. School administrative action is a powerful force that historically often defined teachers as semi- or even non-professionals, incapable of understanding or contributing to the complexity of education environs. Five decades ago, Lowi's (1964) studies on the relationship between policy practice and democratic engagement in soci-ety already showed a dissolution of active citizenry participation, a finding that led her to describe politics and policy thinking in most parts of American society as in a state of "permanent receivership" (p. 75). This concern is central to this chapter and clearly applies to the political realities of music teachers, as permanent receivership is found in our field. We need only consider how methods are at times adopted as if they were music education, itself, or examine the numerous unchanged curricular practices we have continued for decades.

Naturally, this is not the reality everywhere, as much innovation and critical develop-ment are found in the music education field today. At the policy level, however, it should not be controversial to say that music educators experience a state of *permanent receiv-ership*. The results are many, from lack of voice to risk-avert communities that often "play safe." Lowi (1964) observed just such a reality and warned that a lack of policy par-ticipation (what I have called here *policy thought*) facilitates a system where "the stress is on organizational stability," and efforts are made to "eliminate risk or to reduce or share the costs of failure" (p. 280). The reader might have stories of her own that resemble this scenario. Recently, a student teacher reported to me that her cooperating teacher was apprehensive about the circle games she was proposing, as the games presented a risk to "student injury policies" the school had recently implemented. All injury, she told me, even minor bumps, had to be reported, documented, and filed in the school system. The fear of non-compliance was high for this student teacher, and the inability to *talk back* to this policy and its parameters was certainly impacting the nature and quality of instruc-tion in this classroom.

This illustrates how key and urgent the formation of professional dispositions toward policy really is. Pragmatically, it shows the usefulness of policy thought in the process of becoming a teacher, particularly because the issue is not simply a more enlightened leadership. The point is that, in a contested terrain such as a school, understanding limi-tations, alternatives, trends, and under-addressed needs while being able to formulate adaptable possibilities for action is key to success—this is particularly true for often underappreciated subjects such as music.

This vision connects directly to policy thought, as it arms teachers with "a demand for a rights approach as a central component of policy-making" (Barton & Armstrong,

2007, p. 6). These goals are neither utopian nor parts of rogue arguments. Indeed, in the United Kingdom, both the *Rose Report* (DCSF, 2009) and the *Cambridge Review* (Alexander, 2009) speak of the need for better curricular balance with regard to relevance, breadth, and creativity, and how they require teacher voice, as well as active suppression of policies that are de-professionalizing and fostering permanent receivership. Policy thought could help address the findings of these reports. Smart, policy-attuned, teachers understand that the policy process is about communication, about convincing individuals, while dissuading others (see Codd, 1988). They also see visibility as the capacity to raise consciousness and to make something matter in a particular time and context. Central here is the notion that, as dispositions, these ways to communicate value, meaning, and need become generative elements in how we construct voice, either for ourselves, or on behalf of certain ideals or groups of people, such as our students.

While this may sound lofty and abstract, the ground-level representation of these ideas is rather simple. Consider, for example, how social justice thought and policy thought merge when tackling the notion of inclusion. Conceptually, we might see that "inclusion is not simply an end in itself, but a means to an end. It is about contributing to the realization of an inclusive society" (Liasidou, 2012, p. 87). Practically, this discussion begins with self-questioning: Am I an inclusive teacher, who attempts to understand the lives of students with whom I interact? Am I inclusive in the pedagogical approaches I construct with and for my students? Am I inclusive in terms of the musical experiences and conceptions of musical value I foster within my classroom? Do I have an inclusive approach to assessment where peer-to-peer, formative, summative, portfolio-based, critical, and other approaches coexist? A policy disposition then helps teachers to make a connection between the classroom environment and issues *beyond* the classroom, asking, for example: Are we inclusive when it comes to representations of different music productions and consumption? Is my learning community inclusive in terms of practices, language, and opportunities that might have an impact on race interactions, gender challenges, or sexuality issues faced by our students? All this is significant because one of the characteristics of social justice education is the attempt to develop a "vision of democracy through difference" (Barton, 1997, p. 235). The problem is that such a vision remains passive if I, as a teacher and citizen of a school community, do not pursue questions similar to these and attempt to act upon them. Meaningful and sustainable ways to approach such questions depend, to a quite large extent, on policy awareness, savvy, and action.

THE RIGHT TO POLICY AND DOING IT RIGHT

This chapter has argued that, more than ever, a commitment to a socially just music education requires an engagement with policy thought. One way to do so is by engaging with the notion of "idea-based policy change" (McDonnell, 2007, p. 30), in which teacher preparation and professional development directly aid educators to behave as policy thinkers, who can eventually become policy activists. Higher education has a particularly important role in fostering curricular, pedagogical, and conceptual preparation that would better connect teachers to agency. This is a complex undertaking, but it is not out of our reach. My recent research shows that music educators are already attuned to these issues, and teacher preparation and professional development could further help them by focusing on ways to facilitate: (a) self-generated knowledge, (b) intersections between local musical-cultural practices and global aesthetic needs, (c) politically conscious music education leadership, and (d) pedagogical practices situated inside a larger social framework (Schmidt, 2014).

These are initial steps toward policy activism, where the advice is no longer "don't worry you'll have autonomy . . . once you close the door of your classroom you can do whatever you want," but rather, "you will only build autonomy by communicating, interacting, sharing, listening, and challenging those around you and what surrounds you." What I propose in this chapter is a pedagogical approach to policy thinking that rejects permanent receivership and embraces activism. My argument follows the simple set of premises:

(a) No mission, no program!
    We must not simply "advocate" for a limited and prepackaged vision of music education, but seek to create a field that is committed to ample, inclusive, and socially meaningful practices.

(b) No vision, no program!
    This begins by establishing the work of teachers as political work (Danzinger, 1995). Today's pedagogical and policy borrowing has reached "epidemic proportions" as decontextualized ideas are haphazardly copied and applied, regardless of local needs (Levin, 1998, p. 133). Music teacher preparation is rightly concerned with the development of skills and didactic proficiency, but often and wrongly overemphasizes them to the detriment of other "skills" such as capacity toward policy. Critical teacher education must facilitate *critical vision* skills.

(c) No framing, no program!
    This begins with the notion that educational environments are "multidimensional and interactive networks made of structures and actors" (Liasidou, 2012, p. 74). Consequently, communication and the capacity to adapt discourse are essential for music teachers committed to social justice, as equity and access cannot be simply "implemented." Rather, they are established by multiple designs and via contextually appropriate processes. This requires that we constantly frame the issues, frame approaches, and frame dialogue.

(d) No action, no program!
    All participants of an educational community must learn to analyze and foreground educational decisions and their imbalances (Ball, 2003). Consequently, we teachers can and must play a role as policy analysts, establishing action that is informed by our political, intellectual, and communal lives.

These premises are not revolutionary. They are indeed quotidian and foundational to much educational action today. They can be found, for example, in the declared mission of Zelda Glazer Middle School (ZGMS)—a school that serves students with high levels of poverty in Miami—which aims to "nurture a society of thinkers who are knowledgeable and confident."[2] As I interact with ZGMS teachers, I see the recognition of this as policy language and guideline, but I also see how teachers make use of such language to enact their own practices, to justify change, and to challenge themselves as a community. In a recent interview with a governmental agency leader in charge of policy for music schools in Finland, I found a similar disposition. There, she articulated how music educators play an active role in the review of their policy aims and procedures, an example being the current shift in assessment practices in trying to find a balance between *student competencies* and *teacher competencies*, and the subsequent investment in teachers' creative practices, participative pedagogies, and an ultimate emphasis on classroom environs rather than on content delivery. This is in line with Finnish macro policy language that "educational institutions will develop education for democracy," where "instruction will include more contents and procedures which foster participation, influence, and the development of political and societal literacy" (Ministry of Education and Culture Report, 2012, p. 12). Here we see a direct policy aimed at active citizenship and a concern that "equal opportunity is realized when all, whatever their background, have the possibility to pursue education without their background predetermining participation or learning outcome" (p. 10).

It must be emphasized here that it is not sufficient to engage in policy talk for the purpose of simply "advocating" for music or social justice. We all know that educational terms such as "value-added," "best practices," "community partnerships," "collaborative decision-making," and "stakeholder society" have invaded educational discourse and "are now endemic: [they are] learned, practiced, expected, demanded" (Watson, 2003, p. 15). Keeping this in mind, the four premises articulated above are a call to a more robust movement toward policy agency. They are one version of policy thought in action.

We seem to have plenty of evidence that the current displacement of teachers from policy decision-making is a flawed system that desperately needs rethinking. The vast literature on policy and democratic practices (see Moran, Rein, & Goodin, 2006) shows that while it is essential to understand and continuously seek ideals and theories that have framed policy and social justice in various contexts, it is also essential that we dispose ourselves to see them as a living practices that require less communicating and more active construction.

In many ways, the notion of policy thought espoused in this chapter is quite simple and could be summarized in this way: We teachers cannot be simply attuned to history or past practice or borrowing, and our thinking and practices demand a constant and urgent commitment to here and now. Claiming such space fortifies a commitment to a political view of education—not in the sense of party line or ideology, but one in which we understand education as constantly contested—which in turn is a clear and most significant step toward the formation of locally understood, but globally aware, music education for social justice. To engage in policy thought is to nurture our commitment to a political practice, which necessitates our own action and theorizing.

It is also clear that stopping the further devolution of teachers into clerical workers and regaining the professional guise of a civil servant requires that we not only understand the larger politics of the challenges cited above, but also work, daily and actively, to implement, disrupt, and restructure these political policy directives at the local level. Bauman (1997) has argued that every society creates its own sets of strangers. A greater engagement with policy is not a panacea for alienating policies that depict teachers as "estranged" from their own professional environments, but it certainly is an important step toward more informed and active decision-making. This is a call to what Banerjee and Knight (1985) refer to as an *apprenticeship in democracy*, a practice that is key to any attempt at socially just action, and an essential element so that we do not find ourselves strangers in our own profession.

NOTES

1. Charter schools in the United States function with public moneys, just as public schools do, but are organized and administered by private enterprises or coalitions of citizens.
2. See details at http://zgm.dadeschools.net/graphics/2012-13%20Student%20HandbookWeb.pdf.

REFERENCES

Alexander, R. (2009). *The Cambridge primary review.* Retrieved from http://www.primaryreview.org.uk/downloads/Finalreport/CPR-booklet_low-res.pdf.

Armstrong, F., Armstrong, D., & Barton, L. (2000). *Inclusive education: Policy, contexts and comparative perspectives.* London: David Fulton.

Ball, S. J. (2003). The teacher's soul and the terrors of performativity. *Journal of Educational Policy, 18*(2), 215–228.

Ball, S. J. (2009). *The education debate.* Bristol: Policy Press.

Banerjee, B., & Knight, J. B. (1985). Caste in Indian urban labor market. *Journal of Development Economics, 17,* 277–307.

Barton, L. (1997). The politics of education for all. *Support for Learning, 10*(4), 234–261.

Barton, L., & Armstrong, F. (2007). Disability, education and inclusion: Cross-cultural issues and dilemmas. In G. Albrecht, K. Seelman, & M. Bury (Eds.), *The handbook of disability studies* (pp. 34–67). London: Sage.

Berkhout, S. J., & Wielemans, W. (1999). Toward understanding education policy: An integrative approach. *Education Policy, 13*(3), 402–420.

Booth, T., & Ainscow, M. (2000). *The index for inclusion.* Bristol: Centre for Studies on Inclusive Education.

Bowe, R., Ball, S., & Gold, A. (1992). *Reforming education and changing schools: Case studies in policy sociology.* London: Routledge.

Bullough Jr., R. V. (2008). *Counter narratives: Studies of teacher education and becoming and being a teacher.* Albany: State University of New York Press.

Bullough, R. V., Knowles, G., & Crow, N. A. (1998). *Emerging as a teacher.* New York: Routledge.

Coburn, C., & Russell, J. (2008). District policy and teachers' social networks. *Educational Evaluation and Policy Analysis, 30*(3), 203–235.

Codd, J. (1988). The construction and deconstruction of education policy documents. *Journal of Education Policy, 3*(3), 235–247.

Danzinger, G. (1995). Policy analysis postmodernized: Some political and pedagogical ramifications. *Policy Studies Journal, 23*(3), 435–450.

Darling-Hammond, L., & Bransford, J. (Eds.). (2005). *Preparing teachers for a changing world: What teachers should learn and be able to do.* New York: Jossey-Bass.

DCSF (Department for Children, Schools and Families). (2009). *Breaking the link between disadvantage and low attainment: Everyone's business.* Annesley: DCSF.

Dyson, D. (1999). Inclusion and inclusions: Theories and discourses in inclusive education. In H. Daniels & P. Garner (Eds.), *World yearbook of education 1999: Inclusive education* (pp. 36–53). London: Kagan Page.

Foucault, M. (1980). *Power/knowledge: Selected interviews and other writings.* New York: Pantheon Books.

Fulcher, G. (1999). *Disabling policies? A comparative approach to education policy and disability.* London: The Falmer Press.

Gale, T. (2001). Critical policy sociology: Historiography, archeology, and genealogy as methods of policy analysis. *Journal of Education Policy, 16*(5), 379–393.

Grace, G. (1991). *School leadership: Beyond educational management: An essay in policy scholarship.* London: Falmer Press.

Kenworth, J., & Whittaker, J. (2000). Anything to declare? The struggle for inclusive education and children's rights. *Disability and Society, 15*(2), 219–231.

Laes, T., & Schmidt, P. (forthcoming). Activism in Music Education: Working toward inclusion and policy change in the Finnish music school context. *British Journal of Music Education.*

Levin, B. (1998). An epidemic of education policy: (What) can we learn from each other? *Comparative Education, 34*, 131–141.

Liasidou, A. (2012). *Inclusive education, politics and policymaking.* London: Continuum.

Lowi, T. (1964). American business, public policy, case-studies and political theory. *World Politics, 16*, 677–715.

Lowi, T. (1979). *The end of liberalism.* New York: Norton.

Luke, A. (1996). Text and discourse in education: An introduction to critical discourse analysis. *Review of Research, 21*, 3–47.

McDonnell, L. (2007). The politics of education: Influencing policy and beyond. In S. Fuhrman, D. K. Cohen, & F. Mosher (Eds.), *The state of education policy research* (pp. 19–40). Mahwah, NJ: Lawrence Erlbaum Associates, Inc.

Ministry of Education and Culture. (2012). *Education and research 2011–2016: A development plan.* Finland: Ministry of Education and Culture.

Ministry of Culture (2010). Brazil. *Plano Nacional de cultura.* Brasilia.

Moran, M., Rein, M., & Goodin, R. (2006). *The Oxford handbook of public policy.* New York: Oxford University Press.

Ozga, J. (1990). Policy research and policy theory: A comment on Fitz and Halpin. *Journal of Education Policy, 5*(4), 359–362.

Raab, C. (1994). Open government: Policy information and information policy. *The Political Quarterly, 65*(3), 340–347.

Schmidt, P. (2009). Reinventing from within: Thinking spherically as a policy imperative in music education. *Arts Education Policy Review, 110*(3), 39–47.

Schmidt, P. (2014). NGOs as a framework for an education in and through music: Is the third sector a viable option? *International Journal of Music Education, 32*(1), 31–52.

Schneider, A., & Ingram, H. (1997). *Policy design for democracy.* Lawrence: University Press of Kansas.

UNESCO. (2006). *Plan of action: World programme for human rights education.* Paris: UNESCO. Retrieved from http://www.unesco.org/new/en/education/themes/leading-the-international-agenda/human-rights-education/resources/publications/.

Watson, K. (2003). *Doing comparative education research.* Oxford: Symposium.

Wilson, R. (2006). Policy analysis as policy advice. In M. Moran, M. Rein, & R. E. Goodin (Eds.), *The Oxford handbook of public policy* (pp. 153–154). New York: Oxford University Press.

CHAPTER 4

··

FACING THE MUSIC

*Pursuing Social Justice Through Music
Education in a Neoliberal World*

··

STEPHANIE HORSLEY

On September 23, 1987, Margaret Thatcher declaimed that "[t]here is no such thing as society. There is living tapestry of... people and the quality of our lives will depend upon how much each of us is prepared to take responsibility for ourselves... and help by our own efforts those who are unfortunate (quoted by Keay, 1987, http://www.margaretthatcher.org). Thatcher's words set off a public furor that resulted in a rare statement of clarification released by No. 10 Downing Street. It read:

> [Margaret Thatcher] prefers to think in terms of the acts of individuals and families as the real sinews of society rather than of society as an abstract concept. Her approach to society reflects her fundamental belief in personal responsibility and choice. To leave things to "society" is to run away from the real decisions, practical responsibility and effective action. (*Sunday Times*, 1988, http://www.margaretthatcher.org/)

Thatcher's words reflect the neoliberal conception of social welfare, which is built upon the fortitude and industriousness of individuals acting in their own best interests and showing concern for their neighbors, rather than relying on government social programs or policy to ensure a particular quality of life for the citizenry. Neoliberalism and its educational reforms are premised on the importance of individual participation in market practices in order to further one's own well-being, as supported by a conception of social welfare viewed through the lens of *negative justice*. As Sonu (2012) has pointed out, though, social justice education—however we might conceive of it—has three primary aspects that make up one common denominator: "its adherence to the belief that education can cultivate within students a sense of civic responsibility, the duty to care about the plight of others, and the means to work in solidarity to transform the structural and ideological forces that benefit certain communities at the expense of others"

(p. 244). Sonu's conception of social justice education is based on *positive justice*, which, in education, emphasizes the development of democratic, empathetic citizens who are committed to social equity.

Tension arises from between these two conceptions of justice. This chapter begins with a discussion of the conceptions of welfare and social justice as interpreted through neoliberal ideology, which emphasizes negative rights, rather than through the lens of social equity, which emphasizes positive rights. It then turns to a discussion of how education policy in neoliberal public education systems has focused on efficiently achieving equality through standardization and supporting individual economic advancement by securing the academic credentials necessary to support oneself and, subsequently, state and local economies. Such practices, which stress equality over equity, have distinctive implications for how citizens and systems of education are discursively constructed and positioned. This, in turn, affects how music education and its outcomes are structured and perceived within the practices of neoliberal education—a practice that is exacerbated by music education's historical avoidance of issues relating to politics, citizenship, and social justice. The chapter concludes with a discussion of how music education has the potential to balance neoliberalism's negative justice approach to education with one that supports Sonu's emphasis on democracy, empathy, and equity.

WELFARE, NEGATIVE JUSTICE, AND NEGATIVE RIGHTS IN NEOLIBERAL EDUCATION

We generally tend to think of neoliberalism, with its emphasis on the individual, as not particularly concerned with social welfare and justice, a critique often applied to Thatcher's comment that "there is no such thing as society." As an ideology, however, neoliberalism *is* concerned with the question of what individual rights should be and how one may obtain a "good life." Turner (2008) has identified *Welfare* as one of the four core concepts of neoliberalism, the others being the *Market*, the *Constitution*, and *Property*, which interact to form its conceptual underpinnings. Neoliberal ideology requires the state to enact a constitution and set of laws that limit state power to interfere in the freedom of the individual. This is believed to curtail those within government who would pursue their own interests, while also establishing a set of universal rules that ensure that all citizens will be treated equally before the law. Individuals are expected to know the laws, obey them, and use them to their advantage in the pursuit of their own interests in the market (Olssen, 2004; Rose & Millar, 1992). This "freedom from interference," or *negative justice*, promotes what is commonly referred to as *negative rights*.

Negative rights are those that allow individuals to pursue their own fortunes and are meant to foster a society in which individuals are largely responsible for their own welfare and prosperity. They include such rights as the right to own property and the right to engage in a free and open economic market for personal gain. In education, they are tied to the right of parents to make educational decisions about what they consider best for their children. This stands in contrast to social or *positive rights*, which guarantee that certain provisions and standards of living will be provided to all individuals within a state. These include the right to a basic standard of living; to not be discriminated against on the basis of gender, age, or race, and so on; and to public education that ensures students will reach certain outcomes, regardless of one's personal background. Negative rights are meant to remove barriers so that all individuals will have an equal opportunity to succeed in life (assuming that all individuals are able to take advantage of the opportunities that a system of negative rights affords them), while positive rights are meant to lessen the need to compete for social and economic gain and instead foster a base level of social and economic equality among individuals within a state (Hirschl, 2000). The former implies a meritocracy where all students should be treated equally and so succeed based on their respective merits and work ethic, while the latter suggests that all students should be able to succeed in any educational endeavors as long as individual disparities among students and social groups are addressed.

In neoliberal economic and education policy, choice, self-interest, and market participation are positioned as integral to the welfare and rights of individuals. Drawing on the classical economic philosophies of Adam Smith, neoliberals assert that it is through the pursuit of one's individual interests that societies come to flourish (Smith, 1991). The (now famous) example Smith gave is that of buying products from the butcher, brewer, and baker:

> Give me that which I want, and you shall have this which you want, is the meaning of every such offer. . . . It is not from the benevolence of the butcher, the brewer, or the baker, that we expect our dinner, but from their regard to their own interest. We address ourselves not to their humanity but to their self-love, and never talk to them of our own necessities but of their advantages. (p. 13)

The wealth of a nation, then, depends on individual self-interest and market participation. Self-interest is moderated by the desire to achieve our needs and wants, and, in achieving our goal, we help others meet their needs and wants. The wealth gained by individuals through personal market transactions filters through society, creating a "universal opulence" that allows all to prosper (p. 399).

Smith stressed the importance of market evolution in this process and argued that employment would remain high within a state as workers developed new products, services, and ideas to increase the production of goods or to fill (or create) new market "niches" as older products and services fell out of demand or practice. Monopolies should be avoided, as they strangle the cooperative spirit of market exchange. They are self-interest unchecked, as lack of competition means that there is no need to consider the needs of the other in terms of both improving products and services and keeping the cost of goods low.

Smith's ideas about market competition and evolution were refashioned by neoliberals in three primary ways that shaped their conception of social welfare and the structure of education reform: (1) free and open global markets, (2) the knowledge economy and knowledge workers, and (3) educational excellence, facilitated by educational standardization, accountability, and choice. The first was accomplished through the abolishment of trade tariffs, beginning largely with Britain's Thatcher and America's Reagan administrations in the 1980s and continuing through such international policy as the North American Free Trade Agreement and the establishment of the European Union. This resulted in the growing desire by (or perceived necessity of) countries to join supranational economic regulating bodies such as the World Trade Organization (WTO) and the Organisation for Economic Co-operation and Development (OECD), both of which actively promote a neoliberal approach to economics and education (Heron, 2008; Taylor & Henry, 2005). These developments allowed the free movement of skilled workers across international borders and facilitated the relocation of foreign and multinational businesses to open, competitive markets. By the year 2000, the neoliberal approach to economics had become "such a taken-for-granted way to represent and act upon the economic world" that it had reshaped "established social and ideological arrangements along market lines" (Fourcade-Gourinchas & Babb, 2002, p. 534).

The second relevant way in which Smith's ideas are reflected in neoliberalism is in the rise and evolution of the knowledge economy and its workers, which also began in the 1980s and continues today. Faced with a loss in production-related jobs facilitated by open markets that allowed companies to move their businesses to nations where those employed in such work could be paid a much lower wage, industrialized nations such as Canada, Australia, the United States, and England moved to reform their education systems in the hopes of keeping employment high through the production of individuals who would cater to the newly dubbed *global knowledge economy*. In this economy, states with a high standard of living poise themselves as producers of high-technology, high-value goods and suppliers of new, innovative ideas and products (Wilson, 2005).

A knowledge economy is a "value-added" economy where workers (usually referred to as *knowledge workers*) strive to be innovative and or/entrepreneurial in order to create new goods and services or to enhance pre-existing goods and services. Knowledge workers need to be forward thinking, flexible, and team-oriented. Rather than performing a single task at a single job throughout their lives, they are expected to have a set of basic, transferable skills that can be applied as they encounter new situations and problems. They are directly related to the spontaneously evolving knowledge economy, as their primary job is to devise new goods and services that meet the needs of (or to create a need in) society and/or to devise new, more efficient solutions to problems, thereby keeping employment high because of demand for ever-evolving services and products (Waks, 2003). This approach to fostering a mass consumer economy is perhaps best reflected in the culture of planned obsolescence that is particularly prevalent in the electronics industry (Sakiewicz, Nowosielski, Pilarczyk, & Cesarz, 2012), but can also be seen in the ways in which the music industry adopts and exploits various musical cultures, creating an often uncritical and voracious demand for the next great star, hit, dance move, video, or (even better) scandal. In doing so, it often alienates those who initially participated in a specific musical culture and obscures or contradicts the social values of the music in its original context (Moore, 2009). The latter can often happen during the marketization of new products or ideas when musical compositions are co-opted for advertising or political propaganda purposes.

Knowledge workers are expected to be both innovative and entrepreneurial. This relies on particular conceptions of the achievement of educational excellence and what it means to be a well-educated individual. These conceptions are shaped by and through educational standards, accountability, and competition, and thus are related to a third way in which Smith's market competition is invoked through neoliberal ideology: the idea of educational institutions as both a means of efficiently producing economic individuals capable of thriving in the globalized knowledge economy and as a site of market choice. Neoliberal ideology argues that if states are to demonstrate the excellence of their education systems in preparing students for economic prosperity in the knowledge economy, they need a method of assessment and a standard to which such assessment can be held. In most education systems in the Western world, this has led to developing a set of common or core curricula or national standards that clearly state what each child should learn and by when, particularly in the areas of the core skills that support the development of knowledge workers. Thus, standardized curricula and testing to demonstrate student competency were widely developed by state governments over the course of the 1990s and early 2000s, in effect centralizing control over what educational excellence should be and pinning it to literacy, mathematics, science, and technology. These reforms occurred in the midst of a burgeoning growth in international testing and comparison profiles and were meant to establish the competency of a state's students in the fields of literacy, mathematics, and science—all considered necessary for attaining personal and regional economic success in and engagement with a globalized knowledge economy.

Another main concept in the neoliberal discourse of educational excellence, then, is the ability of educational institutions to produce *enterprising* individuals who possess the skills, knowledge, and disposition to actively engage in the market in their own self-interest and who are marketable in and to a world of global enterprise. This has the purported twofold advantage of keeping employment high through local entrepreneurialism and attracting business to the state. As Spring (1998) writes, "in this context, education becomes a form of economic investment and, consequently, the value of education is measured by its contribution to economic growth" (p. 159). In this "human capital accounting" system of measurement, states view funds allocated to education as a social investment that will allow their citizens to better compete in a global market economy, thereby contributing to greater state economic growth and reducing demand on state social services. Prosperous citizens are also citizens who can support the mass consumerism upon which the knowledge economy relies. In a neoliberal state, the *homo economicus* of Smith's classical liberalism is replaced by *manipulated man*, whose actions are directed by the state and its various institutions—including educational institutions—so that they are purposely directed to become entrepreneurial in the interest of the state's prosperity (Apple, 2000; Grimaldi, 2012; Harris, 2007; Roberston, 2009).

As stated earlier, neoliberalism as an economic and social philosophy relies heavily on the individual's involvement in market practices. Just as market choice of physical goods should shape supply and demand, neoliberal education reform depends on competition among individuals and educational providers (usually measured by students' results on standardized tests against specific subjects in a standardized curriculum and also through financial accountability practices) to both raise the quality of services through competition and to ensure that money invested in education is used wisely (Segall, 2006). Cost-saving measures are implemented to encourage greater efficiency in delivering educational services, and per-pupil funding formulas are often implemented in order to ensure that students are given an equal opportunity to access the educational resources needed to learn the curriculum (Horsley, 2014). In some cases, as in England and, to a lesser extent, the United States, parents are allowed school choice for their children. Neoliberalism in these cases asserts that schools must become more "consumer friendly" for parents by improving their standards of education and the efficiency (monetary and otherwise) with which they deliver educational services. When tied to a per-pupil funding formula, such educational schemes make it necessary for schools to focus their educational resources on those accountability measures that are discursively framed as most relevant to school choice, such as league tables in the United Kingdom and Annual Yearly Progress requirements in the United States. Even in cases where parents are not given school choice, the public "naming and shaming" of schools through publication of student test results and budgeting practices is meant to increase school efficiency and achievement (Hursh, 2005).

A neoliberal welfare conception of education, then, relies on three main, state-driven actions: (1) the promotion of individual self-interest and entrepreneurism to ensure that citizens are adequately equipped with the economic skills and interests they need in order to contribute to the economy and avoid relying on the state for a basic quality of life, (2) withdrawal of the state from social welfare programs, and (3) an emphasis on the implementation of cost-saving and "efficiency" measures in those social areas in which the state is still involved (Horsley, 2014). Neoliberal ideology often goes so far as to position the Keynesian welfare state as repressive, rebuffing the positive conception of social justice on the grounds that the markets cannot have planned outcomes. Those who fail to succeed cannot be said to suffer injustice: the market is not sentient and so lacks the intention necessary to foster injustice. The attempts of government to ensure that all citizens lead a high quality of life through social planning and the redistribution of wealth are, in a neoliberal discourse, a violation of the personal freedoms and the negative rights of individuals to succeed through their own merits (Hayek, 1968). During campaigns for neoliberal reform, state services are often framed as fostering a lazy, selfish populace with a sense of entitlement, who fail to recognize the value of hard work and to take personal responsibility for their own welfare, leading to a nation's moral and economic decline (Turner, 2008), as was argued by Thatcher in the opening quote of this chapter. The concepts of welfare and negative rights, then, are essential to the ideology of neoliberalism. It is through these concepts that the idea of economic self-interest (including the acquisition of material goods), personal choice, and responsibility for one's own actions and the consequences of those choices are imprinted on the public consciousness.

Negative Rights, Education, and Music Education

The preceding description of negative rights and the ways in which they frame and are framed by neoliberal education are problematic for those who are interested in a positive conception of social justice education as broadly defined earlier by Sonu (2012). Among them is the "common-sense" rhetoric that is used to justify situating education largely as a means to an economic end, which in turn supports the status quo. For example, Fischman and Hass (2009) have written that neoliberal educational discourse is "articulated as a redeeming narrative, and thus, schools should be apolitical institutions implementing scientifically verified 'best practices,' which will be assessed through standardized testing" (p. 568). Self-interest and its unfettered pursuit are framed as necessary virtues (Ball, 1993). However, educational policy is not value neutral, and neoliberal education policy embodies and shapes specific beliefs about the role of education in society and what constitutes a well-educated, successful citizen (Taylor, 2004). In particular, standards shape the ways in which we conceive of and interact with the world outside school. This includes standards for music education, which "inscribe representations of the world of music that children act on" (Popkewitz & Gustafson, 2002, p. 82). These musical standards, as discussed further below, most often focus on goals that are either specific to the individual or are related to group competitions and thus support the neoliberal emphasis on educational systems as embodying the apolitical.

National needs and individual wants are not necessarily the same thing, even if they are discursively positioned as such in neoliberal education. Further, not all students' needs can be met through a market-driven, seemingly apolitical approach to education (Ball, 1993). Thus, we must view a largely economic framing of education, and the mass consumerism and marketization upon which the knowledge economy depends, through the lens of "manipulated man" described earlier: students and parents are persuaded through rhetoric and educational structures to accept that the main goals of education are to produce economically engaged and eminently employable citizens. Failure of individual students to do so is often attributed not to educational structures and the role that governments play in determining educational goals, values, and policy, but rather to the actions of local administrators and teachers, poor parental choices, or students' failure to take advantage of the rights and opportunities that purportedly allow individuals to acquire the credentials and skills necessary to participate as contributors to and consumers in the knowledge economy (Hursh, 2009).

Indeed, the very notion of "choice" and "equal access" in publicly funded and regulated neoliberal education is not as straightforward as it seems, particularly in relation to subjects such music, which are not considered to contribute overly to those skills identified as "core" (i.e., literacy, mathematics, science, and technology), even, as is the case in the United States, when they are actually labeled as such! Laws such as No Child Left Behind (2001), which designate federal funding for schools that show improvement in literacy and mathematics, help ensure that, while music curriculum policies, documents, and assessment practices may have become standardized, the hierarchical discursive positioning of school subjects that are seen to further neoliberal economic goals give tacit permission for administrators and teachers to overlook music's implementation (Apple, 2003; Eisner, 1998; Horsley 2014). Frierson-Campbell (2007) has pointed out that, as state-developed and sanctioned music curricula are intended to guide the learning of *all* students, a major concern is the equal distribution of resources so that all students can have an opportunity to participate in music education—a goal consistent with neoliberal education discourse. This, however, is usually not the outcome. Research on access to music education in several cases of statewide neoliberal reform has shown that students who live in affluent school districts with strong parental support for the arts and the ability to pay user fees, as well as the ability to raise funds through community and business, consistently have better funded music programs, better teaching resources, and higher teacher retention and student enrolment (Abril & Gault, 2008; Gardner, 2010; Horsley 2014; Pitts, 2000). In this case, social justice might mean just *accessing* the status quo (Frierson-Campbell, 2007), while standardized, compulsory music curricula might become sites for contesting the neoliberal conception of equality of opportunity. Jorgensen (2010) has argued that, instead of focusing on and rewarding success in performance (a model we are all too familiar with due to the North American focus on musical competition), we actively draw attention to the gross inequities in school music provision at the national, state, and local levels. In addition, the diversion of funding from school music programs to other, "tested" subjects has resulted in an increase of public-private partnerships that has allowed, in some cases, businesses and corporations to unduly influence the content and pedagogy of music classes in their own interest. Addressing both of these issues requires music educators to become politically involved with educational policymaking, something they have historically avoided (Woodford, 2005).

Ball (2009), among others, has argued extensively that the effectiveness and implementation of parental choice schemes are impeded by the cultural habitus of one's socioeconomic position. All too often, "those who have the capital—in whatever form: economic, cultural, and social—are in the best position to gain from [school choice]" (Hursh, 2005, p. 12). Boyles, Carusi, and Attick (2009) have pointed out that "all things being equal in school, all things are *not* equal at home and in society in general" (p. 38). The example of the unequal implementation of music education in state-funded schooling is just one such outcome of the limitations of neoliberal "choice." According to Jorgensen (2010), such disparity in music, or in education in general, undermines the historical role that schools have played in facilitating the development of an informed citizenry that engages in democratic practices.

In addition, the question of whose music is officially sanctioned within the school needs to be discussed, as such decisions place limits on the concept of choice. This leads us to consider the historical detachment of music education, particularly in Western cultures, from matters of politics, citizenship, and social justice. Elliott (1995, 2012) has extensively criticized the ways in which music education has divorced musical engagement from the social context in which it is made. Tied as it has been to the Western aesthetic notion of separating music from its sociopolitical context for the purposes of disinterested contemplation, reasoning, and personal introspection, as well as a belief in the superiority of Western "classical" music, music education's aesthetic values "emerged as something individual, self-oriented, inward, and autonomous ... From a less flattering perspective, this aesthetic domain was superfluous, pleasant and agreeable," allowing for the categorization of the musical experience as "losing oneself in the immediacy of the present experience" (Bowman, 2001, p. 13). Woodford (2005) has further argued that ignorance of the social context in which music is produced—an ignorance supported not only by an aesthetic approach to music education, but by the unwillingness of teachers to examine the sources of their musical or pedagogical beliefs or to disturb the status quo by introducing controversial music (which is often the preferred musical choice of students) into the classroom—has contributed to the inability of the citizenry to understand the ways in which music is used to manipulate public attitudes and consumer habits through propaganda and marketization, both historically and in the present. In a neoliberal society that embraces planned obsolescence driven by marketing and the acceptance of a short "shelf life," both in technology and mass media, such an oversight within music education is disturbing. Consider that some of the terms in Bowman's above description of an aesthetic approach to musical engagement might well be applied to the neoliberal citizen's expected engagement with current culture and technology: "autonomous," "superfluous, pleasant and agreeable," and "losing oneself in the immediacy of the present experience." This "self-love" exhibited in the uncritical consumption of music, neoliberals might argue, is part of the freedom and "added value" of a knowledge economy; however, the neoliberal approach to education has been criticized by social justice educators as limiting the ways in which students can think, learn, interact with others, and express themselves. This is attributed in significant part to the narrow focus on an economic purpose for music education, with its emphasis on measurable assessment and outcomes at the expense of creative and critical thinking processes, particularly as the latter relate to addressing broader issues in education and society (Grimaldi, 2012; Leistyna, 2009; Soep, Saavedra, & Kurwa, 2009). As discussed earlier, music education has also focused on the production of technical skills, largely for the goal of succeeding in competitions. Music education's historical practices, then, can implicitly support a neoliberal agenda if teachers and their students continue to focus on a conception of musical experience as either subsumed in competition or as primarily self-centered while, at the same time, failing to confront both music and education as highly influential, value-laden activities. Given this, music educators should be aware of the democratic challenges of their students, who may end up possessing

> musical skills and perhaps a smattering of knowledge of music theory and history yet having no idea of how their perceptions, tastes, values, and understandings of history and current social and political *realities* are often deliberately shaped by other people, organizations, and institutions for their own ends, and how music and music education are sometimes implicated in that process. (Woodford, 2014, p. 39)

To do so fundamentally undermines a positive social justice conception of fostering democratic citizens who can make informed (not manipulated) musical decisions while also engaging in debate about relevant broader social issues, such as which values should underpin music education; what should be the goals of education; and the possible roles of the individual, the state, and industry within public education.

Within the general field of education, others have followed this line of argument and have asserted that neoliberalism establishes a status quo that is fundamentally opposed to education through and for social justice. Rizvi and Engle (2009) have argued that "neo-liberalism promotes and normalizes a 'growth-first' approach to policy, making social welfare concerns secondary" (p. 532). The emphasis on the rights of the individual, coupled with educational structures that pay "lip service" to educational access, limits the distribution of resources necessary to address social inequities that may disadvantage certain students (Grimaldi, 2012). If we re-examine Sonu's very broad definition of social justice education given at the beginning of this chapter, it becomes clear that a neoliberal conception of education based on the negative rights of the self-interested individual is not concerned with any aspect of her basis for social justice education (i.e., democracy, empathy, and equity). Indeed, neoliberal policymakers are sometimes instructed to remove references to gender, race, and socioeconomic status when forming education policy. This decision is guided by the belief that such factors are irrelevant if all students have equal access to the same learning opportunities (Grimaldi, 2012; Pinto, 2012). One is reminded of Stephen Colbert's parody of the neoliberal agenda and his statement that "I don't see race"—an extension of the idea of market competition as rewarding individuals based on their actions, rather than excusing failure on the grounds of social inequities. However, as indicated in the above discussion, inequities *do* exist in home and society (and in education, despite the rhetoric) that result in disadvantaging or alienating particular individuals and groups within education. Neoliberal education, then, must be "reconciled with the broader cultural concerns of education, linked to issues of class, gender, and ethnicity" (Rizvi & Engle, 2009, p. 535), including being linked to a community's culture and traditions. Music education can, and in some cases already does, play an integral role in this. Yet, Fischman and Haas (2009) note that "in most schools, it is nearly impossible to find discourses that emphasize the need for greater democracy or improvement of quality of life not measured in economic terms" (p. 568). Quite the opposite: neoliberal education *constrains* the information needed for democratic participation and choice through its development of "manipulated man."

Pursuing Social Justice Through Music Education in a Neoliberal World

Music educators can address issues of democratic participation and choice, empathy, and equity that surface within a neoliberal ideology of welfare, negative rights, and the role of education in shaping how individuals are conceived of, act, and relate to each other in society. Within the field of music education, however, democracy, empathy, and equity must be seen as interdependent and mutually reinforcing. For example, democracy, as it is discussed below, cannot occur without an empathetic willingness to consider another's point of view and a willingness to defy the status quo in order to do what we might consider equitable (Schmidt, 2007). In addition, as discussed above, social justice education within music education is not possible unless teachers are willing to embrace such an agenda and take a long, hard look at their musical and pedagogical practices and the values upon which they are based. Woodford (2005) argues that "music teachers are probably uniquely positioned to help break down or bridge institutional, social, or cultural barriers through the free exchange and cross-fertilization of ideas in the public sphere" (p. 76), but only if they are aware of the ways in which both they and their students have been constrained by historical and current social and political values and are willing to become politically involved at all levels of educational policymaking. Civic responsibility, then, is not conceived as solely contributing to the economy through one's personal choice (or direction), but as a willingness to engage in respectful and critical engagement in the discussion, reshaping, and "hybridization" of individual and societal values.

Discussion of our musical and relevant social values can foster the types of democratic behaviors desirable for broader public participation and engagement and can uncover attitudes and practices embedded in certain musical practices that may promote social injustices and hinder democratic participation, particularly as they relate to the commodification of music and its political use. For example, Allsup (2003) has explored ways in which democratic participation can be fostered through instrumental music learning, while others have examined how music teaching can become more student-centered and focused either through group decision-making about musical repertoire or the inclusion of musics from the community and students' cultural backgrounds so that the music program reflects cultures relevant to the students and community (Clark, 2005). This, however, means going beyond the common idea of "majority rules" (Bowman, 2007; Schmidt, 2007). Instead, we must see democratic discussion and action as transformative and exposing more choices than what is known to a single individual. We must look beyond what we *think* we need and want and be open to exploring new possibilities that reflect current social, political, and economic trends in or through music, even if we are uncomfortable with the results (Jorgensen, 2007; Väkevä & Westerlund, 2007). In doing so, we are asked to negotiate multiple points of view, which may in turn require us to re-examine our own values and beliefs. This, in itself, can uncover the ways in which we have assumed the "common sense" of the status quo, particularly in relation to whose music should be included in the curriculum, how we engage with the music industry, how we position school music in relation to music outside the school, how music is positioned in relation to other school subjects, and how music may itself be implicated in social and political problems. In doing so, teachers and their students would be better prepared to participate democratically both in administrative and political decisions in relation to music education and in ways that go far beyond choices based on a limited awareness of one's own individual needs.

As discussed above, neoliberal curricula have often removed or overlooked issues of race, socioeconomic status, and gender as a function of the "equal access for all" discourse, while stressing self-interest and a narrow conception of the self as an economic being. In addition, societies across the globe are becoming increasingly diverse, while neoliberalism as an economic policy has sustained and arguably relied upon a structure of economic competition that results in vast economic disparities among countries and socioeconomic classes. Indeed, as discussed above, music education has suffered an "economic disparity" in relation to "core" subjects in the pursuit of neoliberal economic goals that has made it necessary to rely often on the economic "benevolence" of industry. Both students and their teachers should understand that such benevolence is rarely as altruistic as it seems.

Returning to the question of social disparities and differences, music education can play an important role in expanding our understanding of the differences between individuals and cultures and fostering empathy toward them because "as we, along with our students, come to know the music of others, we may better understand our own culture and ourselves" (Jorgensen, 2010, p. 23). Mansfield (2002), for example, discusses how music education can create an awareness of cultural narratives, while at the same time uncovering grand narratives in music education that privilege one culture over another. Uncovering these narratives, particularly within bi- and multicultural nations, can empower excluded or marginalized groups and give them a sense of authority and belonging within the classroom. By fostering an understanding of individual and cultural circumstances and values, it can also negate the blame that a neoliberal approach to education places on certain individuals or groups who do not meet prescribed school standards. We must remember, however, that a discussion of bi- or multiculturalism is not limited merely to understanding the experience of race or ethnicity; it may also include gender (Sands, 2007) and socioeconomic status (Bates, 2011).

Mansfield (2002) has argued that a critical approach to music education as a cultural narrative "would identify dislocation and displacement of the traditional disciplines and play its part in upsetting the granite-like indisputable bodies of knowledge that have confined and disciplined the meaning of 'music' and its subject" (p. 191). Schmidt (2007), expanding on this idea, argues that, by allowing students to create and connect (the typically excluded) music from their outside lives to that within the school, they can come to understand the social, cultural, and political extra-musical realities that underpin musical contexts, genres, and performances and so can be motivated to "imagine a better world through music and dialogue" (p. 167). For example, Kindall-Smith, McKoy, and Mills (2011) give an overview and contextual description of how music teacher education can be restructured to support "culturally responsive" teaching aimed at including segments of society that have been marginalized in the curriculum, particularly urban youth, in order to empower students and give them a place of belonging in schools. Yet, Schmidt's ideas can be turned back on the very mechanisms of neoliberalism that underpin the standardized, outcome-oriented music curricula prevalent in music education today. What are the social, cultural, and extra-political realities of the standardized music curriculum content? How does it reflect neoliberal education ideology and broader neoliberal economic goals? Which musics does it include and exclude and why? Active discussion of these questions within music classrooms can raise students' political awareness of how neoliberalism attempts to shape their conception of how they should engage with music in society, promoting more truly informed choice.

CONCLUSION

Jorgensen (2010) wrote that "difficult though it may be, realizing the important links between the health of our democracy and our culture, as musician-teachers, we need to foster civil discourse, intellectual engagement, and respect for our differences and to struggle against inhumanity and oppression" (p. 26). Choice and the rights of individuals *are* important. Under a neoliberal conception of negative rights, however, choice is largely limited to a focus on the pursuit of one's own economic interest and pleasure in the belief that the combined prosperity of individuals who have chosen well will "trickle down" and result in the general improvement of social conditions. Current economic conditions, the slowly disappearing middle class, and the continuing problems confronted by schools in lower socioeconomic neighborhoods suggest that such an approach to social welfare and individual rights is not working. Instead, we might expand our choices and choose to see music education not just as a platform for developing musical skills and individual engagement, but as an opportunity to broaden notions of what it means to participate in democratic discussion and political action, to make informed choices about the music with which we engage, to foster empathy for those who are not like ourselves, and to uncover and confront the inequities embedded in education systems that insist that race, gender, and socioeconomic status should have no influence on how students participate in and experience schooling.

REFERENCES

Abril, C., & Gault, B. M. (2008). The state of music in secondary schools: The principal's perspective. *Journal of Research in Music Education, 56*(1), 68–81.

Allsup, R. E. (2003). Mutual learning and democratic action in instrumental music education. *Journal of Research in Music Education, 51*(1), 24–37.

Apple, M. (2000). *Official knowledge: Democratic education in a conservative age* (2nd ed.). New York: Routledge.

Apple, M. (2003). Competition, knowledge, and the loss of educational vision. *Philosophy of Music Education Review, 11*(1), 3–22.

Ball, S. J. (1993). Education markets, choice and social class: The market as class strategy in the UK and the USA. *British Journal of Sociology in Education, 14*(3), 3–19.

Ball, S. J. (2009). *Educational policy and social class: The selected works of Stephen J. Ball.* New York: Routledge.

Bates, V. (2011). Sustainable school music for poor, white, rural students. *Action, Criticism, and Theory for Music Education, 10*(2), 100–127.

Bowman, W. (2001). Music as ethical encounter. *Bulletin of the Council for Research in Music Education, 151*, 11–20.

Bowman, W. (2007). Who's asking? (Who's answering?) Theorizing social justice in music education. *Action, Criticism, and Theory for Music Education, 6*(4), 1–20.

Boyles, D., Carusi, T., & Attick, D. (2009). Historical and critical interpretations of social justice. In W. Ayers, T. Quinn, & S. Stovall (Eds.), *Handbook of social justice in education* (pp. 30–42). New York: Routledge.

Clark, S. (2005). Marachi music as a symbol of Mexican culture in the United States. *International Journal of Music Education, 33*(3), 227–237.

Eisner, E. (1998). *The kinds of schools we need: Personal essays.* Portsmouth, NH: Heineman.

Elliott, D. J. (1995). *Music matters: A new philosophy of music education.* Oxford: Oxford University Press.

Elliott, D. J. (2012). Music education as/for artistic citizenship. *Music Educators Journal, 99*(1), 21–27.

Fischman, G. E., & Haas, E. (2009). Critical pedagogy and hope in the context of neo-liberal globalization. In W. Ayers, T. Quinn, & S. Stovall (Eds.), *Handbook of social justice in education* (pp. 565–574). New York: Routledge.

Fourcade-Gourinchas F., & Babb, S. L. (2002). The rebirth of the liberal creed: Paths to neoliberalism in four countries. *The American Journal of Sociology, 108*(3), 533–579.

Frierson-Campbell, C. (2007). Without the 'ism: Thoughts about equity and social justice in music education. *Music Education Research, 9*(2), 255–265.

Gardner, R. D. (2010). Should I stay or should I go? Factors that influence the retention, turnover, and attrition of K-12 music teachers in the United States. *Arts Education Policy Review, 111*(3), 112–121.

Grimaldi, E. (2012). Education and the marginalisation of social justice: The making of an educational policy to combat exclusion. *International Journal of Inclusive Education, 16*(11), 1131–1154.

Harris, S. (2007). *The governance of education: How neo-liberalism is transforming policy and practice.* London: Continuum International Publishing Group.

Hayek, F. (1968). Freedom, reason and tradition. *Ethics, 68*(4), 229–249.

Heron, T. (2008). Globalization, neoliberalism and the exercise of human agency. *International Journal of Politics, Culture & Society, 28*(1–4): 85–101.

Hirschl, R. (2000). "Negative" rights vs. "positive" entitlements: A comparative study of judicial interpretations of rights in emerging neo-liberal economic order. *Human Rights Quarterly, 22*(4), 1060–1098.

Horsley, S. (2014). A comparative analysis of neoliberal education reform and music education in England and Ontario, Canada. (Doctoral dissertation, Western University, London,

Canada). Retrieved from http://network.bepress.com/arts-and-humanities/music/music-education/

Hursh, D. (2005). Neo-liberalism, markets and accountability: Transforming education and undermining democracy in the United States. *Policy Futures in Education, 3*(1), 3–15.

Hursh, D. (2009). Beyond the justice of the market: Combating neoliberal educational discourse and promoting deliberative democracy and economic equality. In W. Ayers, T. Quinn, & S. Stovall (Eds.), *Handbook of social justice in education* (pp. 152–164). New York: Routledge.

Jorgensen, E. (2007). Concerning justice and music education. *Music Education Research, 9*(2), 169–189.

Jorgensen, E. (2010). School music education and change. *Music Educators Journal, 96*(4), 21–27.

Keay, D. (1987, Oct. 31). Aids, education and the year 2000. *Women's Own Magazine,* 8–10. Retrieved from http://www.margaretthatcher.org/document/106689.

Kindall-Smith, M., McKoy, C. L., & Mills, S. W. (2011). Challenging exclusionary paradigms in the traditional music cannon: Implications for music education practice. *International Journal of Music Education, 29*(4), 374–386.

Leistyna, P. (2009). Preparing for public life: Education, critical theory, and social justice. In W. Ayers, T. Quinn, & S. Stovall (Eds.), *Handbook of social justice in education* (pp. 51–58). New York: Routledge.

Mansfield, J. (2002). Differencing music education. *British Journal of Music Education, 19*(2), 189–202.

Moore, R. (2009). *Sells like teen spirit: Music youth culture and social crisis.* New York: New York University Press.

Olssen, M. (2004). Neoliberalism, globalisation, democracy: Challenges for education. *Globalization, Societies and Education, 2*(2), 231–275.

Pinto, L. E. (2012). *Curriculum reform in Ontario: "Common sense" policy and democratic possibilities.* Toronto: University of Toronto Press.

Pitts, S. (2000). *A century of change in music education: Historical perspectives on contemporary practice in British secondary schools.* Aldershot, UK: Ashgate.

Popkewitz, S., & Gustafson, R. (2002). Standards of music education and the easily administered child/citizen: The alchemy of pedagogy and social inclusion/exclusion. *Philosophy of Music Education Review, 10*(2), 80–91.

Rizvi, F., & Engel, L. C. (2009). Neo-liberal globalization, educational policy, and the struggle for social justice. In W. Ayers, T. Quinn, & S. Stovall (Eds.), *Handbook of social justice in education* (pp. 529–541). New York: Routledge.

Rose, N., & Millar, P. (1992). Political power beyond the state: The problematics of government. *British Journal of Sociology, 43*(2), 173–205.

Sakiewicz, P., Nowosielski, R., Pilarczyk, W., & Cesarz, K. (2012). Planned obsolescence: Today's engineering dilemma. *Selected Engineering Problems, 3,* 185–188.

Sands, R. M. (2007). Social justice and equity: Doing the right thing in the music teacher program. *Action, Critcism, Theory, 6*(4), 43–59.

Schmidt, P. K. (2007). In search of a reality-based community: Illusions and tolerance in music, education, and society. *Philosophy of Music Education Review, 15*(2), 160–167.

Segall, W. E. (2006). *School reform in a global society.* Oxford: Roman and Littlefield Publishers.

Smith, A. (1991). *An inquiry into the nature and causes of the wealth of nations.* New York: Everyman's Library.

Soep, E., Saavedra, B. M., & Kurway, N. (2009). Social justice youth media. In W. Ayers, T. Quinn, & S. Stovall (Eds.), *Handbook of social justice in education* (pp. 477–484). New York: Routledge.

Sonu, D. (2012). Illusions of compliance: Performing the public and hidden transcripts of social justice education in neoliberal times. *Curriculum Inquiry, 42*(2): 240–259.

Spring, J. (1998). *Education and the rise of the global economy.* Mahwah, NJ: Lawrence Erlbaum Associates.

Taylor, S. (2004). Researching educational policy and change in "new times": Using critical discourse analysis. *Journal of Educational Policy, 19*(4), 433–451.

Taylor, S., & Henry, M. (2005). Globalization and educational policy making. In B. Lingard & J. Ozga (Eds.), *The Routledge Falmer reader in education policy and politics* (pp. 101–116). London: Routledge.

Turner, R. S. (2008). *Neo-liberal ideology: History, concepts and policies.* Edinburgh: Edinburgh University Press.

Väkevä, L., & Westerlund, H. (2007). The "method" of democracy in music education. *Action, Criticism, and Theory for Music Education, 6*(4), 96–108.

Waks, L. J. (2003). How globalization can cause fundamental curriculum change. *Journal of Educational Change, 4*(4), 383–418.

Wilson, D. (2005). The education and training of knowledge workers. In J. Zaida (Ed.), *The international handbook on globalisation, education and policy research: Global pedagogies and policies* (pp. 49–64). Dordrecht: Springer.

Woodford, P. (2005). *Democracy and music education: Liberalism, ethics, and the politics of practice.* Bloomington: Indiana University Press.

Woodford, P. (2014). Escaping versus confronting reality: Politics and music education in an age of entertainment. In P. Webster & J. Barrett (Eds.), *The musical experience: Rethinking music teaching and learning* (pp. 25–42). New York: Oxford University Press.

CHAPTER 5

EDUCATIONAL POLICY REFORMS AND THE POLITICS OF MUSIC TEACHER EDUCATION

GABRIEL RUSINEK AND JOSÉ LUIS ARÓSTEGUI

EDUCATION is never value-free. Schools and teachers are continuously confronted with problems whose solutions demand either being compliant with the social system they live in or acting to foster critical thinking toward its transformation. Their daily dilemma is whether to contribute to the maintenance of the social status quo or to confront it, and either option will occur, even if teachers are not conscious of the implications of their decisions. This duality between social conformity and change is a reflection of the political nature of education, which has been, is, and always will be in crisis, because education is not a deterministic science but an intrinsically political matter and, therefore, controversial.

Policymakers in democratic societies struggle to establish frames such as national curricula or standards for the social transmission of culture and for the preparation of young people as future workers and members of those societies. These frames have varied everywhere according to the local, regional, and national administrations' political orientations and their more or less conservative or progressive perspectives about the role of education in society. In recent times, however, they are also varying as a consequence of policy recommendations made by international organizations and owing to the impact of comparative assessment campaigns, promoted globally by transnational economic institutions.

Teacher education is challenged with similar problems, as its confrontations are heavily political because of their long-term effects through the pedagogical decisions of trained teachers, which affect many generations of children. Given that ideology is embedded in teacher educators' decided or undecided actions and inactions, to consider teacher education as a neutral and value-free enterprise is in itself, as Cochran-Smith,

Shakman, Jong, Terrell, Barnatt, and McQuillan (2009) proclaim, a flawed assumption. Even though many music teacher educators in the twenty-first century may still have a romantic view of the profession and may see themselves as politically neutral practitioners, or as "artists," we will further argue that music teacher education is also a political enterprise.

In this chapter, we discuss the politics of music teacher education in relation to the major policies that transnational institutions are promoting with respect to national curricular reforms, which influence programs developed by higher education institutions, taking into account the roles that education and music education can play in support of social justice and equity through public schooling. First, we review the impact of international organizations on the reforms of national curricula based on an economic rationale and, within them, on the shaping of a new role for music and arts education in schools. We discuss the case of the European Union as an illustration of the implementation of these policies and the influence they exert on many national curricula. Then, we discuss to what extent higher education institutions in charge of teacher education are assuming these curricular changes, and to what extent the research-based knowledge on music teaching and learning is having an influence on the evolution of music teacher education programs. Finally, we argue that a political interpretation is always present in education, not only with conflicts at the policy level, but also with the many problems faced by music teacher educators at the institutional level in the design, management, and evaluation of a program, and even in the organization of syllabuses or lessons planning.

The Role of Music Education in an Economy-Based Curriculum

Although national educational policies are usually a responsibility of each state's ministry or department of education, in the last decades they have been influenced by the recommendations of global organizations such as UNESCO and regional organizations like the European Union (EU). Moreover, at least for the last 15 years, they have also been heavily influenced by economic institutions such as the Organisation for Economic Co-operation and Development (OECD), the International Monetary Fund, and the World Bank. One of the major contributions of these institutions to education has been to generalize the administration and comparison of standardized assessments of national educational results. Examples of the involvement of these international economic institutions in education are the Programme for International Student Assessment (PISA), the Trends in International Mathematics and Science Study (TIMSS), or the Progress in International Reading Literacy Study (PIRLS). Focused on literacy, numeracy, and science knowledge, they have become pivotal not only for evaluating the effectiveness of different educational systems in relation to the evaluated concepts and skills, but also for the promotion of a specific idea of "educational quality" and its resulting educational interactions.

Correlated with this increasing comparative testing approach, a group of so-called basic school subjects considered crucial for the "knowledge-based economy" (OECD, 1996) is being promoted to the detriment of others. While a recurrent call for a "return to the basics" is not new for teachers and teacher educators, what is new is that today it is supported by an economic rationale. The idea of a "knowledge-based economy" justifies an "economy-based curriculum" with its emphasis on "excellence," "talent," and the development of individual skills, as recommended by the OECD (2012) "Skills Strategy" and the OECD (2010) "Innovation Strategy." This justification is based on the idea of effectiveness in educational systems, where "effectiveness" means, on the one hand, learning outcomes that can be clearly determined and assessed, and, on the other, effectiveness for the economic world. This is how schools should work for the economy, and how the economic rationale is assumed as the only possible curriculum approach in the educational reforms of many countries. The derived discourse, as illustrated, for example, by the EU policies, is that investment in education is essential, not to promote more just societies, but "to boost growth and competitiveness" (European Commission, 2012, p. 2). Within this discourse, a specific type of knowledge is considered the driver of productivity and economic development and therefore must be privileged. Science, technology, engineering, and mathematics—the "STEM" subjects—are thus once again becoming the "core" subjects of many national curricula to the detriment of the rest.

The intentions of these policy reforms are reified in terms of competences, a curricular construct coming from vocational training and originally aimed at the implementation of standards in professional education. The idea of "key competences" was launched in 1997 by the OECD project Definition and Selection of Competencies (DeSeCo) and was eventually included some years later within the European Union recommendations for lifelong learning (European Parliament and Council of the European Union, 2006). That same year, the key competences framework was incorporated into the reform of the Spanish national curriculum (Tiana, 2011), and afterward in the school curricula of most EU countries. From the broader EU viewpoint, the "STEM" knowledge is only one of the eight key competences "which all individuals need for personal fulfillment and development, active citizenship, social inclusion and employment" (European Parliament and Council of the European Union, 2006, p. L394/13). Besides the "STEM" competences, the two communicative competences (in the mother tongue and in foreign languages) and the digital competence, a set of four transversal competences stand in the EU recommendations as a reminder of what should be provided by compulsory education in democratic societies: learning to learn, social and civic competences, sense of initiative and entrepreneurship, and cultural awareness and expression. However, it seems that these transversal competences are usually only nominally included in national curricula because of the difficulty of assessing them. It is symptomatic that recommendations from institutions such as the European Parliament, which pay attention to the social aspects of learning, end up being reduced to an emphasis on "the basics" because of the problems of quantification and assessment. These recommendations tell us that

European society demands space for other competences, even if their nature makes it difficult to determine success in quantitative terms. It is therefore paradoxical that broad curricular perspectives advanced by democratic institutions end up being subverted by narrower "economic-based" perspectives promoted by economic institutions, which are highly political but whose members have not been elected democratically.

A socially just curriculum cannot diminish citizens' rights to learn how to learn, to be entrepreneurs, to be civically competent, or to be aware of their culture and arts because of the limits of the tools to measure the development of these competences. However, the increasing pre-eminence given by standardized evaluations to mathematics, language, and science, together with the difficulties in determining the learning outcomes related to arts experiences through standards, are bringing about a global decline (Aróstegui, 2012, 2016; Burnard, 2010; Burnard & White, 2008), even more accentuated than in the past, of music and the arts as part of compulsory education. For this economy-based curriculum, the question is to what extent music or other subjects are efficient in fulfilling their purposes, a question that, from this rationale, demands measurable evidences.

Among the many existing reviews about the impact of the arts on education, an OECD report (Winner, Goldstein, & Vincent-Lancrin, 2013) analyzes the existing research in many languages with respect to how they could contribute to innovation as one cornerstone of this "economy-based curriculum." Although its authors believe that the arts "are important in their own rights for education" (p. 20), they find that "evidence of any impact of arts learning on creativity and critical thinking, or on behavioral and social skills, remains largely inconclusive, partly because of an insufficient volume of experimental research on these matters and also because of the difficulty of adequately measuring these skills" (p. 256). This might partially explain why music and the arts end up having a secondary place in an "economy-based" curriculum. In the end, the measurement tools and the standard-based evaluations shape the educational policy reforms and determine what is included, and what is considered a "basic" subject, as part of compulsory education.

Music Teacher Education
in an Economy-Based Curriculum

If the preparation of teachers to teach music for music's sake is not a relevant strategy for an "economy-based curriculum," then teacher training programs need to be updated. Although national curriculum reforms and teacher education programs usually coincide in the search for an optimization of "human resources," the demands of the new national curricula are not necessarily acknowledged in college discussions about what music teachers need to know when they are in service. There have been important agreements about the desired learning outcomes of music teacher education, for example, among European higher education institutions (Hennessy, Malmberg, Nierman, & De

Vugt, 2009), but there is still no evidence about an extended application of these agreements. A new vision for music teacher education programs could be expected to adapt the preparation of preservice teachers to the current policy reforms whose challenges they will cope with during their professional careers.

Surprisingly, the data show that there is not too much relation between the policies of the educational reforms implemented virtually all over the world and the design of music teacher education programs. This is at least the conclusion of Aróstegui's (2011) and Aróstegui and Cisneros-Cohernour's (2010) analyses of music teacher education programs across 27 European and 17 Latin American countries, where they did not find clear directions about what a music teacher should be, except for the traditional focus on musical contents and their motivational transmission. Apart from a few exceptions, there is no evidence about whether music teacher education programs have started to become involved in preparing preservice teachers to understand young people's changing needs in a society driven by a knowledge-based society and economy. And not helping teachers to face the problems they will encounter in school settings, we contend, is a potential source of social injustice.

In the field of general teacher education there is an increasing amount of academic debate about the appropriateness of orienting programs toward the promotion of social justice (Bates, 2006; Cochran-Smith, 2010; Gates & Jorgensen, 2009; Kaur, 2012; Spalding, Klecka, Lin, Odell, & Wang, 2010; Ukpokodu, 2007; Weiler & Maher, 2002), with a preponderance of papers from English-speaking countries, and there are also a few research reports about how this orientation has been applied in some programs (Cochran-Smith et al., 1999; Kohl, 2002; McDonald, 2005). Building on philosophical arguments that challenge the relevance of the concept of social justice (e.g., Honneth, 1996; Rawls, 1999; Sen, 2009), Gates & Jorgensen (2009, p. 165) remind us that in the end, it is nevertheless "a relative concept; what is unjust to some, is not unjust to others." From an educational perspective, the problem is how the concept of social justice can be translated into curricular and teacher education discourses, as social injustice presents particular characteristics in each nation, region, or culture, and therefore teacher educators usually face differentiated challenges when designing programs for their contexts. Inequity is different in countries with visible social stratifications linked to extreme poverty, racial discrimination, or the presence of minorities, and in countries where stratification cannot be easily understood because of the blurred frontiers of traditional social class categories. Policymakers, teacher educators, and teachers face different forms of inequity in countries where the funding of public schools derives from local property taxes and in countries where public schooling is nationally funded. And teachers' challenges are also different in countries where standardized testing is an increasing stress on schools because of concomitant threats of funding cuts, and in countries where testing exerts a low pressure or is not linked to funding.

For instance, as teacher educators in Spain, we are concerned about the role of teacher education programs in a European country where social welfare has been nominally well distributed in terms of access to food, housing, health services, and education, but where extended future social injustice is predictable because of a continuing financial crisis. In the third trimester of 2013, according to the National Statistics Institute (INE, 2013a, 2013b), there were 5,904,700 unemployed people in a population of 47.1 million. The Spanish private debt has reached 214% of the GDP (European Commission, 2013), including 800 billion euros of families' mortgages, and the public debt is estimated by Eurostat (2013) as 92.3% of the GDP—and it keeps increasing. We wonder about the relations between low-level entrance and graduation demands for teacher education programs and school failure. We wonder about the relations between the absence of class consciousness and families' lack of trust in schooling as a form of cultural capital (Bourdieu, 1998) for social progress; between an indifference in mainstream teaching practices regarding students' autonomy, critical thinking, creativity or entrepreneurship, and those huge unemployment figures; between a nominally comprehensive, inclusive system where around 30% of students drop out and a society where great quantities of families' mortgages after the real estate bubble exploded are becoming bigger than their houses' current value; and between political corruption and an invisible, but gigantic, economic capital transfer among social groups. And we are particularly concerned about individual teacher educators' possibilities of action toward social justice in a bureaucratized university system wherein responsibility for prospective teachers' excellence is diluted—in all school disciplines, as well as in music—and where improvements at the program level sometimes collide with short-sighted departmental meanness and administrative college inertia.

Cochran-Smith and her colleagues (2009) respond to the critics of a social-justice–oriented teacher education, claiming that such an approach does not need to ignore traditional goals such as a profound knowledge of the subject matter and a responsibility for students' learning. This is crucial in countries where school failure is very high and the efficiency of teacher education cannot be taken for granted. One of the main challenges for social justice in those countries is to promote good quality teacher education programs as a way to provide young people with better opportunities for individual development, employability, and social improvement. In the particular field of music teacher education, an important social justice commitment should be to ensure that music teachers will graduate only after developing the musical and pedagogical expertise necessary to provide their future students with the musical experiences they deserve. However, there is still the possibility that a music teacher education program may contribute to future injustices when, despite providing good musical and instructional training, no attention is paid to the implications of the relation between how music is taught and how it is learned. This is the danger, for example, of the pre-eminent use of the content-centered approaches of twentieth-century "active" music teaching methods, in which students' voices are not allowed to emerge unless they imitate what the teacher says or sings, and where collaborative learning has no place in lesson planning because students are considered empty vessels to be filled, and the teacher is considered the only source of knowledge to be learned and of behaviors to be imitated. Even the names of the specific courses in which preservice teachers are taught to teach music present a kind of hidden curriculum. Whether named "didactics of music," following the German Didaktik tradition (Kertz-Welzel, 2004), or "music methods," following the

North American perspective, the courses' names speak about conservation and transmission of ways of teaching, and not necessarily about understandings of learning and reflections about the implications of how children and adolescents learn. There are still many teacher colleges in which music teaching methods seem to be an unquestioned dogma, the *mantra* of music teacher education, and where any discussion about possible relations between the political regimes where these methods were initially generated and the social interactions they foster (e.g., centered on a fixed sequence to be learned by all, centered on the imitation of a strong leader, or centered on interactions among equals) is perceived as heresy. As teachers tend to apply the teaching procedures they experienced as learners in uncritical manners (Liston & Zeichner, 1991), it is crucial that teacher training programs help preservice teachers reflect on how they learned music and other subjects in school, so that they can understand how the ways they were taught shaped their educational ideas.

For example, among many other topics, preservice teachers are taught how to plan their lessons. Planning comprises the design of learning activities (e.g., teacher-centered, textbook-centered, child-centered, cooperative) as well as cultural selections in relation to repertoire (e.g., classical, pop, world, music composed for the classroom). Failure to encourage preservice teachers to understand the social implications of the cultural selections they will make in their own instructional planning might involve further risks. The emphasis in many secondary schools around the world on teaching *about* classical music is just one example of the lack of reflection on the power of rituals in the reproduction of myths. This power was illuminated in Small's (1998) anthropological description and critique of the classical concert, where it is presented as a ritual for the exploration and affirmation of the beliefs and fears of the industrial societies' middle classes about the stability of the social status quo. A quick visit to many music classrooms, and music classrooms in teacher colleges as well, will show pictures of the classical European orchestra in standardized formation, pictures of instruments, and pictures of mostly dead Western white male composers, as if walls were altars reminding students about *holy* truths to be learned and remembered, and eventually enacted when attending live concerts. The danger resides in not encouraging preservice teachers to critically examine the implications of a content-based teaching that unconsciously prioritizes one cultural model and ignores students' needs. Music teachers should recognize cultural diversity and, therefore, include as many cultures, genres, and ways of musical interaction as possible to expand their students' horizons.

Finally, in this content-based practice of music education, there is another danger when preservice teachers are not encouraged to consider the implications of the different ways in which teachers and students act and interact in the classroom. Music teachers can plan lessons in which primary students play in unison with non-tunable one-piece plastic recorders, or lessons where they sing and dance. They can plan lessons in which secondary students answer written exams about the lives of classical composers, or lessons in which they perform in percussion ensembles, choirs, or bands. In either case, they need to remember their responsibility for preparing children and adolescents for unpredictable futures. A music teacher education program focusing heavily on performance and appreciation but ignoring musical creativity and critical awareness might therefore be helping, intentionally or not, to reproduce a social system in which young people are being trained as consumers or, at most, reproducers of *decaffeinated*, culturally decontextualized adaptations of music created by others and accessed through publishing or record companies.

SOCIAL JUSTICE AND THE NEW CHALLENGES OF MUSIC TEACHER EDUCATION

Social justice is also a concern in the educational reforms promoted by some transnational institutions mentioned earlier as promoters of an economy-based curriculum. The OECD (2011) acknowledges that education policies that promote equity and support disadvantaged students in achieving better academic outcomes may help reduce income inequality in the future and that equity-based education policies can be a key tool for reducing future income inequality. These social challenges can be better faced with a curriculum that is effectively carried out and, at the same time, empowers students for social transformation. To counterbalance inequalities is important not only for social justice, but also for the "knowledge-based economy." As Zeichner (2009) observes, "the potential of educational reform is severely limited unless it is coupled with fundamental changes in the economic, social, and political structures of society" (p. 143).

From the prior discussion presented in this chapter, we identify three major issues for music teacher education in support of social justice. The first is, needless to say, ensuring quality in those programs. Students' educational success and future professional careers are related, among other circumstances, with what happens in classrooms, and this depends mainly on teachers' actions. Thus, a society cannot promote that success without ensuring the quality of teacher education, and if it does not provide this quality, large segments of its population might end up deprived. We contend that music teacher education programs can help to maintain social inequalities when they do not provide appropriate preparation, when candidate music teachers are allowed to graduate without enough musical training in countries where they will eventually be hired, when there is a focus on content and on musical activities for activities' sake, or when music in primary schools is delivered by generalist teachers who are not sufficiently prepared. An inequality of school musical opportunities, thus, derives from an inadequate preparation of music teachers, because in the end it leaves musical participation the privilege of a few.

Music teacher education programs can also contribute to maintaining social injustices when candidate music teachers, with or without enough musical training, are allowed to graduate without sufficient understanding of the cognitive, physical, emotional, and social aspects of music learning, of how and why it has to be assessed, and of its role and the role of the arts in the development of culturally situated human beings. An example of the harmful consequences of this lack of understanding is the emphasis of many general music teachers in some countries on teaching declarative knowledge that cannot be empirically perceived and, consequently, has to be verbally memorized by their students by repeating without understanding (e.g., music theory without musical practice in primary schools, or music theory *and* music history without musical practice in secondary schools). These approaches, unfortunately still common at the beginning of the twenty-first century, might be understood by children as key lessons on the cultural convenience of repeating dogmatic knowledge, complying uncritically with inefficient procedures, and accepting rules as unchangeable, in order to succeed in social life. And in the end, these approaches can also result in a lack of appreciation of music by students and their families, as is documented in some countries (e.g., Gammon, 1996; Lamont & Maton, 2008), thus collaborating with the voices that want to push music out of the school curriculum.

A second issue that music teacher education programs have to consider is the clear demise of the arts as part of compulsory education because many curriculum planners do not value its impact on innovation skills in the new "economy-based" curriculum. From this restrictive perspective, music and the arts seem to be useful only for *talented* students, who will be trained in music schools or conservatories, or for the promotion of social inclusion through community programs. In both cases, teaching occurs outside schools, with the result that not everybody receives artistic knowledge, while elite schools keep arts and music programs to develop their students' cultural capital, which is "the familiarity with precisely those subjects that schools do not teach but that elites value" (DiMaggio, 1982, p. 191).

If we ignore these new social and economic challenges, it is quite probable that music teacher education programs might contribute to the exclusion of music from the curriculum because of their lack of adequacy in meeting students' and schools' changing needs. Music teacher education programs might not be helping teachers to face the demands of the new "economic-based curriculum" if they keep an exclusive focus on musical content, that is, on music for music's sake. The idea of art for art's sake in schools has been confronted by the transnational economic institutions (Winner, Goldstein, & Vincent-Lancrin, 2013), and its corresponding model of music education based on music methods can no longer be supported. Insisting on a model established in the nineteenth century, in correspondence with the spiritual and abstract concept of art from modernity (Baricco, 1999; Gaztambide-Fernández, 2008) far removed from the "economic-based curriculum" fostered by the latest educational policy reforms and from students' social demands, might result in an unequal access to artistic experiences. We are not claiming, by any means, that music teacher education programs should just comply uncritically with the educational policy reforms in the process of implementation virtually all over the world, but rather that we cannot ignore these challenges and that we need to incorporate them as part of the agenda of music education. Music cannot continue to be reified and treated as an artistic matter independent of social context anymore: its teaching must be linked to the real needs of schools.

The presence of music education in schools is no longer a matter of advocacy but of rethinking its role in a new type of curriculum and showing evidence of its contribution to compulsory education. However, in addition to standards and indicators, there must be space for other ways to assess this contribution, for music learning or for any competence whose nature makes it difficult to determine success in quantitative terms. For instance, the "appreciation of the importance of the creative expression of ideas, experiences and emotions in a range of media (music, performing arts, literature and the visual arts)," the cultural competence as defined by the Parliament and the Council of the European Union (2006, p. L394/318), cannot be limited because of the limitations of the tools to measure its development. Thus, a further challenge for music teacher education programs is to ensure that they will prepare preservice teachers to cross from advocacy to evidence when trying to support music and the arts in the curriculum, by training them to find that evidence through qualitative and sociocultural approaches in order to compete with the more restrictive, mainstream, quantitative assessments.

Finally, despite recurrent efforts to persuade teachers and teacher educators that music education is an apolitical, decontextualized, and timeless endeavor, hiding the relation between what is taught and the way it is learned, music education is a social practice that cannot escape from political dilemmas, as some scholars have been advocating (e.g., Green, 2003; Regelski, 2009; Woodford, 2005), and even less the preparation of music teachers. Though this challenge must be faced collegially by music education departments, individual music teacher educators can also make decisions toward the promotion of a social justice education, even if the program in which they participate does not. Many decisions that are made, collegially or individually, will be confrontational because of their political nature and because music education is not a mere entertainment isolated from social milieus, at least if we understand music, as Elliott (1995) suggests, not as sound, but as human interaction through sound, and if we conceptualize school music education as an opportunity to learn about other possible ways of human interaction that should be provided to all children. Hence, both music education departments and individual teacher educators can minimize the risks of promoting further social injustices if, from the very beginning, they help preservice teachers to understand the social nature and the political implications of music teaching and learning in schools.

Acknowledgments

We deeply appreciate all the feedback provided by Paul Woodford, as well as his invaluable support in editing the English text.

References

Aróstegui, J. L. (Ed.). (2011). *Educating music teachers for the 21st century*. Rotterdam: Sense.
Aróstegui, J. L. (2012, July). Neoliberalism and the global decline of music education. Paper presented at the 30th ISME Conference. Thessaloniki (Greece).

Aróstegui, J. L. (2016). Exploring the global decline of music education. *Arts Education Policy Review*, *117*(1).

Aróstegui, J. L., & Cisneros-Cohernour, E. J. (2010). Reflexiones en torno a la formación del profesorado de música a partir del análisis documental de los planes de Estudio en Europa y América Latina. *Profesorado: Revista de Currículum y Formación del Profesorado*, *14*(2), 179–189. Retrieved from http://www.ugr.es/~recfpro/rev142ART14.pdf.

Baricco, A. (1999). *El alma de Hegel y las vacas de Wisconsin: Una reflexión sobre música culta y modernidad*. Madrid: Siruela.

Bates, R. (2006). Public education, social justice and teacher education. *Asia-Pacific Journal of Teacher Education*, *34*(3), 275–286. doi: 10.1080/13598660600927067.

Bourdieu, P. (1998). *Capital cultural, escuela y espacio social*. México: Siglo Veintiuno.

Burnard, P. (2010). Creativity, performativity, and educational standards: Conflicting or productive tensions in music education in England? *Studies in Music from the University of Western Ontario*, *23* (special issue on *Rethinking standards for the 21st century: New realities, new challenges, new propositions*), 18–40.

Burnard, P., & White, J. (2008). Creativity and performativity: Counterpoints in British and Australian education. *British Educational Research Journal*, *34*(5), 667–682. doi: 10.1080/01411920802224238.

Cochran-Smith, M. (2010). Toward a theory of teacher education for social justice. In A. Hargreaves, A. Lieberman, M. Fullan, & D. Hopkins (Eds.), *Second international handbook of educational change* (pp. 445–467). Dordrecht: Springer.

Cochran-Smith, M., Albert, L., Dimattia, P., Freedman, S., Jackson, R., Mooney, J., & Zollers, N. (1999). Seeking social justice: A teacher education faculty's self-study. *International Journal of Leadership in Education*, *2*(3), 229–253.

Cochran-Smith, M., Shakman, K., Jong, C., Terrell, D. G., Barnatt, J., & McQuillan, P. (2009). Good and just teaching: The case for social justice in teacher education. *American Journal of Education*, *115*(3), 347–377.

DiMaggio, P. (1982). Cultural capital and school success: The impact of status culture participation on the grades of US high school students. *American Sociological Review*, *47*(2), 189–201.

Elliott, D. J. (1995). *Music matters: A new philosophy of music education*. New York: Oxford University Press.

European Commission. (2012). *Rethinking education: Investing in skills for better socio-economic outcomes*. Retrieved from http://eur-lex.europa.eu/LexUriServ/LexUriServ.do?uri=COM: 2012:0669:FIN:EN:PDF.

European Commission. (2013). Private debt in % of GDP—non consolidated—annual data. Retrieved from http://epp.eurostat.ec.europa.eu/tgm/table.do?tab=table&plugin=1&language=en&pcode=tipspd10.

European Parliament and Council of the European Union. (2006). Recommendation of the European Parliament and of the Council of 18 December 2006 on key competences for lifelong learning (2006/962/EC). *Official Journal of the European Union*, *30.12.2006*, L394/310-L394/318. Retrieved from http://eur-lex.europa.eu/LexUriServ/LexUriServ.do?uri=OJ:L:2006:394:0010:0018:en:PDF.

Eurostat. (2013). *Eurostat news release: Euro indicators 153/2013*. Luxembourg: Eurostat Press Office. Retrieved from http://epp.eurostat.ec.europa.eu/cache/ITY_PUBLIC/2-23102013-AP/EN/2-23102013-AP-EN.PDF.

Gammon, V. (1996). What is wrong with school music? A response to Malcolm Ross. *British Journal of Music Education*, *13*(2), 101–122. doi: 10.1017/S0265051700003089.

Gates, P., & Jorgensen, R. (2009). Foregrounding social justice in mathematics teacher education. *Journal of Mathematics Teacher Education, 12*(3), 161–170. doi: 10.1007/s10857-009-9105-4.

Gaztambide-Fernández, R. A. (2008). The artist in society: Understandings, expectations, and curriculum implications. *Curriculum Inquiry, 38*(3), 233–265. doi: 10.1111/j.1467-873X.2008. 00408.x.

Green, L. (2003). Why "ideology"is still relevant for critical thinking in music education. *Action, Criticism, and Theory for Music Education, 2*(2), 1–24. Retrieved from http://act.maydaygroup.org/articles/Green2_2.pdf.

Hennessey, S., Malmberg, I., Nierman, F., & De Vugt, A. (Eds.). (2009). *meNet learning outcomes in music teacher training.* Vienna: The European Network for Communication and Knowledge Management of Music Education.

Honneth, A. (1996). *The struggle for recognition: The moral grammar of social conflicts.* Cambridge, MA: MIT Press.

INE. (2013a). Avance de la estadística del padrón continuo a 1 de enero de 2013 Madrid: Instituto Nacional de Estadística. Retrieved from http://www.ine.es/prensa/np776.pdf.

INE. (2013b). Encuesta de población activa (EPA). Tercer trimestre de 2013. Madrid: Instituto Nacional de Estadística. Retrieved from http://www.ine.es/daco/daco42/daco4211/epa0313.pdf.

Kaur, B. (2012). Equity and social justice in teaching and teacher education. *Teaching and Teacher Education, 28*(4), 485–492. doi: http://dx.doi.org/10.1016/j.tate.2012.01.012.

Kertz-Welzel, A. (2004). Didaktik of music: A German concept and its comparison to American music pedagogy. *International Journal of Music Education, 22*(3), 277–286.

Kohl, H. (2002). Developing teachers for social justice. *Radical Teacher, 65,* 5–10.

Lamont, A., & Maton, K. (2008). Choosing music: Exploratory studies into the low uptake of music GCSE. *British Journal of Music Education, 25*(3), 267–282. doi: 10.1017/S0265051708008103.

Liston, D. P., & Zeichner, K. M. (1991). *Teacher education and the social conditions of schooling.* New York: Routledge.

McDonald, M. A. (2005). The integration of social justice in teacher education: Dimensions of prospective teachers' opportunities to learn. *Journal of Teacher Education, 56*(5), 418–435. doi: 10.1177/0022487105279569.

OECD. (1996). *The knowledge-based economy.* Paris: OECD Publishing. Retrieved from http://www.oecd.org/sti/sci-tech/1913021.pdf.

OECD. (2010). *The OECD innovation strategy: Getting a head start on tomorrow.* Paris: OECD Publishing. Retrieved from http://dx.doi.org/10.1787/9789264083479-en.

OECD. (2011). *Divided we stand: Why inequality keeps rising.* Paris: OECD Publishing. doi: 10.1787/9789264119536-en.

OECD. (2012). *Better skills, better jobs, better lives: A strategic approach to skills policies.* Paris: OECD Publishing. Retrieved from http://dx.doi.org/10.1787/9789264177338-en.

Rawls, J. (1999). *A theory of justice* (rev. ed.). Cambridge, MA: Harvard University Press.

Regelski, T. A. (2009). Curriculum reform: Reclaiming "music" as social praxis. *Action, Criticism, and Theory for Music Education, 8*(1), 65–84. Retrieved from http://act.maydaygroup.org/articles/Regelski8_1.pdf.

Sen, A. K. (2009). *The idea of justice.* Cambridge, MA: Harvard University Press.

Small, C. (1998). *Musicking. The meanings of performing and listening.* Middletown, CT: Wesleyan University Press.

Spalding, E., Klecka, C. L., Lin, E., Odell, S. J., & Wang, J. (2010). Social justice and teacher education: A hammer, a bell, and a song. *Journal of Teacher Education*, 61(3), 191–196. doi: 10.1177/0022487109359762.

Tiana, A. (2011). Análisis de las competencias básicas como núcleo curricular en la educación obligatoria española. *Bordón. Revista de Pedagogía*, 63(1), 63–75. Retrieved from http://dial-net.unirioja.es/descarga/articulo/3601025.pdf.

Ukpokodu, O. N. (2007). Preparing socially conscious teachers: A social justice-oriented teacher education. *Multicultural Education*, 15(1), 8–15.

Weiler, K., & Maher, F. (2002). Teacher education and social justice. *Radical Teacher*, 64, 2–4.

Winner, E., Goldstein, T. R., & Vincent-Lancrin, S. (2013). *Art for art's sake? Overview*, Paris: OECD Publishing. doi: http://dx.doi.org/10.1787/9789264180789-en.

Woodford, P. (2005). *Democracy and music education: Liberalism, ethics, and the politics of practice*. Bloomington: Indiana University Press.

Zeichner, K. M. (2009). *Teacher education and the struggle for social justice*. New York: Routledge.

CHAPTER 6

....

THE PROMOTION
OF MULTIPLE CITIZENSHIPS
IN CHINA'S MUSIC
EDUCATION

....

WAI-CHUNG HO AND WING-WAH LAW

DEFINITIONS of citizenship education may vary greatly from country to country, especially when transmitting values across nations. The laws of over half of the nation-states in the world are said to reflect "some forms of multiple citizenship or multiple nationality citizenship" (Kalekin-Fishman & Pitkanen, 2007, p. vii). In this sense, the pedagogical discourse of global citizenship education in schools uses a variety of key terms in different national contexts: citizenship education is also known as cosmopolitan education, multicultural education, democratic education, peace education, human rights education, intercultural education, and multiple citizenship education (Banks, 2004, 2008).

What do multiple citizenships mean to school music education in the twenty-first century? In North America, the long dominant philosophy in music education was Reimer's (1970) music education as aesthetic education, which generally avoided talk of citizenship and other political considerations that were regarded as of only secondary importance in music education, if important at all. However, John Dewey (1859–1952), one of the fathers of the progressive education movement, contended that education should serve a political purpose in preparing children for democratic citizenship (Woodford, 2012a, 2012b). In using Dewey's and other philosophers' views to discuss a "new" and overtly political philosophy of music education for our time, Woodford (2005) argues that "music programs should work to effect social amelioration and contribute to the common or public good.... The purpose of music education ought to be the development of democratic musical citizenship" (personal communication, November 15, 2004, cited in Boon, 2009, p. 17). Given that normative assumptions often connect music education with larger democratic values, Allsup (2010) similarly adopts and explicitly links the term "musical citizenship" to notions of national and, more recently, global citizenship in classroom communities (p. 136). Other music educators (e.g., Allsup, 2004, 2010; Elliott, 2005; Green, 2006) have also examined music teaching and learning as a pedagogy of emancipation and have chosen to use diverse musical cultures, including popular and world music, to initiate or effect education reform leading to social change.

Although the study of citizenship and citizenship education has been established in various disciplines of the humanities and social sciences in other parts of the world, relating citizenship to music education in China is still rare. This chapter discusses the Chinese government's role in defining multiple citizenships in school music education through a new pattern of individual-collective relationships in Mainland China that includes (a) the power of personal values, (b) nation building and filial obedience, and (c) the pursuit of multicultural and global understanding. We argue that, despite giving individuals a greater sense of shared citizenship in learning diverse musical cultures and meanings delineated in song lyrics in school music education, the contemporary Chinese government promotes citizenship education in music education as a means of consolidating its political leadership while maintaining social stability. Before analyzing how the Chinese government shapes and uses music in citizenship education in contemporary China, however, it will be helpful to readers to a have a brief history of how music and music education have previously related to citizenship education in that country.

Contexts and Social Functions of Music Education

Mainland China is a multi-ethnic society, comprising 56 ethnic groups within a population of 1.3 billion people, the largest in the world. The Han ethnic group comprises 92 percent of the population. Although many of the ethnic minority groups have their own languages, the official language is Putonghau, which is based on Beijing pronunciation. Confucianism, the philosophy established by Confucius (551–479 BC), is the cornerstone of traditional Chinese culture and notions of citizenship. The rationale for music education in Imperial China adhered to the discipline of moral education as a way of encouraging citizens to live more virtuously. Because of its close association with the conservative characteristics of Confucian society, music was conceived in terms of ethics, rather than aesthetics.

China has long adopted political-ideology education to serve as a mechanism for political indoctrination. At several turning points in the development of Chinese music education throughout the country's history, songs were used to transmit political ideology. For example, when Mao Zedong (1893–1976) officially proclaimed the founding of the People's Republic of China (PRC) on October 1, 1949, Chinese education served as an instrument for the transmission of the new beliefs and values that helped build a revolutionary communist society. As such, education and music activities had to be strictly in line with the Chinese government's communist Marxist-Leninist-Maoist ideology

(Ho & Law, 2012; Hung, 1996; Perris, 1983). The Cultural Revolution (1967–1976) was launched by Communist Party Chairman Mao Zedong to secure Maoism in China as the state's dominant ideology, but in the end it severely damaged the country's culture, education system, economy, society, and politics.

With the death of Mao in September 1976 and the end of the Cultural Revolution, Deng Xiaoping (1904–1997) began his political comeback. Following the economic boom brought about by the 1978 implementation of the "Open Door Policy," the state minimized the use of education as an instrument of "proletarian politics." To this end, Chinese authorities introduced a series of education reforms, including the 1977 reinstatement of national college examinations (suspended during the Cultural Revolution); the 1977 importation of over 2,000 foreign textbooks from Britain, France, Japan, and the United States to revise China's curriculum (Law, 2013; Lu, 2002); plans to change the curriculum structure and teaching methods; and reinstating English as the first foreign language for junior-secondary to post-secondary school students.

Today, one of the key issues for Mainland China has been how to adapt its revolutionary communist legacy to the increasing pressures of globalization and economic prosperity. Dramatic changes have occurred in education policies and practices and in the larger contexts of the economy, society, and politics. Sociopolitical transitions and ideological shifts have opened the door to education reforms, including the decentralization of education policy, school financing, and administration (Mok, 2000). Education researchers (e.g., Law, 2011; Pan, 2011; Wang, 2008) have examined how global and local events and forces have impacted Chinese education, including a shift, to some extent, from the former Confucian emphasis on the development of moral virtue in children and youths to a new concept of moral education relating to everyday living and the pursuit of personal happiness (Cheung & Pan, 2006; Zhou, Qin, Deng, & Chai, 2011). Chinese cultures value family hierarchy and harmony, which are central concepts in Confucianism, and they continue to be valued in Mainland China. School education in today's China continues to change and evolve in response to curriculum reforms. In the following pages, critical discourse analysis is used to examine these reforms as evidenced in school music curricula and textbooks, government documents concerning education policies and curricula, and other relevant studies as they relate to the tension between national and global interests implicit in the development of multiple citizenships in students, as well as between individualism and collectivism, tradition and change in Chinese music education.

CITIZENSHIP EDUCATION
AND THE POWER OF PERSONAL VALUES

School music education in China has long been criticized for cultivating personal values in a society that has experienced tension between individualism and collectivism in the transmission of both musical and non-musical knowledge (Ho & Law, 2004). Most early studies on individualism and collectivism in China were based on the cultural explanation that describes societies in which people are integrated into groups with strong, cooperative, cohesive, and loyal ties to group orientation (Hofstede, 1984). However, with the political and economic breakthroughs in the past few decades, the younger generations in China have made a gradual shift to individualism, while the older generations have continued to embrace collectivism (Zhang & Shavitt, 2003). According to the 1996 national survey of Chinese youths by the China Youth and Children Research Center, 77.5 percent of the youths recognized the orientation of their self-value as their most prominent feature; in addition, 50.35 percent stated that the major reason they worked hard was to fulfill their own values (Xi & Xia, 2006, p. 98).

With a view to addressing this tension in Chinese society between individualism and collectivism, Chinese authorities have stated their intention to broaden the scope of citizenship education to include this burgeoning individualism among youths by diversifying teaching methods and materials. A new education philosophy, innovative curriculum materials, and the renewal of educational experiences—along with respect for and encouragement of students' independence, individualism, and personal values—suggest a more expansive view toward individualism through the learning of song lyrics in school music education. In 2005, the Shanghai Municipal Education Commission, for example, compiled a list of 100 patriotic songs for secondary schools that included songs that encourage individualism among those with themes of dedication to society and collective values. The most controversial song is "Snail" by the popular Taiwanese singer Jay Chou.[1] The lyrics of this song encourage young people to pursue success in difficult times: "Should I leave my heavy shell and look for a blue sky? . . . I must crawl upwards slowly, waiting for the sun to silently gaze at my face, the tiny sky has a huge dream. . . . One day I will have a piece of sky that is my own. . . ." (translated by the authors). This is a departure from traditional patriotic songs, which were intended to foster in students a sense of collectivism, socialism, and heroism (Zou, 2005).

According to the current national music curriculum in China, popular songs with diverse structures and styles encourage primary school students to adopt a "healthy" (*jiankang*) lifestyle (Ministry of Education, 2012, p. 16). Healthy song lyrics can also help students shape their citizenship and identity, as well as cultivate good social values in secondary school education (Hu, 2011). Despite the different political orientations of Mainland China and Taiwan, some Taiwanese songs have been adopted as suitable for authorized publication, for example, "Invisible Wing" (*Yinxing Di Chibang*), by Taiwanese popular artist Angela Chang (Hunan Literature and Art Publishing House, 2012a, p. 59), "Tomorrow Would Be Better," by Taiwanese popular artist Luo Dayou (Hunan Literature and Art Publishing House, 2012b, p. 59), and "My Tomorrow Is Not a Dream" (*Wodi Weilai Bushi Meng*), by Taiwanese popular artist Zhang Yusheng (Juvenile & Children's Publishing House, 2009, p. 18). Other popular songs, such as "A Flowering Season of a 16-Year Old" (*Shiliu Sui Di Huaji*, the theme song of a popular television drama in Mainland China in the early 1990s) (Shanghai Educational Publisher, 2011b,

p. 10), and "My Heart Will Go On (Love Theme from *Titanic*)," by American musician James Horner (People's Music Publisher, 2010, p. 46), promote the exercise of one's goals, desires, and self-reliance. The introduction of "healthy" popular songs has also been extended to other school subjects. For example, on the first day of China's national college entrance examinations (*gaokao*) in June 2009, Beijing students were required to write at least 800 characters expressing their views on Angela Chang's song "Invisible Wing," because the words "invisible wings, flying toward the distance" were thought to stimulate the students' imagination. In the authors' opinion, the introduction of such songs is intended to temper individualism and to contribute to the understanding of how pro-socialist China copes with the tension between personal autonomy and socialist collectivism.

Citizenship Education in Nation Building and Filial Obedience

Having explained the rise and promotion of individualism relative to collectivism in Chinese citizenship education, this section considers how music education might manage the relationship between personal values (in the context of Chinese communism, Chinese nationalism, Chinese patriotism, Chinese identity, and Chinese soft nationalism) and Confucian values so they can be integrated into citizenship education. The teachings of Confucius stress the interests of the collective and remain the basis of family and societal values, providing norms for work, personal ethical growth, and relationships. As such, the Confucius Institute Project, which began establishing centers for Chinese language instruction in 2004, involves a complex mix of soft power techniques. These teachings are considered a renewed way of projecting soft power, control, and political propaganda with Chinese characteristics in modern China.

In our analysis of the content of citizenship education described by the Communist Party of China (CPC)–led state, China's music education reflects the ruling party's ideologies, infused through national education or patriotic education. After the founding of the PRC in 1949, China invited Soviet experts to visit and provide advice on the construction of a new nation based on the Soviet model of development, and to set up its socialist curriculum for the construction of a new socialist notion of national citizenship and identity. Owing to the special relationship between the PRC and the Soviet Union, Chinese musicians were sent to the Soviet Union and other countries in Eastern Europe to learn their musicianship and other musical training. Many Chinese policies, such as the Great Leap Forward (an economic and social campaign from 1958 to 1961) and the collectivization of agriculture, were presented to the community using Social Realist posters that included communist expressions and slogans.

Collectivism, mass art, and praise of the CPC were strongly emphasized in music and music education. Traditionally, students in China were required to sing monotonous revolutionary songs in the name of patriotic education or to hasten the advent of a "communist utopia." In modern China, however—even though some revolutionary and patriotic songs, such as "The Military Anthem of the Chinese People's Liberation Army" (*Zhongguo Renmin Jiefangjun Junge*) (People's Music Publisher, 2010, p. 28), "A Hymn to My Motherland" (*Gechang Zuguo*) (People's Music Publisher, 2009, p. 3), and "Song for the Common Youth League" (*Gongqing Tuanyuan Zhi Ge*), are still common in music textbooks—the national anthem of the PRC ("March of the Volunteers") and other typical Maoist and revolutionary songs are downplayed in the school music curriculum. Singing the PRC's national anthem, which was once placed at the beginning of music textbooks, used to be compulsory. Today, some textbooks have excluded the national anthem and other revolutionary and communist songs in their present publications in favor of the aforementioned.

As the PRC government has recognized, the continuous praise of the CPC is not sufficient for promoting patriotism among students. As a result, the government has attempted to repackage new Chinese nationalism from "the century of national humiliation," referring to the period of foreign intervention and imperialism by Western powers and Japan between 1839 and 1945. The CPC's propaganda message and the contents of school curricula and textbooks have been amended to account for the blending of Confucianism and the individualism of "Chinese" identity in an effort to adapt to change while ensuring its continuity (Jones, 2005; Vickers, 2007). The identity of "Greater China" is stressed in citizenship education as a means to boost patriotism among students and to guard against attempts by hostile foreign forces to overthrow China's socialist system. For example, even though the Second Sino-Japanese War ended over 65 years ago, anti-Japanese feelings have lingered in the major cities of Mainland China, particularly during the recent anti-Japanese protests over the disputed Diaoyu Islands. Anti-Japanese songs, such as "Protect the Yellow River" (*Baowei Huanghe*) (Lei, 2009a, pp. 48–51), "Non-resistance Is the Only Fear" (*Zhipa Bu Dikang*), and "Military Song for Saving the Nation" (*Jiuguo Junge*) (People's Music Publisher, 2012, pp. 38–39), are still used in class to praise the reconstruction of the nation after Japanese aggression.

As mentioned above, although the PRC government now to some extent downplays patriotic music in the curriculum, it nevertheless continues to use propaganda songs to incorporate traditional notions of Chinese identity into the description of the cultural dimension of "Chinese characteristics." For example, through singing, students are reminded of the roots of Chinese nationalism in China's past. In addition, propaganda songs have placed more emphasis on the legitimacy of their protection of the glorious legacy of China's ancient civilization. To ensure wider cultural circulation, contemporary propaganda songs are closely tied to commercials introducing the concept of a "Greater China." The Opening Ceremony of the 2008 Olympic Games, with its impressive kaleidoscope of China's "four great inventions" from ancient times, highlighted and constructed an ensemble of Chinese cultural characteristics associated with national identity using ancient Chinese musical instruments and music, such as the *Fou* (the most ancient Chinese percussion instrument, made of clay or bronze), the *Ququin* (an ancient stringed instrument), Peking Opera, and Kunqu[2] (CCTV.com, 2008). In recent years, contemporary songs such as "Country" (*Guojia*), which was written to commemorate the sixtieth anniversary of the PRC (October 1, 2009) and was performed by Hong Kong film star Jackie Chan and famous Mainland singer Liu Yuanyuan, have been popularized. The song stresses that each household is tied to the fate of the nation as the populace works together to build a symbolic "country."

The popularity of newer propaganda songs celebrating the rise of China, such as "My Chinese Heart" (*Wo De Zhongguo Xin*), by Hong Kong songwriter James Wong, "The Descendants of the Dragon" (*Long De Chuanren*), by Taiwanese songwriter Hou De Jian, and "Asian Hero" (*Yazhou Xiongfeng*), by Mainland composer Xu Peidong, and the values they espouse reflect both China's modernization and its historic past. Despite the different political perspectives between Mainland China and Taiwan, China's Ministry of Education and schoolteachers have strongly recommended the use of Taiwanese singer Jay Chou's popular songs in their teaching materials for the ethos of Greater Chinese nationalism and patriotism (Cai, 2009; Lu & Fang, 2010). Chou's songs have evoked "Chineseness" together with Western styles by alluding to classical Chinese literature and the use of traditional Chinese musical instruments, such as the Pipa and the Chinese flute, thereby playing a role in the construction of a sense of greater Chinese nationality (Gu, 2008; Zhang, 2011).

In China's citizenship education, nationalism has been almost exclusively directed against the foreign threat that began with Britain in the First and Second Opium Wars (1839–1842 and 1856–1860, respectively), and then notably with the United States and Japan in the twentieth century. As already suggested, but perhaps not emphasized enough, Chinese-style soft nationalism in contemporary China takes pride in Confucian values (Cheung, 2012). In contrast to soft nationalism, the "hard" form of Chinese nationalism is reported to be centered in the CPC's military power. Under Confucianism, all political relationships fall under one of five basic categories: ruler and subject, father and son, husband and wife, elder and younger, and friend and friend. It is believed that Confucian ethics enhance harmonious family rapport. Therefore, Confucianism continues to dominate the content of contemporary China's school music education in terms of the social meanings conveyed in many song lyrics. Popular songs that deal with issues of love, filial obedience, and friendship are recommended in the school music curriculum, and they include songs in praise of home, parenthood, and friendship found in music textbooks, for example, "Little Sheep Have to Return Home" (*Xaioxiao Yanger Yaohui Jia*) (an old Mandarin popular song popularized in Chinese societies since the 1950s) (People's Music Publisher, 2012, pp. 30–31), "Take Me Home, Country Roads" (an American country folk song written and sung by John Denver) (Shanghai Educational Publisher, 2010, p. 18), "A Song for Mother" (adapted from a Japanese song) (Lei, 2009b, p. 35), "Tears in Heaven" (a song sung by British songwriter Eric Clapton that mourns the loss of his four-year-old son in an accident) (Lei, 2007, p. 33), "We Are Friends" (*Women Shi Pengyou*) (Lei, 2007, pp. 2–3), and "Auld Lang Syne" (a traditional Scottish folk song) (People's Music Publisher, 2011, p. 52). These song lyrics represent the paramount guiding ethics regulating social behavior and maintaining good relationships between family members, and as such they continue to serve as the basis for social solidarity, even as the government recognizes the necessity of acknowledging the growth of individualism among youth.

Moreover, with a view to addressing ethnic conflict (particularly in urban, autonomous, and border regions), such as the riots that broke out in Urumqi, the capital of the Xingjiang Uyghur autonomous region in northwestern China on July 5, 2009, both the central and local governments have made efforts to protect and preserve the diverse ethnic cultures of China. For example, the PRC government included education on ethnic unity in the national teaching program for all elementary and high schools, as well as vocational middle schools. The aim of this program was to accelerate the development of the autonomous regions and strengthen Tibetan patriotism. In 1985, the central government launched "Tibetan classes" (*Xizang ban*), which were mainly for Tibetan students who lived in majority-Han areas in China (for details, see Postiglione, 2008, 2009). This practice was extended to other ethnic minorities, such as the Uyghur Muslims in Xinjiang in 2000. Because music had long been used as a political tool in the struggle over ethnic independence movements (see Tibet Information Network, 2004), the "state-sponsored representation of minority groups" was mainly composed of "song and dance troupes" that performed on television (World Music Network, September 21, 2011). Moreover, famous folk songs from different ethnic groups were encouraged, as they were seen as voicing Chinese people's hopes for ethnic unity in the Mainland. Current education policies require schools to address the cultural heritage of ethnic groups in an attempt to promote national unity in education among ethnic minority students.

Similarly, cultivating a love for traditional Chinese music and an understanding of the various styles of China's 56 ethnic groups has been strongly encouraged in order to promote students' cultural understanding (Ministry of Education, 2001, 2011). Launched in December 2000, the three-year "Campaign for Preserving China's Ethnic Folk Songs" was presented in Beijing on March 16, 2004, during the "Fruits of Chinese Ethnic Folk Song Preservation" press conference. Given the ethnic diversity within China, different types of minority music, minority dance, folk instrumental music, Beijing opera, and other arts and regional music were highly recommended across primary and secondary school education (Ministry of Education, 2011, pp. 16–17). As part of that effort, many provincial schools focused on teaching primary and secondary students about ethnic cultures by offering them classes on playing ethnic musical instruments, folk ensembles, and folk dance. Despite their differing ethnic origins, students have been able to share similar values and ethnic music cultures from Tibet, Miao, Mongolia, Qinghai, Shanbei, Shanxi, and Uyghur, among others; this is one of the key strategies that have worked to keep the 56 ethnic groups united in citizenship education (Lei, 2007, 2009a, 2009b; Shanghai Educational Publisher, 2011a).

MUSIC EDUCATION FOR MULTICULTURAL AND GLOBAL CITIZENSHIP

The promotion of global citizenship has also emerged as a common feature of the national school music curriculum, reflecting a shift away from the conception of citizenship as based wholly on the national. The terms "cosmopolitan citizen," "global citizen," and "world citizen" can be seen as other levels of citizenship that join regional, state, and national citizenship, and this joint citizenship is concerned with global issues such as the environment and world peace. In order to respond to the internal and external challenges of globalization and advances in communication technologies, nation-states no longer monopolize the discourse of citizenship (Law, 2007). The encouragement of multicultural and global citizenship through music education is observed in Mainland China with respect to Chinese ethnic music, popular music, and other world music, as well as the delineated reasons for being global citizens found in song lyrics.

Globalization is considered a new stage of development in that it has provided a new perspective for developing China's citizenship education. Students are encouraged to appreciate the quantity and richness of music from other countries by learning world music, and in this way they can develop a greater understanding and respect for other cultures beyond the country's borders (Ministry of Education, 2011, pp. 16–17). Chinese students are introduced to music from around the world through their music textbooks, and they are encouraged to explore the diverse history of musical traditions in Africa, Asia, Europe, and North America (see Juvenile & Children's Publication House, 2010a; Lei, 2007, 2009a; Shanghai Educational Publisher, 2011b). In addition to the PRC's national anthem, students are also encouraged to learn the "Internationale" (one of the most recognizable and popular songs of the socialist movement since the late nineteenth century) and other national anthems from Austria, France, Russia, North Korea, and the United States (Shanghai Educational Publisher, 2011b) to foster respect for cultural and musical values in the name of furthering global development. For example, the Chinese song "The World Would Be Better" (*Shijie Geng Meihao*) (Shanghai Educational Publisher, 2011b, p. 43), written by Mainland composer Lu Jianhua, is deeply concerned with social challenges and building a better world that allows ongoing sharing and collaboration among people to develop global citizenship and human dignity, although it might be seen as propaganda in its pacification of children and youths.

As China becomes more open, it continues to be flooded with all kinds of foreign music and different cultural forms and values. The popularity of digital and cyber cultures in the information age has influenced the entertainment preferences and values of contemporary youths in China. In response, China has increasingly shown its openness toward popular music in both the community and the school. Since the 1980s, Western music genres (largely American and British songs), Mandarin popular songs from Taiwan, and Cantonese popular songs from Hong Kong all became mainstream in Mainland China. The American movie *Breakin'*, shown in 1987, was popular among secondary school students in China; the break dancing culture also introduced Michael Jackson to Chinese youths, among whom he was well received (Zhang, 2005). In the 1990s and 2000s, respectively, China experienced a "Japanese wave" and a "Korean wave" in its conventional media, characterized by the popularity of Japanese and Korean youth fashion, television dramas, and popular music. In modern China, the emergence of a new popular cultural phenomenon related to the ideology of a market economy and the influence of peer groups is evident. As elsewhere, rock 'n' roll and other popular music and the idolization of celebrities (known as "fandom") have become mainstream in popular culture among Chinese youths (Yang, 2006, p. 174; see also Fung, 2009). According to a recent survey questionnaire taken by 1,730 students (ages 12 to 17) and interviews with 60 of these students in 10 secondary schools in Shanghai, most of them said that they enjoy both popular music in their daily lives and learning popular music in school (Law & Ho, forthcoming). The recent educational reforms cover new text-book materials integrating popular songs (but not revolutionary popular songs) and the inclusion of online learning materials and other software for music education.

In addition to foreign languages and overseas studies, many transnational agencies and governments promote the teaching of "learning to live together" through under-standing and respect for other peoples and cultures to create a just, peaceful, harmonious, and sustainable world. In 2010, the Chinese government launched the *National Outline for Medium and Long-term Educational Reform and Development (2010–2020)*, which dictates that the country strengthen education for international understanding and develop cosmopolitan citizenship with the values of peace, respect, and cultural diversity to help students see the world as it is today. The *National Music Curriculum Standard for Full-time School Compulsory Education* (Ministry of Education, 2011) encourages music teachers to exercise openness and sensitivity in curriculum con-tent, resources, and teaching strategies and to adopt various musical styles from both China and other cultures in their teaching. Song literature in the school music curricu-lum is now selected from both Chinese and Western repertoires to encourage students to promote peace and reconciliation. For example, songs such as "Let There Be Peace on Earth," composed by Jill Jackson Miller and Sy Miller (People's Music Publisher, 2011, pp. 67–70), "We Are One," written by Mary Donnelly (Juvenile & Children's Publication House, 2010a, p. 41), "A Whole New World," by Tim Rice (Juvenile & Children's Publication House, 2010b, p. 41), and "Love on the Earth" (*Ai Di Renjian*), by Mainland composer Gu Jianfen (Shanghai Educational Publisher, 2010, p. 12) help students to live in peace and harmony, and cultivate substantial development for the world.

FINAL WORDS

Economic development, political transformation, and cultural change have often occurred together and have influenced, to some extent, a new pattern of citizenship education in China's music education in the global age. The promotion of citizenship education, based on personal values, patriotism, filial piety, and global peace, can be viewed to a large extent as articulating some form of philosophical justification in the school music curriculum. In an era when youth materialism and individualism pose big challenges to national and educational developments, a continuation of traditional norms of family solidarity and filial piety has further promised to consolidate Chinese communism in China's education policy. Such a recommendation is conducive to promoting the greater good of society to encourage students to practice "responsible citizenship" locally, nationally, and internationally. On the one hand, the notion of citizenship in China's music education expresses the relationship between the individual and the wider community. On the other hand, the dynamics of multiple citizenships in school music education foster a sense of cosmopolitanism based on the recognition that individuals may have multiple identities and loyalties, including to family, ethnic or other community, region, country, and the planet. Consequently, there have been questions regarding the introduction of the values and practices of traditional Chinese music, popular music, and other world music in school music education.

Since coming to power in October 2012, the CCP General Secretary and State President Xi Jinping have put forward the slogan "Chinese Dream" (*Zhongguo Meng*) to inspire individuals' personal desires, as well as to describe a set of ideals in the PRC. In his inaugural address as president, Xi grandly laid out his vision of the Chinese Dream as contributing to nation building and leading to the resurgence of China as the center of the world. This slogan went viral in cyberspace after President Xi used it to describe the "great renewal" of the Chinese nation.

The Chinese Dream is not about individual achievement, however; it is about collective efforts and strength for national rejuvenation (Forde, 2013). For example, with a view to cultivating good morals and values among students to contribute to the Chinese Dream, the Beijing Confucian Temple and the Imperial College presented the 2013 National Children's Traditional Culture Festival on July 18, 2013, to introduce traditional culture to children (China Children and Teenagers' Foundation, July 25, 2013). Similarly, the Chinese Academy of Social Sciences, a national center for comprehensive studies and the highest academic research organization in the fields of philosophy and social sciences, has called for proposals to research the Chinese Dream, and the slogan has already inspired a chart-topping folk song (see BBC News, June 5, 2013, http://www.bbc. co.uk/news/world-asia-china-22726375).

Presently, China should attach equal importance to political growth and cultural development, making the Chinese Dream more attainable for national revival and contributing to a new global outlook in school music education. The relationship between Chinese nationalism and multiculturalism, between market competition and social justice, and between individualism and collectivism must be handled properly in the delivery of music contents and materials in school music education. Nonetheless, the concepts of democracy and social justice have never been seriously addressed by the Chinese state. The meaning of democratic music may refer to song lyrics with overt messages of political freedom and/or political pluralism. In this view, the pursuit of social justice requires not only the promotion of diverse ethnic music or folk songs from ethnic groups, but also a removal of any politicization of ethnicity in music education and political control. As Modood (2007) argued (but not from a Deweyan social democratic perspective), "liberal citizenship is not interested in group identities and shuns identitarian politics; its interest in 'race' is confined to anti-discrimination and simply as an aspect of the legal equality of citizens" (p. 69).

Classrooms and schools represent a "culture of power" to the extent that they can mirror unjust social relations that exist in the community. Although there may be a closer correspondence between policy and practice in the highly centralized Chinese system, there may remain great diversity in the practices of schoolteaching as to whether Chinese music teachers conduct their music teaching as prescribed by the CPC-led state. This presents a challenge in devising musical materials and teaching strategies that can help students experience those educational and musical values that are relevant to the notion of multiple citizenship that is part of the Chinese Dream. Teaching social justice engages students, teachers, parents, and the Chinese state in a conversation about music education in a democracy. Emerging themes and concepts on citizenship are being discussed from distinct approaches to school music education from a social justice perspective, as well as those issues related to the importance of promoting education for multiple citizenships within an increasingly heterogeneous and diverse world. How the quest for citizenship empowerment and a genuine break with soft authoritarianism in multiple citizenships for the cultural transformation of values education in China's music education will play out in curricular discourse remains to be seen.

ACKNOWLEDGMENT

The authors would like to express their gratitude to Hong Kong Baptist University for the generous support of the Faculty Research Grants.

NOTES

1. A national survey by China Youth and Children Research in May 2011 of 6,466 students in Grade 3 through Grade 11 from Beijing, Guangdong, Henan, Liaoning, Sichuan, and Shanghai intended to find out who their heroes were. The findings showed that Taiwanese singer Jay Chou was rated as the top figure by a majority of the students polled (Liu, 2012).
2. Kunqu (also known as Kunju, Kun opera, or Kunqu opera) originated in the Kunshan region of Jiangsu Province, and is one of the oldest and most refined styles of traditional Chinese theater performed today. Developed during the early Ming Dynasty in the fourteenth century, it is a synthesis of drama, ballet, opera, poetry recital, and musical recital. In 2001, Kunqu was listed as one of the masterpieces of the Oral and Intangible Heritage of Humanity by UNESCO.

REFERENCES

Allsup, R. (2004). Of concert bands and garage bands: Creating democracy through popular music. In C. X. Rodriquez (Ed.), *Bridging the gap: Popular music and music education* (pp. 204–223). Reston, VA: MENC.

Allsup, R. E. (2010). On pluralism, inclusion, and musical citizenship. *Nordic Research in Music Education Yearbook, 12*, 135–155.

Banks, J. A. (2004). Introduction: Democratic citizenship education in multicultural societies. In J. A. Banks (Ed.), *Diversity and citizenship education: Global perspectives* (pp. 3–15). San Francisco: Jossey-Bass.

Banks, J. A. (2008). Diversity, group identity, and citizenship education in a global age. *Educational Researcher, 37*(3), 129–139.

BBC News. (2013, June 5). What does Xi Jinping's China Dream mean? Retrieved from http://www.bbc.co.uk/news/world-asia-china-22726375.

Boon, I. E. T. (2009). Toward a useful synthesis of Deweyan pragmatism and music education. *Visions of Research in Music Education*. Retrieved from http://www-usr.rider.edu/~vrme/v14n1/vision/Boon.Final.pdf.

Cai, W. P. (2009). Qiantan Zhou Jielun "zhongguofeng" gequ di jiaoyu yiyi [A talk on the educational values of Zhou Jielin's song "Chinese Wind"]. *Art and Literature for the Masses, 11*, 66.

CCTV.com. 2008. (2008). Opening ceremony of the Beijing 2008 Olympic Games. CCTV International Networks Co. Ltd. Retrieved from http://www.cctv.com/english/special/opening/02/index.shtml.

Cheung, C. K. (2012). Away from socialism, towards Chinese characteristics: Confucianism and the futures of Chinese nationalism. *China Information, 26*(2), 205–218.

Cheung, K. W., & Pan, S. Y. (2006). Transition of moral education in China: Towards regulated individualism. *Citizenship Teaching and Learning, 2*(2), 37–50.

China Children and Teenagers' Foundation. (2013, July 25). China promotes traditional culture for children. Retrieved from http://en.cctf.org.cn/html/2013-07/348.html.

Elliott, D. (Ed.) (2005). *Praxial music education: Reflections and dialogues.* New York: Oxford University Press.

Forde, B. (2013, July). Xi's Chinese dream: Collective strength for national rejuvenation. East Asia Forum. Retrieved from http://www.eastasiaforum.org/2013/07/05/xis-chinese-dream-collective-strength-for-national-rejuvenation/.

Fung, A. Y. H. (2009). Fandom, youth and consumption in China. *European Journal of Cultural Studies, 12*(3), 285–303.

Green, L. (2006). Popular music education in and for itself, and for "other" music: Current research in the classroom. *International Journal of Music Education, 24*(2), 101–118.

Gu, X. H. (2008). Zhou Jielun geci zhong di wenhua fuhao [The cultural symbols found in Zhou Jielun's song lyrics]. *Movie Review, 5*, 92–93.

Ho, W. C., & Law, W. W. (2004). Values, music and education in China. *Music Education Research, 6*(2), 149–167.

Ho, W. C., & Law, W. W. (2012). The cultural politics of introducing popular music into China's music education. *Popular Music & Society, 35*(3), 399–425.

Hofstede, G. (1984). *Culture's consequences: International differences in work-related values.* Beverly Hills, CA: Sage.

Hu, Z. B. (2011). Jiyugao xiaoliu xing yinyue jianyu xianzhuang di yixiesikao [Some thoughts on popular music education in senior high schools in the present stage]. *Yinyue Chuangzuo (Music Creation), 2*, 163–165.

Hunan Literature and Art Publishing House. (2012a). *Yinyue [Music]* (Grade 7, vol. 1). Hunan: Author.

Hunan Literature and Art Publishing House. (2012b). *Yinyue [Music]* (Grade 7, vol. 2). Hunan: Author.

Hung, C. T. (1996). The politics of songs: Myths and symbols in the Chinese Communist War, 1937–1949. *Modern Asian Studies, 30*(4), 901–929.

Jones, A. (2005). Changing the past to serve the present: History education in mainland China. In E. Vickers & A. Jones (Eds.), *History education and national identity in East Asia* (pp. 66–100). New York: Routledge.

Juvenile & Children's Publication House. (2009). *Yinyue [Music]* (Grade 7, 2nd term). Shanghai: Author.

Juvenile & Children's Publication House. (2010a). *Yinyue [Music]* (Grade 7, 1st term). Shanghai: Author.

Juvenile & Children's Publication House. (2010b). *Yinyue [Music]* (Grade 7, 2nd term). Shanghai: Author.

Kalekin-Fishman, D., & Pitkanen, P. (2007). Preface. In D. Kalekin-Fishman & P. Pitkanen (Eds.), *Multiple citizenship as a challenge to European nation-states* (pp. vii–xiv). Rotterdam: Sense Publishers.

Law, W. W. (2007). Globalization, city development and citizenship education in China's Shanghai. *International Journal of Educational Development, 27*(1), 18–38.

Law, W. W. (2011). *Citizenship and citizenship education in a global age: Politics, policies, and practices in China*. New York: Peter Lang.

Law, W. W. (2013). Globalization, national identity, and citizenship education: China's search for modernization and modern citizenry. *Frontiers of Education in China, 8*(4), 596–627.

Law, W. W., & Ho, W. C. (forthcoming). Popular music and school music education: Chinese students' preferences and dilemmas in Shanghai, China. *International Journal of Music Education*.

Lei, Y. S. (2007). *Yinyue—Zoujin yinyue shijie [Music—Marching into a musical world]* (Grade 9, vol. 2). Guangdong: Guangdong Educational Publisher and Flower City Publishing House.

Lei, Y. S. (2009a). *Yinyue—Zoujin yinyue shijie [Music—Marching into a musical world]* (Grade 8, vol. 2). Guangdong: Guangdong Educational Publisher and Flower City Publishing House.

Lei, Y. S. (2009b). *Yinyue—Zoujin yinyue shijie [Music—Marching into a musical world]* (Grade 6, vol. 1). Guangdong: Guangdong Educational Publisher and Flower City Publishing House.

Liu, W. G. (2012). Survey reveals youngsters idolize celebrities. All-China Women's Federation. Retrieved from http://www.womenofchina.cn/html/womenofchina/report/139313-1.htm.

Lu, D. (2002). Deng Xiaoping qizhi zhiyin zhongxiaoxue jiaocai gaige huo fazhan [The reform and development of curriculum for primary and secondary schools under the banner of Deng Xiaoping]. In L. B. Gao & Z. S. Zhuang (Eds.), *Jichu jiaoyu kecheng gaige yanjiu [Curriculum reform for basic education in China]* (pp. 3–22). Guangzhou, China: Guangdong Education Publishing House.

Lu, S. H., & Fang, L. (2010). Lun Fang Wenshan di geci yishu [Discussion of Fang Wenshan's song lyrics]. *Journal of Lishi University, 32*(6), 46–50.

Ministry of Education. (2001). *Yinyue kecheng biaozhun [Shiyan ban] [Curriculum standards for primary education and junior secondary education: Music]* [Experimental version]. Beijing: Beijing Normal University Press.

Ministry of Education. (2012). *Yiwu jiaoyu yinyue kecheng biaozhun [Curriculum standards for primary education and junior secondary education: Music]*. Beijing: Beijing Normal University Press.

Modood, T. (2007). *Multiculturalism: A civic idea*. Cambridge, UK: Polity.

Mok, K. H. (2000). *Social and political development in post-reform China*. London: Macmillan; and New York: St. Martin's Press.

Pan, S. Y. (2011). Multileveled citizenhsip and citizenship educaton: Experiences of students in China's Beijing. *Citizenship Studies, 15*(2), 283–306.

People's Music Publisher. (2009). *Yinyue [Music]* (Grade 8, vol. 16). Beijing: Author.

People's Music Publisher. (2010). *Yinyue [Music]* (Grade 7, vol. 13). Beijing: Author.

People's Music Publisher. (2011). *Putong gaozhong kecheng biaozhun shiyan jiaokeshu: Yinyue (Gechang) [Experimental textbook for the ordinary standard curriculum for senior secondary school—music (Singing)]*. Beijing: Author.

People's Music Publisher. (2012). *Yinyue [Music]* (Grade 3, vol. 6). Zhejiang: Author.

Perris, A. (1983). Music as propaganda: Art at the command of doctrine in the People's Republic of China. *Ethnomusicology, 27*(1), 1–28.

Postiglione, G. (2008). Making Tibetans in China: The educational challenges of harmonious multiculturalism. *Educational Review, 60*(1), 1–20.

Postiglione, G. (2009). Dislocated education: The case of Tibet. *Comparative Education Review, 53*(4), 483–512.

Reimer, B. (1970). *A philosophy of music education*. Englewood Cliffs, NJ: Prentice-Hall.

Shanghai Educational Publisher. (2010). *Yinyue [Music]* (Grade 7, 1st term). Shanghai: Author.

Shanghai Educational Publisher. (2011a). *Yinyue [Music]* (Grade 6, 2nd term). Shanghai: Author.

Shanghai Educational Publisher. (2011b). *Yinyue [Music]* (Grade 7, 2nd term). Shanghai: Author.

Tibet Information Network. (2004). *Unity and discord: Music and politics in contemporary Tibet*. London: Author.

Vickers, E. (2007). Museums and nationalism in contemporary China. *Compare, 37*(3), 365–382.

Wang, Z. P. (2008). The impact of existentialism on China's democratic education through globalization. *Intercultural Communication Studies, XVII*(1), 188–196.

Woodford, P. (2005). *Democracy and music education: Liberalism, ethics, and the politics of practice*. Bloomington: Indiana University Press.

Woodford, P. (2012a). Music education as social justice. In C. Philpott & G. Spruce (Eds.), *Debates in music teaching* (pp. 85–101). Abingdon, UK: Routledge.

Woodford, P. (2012b). Dewey's bastards: Mursell, Broudy, McMurray, and the demise of progressive music education. *Visions of Research in Music Education, 21*. Retrieved from http://www.rider.edu/~vrme

World Music Network. (2011, September 21). Ethnic music tests limits in China. Retrieved from http://www.worldmusic.net/news/news/2011-09-21/ethnic-music-tests-limits-in-china/.

Xi, J. Y., & Xia, Y. (2006). Introduction to Chinese youth (with a commentary). *Faculty Publications from CYFS*. Paper 2. Retrieved from http://digitalcommons.unl.edu/cyfsfacpub/2/.

Yang, C. Z. (2006). Popular culture among Chinese youth. In J. Y. Xi, Y. X. Sun, & J. J. Xian (Eds.), *Chinese youth in transition* (pp. 191–192). Aldershot, UK: Ashgate.

Zhang, G. J. (2005). Youth trends in China. *Young Consumers: Insights and Ideas for Responsible Marketers, 6*(2), 28–33.

Zhang, H. B. (2011). Zhou jielun gequ zhong di chuantong wenhua yinzi tanxi [A study of the traditional cultural elements of the songs by Zhou Jielun]. *Writer Magazine, 8,* 196–197.

Zhang, J., & Shavitt, S. (2003). Cultural values in advertisements to the Chinese x-generation. *Journal of Advertising, 32*(1), 21–33.

Zhou, Y. Z., Qin, Z. Q., Deng, X. L., & Chai, X. X. (2011). Study on three-dimensional moral education in universities and its practical approaches. *Asian Social Science, 7*(9), 189–193.

Zou, H. L. (2005). Patriotic songs sing more individualist tune. *China Daily News,* 17 March. Retrieved from http://www.chinadaily.com.cn/english/doc/2005-03/17/content_425967.htm.

CHAPTER 7

WHAT DID YOU LEARN IN SCHOOL TODAY? MUSIC EDUCATION, DEMOCRACY, AND SOCIAL JUSTICE

JOEL WESTHEIMER

What did you learn in school today
Dear little child of mine?
What did you learn in school today
Dear little child of mine?
I learned that Washington never told a lie.
I learned that soldiers seldom die.
I learned that everybody's free,
And that's what the teacher said to me.
That's what I learned in school today,
That's what I learned in school.

—Tom Paxton

IN the fall of 1987, I walked into New York City Public Intermediate School I.S. 44 with a guitar on my back. I had no qualifications whatsoever to teach music, but I wanted to volunteer in the school, with the hope of eventually securing a full-time teaching position, and music was my entrée. Drawing on my amateur experiences songwriting, performing, and cofounding a university student group called *Folksinging Together*, I volunteered to teach folk songs to some of the 6th, 7th, and 8th graders at I.S. 44. We sang Guthrie, Dylan, Ochs, and (Joni) Mitchell. The songs of Peter, Paul, and Mary, Tom Paxton, Malvina Reynolds, and Pete Seeger were regular fixtures. David Mallett's "Garden Song" became a de facto (if somewhat parodic) school anthem. After a few weeks, I benefited from happenstance: when a teacher abruptly left for a district administrative position, I was offered a job as a full-time teacher.

Although I was not a music teacher, music remained a part of my engagement with the school, both within the core subject area classes I taught and through my continued informal folk singing with the children. For example, after sharing the Tom Paxton song shown above with some of my classes, my students and I discussed the relationship between "facts" and "interpretation," gaining a foothold on more complex issues of epistemology and authority. We compared excerpts from textbooks and newspaper articles from different countries around the world that described the same historical events. We asked about the interests embedded in particular narratives and the choice of particular facts and interpretations. We turned a critical lens on the very folk songs we had learned earlier. "What did you learn in school today?" became a popular refrain, recited whenever we were collectively calling into question any presupposed truth.

I recall this now, as I think about the relationship between music education, social justice, and democratic engagement. I am not an expert in music education, and therefore come to this project as an outsider. The other chapters that make up this Handbook will be far better situated in the scholarly work of music education as a field. However, my research in social justice education and the role of schools in democratic societies leads me to recognize music education as one of a number of powerful means by which educators interested in the democratic purposes of schooling might pursue their goals. I agree with Stephanie Horsely, who argues in Chapter 4 of this volume that "musical values can foster the types of social democratic behaviors desirable for broader public participation and engagement...." Those values can be nurtured not only within the music teacher's classroom, but also through the use of musical approaches to teaching in any classroom.

I see at least three ways that music education is salient in this regard. First, music contributes to the overall diversity of pedagogical approaches available to all teachers. Second, music offers a powerful way to connect a variety of academic lessons to the real-world passions that bring those lessons to life. And third, music and those real-world connections and passions it engenders, frequently—although not always—spark broader social, political, and moral questions that might otherwise remain dormant. It is this third characteristic of music in schools with which this chapter is primarily concerned.

Social justice is a contested term in education. It is an old concept under renewed attack in many sectors of society, and schools have not been spared. As many of the chapters in this volume make clear, music education has been subject to the repercussions of a broader shift in education reform that wants to see teaching and learning as a technocratic means to implement increasingly myopic education reform goals. At the same time, growing opposition to these trends can draw particular inspiration from the arts. Music education, therefore, is, perhaps, as threatening as some neoliberal reformers perceive it to be. Indeed, music education holds the possibility for a powerful partnership with all those educators who view education as a profoundly human and liberatory endeavor.[1]

THE DEMONIZATION OF SOCIAL JUSTICE

The history of public education reform is replete with efforts to reduce the gap between the haves and the have-nots in society. Public education has regularly been enlisted as a means to ameliorate poverty, to provide broader employment opportunities to underserved populations, to ensure that students care about those with needs and treat all individuals with respect, and to create policies so that—in more contemporary parlance—"no child is left behind." These efforts, like all educational and social policies, work with varying levels of effectiveness, but few doubt the value of these goals. Indeed, public schooling itself could be considered one of the greatest experiments in social justice, based on the idea that all children, regardless of their socioeconomic background, are entitled to quality education.

At the same time that there is considerable unity around these goals, the term "social justice" has frequently drawn criticism. In one of the more well-known battles around the pursuit of social justice in American education, the National Council for the Accreditation of Teacher Education (NCATE) was forced to drop all language related to social justice from its accrediting standards (Wasley, 2006). The Council was responding to pressure from officials in the US Department of Education. Conservative groups, such as the American Council of Trustees and Alumni, the National Association of Scholars, and the newly formed Foundation for Individual Rights in Education, led the charge. NCATE's guidelines had simply required that teacher candidates in education programs "develop and demonstrate knowledge, skills, and dispositions resulting in learning for all P–12 students" (2001, p. 25). Then, in an appended glossary of terms, they suggested that these dispositions *might* include "beliefs and attitudes related to values such as caring, fairness, honesty, responsibility, and social justice" (p. 30). NCATE never said that teachers must be committed to social justice. And they certainly did not say that a commitment to social justice was associated with particular political perspectives. The appended reference to social justice as a goal was enough to provoke a threat of censure until the reference was removed.

Conservative pundits have also waged a withering attack on social justice in education. Manhattan Institute Senior Fellow Sol Stern, for example, writing for *Front Page Magazine*, charged that schools are "openly infusing the themes of 'social justice' throughout the curriculum" (Stern, 2006). To make his case, he cites the various teacher education and high school courses that mention "social justice" or mention words that Stern identifies as smacking of social justice; for Stern and like-minded critics, any mention of "diversity" is a call to arms, as is the concept of "peace." In short, the idea that teachers and students might tie knowledge to social ends is anathema to any conception of a good educational program.

Set against this broader context, it seems inevitable that music educators interested in social justice face an uphill road when seeking to broaden the educational goals of teaching music beyond the aesthetic goals of music appreciation and the technical skills of music performance. Yet, fostering classrooms that enlist music in the pursuit of social justice should not be a controversial commitment. To say that one supports music education for social justice is simply to say that one supports the idea of enlisting music education in the service of improving society by making it more just, preparing students to use the knowledge and skills they develop in the music classroom to identify ways in which society and societal institutions can treat people more fairly and more humanely.

At the same time that conservative attacks on social justice have hindered reforms aimed at tying the school curriculum to social ends, a recurring educational preoccupation with standardization has further marginalized efforts to make artistic development and imagination central to students' school experiences.

STANDARDIZATION AS THE ENEMY OF ARTISTIC IMAGINATION AND SOCIAL JUSTICE

In a popular scene from the 1989 movie *Dead Poets Society*, the eccentric Mr. Keating (played by Robin Williams) asks one of his students to read aloud from the preface of a high school poetry textbook:

> To fully understand poetry, we must first be fluent with its meter, rhyme and figures of speech, then ask two questions: 1) How artfully has the objective of the poem been rendered and 2) How important is that objective? Question 1 rates the poem's perfection; question 2 rates its importance. And once these questions have been answered, determining the poem's greatness becomes a relatively simple matter. If the poem's score for perfection is plotted on the horizontal of a graph and its importance is plotted on the vertical, then calculating the total area of the poem yields the measure of its greatness.

The fictional author of the text, Dr. J. Evans Pritchard, PhD, continues with an example: "A sonnet by Byron might score high on the vertical but only average on the horizontal. A Shakespearean sonnet, on the other hand, would score high both horizontally and vertically, yielding a massive total area, thereby revealing the poem to be truly great." Pritchard concludes by asking students to practice this rating method (using the provided rubric) because "[a]s your ability to evaluate poems in this matter grows, so will your enjoyment and understanding of poetry."

Although both the textbook and its author are fictional, the satire is worrisomely apt. In fact, the fictional passage was based closely on a real text found in a popular 1950s poetry textbook currently in its twelfth edition and still used by high school students across the country: Laurence Perrine's *Sound and Sense: An Introduction to Poetry*. In other words, the demand for standardized measures of quality and success in education has not abated but increased. Could we imagine a similar scene substituting music for poetry? Indeed, virtually every component of the school experience has been subject to an agenda that elevates standardization above local knowledge, experience, and imagination.

The relatively uncritical and universal acceptance among school reformers of the importance of so-called standards, rubrics, and uniform assessment tools for teaching and learning is at once predictable and misguided. It is predictable because the idea that we should clearly articulate educational goals and then devise methods for determining whether those goals are met is irresistibly tidy. After all, how can teachers pursue high-quality lessons if they do not know what they are trying to teach and whether students are learning? Uncritical acceptance of even such a seemingly commonsensical idea, however, is misguided for the following reason: education is first and foremost about human relationship and interaction, and as anyone who has tried to create a rubric for family fealty or for love or for trust would discover, any effort to quantify complex human interactions quickly devolves into a fool's errand. Nowhere is this more true than in the traditionally "non-academic" (although I do not like that distinction) scholastic domains such as music, art, and physical education.

Standardization also hinders the ability of teachers to employ the arts as a tool for democratic engagement and critique because standardization precludes rooting instruction in the local context, thereby allowing teachers to work within their own specific surroundings and circumstances. It is not possible to teach democratic forms of thinking without providing an environment to think about.

I do not mean to imply that there is no place for evaluation or standards or testing in school subject areas such as music and art. I have rarely met a teacher who did not have standards; most have their own forms of rubrics or evaluative frameworks as well. But "No Child Left Behind" and "Race to the Top" legislation and related reforms that call for ever-more standardized rubrics and frameworks have severely restricted teachers' abilities to draw on individual strengths and experiences. In the process, opportunities for education that strives for critical analysis of social and political concerns are diminished.

Finnish educator Pasi Sahlberg (2012) calls the kind of school reform that elevates the pursuit of rubrics and standardization above all other educational considerations "GERM" (for Global Education Reform Movement). He describes GERM as follows:

> It is like an epidemic that spreads and infects education systems through a virus. It travels with pundits, media and politicians. Education systems borrow policies from others and get infected. As a consequence, schools get ill, teachers don't feel well, and kids learn less. (2012, n.p.)

Not only do kids learn less. What they learn also tends to follow prescriptive formulas that match the standardized tests. In the process, more complex and difficult-to-measure learning outcomes get left behind. These include creativity and emotional and social development, as well as the kinds of thinking skills associated with robust civic engagement and social justice.

Almost every school mission statement these days boasts broad goals related to multiple intelligences (including musical, rhythmic, and harmonic intelligence). Yet beneath the rhetoric, increasingly narrow curriculum goals, accountability measures, standardized testing, and an obsession with sameness have reduced too many classroom lessons to the cold, stark pursuit of information and skills without context and without social meaning—what the late education philosopher Maxine Greene called "mean and repellent" facts.[2] It is not that facts are bad or that they should be ignored. But democratic societies require more than citizens who are fact-full. They require citizens who can think and act in ethically thoughtful ways. Schools need the kinds of classroom practices that teach students to recognize ambiguity and conflict in "factual" content and to see human conditions and aspirations as complex and contested. The arts, to be sure, are exceedingly well-suited to this task.

Imagination and Creativity as the Enemy of Standardization

Education scholars often talk about how standardization of the curriculum is the enemy of creativity and imagination (Eisner, 2004; Greene, 2000, 2001; Kohn, 2004; Meier, 2002; Robinson, 1982). But scholars of arts and music education, including many of the authors of chapters in this Handbook, remind us that the reverse is also true: that creativity and imagination are the enemies of standardization, powerful counter-forces to the dull and the dreary, worthy adversaries against uniformity and conformity. They push us to recognize education as a richly human enterprise, built not on disconnected and disembodied facts but on the language of freedom, beauty, art, poetry, and music.

Indeed, education goals, particularly in democratic societies, have always been about more than narrow measures of success, and music education should be central to these concerns. Saul Alinsky (1965) called dissonance the "music of democracy," and although his use was metaphorical, the connections between music and democracy, I believe, can also be literal. Teachers are called on and appreciated for instilling in their students a sense of purpose, meaning, community, compassion, integrity, imagination, and commitment—all features of a robust music education. Educators in a democratic society have a responsibility to create learning environments that teach students a broad variety of lessons—including, but not limited to, the kinds of learning goals easily captured by standardized assessments.

You may recall in *Dead Poets Society* that after allowing his students to listen attentively to the detailed instructions on measuring the quality of poetry (even drawing a graph on the blackboard to show just how to execute the formula for evaluation), Keating proceeds to demand that students rip out that entire chapter from the text. "Be gone J. Evans Pritchard, PhD!" he exclaims to the sound of students tearing out the offending pages. He was asking them, of course, to revel in the radical possibility of teaching and learning that cannot be standardized, the kind of teaching and learning that poetry and music inspire.

Music Education
and the Power of Hope

My teacher education students sometimes get annoyed with me for pointing out all the problems with schooling in North America. They learn that in the past two decades, education goals, broadly speaking, have become increasingly technocratic, individualistic, and narrowly focused on job training. As teachers about to enter the profession, they do not want to assume that too many of the lessons that inspire hope have been put on the back burner. They recognize that there are many wonderful teachers doing wonderful work, but they worry that the kinds of lessons in participation and democratic action that give meaning to teaching and learning tend to be opportunistic rather than systematic—based on an individual teacher's courage, rather than on programmatic muscle—and episodic rather than consistent and enduring.

Educators face many obstacles to improving schooling. Today, we trust teachers less and less and standardized tests more and more. Reform policies at the highest levels are made without any evidence that they will work. And students are treated alternately as blank slates waiting to be trained, as clients waiting to be served, or as consumers waiting to buy. With those kinds of anemic educational goals, the music educator's work is bound to be both undervalued and constrained. In some schools, the entire school day is reduced to almost nothing but test preparation in only two subject areas: math and literacy. At the same time (and I think not unrelatedly), reported rates of depression and alienation among young people have skyrocketed. Accordingly, we prescribe medications to a shockingly high percentage of students to make them attentive and "normal." In a phenomenon reminiscent of Garrison Keillor's Lake Wobegone, where all children are above average, some schools have now deemed the majority of students "not normal." Meanwhile, elaborate reward and punishment systems are instituted to keep students engaged. It sometimes seems that in the quest to improve students' focus and interest, the only thing we are not trying is to actually make the curriculum interesting and worth focusing on.

In the face of these conditions, it would seem easy to lose hope. I would like to suggest two reasons that we do not have to. First, overall reform trends *never* dictate what is possible in individual classrooms. In the end, it is the teacher who is with students day in and day out. And we all know that teachers, especially those powered by hope and possibility, can and do make tremendous differences in children's lives. Moreover, teachers of regrettably marginalized subject areas such as music, ironically, are also those who are more able to work under the radar of the education reform juggernaut. Music educators can (and many do) work within the interstices of educational programs that are otherwise reduced to uniformity and blandness.

Second, as the playwright and statesman Vaclav Havel observed, hope is not the same as choosing struggles that are headed only for success: "Hope . . . is not the conviction that something will turn out well," he wrote, "but the certainty that something makes sense, regardless of how it turns out" (2004, p. 82). Hope requires, as the historian Howard Zinn eloquently wrote, the ability "to hold out, even in times of pessimism, the possibility of surprise" ([1980]2010, p. 634). From orchestral scores to jazz to folk, gospel, and hip-hop traditions, music has often served similar aims.[3] The singer-songwriter-activist Holly Near expressed this artfully in her anthem to the many social change movements that have existed for as long as there have been things to improve. Change does not always happen at broadband speeds, but knowing that one is part of a timeless march toward good goals makes much of what we do worthwhile. In her song *The Great Peace March*, Near (1990, track 8) sings: "Believe it or not / as daring as it may seem / it is not an empty dream / to walk in a powerful path / neither the first nor the last . . . ." Neoliberal education reforms have hindered efforts to fully articulate an education agenda that recognizes social justice and democracy as important curricular goals and that sees music and the arts as an inextricable part of human experience. If I could hope for one certainty in anyone's arc as an educator, it would be this: the knowledge that—whether in the face of successes or setbacks—we are walking in a powerful and worthwhile path. Music and music education have an important role to play.

NOTES

1. I would like to thank Matt Brillinger and Karen Emily Suurtamm who provided excellent research assistance with this chapter and Joan Harrison who prompted my thinking about music education and democratic citizenship.
2. Maxine Greene (2006) credits John Dewey with reminding us that "facts are mean and repellent things until we use imagination to open intellectual possibilities" (p. 1).
3. Although I refer here to the innumerable examples of music being employed in the service of hope and possibility for social justice, music, of course, has also served less noble aims, including totalitarianism and oppression.

REFERENCES

Alinsky, S. (1965). The war on poverty—political pornography. *Journal of Social Issues, 11*(1), 41–47.

Eisner, E. (2004). *The arts and the creation of mind.* New Haven, CT: Yale University Press.

Greene, M. (2000). *Releasing the imagination: Essays on education, the arts, and social change.* New York: Teachers College Press.

Greene, M. (2001). *Variations on a blue guitar: The Lincoln Center Institute Lectures on Aesthetic Education.* New York: Teachers College Press.

Greene, M. (2006). Jagged landscapes to possibility. *Journal of Educational Controversy, 1*(1), 1.

Havel, V. (2004). An orientation of the heart. In P. Loeb (Ed.), *The impossible will take a little while: A citizen's guide to hope in a time of fear* (pp. 83–89). New York: Basic Books.

Kohn, A. (2004). *What does it mean to be well educated? And other essays on standards, grading, and other follies.* Boston: Beacon Press.

Meier, D. (2002). *The power of their ideas: Lessons for America from a small school in Harlem.* Boston: Beacon Press.

National Council for Accreditation of Teacher Education. (2001). *Standards for professional development schools.* Retrieved from http://www.ncate.org/documents/pdsStandards.pdf.

Near, H. (1990). Great peace march. On *Singer in the storm* [CD]. Hawthorne, CA: Chameleon Music Group.

Perrine, L. (2008). *Sound and sense: An introduction to poetry.* 12th ed. Stamford, CT: Wadsworth.

Robinson, K. (1982). *The arts in schools: Principles, practice and provision.* London: Calouste Gulbenkian Foundation.

Sahlberg, P. (2012). How GERM is infecting schools around the world. *The Washington Post.* [The Answer Sheet web log by Valerie Strauss]. Retrieved from http://www.washingtonpost.com/blogs/answer-sheet/post/how-germ-is-infecting-schools-around-the-world/2012/06/29/gJQAVELZAW_blog.html.

Stern, S. (2006). "Social justice" and other high school indoctrinations. *Front Page Magazine,* April 14, 2006. Retrieved from www.psaf.org/archive/2006/April2006/SolSternSocialJusticeandotherIndoct041306.htm.

Wasley, P. (2006, June 16). Accreditor of education schools drops controversial "social justice" standard for teacher candidates. *Chronicle of Higher Education.* The Faculty, A13.

Zinn, H. ([1980]2010). *A people's history of the United States: 1492–present.* New York: Harper & Row.

SECTION II

RECLAIMING DIFFERENCE IN MUSIC EDUCATION

INTRODUCTION

Beyond Toleration Facing the Other

CATHY BENEDICT, SECTION EDITOR

The question is not one of exercising "tolerance," but of making present the roots of community and its ramifications, of so experiencing and living in the trunk . . . that one also experiences, as truly as one's own, where and how the other boughs branch off and shoot up. (Burber, 1957, p. 102)

IT felt appropriate to incorporate the words "tolerance" and "other" in the title of this section. Both terms seem innocuous enough; stealth-like in character, they almost transcend examination. The authors in this book, and particularly in this section, however, insist on the interrogation of each, both in their words and deeds. "Tolerance" is a word that, when used, rarely raises attention. It enters the discursive space as a sleight of hand, making it almost impossible to stop and ask for clarification or intent. The "other" is perhaps, more obviously, a problematic term, as it is more often than not used specifically to divide and delineate. The above quote of Burber's exemplifies the beliefs of the authors in this section, all of whom, in one way or the other, grapple with "what makes it bearable for us to live with other people, strangers, forever, in the same world, and makes it possible for them to bear with us" (Arendt, 1994, p. 322). These authors, through personal stories, historical reflections, and empirical research tease out this complexity as they enter into and make their way from seemingly obvious topics to those that may not immediately come to mind as we think of social justice.

The voice of the feminist scholar in music education is one that is both acknowledged and reclaimed in this section. Why remember the stories of women in the field of music education—surely we have grown and moved beyond that need? To begin with, the task is not one of remembering, but rather of contending with the context and ideological discourse that has shaped and shapes erasure. Roberta Lamb and Niyati Dhokai in Chapter 8 remind us that lived stories are too easily forgotten or are simply not known, particularly when these stories were lived during times when these voices were hidden and silenced—indeed, were deemed non-voices. As multigenerational authors, they bring their diverse perspectives and experiences as they read feminism, feminist theory, feminist geographies and cultures through the lens of historical and ethnomusicological viewpoints. Both share personal and public experiences, thinking through their own identity development and those of their students, confronting narratives of institutional power and production. In doing so, they remind us that we might and should engage in the "creation of flexible definitions and include practice-based knowledge and community activism."

Great power is to be found within the words of our second author, as we are drawn away from the predictable narrative of traditional scholarly work into a world of music and poetry. Seeking to challenge, indeed dismantle, the narrative structure of both the history of social justice and music education, Elizabeth Gould in Chapter 9 chooses to shape a story with the use of historical narrative interwoven with personal reflections. Calling our attention to those ways in which texts work on us, she disrupts the entitlement of "benevolence" we may feel as we read through this Handbook. Flights of deterritorializations allow her to present us movement through ideologies, philosophies, misogyny, racism, and heterosexism as she "cuts loose feminism" so as to "create potentialities of lives worth living."

While the phrase "minority" continues to function (in many cases) as a label that reproduces social standing and status quo, it is no longer a word that accurately represents the Latino population in the United States. Certainly Carlos Abril and Jacqueline Kelly-McHale, the authors of Chapter 10, are not suggesting that this is why we need to attend to this particular population. Rather, their concern is with the ways that "current pedagogical practices misalign with the values of many Latino students and families, and may contribute to the alienation of Latino families from schools." They challenge the "access equals equity" paradigm when access is determined and even provided by the dominant culture. Pointing to givens such as competition, the nature of school ensembles, after- and before-school time commitment, musical and cultural identity, and teacher beliefs and attitudes, they help us understand that culturally relevant pedagogy is much more than simply teaching "differently." They do this by providing examples of teachers who have had both successes and failures as they grapple with these issues in their own particular contexts.

Reminding us that music education often exists in places we might not immediately identify, Kathy Marsh in Chapter 11 calls our attention to music in the lives of refugees and newly arrived immigrant populations. Working with children and arts groups in refugee camps in Sydney, Australia, she documents the lives of children who are marginalized within the already marginalized. She finds that participation in rehearsals and final performances provides "participatory parity, cultural justice, and social inclusion" in ways that, while not at all fluid or simple, do further cultural identity development, and belonging.

Few would ever desire to be called racist or to be thought to engage in acts of racism. We know better as caring individuals, and we certainly know better as music educators. We feel we know this so well that we often believe we don't need to talk about race or racism—talking about it just brings it out into the open and stirs the pot. In Chapter 12, Deborah Bradley dispels this notion and insists that it is our responsibility to interrogate both terms and to attend to those ways that race and racism hide in our inability to address these issues. She addresses "Whiteness," "music is a universal language," "color-blind teaching," and "authenticity" as constructs, platitudes, and pedagogical givens in order for us to take a "serious, introspective look" at what it is we do and don't do in furthering an agenda of racism.

Social injustices are perpetuated among multiple peoples and communities. This may be more obvious in some instances than others. Alice-Ann Darrow in Chapter 13 reminds us that historically, persons with disabilities have been marginalized, overlooked, ignored, mocked, and even expunged from society. While benefiting from past civil rights legislation, persons with disabilities continue to gain acceptance in schools and society. However, teachers need to continue to insist on due process and rights for their students, as well as recognize the importance of understanding disability culture and ways in which stereotyping and stigmatizing continue to take place. She challenges the media representations of persons with disabilities and how the arts can play an important role in either reproducing representations or challenging them.

Extending the conversation of othering and other into gender and sexual diversity in the context of public schooling and music education, Louis Bergonzi in Chapter 14 uses the work of Kumashiro to help provide us with the tools to dismantle those ways we continue to benefit from the gender and sexual status quo. Schools are particularly problematic sites, as they too often further and constitute dominant discourses about identity. To that end, activist theory and anti-oppressive education can help to play an integral role in compelling us to recognize the erroneous framing of heterosexuality as "normal."

In Chapter 15, Richard Matthews concludes this section with his scholarly positioning as a political philosopher and peace scholar. He observes how constructs of privilege and oppression, cultural imperialism, and the legitimation of exploitation are reflected in the words of the authors of these chapters, and reminds us that we are "not condemned to replicat[e] oppression." Rather, as we think and act upon the issues that were raised, we are in a "powerful position to aid in the promotion of socially just states of affairs."

These multiple voices, from multiple scholarly traditions, help us to navigate the terrain of difference and otherness. Reflection, reflexivity, care, and agency "[make] present the roots of community" (Burber, 1957, p. 102) so that we might see and know those with whom we share and take responsibility.

REFERENCES

Arendt, H. (1994). Understanding and politics (the difficulties of understanding). In H. Arendt & J. Kohn (Eds.), *Essays in understanding 1930–1954* (pp. 307–327). New York: Harcourt, Brace.

Burber, M. (1957). *Pointing the way.* New York: Harper & Brothers.

CHAPTER 8

DISJUNCTURED FEMINISMS

Emerging Feminisms in Music Education

ROBERTA LAMB AND NIYATI DHOKAI

SOCIAL justice is currently a hot topic in music and education; as educators invoke it with ease, there is concern that the historical, sociological, and philosophical origins of the social justice story need exploration in general and in specifics. While this chapter is one of many engaging in such exploration, we welcome this opportunity to document some aspects of feminism relevant to music education. From publications that served as precursors to the social justice topics of the second decade of the twenty-first century, including feminist theory and its development into gender and sexuality studies, to emerging feminisms across many cultural and geographic contexts, we take historical and ethnomusicological viewpoints to demonstrate the values of feminism in the current era. In order to do so, we employ feminist and ethnographic methodologies to unpack our individual experiences and understandings. To that end, we hope to demarcate a lineage that may be helpful to many people who study, teach, and participate in musical cultures.

THE AUTHORS

Although we wrote this chapter together, we necessarily identify our authorial voices separately at certain points, in order to make evident the two different persons and the lives we live. We attempt to model authentic dialogue across these differences without erasing the actual experiences of actual people. Where we do not identify individual authorship, we wrote and edited together to indicate the outcome of dialogue.

Roberta Lamb

I write from my perspective as a music educator, lesbian-feminist, and union organizer. I grew up in the United States, shaped by the Civil Rights movement, the

Vietnam War, and the Women's Liberation movement. I trained in the Western Art Music classical tradition and loved it! I taught music in the schools until I could no longer live with the very real fear that my sexual orientation would become public and I would not be able to continue as a music educator in the schools. Once I completed my doctorate in the 1980s, I took a position in Canada because the feminist perspectives represented in my scholarship were not as "scary"[1] to the Canadian university that hired me. Canada appeared as the "Promised Land" where I could integrate all aspects of my life. This freedom gave me space to write honestly regarding music education in the context of the social and political, particularly as experienced by women. At the time of this writing I am over 60, a grandmother nearing retirement after 30 years of university teaching.

Niyati Dhokai

My perspective is that of an ethnomusicologist and a music educator, an Indian-American woman, and a formerly hesitant feminist. Until I completed preliminary fieldwork in India in 2008, my experience of "feminism" was not something that I recognized as such, especially when compared to the feminism of my Western counterparts in North America. I returned to graduate school with a desire to further examine cross-cultural "gendered" experiences from the field and a way to discuss these experiences with my Western counterparts. I also wanted to become better equipped with theoretical tools through which I could examine gender relations that I would explore in future academic work. It was also important to me to include my undergraduate students into the discussion, many of whom did not relate to "feminism."

Although we come from different ethnic and cultural backgrounds, generations, and career paths, our collaboration grew from an interest in understanding each other's experience of feminism and its impact on our pedagogical practices. We met through the Society of Ethnomusicology (SEM) Section on the Status of Women and began to follow each other's work, eventually agreeing to collaborate on this chapter.

GROUNDWORK

Canadian feminist sociologist Dorothy E. Smith[2] begins her 2010 lecture to students at the University of Oregon by acknowledging the centrality of the women's movement of the 1970s to the current practices of Institutional Ethnography:

> Our experiences in the early days of the women's movement are ones you cannot have any more. The completeness of women's exclusion from the intellectual, political and cultural life of the society was extraordinary, and something that we in a sense had internalized. In beginning to transform ourselves, and in the process, transform

society, transform our culture, transform its intellectual life, in some way that admitted women as significant subjects and gave us presence, was a major transformation in our lives. Some of how we went about it was from talking, from learning from each other's experiences. We didn't have a language. We didn't have what we have come to take for granted, concepts like gender, for example. (Smith 2010, transcribed by Lamb)

The extent of this transformation and its impact on us as individuals, as well as on public institutions, such as music education, should not be underestimated. We who taught music during the 1970s and 1980s are not the same teachers we were then. Obviously, generations of students who then entered our classes have graduated and borne children. This generational cycle is ongoing. It is magnificent, it is painful—simultaneously.

If we are to approach a world where we embrace equity and equality with commitment and compassion, we must start with the recognition of actual people and their experiences within this cycle.[3] As scholars and students of music and music education, we must recognize what we do not know. We must acknowledge the relationships that bring about the transformations that we do not yet recognize as transformations, rather than seeing them as the way things are and always have been.

We notice that the music education profession does not engage easily in this project of acknowledgment. The music education profession tends to take a digital image of the moment, erase the historical traces and social relations that brought the image into focus, and present the moment as if it had always, and already, existed. Accordingly, part of the reason for this historical and social erasure is that "our experiences in the early days of the women's movement are ones you cannot have any more" (Smith 2010, transcribed by Lamb). Therefore, one cannot now experience what many experienced during the 1970s or before Stonewall (1968) or before the US Voting Rights Act (1964) or before the Canadian Charter of Rights and Freedoms (1985). Based on current context, it may appear that those earlier experiences are implausible, not real, and not true.

This process of acknowledgment can also be challenging, as the music education profession is practical and often focuses on producing a current product, concert, or show. The past, beyond the lineage of gurus/master teachers, is not relevant for such technical skills. A third case for historical and social erasure in music education is the emphasis on grand narrative within "foundations" of music education. This grand narrative, historically written by white, Anglophone heterosexual men, systemically ignored individuals who wrote a different narrative. This systemic erasure becomes obvious in the texts historically assigned to students, the lack of citation of scholars who are feminists, anti-racists, and those not from the Northern and Western Hemisphere.

We are interested in considering the role of emerging feminisms, particularly the integration of individuals of all genders and orientations who participate in feminist movements now. As educators and scholars, we aspire to a feminism that allows people to begin where they are (especially upon entering a classroom setting), and that takes into consideration different experiences brought to feminist dialogue. We are interested in how we express cross-cultural experiences through transnational and global contexts; however, we do not want to lose the relevance of feminist messages. It is the disjuncture in feminism that concerns us—the asking of academic questions that remain unanswered, while the situations of women globally vary so wildly. Although some voices within music education declare feminism as divisive and irrelevant, we see feminism at the heart of struggles to ensure girls' education and women's rights worldwide. "Although feminisms, in some organized fashion, are alive and well in more parts of the world today than at any other time, the lives of most women around the world are mired with poverty, ill-health, and injustice," states Manisha Desai (2007, p. 800). We are concerned with poverty, ill health, and injustice, whether it is found in North America, India, or anywhere in the world. How do we work with these issues, especially when the social, political, religious, and educational are so messily intertwined? We turn to lived experiences as one way to navigate the complex terrains of disjunctured feminisms. What Dorothy E. Smith reminds us of the past, ". . . some of how we went about it was from talking, from learning from each others' experiences . . ." (Smith 2010, transcribed by Lamb) is a strategy that we wish to employ now. We talk with each other and extend feminist conversations into more locations where music education is part of our lives. We invite you to join us in this conversation.

As we write, we hope that some among you will become interested enough in the historical traces and social relations to follow the centrality of emancipatory movements, especially the Civil Rights movement in the United States and the early Women's Liberation movement worldwide, and, thus, make connections from these earlier political actions to your life today. If we are able to present you, the reader, with an adequate map and you are able to take these tracings into your future, then we all have the opportunity for comprehending the ruling relations[4] of music education. Ruling relations of music education include, but are not limited to, our professional associations, ministries/departments of education, curricula, and textbooks. These ruling relations coordinate our social relations within classrooms and among teachers, even when we do not realize that is what is happening. When we comprehend the ruling relations and understand how they work, then we have the opportunity to engage in music education for people, just as Dorothy E. Smith (2005) encourages us to engage in sociology for people.

We reconsider the role of the music educator in encouraging students to engage in feminist dialogue within the classroom. By examining the role of the educator, considering the classroom setting and its dynamics, and engaging in a reflexive, ethnographic study on the role of the educator, we might be able to provide constructive ideas and encouragement for the classroom instructor who may be searching for a new space for feminism in the classroom.

MEMORY (ROBERTA LAMB)

First Memory

> My starting point for feminist analyses for music education was to consider the addition of women to the content of music teaching and learning [Lamb, 1987]; however, I soon found that project to be lacking, both in theoretical substance and as a means for conceptualizing change. Being a feminist musician, I wondered about how we teach as well as what we teach. This led me into considerations of feminist criticisms and theories in relation to music and music education. (Lamb, 1993–1994, p. 5)[5]

Thus, I began "Aria senza acompagnamento," a 1994 publication, although today it is a 20-year-old memory. Yet, this essay was a memory in itself. The 1994 piece was written four years earlier, but because this "Sex-equity in Music Education" special issue (1993–1994) was the first time the music education profession highlighted feminist scholarship, it was important to allow the article to be published as it was written. "The general field of education and the specific discipline of musicology have been more willing to interact with feminist theory in music education than has music education itself" (Lamb, 1993–1994, p. 5). This statement resonates today, perhaps because music education as a field does not have much memory. Tracing origins and making connections are not so significant when the fundamental concern is in today's classroom. Yet, the lack of memory standardizes the educational process by smoothing out the interesting contours and ruptures and eliminating what does not "fit," minimizing diverse values. This standardization removes the earlier research from current thinking. Thus, today's young scholars do not know what Betty Atterbury (1993–1994), Virginia Caputo (1993–1994), Judith Delzell (1993–1994), Vicki Eaklor (1993–1994), Julia Koza (1993–1994), Roberta Lamb (1993–1994), Patricia O'Toole (1993–1994), Laree M. Trollinger (1993–1994), Molly Weaver (1993–1994), and Charlene Morton (1996) contributed to social justice 20 years ago. Consequently, new researchers repeat many of these ideas, especially of gender stereotypes of instruments and male choristers, without recognition of long-standing social inequities, or they ignore this research completely.

Charlene Morton completed her philosophical dissertation examining the obstacle of music as feminine and music education as feminized in 1996. This dissertation laid out issues in theoretical reasoning touched upon in the following articles. Laree M. Trollinger reviewed literature published in recognized peer-reviewed journals from 1968 to 1992. "This period coincides with the rebirth of the feminist movement, which has led to increased awareness of sex differences and gender roles, as well as to far-reaching social changes" (Trollinger, 1993–1994, p. 22). Historian Vicki L. Eaklor "provide[s] a sketch of what developed" during 1838–1911, "in order to suggest some directions in thinking about America's gender paradoxes on the subject of music and musicians" (Eaklor, 1993–1994, p. 40). Betty Atterbury brilliantly turned a book review into an analysis of workplace inequity:

It is too easy for women in academia, who have been socialized throughout their lives to be submissive, to accept the denial of tenure or promotion as a personal problem, one resulting from a situation they themselves created.... There are much deeper and more complicated forces at work which must see the light of day before the ideal world of equality for female professors will ever exist. (1993–1994, pp. 103–104)

Both Judith K. Delzell and Molly Weaver examined workplace conditions. Delzell's 1993–1994 study identified the gender of US high school and university band directors and discussed recommendations to increase female representation in these positions. Weaver surveyed gender differences in the US "Big Ten" universities and noted, "Policies in the interest of gender equity in higher education serve not only the interests of women; they benefit everyone" (1993–1994, p. 99). She listed areas requiring further research: salary increments, tenure, length of service, frequency of promotion, and the impact of childbirth, dependent-care responsibilities, and sexual harassment of women academics. We continue to need such research and elimination of barriers for those who are different.

Virginia Caputo, Julia Koza, and Patricia O'Toole turned their early feminist research to music classrooms. Caputo studied "non-technical issues surrounding music technology" to discover that "the educational use of computers may be driven by factors such as market forces that obscure other issues more pertinent to the educational success of our female as well as male students" (1993–1994, p. 89). Koza analyzed choral music education textbooks and found that they "reinforced systems of ideas that tend to perpetuate unequal power relations and that foster the continued oppression of women and gay men" (1993–1994, p. 61). Koza states, "We constantly need to scrutinize the larger systems of ideas upon which our understandings and solutions are built" (p. 61). She notes that those "working in gay/lesbian studies speak of alternative ways of thinking about males, females, gender, and sexual orientation" (p. 62). Although O'Toole (1993–1994) did not know the sociological terminology (because it did not come into use until the end of the 1990s), she clearly identified ruling relations in her study of choral music education experiences:

Because it is impossible to blame director or singer, I argue that it is the system of beliefs, the conventions of choral pedagogy which determine the interaction between director and singer, that must be questioned. This re-vision is not a simple task, as exemplified in my story. Even though many choir members were dissatisfied with rehearsals, they did not question the system of rules that created this situation. (p. 76)

Second Memory

The second memory refers to the negative fallout to initial feminist analyses in music education. Music education as a profession did not participate in contemporary social movements, and professional organizations, particularly Music Educators National

Conference (MENC)[6] in the United States, dictated sanitized, white middle-class values to the profession. During the early 1990s, the staff at MENC told us that music educators were not interested in issues such as sexism and racism.[7] Throughout the mid-1990s, it was not possible to talk about feminism or sexuality in a way that music education could recognize and understand what was being said. Even so, Elizabeth Gould continued an impressive feminist and queer philosophical project in music education. Gould's (2011) critique of "Tone Deaf" (Lamb, 1995) demonstrated the complete bifurcation between scholarship in women's studies and music education. Some women preparing feminist research were afraid; they did not want to take the risk of being associated with feminism or lesbians; their academic advisors told them they would never get jobs as feminists.[8] Although this fear of feminists lessened over the decades, it has not disappeared completely. "And as a struggle, it requires creative responses so that gender issues may become legible in the profession as something more than a personal concern or special interest" (Gould, 2011, p. 880).

Today it is hard for us to understand how it was impossible to write feminism in music education during the 1990s. That era in music education was another one of those contexts, like Smith's description of the early Women's Liberation movement, where we did not have the concepts or the words for the text; we were not legible. Although the concepts are more accessible today, Elizabeth Gould's analysis of "Tone Deaf" (Lamb, 1995) did not see publication until 2011, indicating that the profession is not as open to full discussion of feminism and sexualities as current discourse might suggest. In general, music education continued, where gender is concerned, to avoid complexities and

> ... focus solely on research of gender issues and music education, including studies of gender and identity, experiences of boys and girls in musical achievements, and gender stereotypes in relation to musical preferences, and gender and musical performance. (Olsson, 2007, p. 996)

Another second memory example arises from "a firestorm of criticism" documented by Koza (2012, p. 97) when the ruling relations of music education were uncovered and demonstrated that gendered and raced power structures in music education associations from the early 1900s throughout 2009 reveal histories differing from their official representations (Lamb, 2009):

> Some of us have survived ... recently published histories and philosophies of music education have had little or nothing to say about the significant contributions of female feminist academics, and, ... what is said tends to be negative. Thus, *silence* has been one way to support the assertion that women academics of my generation have done nothing. (Koza, 2012, pp. 101–102)

This is not so different from Atterbury's assertion, 20 years earlier, regarding complicated forces, the ruling relations, which deem our lack of progress a personal problem, which we women created.[9] It is not only the women who notice this phenomenon. Bengt Olsson (2007) says:

> Wide acceptance of these changes has yet to be achieved.... The changes demand teaching in new subject areas, developing new modes of education founded on diversity, shared responsibility, opportunities for all voices and orientation to action. (p. 997)

Drama (McCammon, 2007), dance, visual art, and creative writing moved forward more quickly into these new modes of education. Introducing the social and cultural issues broadly conceived within arts education, dance educator Doug Risner and art educator Tracie E. Costantino (2007) write:

> Feminist theory in education is ... an approach to or perspective on issues not otherwise adequately addressed in educational literature, such as gender equity, the body, and individuals and groups considered ignored or peripheral. It is characterized by narrative and dialogical communication. (p. 942)

While narrative research gains popularity, we have yet to successfully engage in dialogical communication within music education. An era of "social justice" requires diverse values, experiences, and peoples engaged in narrative and dialogical communication in order to accomplish the spirit of the term. Women feminist scholars active since the 1980s began from our experiences of being women and then worked through these issues in social groups, not as solitary individuals. This led us to explore the politics of gender, race, sexualities, and class. We were constantly self-critical, as bell hooks (2000) wrote, "There has been no other movement for social justice in our society that has been as self critical as feminist movement" (p. xiii), thus expanding our thinking through this analysis. Yet, the systemic censure of feminist scholarship in music education, combined with the media misrepresentations of feminist movements, ensures that depictions of feminism are caricatures: feminism is negative, for women only, and not relevant to anyone who is not a particular kind of woman. In actuality, feminisms are such profound movements for social change precisely because they have developed as movements for creating more equality in everyone's lives. Although past music education focused on individual talent, and thus assumed separation from other spheres of living, now music must embrace the disparate world if it is be a meaningful part of social justice.

Embracing this disparate world means acknowledging that feminism is relevant and significant wherever people live. Women and children do not live in universally safe environments or enjoy equal access to education, work, healthcare, and basic human rights. "Violence against women exists in every country in the world as a pervasive violation of human rights and a major impediment to achieving gender equality, development and peace" (UNODC, 2012, p. 13). We read weekly news stories that demonstrate the stark reality of the lives of most women and children throughout the world. The decades-old feminist critique of education may be more relevant today than it was in

1993. It appears impossible to consider the contemporary idea of social justice as meaningful without feminism.

How have we in music education agreed to those ruling relations that erase so much of our history? One way we do so is by putting the music first. We teach something we engage in with passion, so we believe we do not see differences and we do not oppress. Such lack of awareness is one aspect of the ruling relations. However, social justice points to an equitable society and suggests a liberatory pedagogy; therefore, we in music education need to acknowledge the cycles of past inequities and make clear breaks with exclusionary practices. We tend to pretend that such a past never existed, but we help ourselves and our students more if we accept the damage and oppression that is our past in order to see it clearly and transform music education. We do not help our profession by restating history as a denial of bad memories, or suggesting there was nothing from which to be liberated. It is not helpful to suggest that no one has thought previously about or acted upon such issues as queer identity, because a particular journal has not published them before a specified date. It is good news to know from Patrick Freer, recent editor of *Music Educators Journal*, that he does not reject certain topics[10]—we celebrate this!—yet, that welcome fact does not negate past practice, when editors did make rejections based on topic.

Another way we participate in the ruling relations that erase our history is in the way we cite (or do not cite) our lineage. We tend to look very narrowly at our topics and do not see any correspondence between different areas that fall underneath the "social justice" umbrella. For example, feminist scholars have heard statements from those interested in queer research to the effect, "I never read your feminist work because it has nothing to do with me." This narrow perspective fails to recognize that aspects of queer theory grew out of lesbian feminist struggles with sexism, racism, class oppression, and sexualities into a more complex discernment of identification in change. Risner and Costantino (2007) demonstrate recognition in their summary of current queer theory in arts education:

> Queer theory asserts that identities are not fixed or based on a dominant characteristic but complex and changing. It may be applied to any social and cultural issue related to identity, not just lesbian, gay, bisexual, or transgendered concerns. (p. 942)

Risner and Costantino are clear that cultural and social justice issues develop along complex lines of thought that do not exclude. Further, issues of sexuality and sexual orientation have been fundamental to feminist research from the first publications. Eaklor (1993–1994) notes extreme gender dichotomy in Victorian United States as a factor toward intolerance of homosexuality and high crime rates against women. Lamb (1993–1994) refers to lesbian desire and phallogocentrism. Homophobia, in conjunction with misogyny and feminism, are Koza's (1993–1994) topics. It is a significant progressive step for us to begin tracing our history through the women, people of color, and others deemed not as fundamental as white, heterosexual men.[11]

Today we have opportunities to encounter many approaches for emancipatory practices in music education, including acknowledgment of our foremothers as well as forefathers. We can notice and learn from those among us who persevere, incorporating social and cultural issues through the varied lenses of feminism, sexualities, anti-racism, and cross-cultural perspectives while embracing musicking in diverse contexts. This ability to explore diversity and uncover feminism is the standpoint presented in the next section.

Exploring Diversity and Uncovering Feminism in the Classroom (Niyati Dhokai)

Feminism is a process that I have been able to discover easily in the realm of fieldwork in diasporic settings in the United States and in urban and rural settings in India. Bringing the complex definitions and processes of Indian feminisms that I experienced in the field back into the classroom has often resulted in a complex, cross-cultural, and integrative dialogue, rather than a linear narrative. This dialogue aims to be productive and forward moving in a limited amount of time. Situating myself, students, colleagues, primary and secondary sources, and the institution that serves as our setting often requires a complex background survey that encompasses a plurality of experiences,[12] many of which are feminist but are not always conventionally recognized as such. Often, these social and political topics surrounding feminist issues become easier to discuss, relegating feminism to a secondary subject. How feminist experiences have been conceived by students before they enter the classroom affects how, or whether, these experiences are seen as being worthy of being discussed in the classroom; often, feminist topics are dismissed or overlooked. Worse, individuals see "women's issues" as divisive when they become reduced to a trajectory that appears to be no longer (broadly) meaningful. This divisiveness is unfortunate, especially since many of the symbols and signifiers of the North American feminist movements during the twentieth century remain relevant in new contexts and with different definitions cross-culturally. Simultaneously, these contexts and definitions continue to be identified and modified.

In this section, I wish to examine the relationship between the perception of gender and identity in music education and the perception of feminism during the era of globalization.[13] As the "Memory" section demonstrates, individuals, institutions, and discourse that become increasingly multilayered and complex shape the identity and experience of the feminist scholar. Navigating these complexities while dealing with the gendered experiences of the classroom can be a rather daunting task for the classroom instructor; therefore, through this examination, I hope to propose strategies that may allow for the classroom instructor to discuss feminism in a way that is more integrative to the multitude of gendered experiences that may be present in the classroom. These strategies include exploration of identity through discussions of professional and personal identity development during university education, the negotiation of different elements of identity (especially gender) and how these elements affect one's approach to others, the consideration of social processes and how they vary in different cultural and social backgrounds, and the consideration of integrating plural experiences within the classroom and identifying common themes for mutual understanding and conversation.

Examining the dynamics of music education and gender begins with analyzing the identity, and subsequent role, of the music educator. I propose an investigation of the identity contradictions that music educators face. Many music educators begin to explore their identities within music education as music students. These ideas continue to change within university settings, through experiences with student teaching, and finally as an independent music educator. At each level, social authority and identity placement are based on the role one inhabits, and this affects how gender is perceived at each level of the music educator's development.

Music educator identity is the point through which elements of curriculum are filtered to the music students. Daniel S. Isbell (2008) investigated the "socialization and occupational identity of undergraduate music education majors enrolled in traditional preservice teacher education programs" (p. 162) by first examining the primary socialization of these individuals within the home, through school music teachers, and private lesson instructors. He then compared these to the secondary socialization of the same individuals in the university setting where they "must reconcile the expectations, beliefs, and values espoused by faculty with those of high school music ensemble directors, private lesson instructors, and other significant people from their past" (pp. 163–164). In Isbell's findings, "experiences associated with secondary socialization in particular are a consistently significant predicator of occupational identity" (p. 176). Isbell explains that occupational identity is a "complex construct," and "teacher and musicians represent two distinct aspects of identity" (p. 175) that do not function in a similar manner, so he recommends "dialogue with student teachers regarding self-perceptions and how these may or may not correspond to the views from significant others" (p. 176).

The negotiation of identities is an ongoing process that teachers and ethnographers both undergo. The ethnographer often deals with being perceived through the lens of the group that he or she is studying. As Kathleen DeWalt and Billie DeWalt (2002) state, "Men and women have access to different settings, different people, and different bodies of knowledge. Our own experience has been that having a man and woman involved in fieldwork at the same time has provided a more balanced view of community life, of key relationships, and of the interaction of households and families than we would have had if we had worked alone" (p. 86). How these experiences are managed, especially by a feminist, is a complex terrain, especially when it comes to bridging the temporal differences of cultural history. About this, Kumkum Sangari and Sudesh Vaid (1989) state,

Cultural history seems to be the richest, most integrated, and yet most difficult form available for feminist historiography. Both its difficulty and energy are, in one sense, generated by the obtuseness of the present situation. In order to understand the construction of gender difference—through ideologies, concepts and behavior—and their relation to class and colonial economy, it is necessary to press against the boundaries of established disciplines. This not only involves knowledge of and working at interface of various disciplines, but also a simultaneous questioning of the histories and assumptions of these disciplines. The act of understanding our construction as agents and subjects of social processes is itself a kind of intervention in the creation of exclusive knowledge systems. (p. 3)

Through the case of feminism and music education, I demonstrate how ethnographers who work through issues of gender in the field to produce narrative and analytical writing transfer similar skills to the classroom. In this way, we might reach students of music education to make topics of feminism, gender, and sexuality more accessible. In his discussion of Peircian semiotic theory, Thomas Turino (1999) emphasizes "signs of Secondness, indices and dicents as signs of reality connections, social relations, and direct experience" (p. 249). Uncovering these relations and representations within the classroom through the fractured identities that emerge within the classroom, one of which is gender, helps educators utilize the lived experiences that students bring to the classroom.

During my experience as an educator addressing topics of hip-hop culture within a popular music course in the university classroom, I found that the lived experiences of my students provided the best point of reference through which to connect to the material being covered in the class. This was more effective for critical study than overstating the vantage point of the performers and/or composers that we were studying (Dhokai, 2012). As a feminist, I believe such critical study is more complex, because of the many layers of meaning that feminism contains for each generation that encounters feminism, as well as the degree to which sexuality and gender are a personal subject, particularly when compared to the public nature of a classroom setting. Furthermore, the history of feminism can be somewhat deceptive; often, history homogenizes in its retelling. We believe that it is important for educators to emphasize the necessity for each generation to make feminism relevant to its own situation. I believe that it is crucial to remember that the signs and symbols of feminism often continue to be relevant, but it is how they hold meaning that may change for individuals of different backgrounds.

Pamela Aronson's (2003) extensive research indicates that "young women's development of a feminist perspective and identity is tied closely with institutions . . ." but that "although the women of color that I interviewed were supportive of equality, most distanced themselves from the identity of feminist, suggesting that the institutional supports for women may be more appealing or available to white women" (p. 919). Aronson also states, "whether or not young women call themselves feminists, they support feminist goals" (p. 919). Feminism presents a great deal of promise. As Manisha Desai (2007) explains, "feminists scholars have written either about gender and globalizations or about transnational feminisms but rarely examined the relationship between them" (p. 797), and she recommends pragmatism and plural feminisms as ways to utilize "one of the strengths of feminism," which has been "openness to self-critique and change" (p. 801).

The greatest promise for feminism lies in the feminist educator's awareness of the plurality of experiences that current students bring to the classroom. With skill we can draw these experiences toward an inclusive and comprehensive feminism that recognizes how each individual's experience contributes to feminist diversity.

Conclusion: What Feminist Thinking Has to Offer the "Social Justice" Umbrella

As our chapter demonstrates, feminism in the music classroom changed greatly during the past few decades. We singled out progress through complexity, disjuncture, and emergence. As we reflect on the history, identities, and experiences of feminisms, shaped by discourse and institutions, and consider how feminism in music education will continue to develop, questions begin to arise about the "packaging" of the message. Based on an issue of *Elle Magazine*, Laurie Penny (2013) recently discussed the "rebranding" of feminism. She asks how much women are willing to sacrifice to make the feminist message more agreeable. Penny raises an important issue. We, too, do not believe that feminism needs "rebranding." Instead, we ask this question: How can we introduce feminism to a new generation of men and women whose gendered experiences may be waiting to emerge in the feminist dialogue?

In the case of the music classroom, we believe that a reintroduction of feminism can provide what Lise C. Vaugeois (2009) calls "a practice of thinking beyond the authority of texts, single leaders, and institutional structures" rather than "what Foucault calls *docile bodies*" (p. 19). This is not to say that what is being recommended in this chapter is without its challenges—the inherent errors of being inclusive, in ways that make differences disappear, are not be to overlooked or dismissed. In such cases, being inclusive comes at the risk of being less critical; however, being inclusive in ways that make room for more nuanced feminist approaches, while avoiding the risks of overstating particular feminist experiences or terms, advances our thinking. We need to do so because individuals (and groups) come to feminism from their own unique experiences. The dialogue that may emerge from errors, and the constructive solutions that may become apparent, are well worth the hazards and risks, especially when these risks lead to the creation of flexible definitions and include practice-based knowledge and community activism. Furthermore, the enactment of social justice is uniquely constructed in each setting, even in those settings that do not seem so different from each other, such as Canada and the United States. Nuanced differences affect how feminism performs in the classroom; therefore, we propose a second question for our discussion of feminism in music education: How does feminism function in different contexts?

For example, feminism in the urban areas in Gujarat, India, requires the negotiation of public and private spaces where gender roles are often relational and not individualized. Social authority and identity placement are constructed through the different roles that individuals have, based on the needs of each social situation. Therefore, analyzing how feminism functions in these contexts requires inter-subjectivity that does not always allow for a concise point of analysis. In the case of women's transnational activism, Manisha Desai (2009) states that engendering politics "is for everyone, so that all can recognize how gender operates in all power relations and how people, as gendered beings, need to think about what gender relations ought to be" (p. 95). Therefore, as gendered music educators, we must be aware that it is up to us to negotiate gender relations, and their complexities, within the classroom. We should be willing to engage in the process of trial and error to determine which teaching practices work best for the demographic and location with which we engage.

Due to the transformations that feminist, anti-racist, and LGBT movements have made in human rights, our current experiences are different from those in 1993. Then, the idea of gay marriage and a black president of the United States were distant dreams, maybe not even imagined.[14] Although many people still experience crises in coming out, university students do not socially segregate by sexuality in many Northern Hemisphere societies. Simultaneously, violence against LGBT people is sanctioned in other regions. We live in a time of equal human rights, but racism still functions in our societies to limit opportunities and promote intimidation and/or violence against many people who are not white. In Canada, living conditions on many northern First Nations reserves are as bad as those in countries with a lower standard of living. Women, particularly in the Southern Hemisphere, face violence and poverty as forms of gender discrimination. Given the worldwide variability of social justice, we face great challenges in finding ways to understand each other. It is only through increased understanding that we can reduce conflicts, both globally and locally. As music educators, we need to increase understanding among all of us. The dialogical communication referenced earlier (Risner & Constantino, 2007; Smith, 2005, 2010) is a starting point. Feminism provides a useful model for this communication, wherein embodied knowledge is recognized and the embodied knower respected for what she or he knows. Through these feminist dialogical communications, we can map the ruling relations we participate in and work through the challenges of social justice together.

Emerging feminism is where we have these conversations that are intergenerational, cross-cultural, translocal, and global. We hope that our chapter begins such conversations that can continue into many classrooms, encouraging the examination of the messily intertwined social, political, and religious facets of music education, while the identity and experience of feminist scholars, shaped by individuals, institutions, and discourse, becomes increasingly multilayered and complex. Therefore, by being mindful of the functions of feminism, we can draw these experiences toward an inclusive and comprehensive music education that recognizes how each individual's experience contributes to feminist diversity and social justice.

NOTES

1. About a year after moving to Canada, I met a member of the hiring committee from a university that rejected me. He said he was intrigued by my work, but the committee found my feminist scholarship to be scary.
2. The first time we mention any author we use their full name in order to ensure that women do not disappear from the historical record through our formal systems of citation. Using only the given name initial in APA style eliminates many chances of discovering gender identity of the author.
3. Froehlich (2006) makes a similar proposal that we "examine structures of hegemony, power, and exclusion where they are perceived as negative forces in the script called music education," and analyze "the part each of us has played in the complexity of power structures of which we are or were an integral part" (p. 4).
4. "Ruling Relations: D. Smith (1999) and Campbell and Manicom (1995) adopted the term 'ruling relations' in order to develop language that moves beyond traditional concepts of power and the state. Ruling relations demonstrate the connections between the different institutional relations organizing and regulating society. Ruling relations combine state, corporate, professional, and bureaucratic agencies in a web of relations through which ruling comes to be organized. Key to linking together these different institutional relations are the use of ruling texts in coordinating action in these sites" (Frampton, Kinsman & Thompson 2006, p. 37).
5. The 1993–1994 publication date is accurate because this is how the original journal listed the double issue. To assure future generations that this journal, which ceased publication in 1997, would remain available, *Visions of Research in Music Education* (http://www-usr. rider.edu/~vrme/) reprinted all of these articles online as pdfs.
   Frank Abrahams, senior editor of VRME wrote:

   > It is with pleasure that we inaugurate the reprint of the entire seven volumes of The Quarterly Journal for Music Teaching and Learning. The journal began in 1990 as The Quarterly. In 1992, with volume 3, the name changed to The Quarterly Journal of Music Teaching and Learning and continued until 1997. The journal contained articles on issues that were timely when they appeared and are now important for their historical relevance.

6. Now known as the National Association for Music Education (NAfME).
7. Julia Koza and I organized the early meetings of Gender Research in Music Education (GRIME) at MENC conferences. At the Kansas City (1996) conference, I investigated why our room reservation for the meeting had been canceled, and was explicitly told by the MENC conference staff that delegates were not interested.
8. In 1985–1986, when I began looking for university jobs, my dissertation supervisor suggested I take the feminism out of my resumé in order to make it easier for me to obtain a position. I did not do so, but I heard from other feminists of my generation who did. Here are several examples of the type of fear prevalent during the 1990s: First, a graduate student called me to discuss her plans for a dissertation. She whispered,

even though she was calling from her office. She did not want any of her office companions to hear her talk about her proposal for feminist research. She feared that if this plan reached a music education professor other than her advisor, she would be branded as a man-hating lesbian, even though she was heterosexual, and her ideas would be trashed before she had the opportunity to develop them into an appropriate proposal. Second, during our early GRIME meetings at MENC, women wanted to take the word "feminist" out of any of our statements because it would be considered inflammatory and would have a negative impact on their career aspirations and the organization. Last but not least, at an MENC conference, I was having a conversation with a woman in a tenure-track position when she suddenly walked away from me in mid-sentence. Later she apologized to me, but said that she had to walk away because a senior professor who would be judging her tenure case appeared in the hallway and she could not risk being seen talking with me.

9. See Atterbury quotation cited earlier in this chapter.

10. Patrick Freer reiterated this statement throughout Establishing Identity: LGBTQ Studies and Music Education II, University of Illinois, October 18–19, 2012.

11. See fn 2. We also tend to cite the male lineage more than the female. Citing the men becomes more important than citing the women, and so, the women disappear from the record.

12. I draw on this idea of situating vantage points from Qureshi (1995), which is also summarized in Dhokai (2012), on p. 113.

13. This term is not used in the context of new liberal market-based issues. I am utilizing Manisha Desai's definitions of globalization(s), which are "plural processes" that are "economic, political, and cultural" (2007, p. 802).

14. Although *Egan v. Canada* 2 S.C.R. 513 would not be decided by the Supreme Court of Canada until 1995, Canadians were already using *Section 15* of the *Canadian Charter of Rights and Freedoms* to assert LGBT rights as human rights protected by the Charter. Many legal cases were in progress in different jurisdictions and the *Quebec Charter of Rights and Freedoms* has prohibited discrimination on the basis of sexual orientation since 1977.

References

Aronson, P. (2003). Feminist or "Postfeminists"?: Young women's attitudes toward feminism and gender relations. *Gender and Society, 17*(6), 903–922.

Atterbury, B. (1993–1994). What do women want? *The Quarterly Journal of Music Teaching and Learning, 4–5*(5–1), 100–104. (Reprinted with permission in *Visions of Research in Music Education, 16*(5), Autumn 2010). Retrieved from http://users.rider.edu/~vrme/.

Bell, h. (2000). *Feminist theory: From margins to center.* London: Pluto Press.

Campbell, M., & Gregor, F. (2002). *Mapping social relations: A primer in doing institutional ethnography.* Aurora, ON: Garamond Press.

Caputo, V. (1993–1994). Add technology and stir: Music, gender and technology in today's music classrooms. *The Quarterly Journal of Music Teaching and Learning, 4–5*(5–1), 85–90. (Reprinted with permission in *Visions of Research in Music Education, 16*(5), Autumn 2010). Retrieved from http://users.rider.edu/~vrme/.

Delzell, J. K. (1993–1994). Variables affecting the gender role stereotyping of high school band teaching positions. *The Quarterly Journal of Music Teaching and Learning, 4–5*(5–1), 77–84.

(Reprinted with permission in *Visions of Research in Music Education*, 16(5), Autumn 2010). Retrieved from http://users.rider.edu/~vrme/.

Desai, M. (2007). From the SWS president: The messy relationships between feminism and globalizations. *Gender and Society*, 21(6), 797–803.

Desai, M. (2009). *Gender and the politics of possibilities: Rethinking globalization*. Plymouth, UK: Rowan & Littlefield.

Dewalt, K., & Dewalt, B. (2002). *Participant observation: A guide for fieldworkers*. Walnut Creek, CA: AltaMira Press.

Dhokai, N. (2012). *Defining regionalism through genres: Situating Gujarati identity in India through urban music culture* (Doctoral dissertation, University of Alberta).

Dhokai, N. (2012). Pedagogical ideas on sonic, mediated and virtual musical landscapes: Teaching hip hop in a university classroom. *International Journal of Music Education*, 30(2), 111–119.

Eaklor, V. L. (1993–1994). The gendered origins of the American musician. *The Quarterly Journal of Music Teaching and Learning*, 4–5(5–1), 40–46. (Reprinted with permission in *Visions of Research in Music Education*, 16(5), Autumn 2010). Retrieved from http://users.rider.edu/~vrme/.

Frampton, C., Kinsman, G., & Thompson, A. (2006). *Sociology for changing the world: Social movements/social research*. Winnipeg, MB: Fernwood.

Froehlich, H. (2006). Mirror, mirror on the wall . . . Or the challenge of jumping over our own shadows. *Action, Criticism, and the Theory for Music Education*, 5(2), 2–22.

Gould, E. (2011). Writing Trojan horses and war machines: The creative political in music education research. *Educational Philosophy and Theory*, 43(8), 874–887.

Gould, E., Morton, C., Countryman, J., & Rose, L. S. (2009). *Exploring social justice: How music education might matter*. Waterloo, ON: Canadian Music Educators Association.

Isbell, D. (2008). Musicians and teachers: The socialization and occupational identity of pre-service music teachers. *Journal of Research in Music Education*, 56(2), 162–178.

Koza, J. E. (1993–1994). Big boys don't cry (or sing): Gender, misogyny and homophobia in college choral methods texts. *The Quarterly Journal of Music Teaching and Learning*, 4–5(5–1), 48–64. (Reprinted with permission in *Visions of Research in Music Education*, 16(5), Autumn 2010). Retrieved from http://users.rider.edu/~vrme/.

Koza, J. E. (2012). Someday they will dance. *Women and Music: A Journal of Gender and Culture*, 16, 97–112.

Lamb, R. (1987). Including women composers in music curricula: Development of creative strategies for the general music classes, gr. 5–8 (Doctoral dissertation, Teachers College, Columbia University, New York).

Lamb, R. (1993–1994). Aria senza accompagnamento: A woman behind the theory. *The Quarterly Journal of Music Teaching and Learning*, 4–5(5–1), 48–64. (Reprinted with permission in *Visions of Research in Music Education*, 16(5), Autumn 2010). Retrieved from http://users.rider.edu/~vrme/.

Lamb, R. (1995). Tone deaf/symphonies singing: Sketches for a musicale. In J. Gaskell & J. Willinsky (Eds.), *Gender In/forms Curriculum: From enrichment to transformation* (pp. 109–135). New York: Teachers College Press.

Lamb, R. (2009). Ethnomusicology, feminism, music education: Telling untold tales. In V. Kurkela & L. Vakeva (Eds.), *De-canonizing music history* (pp. 141–161). Newcastle, UK: Cambridge Scholar Publishing.

McCammon, L. A. (2007). Research on drama and theatre for social change. In L. Bresler (Ed.), *International handbook of research in arts education* (pp. 945–964). New York: Springer.

Morton, C. (1996). The "status problem": The feminized location of school music and the burden of justification. (Doctoral dissertation, University of Toronto, Department of Graduate Studies in Education).

Olsson, B. (2007). Social issues in music education. In L. Bresler (Ed.), *International handbook of research in arts education* (pp. 989–1002). New York: Springer.

O'Toole, P. (1993–1994). I sing in a choir but I have "no voice." *The Quarterly Journal of Music Teaching and Learning, 4–5*(5–1), 65–76. (Reprinted with permission in *Visions of Research in Music Education, 16*(5), Autumn 2010). Retrieved from http://users.rider.edu/~vrme/.

Penny, L. (2013, October 7). If you're a feminist you'll be called a man-hater. You don't need rebranding. *The Guardian*. Retrieved from http://www.theguardian.com/commentisfree/2013/oct/07/feminism-rebranding-man-hater.

Qureshi, R. B. (1995). *Sufi music of India and Pakistan: Sound, context and meaning in qawwali*. Chicago: University of Chicago Press.

Risner, D., & Costantino T. E. (2007). Social and cultural perspectives. In L. Bresler (Ed.), *International handbook of research in arts education* (pp. 941–944). New York: Springer.

Sangari, K., & Vaid, S. (1989). Recasting women: An introduction. In K. Sangari & S. Vaid (Eds.), *Recasting women: Essays in Indian colonial history* (pp. 1–26). New Brunswick, NJ: Rutgers University Press.

Smith, D. E. (2005). *Institutional ethnography: A sociology for people*. Walnut Creek, CA: AltaMira Press.

Smith, D. E. (2010, July 14). *Institutional ethnography* [Video File]. Retrieved from http://www.youtube.com/watch?v=1RI2KEy9NDw.

Trollinger, L. M. (1993–1994). Sex/gender research in music education: A review. *The Quarterly Journal of Music Teaching and Learning, 4–5*(5–1), 22–39. (Reprinted with permission in *Visions of Research in Music Education, 16*(5), Autumn 2010). Retrieved from http://users.rider.edu/~vrme/.

UNODC (2012). United Nations Office on Drugs and Crime Thematic Programme: Crime prevention and criminal justice reform, 2012–2015. http://www.unodc.org/unodc/en/justice-and-prison-reform/index.html?ref=menuside.

Vaugeois, L. (2009). Music education as a practice of social justice. In E.Gould et al. (Eds.), *Exploring social justice: How music education might matter* (pp. 2–22). Waterloo, ON: Canada Music Association.

Weaver, M. A. (1993–1994). A survey of big ten institutions: Gender distinctions regarding faculty ranks and salaries in schools, divisions, and departments of music. *The Quarterly Journal of Music Teaching and Learning, 4–5*(5–1): 91–99. (Reprinted with permission in *Visions of Research in Music Education, 16*(5), Autumn 2010). Retrieved from http://users.rider.edu/~vrme/.

CHAPTER 9

....

A JAZZ FUNERAL
IN MUSIC EDUCATION

....

ELIZABETH GOULD

Alfonso Cuarón's 2013 movie, *Gravity*, vividly demonstrates the potentialities of the terrible power of gravity in territorialized human existence. Out of control, its capacity to kill is boundless, as those who have hurtled through space toward earth, or have attempted earth-bound deterritorializations over material and metaphorical edges, know. This is the gravity of physics, of science, the gravity of scholarly discourse in the academy that demands reason in response to *un*reasonable worlds of social *in*justice. Discounting the material effects of reason that create social injustice, gravity conceals itself—"pay no attention to that man behind the curtain"—as rationality, directing readers to focus on what texts *mean* in order to divert them from paying attention to what texts *do*. Resistance, defying gravity, requires oxygen, air to leap, breath to reject reason and its grounded territorializations. Indeed, if *social justice* handbooks in music education, oblivious to material effects of reason as their very construction, are to mean *anything*, they must do *something*—in the Deleuzian sense of becoming as transformative potentialities actualizing difference (Gould, 2007, 2012a, 2012b). My attempted experiment to *do* something throughout the rest of this chapter consists of mixing tenses in order to disrupt linear time, and of using the second person (you) as a literary "apostrophe" to address nonspecific absent person(s) who "cannot respond to or even hear the speech," which includes me as well as readers, in order to disrupt the "'proper function'" (McLaughlin, 1995, p. 83) of address in ways that extend (different) spaces and stances for reading. How the chapter, situated in an apparently reasonable handbook tethered by academic necessity to the violence of reason expressed in and as dualisms (Finn, 1996; Plumwood, 1993), might *actually* defy gravity remains a mystery. Paradoxes proliferate.

"Kiss me goodbye, I'm defying gravity."[1]

Stepping Off[2], Grand Marshals

Julia Koza, Roberta Lamb, Patricia O'Toole, Estelle Jorgensen

You[3] wake up one morning and you know how it ends; not the details, of course, but the contours, the arc, the final deterritorializing line of flight reterritorialized at last. What is never written; stories you are told that you cannot re-present, your responses of outrage expressed (only) as white, middle-class academic publications in music education that by definition—do not rock. Not the boat, not the white, middle-class, heterosexual profession, even as your writing would call those who do. Your stories narrativize lives in ways that articulate subjectivities, how you experience the world. They are always in process, always undergoing construction and deconstruction, resignifications that reflect continuous negotiations of meaning in which you engage with the world and those who inhabit it. Ideologies, philosophies, sciences, and arts all compete to shape and wrench them from you—in death rolls of (at least) misogyny ("you can't use that word in discussions of social justice"),[4] racism ("you cannot speak that word in the Manitoba Legislative Assembly"),[5] and heterosexism ("you are hurtful when you say that word").[6] But you hang on, not brave enough to cut loose; instead, hearing the music of jazz funerals re-played, you look for deterritorializations defying gravity.

New Orleans Jazz Funeral

You think you know how it goes—at least to the extent of how and why it will not, cannot go here—the traditional New Orleans jazz funeral.[7] Ubiquitous since at least the mid-nineteenth century in a city uniquely enriched by "exceptional levels of diversity, interaction, racial mixing, and cultural creolization" (Sakakeeny, 2011, p. 294), jazz funerals, in which white and non-white musicians participated, were a function of the brass band, one of many musical ensembles that flourished in antebellum New Orleans. These bands were based on European military models, including community brass bands composed of mostly Creole men[8] until the turn of the twentieth century, when post–Civil War African-American migration from rural plantations brought to New Orleans new musical forms and a critical mass of black musicians,[9] as well as, not insignificantly, black music teachers,[10] most of whom were women.

African-American bands first appeared in New Orleans around 1870 (Burns, 2006), and gradually altered brass band performance practices by reducing instrumentation for financial reasons and, importantly, to facilitate what would become their signature simultaneous group improvisation. This "hot" playing style, associated with the Tuxedo Brass Band around 1910 (Knowles, 1996), is precisely what distinguishes black New Orleans brass bands (Burns, 2006), as they discarded stock arrangements in favor of "'head' arrangements transmitted by ear [as] the brass band developed into a black musical form and funerals with music became indelibly linked to black New Orleanians" (Sakakeeny, 2011, p. 313). Exchanging military-style uniforms for black suits (with or without jacket), white shirts (with or without black tie), and visored hats on which the band's name was displayed (Schafer, 1977), African-American bands took great pride in their appearance. Particularly resplendent was the grand marshal, "who might be a man or a woman," dressed in tuxedo or tails with an elegant sash bearing the band's name, "carry[ing] a baton or walking stick" (Osbey, 1996, p. 100). The procession from the funeral home to the cemetery, accompanied by dirges, was critical to the process of communal grieving.

> Typically the procession went past the deceased's favorite haunts: the family home, a particular school or church, a barroom or pool hall, a godmother's house.... At these points, the marshal would step away from the band, take an especially graceful turn in the middle of the road, placing her or his derby or tall hat solemnly across the breast in a show of knowing consideration and respect. At each of these stations, the people would come out of their homes and businesses and look on in appreciation. And thus the procession moved along, reverently guiding the remains of the deceased to their ultimate dwelling-place, both apart from and at a fitting proximity to the community of the living. (Osbey, 1996, p. 101)

At the cemetery, the body of the deceased was "cut loose." Final words were said, and music appropriate to the deceased's personality or life was played. Leaving the cemetery, the grand marshal switched his or her sash from mourning to the decorated side, and "at a respectable distance from the gravesite, the music's tempo and the crowd's general attitude morph[ed] into an upbeat celebration" (Atkins, 2012, p. 169).

These traditional New Orleans jazz funerals disappeared approximately 40 years ago, however, as audiences for brass bands dwindled, and traditional jazz became increasingly unpopular and so was considered to be irrelevant (Osbey, 1996). Consequently, the "canonical form of the traditional jazz funeral is [on the one hand] being reified by documentarians, represented as timeless ritual or 'dying tradition,' and packaged as a nostalgic commodity" (Regis, 2001, p. 754) and, on the other hand, staged in a stripped-down version akin to minstrelsy for (typically) white New Orleans residents and tourists (such as those attending music education or ethnomusicology conferences) who are unwilling to visit black neighborhoods (Regis, 1999). These static and rigid "ersatz jazz funeral[s] of largely white conventioneers" (Stow, 2008, para. 22) function as "mock jazz funerals" that include a brass band and a small procession of people carrying umbrellas and waving white handkerchiefs led by a single grand marshal ("standing in") for all the "traditional" mourners (Regis, 2001). Participating in order to earn a living[11] in a city ever more clearly defined geographically in terms of "racialized patterns of poverty, underemployment, and murder risk" (Regis, 1999, p. 476)—which is to say, "Spatial Apartheid"—performers consciously decide what they share and what they withhold from outsiders in a practice that deliberately leads "a certain group of people" to "misread" the spectacle (Okoye, 1998, quoted in Regis, 1999, p. 475).

By contrast, contemporary "funk-brass" (Osbey, 1996) jazz funerals enacted in black neighborhoods as expressions of resistance, remembrance, and renewal, in response to histories of racism, oppression, and unbridled brutality, flourish as part of an ongoing "brass band renaissance" (Burns, 2006), interrupted in 2005 by the forced dispersion of musicians in the wake of Hurricane Katrina. These funerals, a type of second line parade, in that they omit the traditional dirge portion, begin celebrating immediately upon leaving the funeral home.

> The term *second line* is ambiguous, pointing to multiple dimensions of the same phenomenological reality. It refers to the dance steps, which are performed by club members and their followers during parades. It also refers to a distinctive syncopated rhythm (Riley and Vidacovich 1995) that is said to have originated in the streets of New Orleans. More importantly, *second line* means the followers, or joiners, who fall in behind the "first line," composed of the brass band and the social club. . . . Second liners are a massive and heterogeneous group of individuals drawn from all walks of life. The distinctive interaction between the club members, musicians, and second liners produces a dynamic participatory event in which there is no distinction between audience and performer. . . . It is only by plunging into the crowd that one can begin to apprehend the complex experiential reality of "the line." . . . When jazz funerals elicit mass participation, they too are second lines. (Regis, 2001, p. 755)

Organized and sponsored by African-American social clubs and benevolent societies, "back of town" second line parades are "massive moving street festivals" that attract as many as 5,000 people at each of a series of events that occur year-round (Regis, 1999). Propelling participants on a four-hour journey through many distinct neighborhoods in which they stop at bars and restaurants to refresh, and at the homes of deceased club members to pay respect, second line parades "own" the streets as they map the social and geographical "landscapes" in which participants live. This has only taken on more urgency since the disastrous governmental and military response to Hurricane Katrina (Sakakeeny, 2006),[12] lending unprecedented historical significance to second line parades.

Incorporating both the formalized role of first line grand marshals, who maintain order in chaos by controlling every aspect of the parade, and the spontaneous role of second line provocateurs whose daring dancing and "highly individualized [antics that] play, parody, and burlesque" (Regis, 1999, p. 486), second line parades delight and entertain even as they scandalize. Impeccably dressed grand marshals, men or women (Flaherty, 2010),[13] are "master strutters" who improvise controlled and dignified dance moves that "invite the community into an exploration of new group possibilities" (Atkins, 2012, p. 173), while adventurous (men) "daredevils" perform intricate dance moves on telephone poles, car hoods, and front porches, "activating unused spaces . . . in the attempt to draw out the community" (p. 174). The dance moves of grounded daredevils or "clowns" (Regis, 1999) are wildly sexual, "violating some members' sense of decorum" (p. 486), acting not only as "agent[s] of desire, but . . . also a sacred reminder of the cyclical rhythm of birth, death, rebirth" (Atkins, 2012, p. 176). In combination, the two roles (daredevils and clowns) function as "symbols of communal uplift and as creative articulations of African-American masculinity" (p. 177). This is particularly salient in relationship to the so-called "lost generation" of young African-American men "who are most vulnerable to the violence of contemporary urban life" (Regis, 2001, p. 754) in pre- and post-Katrina New Orleans. With their young women contemporaries, "re-appropriating and refashioning" traditional jazz funeral practices in ways that express their experiences and local subjectivities, second liners "improvise on the standard lyrics of the brass-band [*sic*] tunes," and use sticks to loudly bang on street signs in

> gestures of defiance as musical appropriations of space. As tokens of the law, signs mandate specific uses of space, regulating traffic with directions to "stop," "yield," and obey "one-way" flow. Hitting the signs constitutes an essential signifying practice for many young boys who participate in parades. The second line does not stop or yield at intersections, but rather floods traffic lanes on major avenues, blocking intersections.... "Bang!" The second line supersedes quotidian routines and traffic laws. (p. 757)

Like second lines parades that incorporate music styles such as funk, hip-hop, and rhythm and blues, contemporized jazz funerals are played typically by young men[14] who combine traditional New Orleans street jazz, in which they are steeped, with newer, hipper music (Osbey, 1996). These funerals often memorialize non-musicians, women, or people who died violently. As expressions of "the communal outrage over casualties of drug wars who are buried with brass band accompaniment" (Raeburn, 2007, p. 813), these so-called "crack funerals" include young mourners who carry signs and wear personalized memorial T-shirts that feature a color picture of the deceased, along with nickname, birth and death dates (referred to as "sunrise" and sunset"), as well as messages that address the deceased in the second person (Regis, 2001, p. 764) (see Figure 9.1).

**Missing
you.
Loving
you.**

Other messages interrogate the economic and sociopolitical circumstances of their lives (Regis, 2001, p. 765) (Figure 9.2). As "tactics of memory," the shirts clothe young bodies in death even as those very alive bodies make present the absence of the dead. In this way, second liners "fashion their own generation's intervention in the national discourse of blackness" (p. 765), exemplified perhaps most eloquently in the message on a young women's shirt (p. 759) (Figure 9.3).

Does heaven have a ghetto?

Life makes truth possible. Death makes truth necessary

Remembering that it's all about the band, that it has always been about the band for you—playing this music of your childhood, hearing it in your head even now, music that you study and practice and eventually play well enough that from time to time you fool them ("Hey—you play with balls!" Click![15] "Whoa—no chicks on the bandstand!" Click!)—what can only go here, with profound respect, is memory, remembering, and re-membering—not to (mis)appropriate or valorize,[16] but to hold in regard, to acknowledge what made and continues to make music possible, what enlivens it, sounding and re-sounding (Sakakeeny, 2006)—after death rolls that would drown, swamp the profession—not with repeated flooding of biblical proportions precipitated by systemic racism—but with disdainful disregard, disguised as benevolence. Mapping Deleuzian lines of flight, this music functions here as relays, a soundtrack-ed memory second-ed.

"It Don't Mean a Thing If It Ain't Got That Swing"
Duke Ellington, music; Irving Mills, lyrics; 1931
performed by Ella Fitzgerald, 1957
Roy Eldridge, trumpet
Oscar Peterson, piano
Herb Ellis, guitar
Ray Brown, bass
Papa Jo Jones, drums
http://www.youtube.com/watch?v=PrVu9WKs498

The music wakes you—music not unlike what Mother plays on her LP record player. Its irresistible pull overtakes your terminal shyness and you sneak down the stairs in your brown puppy pajamas with the feet attached. Reaching the basement unnoticed, you slink along the wall, stopping next to the drummer sitting atop his throne behind the drum set. Laughing, he scoops you up with one arm, sets you on his knee controlling the high hat, and hands you a brush. But you are captivated by the tenor saxophone player who is in the midst of playing an improvised solo, and can only hold the brush, suspended, in mid-air. When he finishes the solo, you drop the brush, squirm to the floor and tentatively reach up to touch the saxophone. The sax player meets your eyes, smiles and kneels. Balancing the instrument on his knee, he shows you how to place your tiny hands on the keys. Upon doing so, you practically pass out.

I hung around the bandstand in the summertime and practically passed out when they played "Custer's Last Stand"; with the red fire and everything. Naturally, I wanted to play in the band someday. (Willson, [1949]1975, p. 16)

So that she could bring the band—and party—home after the gig, Mother teaches herself to read blueprints, hires and supervises contractors, and remodels the basement.

"Alice Gould is your Mother? She was the singer for a couple of bands I played in years ago. You know, she was a lot of fun."

She tells you about her desire to become an engineer. Her mother sends her to a two-year women's college to study voice. Years later, she develops alcoholism, sings the gig, sleeps past noon, greets you after school with a snack (your favorite chocolate cake), cooks supper as you watch TV, and joins you—along with three brothers, two sisters, and Dad—to eat. When your kitchen chores are complete, you sit with her as she applies her makeup: "putting on my face," she calls it, in preparation for that night's gig. She favors red lipstick and nail polish, dresses that show off her figure, and three-inch spike heels. You watch, smell her perfume, and ask about the band. She goes out the door with a flourish, driving away in her purple Pontiac.

More than a decade later, you're sitting with her in a tiny jazz club. She drives and pays, you drink, both listen.

"You know, I'm a sober drunk now. But I still know how to have fun."

She's right—on both counts. Mother remains sober for 18 years before her suicide, the final effect of bipolar disorder, of which alcoholism is a symptom, not a cause. And she *is* fun, gregarious, still beautiful. She drives her red Toronado to this particular club, not only to hear the three-piece jazz combo playing there, but so she can introduce you to the tenor saxophone player, a middle-aged black man who readily agrees to sponsor you in joining the musicians' union. He greets her warmly, turns to you and says,

"You know, Alice Gould's singing could bring down the house."

Appearing with combos and big bands, she specializes in ballads, torch songs for which she has some affinity: "All of Me," "My Man." You play them, too, during the years that you gig with combos and big bands.

> "When the Saints Go Marching In"
> 19th-century Protestant hymn
> performed by Lorraine and the Polka Queens, featuring Liz Gould, 1975
> Spectrum, NR6775-2

Lorraine and the Polka Queens is a fairly well known all-women's polka band. They are seeking a saxophone player, and are genuinely pleased when they hear you play. Teaching you polka style, they make music-specific suggestions, sing melodic lines and rhythms, and actively shape each song's arrangement. You are genuinely pleased when they—easily—keep up with the bebop tempo you set for "Yakety Sax," a novelty piece you know from a recording by Boots Randolph, and which you find no more banal than Glenn Miller's maudlin "Sentimental Journey," a staple of far too many big bands that you play with. Indeed, by comparison "Yakety" is fun to play, raucous and ridiculous, a frenetic frenzy that actually halts the dancing—couples, paired in all conceivable combinations, turn, listen, and cheerfully clap along.

Lorraine plays concertina; it's her band. Her composition, "Lorraine's Polka," is the Polka Queens' signature piece. They play it with real verve—that and virtually every polka imaginable, in addition to a variety of country songs and a few popular standards—all of which you play from memory. Leona sings lead and plays bass. She drives you and Pat, the band's drummer and backup singer, to and from gigs in her Pinto wagon. Playing with these creative and generous women for enthusiastic audiences who dance energetically in large well-lit halls is both enjoyable and satisfying. The music is noticed and appreciated; the musicians are capable and musical, and so Lorraine and the Polka Queens produce a 45 record: on the A side, "Lorraine's Polka;" on the B side, "When the Saints Go Marching In"—featuring Liz Gould. A polka "Saints": completely consistent with New Orleans, where "fans dance with unbridled joy, regardless of circumstance," and with the song's history in which "every artist has his or her own approach" (Marsalis, 2013, n.p.).

"Mountain Song"
Holly Near, words and music, 1976
performed by Holly Near and Cris Williamson, 2003
Cris and Holly
HC Records, H&C6201

You know her—at least you know her philosophical writing on dualisms, having read about it in music education literature. Paddling a canoe in Kakadu National Park, Australia, feminist environmental philosopher Val Plumwood, eminently experienced in the bush, finds her course rapidly intersecting with that of an approaching crocodile, which, she thinks, doesn't look especially large. Assured that she will be safe as long as she remains in the canoe, Plumwood is unprepared for the crocodile's sudden attack that threatens to capsize the craft, and paddles furiously toward a paperbark tree onto which she intends to escape. As she begins to leap, the crocodile's "flecked golden eyes looked straight into [hers]" just before it "seized [her] between the legs in a red-hot pincer grip and whirled [her] into . . . suffocating wet darkness" (Plumwood, 2008, para. 8).

> Few of those who have experienced the crocodile's death roll have lived to describe it. It is, essentially an experience beyond words of total terror. The crocodile's breathing and heart metabolism are not suited to prolonged struggle, so the roll is an intense burst of power designed to overcome the victim's resistance quickly. The crocodile then holds the feebly struggling prey underwater until it drowns. The roll was a centrifuge of boiling blackness that lasted for an eternity, beyond endurance, but when I seemed all but finished, the rolling suddenly stopped. (para. 10)

The crocodile executes a total of three death rolls with Plumwood in its jaws. She survives by pulling free from the exhausted predator as it relaxes its grip—for the second time. Instead of attempting for a third time to climb the paperbark tree, she claws up the steep muddy bank of the river. The crocodile does not pursue her.

After several hours of walking and finally crawling in the dark to a place where she knows her chances of being found are greatest, Plumwood is rescued by the park ranger who had loaned her the canoe. During the 13-hour transport to the hospital, she repeatedly insists that no one attempt to hunt and kill the crocodile. Her concern is not that the animal—now narrativized as "monster"—was following its (ultimately uncontrollable) instinct to hunt and kill, but that the master narrative of monster inexorably unfolding after such an attack would lead to wholesale slaughter of saltwater crocodiles in Australia, as had happened following previous attacks in the land of "Crocodile Dundee." Consequently, Plumwood attempts to minimize publicity about the attack—with little success, as "hospital authorities, whose phone lines had been jammed for days" (para. 4) insist that she give a press interview. Despite her remonstrations otherwise, the "masculinist monster myth: the master narrative" (para. 21) quickly emerges in the media.

> The imposition of the master narrative occurred in several ways: in the exaggeration of the crocodile's size, in portraying the encounter as a heroic wrestling match, and especially in its sexualization. The events seemed to provide irresistible material for the pornographic imagination, which encouraged male identification with the crocodile and interpretation of the attack as sadistic rape. (para. 23)

It is nine years before Plumwood can "repossess [her] story and write about it in [her] own terms" (para. 25). During the terror of the attack and the horrible hours spent crawling through the swamp, Plumwood reflects that she caught a glimpse of "our frameworks of subjectivity," which are predicated on what she describes as a subject-centered view of the world "'from the inside,' structured to sustain the concept of a continuing, narrative self." This narrative supports the myth of human exceptionalism, which in the midst of the attack she suddenly sees "'from the outside,' as a world no longer my own, an unrecognizable bleak landscape composed of raw necessity, indifferent to my life or death" (para. 9). In other words, Plumwood suddenly sees herself, through what she describes as "terminal incredulity," as nothing more than "a mere piece of meat" (para. 29)—which is to say, as prey.

Locating herself as an intruder in that wild place, and despite—or perhaps because of—her extensive experience, Plumwood commits two crucial mistakes. Before embarking on the trip, she fails to seek the advice of the indigenous Gagadgu owners of Kakadu, who likely could have told her about the flooding already occurring well upstream that in just 24 hours would leave the area where she intended to canoe under six feet of water. She also refuses to succumb to "timidity, in philosophy or in life" (para. 2), and disregards her intuition and feelings of unease as the trip progresses. In the end, Plumwood's narrative, in contradistinction to the master's monster narrative, is framed as "a humbling and cautionary tale about our relationship with the earth, about the need to acknowledge our own animality and ecological vulnerability" (para. 31), particularly in the presence of large predators. Not so much that humans are like animals, but that we are interconnected, codependent, and if we are lucky, co-present (Haraway, 2008) with and to animals as well as each other. Plumwood notes that the integrity of an ecosystem can be measured by its ability to support large predators, and for humans the challenge of living alongside them in these ecosystems is an indicator of "our preparedness to coexist with the otherness of the earth" (para. 30), and with those we conceive as radically other. Successful coexistence—flourishing (Haraway, 2008)—is dependent upon dismantling the master narrative, upon telling other stories.

Social justice has nothing to do with this—for crocodiles or music education. Rather, social justice is a red herring, a mandated curricular and/or pedagogical requirement at worst, or naïve aspiration at best, that would maintain the master narrative of "justice." As a function of adjudication, justice is constructed in liberal democracies as adversarial, making it quite literally a lost cause, a zero sum game in which the master inevitably wins. Rather than justice, the issues Plumwood raises are deeply ethical, grounded in respect, concern for others, looking back—*respecere*, as Donna Haraway (2008) describes it. That Plumwood and Haraway, both feminist philosophers—Plumwood an Australian environmental activist with legendary knowledge of the natural world where she lived; Haraway an American biologist legendary for her "Manifestos" ("Cyborg" in 1991; "Companion Species" in 2003)— take up human-implicated ethics in and through inhabitants of the natural world (Plumwood's [2008] concern with large predators living free; Haraway's [2008] concern with laboratory animals living unfree), vis-à-vis the culture/nature dualism, is a function of the impossibility of conceiving any form of ethics (or justice, for that matter) on exclusively human terms, which is to say, from the standpoint of human subjectivity, the "inside view" that Plumwood identifies.

After their divorce, she changes her name from that of her second husband to Plumwood, for Plumwood Mountain (itself named for the tall plumwood tree) located in the temperate rainforest in southern Australia, where she continues living in the stone house they had built together. Rather than solitary, she sees "herself as a member of a convivial biotic community of animal and plant beings who provided daily drama, delight, excitement and opportunities for discovery" (Mathews, 2008, para. 6), much as musicians engage with the musical world in their daily lives. Plumwood died—quickly and likely quietly—of a stroke while walking alone on Plumwood Mountain. A vegetarian before and after the crocodile attack, not because she considered "predation itself [to be] demonic and impure, but because [she] object[ed] to the reduction of animal lives in factory farming systems that treat them as living meat" (para. 29), Plumwood was similarly "critical of academic orthodoxy" (para. 8), and worked as an independent scholar by choice. She honored all sentient beings in an ethics of respect, undertaken as worldly entanglements where "earthly heterogeneous beings are in this web together for all time, . . . [and] no one gets to be Man" (Haraway, 2008, p. 82).

Except, apparently, in music education, where "Man" smiles as he says, "I get along with you because you're the only feminist in music education with a sense of humor!"[17] Click! "Man" in music education publishes widely, writing in and editing (hand)books while "persuad[ing himself] that deciding what [he] like[s] or do[esn't] like about what's happening is the same thing as actually intervening in its production" (Sedgwick, 1993, pp. 132–133) (see Figure 9.4), and

**He calls
that
social justice.**

When her body is discovered in the rainforest on Plumwood Mountain, it is widely—and incorrectly—reported that Val Plumwood died from the effects of a poisonous spider bite she sustained during her daily perambulation that for years she had safely navigated by carefully detaching and reattaching their webs along her path (Figueroa, 2008, para. 1).

"Wild Things"
written and performed by Cris Williamson, 1975
The Changer and the Changed
Olivia Records, ORCD904

So, *this* is how it ends: cutting loose feminism, deterritorializations hinted at but not actualized in a music education still "to come" (Deleuze & Guattari, 1994); one to move the body, to incite passion, to affirm life in feminist critiques of inclusions and exclusions, to enable and to value contingent alternatives, to queer perspectives, to open potentialities of multiple subjectivities, to create potentialities of lives worth living—a music education to matter (Figure 9.5).[18]

In memoriam
Jean Anyon (1941–2013)
Ghetto Schooling: A Political Economy of Urban Educational Reform (1997)
Radical Possibilities: Public Policy, Urban Education, and a New Social Movement (2005)
Marx and Education (2011)[19]

ACKNOWLEDGMENTS

I am grateful to editor Cathy Benedict for her invaluable insight, wit, and intelligence, without which the chapter *would not* have been written, and for her indomitable patience, passion, and compassion, without which it *could not* have been written.

NOTES

1. From the song "Defying Gravity," which closes the first act of the musical *Wicked*. In the show-stopping number, green-skinned witch Elphaba, smart and political, declares her rebellion against and freedom from the ("great and powerful") wizard's authority. She is propelled high above the stage while triumphantly singing, "It's me!"—defying gravity. As she moves into and occupies the space, "flying solo," Elphaba defiantly belts, "And nobody is ever going to bring me down!" Lyrics are quoted from a Broadway performance featuring Idina Menzel and Kristen Chenowith posted on YouTube, http://www.youtube.com/watch?v=8-ncy4gzM4I. Based on Gregory Maguire's 1995 novel, *Wicked*, the musical (music and lyrics by Stephen Schwartz, book by Winnie Holzman, original Broadway production directed by Joe Mantello), opened in 2003 to mixed reviews, but quickly developed a fiercely loyal fan base of mostly adolescent girls.

2. In New Orleans, social clubs and benevolent societies sponsor contemporary jazz funerals and each club's anniversary parade. Grand marshals lead the procession by stepping off; their reputation and dancing skills not only "counter damaging stereotypes," but are indicative of the club's status, as the most prestigious "employ three, four, or more grand marshals to lead the way" (Atkins, 2012, p. 172).

3. My deployment of the literary apostrophe here most emphatically does *not* address any named person in this chapter; specifically, I am *not* addressing Julia Koza, Roberta Lamb, Patricia O'Toole, or Estelle Jorgensen.

4. Spoken communication.

5. In 1995, Oscar Lathlin, a Cree Member of the Opposition was expelled from the House for "refusing to retract his use of 'racist' [as 'unparliamentary language'] from an earlier critique of provincial government policy and programs affecting Aboriginal communities. The Speaker's parliamentary ruling insisted on the performance of a racism-free Manitoba" (Gill, 2002, p. 159).

6. Spoken communication.

7. According to jazz historian Bruce Raeburn (2007), *jazz funeral* is a term used by tourists—as opposed to musicians, who refer to it as a "brass band funeral" because jazz is played only during the return trip from the cemetery while dirges are played on the way to the gravesite. Matt Sakakeeny characterizes *jazz funeral* as a neologism produced by musicians, audiences, and others that "localizes funerals with music by rooting them in the birthplace of jazz" (2011, p. 320).

8. Sakakeeny (2011) describes the Creole population as "a prominent mixed-race group whose in-between status had long been recognized within New Orleans's three-tiered racial hierarchy that was as much Caribbean as North American.... [A]s a group they were distinguished by language (French), religion (Catholicism), location (concentrated downtown in the historically French districts of the Tremé and the Seventh Ward), occupation (doctors, lawyers, educators, entrepreneurs, artisans, and skilled crafts people), and a Eurocentric view of culture as the fine arts.... Creole musicians who performed in the opera houses, symphonies, dance orchestras, and brass bands of the city were often trained professionals who mastered techniques associated with Western classical music" (p. 308).

9. While "the black population of New Orleans quadrupled and the number of black musicians and music teachers more than doubled" (Sakakeeny, 2011, p. 309) in the half-century between 1860 and 1910, the increase among the latter (between 1880 and 1910) is mostly attributable to women music teachers, almost none of whom were professional musicians

(Gushee, 1994, p. 7n4). Migrating to New Orleans from "rural Southern plantations, the majority were Prostestant (Baptist, Methodist, and Sanctified), worked primarily as laborers and domestics, and settled above Canal Street in the uptown district" (Sakakeeny, 2011, p. 309).

10. For a detailed discussion about music teaching in New Orleans public schools, see Al Kennedy, *Chord changes on the chalkboard: How public school teachers shaped jazz and the music of New Orleans* (Boston, Scarecrow Press, 2002).

11. Sakakeeny (2011) describes the life of brass band musicians living in New Orleans today as "a balancing act between *tradition* (community-based parades and performances) and *heritage* (staged exhibitions of tradition)" (p. 321).

12. For a powerful firsthand account, see Jason Flaherty, *Floodlines: Community and resistance from Katrina to the Jena Six* (Chicago: Haymarket Books, 2010).

13. The Lady Buck Jumpers, "a strong, powerful group of women of all ages ... dance harder and better than any other secondline [*sic*] crew" (Flaherty, 2010, p. 9), lead one of the largest annual parades of the year.

14. For a documentary about sexism and racism enacted against women jazz musicians generally during the 1930s and 1940s, see *Girls in the Band*, written and directed by Judy Chaikin, distributed by Independent Pictures; An Artist Tribe/One Step Production.

15. Jane O'Reilly coined the term "Click!" in "The Housewife's Moment of Truth," published in the 1972 debut issue of *Ms. Magazine*, to describe the ah-ha moment women experience when "realizing unfairness" (Steinem in Pogrebin, 2011, n.p.)—otherwise known as sexism—in personal and professional gender relations. For additional contemporary accounts of Click! moments, see Courtney E. Martin and J. Courtney Sullivan (Eds.), *Click: When we knew we were feminists* (Berkeley, CA: Seal Press, 2010).

16. See Simon Stow (2008) for an insightful discussion of how, in the aftermath of Hurricane Katrina, George W. Bush managed to do both, perhaps most egregiously by not only deploying this strategy of remembering inaccurately, but by deploying it as part of his strategy of forgetting.

17. Spoken communication.

18. Kathleen Casey, *I answer with my life: Life histories of teachers working for social change* (New York, Routledge, 1993).

19. First and last names of authors, editors, translators: Jean Anyon; Jennifer Atkins; Mick Burns; Kathleen Casey; Judy Chaikin; Alphonso Cuarón; Gilles Deleuze and Félix Guattari; Hugh Tomlinson and Graham Burchell (Trans.); Robert Melchoir Figueroa; Geraldine Finn; Jordan Flaherty; Sheila Dawn Gill; Sherene Razack (Ed.); Lawrence Gushee; Donna J. Haraway; Al Kennedy; Richard Knowles; Wynton Marsalis; Cortney E. Martin and J. Courtney Sullivan (Eds.); Freya Mathews; Thomas McLaughlin; Frank Lentricchia and Thomas McLaughlin (Eds.); Ikem Okoye; Brenda Marie Osbey; Val Plumwood; Abigail Pogrebin; Bruce Boyd Raeburn; Helen A. Regis; Herlin Riley and Johnny Vidacovich; Matt Sakakeeny; William J. Schafer and Richard B. Allen; Eve Kosofsky Sedgwick; Susan Gubar and Jonathan Kamholtz (Eds.); Simon Stow; Meredith Willson.

REFERENCES

Anyon, J. (1997). *Ghetto schooling: A political economy of urban educational reform.* New York: Teachers College Press.

Anyon, J. (2005). *Radical possibilities: Public policy, urban education, and a new social movement*. New York: Routledge.

Anyon, J. (2011). *Marx and education*. New York: Routledge.

Atkins, J. (2012). Class acts and daredevils: Black masculinity in jazz funeral dancing. *The Journal of American Culture, 35*(2), 166–180.

Burns, M. (2006). *Keeping the beat on the street: The New Orleans brass band renaissance*. Baton Rouge: Louisiana State University Press.

Casey, K. (1993). *I answer with my life: Life histories of teachers working for social change*. New York: Routledge.

Chaikin, J. (2013). *Girls in the band*. Independent Pictures. An Artist Tribe/One Step Production.

Cuarón, A. (2013). *Gravity*. Esperanto Filmoj & Heyday Films. United States & United Kingdom: Warner Brothers Pictures.

Deleuze, G., & Guattari, F. (1994). *What is philosophy?* H. Tomlinson & Graham B., (Trans.). New York: Columbia University Press.

Figueroa, R. M. (2008, February 29). A day on Plumwood Mountain. *Val Plumwood (11 August 1939—29 February 2008)*. Retrieved from http://enviroethics.org/2008/02/29/val-plumwood-11-august-1939-%E2%80%93-29-february-2008/.

Finn, G. (1996). *Why Althusser killed his wife: Essays on discourse and violence*. Atlantic Highlands, NJ: Humanities Press International.

Flaherty, J. (2010). *Floodlines: Community and resistance from Katrina to the Jena Six*. Chicago: Haymarket Books.

Gill, S. D. (2002). The unspeakability of racism: Mapping law's complicity in Manitoba's racialized spaces. In S. Razack, (Ed.), *Race, space, and the law: Unmapping a white settler society* (pp. 157–186). Toronto: Between the Lines.

Gould, E. (2007). Social justice in music education: The problematic of democracy. *Music Education Research, 9*(2), 229–240. Retrieved from http://dx.doi.org/10.1080/14613800701384359.

Gould, E. (2012a). Homosexual subject(ivitie)s in music education: Deconstructions of the disappeared. *Philosophy of Music Education Review, 20*(1), 45–62. doi 10.1353/pme.2012.0006.

Gould, E. (2012b). Uprooting music education pedagogies and curricula: Becoming-musician and the Deleuzian refrain. *Discourse: Studies in the Cultural Politics of Education, 33*(1), 75–86. Retrieved from http://dx.doi.org/10.1080/01596306.2012.632168.

Gushee, L. (1994). The nineteenth-century origins of jazz. *Black Music Research Journal, 14*(1), 1–24.

Haraway, D. J. (2008). *When species meet*. Minneapolis: University of Minnesota Press.

Kennedy, A. (2002). *Chord changes on the chalkboard: How public school teachers shaped jazz and the music of New Orleans*. Boston: Scarecrow Press.

Knowles, R. (1996). *Fallen heroes: A history of New Orleans brass bands*. New Orleans: Jazzology Press.

Marsalis, W. (2013, February 2). The rich history of "When the saints go marching in." *CBS This Morning*. Retrieved from http://wyntonmarsalis.org/videos/view/the-rich-history-of-when-the-saints-go-marching-in-cbs-this-morning.

Martin, C. E., & Sullivan, J. C. (Eds.). (2010). *Click: When we knew we were feminists*, Berkeley, CA: Seal Press.

Mathews, F. (2008, March 26). Val Plumwood: Australian philosopher devoted to an ethic that regarded people as part of nature. *The Guardian*. Retrieved from http://www.theguardian.com/education/2008/mar/26/australia.world.

McLaughlin, T. (1995). Figurative language. In F. Lentricchia & T. McLaughlin, (Eds.), *Critical terms for literary study*, 2nd ed. (pp. 80–90). Chicago: The University of Chicago Press.

Okoye, I. (1998, April 10). Contra-history: A recalcitrant architecture of Umunri. Paper presented at the Arts Council of the African Studies Association, New Orleans.

Osbey, B. M. (1996). One more last chance: Ritual and the jazz funeral. *The Georgia Review*, 50(1), 97–107.

Plumwood, V. (1993). *Feminism and the mastery of nature*. London: Routledge.

Plumwood, V. (2008). Being prey. *Remembering Val Plumwood*. http://valplumwood.com/2008/03/08/being-prey/.

Pogrebin, A. (2011). How do you spell Ms.: Forty years ago, a group of feminists, led by Gloria Steinem did the unthinkable: They started a magazine for women, published by women—and the first issue sold out in eight days. An oral history of a publication that changed history. *New York*, 7 November. Retrieved from http://search.proquest.com.myaccess.library.utoronto.ca/docview/901209707/140AC7B3BA0434124ED/12?accountid=14771.

Raeburn, B. B. (2007). "They're tryin' to wash us away": New Orleans musicians surviving Katrina. *The Journal of American History*, 94(3), 812–819.

Regis, H. A. (1999). Second lines, minstrelsy, and the contested landscapes of New Orleans Afro-Creole festivals. *Cultural Anthropology*, 14(4), 472–504.

Regis, H. A. (2001). Blackness and the politics of memory in the New Orleans second line. *American Ethnologist*, 28(4), 752–777.

Riley, H., & Vidacovich, J. (1995). *New Orleans jazz and second line drumming*. New York: Manhattan Music.

Sakakeeny, M. (2006). Resounding silence in the streets of a musical city. *Space and Culture*, 9(1), 41–44.

Sakakeeny, M. (2011). New Orleans music as a circulatory system. *Black Music Research Journal*, 31(2), 291–325.

Schafer, W. J. (with assistance from R. B. Allen). 1977. *Big bands and New Orleans jazz*. Baton Rouge: Louisiana State University Press.

Sedgwick, E. K. (1993). Socratic raptures, Socratic ruptures: Notes toward queer performativity. In S. Gubar & J. Kamholtz (Eds.), *English inside and out: The places of literary criticism* (pp. 122–136). New York: Routledge.

Stow, S. (2008). Do you know what it means to miss New Orleans? George Bush, the jazz funeral, and the politics of memory. *Theory & Event*, 11(1), 1. Retrieved from http://search.proquest.com/docview/210779359?accountid=14771.

Willson, Meredith. 1949/1975. *And there I stood with my piccolo*. Westport, CT: Greenwood Press.

CHAPTER 10

....

THE SPACE
BETWEEN WORLDS

Music Education and Latino Children

....

JACQUELINE KELLY-MCHALE
AND CARLOS R. ABRIL

ONE of the most discussed demographic changes in the United States in the last two decades has been the rise of the Latino population, which is the fastest-growing, largest, and youngest ethnic group in the country (Casellas & Ibarra, 2012). According to the US Census Bureau (2012), by 2050 Latinos are projected to represent approximately 25 percent of the US population. It should come as no surprise, then, that the population of Latino students in schools has also risen tremendously: from 1990 to 2011 enrollment in public schools for Latino students increased from 7.7 million (16 percent of the student population) to 11.4 million (23 percent) (National Center for Educational Statistics, 2013a). These latest figures indicate that Latinos are the majority student population in the two largest states, California and Texas, and many, even if they were born in the United States, enter school as English language learners (ELLs) and remain socially connected to the Latino culture (NCES, 2013b).[1]

The term "Latino" is used in the United States to describe and categorize people of diverse races, geographical origins, socioeconomic conditions, political affiliations, and traditions—a people united by language and a Spanish colonial heritage (Dutwin et al., 2005; Marotta & Garcia, 2003; US Census, 2012). Clearly, a single, monolithic designation is problematic. On the one hand, it serves to categorize a group of people who speak the Spanish language, and is used by the US Census to classify individuals broadly and more specifically by country or territory of affiliation. On the other, it over-generalizes and does not capture individual or subgroup nuances and differences, even of those from the same country of origin. Recognizing these problematics, we will, however, use the term "Latino" throughout the rest of the chapter. When clarification or exemplification becomes necessary, this will be noted in the text.

In this chapter we choose to bring into focus issues that impact Latino students in school music programs in the United States. Specifically, we will examine the ways current pedagogical practices misalign with the values of many Latino students and families, and may contribute to the alienation of Latino families from schools. We will also consider teacher beliefs and attitudes toward Latinos, as a way of understanding how they are or are not being served by a school music culture—a culture that seems to emphasize materials, skills, and repertoire over people. We assert that attending to the unique needs of Latino students in music education is a moral imperative, one of social justice and equity pedagogy. We further propose that access is often used to claim equity; however, access does not necessarily create equity, especially when access is viewed through the lens of the dominant culture. In the case of music education, the reliance on Western European practice, repertoire, and curriculum and course design creates inequitable experiences and contributes to the marginalization of Latino students in music classrooms.

Latino Students and Music Education Programs in the United States

Taking into consideration the continued increase in the numbers of Latino students in US schools, we would expect to see a concomitant rise in their school music participation, but this is not the case. Elpus and Abril (2011) found a notable gap between Latino students and their White counterparts with regard to per capita participation in high school music programs across the country. Students who speak a language other than English (most commonly Spanish), are in low socioeconomic groups, and have parents with the lowest levels of education, were also found to be significantly underrepresented in high school music programs. This gap in high school music participation for Latino students has not been fully explained by the research literature. However, potential reasons for the gap might be due to limited access to elective music courses, a lack of support from school districts, insufficient family economic resources, or the perception that school-based music programs lack relevance and importance in their lives due to the nature and structure of large performing ensembles—which comprise the vast majority of music education offerings in secondary schools (Abril & Gault, 2008).

For instance, an example of the impact of parent involvement and financial support on band programs has been explored through the study of a large Texas school district. Costa-Giomi and Chappel (2007) reported that of the 25 band programs in one school district, the bands with larger numbers of Latino and Black students had fewer financial resources, less adequate facilities, and less parental involvement than those band programs in schools with fewer Latino and Black students. The study emphasized that equal access to an instrumental program does not guarantee equal program quality, and raised the question of how parent support and financial issues, such as ability to fundraise, the existence of booster clubs, the ability to afford private lessons, and the space and configuration in the home for instrumental practice (Costa-Giomi & Chappel, 2007), play more of a role in the quality of a program than the music educator.[2]

In schools with a high population of Latino students, the nature of school ensembles may also pose a problem of relevance and access. Many school music programs with large Latino and minority populations continue to replicate the musical practices of the past, in terms of traditional ensemble structure, style, and repertoire. While school-based ensembles may play music inspired by the sounds of or folk tunes from Latin American countries, the vast majority of the repertoire is disconnected from the musical traditions of Latino families.

There are other aspects of secondary ensembles that may also be incompatible with Latino culture. The competitive nature of ensembles (e.g., students competing for positions in the ensemble) stands in stark contrast to the concept of allocentrism, which emphasizes collaboration and cohesiveness among groups—a common approach within the Latino family (Kagen, 1986). While the large financial obligation has already been mentioned, the time commitment of ensemble participation may make participation impossible. In some Latino families, students who are of working age are expected to contribute financially by working after school, which makes daily after-school rehearsals impossible. There may also be resistance from students, based on their perception that what they are learning in school ensembles has little to do with their musical and cultural identities.

Participation in school music programs at the elementary level is most commonly compulsory. Therefore, unlike Latino participation in secondary school music programs, participation should be equally dispersed across ethnicity. However, there is often a lack of or inconsistent availability of music education programs in elementary schools in school districts and states with large concentrations of Latino and Black students. We must be vigilant, then, of other ways in which access does not necessarily translate to equity, even when music programs are offered. For example, students who are English language learners (most of whom are Latino in the United States) are, in many districts, systematically excluded from music instruction for additional instruction in other subject areas. In many instances, they are pulled from "specials" in order to have extra test preparation, speech or language instruction, or simply for "extra help." This not only prevents these students from arts engagements but also serves to disrupt the music curriculum and community building for all students within the school.

There are other issues facing Latino students in the elementary school music program. Elementary music curricula are often based on specific teaching methods. The four most prominent approaches in US elementary general music programs are Orff, Kodály, Dalcroze, and Gordon (Brophy, 2002). These approaches are based on the belief that musical play is the path to the development of musical competency, and that all children have the ability to learn and enjoy music (Choksy, Abramson, Gillespie, & Woods, 1986; Shamrock, 1997). Yet, each of these approaches was developed based upon the Western European music paradigm, using repertoire, notation, and a reverence for that art music tradition. Kelly-McHale (2011) proposed the designation of "sequence-centered"

(p. 277) to describe classroom practice that is dependent upon a sequence of skills or an approach to teaching. Analogous to this would be ensemble contexts where a "score-centered" approach is adopted and the focus is on the performance of a piece of music (Thibeault, 2009). In music classrooms that are sequence- or score-centered, diversity is often approached from an additive perspective, meaning that any repertoire chosen to represent diversity is either disconnected from the curriculum, presented as something extra, or tied to a holiday or special occasion (Banks, 2004). The problem of an additive approach is that it takes the viewpoint of the dominant cultural group and presents the diverse material through a Western European lens, allowing little room for alternative perspectives. Thus, the reliance on a Western European view can alienate students and, in music class, can contribute to a feeling of musical isolation.

Recognizing that music education is predominantly structured around a Western European paradigm, and that practices in schools largely reflect these cultural practices, questions of how and if to adapt instruction to meet the needs of culturally and linguistically diverse students remain. The actions of music educators and administrators that either fail to financially support school programs where Latinos represent that majority, or through an overreliance on Western European practices, traditions, and repertoire ignore cultural practices and beliefs, continue to sustain a canonically based system of music education. This system can alienate and marginalize Latino students (Abril, 2010; Carlow, 2004; Kelly-McHale, 2013). However, understanding the role of teacher beliefs and practices in conjunction with the cultural beliefs and practices of Latino students can provide opportunities for all stakeholders to reimagine practice and create more inclusive musical opportunities.

TEACHER BELIEFS AND ATTITUDES

A teacher's view toward a specific group of students is largely framed by that teacher's personal experiences outside school (Nieto, 1994). Community perception of culturally diverse populations can also shape how teachers act and react toward these students in the classroom (Freeman & Freeman, 2001). While teachers may believe that they hold a positive view of culturally or linguistically diverse students, they must develop an understanding of how the traditional structure of schools "reproduce existing social inequalities while giving the illusion that such inequalities are natural and fair" (Villegas & Lucas, 2002, p. 23). These inequalities occur when success is viewed as an individual accomplishment not tied to the role of the institution. Teachers, in order to develop the understanding necessary to respond to students who are marginalized in society, need to recognize that the current structure of schools benefits those who are already advantaged (2002).

Deficit-based practices and cultural responsiveness represent dichotomous praxis regarding the cultural and linguistic diversity of Latino students. Delpit (2006) believes that students are the products of their homes; therefore, any preconceived notion that a teacher may have about how that home functions becomes the baseline for that teacher's attitude toward the student. Teacher education programs that focus on the research tying failure in schools to socioeconomic status, cultural differences, and single-parent households promote an insidious practice that further impacts the negative aspects of deficit-based perspectives. Delpit (2006) argues that "to counter this tendency, educators must have knowledge of children's lives outside of school so as to recognize their strengths" (p. 172).

Culturally responsive teaching is an approach that can guide teachers in meeting the needs of diverse student groups. This approach to teaching requires that teachers not only acknowledge and understand diverse cultures represented in the classroom, but that they act upon their understanding through all interactions with students and their families. Culturally responsive teaching strategies in the classroom have been shown to improve student academic achievement and attitude toward schooling (Foster, 1995). Other studies have found that students who maintain their cultural identity while working to adopt the ideals of the US public school system are successful in school (Gibson, 2002; Matute-Bianchi, 1991; Rumbaut & Ima, 1988; Suárez-Orozco, 1987). In the following sections, we will further define deficit-based practices and culturally responsive teaching and then discuss the role of teacher education programs in the development of teacher attitudes toward diversity.

DEFICIT-BASED PRACTICES

Deficit-based practices in education are rooted in the view that students from minority cultures enter schools without the necessary skills and experiences needed to succeed (Nieto, 1994). Based on this perspective, students need to be taught how to effectively function within a white middle-class norm in order to break a cycle of poverty or overcome a language or cultural deficiency. Ford and Grantham (2003) describe the deficit perspective as being a lens through which teachers (or others) view students of ethnic, racial, and linguistic backgrounds that differ from a white, Christian, straight, English-language perspective. They further assert that this perspective serves to continue the propagation of stereotypes and negative, counterproductive views regarding marginalized groups in US society. Teacher's beliefs must be questioned or challenged so that they are aware of the need to directly address issues of racism, language discrimination, and other biases that exist within the school culture, and as a way to facilitate their ability to establish effective educational environments (Nieto, 2002).

The idea of being *color-blind*[3] in the classroom is also directly related to deficit-based perspectives of teaching and learning. DeLorenzo (2012) reminds us that "to ignore color is to ignore identity. Ignoring identity is tantamount to rendering a child invisible" (p. 45). *Color-blindness* is a term used to describe educational practice that takes the perspective of the dominant cultural group as the norm and assumes that the goals of schooling are to maintain the primacy of the dominant group—in effect, practice that seeks to bring all students to "the normalized White standard" (Williams & Land, 2006, p. 579). Color-blindness in schools is predicated on the idea that the United States is a product of Western Europe and should therefore represent its cultural norms (Howard, 2006; McCarthy, 1995). This paradigm "assumes that we can erase our racial catego-ries, ignore differences, and thereby achieve an illusory state of sameness or equality" (Howard, 2006, p. 57).

Deficit and color-blind views are entrenched in the *absolute democracy* paradigm, which posits that good teaching is all that is needed to generate success in a classroom (Finney & Orr, 1995; Sleeter, 1992). This gives credence to the idea that student expe-riences and cultural beliefs are not relevant to the educational process. Teachers who draw on a deficit or color-blind view in their approach within the classroom may do so with good intention; however, the intentions are based on inward reflection of what is *good*, as opposed to understanding that what is *just* is based on understanding and respecting what the students in front of them need to know and learn. The implied goal of instruction that is based on deficit and color-blind views is the assimilation of the student population to the norms and mores of the dominant cultural majority. Practices in the music classroom that privilege the norms and expectations of the dominant cul-tural group, through repertoire, approaches, and perspectives, legitimize a hegemonic perspective toward students who are not in the dominant group (Kelly-McHale, 2011). Pluralistic approaches to education, such as culturally responsive instruction, embrace the diversity of the American school system and seek to enable all students the opportu-nity to "become American" rather than to "be American" (Nieto, 2002, p. 111).

CULTURALLY RESPONSIVE INSTRUCTION IN GENERAL EDUCATION

Culturally responsive instruction is predicated on the belief that culture influences the manner in which students construct knowledge and learn through the tools acquired from their position in society. Culture shapes what we learn, how we learn it, and what is perpetuated in a cultural group or society at large (Erickson, 2004; Samovar & Porter, 1991). Culturally responsive teaching, then, aims to create instructional contexts that teach "to and through the strengths" of the students as it seeks to be culturally "validat-ing and affirming" (Gay, 2000, p. 29).

Gay (2000) defines five essential elements that are required within culturally respon-sive teaching contexts: (1) the development of a knowledge base about diversity, (2) the inclusion of ethnic and culturally diverse content, (3) demonstrating caring and work-ing to build a learning community, (4) developing cross-cultural communication, and (5) subsuming cross-cultural congruity with instruction. Each of these elements speaks to the role of the school as an agent of instruction. The literature on culturally responsive teaching provides a glimpse into the power of instruction when focused on the development of cultural awareness. As previously stated, students who are taught by teachers employing culturally responsive practice succeed, and the reliance on deficit-based instruction prohibits the growth of cultural identity. Thus, there needs to be a two-way interaction between the teacher and student, between culture and knowledge. Understanding how this interaction can be facilitated in classrooms is the responsibility of teacher education programs and is dependent upon the recognition that difference is not a problem to be solved; it is a positive contribution for all students in the classroom.

Addressing Diversity in Teacher Education

The changing demographic landscape in American public schools has necessitated that teacher education programs address issues of diversity. University teacher preparation programs may require a single course that examines culture, implement a program mission that seeks to engage students in multicultural awareness, or offer classes that emphasize the development of cultural sensitivity and the development of positive attitudes and beliefs toward diverse populations (Garmon, 1996). The impact of a single course, designed to shape attitudes and beliefs, has been widely, yet inconclusively, studied. The research literature in teacher education presents contradictory findings regarding the efficacy of coursework on the development of attitudes toward diversity. Studies that have reported positive changes in students' views of diversity (Artiles & McClafferty, 1998; Delany-Barmann & Minner, 1997; Ross & Smith, 1992; Tran, Young, & DiLella, 1994) stand in contrast to those that have found no change in students' attitudes (Causey, Thomas, & Armento, 2000; Cockrell, Placier, Cockrell, & Middleton, 1999; Garmon, 1996; Haberman & Post, 1998; McDiarmid, 1992). The reason for these conflicting findings has been based on the idea that previously held beliefs are reinforced and are not confronted through coursework (Kagan, 1986).[4]

However, teacher education programs that implement a program-wide mission based on culturally responsive teaching, social justice, or multicultural approaches to teaching have not been as widely studied. Cochran-Smith (2009) found that graduates of a teacher education program that emphasized social justice were acting on some of the social justice tenets they had learned, such as maintaining high expectations for students and drawing upon the student's culture in lesson design, but other elements, such as activism, were not observed. Whipp (2013) found that two primary groups emerged from among teachers who studied in a teacher education program that had a social justice orientation. The first group, those who exhibited teaching behaviors rooted in understanding the structural influences that impact education as well as the needs of the students, drew upon culturally responsive teaching approaches, high classroom expectations, parent connections, consciousness-raising, and advocacy. The second group of teachers from the same program, those who exhibited more individually focused behavior, demonstrated teaching practices that were rooted in correcting deficits, color-blind views of students, and teaching for skills and content. Despite coming from the same teacher education program, there were differences in how these teachers interacted with their students. Whipp (2013) theorized that the differences between the two groups of teachers could be the result of in-service mentoring and professional support and development. Whatever the differences, it is clear that the teacher preparation program itself was not enough to prepare teachers to create responsive environments. The educational process for teachers must continue into the practice of teaching in order for the experiences had and knowledge gained within the teacher preparation program to be codified.

Culturally Responsive Teaching in Music

Research in music education focusing specifically on culturally responsive instruction has examined teacher practice and students' expressed experiences (Abril, 2010; Carlow, 2004; Lum, 2007; Lum & Campbell, 2009; Robinson, 2006; Thibeault, 2009). Robinson (2006) examined the practice of three White teachers in culturally diverse settings using Geneva Gay's (2000) five essential elements of culturally responsive teaching. Teachers in the study were described as being successful in their work with students of diverse cultural backgrounds because the teachers accepted the linguistic and cultural diversity of their classroom as normal and expected. Robinson described how the teachers worked to create a sense of community in their music classrooms and chose materials that reflected their students' backgrounds while expanding the students' knowledge.

The study of diverse students' musical experiences has yielded the understanding that teachers who approach instruction from their cultural and past educational perspective often create a sense of isolation for their students (Carlow, 2004; Lum, 2007). Carlow (2004) found that a lack of cultural and language understanding, combined with teachers' reliance on contextual language for musical instruction, created an unfair learning environment for culturally and linguistically diverse students. Lum (2007) investigated the musical lives of primary-aged children representative of the ethnic diversity found in Singapore. Based on his findings, he recommended that teachers should adopt a constructivist approach that begins with the musical world of each child, so as to have a positive impact on the musical identity development of the child.

Thibeault (2009) identified a disjuncture between school- and life-based musical activity that highlighted isolation in school music practices. He describes a student who had participated in bluegrass music outside school as having musical experiences that were setting-based, or shaped through the interaction she had with music as a process. The student's school music experiences, on the other hand, were defined as being score-based, and organized around the music as object, using notation and reliance upon a conductor or teacher. The relevance of this research to the discussion of Latino students in American music programs rests in the reality that score-centered practices are based in the Western European paradigm and do not necessarily take into account musical practices that are setting-based. We do well to consider, then, that continuing to teach in the manner that has been codified within the US school system quite possibly contributes to feelings of alienation, especially for those for whom music is shared and created in aurally based practices.

Latino Students and Culturally Responsive Music Education: Failures and Successes

Through efforts to be more culturally responsive, teachers often approach difference through surface experiences, such as food, clothing, and music. This narrows the spectrum of understanding and also furthers stereotypes within the community. These may be outward expressions of culture; however, the practices and values of a family go well beyond these manifestations and require deeper understanding. An examination of the cultural practices and values more commonly found in Latino families can help educators better understand the ways Latino students may make meaning. hooks (1994) writes, "multiculturalism compels educators to recognize the narrow boundaries that have shaped the way knowledge is shared in the classroom. It forces us all to recognize our complicity in accepting and perpetuating biases of any kind" (p. 44). The reliance on methods of teaching rooted in White cultural beliefs disadvantages Latino students who have not completely acculturated to the normalized standards in American public schools and thus perpetuates bias.

The perspective of Latino students with regard to musical experience (Lum & Campbell, 2009) and the musical decisions made by teachers have been examined in recent years (Abril, 2009; Kelly-McHale, 2011). Lum and Campbell (2009) describe the ways a young Mexican-American student interacted with music in all facets of her life. Their findings highlight the multiple ways that students interact with music within and outside school. The student in this study, Mirella, led a rich musical life in which she experienced *Tejano* music with her father, popular Spanish-language music through the radio, "Jesus songs" at church, and popular American music such as hip-hop and rhythm and blues with her friends. Each musical experience was transmitted primarily through technology, underscoring the role of technology in children's musical experiences. This study not only demonstrates the importance of music in children's lives, it also demonstrates the lack of connectivity between school and home experiences, suggesting that the school experience can potentially become irrelevant in the life of a child.

Disjuncture Between Practice and Latino Culture

In a study examining the musical identity of Latino students in an elementary music classroom, Kelly-McHale (2011) found that the teacher's reliance on her curriculum and pedagogical structure created an isolated musical experience for the students. Participating students shared that music was something you did in the classroom and that school music experiences were not independently extended or applied to the students' musical experiences outside school. The primary reason for the isolation was the teacher's reliance upon a curriculum based on a Western European approach to music education.

Kelly-McHale (2011) found that these pedagogical and repertoire decisions implicitly denied the existence of the students' common ethnic roots, and positioned Western European–based folk repertoire as the musical mother tongue in the classroom. The music teacher did include a few songs in the students' primary language, but those choices did not create a multicultural or multilingual environment, nor did they broaden the concept of musical mother tongue. The focus on songs that were English-language in origin sustained a monolinguistic environment. Students were not allowed to experience the folk song culture embedded in their primary language, and developed a distaste for singing in their primary language in the general music classroom.

As Delpit (2006) states, the member of the culture of power (in this case a White middle-class teacher) considers those who do not have power or an understanding of the teacher's "expert knowledge" as being at a deficit, and in doing so "disempowers" the students (p. 33). It is important to note that the teacher did not seek to "disempower" her students; her goals of teaching them to sing well and become notationally literate were based on her experiences as a musician and a teacher, and her musical and pedagogical beliefs.

Responding to Latino Populations through Music Curriculum and Instruction

Some teachers are responding to the noticeable rise in the Latino population in their schools through curriculum and instruction. In one case study (Abril, 2009), a music teacher's awareness of a dramatic rise in the Latino population in her middle school (a rise not reflected in her instrumental classes) led her to create a Mariachi program in the hopes that it would interest the Latino students in her school, most of whom were Mexican. Some have recommended the inclusion of Mariachi programs in schools because they are thought to be of interest to Latino students and parents.[5] Bryce (1996) found that Latino parents are positive toward the study of Mariachi in schools because they see it as a form of vocational training, which leads to employment. In the case of the Mariachi ensemble study in the aforementioned case, Abril (2009) writes:

> While important to start thinking beyond a particular nation's music education traditions, creating a new school music ensemble with the purpose of drawing a certain ethnic population into the music programme can prove problematic. Although Mariachi ensembles in schools are popular in some regions of the U.S. with large Mexican populations, the ensemble music presents only one style of Mexican music . . . which may not always be culturally relevant to adolescents—Mexican or not. (p. 88)

Incorporating repertoire has been one of the most common ways music teachers throughout history have responded to demographic shifts (Abril, 2006; Campbell, 2002). In the above cases, the choice of instrumental ensemble and repertoire proved problematic on some levels. In each study, the isolation between Latino students and school-based music instruction was connected to the lack of cultural responsiveness within the classroom. In both instances, teachers reported that they had little to no understanding of the students' home culture, especially with regard to music, or made sweeping generalizations that were more closely related to Latino stereotypes.

Caring and Responsive Music Instruction

> If you can show me how I can cling to that which is real to me, while teaching me a way into the larger society, then and only then will I drop my defenses and hostility, and I will sing your praises and help you to make the desert bear fruit. (Ellison, 1995, p. 551)

Teaching is about learning, but learning is not necessarily a prescriptive endeavor. Ellison's quote reminds us that the foundation of culturally responsive teaching is caring. The content within the classroom, the skill development, and the pedagogical choices, no matter how responsive to the culture of the students, become irrelevant when the classroom environment is not built upon caring.

Powell's (1996) cross-case analysis of the practices of successful teachers in diverse school settings found that (a) teachers worked from the position of facilitator, guide, and risk-taker, rather than leader; (b) they worked to reinvent the curriculum, aligning their practice more closely with their students' experiences and knowledge; and (c) the teachers sought to show their understanding of the students' culture. Of the four teachers in the study, one was a music educator. Powell surmised that the teachers' intuitive practice and a compassionate disposition for teaching and learning were at the root of their successes.

Studies of two school districts in Texas have shown that when schools begin with caring and then acknowledge and incorporate strategies that are congruous with Latino values, students benefit and succeed (Reyes, Scribner, & Scribner, 1999;

Valenzuela, 1999). Valenzuela (1999) profiled a band director who came to realize that in order for his marching band to function with some measure of adequacy, students had to be well nourished. Many of the students came from impoverished households and were not eating regular meals. The band director began making *taquitos* for his students in an effort to address the issue. This act of caring became foundational to the growth and success of his band program, as the students recognized that the band director cared for them as people. His responsiveness to the students' needs contributed to the students' development of a more positive attitude toward band and school in general.

Each of these previous examples demonstrated the importance of care and community building in music classrooms. Returning to Gay's (2000) five essential elements of culturally responsive teaching, it becomes clear that the ability to create opportunities for students to participate and to be provided with experiences that are equitable is greatly influenced by instructional practice that is informed by culturally responsive teaching. The above accounts of teacher practice demonstrate why understanding diversity, including content that is reflective of diversity, and creating classroom communities that are caring are foundational to fostering access and equity in music education.

IMPLICATIONS

Issues addressed in this chapter bring to bear questions of attitudes, access, and equity. The vast majority of elementary schools do provide instruction in music taught by a specialist, meaning that students participate, regardless of choice or other factors such as socioeconomic status, race, and ethnicity. However, other barriers to access (many of which were discussed in this chapter) need to be addressed and studied further, as does the concern that participation drops and becomes elective in secondary schools. As was reported in prior research (Abril, 2009; Kelly-McHale, 2011; Lum, 2007), the curricular choices made by the music teacher have an impact on student experience in the music classroom, and perhaps contribute to poor representation in the secondary years.

Thibeault (2009) contends that music educators need to understand that the inclusion of setting-centered practices can "bring a different set of emphases, and can allow performers to engage in conversations that seem to have ended by the time a score usually reaches them" (p. 272). Extending this thought, it also follows that music teachers can reach more diverse populations when they include practices and repertoire that are more representative of the ways that their students engage with music. However, materials and practices cannot be the only factors considered because these elements can become cursory at best and offensive at worst. Building connections with students, showing respect and understanding, and creating a culture of caring in the classroom need to take precedence. This can only occur when music educators are taught how to see their students as individuals, while also providing musical experiences that enable students to grow and build community.

Conclusion

Recent publications and articles have sought to reimagine what occurs in music classrooms, placing an emphasis on adopting setting-centered or popular music–based approaches to music instruction (Folkestad, 2006; Tobias, 2013). This work has sought to reinvigorate music education practice. Yet, embedded in many of these conversations is the perspective that materials, repertoire, and musical behaviors are the most important elements to consider when questioning or challenging the music education paradigm. Throughout this chapter we have suggested that questions and challenges need to focus on issues of teacher knowledge, beliefs, and attitude toward culturally diverse students and how instruction is designed and delivered in ways that are respectful to and knowledgeable about the differences students bring to our classrooms. The reality is that no matter how many studies are conducted and policies created, issues of equity and access that have negatively impacted the music participation and experience of Latino students in the United States will not change until music teacher education programs seek to adopt culturally responsive practices that require music education students to recognize that family and family values reside just as powerfully within cultures that aren't necessarily their own.

Notes

1. In the United States, the vast majority of Latinos are of Mexican origin, followed by Puerto Rican, Cuban, Salvadoran, Dominican, and Guatemalan (US Census Bureau, 2012).
2. It is important to note that there was no correlation found between school socioeconomic status and music teacher quality.
3. The term *color-blind* is used in this chapter to frame the perspective that good teaching creates an equal opportunity for all children, and that racial and ethnic differences are not important in education. A discussion of the misrecognized nature of the term can be found in Bradley's Chapter 12 in this volume.
4. Pohan (1996) investigated the relationship between personal and professional beliefs of 492 preservice teachers regarding diversity. A significant relationship between personal and professional beliefs was discovered. She reported that preservice teachers' previous experiences with diversity influenced their professional beliefs, thus confirming Kagen's observation.
5. The National Association for Music Education (NAfME) offers professional support for music teachers interested in developing Mariachi programs in their schools. http://musiced.nafme.org/mariachi/.

References

Abril, C. R. (2006). Music that represents culture: Selecting music with integrity. *Music Educators Journal*, 93(1), 38–45.

Abril, C. R. (2009). Responding to culture in the instrumental music program: A teacher's journey. *Music Education Research, 11*(1), 77–91.

Abril, C. R. (2010). Opening spaces in the instrumental music classroom. In A. Clements (Ed.), *Alternative approaches in music education.* Lanham, MD: Rowman & Littlefield.

Abril, C. R., & Gault, B. M. (2006). The state of music in the elementary school: The principal's perspective. *Journal of Research in Music Education, 54*(1), 6–20.

Abril, C. R., & Gault, B. M. (2008). The state of music in secondary schools: The principal's perspective. *Journal of Research in Music Education, 56*(1), 68–81.

Artiles, A. J., & McClafferty, K. (1998). Learning to teach culturally diverse learners: Charting change in preservice teachers' thinking about effective teaching. *The Elementary School Journal, 98*(3), 189–220. http://www.jstor.org/stable/1002257.

Banks, J. (2004). Multicultural education: Historical development, dimensions, and practice. In J. A. Banks & C. A. M. Banks (Eds.), *Handbook of research on multicultural education* (2nd ed., pp. 3–29). San Francisco: Jossey-Bass.

Brophy, T. S. (2002). Teacher reflections on undergraduate music education. *Journal of Music Teacher Education, 12*(1), 10–16.

Bryce, R. (1996). Forget the Macarena: Texas high schools do the Mariachi. *Christian Science Monitor, 88*(221), 3.

Campbell, P. S. 2002. Music education in a time of cultural transformation. *Music Educators Journal, 89*(1), 27–32.

Carlow, R. (2004). *Hearing others' voices: An exploration of the music experience of immigrant students who sing in high school choir* (Unpublished doctoral dissertation, University of Maryland, College Park).

Casellas, J. P., & Ibarra, J. D. (2012). Changing political landscapes for Latinos in America. *Journal of Hispanic Higher Education, 11*(3), 234–258.

Causey, V. E., Thomas, C. D., & Armento, B. J. (2000). Cultural diversity is basically a foreign term to me: The challenges of diversity for preservice teacher education. *Teaching & Teacher Education, 16*, 33–45.

Choksy, L., Abramson, R. M., Gillespie, A. E., & Woods, D. (1986). *Teaching music in the twentieth century.* Englewood Cliffs, NJ: Prentice-Hall.

Cochran-Smith, M. (2009). Toward a theory of teacher education for social justice. In *Second international handbook of educational change* (pp. 445–467). Dordrecht: Springer.

Cockrell, K. S., Placier, P. L., Cockrell, D. H., & Middleton, J. N. (1999). Coming to terms with "diversity" and "multiculturalism" in teacher education: Learning about our students, changing our practice. *Teaching and Teacher Education, 15*(4), 351–366.

Costa-Giomi, E., & Chappell, E. (2007). Characteristics of band programs in a large urban school district: Diversity or inequality? *Journal of Band Research, 42*(2), 1–18.

Delany-Barmann, G., & Minner, S. (1997). Development and implementation of a program of study to prepare teachers for diversity. *Equity and Excellence in Education, 30*(2), 78–85.

Delpit, L. (2006). *Other people's children: Cultural conflict in the classroom* (2nd ed.). New York: Norton.

DeLorenzo, L. C. (2012). Missing faces from the orchestra: An issue of social justice? *Music Educators Journal, 98*(4), 39–46.

Dutwin, D., Brodie, M., Herrmann, M., & Levin, R. (2005). Latinos and political party affiliation. *Hispanic Journal of Behavioral Sciences, 27*(2), 135–160.

Ellison, R. (1995). *The collected essays of Ralph Ellison.* New York: Random House.

Elpus, K., & Abril, C. R. (2011). High school music ensemble students in the United States: A demographic profile. *Journal of Research in Music Education, 59*(2), 128–145.

Erickson, F. (2004). Culture in society and in educational practices. In J. Banks & C. A. M. Banks (Eds.), *Multicultural education: Issues and perspectives* (5th ed., pp. 31–60). Hoboken, NJ: Wiley.

Finney, S., & Orr, J. (1995). "I've really learned a lot but...": Cross-cultural understanding and teacher education in a racist society. *Journal of Teacher Education, 4,* 129–138.

Folkestad, G. (2006), Formal and informal learning situations or practices vs formal and informal ways of learning. *British Journal of Music Education, 23,* 135–145.

Ford, D. Y., & Grantham, T. C. (2003). Providing access for culturally diverse gifted students: From deficit to dynamic thinking. *Theory into Practice, 42,* 217–225.

Foster, M. (1995). African American Teachers and Culturally Relevant Pedagogy. In J. A. Banks & C. A. M. Banks (Eds.), *Handbook of research on multicultural education* (pp. 570–581). New York: Macmillan.

Freeman, D. E., & Freeman, Y. S. (2001) *Between worlds: Access to second language acquisition* (2nd ed.). Portsmouth, NH: Heinemann.

Garmon, M. A. (1996). *Missed messages: How prospective teachers' racial attitudes mediate what they learn from a course on diversity.* East Lansing: Michigan State University.

Gay, G. (2000). *Culturally responsive teaching: Theory, research, and practice* (Vol. 8). New York: Teachers College Press.

Gibson, M. A. (2002). The new Latino diaspora and educational policy. In S. Wortham, R. G. Murillo, & E. T. Hamann (Eds.), *Education in the new Latino Diaspora: Policy and the politics of identity* (pp. 241–252). Westport, CT: Ablex.

Haberman, M., & Post, L. (1998). Teachers for multicultural schools: The power of selection. *Theory into Practice, 37*(2), 96–104.

hooks, B. (1994). *Teaching to transgress: Education as the practice of freedom* (Vol. 4). New York: Routledge.

Howard, G. R. (2006). *We can't teach what we don't know: White teachers, multiracial schools* (2nd ed.). New York: Teachers College Press.

Kagan, S. (1986). In sociocultural factors in schooling. In C. Cortes (Ed.), *Beyond language: Sociocultural factors in schooling in language minority students* (pp. 282–285). Berkeley: University of CA Press.

Kelly-McHale, J. (2013). The influence of music teacher beliefs and practices on the expression of musical identity in an elementary general music classroom. *Journal of Research in Music Education, 61*(2), 195–216.

Kelly-McHale, J. L. (2011) *The relationship between children's musical identities and music teacher beliefs and practices in an elementary general music classroom* (Unpublished doctoral dissertation, Northwestern University, Evanston, IL).

Lum, C. H. (2007). *Musical networks of children: An ethnography of elementary school children in Singapore* (Unpublished doctoral dissertation, University of Washington, Seattle).

Lum, C. H., & Campbell, P. S. (2009). "El Camaleon": The musical secrets of Mirella Valdez. In C. Abril & J. L. Kerchner (Eds.), *Musical experience in our lives: Things we learn and meanings we make* (pp. 113–126). Lanham, MD: Rowman & Littlefield.

Marotta, S. A., & Garcia, J. G. (2003). Latinos in the United States 2000. *Hispanic Journal of Behavioral Sciences, 25*(1), 13–34.

Matute-Bianchi, M. (1991). Situational ethnicity and patterns of school performance among immigrant and non-immigrant descent students. In M. A. Gibson & J. U. Ogbu (Eds.), *Minority status and schooling: A comparative study of immigrant and involuntary minorities* (pp. 397–432). New York: Garland.

McCarthy, C. (1995). Contradictions of identity: Education and the problem of racial absolutism. *The Clearing House, 68,* 297–300.

McDiarmid, G. W. (1992). What to do about differences? A study of multicultural education for teacher trainees in the Los Angeles Unified School District. *Journal of Teacher Education, 43*(2), 83–93.

National Center for Educational Statistics. (2013a). https://nces.ed.gov/programs/coe/index.asp.

National Center for Educational Statistics. (2013b). *Mega-states: An analysis of students' performance in the five most heavily populated states in the nation.* Washington, DC: US Department of Education, NCSE 2013–2450.

Nieto, S. (1994). Lessons from students on creating a chance to dream. *Harvard Educational Review, 64*(4), 392–426.

Nieto, S. (2002). *Language, literacy, and culture: Intersections and implications.* Mahwah, NJ: Lawrence Erlbaum.

Pohan, C. A. (1996). Preservice teachers' beliefs about diversity: Uncovering factors leading to multicultural responsiveness. *Equity and Excellence in Education, 29*(3), 62–69.

Powell, R. R. (1996). "The music is why I teach": Intuitive strategies of successful teachers in culturally diverse learning environments. *Teaching and Teacher Education, 12,* 49–61.

Reyes, P., Scribner, J. D., & Scribner, A. P. (1999). *Lessons from high-performing hispanic schools: Creating learning communities.* Critical Issues in Educational Leadership Series. New York: Teachers College Press.

Robinson, K. M. (2006). White teachers, students of color: Culturally responsive pedagogy for elementary general music in communities of color. In C. Frierson-Campbell (Ed.), *Teaching music in the urban classroom: A guide to survival, success, and reform* (Vol. 1, pp. 35–53). Lanham, MD: Rowman & Littlefield.

Ross, D. D., & Smith, W. (1992). Understanding preservice teachers' perspectives on diversity. *Journal of Teacher Education, 43*(2), 94–103. doi: 10.1177/0022487192043002003.

Rumbaut, R. G., & Ima, K. (1988). *The adaptation of southeast Asian refugee youth: A comparative study.* Washington, DC: US Office of Refugee Resettlement.

Samovar, L. A., & Porter, R. E. (1991). Basic principles of intercultural communication. In L. A. Samovar & R. E. Porter (Eds.), *Intercultural communication: A reader* (pp. 5–22). Belmont, CA: Wadsworth.

Shamrock, M. (1997). Orff-Schulwerk: An integrated foundation. *Music Educators Journal, 83*(6), 41–44.

Sleeter, C. E. (1992). White racism. *Multicultural Education, 1*(4), 5–8, 39.

Suárez-Orozco, C. (1987). Towards a psycho-social understanding of Hispanic adaptation to American schooling. In H. Trueba (Ed.), *Success or failure? Learning and the language minority student* (pp. 156–168). Cambridge, MA: Newberry House.

Thibeault, M. D. (2009). The violin and the fiddle: Narratives of music and musician in a high-school setting. In C. Abril & J. L. Kerchner (Eds.), *Musical experience in our lives: Things we learn and meanings we make* (pp. 255–276). Lanham, MD: Rowman & Littlefield.

Tobias, E. S. (2013). Toward convergence: Adapting music education to contemporary society and participatory culture. *Music Educators Journal, 99*(4), 29–36.

Tran, M. T., Young, R. L., & Dilella, J. D. (1994). Multicultural education courses and the student teacher: Eliminating stereotypic attitudes in our ethnically diverse classroom. *Journal of Teacher Education, 45*(3), 183–189.

US Census Bureau. (2012). http://www.census.gov/newsroom/cspan/hispanic/2012.06.22_cspan_hispanics.pdf.

Valenzuela, A. (1999). *Subtractive schooling: US-Mexican youth and the politics of caring.* Albany: State University of New York Press.

Villegas, A. M., & Lucas, T. (2002). Preparing culturally responsive teachers rethinking the curriculum. *Journal of Teacher Education, 53*(1), 20–32.

Whipp, J. L. (2013). Developing socially just teachers: The interaction of experiences before, during, and after teacher preparation in beginning urban teachers. *Journal of Teacher Education, 64*(5), 454–467.

Williams, D. G., & Land, R. R. (2006). Special focus: The legitimation of Black subordination: The impact of color-blind ideology on African American education. *The Journal of Negro Education, 75,* 579–588.

CHAPTER 11

MUSIC, SOCIAL JUSTICE, AND SOCIAL INCLUSION

The Role of Collaborative Music Activities in Supporting Young Refugees and Newly Arrived Immigrants in Australia

KATHRYN MARSH

My name is "Sia."[1] I come from Freetown, Sierra Leone, Africa. I live with my family. I have two sisters, but during the war I lost my parents. My life in Sierra Leone was very hard for me and my family because my mother had no money to pay our school fees. So we studied at home without going to school. It was not simple for us.

In January 1999 the rebels attacked the city all over. I was four years old. The next day they came to our street shouting "Mr. and Mrs. K!" My father and mother went outside and my father said, "Don't go outside—stay here." We hid under the bed. The rebels' leader asked my father for money. My father said, "There is no money here." The rebels' leader said, "If there is no money we are going to shoot you and your wife." He pointed the gun at my father and shot him. Then they shot my mother. When they went to the next street my mother's sister came and took us away. We were crying because we had lost both of our parents.

My mother's sister took us to the Red Cross and they helped us to travel to another country by boat. We took two days in the sea without food or water. My Aunty looked after us and her daughter helped us come to Australia. I was so happy, but sad because we had lost our parents during the war. I always think about the past and the way we suffered. I say "Thank you" to my Aunty and her daughter for what they have done for me and my sister. I want to do the best that I can to repay them and to make them proud of us.[2]

The story of "Sia," one of the young refugees who are the focus of this chapter, exemplifies the traumatic events that may result in the forced migration of children, young people, and their residual families, and some of the attendant difficulties relating to their lives pre-migration, en route, and following resettlement in a host country. Sia's story is a testament to young refugees' resilience and determination to succeed.

This chapter investigates this resilience and determination and the role of music in developing social inclusion, maintaining cultural traditions, and creating opportunities for participating in activities that connect refugee and newly arrived immigrant young people with others in Australian society. These issues, including the difficulties and rewards of implementing socially just and inclusionary music programs, are explored through the stories of Sia and others so that we may have a better understanding of how participation in musical activity has the potential to develop ongoing forms of social inclusion for marginalized participants.

The Sociopolitical Context of Refugees and Newly Arrived Immigrants in Australia

A refugee is defined as any person who is "unable or unwilling to return to their country of origin owing to a well founded fear of being persecuted for reasons of race, religion, nationality, membership of a particular social group, or political opinion" (United Nations High Commissioner for Refugees, UNHCR, 2010, p. 3). In the years 2009–2010, Australia granted 13,077 visas under the Humanitarian (refugee intake) program (Department of Immigration & Citizenship, 2011b). At the end of 2012, UNHCR data documented a population of 30,083 refugees and asylum seekers residing in Australia, although this constitutes a very small proportion of the total international refugee population of 35,844,480 (UNHCR, 2013). Australia has a history of extensive immigration, and has provided permanent settlement for a large number of refugees relative to its population (Bhabha & Crock, 2007; Castles & Miller, 2009). For example, in the 1970s and 1980s, during the post–Vietnam War flight of refugees, Australia resettled more refugees per capita than any other nation (McMaster, 2001).

As a result of general immigration and humanitarian programs, the population of Australia is drawn from more than one hundred birthplace groups, with Australian people identifying with more than 270 ancestral groups and speaking over 260 languages (Department of Immigration and Citizenship, 2011a). Notwithstanding the cultural and linguistic diversity of Australia, and the principle of multiculturalism being enshrined in Australian law and institutions since the 1970s, xenophobia is also evident in political debate and is reported and promulgated, sometimes vehemently, by the Australian media. Since the beginning of the twenty-first century, this has been manifested by concerted campaigns to reject asylum seekers and refugees arriving visibly and literally on Australian shores in the form of "boat people," despite the success of the previous Indo-Chinese "boat people" resettlement program during the 1970s and 1980s (Castles & Miller, 2009; Vasta & Castles, 1996). Issues of "illegal" access to asylum, "queue jumping," and mandatory detention of asylum seekers arriving by boat have divided social and political opinion among the Australian population. Most recently, "offshore processing," the removal of such asylum seekers from the Australian mainland to Papua New Guinea and Nauru to have their claims processed, thereby rendering them relatively invisible, and with scant hope of resettlement in Australia, has further polarized opinion. Such draconian political provisions coexist with strong social justice movements and represent the uneasy sociopolitical background to current refugee and immigrant settlement in Australia.

For refugees and asylum seekers in particular, the need for procedural justice "that extends to everyone an unrestricted right to speak, to be heard, to be taken seriously and to withhold assent" (Bowman, 2007, p. 8) is of immediate concern. The most recent Australian Government Multicultural Policy (Department of Immigration and Citizenship, 2011a) states that "[t]he Australian Government is committed to a just, inclusive and socially cohesive society where everyone can participate in the opportunities that Australia offers" (p. 5). The policy endorses multiculturalism, as it "speaks to fairness and inclusion," "embraces our shared values and cultural traditions," and "allows those who call Australia home the right to practise and share in their cultural traditions and languages" (p. 2). It states that an "enduring theme of Australia's multicultural policy is that everyone belongs" and that "Australians of all backgrounds can participate in our society" (p. 5). In contrast to the xenophobic rhetoric surrounding the arrival of asylum seekers, the Australian multicultural policy thus articulates an ethos of "participatory parity," a socially just view requiring "social arrangements that permit all to participate as peers in social life" (Fraser, 2007, cited in Keddie, 2012, p. 13). It also promotes ideals of "cultural justice," where "minority culture is recognised and valued" (Keddie, p. 16). In the following sections I address the trauma of relocation and resettlement and the ways in which differing musical engagements and activities can provide participatory parity and can assist with fulfilling the varied needs of refugee and immigrant children.

MUSIC AND SOCIAL PARTICIPATION OF REFUGEES AND NEWLY ARRIVED IMMIGRANTS

Refugees face a range of social, emotional, and cultural challenges related to geographical and cultural displacement and trauma, experienced in the country of origin, en route, and during relocation and resettlement (Aroche & Coello, 2002; Berry, 1997, 2001;

Fazel & Stein, 2002; Hamilton & Moore, 2004; Jones, Baker, & Day, 2004). Although the level of trauma may not be as marked, many similar issues of social integration, identity construction, cultural maintenance, change, and associated stresses are also experienced by newly arrived immigrants (Howell, 2009). In their final place of settlement, both refugee and newly arrived immigrant children must adapt to a new country and culture, despite possible language problems, culture shock, racism, changes in family structure and roles, and social isolation (Fazel & Stein, 2002; Frater-Matheison, 2004; Hodes, 2000).

Music participation may be seen to facilitate "the management of social relationships within situations of social uncertainty" (Cross & Woodruff, 2009, p. 113), including major life transitions, circumstances requiring the reaffirmation of the integrity or stability of a community, "the management of inter-group relationships, and conditions relating to the formation of within-group identity (pp. 113–114). Such "situations of social uncertainty" are well represented in the lives of refugees and newly arrived immigrants.

A number of studies have investigated the role of music activity among refugee populations to assist in developing varying forms of communication where verbal communication is limited, a sense of belonging and empowerment, and as a contribution to cultural maintenance, identity construction, stress relief, and integration within the host country (Diehl, 2002; Heidenrich, 2005; Jones, Baker & Day, 2004; Ladkani, 2001; Marsh, 2012, 2013; Osborne, 2009; Pesek, 2009; Reyes, 1999; Sebastian, 2008; Socolov & Hamilton, 2006; Sutton, 2002; Turpin, 2004). Additional studies have explored children's intercultural transmission of music within a social framework and the role of music in the creation of transitional identities for immigrant and bicultural children (Campbell & Wiggins, 2013; Karlsen, 2013; Lum, 2008; Marsh, 2001, 2008, 2011, 2012, 2013; Saether, 2008). This chapter discusses selected findings of an ethnographic research study investigating the role of music in the lives of refugee and newly arrived immigrant children aged 0–18 in a number of communities in Sydney, Australia.

THE STUDY

Several community- and school-based programs formed the basis of case studies for this project, but this chapter centers on the case of a Sierra Leone Youth Group, which also had links with music, drumming, and hip-hop activities in an Intensive English Centre (a specialist secondary school in which newly arrived children with minimal English begin their education, at the same time developing communicative ability in English). The research team, consisting of the author and two research assistants, Laura Corney and Samantha Dieckmann, observed and video recorded young people and facilitating adults when engaged in musical activities in community or formal educational settings and conducted both formal and informal interviews in the context of the activities. As the project developed, what had originally been envisaged as non-participant observation by the research team within the different contexts rapidly evolved into a reciprocal partnership between the researchers and the other participants, so that all became participants in a joint venture. This was most evident in the involvement of multiple actors in the overlapping activities of the Intensive English Centre (henceforth designated IEC) and the Sierra Leone Youth Group. This set of activities and relationships forms the focus of the following discussion.

SIERRA LEONE YOUTH GROUP

Sierra Leone is located on the west coast of Africa and has a population of approximately six million people, consisting of more than 15 ethnic groups. Following independence from Britain in 1961, and a brief period of stable government, Sierra Leone has experienced a high level of political instability since 1964, and 10 years of civil war from 1991 to 2002 (Bingley, 2011; Olonisakin, 2008). As a result of this and the primarily agrarian economy, Sierra Leone is currently ranked 177 of 186 countries in the world Human Development Index (United Nations Development Program, 2013), with continuing poverty and poor levels of health and education. The large numbers of refugees who fled the country during the civil war have sometimes spent many years in transit in refugee camps or living with relatives in neighboring countries (Cassity & Gow, 2006), so the process of resettlement has continued until the present. Other family members have subsequently migrated to Australia under the family reunion program. At the time of my involvement with the Sierra Leone Youth Group, many of the children and young people in the group had arrived relatively recently, some within the period of the study.

The youth group had been initiated by two Sierra Leonean refugees in collaboration with a Salvation Army church in order to provide a safe and social space for Sierra Leonean young people, aged from approximately 5 to 18 years, though a number of younger children occasionally attended. Although some young children had been born in Australia, many of these children and young people were refugees and immigrants, having experienced varying degrees of trauma in their past and present resettlement, as exemplified by Sia's description of her past life at the beginning of this chapter. The purpose of the group, then, included the provision of social benefits, including "deeper" forms of "social goods" that afforded varying forms of extrinsic and intrinsic satisfaction to its members (Elliott, 2007, p. 5). The group met weekly on Saturdays in a Salvation Army hall to engage in drumming, dancing, and drama activities that provided avenues for emotional release for the children. Max, the dynamic instigator and coordinator of the group, was employed as a school learning support officer (SLSO), a bilingual and bicultural staff member who assisted students and teachers within the IEC. In this capacity, Max was generally responsible for students from Sub-Saharan Africa. Sierra Leonean students from the IEC, ex-students who had graduated to other high schools, and some younger children from the Sierra Leonean community were invited to attend. Participation of younger children tended to occur sporadically, and the discussion in this chapter centers on the adolescent members of the youth group.

Musical Activities in the Youth Group

When I was initially invited to visit the youth group, the principal activities were drama-based, with a focus on improvisatory dramatic activity designed to address issues of social difficulty and belonging in a school situation. The adolescents participated in play-building with the assistance of a drama teacher from the IEC, who volunteered her time for this purpose. In addition, the activities included some West African drumming (mostly for boys) and dance, mostly enacted by girls. When I asked about this choice of activities, Max discussed their inception in the drumming activities that were taught at the IEC by Soemadi, an Indonesian SLSO who was an accomplished professional jazz drummer and who acted as a music teacher at the school.

> M: Probably you know that I wasn't a drummer.... So I actually started not playing drum but used to go sit watching the drumming with the kids. And... whilst he's [Soemadi's] doing the drumming, he get to bring in song that sort of take memories back to Africa. When I get to sit there and listen 'cause my mum was more into cultural aspect which is the drumming and dancing.... I started getting involved in the dancing aspect. That's where I actually started, the dancing. Showing the kids steps and all the movement we used to have in African kids. So I would show them some of the African moves and all that. Then from African moves, for me to be able to match the African moves to the beat, that's when I start coming in to drumming. (interview, Max, September 23, 2011)

For Max, a Mende[3] man, there was a clear impetus to connect with homeland culture, although his own knowledge of traditional drumming and dance in this area was not highly developed, despite lengthy exposure in his childhood. To meet this purpose within the Sierra Leonean group, Max utilized the expertise of a group of Sierra Leonean girls called the "Sensational Sisters," who had formed a dance troupe specializing in Sierra Leonean dance, but who also drew on multiple African and other dance traditions. The core of the group comprised several Temne sisters and others, linked by friendship and kinship affiliations, who demonstrated considerable dancing skill and enjoyment. The Sensational Sisters, supported by their Sierra Leonean mothers, performed mostly what they termed "culture dances," but also hip-hop styles, at weddings and church. In the Saturday youth group sessions, Aminata, the oldest of the sisters, took on a leadership role, and the Sensational Sisters formed the nucleus of a larger group of dancers as other members of the youth group joined in. In utilizing the combined dancing skills of the Sisters, Max was recognizing and valuing the "funds of knowledge" of what might be conceived of as a marginalized group (Keddie, 2012, p. 17), thereby instituting "cultural recognition" (p. 24), a tenet of cultural justice.

Particular drumming patterns were required for the dances to proceed appropriately, but early in the group's development there were no drummers proficient in the traditional drumming patterns and only a limited number of drums provided by the

Salvation Army. At this point, our transition into acknowledged participants in the field began. Laura, one of the project's research assistants, had studied West African drumming both in Sydney and in Ghana, and willingly brought her drum to assist with the appropriate techniques and rhythms. Each week I brought a set of djembes that had been purchased for student use by the Music Education Unit at the university, so that there were sufficient drums for the boys in the youth group to participate. Abdullah, the co-initiator of the group, mentioned the importance of this support and that of the IEC teachers and the Salvation Army to the success of the venture, noting that they had tried to start the group several years earlier but it had failed because of lack of external backing (conversation, October 17, 2009).

However, cultural recognition did not ensure social cohesion or social inclusion within the group. Recently arrived Sia, who had been discovered at the IEC to be an accomplished dancer, was invited to join the youth group, along with her sister, Elissa, and newly arrived Suzan and her younger brother David, both from Freetown, the capital city of Sierra Leone. David was initially very withdrawn, and neither he nor his sister was used to dancing, so their initial involvement was quite inhibited. David tended to observe from the sidelines, though his sister joined in with the culture dances. Although Sia was an exceptionally good dancer, she was initially shunned by the members of the Sensational Sisters. The dances consisted of a number of choreographed steps that were modeled by the experienced dancers, with a segment where individual dancers in turn improvised a movement sequence to demonstrate their prowess. Sia's improvised solo, though extremely virtuosic, was quite different stylistically from that of the others and produced laughter from many of the other dancers.[4] Although she emulated the other dance movements well, she was clearly not accepted socially into the group and was often isolated. Suzan's non-idiomatic movements as a neophyte dancer were also greeted with laughter.

When I asked Max about this initial lack of acceptance, which I thought might be attributable to ethnic difference and resultant differences in cultural practice, he indicated that it was because Sierra Leoneans "sort of integrate based on sometimes how we arrived in the country."

> M: Sensational Sisters and their family if you notice, they have been in Australia for quite a long time.
> K: Right.
> M: David, Suzan, Sia and . . . Elissa, they *just* got into the country then. So they weren't friends. Through the program, this program, the Conservatorium thing we did, because of we meeting at . . . the Salvation Army, then they clicked. Then they knew that I was into the tradition. "Oh we from Sierra Leone, this, that, blah blah blah." So through the dancing there was a connection. (interview, Max, September 23, 2011)

The establishment of this "connection" and development of social inclusion for Sia and other participants is discussed in the following section.

Musical Collaborations

The process by which this connection developed occurred as a result of a joint initiative of the IEC, the Sierra Leonean Youth Group, and the Sydney Conservatorium of Music research team. The IEC principal, Martin, music teacher Soemadi, Max, and the counselor at the IEC who had particular responsibility for the psychological well-being of students asked if the research team could assist the school and the youth group in mounting a joint performance in a large venue at the Conservatorium to celebrate Harmony Day.[5] Soemadi and the counselor had earlier talked about the benefits of musical involvement they saw for these young people. These included a sense of belonging and also looking forward, planning positively for musical performances in the future, instead of looking back to their sometimes traumatic past. Other perceived benefits included the development of young people's courage to do things on their own, in interpolated musical solos, and the confidence to do this. Counterbalancing this was collaboration and the feeling of being a necessary part of a musical whole, which required interdependence of individual parts and individual responsibilities (fieldnotes, August 6, 2009). For Martin, the goals of such activities were closely linked to social and cultural inclusion:

> Group practice and performance brings confidence, acknowledgment, friendship and enjoyment. . . . [Performances] help to build bridges with the broader community. . . . Benefits to all students include team building, confidence, joy, relaxation, affirmation of cultural identity, communication. (email interview, December 18, 2011)

Over the months from September to the following March, various forces were mobilized to assist in the transformation of what were initially conceived as predominantly social activities into musical activities with an additional performance-based outcome. Students from the IEC (who came from a variety of ethnic and cultural backgrounds) joined the Sierra Leone Youth Group sessions on Saturdays to rehearse these performances. Some of the performances, including hip-hop routines with accompanying drumming, had been developed at the school as stand-alone activities. Others, including the Sierra Leone culture dances with drumming accompaniment, involved only the Sierra Leonean Youth Group members. Still others combined both groups, in particular for a joint choral rendition of the Michael Jackson song "You Are Not Alone" (Kelly, 1995, Track 9), which was the planned culmination of the concert.

Soemadi came every week to assist with drumming, and two other teachers from the school joined in to work with the dancers. The university research team was involved in rehearsing the choir and vocal soloists, both in the Sierra Leone Youth group sessions and at the IEC, participating in the drumming, and also giving practical support, helping to prepare lunch for the group and providing transport for some of the young people. The latter activities enabled me to have informal and relaxed conversations with the group participants and with other students from the IEC. As we made lunch together, Sia told me her story, talking about her separation from siblings who had been settled in other countries and how she missed them and her parents. Similarly, as I drove Sia, Elissa, Suzan, and David home from the group each week, they talked animatedly about the group activities and their relationships with the other group members.

Value Differences and Difficulties

Although the performances progressed, and had many positive aspects, there were tensions arising from the changing focus of the group from social to performative. These tensions can be encapsulated in Turino's (2008) definitions of participatory and presentational performance. Turino states:

> Participatory performance is a particular field of activity in which stylized sound and motion are conceptualized most importantly as heightened social interaction. In participatory music making one's primary attention is on the activity, on *the doing*, and on the other participants, rather than on an end product that results from the activity. (p. 28)
>
> Presentational performance, in contrast, refers to the situation where one group of people, the artists, prepare and provide music for another group, the audience, who do not participate in making the music or dancing. (p. 26)

While participatory performance can be seen to exhibit features of participatory parity, presentational performance is more hierarchical in nature. Turino notes that while musicians in a participatory performance will find a role that matches their level of capability and take part in ways in which they are most comfortable, presentational performance aspires to forms of perceived excellence, and therefore requires rehearsals that are "much more goal oriented and detail oriented" (p. 53).

The clearest example of this contrast was in the development of a sequenced dance performance from what was a spontaneous social activity. Early in the youth group's existence, there had been a dance rehearsal with both boys and girls dancing a routine to popular music, led by Aminata. During a break, one member of the group attached her mobile phone to a speaker, playing the music that was on her playlist. All members of the group immediately began dancing to the song, Awilo Longomba's "Karolina" (2004), an example of the popular *soukous* dance music genre that originally emanated from the Congo but which is now popular across Sub-Saharan Africa (Stewart, 2004). Each person danced entirely idiosyncratically with very different dance steps performed at their own pace, reflecting myriad stylistic influences, gained in home and transit cultures, and mediated sources in the final place of settlement. Max cited dance steps learned from their parents, dance in Guinea (a transit country), and the influence of Beyonce, JayZ, Lady GaGa, and the Nigerian movies popular with the Sierra Leonean diaspora (interview, September 23, 2011). In this spontaneous dance, all of the group members were performing individually and in ways that were self-determined, but also as part of a joyous whole.

In contrast, when this song was adopted for use in a choreographed dance sequence, the dance steps, incorporating those idiomatic to *soukous*, were determined by Aminata and imitated by the whole group in synchrony. The group members still enjoyed mastering the dance steps, and Suzan and David joined in and began to develop more kinesthetic freedom and prowess as the rehearsals continued. Aminata was empowered by the opportunity to demonstrate her considerable dance skills and to lead the performance. Nevertheless, the freedom of the spontaneous dance response to the music was lost. There was further movement away from spontaneity when the schoolteachers began to give instruction in the dance rehearsals to tighten up the dance routine for public performance. This was done with both the *soukous* contemporary dance and the culture dance, and caused some resentment among the performers, particularly of the culture dance, as the Sierra Leonean young people no longer had complete ownership of the dance and their "funds of knowledge" were temporarily subsumed within the values of presentational performance.

What was important to the dancers was also not always understood by those who were endeavoring to assist. Thus, there was heated discussion of the rhythms needed for the culture dance to proceed effectively, as Soemadi (who began to lead the drummers when Laura moved away to study) did not have this knowledge. This problem was later explained by Max, who frequently took on the role of intermediary between the members of the youth group and adults who were assisting the enterprise:

> M: OK Soemadi, if you want the kids to dance—'cause you say "I want the kids to dance African dance," fine. But if you want the kids to dance like this, this is how we have to beat because this is the beat they're used to. (interview, Max, 23 September, 2011)

The values of the adults, who were concerned with producing a successful performance in Western presentational terms, did not coincide with the values of the dancers, whose understanding of dance, and its meaning and importance, was derived from participatory values that were culturally contextualized.

Also, although I was unaware of this during the period of rehearsals, there was some dissension with some of the parents regarding the value of the activities.

> M: It was not easy. But I guess, if you have passion for something, if you believe in something, sometimes they do work. . . . . Getting the parents to accept their kids to come to Salvos on every Saturday 10am. It wasn't an easy task. . . .
> K: Yeah. Why were they hard to convince?
> M: Because one, for us they say, in our culture, very few people are more into that. You have to be culturally inclined for you, for your parents to really accept you to do things like that. Back home, from the little knowledge I have, if you're more into something like that you are classified differently. Probably as a low class or something like that. So very few people like really embrace the cultural aspects.
> K: So is that because it's more important to be seen to be doing you know, modern . . .

M: Schooling, yes.

K: Modern things, or education?

M: It's more education. . . . Sierra Leone parents that I know hear you say, "I want to dance," to them you're a foolish person. Dancing, it doesn't matter what kind of dancing. You're a foolish person. They, all they think is school. And even, let's say dancing it's part of that school activity, to them no. They believe it's the writing, the reading and stuff like that. (interview, Max, September 23, 2011)

There were also conflicting priorities of parents of a number of the dancers from the core group of Sensational Sisters, although they supported this maintenance and dissemination of dance traditions and provided costumes imported from Sierra Leone. Because these dancers were often given money for their performances, the parents were reluctant for the performance to proceed without financial benefit.

M: 'Cause I try to tell them that, "Hey look, this is not about money this is about harmony. It's not just about harmony it's about giving your kids the opportunity to express themselves in like music, dancing and stuff like that. So this is what this is about. And we never know what the future holds. Some of them might end up becoming dancers, singers or something. So it's just an opportunity." . . . 'Cause to me these kids, it's not about money. From what I know about them. They not dancing for money. They dance because they enjoy. I wish I can describe what world they in when they dance. (interview, Max, September 23, 2011)

One of the members of the group, 14-year-old Selina, alluding to the transformative power of dance, told me, "Dance is my passion. . . . When I dance there is only me" (conversation, September 26, 2009). Sia also discussed the power of drumming and dance, stating that "African drums draw you to dance. Even if you don't want to dance they draw you to dance" (conversation, March 13, 2010). It was evident, then, that the cultural traditions were multifaceted and that they also vied with current intergenerational aspirations and personal proclivities.

Transformative Power of Music and Dance

Despite the difficulties created by conflicting values and priorities, it seemed that this power of music and dance to transport the performers into a state where disagreements and affronts did not matter, in combination with external adult support (even if sometimes unwelcome) and Max's considerable diplomatic and persuasive skills, resulted in developed performances with great verve and energy. Drawing on further "funds of knowledge" from the community, Max had secured the assistance of an experienced Sierra Leonean drummer, Gabriel, who focused and unified the drummers and dancers, as I witnessed in a rehearsal in the week preceding the performance:

As the girls waited behind the screen to start again, the drumming really started to get going and this seemed to have an immediate impact on the girls, who could be seen spontaneously dancing as they waited. When they came in a second time they were much more energetic and the energy seemed to build through this and subsequent performances. [Although Sia's improvised solo still drew comment] . . . even this dissension seemed to melt away as the drumming became more intense and the girls' dancing increasingly energised. By the end of the dance some of the boys who were drumming were also up and dancing with the drums. . . . The performance had become quite electrifying with Gabriel's leadership. (fieldnotes, March 13, 2010)

Although social unification was still not completely evident, there was ultimately acceptance of the individual contributions that each member of the group could make to the final performance. Within the performative space of the dance, Sia and Suzan became part of a coherent whole, within which they were able to contribute individually, Sia with ethnically different dance movements and Suzan with greatly improved kinesthetic skill. As Osborne (2009) states, "music may also entrain, coordinate and synchronize movement between individuals, offering the excitement, satisfaction, security, comradeship and cohesion of playing and moving rhythmically together" (p. 344).

By the time of the performance, the commitment of the performers to a joint endeavor was very evident. A dress rehearsal in the Salvation Army chapel, with the almost entirely white Anglo Australian church congregation as audience, had an enthusiastic reception, in some ways endorsed by the chapel banner under which they performed: "With God All Things Are Possible," though this performance was made possible by the combined efforts of many people, most significantly the young people themselves.

The final performance at the Sydney Conservatorium of Music, traditionally a "high culture" venue, was polished and very exciting for both performers and audience. The joint enterprise that framed the performance was clearly evident in the lineup of items, which included several jazz and solo performances by current and past IEC students; a Javanese *anklung* group, connected to the school through the Indonesian Consulate; a performance of both the Sierra Leonean culture dance and contemporary *soukous* dance with drumming; and a Sierra Leonean hunting dance, involving the boys in the youth group and several adult male members of the Sierra Leonean community. The two items that opened and closed the performance symbolically combined IEC students and Sierra Leone Youth Group members. These items included the hip-hop dance developed by its Vietnamese, Chinese, Croatian, and Sierra Leonean performers (including Sia) and the culminating choral rendition of Michael Jackson's anthemic song "You Are Not Alone," which involved all the young people. Sia's confident vocal solo as part of this final rousing performance demonstrated her determination to "do the best that I can" to make her residual family proud of her, through multiple performance opportunities provided by the IEC and the Sierra Leone Youth Group. Her virtuosic involvement was finally accepted as a valuable contribution to the event by the members of the youth group, and the performers in turn were endorsed by the audience. Soemadi summarized the resultant feeling of social inclusion that such performance opportunities bring.

> If new arrivals coming to Australia . . . because everything new they feel like isolated. They feel shy, they feel don't have any confidence. And through all the performance thanks to the school we going like to the mainstream. And they see. They perform, the audience accept them. They applaud them. You know? They feel really good they said, "Wow! This is related [gestures between himself and outwards to others]. I feel now sort of like belonging to the wide . . . society." (interview, September 23, 2011)

CONCLUSION

In outlining the complexities of multiple forms of social justice, Elliott (2007) cites Alwin's (2000) definition of social justice as being "the realm of status, respect, and the sense of worth given and received in social interaction or in relation to society" (p. 61). In the case of the Sierra Leonean Youth Group and the Intensive English Centre, the process of developing a range of music and dance activities and performance opportunities in which young refugees and newly arrived immigrants could develop and demonstrate their capabilities in a joint venture led to acceptance of marginalized participants both within a performative group and by a mainstream audience in a venue with significant status in the host culture. As stated by Elliott (2007), this example of music education for social justice required "personal and political persistence over a long period, the skills of building musical community solidarity, specific social and musical-social aims" (p. 84) and the collaborative employment of the skills of a range of people. At the culmination of the final song, as the audience applauded enthusiastically, members of the group called out "Yes, we done it! Yes we done it," demonstrating the sense of achievement and extrinsic and intrinsic satisfaction emanating from the culmination of this lengthy process.

This performative and social outcome was made possible partly by the strong disposition of many of the key participants (both performers and facilitators) to incorporate culturally responsive forms of cultural recognition as central tenets of the endeavor. However, as previously discussed, enacting cultural justice in this way is not necessarily straightforward, because culture is multifaceted, situated, and individually differentiated. As Keddie (2012) states, cultural recognition in educational settings

> is about teaching and learning that is respectful of, and responsive to, the norms of the settings students represent. Culturally responsive teachers are able to use the cultural knowledge, prior experiences, frames of reference, and performance styles of students to make learning encounters more relevant to and effective for marginalized students. (p. 24)

In creating a successful presentational performance, with all of its attendant feelings of social inclusion, self-esteem, confidence and social acceptance, the democratic participatory values of participatory performance may sometimes be given lesser emphasis, particularly in the final stages of the process. Music educators therefore must walk a fine line in ensuring that both sets of values, approached from the viewpoints of all participants, can be accommodated.

Whether outcomes such as those described go on to engender further success will depend not only on individuals and their circumstances, but also on the continuation of support and opportunity. Although the Sierra Leone Youth Group did not continue for a lengthy period of time following this performance, the social and performative opportunities offered by the IEC to members of the group enrolled at the school did continue. Several months later, I witnessed dancing by Sia, Suzan, and several other members of the group, accompanied by drumming IEC students at a large public stage event in the Sydney CBD associated with the 2010 Football World Cup (FIFA Fanfest). Offstage, Sia and Suzan were chatting comfortably and amicably with groups of other performers, clearly socially accepted and included and with the confidence partly developed as a result of performative accomplishment. Suzan has made a positive transition to high school, while Sia has gone on to pursue nursing training, thereby fulfilling her own aspirations to succeed in order to reciprocate the support that she has received. The continued application of policies of cultural justice as an aspect of social justice within the context of participation in musical activity therefore has the potential to develop ongoing forms of social inclusion for marginalized participants.

Acknowledgments

I am deeply grateful to the members of the Sierra Leone Youth Group, the staff and students of the IEC, and to my research assistants, Samantha Dieckmann and Laura Corney. The project was supported by a research grant from the Sydney Conservatorium of Music, University of Sydney.

Notes

1. Names have been abbreviated or changed to preserve anonymity of participants within the reported activities.
2. Sia's story has been reproduced from a school website, with permission.
3. The Sierra Leonean ethnic groups represented in the youth group included Mende and Temne, the two dominant groups in Sierra Leonean society, in addition to Kono, Susu, and Limba.
4. I was unable to confirm the ethnic derivation of Sia's dance movements, though Max stated that Sia was Kono.

5. Harmony Day, held throughout Australia on March 21 each year, is a celebration of Australia's cultural diversity. The day is also the United Nation's International Day for the Elimination of Racial Discrimination. Harmony Day encourages community participation, inclusiveness, and respect (Department of Immigration and Citizenship, 2011b).

References

Alwin, D. (2000). Social justice. In E. Borgatta & R. Montgomery (Eds.), *Encyclopedia of sociology* (Vol. 4, pp. 2695–2711). New York: MacMillan.

Aroche, J., & Coello, M. (2002). *Towards a systematic approach for the treatment rehabilitation of torture and trauma survivors in exile.* Retrieved from http://www.startts.org.au/default. aspx?id=116.

Bhabha, J., & Crock, M. (2007). *Seeking asylum alone: Unaccompanied and separated children and refugee protection in Australia, the U.K. and the U.S.* Annandale, Australia: Themis Press.

Berry, J. W. (1997). Immigration, acculturation, and adaptation. *Applied Psychology: An International Review, 46*(1), 5–68.

Berry, J. W. (2001). A psychology of immigration. *Journal of Social Issues, 57*(3), 615–663.

Bingley, K. (2011). Bambeh's song: Music, women and health in a rural community in post-conflict Sierra Leone. *Music and Arts in Action, 3*(2), 59–78.

Bowman, W. (2007). "Who's asking? (Who's answering?): Theorizing social justice in music education. *Action, Criticism, and Theory for Music Education, 6*(4), 1–20.

Campbell, P. S., & Wiggins, T. (Eds.) (2013). *Oxford handbook of children's musical cultures.* New York: Oxford University Press.

Cassity, E., & Gow, G. (2006). *Making up for lost time: Young African refugees in western Sydney high schools.* Sydney: Centre for Cultural Research, University of Western Sydney.

Castles, S., & Miller, M. J. (2009). *The age of migration: International population movements in the modern world* (4th ed.). Basingstoke, UK: Palgrave Macmillan.

Cross, I., & Woodruff, G. E. (2009). Music as a communicative medium. In R. Botha & C. Knight (Eds.), *The prehistory of language* (Vol. 1, pp. 113–144). Oxford, UK: Oxford University Press.

Department of Immigration and Citizenship. (2011a). *The people of Australia: Australia's multicultural policy.* Canberra: DIAC, Australian Government. Retrieved from https://www.dss.gov.au/sites/default/files/documents/12_2013/people-of-australi a-multicultural-policy-booklet_print.pdf.

Department of Immigration and Citizenship. (2011b). *About Harmony Day.* Retrieved from http://www.harmony.gov.au/harmony-day/about-harmony-day.htm.

Diehl, K. (2002). *Echoes from Dharamsala: Music in the lives of a Tibetan refugee community.* Berkeley & Los Angeles: University of California Press.

Elliott, D. (2007). "Socializing" music education. *Action, Criticism and Theory for Music Education, 6*(4), 60–95.

Fazel, M., & Stein, A. (2002). The mental health of refugee children. *Archives of Disease in Childhood, 87*(5), 366–370.

Fraser, N. (2007). Identity, exclusion and critique: A response to four critics. *European Journal of Political Theory, 6*(3), 305–338.

Frater-Matheison, K. (2004). Refugee trauma, loss and grief: implications for intervention. In R. Hamilton & D. Moore (Eds.), *Educational interventions for refugee children: Theoretical perspectives and best practice* (pp. 12–34). London: RoutledgeFalmer.

Hamilton, R., & Moore, D. (Eds.) 2004. *Educational interventions for refugee children: Theoretical perspectives and best practice.* London: RoutledgeFalmer.

Heidenrich, V. (2005). Music therapy in war-effected [*sic*] areas. *Intervention, 3*(2), 129–134.

Hodes, M. (2000). Psychologically distressed refugee children in the United Kingdom. *Child Psychology and Psychiatry Review, 5*(2), 57–68.

Howell, G. (2009). *Beyond words: Newly-arrived children's perceptions of music learning and music making* (Unpublished Master's thesis, University of Melbourne).

Jones, C., Baker, F., & Day, T. (2004). From healing rituals to music therapy: Bridging the cultural divide between therapist and young Sudanese refugees. *The Arts in Psychotherapy, 31*(2), 89–100.

Karlsen, S. (2013). Immigrant students and the "homeland music": Meanings, negotiations and implications. *Research Studies in Music Education, 35*(2), 161–177.

Keddie, A. (2012). *Educating for diversity and social justice.* New York: Routledge.

Kelly, R. (1995). You are not alone [Recorded by Michael Jackson]. On *HIStory: Past, present and future, Book 1* [CD]. New York: Sony, Epic Records.

Ladkani, J. L. (2001). *Dabke music and dance and the Palestinian refugee experience: On the outside looking in* (Unpublished doctoral dissertation, Florida State University, Tallahassee).

Longomba, A. (2004). Karolina. *Mondongo.* Retrieved from http://www.allmusic.com/artist/awilo-longomba-mn0001216061/discography.

Lum, C. H. (2008). Home musical environment of children in Singapore: On globalization, technology, and media. *Journal of Research in Music Education, 56*(2), 101–117.

Marsh, K. (2001). It's not all black or white: The influence of the media, the classroom and immigrant groups on children's playground singing games. In J. C. Bishop & M. Curtis (Eds.), *Play today in the primary school playground* (pp. 80–97). Ballmoor, Buckingham, UK: Open University Press.

Marsh, K. (2008). *The musical playground: Global tradition and change in children's songs and games.* New York: Oxford University Press.

Marsh, K. (2011). Meaning making through musical play: Cultural psychology of the playground. In M. Barrett (Ed.), *A cultural psychology of music education* (pp. 41–60). Oxford: Oxford University Press.

Marsh, K. (2012). "The beat will make you be courage": The role of a secondary school music program in supporting young refugees and newly arrived immigrants in Australia. *Research Studies in Music Education, 34*(2), 93–111.

Marsh, K. (2013). Music in the lives of refugee and newly arrived immigrant children in Sydney, Australia. In P. Campbell & T. Wiggins (Eds.), *Oxford handbook of children's musical cultures* (pp. 491–509). New York: Oxford University Press.

McMaster, D. (2001). *Asylum seekers: Australia's response to refugees.* Melbourne: Melbourne University Press.

Olonisakin, F. (2008). *Peacekeeping in Sierra Leone: The story of UNAMSIL.* London: Lynne Rienner Publishers.

Osborne, N. (2009). Music for children in zones of conflict and post-conflict: A psychobiological approach. In S. Malloch & C. Trevarthen (Eds.), *Communicative musicality: Exploring the basis of human companionship* (pp. 331–356). Oxford: Oxford University Press.

Pesek, A. (2009). War on the former Yugoslavian territory. Integration of refugee children into the school system and musical activities as an important factor for overcoming war trauma. In B. Clausen, U. Hemetek, & E. Saether (Eds.), *Music in motion: Diversity and dialogue in Europe* (pp. 359–370). Bielefeld, Germany: Transcript Verlag.

Reyes, A. (1999). *Songs of the caged, songs of the free: Music and the Vietnamese.* Philadelphia: Temple University Press.

Saether, E. (2008). When minorities are the majority: Voices from a teacher/researcher project in a multicultural school in Sweden. *Research Studies in Music Education, 30*(1), 25–42.

Sebastian, S. (2008). *A multicase study of the ways music learning is used to meet the social, emotional and cultural challenges experienced by refugees and asylum seekers in Sydney* (Unpublished Honours thesis, Sydney Conservatorium of Music).

Socolov, E., & Hamilton, G. M. (2006). Immigrant arts in collaboration: Current community cultural initiatives. *Voices, 32*(1), 28–32.

Stewart, G. (2004). *Rumba on the River: A history of the popular music of the Two Congos.* London: Verso Books.

Sutton, J. P. (Ed.). (2002). *Music, music therapy and trauma.* London: Jessica Kingsley Publishers.

Turino, T. (2008). *Music as social life: The politics of participation.* Chicago: University of Chicago Press.

Turpin, L. (2004). *Traces of places: A vicarious journey into memories of the homeland in a Lao-American community* (Unpublished doctoral dissertation, California Institute of Integral Studies, San Francisco).

United Nations Development Program (2013). *Summary Human Development Report 2013. The rise of the south: Human progress in a diverse world.* Retrieved from http://hdr.undp.org/en/media/HDR2013_EN_Summary.pdf.

United Nations High Commissioner for Refugees. (2010). Convention and protocol relating to the status of refugees. Retrieved from http://www.unhcr.org/3b66c2aa10.html.

United Nations High Commissioner for Refugees. (2013). UNHCR global trends 2012. Retrieved from http://www.unhcr.org/pages/49c3646c4d6.html.

Vasta, E., & Castles, S. (1996). *The teeth are smiling: The persistence of racism in multicultural Australia.* St Leonards, Australia: Allen & Unwin.

CHAPTER 12

....

HIDDEN IN PLAIN SIGHT

Race and Racism in Music Education

....

DEBORAH BRADLEY

WITHIN any discursive terrain, the concepts of *race* and *racism* provide challenges for those willing to engage in such discussion. This is as true in music education as in any other discourse, perhaps even more so due to the nature of music and commonplace statements about its universality. Yet the twin concepts of race and racism are important pieces of the puzzle for music education in the twenty-first century.

In a desire to correct the under-representation of peoples of color and their musics within traditional music education curricula, an interest in multiculturalism began to take root in North America, and elsewhere, in the 1960s. Multiculturalism promised to help develop understandings across cultures that could alleviate racial prejudices. Yet even as many music educators took up the mantle for multicultural music education, more than 50 years later, inequities persist along color lines. Within traditional paradigms of band, choir, and orchestra, participating students continue to be predominantly White,[1] even in multi-ethnic, multi-racial schools and communities (Bradley, 2007; Koza, 2008). Curriculum continues to focus predominantly on Western classical and art musics; other forms of music making, even when included in the curriculum, are sometimes denigrated through language suggesting that they are "primitive" or "simple." Compounding this problem is the fact that teachers often enter the profession with misguided notions of "saving the unfortunate," an unacknowledged bias that may lead to friction in the classroom (Dei, James, James-Wilson, Karumanchery, & Zine, 2000; Ladson-Billings, 1996, 2009; Marx, 2006).

This chapter seeks to tease out some of the challenges related to issues of race and racism that lurk below the surface within music education. I will discuss the slippery nature of the concept of race, the complex nature of racism, and the ideology of Whiteness that informs much current music education practice, including those practices considered to be "multicultural." The chapter proposes that issues of race and racism remain hidden under such common-sense narratives as "music is a universal language," which operate in tandem with "color-blind" racism. Racism also hides within the myth of "authenticity" in music education practices, which too often serves as a barrier that prevents the inclusion of musics other than Western art musics in the curriculum. By interrogating some of the ways in which cultural Whiteness operates as racism within music education, I hope to shed light on ways of thinking that enable racism to be hidden in plain sight. Once these hiding places are recognized, we may begin to engage in a music education that values all students and all musics.

The Slippery Notion Called Race

The term *race* is one that at first seems to signify something of distinction—a system to help humankind determine its similarities and differences. Humans have a predisposition for categorizing, for labeling, and have done so since the beginning of time. There is an advantage in labeling, in that it provides humans with a general sense of what is what (for example, edible foods versus those that are poisonous), yet when applied to notions of *who is who*, the practice of labeling becomes fraught with malevolent potential. Labeling human beings according to an ever-changing set of general characteristics has brought into existence an apparatus for humans to behave at their worst: to enslave, to sell as chattel, to abuse, or to murder en masse their fellow human beings. Whoever has the power to create and enforce the labels categorizing *who is who* indeed holds a frightening advantage over those without such power.

In this chapter, I use the term *race* as a word that has no fixed meaning. As a term, it has often been used to designate people of similar skin color, but it may also group people together for reasons not necessarily related to skin color (for example, the category *Hispanic* refers to a linguistic heritage applied as racial category). By employing the social construct of race, humans designate *Otherness* through the labels they attach. The concept of race may categorize people according to physical characteristics (including skin color), by ethnic heritage, by shared language, by religion, by geographic location—it is a long and fluid list of factors determining who currently makes up any society's Others. Yet these categories are not rigid, and the meaning of the term *race* is not constant; groups designated as Other may eventually move out of that category, but to do so sometimes takes years of political and economic maneuvering, as Roediger (2007, p. 16) chronicles in *The Wages of Whiteness*. The social construct that labels any particular group of people as a race is subject to change based on political or economic agendas, or on changes to societal attitudes that occur over time.

The difficulties related to defining race also extend to academic engagements. The observation that race is a theoretically and empirically meaningless term has given rise to the practice of discarding it as a concept in academic studies. The argument suggests that if we stop acknowledging race, racism will cease to exist. Yet in such an argument, the tyranny of theory asserts its own unacknowledged, insidious racism. Racism is a systemic issue that goes far beyond individual expressions of prejudice toward others. "The fight against racial inequality cannot be predicated on the abolition or minimization of race. Race has profound social, material, and political consequences" (Dei, 2000, p. 14). As Dei argues, race is not usually itself the source of conflict; rather, conflict stems from the institutional and social practices that create and sustain injustice and inequality among groups.

Another difficulty related to academic engagements with ideas of race results from a common slippage—the ease with which discussions of race turn to issues of gender and class—both of which may be part of an issue better identified as racism (depending on the context), but for a variety of reasons subsume race discursively. As Dei (2000) writes, "In conventional discourses articulating a multiplex of oppressions, race is the category that often gets lost" (p. 16). This may in part be the result of what Morrison (1992) has termed the "graceful, liberal gesture" of avoiding topics related to race, since "to notice is to recognize an already discredited difference" (p. 10). Our aversion to the topic of race has led to a situation of near incoherence among Whites attempting to talk about racially sensitive matters "in a period in which certain things cannot be uttered in public" (Bonilla-Silva, 2003, p. 54), rendering us "colormute" (Pollock, 2004). Nor is this silence on matters of race all that recent; it has become an ingrained social convention. Over one hundred years ago, in 1903, W. E. B. DuBois made note of the awkwardness created by the rhetorical aversion to naming race: "Between me and the other world there is ever an unasked question: unasked by some through feelings of delicacy; by others through the difficulty of rightly framing it. All, nevertheless, fluttering round it" (Du Bois, 2005, p. 7). This chapter seeks to draw from the work of those who have bravely ruptured the silence on race and racism, in order to further our understanding of racism within the discipline of music education. My project is to expose how racism frequently hides within, and thus thwarts, our efforts toward accomplishing those original, crucial goals of multicultural education—the reduction of prejudice through cross-cultural understanding.

THE COMPLEX NATURE OF RACISM

Racism has been defined as "a system of advantage based on race" that "clearly operates to the advantage of Whites and to the disadvantage of people of color" (Tatum, 1997, p. 7). In this definition, skin color holds prominence, yet when one reviews recent events of racism in the world, skin color was not always the predominant factor at play. Definitions such as Tatum's that focus exclusively on skin color are helpful in calling attention to racism as a system, but simultaneously tend to overlook the many other ways in which racism may manifest in human behavior. Racism as a system may be based upon religion, language, ethnicity, even sexual orientation, and with this perspective, may be understood in a more encompassing way as a system that benefits some and disadvantages others (Marx, 2006, p. 5). For example, in Nazi Germany, religion served as the determining factor for state-sanctioned racism against the Jews, supported by descriptions of contrived common physical characteristics. Color and religion combined to designate the Jews as Others to be hated. Yet the Third Reich also levied its racist venom against homosexuals[2] and the Romani, who, like the Jews, were forced into concentration camps and exterminated en masse.

In the former Yugoslavia, differences in ethnicity, made complex by religious intolerance, gave rise to a horrific genocide against people who looked more or less the same as the perpetrators (Longinovic, 2000). The term employed in that conflict, "ethnic cleansing," masked racism as the motivation behind the killings. In Rwanda, tribal affiliation provided the excuse for mass exterminations that took place as the rest of the world watched in near silence—a shameful display of passive racism. During the fall of colonialism, as Africa's former colonies sought to establish independence, language often provided the terrain on which racism marched (Blommaert, 1999).

The examples above share a common response: the major political powers of the world watched, at least for a significant period of time, without taking action. Some have claimed that the lack of response from Europe, the United States, and Canada is an indication of color-blind racism (Bonilla-Silva, 2003). Considering that the populations of these world powers are predominantly White, the hands-off response may have subtly indicated that people in the conflict areas were not considered human enough to risk intervention. While the Yugoslavian and African conflicts did not provide any obvious advantage to White people, Whites enjoyed the privilege of observing the horrors from afar, while simultaneously being able to talk about "those people" as barbaric, cruel, and uncivilized.

We somehow take comfort in naming acts of racism associated with war or civil unrest as aberrant human behavior. Think of the Holocaust, which now stands in most curricula as history's "worst example" of violence against fellow humans. Yet within a few short years of that trauma, the world witnessed both Yugoslavia's devolution into ethnic cleansing and the Rwandan genocide. People of First Nations heritage are usually quick to point out that genocides against them began shortly after European contact in the fifteenth century. In Canada, cultural genocide continued until 1996, when the last residential school for indigenous children closed. The United States has a similar history of physical and cultural genocide. The lynching of Blacks in the United States in the early twentieth century goes practically unmentioned in history texts, yet caused the deaths of over 4,700 people between 1880 and 1951. In Canada, the razing of Africville[3] similarly goes unmentioned, and remains a little known fact for most White Canadians. Horrific, yes; anomalous, sadly not.

These examples from history deceive us, however, when we assume them to be exceptional. The fuses leading to such explosions of active racism were lit long before we heard the first rumble. While such events are without question like the eruption of a volcano, what bubbles under the mountain is a normalized, institutional, passive, color-blind racism (Bonilla-Silva, 2003) that affects everyone in society (including global society). No matter whether predicated on skin color, religion, language, or other factors, racism is a systemic issue benefiting some and victimizing others (Marx, 2006, p. 5). Racism is so normal that it is typically invisible to those who benefit daily from it (McIntosh, 1990). Institutionalized in the way society functions (education and hiring practices, to name just two), it becomes increasingly difficult for those who benefit from White privilege, which I will discuss in the next section of this chapter, to see how racism operates to disadvantage those on the other side of the "color line" (Du Bois, 2005). Myths of meritocracy blind us to the fact that the playing field has never been level for some people, or to the realization that success results from hard work most often for those who have the advantage of Whiteness. As race scholar Derrick Bell has written, racism is likely a permanent element of society (Leonardo & Harris, 2013); our goal as educators is to do whatever we can to make its existence visible, to ameliorate its devastating impact on lives. When we can see it, it becomes more difficult to ignore.

The point I wish to make clear here is that when we confine our concept of racism solely to issues of skin color, we allow ourselves to remain blind to its many subtle machinations and manipulations, a point that hopefully will become clear as the chapter progresses. And yet, those who benefit most often from systemic racism tend to share what is perceived as a common "White" skin color, or more accurately, share cultural Whiteness. Music education in North America has a history of promoting Western art music, part of an obvious agenda of cultural Whiteness. What is less obvious, however, is how our efforts at multicultural education may unintentionally support that same agenda.

WHITENESS AND IDEOLOGIES OF RACISM IN MUSIC EDUCATION

Defining Whiteness

Before looking at the ideologies common to Whiteness as a racial perspective within music education, it may be helpful to define the term. Like the slipperiness of race as a concept, the actions and beliefs that characterize Whiteness at any given time are subject to change. It is also necessary in this discussion to separate *Whiteness* from White people. Whiteness is a racial discourse; the category *White people* is a socially constructed identity usually premised on skin color (Leonardo, 2002, p. 31). Since Whiteness by its nature benefits White people, it is impossible for a White person to completely escape the influence of Whiteness, although White people can learn "to be critical of it and to work against the racism related to it" (Marx, 2006, p. 6). Leonardo describes Whiteness as a "racial perspective or world-view" that is supported by material practices and institutions. While many White people have disavowed Whiteness to fight for racial justice, Leonardo reminds us that historically, "the assertion of a White racial identity has had a violent career . . ., whenever Whiteness, as an imagined racial collective, inserts itself into history, material and discursive violence accompanies it" (Leonardo, 2002, p. 32). Whiteness as a racial category is connected to White culture through historical association. It is perhaps best thought of as a social concept rather than a singular culture. Marx (2006) posits Whiteness as "an amalgamation of qualities including the cultures, histories, experiences, discourses, and privileges shared by Whites" (p. 6). As such, it represents the combining of various White ethnic cultures into a single entity for purposes of racial domination. Aspects of White culture assume superiority over others, and it is this historical record that must not fade from our memory (Leonardo, 2002, p. 32). One need not look far to see the assumption of cultural superiority at work in many school music programs, particularly those whose curricula rarely venture beyond Western art musics. If such musics are included in the curricula, they often tend to perpetuate the sense of "different or exotic" (Campbell, 1994), rather than musics as equally important components of the curriculum.

The Luxury of Ignorance

Howard calls "the luxury of ignorance" one of the distinguishing characteristics of Whiteness. Because White people often live in segregated neighborhoods, many move about freely in society without coming into direct contact with people of color. As the "members of the dominant group in society, [they] do not necessarily have to know anything about those people who are not like them" (Howard, 2006, p. 14). Although the increasing diversity in many urban centers makes the luxury of ignorance less sustainable, there are still many places, both rural and suburban, where people only see others of similar racial or ethnic background in their daily interactions, and as a result, may choose to learn about only those people or the culture found in their immediate surroundings.

The luxury of ignorance certainly exists among those in the music teaching profession. Believing that racism is no longer widespread, they teach from a perspective of Whiteness as ignorance, ignoring the realities of lived experience for children of color or those who are minoritized for other reasons, and/or ignoring other forms of music that may be more relevant to the students in their charge. Having never experienced music outside the Western canon, or only superficially so, teachers may react defensively at the very suggestion of including music from another culture or musical tradition. This is particularly noticeable among preservice teacher candidates (Marx, 2006). They complain that they do not know anything about other musics; in the extreme, some argue that the movement to teach from a multicultural perspective is an attempt to erase the Western canon from the curriculum, a defensive position that suggests unacknowledged racism. While many teachers embrace multicultural music education wholeheartedly, without exoticizing or tokenizing, there are also those who refuse to venture beyond what they already know, remaining shrouded in the luxury of ignorance, perpetuating an agenda of cultural Whiteness in their classrooms.

The Myth of Music as a Universal Language

The luxury of ignorance has given rise to reliance on the cliché, "music is a universal language." Even those who point to how well music "travels" admit that the belief in music's abilities to transcend boundaries is naïve (Schippers, 2010, p. 54). While there are good arguments to be made on all sides of the debate about music's universality, most of these overlook the fact that in order for music to communicate (as language), both performers and listeners need at least a basic understanding of cultural context. Koza (2001) writes that

> although music is a universal phenomenon, it is bound to social context, and thus, the culture that produces the music also constructs its meaning. Therefore, rather than sending a universally understood message, the music of a particular culture may sound alien and incomprehensible to an uninitiated listener. (p. 242)

I would add to Koza's argument that music heard as "alien and incomprehensible" may also reinforce any stereotypes about people and culture already held by those listeners. Music viewed as an entity apart from the culture from which it springs cannot begin to transcend cultural boundaries or break down racial prejudices. "Music for music's sake" supports color-blind ideologies. As teachers, unless we make it clear that music is the product of human activity, and encourage students to learn about the humans who make particular kinds of musics, that music falls on ears unprepared to hear and understand, and may be filtered through prejudicial beliefs or misinformation about people and cultures.

Those who accept the myth of music's universality often fail to acknowledge that the choice of *what music* cannot be separated from the issue of *whose music* to include in the curriculum. By overlooking this important connection, music teachers may teach only what they know best (the Western canon), believing they are reaching all children because of their reliance on the myth of music as a universal language.

Color-Blind Racism and Music Education

The myth of music as a universal language works hand in hand with one of the most distinguishing characteristics of Whiteness—that of color-blind racism, or "the new racism" (Bonilla-Silva, 2003). By hiding behind the statement, "I don't see color, I only see children (or people)," White people are able both to distance themselves from obvious racisms around them, and at the same time feel self-congratulatory for not being racist themselves. This dynamic of Whiteness may be likened to viewing a shadow projected onto a screen. Those who experience racism as lived reality see the original object. The other group sees only the shadow. Through their learned experiences, one group understands race and racism as lived realities. The other group, from their (White) vantage point, sees racism as "an outlier of sorts, an inconvenient experience, the result of overly sensitive minorities looking for any excuse to be aggrieved, or as an example of a simple misunderstanding where race is not truly operative as a relevant variable" (Deis, 2009, p. 1).

Color-blindness provides a mask for racist thoughts, actions, and beliefs while allowing White people to appear reasonable, even moral (Bonilla-Silva, 2003, p. 28), in their opposition to policies to promote multiculturalism, for example. Often, however, these same folks who proclaim color-blindness fail to see that they make determinations about other people based upon their skin color, ethnicity, language, sexual orientation, or socioeconomic status. For example, comments about students who live in public housing, or about parents from certain ethnic groups, often find their way into negative discussions in the teachers' lounge. These statements are often prefaced with phrases such as, "I am not a racist, but . . ." (p. 57), as if the declaration absolves the speaker from the racist statement that is almost certain to follow.

Color-blindness is an insidious form of racism because it erects a wall of denial that prevents White people from interrogating their Whiteness or their racist attitudes. Marx discovered in her research with preservice teachers that a major factor preventing White teachers from being able to see and to name their own color-blind racism is that they most often see themselves as "good people." Good people cannot be racist because racism suggests hate, and hate is an unacceptable emotion, particularly for teachers (Marx, 2006, p. 85).

The color-blind mantra of "treating everyone the same" assumes that all children are the same; the ideology behind this assumption, when asserted by those whose "vision is filtered by a White lens," in reality assumes that all children are White children (p. 86), and that the teacher has no real need to understand the cultural backgrounds or lived realities of the students in her charge. For those teaching music, subscribing to the belief in music as a universal language may feed this sense of treating all children as if they were White. By teaching only "the best" music, one can easily hide behind a misguided sense of providing children with an equitable music education, overlooking the fact that such musical curricular choices represent a specific and narrow cultural perspective.

Even when teachers incorporate multicultural and global musics into their curricula, the ways in which musical cultures and characteristics are taught may inadvertently reinforce cultural Whiteness. By superimposing Western concepts such as notation on musics typically learned aurally or through immersion in the musical practice, teachers fail to take into account that Western music learners infer from notation many non-written aspects of music that have been learned through their enculturation into Western society. Yet these non-written aspects of music "do not complement the notation when reading music of unknown traditions" (Schippers, 2010, p. 76). In other words, notation itself conveys cultural information that may confuse and distort the music of cultures not dependent upon notation. This is a musical variation on color-blindness, in which the use of notation is justified as providing a common starting place for all children in the classroom. While some situations may indeed justifiably call for using notation to teach musics typically learned through aural transmission, compromises result and need to be understood as such. Avoiding notation's tendency to "Whitewash" global musics can only be accomplished when teachers have a good understanding of the musical culture being taught, so that the Western cultural messages implied by notation may be deconstructed and replaced with more culturally appropriate musical understandings.

CURRICULUM AS THE HIDDEN COLONIZER

Education—particularly public schooling—has long been used to socialize students into the presumed way of life of the nation, to "naturalize" (the term previously used in the United States for the process of citizenship acquisition by those from other lands). Within this process of socialization, schools often employ strategies that categorize and exclude those perceived as "different." As such, schools are key institutions for the ideological processes through which inequality may be made to seem legitimate. "Schools have been instrumental in maintaining a hegemonic legacy via a variety of structures and mechanisms, especially curriculum" (Goodwin, 2010, p. 3110).

I use the term *curriculum* to include not only the textbooks, materials, and instructional procedures that outline what students learn but also as

> society's implicit consensus around what is worth knowing and what is worthwhile; it shapes and defines students' learning experiences, speaks to or ignores who they are, and ultimately influences (some theorists might argue "determines") their vocational choices and options. (Goodwin, 2010, p. 3111)

Thus curriculum has the potential to emancipate or to colonize. As Apple (2004) writes, the knowledge deemed worth knowing—that which becomes part of the curriculum—is not random, but represents the "economic and social interests" of the dominant group, those who hold power in curricular decision-making. The interests of those living in society's margins may be overlooked in making curriculum decisions. Some theorists argue that the oversights are not accidental; for example, see Gillborn (2008), who suggests that those making curricular and educational policy decisions are not acting blindly, but with a realization of the negative outcomes that may result for marginalized students.

With the understanding that colonialism is a "distinctive kind of political ideology" operating through cultural exploitation that "marks people of color and indigenous peoples as inherently inferior" (Goodwin, 2010, p. 3114), we can begin to look at the music curriculum as one that colonizes as often as it emancipates. Particularly within the traditional paradigms of choir, band, and orchestra, repertoire heavily focused on European classical and the Euro-American canon represents *the* curriculum, with little if any allowance for exploration of other musical practices. The choice of *what music* in such settings may be understood clearly as a choice of *whose music*, with the implication that only the music of some people is worthy of inclusion in the curriculum; the rest is unworthy of being taught in schools.

Unlike Gillborn, I am not suggesting that those making the decisions about music curricula are deliberately attempting to colonize students in band, choir, and orchestra, or to exclude those students who may prefer other types of musical engagement, yet the result is that all are colonized by curriculum's visible and invisible cultural biases. In reality, this colonizing may extend beyond curricular materials, infusing pedagogical environments with colonial attitudes about cultural superiority. As students ascend through grade levels, participation in traditional ensembles "Whitens" noticeably as students of color choose not to participate (Lundquist, 2002, cited in Gurgle, 2013, p. 2). Gurgle's research suggests that among the Grade 7 choir students she interviewed, the White teacher's subtle cultural messages about body comportment had a colonizing affect on the diverse student population in her classroom. Despite the inclusion of "the students' music" in her curriculum, and her well-meaning attempts to employ a culturally relevant pedagogy, the teacher unintentionally conveyed the belief that proper performance behavior equated to notions of cultural Whiteness. The teacher was oblivious to this; she did not understand that her instructions to "stand still with hands at your sides," "no unnecessary movement," and so on, embodied Whiteness (Gustafson, 2008). The students trusted their teacher's instructions regarding stage appearance so much that even when she attempted to encourage movement for a gospel-style piece, the students maintained their traditional choir stances, fearing that any movement would make them appear disorganized to their audience or cause them embarrassment (Gurgle, 2013, p. 159). Gustafson (2008) writes that the cultural differences implicit in music pedagogies unwittingly insert demographic divides, creating boundaries to meaningful participation—in this case, the boundary discouraged moving to/with the music—(p. 269); similarly, the cultural messages inherent in music education pedagogies may cause students to infer abilities from comportment, gesture, and speech, often precipitating judgments (against themselves and others) of inadequacy (p. 270). As students progress in school, they come to understand intuitively that participation in traditional music ensembles is really the domain of those who identity as culturally White.

"Authenticity" as a Colonizing Concept

In my own work with preservice music teachers, one word seems to represent a significant barrier to engaging respectfully with multicultural and global music education: *authenticity*. Authenticity as a barrier serves to maintain a predominantly Eurocentric musical focus. Likewise, it holds an unattainable standard up as "necessary" for engaging with world musics. Each year, I meet students in my classes who express their fear that if they cannot teach a genre of music, or even a single song, authentically, they will cause offense. The fear of cultural *faux pas* is so strong that it paralyzes many in their attempts to learn other musics, and for some, the fear of inauthenticity serves as a (color-blind) excuse to stay within the musical status quo by explaining that "once you take the music out of its cultural context, it's no longer authentic" (Schippers, 2010, p. 52). These overly rigid concerns for authenticity may have been the unintended consequence emerging from the early days of multicultural music education, influenced by ethnomusicologists and well-meaning educators who themselves were anxious to "get it right" in performance. Music educators took the concerns to heart to the extent that for many, achieving authenticity became an impossible goal. The fear of inauthenticity encouraged clinging to the curricular status quo. Rather than abandoning the need to achieve absolute authenticity, many chose to abandon the inclusion of world musics. The impossibility of authenticity became part of the language of Whiteness in music education that now colonizes teachers and students alike. The word seems to have a remarkably strong influence on music educators, and not usually in a productive way. While it is widely believed that inauthentic presentations reiterate stereotypes, "an ill-chosen 'authentic' performance is at least as likely to confirm stereotypes" (Schippers, 2010, p. 59).

The fear of inauthenticity and its twin, overly prescriptive concerns about authentic presentation, have served to colonize students and educators by preventing us from engaging with musics that might genuinely broaden our understanding and respect for other people and cultures. As Schippers writes, "almost all music is transmitted out of context. Our entire formal education system—for music and all others subjects—is a major exercise in recontextualization" (p. 59). I suggest that if we can break away from our fears of committing offense, and find ways to engage other music cultures with the intent of disrupting the curriculum's White cultural agenda, we may begin to free ourselves from a colonial brainwashing that suggests to White teachers that they are not capable of authentic presentation. Shifting the focus from authenticity to respectful engagement and performance of the music encourages exploration and provides teachers and students alike with a better understanding of music's dynamic nature.

A focus on strict authenticity usually pairs with a focus on "traditional" music, a word that conjures up images of static practice and unchanging ritual, a "museum" approach to music and music education, particularly noticeable in our engagements with world music. Yet traditions are themselves dynamic, changing over time according to societal needs or the needs of the group that calls it theirs. The idea that tradition is static is yet another colonizing concept. Labeling anything as "traditional" may heighten fears of causing offense. The discourse of cultural Whiteness suggests it is best to avoid the uncomfortable and thus exerts its disciplinary power on teacher and student behavior. Yet as Schippers (2010) points out,

> a powerful piece of music presented "inauthentically" out of context may engage learners more than an academically approved, representative traditional piece, especially if the connection with the learners is well conceived and carefully presented. (p. 59)

Much has been written about the ways teachers can resolve the authenticity dilemma: bringing in culture bearers and having students themselves share their cultural knowledge are but two oft-cited suggestions. Teacher workshops and self-study often help teachers cross the bridge over fear to explore musical cultures not previously familiar to them; however, in these approaches, the goal needs to be an immersion in the music, the culture, and the people, rather than a focus on learning to perform the music "authentically." When authenticity serves as the goal for musical engagement, it operates as a tool of Whiteness to maintain the curricular status quo.

Rather than maintaining tunnel vision on authenticity, an approach focused on culturally relevant pedagogy (Ladson-Billings, 1995, 2000, 2009) allows music educators to understand that there is no set of unambiguous guidelines related to teaching music from a multicultural perspective. Culturally relevant pedagogy finds the media and methods that best connect with the students in the room. As Ladson-Billings (1995) explains, a culturally relevant pedagogy helps students "accept and affirm their cultural identity while developing critical perspectives that challenge inequities that schools (and other institutions) perpetuate" (p. 469). A slavish devotion to achieving authenticity may result in the teacher's imposition of musics with which students have very little connection, and may foreclose possibilities for developing critical perspectives; the freedom to recontextualize both maintains necessary respect for culture, while it allows for crucial connections to students' own cultural identities.

OUT OF HIDING

I have attempted in this chapter to bring out of hiding some of the subtleties of racism in music education. The very definition of race itself, along with whose bodies are seen as racialized, is an amorphous concept that seemingly changes on a political whim; likewise, the racisms that emerge from the shifting concept of race also take many forms. Some, like genocide or overt acts of prejudice, are easy to identify, although difficult to prevent, if recent history teaches us anything. This chapter, however, has sought to look specifically at the color-blind racism associated with Whiteness, and its near-invisibility within music education discourses. I have argued that commonly accepted platitudes, such as *music is a universal language*, and concepts of *authenticity* rigidly applied in world music teaching, may support an agenda of cultural Whiteness, particularly when educators are unaccustomed to looking past the surface meanings. By looking more deeply into accepted practices and common-sense language, we may begin to realize how an agenda of cultural Whiteness imbues much of what music teachers often take for granted as "good teaching." Taking a serious, introspective look into Whiteness is never easy, particularly when the image in the mirror is our own. The first step in learning to live with the realities of racism (Leonardo & Harris, 2013) is to be able to see it, to name it, and to begin to change the behaviors that enable it, including the color-blind teaching practices and discourses that obscure racism from our sight.

NOTES

1. I use the term *White* to signify skin color as well as the ideology of "Whiteness," the cultural norms prevalent in North American societies that presume that the customs and

practices of White people are both "normal" and "correct." Associated with Whiteness is the concept of "White privilege," which enables Whites to benefit, sometimes without realization, from their position as Whites, while simultaneously disadvantaging others. These concepts will be discussed in greater detail throughout the chapter.

2. I use the term *homosexuals* in this setting, rather than the terms commonly used in today's vernacular (gay, lesbian, queer, transgendered). These terms would be anachronistic to the time period (mid-twentieth century) of the discussion. In addition, the term *homosexual* in this usage references the pathology assumed by the Nazis to justify persecution of anyone they believed was homosexual.

3. Africville, a small seaside community outside of Halifax, Nova Scotia, was bulldozed between 1965 and 1970 as part of a program of "urban renewal," displacing its Black residents. An announcement appearing in the local newspaper reflected the attitudes of White Haligonians toward the community's destruction: "Soon, Africville will be but a name. And in the not too distant future, that too, *mercifully*, will be forgotten" (*Africville: A community displaced*, http://www.collectionscanada.gc.ca/northern-star/033005-2601-e.html, italics added).

References

Africville: A community displaced. (2008). Ottawa: Library and Archives Canada. Retrieved from http://www.collectionscanada.gc.ca/northern-star/033005-2601-e.html.

Apple, M. W. (2004). *Ideology and curriculum* (3rd ed.). New York: Routledge Falmer.

Blommaert, J. (1999). *Language ideological debates* (Vol. 2). New York: Mouton de Gruyter.

Bonilla-Silva, E. (2003). *Racism without racists: Color-blind racism and the persistence of racial inequality in the United States*. Lanham, MD: Rowman & Littlefield.

Bradley, D. (2007). The sounds of silence: Talking race in music education. *Action, criticism, and theory for music education*, 6(4). Retrieved from http://act.maydaygroup.org/articles/Bradley6_4.pdf.

Campbell, P. S. (1994). Musica exotica, multiculturalism, and school music. *The Quarterly Journal of Music Teaching and Learning*, 5(2), 65–75.

Dei, G. J. S. (2000). *Power, knowledge and anti-racism education*. Halifax: Fernwood Publishing.

Dei, G. J. S., James, I. M., James-Wilson, S., Karumanchery, l. L., & Zine, J. (2000). *Removing the margins: The challenges and possibilities of inclusive schooling*. Toronto: Canadian Scholars' Press.

Deis, C. (2009). Why can't we have a smart conversation about race? *AlterNet* (August 3, 2009), 1–6.

Du Bois, W. E. B. (2005). *The souls of Black folk: Essays and sketches*. New York: Fine Creative Media.

Gillborn, D. (2008). *Racism and education: Coincidence or conspiracy?* London: Routledge.

Goodwin, A. L. (2010). Curriculum as colonizer: (Asian) American education in the current U.S. context. *Teachers College Record*, 112(12), 3102–3138.

Gurgle, R. E. (2013). *Levels of engagement in a racially diverse 7th grade choir class: Perceptions of "feeling it" and "blanked out"* (Ph.D. dissertation, University of Wisconsin-Madison).

Gustafson, R. (2008). Drifters and the dancing mad: The public school music curriculum and the fabrication of boundaries for participation. *Curriculum Inquiry*, 38(3), 267–297.

Howard, G. R. (2006). *We can't teach what we don't know: White teachers, multiracial schools* (2nd ed.). New York: Teachers College Press.

Koza, J. E. (2001). Multicultural approaches to music education. In C. A. Grant & M. L. Gomez (Eds.), *Making schooling multicultural: Campus and classroom* (pp. 239–258). Englewood Cliffs, NJ: Prentice-Hall.

Koza, J. E. (2008). Listening for Whiteness: Hearing racial politics in undergraduate school music. *Philosohy of Music Education Review, 16*(2), 145–155.

Ladson-Billings, G. (1995). Toward a theory of culturally relevant pedagogy. *American Educational Research Journal, 32*(3), 465–491.

Ladson-Billings, G. (1996). "Your blues ain't like mine": Keeping issues of race and racism on the multicultural agenda. *Theory into Practice, 35*(4), 248–255.

Ladson-Billings, G. (2000). Racialized discourses and ethnic epistemologies. In N. Denzin & Y. Lincoln (Eds.), *Handbook of qualitative research* (2nd ed.). Thousand Oaks, CA: Sage Publications.

Ladson-Billings, G. (2009). *The dreamkeepers: Successful teachers of African American children.* San Francisco: Jossey-Bass.

Leonardo, Z. (2002). The souls of White folk: Critical pedagogy, Whiteness studies, and globalization discourse. *Race Ethnicity and Education, 5*(1), 29–50.

Leonardo, Z., & Harris, A. P. (2013). Living with racism in education and society: Derrick Bell's ethical idealism and political pragmatism. *Race Ethnicity and Education, 16*(4), 470–488.

Longinovic, T. (2000). Music wars: Blood and song at the end of Yugoslavia. In R. Radano & P. Bohlman (Eds.), *Music and the racial imagination* (pp. 622–643). Chicago: University of Chicago Press.

Marx, S. (2006). *Revealing the invisible: Confronting passive racism in teacher education.* New York: Routledge.

McIntosh, P. (1990). White privilege: Unpacking the invisible knapsack. *Independent School, 49*(Winter 1990), 31–36.

Morrison, T. (1992). *Playing in the dark: Whiteness and the literary imagination.* New York: Vintage Books.

Pollock, M. (2004). *Colormute: Race talk dilemmas in an American school.* Princeton, NJ: Princeton University Press.

Roediger, D. R. (2007). *The wages of Whiteness: Race and the making of the American working class* (Rev. ed.). London; New York: Verso.

Schippers, H. (2010). *Facing the music: Shaping music education from a global perspective.* New York: Oxford University Press.

Tatum, B. D. (1997). *Why are all the Black kids sitting together in the cafeteria?and other conversations about race* (1st ed.). New York: Basic Books.

CHAPTER 13

ABLEISM AND SOCIAL JUSTICE

Rethinking Disability in Music Education

ALICE-ANN DARROW

INTRODUCTION

ALL learners exist somewhere on the continuum of human diversity, although educational institutions often attempt to categorize them based on one or more of their learner characteristics, and students often group themselves through their elective participation in academic, social, or cultural organizations. Despite the various educational practices that attempt to classify students, they remain unique in many important respects. Society—and schools in particular—is increasingly invested in respecting differences and supporting diversity. Today's teachers must educate students varying in culture, language, and religious beliefs, as well as many other characteristics (Gollnick & Chinn, 2002).

> To meet this challenge, teachers must employ not only theoretically sound, but also culturally responsive pedagogy. Teachers must create a classroom culture where all students, regardless of their cultural and linguistic backgrounds, are welcomed and supported, and provided with the best opportunity to learn. (Richards, Brown & Forde, 2007, p. 64)

Diversity is generally considered a composite of racial, ethnic, gender, LBGT, or class representation. Unfortunately, disability representation is often forgotten, dismissed, or overlooked as an important part of what we consider to be diversity.

People with disabilities constitute a large segment of American society. According to the US Census Bureau in 2010, nearly 20 percent of the non-institutionalized US population had a disability, with advancing age as a significant factor in the acquisition of a disability. Despite the prevalence of disability, most people report a fear of becoming disabled. Most of the literature on this population conceives disability as a form of deviance from the norms of society (Smart, 2009). More contemporary authors have reconceptualized disability as simply a form of diversity or human variation, much like race or gender (Darling, 2013). The consistent inclusion of disability as a form of diversity would do much to combat ableism and to promote the identity of persons with disabilities.

Education is a major force in the early development of self-identity and in the conceptualization of others. Students with disabilities often share a group identity—an identity that developed due to the physical, sensory, or cognitive nature of their disabilities, or because of a shared education history that resulted in time spent together in self-contained classrooms and resource rooms. For many years, students were segregated by their disability, and continue to be in some educational contexts. Compared to public rhetoric protesting racial segregation, exclusion based on disability is still seen as acceptable, and often warranted (Hallahan, Kauffman, & Pullen, 2012). Academic segregation is an important part of the history of oppression experienced by many students with disabilities.

DISABILITY HISTORY AND EDUCATIONAL REFORM

During most of the 1800s, students with disabilities were not considered eligible for an education. If they were educated at all, they were educated in segregated institutions. By the early 1900s, there were state schools for students who were deaf or blind, and some schools for students with intellectual disabilities. Children left home to attend and to live in dormitories at these schools, often at the age of only four or five years. In larger metropolitan areas, some parents were able to find a private school that would accept their child; however, they often had to pay an expensive tuition fee and drive their child long distances to school each day. It is not difficult to understand, then, why some parents, particularly those of children with severe disabilities, felt that, even though most were under-funded and conditions were inhumane, the best placement for their child was in a state residential institution, a facility where they believed their child would be cared for and would receive educational training.

Until the mid-1970s, public schools educated approximately only one in five children with disabilities (Winzer, 1993). Most children with disabilities were denied access to their neighborhood schools. Parents of children with disabilities paid the same taxes their neighbors paid, but they were unable to send their children to the schools supported by those taxes. Many public school administrators believed that their schools' facilities and faculty were inadequate to provide services to students with disabilities; in most cases, they were correct. More disturbing, though, was the fact that many school officials also doubted the value of education for students with disabilities (Stainback, Stainback, & Bunch, 1989).

Following the racial desegregation of schools during the 1960s, early advocates reasoned that if schools should not segregate students by race, they should also not segregate them by their abilities and disabilities. As a result of their efforts, lawsuits were filed and legislation was passed on behalf of students with disabilities. The Education for All Handicapped Children Act, now known as the Individuals with Disabilities Education Act (IDEA, 2004), was passed in 1975. This law guaranteed a free, appropriate, public education (FAPE) to every child with a disability.

The 1980s brought increased legal pressure to provide more integrated educational opportunities for students with disabilities. From this time to the present, varying educational models have been employed to provide more normalized and inclusive experiences for students with disabilities. In the mid-1980s, the Regular Education Initiative (REI) was introduced as a model to improve educational services for students with disabilities. Proponents of the REI called for a dismantling of the dual system of education (general education and special education) in favor of a unified system. This movement challenged educators to re-evaluate current educational practices related to all students with disabilities. The REI served as a catalyst for change, moving education from a segregated system to a more inclusive and integrated system (Adamek & Darrow, 2010).

THE ROLE OF MUSIC IN THE EDUCATIONAL HISTORY OF STUDENTS WITH DISABILITIES

Music education, like all education for students with disabilities, has moved from an exclusion model, with limited access to music programs, to an inclusion model, in which students with disabilities have the right to a free and appropriate music education in the least restrictive environment. Each year, increasing numbers of students with disabilities participate in school music programs (Adamek & Darrow, 2010). As far back as the early 1800s, when Jean-Marc-Gaspard Itard (1775–1838) and others utilized music in the diagnosis and treatment of speech and hearing disorders, music has played an important role in the education of students with disabilities. In addition, music was found to be effective to teach auditory and speech skills to students with cognitive disabilities (Solomon, 1980). Early uses of music in special education settings were primarily with children who had intellectual or sensory disabilities. Music was used as a way to facilitate learning and to reinforce students' academic achievements.

Opportunities for students with disabilities to participate in music experiences increased concurrently with the growth in overall educational opportunities. Schools for children who were deaf or blind included singing, rhythm activities, and instrument playing (Solomon, 1980). Music was also a part of the programming in institutions for children who had intellectual disabilities. Music education was provided so that these students had opportunities to develop useful leisure skills that might, in turn, allow them to assimilate more easily into their communities (Adamek, 2002). Thus, music was seen as a facilitator for integration, and in many of these accounts of music with students with various disabilities, the primary goal of the activities was non-musical.

Many of the early music programs included opportunities for students with disabilities to participate in musical ensembles. There are numerous accounts of musical organizations specifically for students with various disabilities (British Deaf Band Tour in North America, 1991; Darrow, 2006; Sheldon, 1997). Such groups participated in "Very Special Arts Festivals"[1] across the country during the 1970s, 1980s, and into the 1990s. Though segregated, such performing groups helped to cultivate a social and musical identity for their members (Smith & Plimpton, 1993).

DISABILITY CULTURE AND SOCIAL IDENTITY

All individuals share and create culture; like those from other cultures, persons with disabilities share a common bond of experiences and resilience. This common bond has resulted in what has been termed "disability culture" (Jones, 2002). Culture shapes how we see the world, influences our behaviors, and defines how we see others and ourselves. Likewise, culture also determines how we make sense of disability and respond to people with disabilities. Persons with disabilities are viewed very differently depending upon where they live in the world. In some countries, people with disabilities are still segregated and lack access to education (Charlton, 2000). Even in the United States, individuals with disabilities have had to battle discrimination in terms of employment, housing, education, and access to public buildings and services (Americans with Disabilities Act, 1990). Brown (2002), the most noted author on the topic of the disability culture, shares his perspective regarding this term:

> Those of us working the field of disability culture probably all agree on several basic points. First, disability culture is not the same as how different cultures treat different disabilities. Instead disability culture is a set of artifacts, beliefs, expressions created by disabled people ourselves to describe our own life experiences. It is not primarily how we are treated, but what we have created. Second, we recognize that disability culture is not the only culture to which most of us belong. We are also members of different nationalities, religions, colors, professional groups, and so on. Disability culture is no more exclusive than any other cultural tag. (p. 49)

Numerous authors have discussed disability identity as a social construct and the resulting limitations (Epp, 2000; Riddell, Baron, & Wilson, 2001). Riddell, Baron, and Wilson (2001) conjecture that people with disabilities often have a restricted range of self-identities because of limiting societal labels and ascriptions. As Brown (1996) points out in the above quote, people with disabilities have forged a group identity. They have fought for anti-discrimination and entitlement laws that have served to protect their educational, employment, and accessibility rights; however, civil rights do not equate with social rights or acceptance. In 1983, Wright reported that, in social interactions between persons with and without a disability, those without a disability exhibited the following behaviors: they terminated conversations more quickly, smiled less, showed more signs of discomfort or restlessness, made less eye contact, and maintained greater physical distance. In the 30 years since, researchers still cite social acceptance as a major obstacle for people with disabilities (Michalko, 2002; Putnam, Greenen, Power, Saxton, Finney, & Dautel, 2003; Smart, 2009).

Although persons with disabilities compose a growing segment of society, when compared with other aspects of diversity, such as race or gender, disability has received little research attention. Johnson and Darrow (2003), as well as McLaughlin, Bell, and Stringer (2004), evaluated the role of disability type (AIDS, cerebral palsy, stroke, etc.) and the related stigma in the acceptance of coworkers and students with disabilities. They found that it is the stigma associated with a particular disability—which varies across disability types—that influences acceptance. Participants' categorizations of individuals with disabilities evoked stereotyping, which in turn affected their affective responses to individuals with particular disabilities. How then are such stereotypes formed? A number of authors suggest that popular media are greatly influential in how we perceive persons with disabilities, as well as other minority groups (Norden, 1994; Safran, 1998).

THE MEDIA'S INFLUENCE ON PERCEPTIONS OF PERSONS WITH DISABILITIES

To eliminate stereotypes, they must first be recognized and then challenged. The media have incredible power to influence our perception of others, particularly those with whom we have little contact. Students are one of the most active consumers of popular media, and are consequently subject to their influences. Unfortunately, depictions of persons with disabilities are rarely written or portrayed by persons with disabilities, thus making such depictions subject to the non-disabled perspective (Haller, Dorries, & Rahn, 2006).

The arts are an important part of the media, which continue to be a major public information source about disabilities. Darrow (2011) examined selected lyrics related to disability in the popular Broadway musical *Wicked*. The lyrics were analyzed and placed in the context of disability literature, common disability stereotypes, historical and contemporary uses of disability as a metaphor in film and literature, and portrayals of persons with disabilities in the popular media—specifically the arts. She found stigmatizing views of disability that included self-pity, pity, dependence, bitterness, resentment, loneliness, and wickedness. Darrow (2012) also examined *Glee*, a popular television show in the United States about a school choir and the adventures of its members. She found not only stigmatizing depictions of disability, but also misinformation about disabilities, such as in one episode (*The Purple Piano Project*) when a new character, Sugar Motta, enters the practice room with the line, "I have self-diagnosed Asperger's, so I can pretty much say whatever I want." The freedom to say whatever one wishes is not a character-istic of Asperger's, which is diagnosed by a professional after extensive observations of a student and interviews with parents, teachers, and others who interact with the indi-vidual on a regular basis. While likely unintentional, early episodes of *Glee* prompted numerous commentaries regarding its missteps in representing persons with disabilities (Darrow, 2012; Elber, 2009).

Disability portrayals in the media are a fact of life. Safran (1998) found that 43 per-cent of Best Picture, Best Actor, and Best Actress awards during the 1990s involved disability-related films. Some portrayals, though not negative, depicted the person with a disability as superhuman—a different type of stereotype that can also create unrealistic expectations regarding persons with disabilities. Motion pictures, regard-less of their accuracy, remain one of the major public information sources about dis-abilities (Norden, 1994). Television, film, and musical scripts will continue to be written by persons who have little experience with disability, and disability roles will continue to be played by (for the most part) actors without disabilities; and thus it is likely that the popular media will continue to perpetuate stereotypical portrayals of people with disabilities.

Clearly, the arts constitute a major segment of the popular media. It is imperative, then, that music educators learn to recognize discriminating and/or stereotypical por-trayals of persons with disability in the arts, to question these stereotypes, and to be mindful never to propagate such stereotypes in their teaching and writing. Most impor-tant, teachers must take advantage of every opportunity to highlight portrayals of per-sons with disabilities that are realistic and affirming. The acceptance of persons with disabilities will be positively influenced if educators, and the students they teach, con-tinue to challenge stigmas associated with disabilities.

REFERRING TO PERSONS WITH DISABILITIES

Language is important, as it can influence our perceptions of others. Questions have been raised about the terminology used to refer to many minority groups. As early as 1960, Beatrice Wright in her landmark text, *Physical Disability: A Psychological Approach*, claimed that the language used to refer to people with disabilities can be either empowering or devaluing. Educators understand that words have power, and a teacher's use of inappropriate disability-related terminology is generally inadvertent, reflecting a lack of awareness, not maliciousness.

As with any term used to describe a group of people, deference is usually given to those being described (American Psychological Association, 2009). For example, the evolution of terms used to describe groups of individuals based upon race and/or sexual orientation is well known. This evolution was the result of public education and self-advocacy by these groups. Guidelines for reducing biases in language have been updated over the years, and provide practical advice for writing about disability status.[2] The World Institute on Disability (Berkeley, CA), National Organization on Disability (Washington, DC), and Disabilities Research and Information Coalition (Seattle, WA) are some of the organizations that have actively advocated for the use of appropriate non-discriminatory terminology to describe persons with a disability. Defining persons by their disability fails to recognize their humanness; what words would be used to describe the individual if he or she did not have a disability?

Most music educators today are aware of "person-first" language, putting the person before the disability, saying, for instance, "a student with autism" instead of "the autistic student." Rather than seeing the person as the disability, person-first language demonstrates that the person has many characteristics and qualities, of which a disability might be one. The purpose of this approach is not to minimize or deny a disability, but to affirm that a student is more than his or her disability, so that the disability does not supersede all of the other attributes the student possesses (Adamek & Darrow, 2010; Turnbull, Turnbull, & Wehmeyer, 2010). As a professional working in schools, it is important to know and use appropriate terminology when communicating with other professionals, parents, and school administrators. Using labels and other terminology unique to special education demonstrates an understanding of related laws, school culture, and recent developments in the field (Darrow, 2013). Using appropriate language also demonstrates a respect for persons with disabilities.

ABLEISM AND SCHOOLS

"Ableism," sometimes referred to as "handicapism," has various definitions, although all are based on the discrimination and oppression that people with disabilities experience in our society (Ferri & Connor, 2005; Hehir, 2002). Ableism "operates on individual, institutional, and cultural levels to privilege 'temporarily able-bodied people' and disadvantage people with disabilities" (Adams, Bell, & Griffin, 2007, p. 335). "Temporarily able-bodied" refers to the notion that nearly all people will experience disabling conditions due to aging, if not by other means. Ableism in schools occurs when physical, attitudinal, social, or educational barriers are posed that prevent students with disabilities from successful inclusion. Much progress has been made in the past three decades to improve the quality of education for students with disabilities; however, forms of ableism, both overt and subtle, remain. Ableism is often overlooked as one reason that students with disabilities often experience difficulties in school. Being aware of forms of ableism is the most important precursor to bringing about social justice for students with disabilities. Several sources of prejudice against persons with disabilities should be of particular concern to educators: bullying in schools, educational economics, the nature and etiology of disability, fear of acquiring a disability, societal emphasis on beauty and fitness, and the inferred emotional consequences of disability. In the following sections, I discuss each of these sources of prejudice against persons with disabilities and the resulting consequences of these prejudices for students.

Bullying in Schools

The effects of bullying are long-lasting and extremely detrimental to the academic success of victims. The implications of bullying for students include poor academic performance, absenteeism, depression, anxiety, and even suicide (Flynt & Morton, 2004; Ross, 2003). Carter and Spencer (2006) reviewed current research in order to examine the risk factors and the degree and nature of bullying experienced by students with disabilities. They found that students with disabilities were at greater risk of being victimized than their non-disabled peers. Forms of bullying included name-calling, teasing, physical attacks, verbal abuse, threats, taking belongings, imitating, and making fun of students with disabilities. Students with disabilities also tended to be less popular, to have fewer friends, and to struggle with loneliness.

Educational Economics

Educational services for students with disabilities, particularly for those with severe disabilities, are often expensive. Public schools spend an average of two to three times more on each student eligible for special education than they do for students without disabilities (Aron & Loprest, 2012). Under the Individuals with Disabilities Education Act, public schools are obligated to provide a free and appropriate education for every child with a disability, and regardless of cost, students must be placed in an environment that provides the fewest restrictions to their success. Some legislators and school officials consider special education services to be a hardship and not cost-effective because many students with disabilities graduate and then are underemployed or never find employment at all (Hahn, 2005; Longmore, 2003). However, only 35 percent of persons with disabilities reported being employed full- or part-time, compared with 78 percent of those without disabilities (Smart, 2009). From a social justice perspective, cost-benefit analysis should not be the major factor in assessing the value or worthiness of educating students with disabilities.

The Nature and Etiology of Disability

Some disabilities are more or less stigmatizing than others depending on the nature of the disability and on the etiology of disability. Disabilities that can be seen, such as blindness, are more stigmatizing than those that cannot be seen, such as deafness. Additionally, physical disabilities are less stigmatizing than mental health disabilities (Spencer, 2006). The etiology of disabilities also plays a role in the social acceptance of students with disabilities. Students who acquire a disability due to an athletic injury, or a nationally publicized event, such as a school shooting or a bombing, are often celebrated, and always are afforded a higher status than students who have identical disabilities that are congenital (Smart, 2009).

Fear of Acquiring a Disability

Most people have a fear of becoming disabled, and the presence of a person with a disability can serve as a reminder that acquiring a disability is always a possibility. As a result, people often feel the need to personalize disability and to express sentiments such as, "I wouldn't want to live if I lost my sight, or I would rather die than have to use a wheelchair." These and similar comments devalue the lives of persons with disabilities. Students with disabilities who hear these types of comments from peers find them to be demoralizing and depressing (Marks, 1999).

Emphasis on Beauty and Fitness

It is well known that attractiveness and athleticism are positively related to acceptance and popularity (Remland, 2009). People who are attractive and able-bodied earn more money, receive more social benefits, and experience less rejection than those who are not (Knapp & Hall, 2010). These effects are particular salient in the school environment, where personality, intelligence, and the content of one's character are generally not as highly regarded as beauty and athleticism. Certainly, students with disabilities can be considered attractive, but researchers have found that beauty is most often defined by facial and bodily symmetry and physical fitness (Remland, 2009).

Inferred Emotional Consequences of Disability

Many persons without disabilities assume that people with disabilities lead sad or tragic lives, a stereotype conveyed in the lyrics of the popular musical *Wicked* (Darrow, 2011). People without disabilities often spend more time thinking about a person's disability than the person with the disability. Most students with congenital disabilities are not mindful of their disabilities, and find them to be inconsequential to their happiness, or to their academic life. They are often reminded of their disability only when others make reference to it.

COMBATING ABLEISM
AND EMBRACING SOCIAL JUSTICE

As the previous sections suggest, ableism is rooted in negative cultural assumptions about disability (Hehir, 2002), and disability is generally seen as a negative condition that is characterized by deficiency, dysfunction, or disorder, and sometimes "a tragedy" (Darrow, 2011). Such perspectives contribute to disability as a social construct and thus to the marginalization of persons with disabilities. Some authors have identified educational policies, and special education policies in particular, as factors contributing to institutionalized and systemic ableism in schools (Danforth, 2004). Nevertheless, schools have historically served as an effective catalyst for social change, as in the landmark US Supreme Court case *Brown v. Board of Education* (1954). Clearly, education can play an important role in combating ableism and creating a new disability paradigm.

Reframing disability as a natural form of human variation—one characteristic among many possible human characteristics—can recast the image of people with disabilities, and consequently can promote their assimilation into the majority culture. During the late 1960s and the 1970s, the earliest conceptualization of multicultural education was defined, but it did not include disability (Davidman & Davidman, 1997). Music educators can help propel the social justice movement forward by including disability as part of their multicultural education practices. To combat ableism, music educators can start by creating equal music education opportunities for students with disabilities, and by promoting a positive image of individuals with disabilities.

The arts comprise a content area that lends itself well to infusing disability-related information. Several authors have suggested ways of bringing disability into the curriculum, and have provided recommendations to combat ableism that can be easily applied to the music classroom (Ferguson, 2001; Hehir, 2007; Storey, 2007).

- Ability awareness: Teachers and students can participate in music activities while simulating a disability, particularly disabilities experienced by fellow classmates. Research indicates that disability simulations during music activities can increase sensitivity toward persons with disabilities (Colwell, 2012). However, some disability advocates have suggested that such simulations often reinforce stereotypes and emphasize a "deficit" model of disability (Ferguson, 2001).
- Disability content in school curriculum and activities: The study of disability should be included in school curricula, as is the study of other minority and cultural groups. Such curricular information can influence music students' perceptions of persons with disabilities (Colwell, 1999; Johnson & Darrow, 1997). Persons with disabilities have been and are well represented in the musical arts, and studying these musicians, as well as recognizing student musicians with disabilities, is one way to infuse disability information into the music curriculum (Storey, 2007).

- Teacher in-service: Education programs addressing disability and ableism have been shown to positively influence music educators' attitudes and actions (Wilson & McCrary, 1996).
- Disability literature: Literature about various cultures is often integrated into school curricula. Books about musicians with disabilities, such as *Extraordinary Measures: Disability in Music* (Straus, 2011), as well as works written by persons with disabilities, can be included in the music curriculum.
- Use of role models: Students with disabilities need positive role models. There are numerous well-known composers and artists, such Beethoven, Itzhak Perlman, and Andreas Bocelli, who have disabilities, and those who are less well known, such as Thomas Quasthoff and Adrian Anantawan. These individuals, as well as fellow student musicians, can serve as positive role models, not only for students with disabilities, but for all students.
- Hiring teachers with disabilities: Teachers are often hired to represent a range of diversity, particularly in terms of ethnicity and gender. It is not as commonplace to hire an educator who has a disability (Storey, 2007, pp. 57–59).

A number of authors have emphasized the importance of understanding the causes and characteristics of disabilities commonly represented in the school population (Adamek & Darrow, 2010; Hehir, 2007). Making an effort to understand a student's disability demonstrates that the music educator is invested in that student. Knowledge about a disability also increases the likelihood that the music educator can adapt instruction to the needs of the student. Reading and understanding a student's Individual Education Plan (IEP), and conferring with IEP team members and family members, as well as the student, are all excellent resources to consider when searching for ways to adapt instruction. Many students with disabilities learn differently, and they are often capable of relaying the kinds of assistance or adaptations that have served them well in the past (Adamek & Darrow, 2012; Malian & Nevin, 2002). There is a considerable body of research indicating that inclusive practices are beneficial to both students with and without disabilities (US Department of Education, 1999), and that the types of adaptations a music teacher makes for a student with a disability will ultimately benefit other students as well.

Inclusive education is based on the principles of social justice, equity, tolerance, pluralism, and individual rights (Ayers, Quinn, & Stovall, 2009). Educational equity implies that music educators should have high expectations for all of their students, including those with disabilities. All music students should be expected to make progress over the course of instruction. The German poet Wolfgang Goethe posited, "If you treat an individual as he is, he will stay as he is; but if you treat him as if he were what he ought to be and could be, he will become what he ought to be and could be." High expectations for all students, however, requires that all students have equal access to instruction and the curriculum. One instructional approach that has been useful in addressing learner diversity is Universal Design for Learning, a researched-based framework that provides students with multiple ways of accessing the curriculum.

Universal Design for Learning in Music Education

Universal Design for Learning (UDL) operates on the premise that the planning and delivery of instruction, as well as the evaluation of student learning, can incorporate inclusive attributes that accommodate students with the widest range of learner characteristics. Universal Design for Learning offers an egalitarian education in which students are not marginalized by their differences. If the principles of Universal Design are applied appropriately, accommodations for students of varying abilities are imperceptible to the casual observer. When applying the principles of Universal Design, music educators have options in the approaches they will use to meet students' diverse needs, and learners have options in how they will respond to these instructional approaches. Application of Universal Design suggests (1) multiple means of representation (options for perceiving and comprehending information), (2) multiple means of action and expression (options for learners to navigate a learning environment and express what they know), and (3) multiple means of engagement (options to capture learners' interest, challenge appropriately, and motivate) (Rose & Meyer, 2006). Application of UDL principles to music education practices reduces barriers to learning by accommodating students with varying skill sets (Darrow & Adamek, 2012).

Most often, music educators address diversity by modifying an existing curriculum. Applying the principles of UDL requires that educators engage in a new way of thinking about and planning for instruction. A UDL music curriculum is designed from inception to meet the needs of as many students as possible. Doing so eliminates the need for after-the-fact adaptations and modifications. A universally designed curriculum also reduces the likelihood that a student will be stigmatized by disability-specific adaptations that highlight the learner's differences.

The application of UDL to any curriculum improves access, participation, and student advancement. The flexibility of UDL has the potential to increase access to the music curriculum for all students, but particularly for those with disabilities. Rose and Meyer (2002) promote the notion that the malleability of a curriculum rich in contemporary digital media and technology tools would support the needs of all learners. A curriculum that is fixed or static has proved to be inadequate for many students, and is particularly inaccessible to students who learn differently or who have sensory, cognitive, or physical challenges.

Any curriculum can be presented in ways that promote the learning of all students. The principles of UDL can be applied to all music curricula, provided music educators are aware of and understand the principles of UDL, are conscious of the many learner differences represented in their classrooms, and are aware of all the resources available to make a curriculum accessible to all students. All music educators would do well to adopt Kodály's belief that "music belongs to everyone." Music can only belong to everyone when everyone has an equal opportunity to learn (Darrow, 2015).

Conclusion

Over the past decade, increasing numbers of students with disabilities have been placed in the music classroom. As music educators, we can do much to combat ableism and to promote the image of students with disabilities in our schools. We can begin by

- understanding the history of disability oppression,
- recognizing and appreciating disability culture,
- challenging stereotypic views of disability played out in the media,
- using appropriate terminology in our teaching and communications with others, and
- employing instructional strategies that promote the inclusion of students with disabilities.

When teachers create accepting environments, and utilize terminology and practices that affirm all students, musical learning is more likely to take place. All students learn better when they are respected and accepted for their individuality.

Educators are obligated to confront injustices and to combat discrimination in the classroom. By advocating for social justice, educators can aptly serve as agents for change. The arts provide a powerful platform for discussing and promoting social justice. We must teach our students not to perpetuate injustices against those with disabilities, but sadly, it is likely such injustices will remain in the world; therefore, we must also teach our students with disabilities how to respond to incidents of prejudice with grace and dignity. Consider recent media reports of racism, even though we have actively combated racial discrimination for over 50 years. Social justice requires that we make a commitment to *all students*. When music educators model inclusive practices that honor human diversity, students are more likely to act in service of a more just society in their adult lives.

Notes

1. Very Special Arts (VSA) was an international organization founded in 1974 by Jean Kennedy Smith, sister of President John F. Kennedy. The purpose of the organization-sponsored festivals was to provide people with disabilities opportunities to share their talents with the public.
2. See, for instance, American Psychological Association (2009), pp. 70–77, and Research and Training Center on Independent Living (2008).

References

Adamek, M. (2002). In the beginning: A review of early special education services and legislative/regulatory activity affecting the teaching and placement of special learners. In B.

Wilson (Ed.), *Models of music therapy interventions in school settings* (2nd ed.). Silver Spring, MD: American Music Therapy Association.

Adamek, M. A., & Darrow, A. A. (2010). *Music in special education* (2nd ed.). Silver Spring, MD: American Music Therapy Association.

Adamek, M., & Darrow, A. A. (2012). Music participation as a means to facilitate self-determination and transition to community life for students with disabilities. In Sharon M. Malley (Ed.), *Intersection of arts education and special education* (pp. 101–112). Washington, DC: John F. Kennedy Center for the Performing Arts.

Adams, M., Bell, L. A., & Griffin, P. (2007). *Teaching for diversity and social justice* (2nd ed.). New York: Routledge/Taylor Francis Group.

American Psychological Association (APA). (2009). *Publication manual*. Washington, DC: APA.

Americans with Disabilities Act of 1990, Pub. L. No. 101–336, § 2, 104 Stat. 328 (1991).

Aron, L., & Loprest, P. (2012). Disability and the education system. *The Future of Children*, 22(1), 97–122.

Ayers, W., Quinn, T., & Stovall, D. (2009). *Handbook of social justice in education*. New York: Routledge.

British Deaf Band Tour in North America. (1991, February). *Silent News*, p. 5.

Brown, S. E. (1996). We are who we are . . . So what are we? *Mainstream: Magazine of the Able-Disabled*, 20(10), 28–30, 32.

Brown, S. E. (2002). What is disability culture? *Disability Studies Quarterly*, 22(2), 34–50.

Brown v. Board of Education, 347 U.S. 483 (1954).

Carter, B. B., & Spencer, V. G. (2006). The fear factor: Bullying and students with disabilities. *International Journal of Special Education*, 21(1), 11–23.

Charlton, J. I. (2000). *Nothing about us without us*. Berkeley: University of California Press.

Colwell, C. (1999). Effects of information on elementary band students' attitudes toward individuals with special needs. *Journal of Music Therapy*, 35(1), 19–33.

Colwell, C. M. (2012). Reflections on a disability simulation by pre-service music educators and student music therapists. In Lyn E. Schraer-Joiner (Ed.), *Proceedings of the 18th International Seminar of the Commission on Music in Special Education, Music Therapy, and Music Medicine* (pp. 9–24). Nedlands, WA: International Society for Music Education, 2012.

Danforth, S. (2004). The "postmodern" heresy in special education: A sociological analysis. *Mental Retardation*, 42(6), 445–458.

Darling, R. B. (2013). *Disability and identity: Negotiating self in a changing society*. Boulder, CO: Lynne Rienner Publishers.

Darrow, A. A. (2006). Sounds in the silence: Research on music and deafness. *Update: Applications of Research in Music Education*, 25(1), 5–14.

Darrow, A. A. (2011). What's so wicked about *Wicked*? *Florida Music Director*, 64(6), 14–18.

Darrow, A. A. (2012, November). Keynote address: No *Glee* for students with disabilities. American Choral Directors Association, Lake Mary, FL.

Darrow, A. A. (2013). What's in a name? Referring to students with disabilities. *Orff Echo*, 45(3), 11–14.

Darrow, A. A. (2015). Applying the principles of Universal Design for Learning to approaches in general music. In C. Abril & B. Gault, (Eds.), *Oxford handbook on approaches to teaching general music: Methods, issues, and viewpoints*. Oxford: Oxford University Press.

Darrow, A. A., & Adamek, M. (2012). Integrating students with disabilities in music education. In A. Ockleford & G. McPherson (Eds.), *Oxford Handbook of Music Education* (Vol. II, pp. 81–96). Oxford, England: Oxford University Press.

Davidman, L., & Davidman, P. (1997). *Teaching with a multicultural perspective: A practical guide.* New York: Longman.

Education for All Handicapped Children Act of 1975, P.L. 94–142, 20 U.S.C. 1400 et seq.

Elber, L. (2009, November). *Glee* wheelchair episode upsets disabled. *Huffington Post.* November 10, 2009. Web. Accessed January 8, 2014.

Epp, T. (2000). Disability: Discourse, experience and identity. *Disability Studies Quarterly,* 20(2), 134–144.

Ferguson, P. (2001). On infusing disability studies into the general curriculum. Washington, DC: Special Education programs (ED/OSERS). Retrieved from http://www.urbanschools. org/pdf/OPdisability.pdf.

Ferri, B. A., & Connor, D. J. (2005). Tools of exclusion: Race, disability, and (re)segregated education. *Teachers College Record,* 107(3), 453–474.

Flynt, S. W., & Morton, R. C. (2004). Bullying and children with disabilities. *Journal of Instructional Psychology,* 31(4), 330–333.

Gollnick, D. M., & Chinn, P. C. (2002). Multicultural education in a pluralistic society (6th ed.). New York: Merrill.

Hahn, H. (2005). Academic debates and political advocacy: The U.S. disability movement. In G. E. May & M. B. Raske (Eds.), *Ending disability discrimination: Strategies for social workers* (pp. 1–24). Boston: Pearson Education, Allyn & Bacon.

Hallahan, D. P., Kauffman, J. M., & Pullen, P. (2012). *Exceptional learners: An introduction to special education* (12th ed.). Boston: Allyn & Bacon.

Haller, B., Dorries, B., & Rahn, J. (2006). Media labeling versus the U.S. disability community identity: A study of shifting cultural language. *Disability & Society,* 21(1), 61–75.

Hehir, T. (2002). Eliminating ableism in education. *Harvard Educational Review,* 72(1), 1–32.

Hehir, T. (2007). Confronting ableism. *Educational Leadership,* 64(5), 8–14.

Individuals with Disabilities in Education Act of 2004, P.L. 108–446, 20 U.S.C.1400 et seq.

Johnson, C. M., & Darrow, A. A. (1997). The effect of positive models on band students' attitudinal statements regarding the inclusion of students with disabilities. *Journal of Research in Music Education,* 45, 173–184.

Johnson, C. M., & Darrow, A. A. (2003). Attitudes of junior high school music students from Italy and the USA toward individuals with a disability. *Bulletin of the Council for Research in Music Education,* 155, 33–43.

Jones, M. A. (2002). Deafness as culture: A psychosocial perspective. *Disability Studies Quarterly,* 22(2), 51–60.

Knapp, M. L., & Hall, J. A. (2010). *Nonverbal communication in human interaction.* New York: Wadsworth Publishers.

Longmore, P. K. (2003). *Why I burned my book on disability and other essays on disability.* Philadelphia: Temple University Press.

Malian, I., & Nevin, A. (2002). A review of self-determination literature: Implications for practitioners. *Remedial and Special Education,* 23(2), 68–74.

Marks, D. (1999). *Disability: Controversial debates and psychosocial perspectives.* London: Routledge.

McLaughlin, M. E., Bell, M. P., & Stringer, D. Y. (2004). Stigma and acceptance of persons with disabilities: Understudied aspects of workforce diversity. *Group & Organization Management, 29*(3), 302–333.

Michalko, R. (2002). *The difference disability makes.* Philadelphia: Temple University.

Norden, M. F. (1994). *The cinema of isolation: A history of physical disabilities in the movies.* New Brunswick, NJ: Rutgers University Press.

Putnam, M., Greenen, S., Powers, L., Saxton, M., Finney, S., & Dautel, P. (2003). Health and wellness: People with disabilities discuss barriers and facilitators to well being. *Journal of Rehabilitation, 69,* 37–35.

Research and Training Center on Independent Living. (2008). *Guidelines for reporting and writing about people with disabilities* (7th ed.) [Brochure]. Lawrence, KS: Author.

Remland, M. S. (2009). *Nonverbal communication in everyday life.* New York: Pearson Educational.

Richards, H., Brown, A., Forde, T. (2007). Addressing diversity in schools: Culturally responsive pedagogy. *Teaching Exceptional Children, 23*(3), 64–68.

Riddell, S., Baron, S., & Wilson, A. (2001). The significance of the learning society for women and men with learning difficulties. *Gender and Education, 13*(1), 57–73.

Rose, D., & Meyer, A. (2002). *Teaching every student in the digital age: Universal Design for Learning.* Alexandria, VA: Association for Supervision and Curriculum Development.

Rose, D. H., Meyer, A., & Hitchcock, C. (Eds.). (2006). *A practical reader in universal design for learning.* Cambridge, MA: Harvard Education Press.

Ross, D. M. (2003). *Childhood bullying, teasing, and violence: What school personnel, other professionals, and parents can do* (2nd ed.). Alexandria, VA: American Counseling Association.

Safran, S. P. (1998). Disability portrayal in film: Reflecting the past, directing the future. *Exceptional Children, 64,* 227–238.

Sheldon, D. A. (1997). The Illinois School for the Deaf band: A historical perspective. *Journal of Research in Music Education, 45*(4), 580–600.

Smart, J. (2009). *Disability, society, and the individual.* Austin, TX: Pro-Ed.

Smith, J. K., & Plimpton, G. (1993). *Chronicles of courage: Very special artists.* New York: Random House.

Solomon, A. (1980). Music in special education before 1930: Hearing and speech development. *Journal of Research in Music Education, 28,* 236–242.

Spooner, F., Baker, J. N., Ahlgrim-Delzell, L., Browder, D., & Harris, A. (2007). Effects of training in universal design for learning (UDL) on lesson plan development. *Remedial and Special Education, 28*(2), 108–116.

Stainback, W., Stainback, S., & Bunch. G. (1989). Introduction and historical background. In S. Stainback, W. Stainback, & M. Forest (Eds.), *Educating all students in the mainstream of regular education* (pp. 3–14). Baltimore, MD: Paul H. Brookes.

Storey, K. (2007). Combating ableism in schools. *Preventing School Failure, 53*(1), 56–58.

Straus, J. N. (2011). *Extraordinary measures: Disability in music.* New York: Oxford University Press.

Turnbull, A., Turnbull, R., & Wehmeyer, M.L. (2010). *Exceptional lives: Special education in today's schools.* (6th ed.). Upper Saddle River, NJ: Merrill.

US Census Bureau, Washington, DC. (2010). *Americans with disabilities: 2010.* Retrieved from http://www.census.gov/people/disability/publications/sipp2010.html.

US Department of Education. (1999). *To assure the appropriate public education of all children with disabilities. Twenty-first annual report to Congress on the implementation of the Individuals with Disabilities Education Act.* Washington, DC: Author.

Wilson, B., & McCrary, J. (1996). The effect of instruction on music educators' attitudes toward students with disabilities. *Journal of Research in Music Education, 44*(1), 26–33.

Winzer, M. (1993). *The history of special education: From isolation to integration.* Washington, DC: Gallaudet University Press.

Wright, B. A. (1960). *Physical disability: A psychological approach.* New York: Harper & Row.

Wright, B. A. (1983). *Physical disability: A psychological approach* (2nd ed.). New York: Harper & Row.

CHAPTER 14

GENDER AND SEXUAL
DIVERSITY CHALLENGES
(FOR SOCIALLY JUST) MUSIC
EDUCATION

LOUIS S. BERGONZI

THE purpose of this chapter is to explore music education's relationship to social justice for sexual-diverse and gender-diverse (hence, gender-sexual diverse) persons and communities. I have chosen to complicate this discussion by focusing on music education in the context of public schools because schools are critical sites for social justice and social justice education, particularly as related to gender and sexual diversity (Britzman, 1997; Epstein, O'Flynn, & Telford, 2000, 2003; Ferfolja, 2007; Macgillivray, 2004; Meyer, 2010). The relationship between gender-sexuality and education is currently evidenced in legal discourse around gender-sexuality and employment discrimination (Biegel, 2010), student safety (Ali, 2010; Patterson, 2013), right to assembly (i.e., gay-straight alliances and other student clubs) (Green, 2004), sex education programs (Mayo, 2004), and freedom of speech (i.e., being out) within school-as-public-square (Biegel, 2010; Macgillivray, 2004). With regard to schools, particularly those in the public sector, gender-sexual diversity is most evident within issues of curriculum, extracurricular activities, and school climate (Meyer, 2010).

Liberal and democratic frameworks of social justice award functional capability for securing social justice to educational, legal, and judicial systems as mechanisms of democratic values such as freedom and equality of opportunity.[1] However, scholars working from feminist, multicultural, and critical pedagogies of social justice see a more limited capacity for those systems to dismantle oppressive systems. Thus for those scholars, social justice *education* incorporates the "unlearning of cultural biases that privilege dominant groups and perspectives and existing educational structures" (Meyer, 2010, p. 18). However, both critical and feminist theories, as well as democratic ideals, are reflected in the goal for social justice education offered by Bell (2002), for whom the project of social justice is

> to enable people to develop the critical analytical tools necessary to understand oppression and their own socialization within oppressive systems, and to develop a sense of agency and capacity to interrupt and change oppressive patterns and behaviors in themselves and in the institutions and communities in which they are a part. (p. 2)

I center my examination of social justice and social justice education on the notion of oppression-privilege. Consequently, in this chapter, I position gender-sexual diversity within social justice education work, specifically as anti-oppressive education, and will offer observations of music education practice and research as anti-oppressive education with specific regard for gender-sexual diversity.

Oppression as Social Justice Violation and System

Social injustices are more oppressive than discrimination, bigotry, and prejudice because they infiltrate not only individual consciousness, but also social institutions (Bell, 2007). Whereas fear is the basis of homophobia (Lipkin, 1999), it is non-recognition, disrespect, and marginalization—as components of oppression (Ayers, 2010)—that underlie heterosexism and heteronormativity. When social justice violations are loaded onto individual and group identities and experiences, they constitute the situated oppression of Other.[2]

Oppression, then, is "the fusion of discrimination, personal bias, bigotry and social prejudice in a complex web of relationships and structures that shade most aspects of life" (Bell, 2007, 3). Historical systems of oppression can be related to immigrant status, racism, and white privilege; religious oppression and anti-Semitism; classism, ableism, ageism/adultism; and heterosexism-transgender experiences (Bell, 2007, pp. 3–7).[3]

However, in most contemporary Western societies, oppression is no longer commonly evident as a totalistic use of power, but rather as the more-difficult-to-discern "everyday practices of a well-intentioned liberal society ... [and with its causes] embedded in unquestioned norms, habits, and symbols, in the assumptions underlying institutional rules, and the collective consequences of following those rules" (Young, 1990, p. 56). Oppression depends on subtle and repeated associations across personal and group identities, or "citations" as Butler has noted (as cited in Kumashiro, 1999), that are detrimental to social justice. Female, for example, is often cited as weakness.

Two citations significant to this chapter are heterosexuality and humanity, as related to homophobia (Rodriguez, 1998, p. 154); and heterosexuality and normal, as the requirement for and the result of heteronormativity and heterosexism. Not merely theoretical conventions, these citations endow the derogatory phrases, "that's so gay" and "you're so gay" that are pervasive in schools (Interactive & GLSEN, 2005; Kosciw et al., 2012) and music classrooms (Bergonzi, 2013a), with the power to distress not only students who identify as lesbian, gay, bisexual, or transgender (LGBT) [4] (Kosciw et al., 2012), but also heterosexual students who are perceived as LGBT (Swearer, Turner, Givens, & Pollack, 2008).[5] These identifications are not only subjects for oppressive power, but are the partial product of the very dualistic assumptions on which they depend. For example, heterosexism is possible only when "heterosexual-homosexual" is held as the exclusive, binary option for human sexuality.

This imposition of categorical and reflexive conceptual limits around identity moves oppression from construct of sanctioned practices and behaviors to "a dynamic [system] in which certain ways of being (or, having certain identifications) are privileged in society while others are marginalized" (Kumashiro, 2002, p. 31). The privilege-oppression dyad is central to the work of educators and educational researchers in gender studies, critical theories, multicultural paradigms, as well as queer and other post-structural perspectives (Gereluk, 2009; Kumashiro, 2002; Young, 1990). Drawing from gender theory, critical race theory, social justice, and LGBT studies, intersecting identifications represent and result from the complex situated nature of lived identity (Hardiman & Jacob, 2007, p. 42).

Schooling as Heteronormative System

Schooling not only reflects dominant discourses about identities, but constitutes them. Systems of heteronormativity and heterosexism rely on the myths and misconceptions surrounding gender-sexual diversity commonly found in schools. These views, when allowed to persist, create and sustain hostile climates toward LGBT individuals and families. Four are identified by Meyer (2010), based on 15 years of grassroots social justice work with educators, students, and parents.

First, a popular misconception is that simply talking about diversity with specific regard to sexuality or gender means teaching about homosexuality and sexual behaviors. After all, as this thinking goes, promoting diversity or implementing anti-discrimination policies that include gender-sexual diversity are just ways to advance surreptitiously *the homosexual agenda* (Macgillivray, 2004). A second misconception is that knowledge and consideration of gender-sexual diversity is not relevant for education professionals and others who work with children and youth. (This has implications for teacher education, as will be discussed later.) Perhaps more controversial than this misconception is the opinion that explicit teaching of gender and sexual diversity should be avoided in schools. This position is contingent on "myths of childhood innocence" (Epstein et al., 2000) and requires an ongoing blindness to the very basic and observable ways that gender and sexual diversity have always been present in school curricula, extracurricular activities, and routines (Meyer, 2010)—from preschool (Blaise, 2005) to higher education (Daniels & Geiger, 2010; Epstein et al., 2003; Wickens & Sandlin, 2010). Finally, deeming sexual diversity as a concern of social justice education has been said to violate some students' cultural or religious views. When the latter is misunderstood as a violation of a constitutionally protected right, some parents invoke the libertarian tenant of government nonintervention in raising their children (Macgillivray, 2004).

CHALLENGING OPPRESSION
OF GENDER-SEXUAL DIVERSITY
IN MUSIC EDUCATION

In this section, I use Kumashiro's work in social justice education, specifically his activist theory of anti-oppressive education (Kumashiro, 2000, 2002, 2008), to bring together key ideas about social justice and gender-sexual diversity as they relate to music education theory and practice. My purpose here is to provide the reader with a way to consider and question the intentions, choices, priorities, and processes that constitute the "common sense" of music education as it relates to gender-sexual diversity. I chose Kumashiro's theory in part because it provides a variety of manageable entry points, including some recognizable theoretical and empirical junctions with established music education and education (hence, music/education) discourse. Additionally, Kumashiro requires more than recognition and remediation of oppression in the process of social justice work. He insightfully awards key theoretical ground to the crucial nature and essential role of personal discomfort, or even crisis, to the work of social justice education. Kumashiro's theory incorporates a necessary and difficult "coming out" to one's complicity in the oppression of multiple Others via marginalization and silencing.

As a queer theorist, Kumashiro relies on the deconstruction of alterity, followed by analysis of functional privilege and reconstruction (Kumashiro, 2000).[6] Kumashiro's theory is based on an analysis of empirical and theoretical literature and resembles the tripartite structure (safety, equity, and critical theory) of LGBT-inclusive education similarly derived by Szalacha (2004). For Kumashiro, there are four overlapping ways to conceive (theory), and contest (act) oppression in education: Education for the Other, Education about the Other, Education that is critical of privileging and Othering, and Education that changes students and society (2000, 2009).[7]

In the following sections, from within each of the four components, I describe how oppression is constructed and sustained, and how oppression can be problematized and responded to within music education/education. I also indicate how the components, although essential parts of a whole, each have conceptual and practical deficiencies as means of anti-oppression education.

EDUCATION FOR THE OTHER

Anti-oppressive education is held first as education for the benefit of Other, or simply Education for the Other (EfO). Under EfO, oppression is the harmful mistreatment of the Other characterized by (1) either inaction (i.e., not providing adequate funding, or materiel) or action (e.g., harassment, verbal or physical abuse); and (2) the existence of educational actors' assumptions and expectations about what constitutes normal behavior and expressions, including those required not to be Other. EfO as social justice calls for the existence of physical and learning spaces by which Other is identified, made safe, and affirmed. A strength of EfO is that it calls upon educators to identify diversity among students and to consider oppression of students who are not White, American, male, hegemonically masculine, heterosexual, and middle-class or wealthy.[8] Included under EfO are culturally responsive pedagogies (e.g., Ladson-Billings, 1994) and research related to the description, prevention, and intervention of bullying and other forms of student victimization.

Relative to gender and sexual diversity, EfO would do more than make visible and integrate the needs of students and teachers from gender and sexual minority groups among those of all students and teachers. Also valued under EfO would be curricular space for LGBT-inclusive instructional content and materials, as well as safe, affirming physical spaces, for example, gay-straight alliances.[9]

A space that is safe can make an important difference to a single student, especially one whose life is lived mostly as Other. Fitzpatrick and Hansen's multiple case studies of undergraduate music education majors and their reflections on their high school experiences inform us how gay music students seek out music spaces to find community and safety, and generally see music classes, musicians in society, and musical communities as relatively accepting of gay individuals, the gay community, and gay culture (2010).

The sense of music programs as a safe space inside high schools is supported by results from studies involving nationally representative samples of students. In the two most recent administrations of the National School Climate Survey, music (here, "band, orchestra, chorus, choir") was the most popular extracurricular activity among LGBT students, with at least 6 out of 10 participating or occupying a leadership in these ensembles (Kosciw et al., 2012, p. 47; Kosciw, 2014, p. 58). Furthermore, it appears that music students need a space in which to be safe from bullying. From analyses of data from the National Crime Victimization Survey, Elpus and Carter (under review) determined that music (band, choir, orchestra) and theater students were significantly more likely to have been victims of bullying, here expressed as a composite indicator of in-person (physical, verbal, relational) and cyber bullying.

Affirming classrooms and programs are not only spaces of safety, but also spaces where Otherness is embraced, and where normalcy is not assumed, but contested. This could be something as simple as labeling choral ensembles in ways that detach gender expression from vocal range and choral part, that is, not naming a group that sings SSA (soprano 1, soprano 2, alto) repertoire as "Women's Choir." Music education for gender-sexual diverse Others would also anticipate choral opportunities for student singers who are transgender, develop travel and housing policies that are gender-sexual diverse, and consider gender expression in selecting ensemble concert "dress." To be an agent of social justice under EfO, music teachers would contest "gender-sexual common sense" in these ways, whether or not there were music students who were transgender or gender non-conforming in their classrooms.

However, because identity is multidimensional and situated, there can be no single approach to creating safe and affirming spaces. This is a limitation of relying simply on EfO's recommendations to address oppression based on gender-sexual diversity.

EDUCATION ABOUT THE OTHER

Education about the Other (EaO) moves the focus from a rethinking of oppressive assumptions, expectations, and interactions to expanding students' understanding of other ways of being *in* and being recognized *by* the world as "fully human" (Ayers, 2010, pp. 792–793). EaO attempts to address knowledge and understandings that are incomplete due to suppression and distortions based on stereotype and myth.

Here, teacher preparation programs can assist preservice teachers in identifying the need for and means of Education about the Other. Regarding gender-sexual diversity, however, it seems there is little opportunity for this to happen (Gorski, Davis, & Reiter, 2013; Szalacha, 2004). Even when gender-sexual diversity is considered—usually as a subtopic of social justice (Ferfolja 2004)—it is often decontextualized to the extent of protecting heteronormativity (Gorski et al., 2013).

The promise, goals, and limitations of Education about the Other mirror those of multicultural education. Both frameworks seek curricular diversification as means to represent and move to the center the cultural ways of being of communities positioned outside the mainstream. In fact, some multicultural theorists incorporate gender and sexual diversity into multicultural education theory and actions (e.g., Banks & Banks, 2001; Steinberg & Kincheloe, 2009), but advisably not as proxy or replacement for race/ethnicity (Gay, 2010).

One of the reasons that LGBT concerns[10] are silenced within the education enterprise is a broadly held misconception that learning about gender and sexuality is not relevant for education professionals and others who work with youth (Meyer, 2010). However, this does not appear to be the view and experience of music/educators and music/teacher educators, as the following research suggests.[11]

From a review of the literature, Szalacha (2004) found LGBT concerns were brought to teachers' attention more during in-service than preservice work. From multiple studies involving teacher educators from across New South Wales (Australia), it is clear that teacher educators consider anti-homophobia education for preservice teachers, particularly in secondary settings, as important and relevant (Ferfolja, 2007; Ferfolja &

Robinson, 2004; Robinson & Ferfolja, 2008). This was often from a view of teachers as positive role models, and liberal-tolerance perspectives, despite evidence of "strong theoretical presence of feminist post structuralism" among other responses (Ferfolja & Robinson, 2004, p. 20). Anti-homophobia education was thought less important for teachers of younger students, and when compared to the need to address race and Indigenous issues in teacher education (Robinson & Ferfolja, 2008). Nonetheless, these researchers argue that anti-homophobia education is needed to affirm social inclusivity and to counterbalance the important biases and power inequities that exist across society that are learned, even during early childhood (e.g., Blaise, 2005).

In music education, the need to include issues of sexual orientation as part of teacher education has also been voiced (e.g., Garrett, 2012; Haywood, 2011; Sweet & Paparo, 2011) and suggestions for their incorporation made (Garrett, 2012). From a survey of coordinators of undergraduate music education programs, Spano (2011) reports that in 64 percent of music education programs the topic of sexual orientation is included in undergraduate course work. In a follow-up study (Spano, 2012) involving music education undergraduates drawn from a nonprobabilistic sample, survey respondents were about evenly split in reporting that LGBT2Q[12] concerns in music education were included as part of course content related to diversity.[13]

Although EaO may help develop empathy for the Other (Britzman, 1998), it does not necessitate seeing the Other as "equal, but on different terms"; it does not bring about any expansion of *normal*. Although difficult, such a reorientation has been part of recent music education research and practice.

In music education, a progressive resetting of "normal" (which, as we will see, exemplifies the next component of Kumashiro's framework) has occurred related to oppression based on age, or ageism. For much of modern music education history, particularly music education in college and universities where teachers are prepared, *beginners* were supposed to be young, of school age. Adult learners and their concerns were at the margin of music education research and practice. However, with the advent of New Horizons Music Programs (NHMP) in 1991, adult instrumentalists of all abilities are now welcomed into large ensemble music making. New Horizons Music Programs have since been the subject of research for graduate students and faculty members in music education owing to professional networks and faculty leadership, both musical and organizational. Indeed, there is much about the NHMP movement that has to do with social justice education.[14]

EDUCATION THAT IS CRITICAL
OF PRIVILEGING AND OTHERING

Education that is critical of privileging and Othering (EcpO) goes beyond examination of prejudicial dispositions toward the Other, or incomplete knowledge about the Other.

EcpO requires identifying, problematizing, and transforming the social structures and cultural ideologies that sustain privilege-oppression, and helping students to become aware of, to critique, and to challenge them (Epstein et al., 2000; Kumashiro, 2004; Meyer, 2010).

Anti-oppressive work is made more difficult when attempted in schools as institutions that both receive and transmit oppressive ideologies. EcpO confronts what is understood about and in schools as "common sense," that is, just the way things are, the way they should be, or the way they have always have been. "Common sense narrowly defines what is considered to be consistent within the purposes of schooling" (Kumashiro, 2008, p. 4).

In many educational sites, common sense about sexual and gender conformity is based on an assumption that heterosexuality and gender congruence are normal, natural, moral, simply better for kids, or even God's plan. Education that is socially just for gender-sexual diverse individuals is impossible without seeing and accepting the fact that sexuality as heterosexual privilege has always been present, even in music education (Bergonzi, 2009), and without contesting the educational common sense that sexuality has no place or purpose in schools. Two examples of common music education sense that neither recognize nor problematize *normal* with regard to gender conformity or sexual diversity follow.

Straightening out "that's so gay!" Music teachers regularly tell me that they do not allow phrases like "no homo," and "you're so gay" in the music classroom; and they assure me that when they hear such comments their response is swift and clear.[15] Their stated responses to these micro-aggressions (Pierce, Carew, Pierce-Gonzalez, & Wills, 1977) toward gender-sexual Others generally seem to be variants of "there's no name-calling in my class." Their intent is clear, and I have little doubt that students' behavior is extinguished, at least for that moment, in front of that teacher.

Rather than constituting anti-oppressive acts, responses like this, especially as called for by a school's "anti-bullying" program, do little more than sustain heterosexual privilege by "straightening up"[16] classroom discourse within a framework of classroom management. What students learn from this closeting of gender and sexual Other is that school is a place where they will not be asked to engage with the varied constructions of "gay" or "homo" that exist inside and outside school, and that regardless of the unjust, and at times even unsafe, spaces in which gender and sexually diverse students must live, schools will not only police the boundaries that privilege traditional gender-sexual norms, but will protect everyone at school from the queering of a non-sexual, gender-binarized reality (Pinar, 2004; Rodriguez & Pinar, 2007).

Missing males or invisible males? Common sense about "the missing males" in choral programs has been persistent within music education discourse for almost a century (Harrison, 2008; Koza, 1993). As a topic that has preoccupied researchers, "missing males" has been addressed from perspectives of gender studies and critical sociological theory (Koza, 1993–1994), post-structural gender theory (Koza, 1993), post-feminist theory (Harrison, 2007), and critical theory (Abrahams, 2012). This issue has also been worked as narrative-based exploration of males singers' cognitive sense of their possible selves (Freer, 2009).

Oppressive strains of gender-sexual normativity and privilege-oppression are explicitly and implicitly found in the well-worn recommendation that choral teachers "butch up" both singing and the choral music experience via various means in order to recruit more male-identified students to sing voice parts traditionally reserved for lower (read, *male*) voices. Two commonly endorsed strategies are recruiting student athletes into choir and importing older male singers to interact with current and potential students as role models.[17] The general approach here is to de-couple singing from female and things feminine/not male.[18]

This discourse does not even suspect, let alone contest, how the male-female binary regularizes heterosexuality.[19] Key questions are left at the margin: Why are the boys already in choir not "present"? Is it because they are not considered authentically male—not as normal as the other (!), "red blooded, manly men" (Koza, 1993–1994)? How is it that athletes and other "real" males, when recruited to choir (or other feminized spaces), are inoculated against feminization or narrowed masculinity (Anderson, 2013; Connell, 2008; Hall, 2008; Harrison, 2003)?

EDUCATION THAT CHANGES STUDENTS AND SOCIETY

From post-structuralist and psychoanalytical perspectives, the general direction of Kumashiro's fourth component is toward a queering of education and social justice through an emphasis on a continuous problematizing of knowledge and searching of the margins for oppressively veiled individuals, knowledges, and pedagogies discursively constructed (Pinar, 2003; Rodriguez & Pinar, 2007).[20] This is a complex and arduous quest because of the partial, privileged nature of knowledge and the complexities of identity.[21] To address the latter, Kumashiro (2002) turns to psychoanalytic theory and identifies the need to adopt a "pedagogy of crisis" to create curricular space for a necessary *working through*, in the psychological sense (Kumashiro, 2002, pp. 53–62).

(Now) Visible Music Students and Oppression

The queer education theorist Nelson Rodriguez (1998) proposes that we recognize how queer youth engage in a practice that is both political and pedagogical and that holds potential for connecting youth to larger democratic and social justice goals:

> the ways in which youth politically use and appropriate their bodies, language, culture, and myriad public spheres to contest dominant cultural practices, as well as

dominant representations and ideologies, suggests that they are engaging in a peda-gogical enterprise that wishes to educate us [that] any particular practice can be (re) appropriated by a subcultural group and "rearticulated" according to its own specific political meanings and values. (1998, pp. 147–148)

Consider how openly LGBTQ2 school music students embody the potential "to change students and society" by "musicianly" troubling gender-sexuality conformity. Due to the entrenched nature of homophobia in schools, this contestation is likely to be seen by some as (inappropriately) aggressive; but it is also compelling in ways that force us to consider how it advances social justice by rewriting the oppressive strains of gender-sexual normativity and oppression-privilege. Within school-based music edu-cation, gender-queer singers operate in a double-gendered context because, as contends Gould (2012), they are engaged in study of a feminized subject within a feminized social institution.[22] In ways only they can do, LGBTQ school music students contest compul-sory heterosexuality (Rich, 1983) and hegemonic masculinity. Furthermore, they dare to declare this in social institutions charged with establishing and policing narrow and oppressive conformations of gender and sexual identities. Finally, by rejecting the pro-tection offered by *str8* camouflage, openly LGBT2Q school music students outwardly *re-cite* the nineteenth-century "queer-musician" narrative of pathological deviance and emotional/feminine instability (Brett & Wood, 2009). Under education that changes students and society, and with respect to the ultimately unknowable nature of all theory and practice, including social justice education, one can see how these music students may even contest the victimization narrative that frames so much of contemporary dis-course around LGBT2Q students in schools.[23]

Close: Troubling Knowledge Creates Troubling Knowledge

Nadine Hubbs is a musicologist and a specialist in women and gender studies. She also has a personal background in school-based music education. In her keynote address at the 2010 symposium, "Establishing Identity: LGBT Studies and Music Education," she made the following observation and prediction:

There's no realm of American school life more universally associated with "fag" taunting than school music. It's particularly attached to student ensemble member-ship: we've all heard of the band fag, choir fag, and orchestra fag. This scenario sug-gests one reason that music education has stronger impetus than many other fields to open channels of inquiry and dialogue with LGBT studies. But it also predicts defensive reactions and denial among members of the music education community who don't identify with feminizing and minoritizing sexual identity labels and resent being associated with them. (Hubbs, 2010, p. 9)

Throughout this chapter, I have tried to silhouette the relationship between music education and social justice as it pertains to gender and sexual diversity. I focused my discussion of gender-sexual diversity within social justice education, specifically Kumashiro's conception of anti-oppressive education that involves both conception and action. I hope to have illustrated how social justice requires that intentions be placed against personal awareness and readiness. As stated by Allsup and Shieh (2012), "social justice education begins with adopting a disposition to perceive and then act against indecencies and injustices" (p. 47). So, how willing are we to take on such dispositions?

> Racism and homophobia are real conditions of all our lives in this place and time. I urge each one of us here to reach down into that deep place of knowledge inside herself and touch that terror and loathing of any difference that lives here. See whose face it wears. Then the personal as the political can begin to illuminate all our choices. (Lorde, 1984, pp. 110–114)

Lorde reminds us that racism and homophobia are simply not the responsibility of a few, and not merely an existential condition for some. We all condition and have been conditioned by the multiplicity of others. So, I ask: In what ways is the music education community ready to recognize the nature of the relationships among diverse gender-sexual identities and musicianhood, or the inherent place of sexuality and gender in music education and schools? How ready are we to challenge the oppressive structures that render claims of social justice for gender-sexually diverse music students, teachers, and families unfulfilled? For if there is one assumption upon which social justice education, including anti-oppressive education depends, it is a willingness to pose the question: What if we are the problem?

NOTES

1. Even though social justice cannot be ensured even by means of legal justice (see Sadurski, 1984).
2. The idea of "Other" in this chapter is fixed to the notion of privilege (McIntosh, 1988). "Other" will be used to refer to those groups that are traditionally marginalized, denigrated, or violated (i.e., Othered) in society, including students of color and students from under- or unemployed families. Gender and sexual Others would be students who are female, or male but not stereotypically *masculine*, and students who are or are perceived to be queer. They are often defined in opposition to groups traditionally favored, normalized, or privileged in society, and as such, are defined as other than the idealized norm (Kumashiro, 2002, p. 32).
3. Young (1990) identifies five types of oppression: powerlessness, exploitation, marginalization, cultural imperialism, and violence. In music education, these categories have been used in social justice examinations by Elliot (2007) and Abrahams (2009).
4. There are various acronyms used and terminology used in popular, professional, and theoretical literatures to refer to gender-sexual diverse individuals and communities. In this chapter, my choice of acronyms or term most often was the one employed by the author or

authors whose work I am referencing. In a few instances, for reasons of parsimony, I made a choice based on the work's theoretical grounding: specifically, whether a study was more firmly in LGBT Studies or Queer Theory, with *queer* being reserved for the latter.

5. Other researchers also found that these comments are likely to be heard more frequently by students who were White, LGBT, and from higher socioeconomic backgrounds relative to their counterparts in each of these subgroups (Interactive & GLSEN, 2005, p. 19).

6. Because the word "queer" has a long history as a derogatory term (Jagose, 1996; Meyer, 2007), some scholars and educators have an aversion to its use. To others, including members of the LGBTQ community, to use the word is to reclaim it as self-affirmation and an act of empowerment (Butler, 1993; Carlson, 1998; Kumashiro, 2002; Pinar, 1998; Tierney & Dilley, 1998).

7. I will not delineate the theoretical and practical research that underlies each approach because many readers will be able to infer these connections from my discussion; my focus is music education and gender and sexual diversity; and finally, space does not permit.

8. Working from a broad, non-oppressive orientation to social justice in music education, hegemonic masculinity is not among the barriers to music education identified by Jorgensen (2007).

9. GSAs are affirming and safe spaces for gender and sexual diverse groups. A GSA's presence in a school has been shown to positively affect school experiences and well-being of sexual minority students (Goodenow, Szalacha, & Westheimer, 2006; Kosciw et al., 2012). As such, they can be seen as an anti-oppressive mechanism of Education for the Other.

10. *LGBTQ concerns* in this case refers to identities claimed, the oppressions experienced, and the resistances enacted by LGBT2Q people and those committed to eradicating heterosexism (Gorski et al., 2013, p. 226).

11. Please note that this research from music education and education is limited to LGB (cisgender) individuals.

12. LGBT2Q = lesbian, gay, bisexual, transgender, queer/questioning.

13. Spano acknowledges the problematic nature of the sample used in this study.

14. Unfortunately, a comparable widening of the circle to include LGBTQ concerns has not occurred (Bergonzi, 2013b; Lamb, 2010). Although, Gala Choruses Inc., and the Lesbian and Gay Band Association began nine years before the inception of NHMP, the music teaching/learning, and the community building that one can only assume takes place inside these music education projects has not been considered to the same extent by music education scholarship and research, as has that within NHMP in less time.

15. At the time this book was published I could find no empirical research on music educators' response to verbal harassment based on sexual orientation or gender-expression inside or outside the music classroom.

16. Straightening-up: "When a homosexual or bisexual person alters the appearance of his or her domicile in order to hide from view any objects that could be construed as 'gay.' This is done in anticipation of the arrival of guests who are unaware of or uncomfortable with the individual's sexual orientation" (see entry "straighten up" at urbandictionary.com).

17. See summary in Freer (2010).

18. An exception is the work of Freer, in which constructions and expressions of gender or sexuality work are given much less attention than are the psycho-social learning and developmental needs of adolescents, especially those over which educators have control and about which boys have provided insight through narratives (Freer, 2007, 2012).

19. Only Koza (1993–1994) identifies the oppressive function of sex-gender norms on female and gay students, and calls for examining how "normal" casts femininity, females, and homosexuality as detrimental to the *de facto* goal of music education in the early twentieth century (and perhaps beyond): meeting the needs and interests of males and men. From a feminist perspective the question asked is: When professional discourse recurrently ignores or subjugates females and women, how is it that we view the males as missing (p. 227)?

20. To queer education means to question the nature of knowledge and pedagogy (Britzman, 1995). Queer theory creates—if not requires—a permanent reorienting of the tension between knowledge and pedagogy in its effort to bring the boundaries between the two as close to collapse as possible.

21. See Benedict and Schmidt (2007) for discussion, conveyed through and as conversation of social justice knowledge as an "interminable question" (Luhmann, 1998) and its relationship to music education.

22. This places them within school repertory, and thus distances them from rock and pop music, which are positioned differently with regard to gender and masculinity (see Harrison, 2008, Chapter 5, "Gender in Music Education," for summary).

23. This is certainly not to suggest that LGBT2Q individuals are not victimized.

References

Abrahams, F. (2009). Hosanna, hanukah, and hegemony: Anti-semitism in the music classroom. In E. Gould & J. Countryman (Eds.), *Exploring social justice: How music education might matter* (pp. 325–342). Toronto: Canadian Music Educators' Association.

Abrahams, F. (2012). Changing voices—voices of change: Young men in middle school choirs. In S. D. Harrison, G. F. Welch & A. Adler (Eds.), *Perspectives on males and singing* (Vol. 10, pp. 79–93). New York: Springer.

Ali, R. (2010). *Dear colleague letter: Harassment and bullying.* Washington, DC: Retrieved from http://www2.ed.gov/about/offices/list/ocr/letters/colleague-201010.pdf.

Allsup, R. E., & Shieh, E. (2012). Social justice and music education: The call for a public pedagogy. *Music Educators Journal, 98*(4), 47–51.

Anderson, E. (2013). *Sport, masculinities, sexualities.* New York: Taylor & Francis.

Ayers, W. (2010). Social justice. In *Encyclopedia of curriculum studies* (pp. 792–793). Thousand Oaks, CA: SAGE Publications. Retrieved from http://dx.doi.org/10.4135/9781412958806.

Banks, J. A., & Banks, C. A. M. (2001). *Handbook of research on multicultural education.* San Francisco: Jossey-Bass.

Bell, L. A. (2007). Theoretical foundations for social justice education. In M. Adams, L. A. Bell, & P. Griffin (Eds.), *Teaching for diversity and social justice* (2nd ed., pp. 1–14). New York: Routledge.

Benedict, C., & Schmidt, P. (2007). From whence justice? Interrogating the improbable in music education. *Action, Criticism, and Theory for Music Education, 6*(4), 21–42.

Bergonzi, L. S. (2009). Sexual orientation and music education: Continuing a tradition. *Music Educators Journal, 96*(2), 21–25.

Bergonzi, L. S. (2013a). *Instructional climate in secondary school music classrooms reported by engaged music students: A comparison of school and music camp settings.* Paper presented at the Research in Music Education Symposium, Exeter, UK.

Bergonzi, L. S. (2013b). ". . . not just for 'the gays'": LGBT and queer studies' potential to inform music education practice and research. MayDay Group Colloquium 25, Music Education and Political Agency. Conference paper. University of British Columbia, Vancouver.

Biegel, S. (2010). The right to be out: Sexual orientation and gender identity in America's public schools. Minneapolis: University of Minnesota Press.

Blaise, M. (2005). Playing it straight: Uncovering gender discourses in the early childhood classroom. New York: Routledge.

Brett, P., & Wood, E. (2009). Gay and lesbian music. Grove Music Online. Oxford Music Online. Oxford University Press. Retrieved from http://www.oxfordmusiconline.com/subscriber/article/grove/music/42824.

Britzman, D. P. (1995). Is there a queer pedagogy? Or, stop reading straight. Educational Theory, 45(2), 151.

Britzman, D. P. (1997). What is this thing called love? New discourses for understanding gay and lesbian youth. In S. De Castell & M. Bryson (Eds.), Radical interventions: Identity, politics, and difference/s in educational praxis (pp. 183–208). Albany: State University of New York Press.

Britzman, D. P. (1998). Lost subjects, contested objects: Toward a psychoanalytic inquiry of learning. Albany: State University of New York Press.

Butler, J. (1993). Bodies that matter: On the discursive limits of "sex." New York: Routledge.

Carlson, D. (1998). Who am I? Gay identity and a democratic politics of the self. In W. F. Pinar (Ed.), Queer theory in education (pp. 107–119). Mahwah, NJ: Lawrence Erlbaum Associates.

Connell, R. (2008). Masculinity construction and sports in boys' education: A framework for thinking about the issue. Sport, Education & Society, 13(2), 131–145.

Daniels, J. R., & Geiger, T. J. (2010). Universal design and LGBTQ (lesbian, gay, transgender, bisexual, and queer) issues: Creating equal access and opportunities for success. Paper presented at the Annual Meeting of the Association for the Study of Higher Education, Indianapolis, IN. http://files.eric.ed.gov/fulltext/ED530463.pdf.

Elpus, K., & Carter, B. (under review). Bullying victimization among music ensemble and theater students in the United States.

Epstein, D., O'Flynn, S., & Telford, D. (2000). "Othering" education: Sexualities, silences, and schooling. Review of Research in Education, 25, 127–179.

Epstein, D., O'Flynn, S., & Telford, D. (2003). Silenced sexualities in schools and universities. Stoke-on-Trent, Staffordshire, UK: Trentham Books.

Ferfolja, T. (2007). Teacher negotiations of sexual subjectivities. Gender and Education, 19(5), 569–586.

Ferfolja, T., & Robinson, K. H. (2004). Why anti-homophobia education in teacher education? Perspectives from Australian teacher educators. Teaching Education, 15(1), 9–25.

Fitzpatrick, K. R., & Hansen, E. (2010). Off the radar: Reflections of lesbian and gay undergraduates on their experiences within high school music programs. Paper presented at the Establishing Identity: LGBT Studies & Music Education, Urbana, IL.

Freer, P. K. (2007). Between research and practice: How choral music loses boys in the "middle": We can use research-based knowledge and instruction to attract and keep boys in middle school choir. Music Educators Journal, 94(2), 28(27).

Freer, P. K. (2009). 'I'll sing with my buddies'—fostering the possible selves of male choral singers. International Journal of Music Education, 27(4), 341–355.

Freer, P. K. (2010). Two decades of research on possible selves and the 'missing males' problem in choral music. International Journal of Music Education, 28(1), 17–30.

Freer, P. K. (2012). From boys to men: Male choral singing in the United States. In S. D. Harrison, G. F. Welch, & A. Adler (Eds.), *Perspectives on males and singing* (Vol. 10, pp. 13–25). New York: Springer.

Garrett, M. L. (2012). The LGBTQ component of 21st-century music teacher training: Strategies for inclusion from the research literature. *Update: Applications of Research in Music Education, 31*(1), 55–62.

Gay, G. (2010). Multicultural curriculum. In C. Kridel (Ed.), *Encyclopedia of curriculum studies* (pp. 587–591). Thousand Oaks, CA: SAGE Publications. Retrieved from http://dx.doi.org.proxy2.library.illinois.edu/10.4135/9781412958806.n316.

Gereluk, D. (2009). Education for social justice. In E. F. Provenzo, Jr., J. Renaud, & A. B. Provenzo (Eds.), *Encyclopedia of the social and cultural foundations of education* (pp. 729–733). Thousand Oaks, CA: SAGE Publications.

Goodenow, C., Szalacha, L., & Westheimer, K. (2006). School support groups, other school factors, and the safety of sexual minority adolescents. *Psychology in the Schools, 43*(5), 573–589.

Gorski, P. C., Davis, S. N., & Reiter, A. (2013). An examination of the (in)visibility of sexual orientation, heterosexism, homophobia, and other LGBTQ concerns in U.S. multicultural teacher education coursework. *Journal of LGBT Youth, 10*(3), 224–248.

Gould, E. (2012). Homosexual subject(ivitie)s in music (education): Deconstructions of the disappeared. *Philosophy of Music Education Review, 20*(1), 45–62.

Green, B. I. (2004). Discussion and expression of gender and sexuality in schools. *Georgetown Journal of Gender & the Law, 5*(1), 329–341.

Hall, M. A. (2008). Sport, sexualities, and queer/theory. *Sociology of Sport Journal, 25*(2), 281–283.

Hardiman, R., & Jacob, B. A. (2007). Conceptual foundations for social justice education: Conceptual overview. In M. Adams, L. A. Bell, & P. Griffin (Eds.), *Teaching for diversity and social justice* (2nd ed., pp. 471). New York: Routledge.

Harrison, S. D. (2003). Music versus sport: What's the score? *Australian Journal of Music Education, 1*, 10–15.

Harrison, S. D. (2007). A perennial problem in gendered participation in music: What's happening to the boys? *British Journal of Music Education, 24*(03), 267–280.

Harrison, S. D. (2008). *Masculinities and music: Engaging men and boys in making music.* Newcastle, UK: Cambridge Scholars Publishing.

Haywood, J. (2011). *LGBT self-identity and implications in the emerging music education dialogue.* Paper presented at the Establishing Identity: LGBT Studies & Music Education, Urbana, IL.

Hubbs, N. (2010). *Visibility and ambivalence: Thoughts on queer institutionalization.* Paper presented at the Establishing Identity: LGBT Studies and Music Education, Urbana, IL. http://bcrme.press.illinois.edu/proceedings/Establishing_Identity/16_Hubbs.pdf.

Interactive, H., & GLSEN. (2005). *From teasing to torment: School climate in America.* New York: Gay, Lesbian, and Straight Education Network.

Kosciw, J. G., Greytak, E. A., Bartkiewicz, M. J., Boesen, M. J., Palmer, N. A., Gay, L., et al. (2012). *The 2011 National School Climate Survey: The experiences of lesbian, gay, bisexual and transgender youth in our nation's schools.* New York: Gay, Lesbian and Straight Education Network (GLSEN).

Kosciw, J. G., Greytak, E. A., Palmer, N. A., & Boesen, M. J. (2014). *The 2013 National School Climate Survey: The experiences of lesbian, gay, bisexual and transgender youth in our nation's schools.* New York: Gay, Lesbian & Straight Education Network (GLESN).

Koza, J. E. (1993). The so-called missing-males and other gender issues in music-education: Evidence from the music-supervisors-journal, 1914–1924. *Journal of Research in Music Education, 41*(3), 212–232.

Koza, J. E. (1993–1994). Big boys don't cry (or sing): Gender, misogyny, and homophobia in college choral methods texts. *The Quarterly: Journal of Music Teaching and Learning, 4–5,* 48–64. http://www-usr.rider.edu/~vrme/.

Kumashiro, K. (1999). Supplementing normalcy and otherness: Queer Asian American men reflect on stereotypes, identity, and oppression. *International Journal of Qualitative Studies in Education, 12*(5), 491–508. doi: 10.1080/095183999235917.

Kumashiro, K. (2000). Toward a theory of anti-oppressive education. *Review of Educational Research, 70*(1), 25–53.

Kumashiro, K. (2002). *Troubling education: Queer activism and antioppressive education.* New York: RoutledgeFalmer.

Kumashiro, K. (2004). *Against common sense: Teaching and learning toward social justice.* New York: RoutledgeFalmer.

Kumashiro, K. (2008). *The seduction of common sense: How the right has framed the debate on America's schools. Teaching for social justice.* New York: Teachers College Press.

Kumashiro, K. (2009). *Against common sense: Teaching and learning toward social justice* (2nd ed.). New York: Routledge.

Ladson-Billings, G. (1994). *The dreamkeepers: Successful teachers of African American children* (Vol. 1). San Francisco: Jossey-Bass Publishers.

Lamb, R. (2010). Music as sociocultural phenomenon: Interactions with music education. In H. F. Abeles & L. A. Custodero (Eds.), *Critical issues in music education: Contemporary theory and practice* (pp. 23–38). New York: Oxford University Press.

Lipkin, A. (1999). *Understanding homosexuality, changing schools: A text for teachers, counselors, and administrators.* Boulder, CO: Westview Press.

Luhmann, S. (1998). Queering/querying pedagogy? Or, pedagogy is a pretty queer thing. In W. Pinar (Ed.), *Queer theory in education.* Studies in Curriculum Theory Series (pp. 141–155). Mahwah, NJ: Lawrence Erlbaum Associates.

Macgillivray, I. K. (2004). *Sexual orientation and school policy: A practical guide for teachers, administrators, and community activists.* Lanham, MD: Rowman & Littlefield.

Mayo, C. (2004). Queering school communities: Ethical curiosity and gay-straight alliances. *Journal of Gay & Lesbian Issues in Education, 1*(3), 23–36.

McIntosh, P. (1988). *White privilege and male privilege: A personal account of coming to see correspondences through work in women's studies* (Vol. 189). Wellesley, MA: Wellesley College, Center for Research on Women.

Meyer, E. J. (2010). *Gender and sexual diversity in schools: An introduction* (Vol. 10). Dordrecht: Springer.

Patterson, C. J. (2013). Schooling, sexual orientation, law, and policy: Making schools safe for all students. *Theory into Practice, 52*(3), 190–195.

Pierce, C. M., Carew, J. V., Pierce-Gonzalez, D., & Wills, D. (1977). An experiment in racism: TV commercials. *Education and Urban Society, 10*(1), 61–87.

Pinar, W. F. (1998). *Queer theory in education.* Mahwah, NJ: Lawrence Erlbaum Associates.

Pinar, W. F. (2003). Queer theory in education. *Journal of Homosexuality, 45*(2), 357–400.

Pinar, W. F. (2004). *What is curriculum theory?* Mahwah, NJ: Lawrence Erlbaum Associates.

Rich, A. (1983). Compulsory heterosexuality and lesbian existence. In E. Abel & E. K. Abel (Eds.), *The Signs Reader: Women, Gender and Scholarship* (pp. 139–168).

Robinson, K. H., & Ferfolja, T. (2008). Playing it up, playing it down, playing it safe: Queering teacher education. *Teaching and Teacher Education*, 24(4), 846–858.

Rodriguez, N. M. (1998). (Queer) youth as political and pedagogical. In W. F. Pinar (Ed.), *Queer theory in education* (pp. 173–185). Mahwah, NJ: Lawrence Erlbaum Associates.

Rodriguez, N. M., & Pinar, W. F. (2007). *Queering straight teachers: Discourse and identity in education* (Vol. 22). New York: Peter Lang.

Sadurski, W. (1984). Social justice and legal justice. *Law and Philosophy*, 3(3), 329–354.

Spano, F. P. (2011). The inclusion of sexuality topics in undergraduate music teacher preparation programs. *Bulletin of the Council for Research in Music Education. Special issue: Conference Proceedings: Establishing Identity: LGBT Studies & Music Education*, 189, 45–50.

Spano, F. P. (2012). *Preservice music teachers' perceptions of LGBTQ topics*. Paper presented at the National Association for Music Education 2012 Conference, St. Louis, MO.

Steinberg, S. R., & Kincheloe, J. (2009). More than one way to be diverse and multicultural *Diversity and multiculturalism: A reader*. New York: Peter Lang.

Swearer, S. M., Turner, R. K., Givens, J. E., & Pollack, W. S. (2008). "You're so gay!": Do different forms of bullying matter for adolescent males? *School Psychology Review*, 37(2), 160.

Sweet, B., & Paparo, S. A. (2011). *Starting the conversation in music teacher education programs*. Paper presented at the Establishing Identity: LGBT studies and music education, Urbana, IL.

Szalacha, L. A. (2004). Educating teachers on LGBTQ issues: A review of research and program evaluations. *Journal of Gay & Lesbian Issues in Education*, 1(4), 67–79.

Tierney, W. G., & Dilley, P. (1998). Constructing knowledge: Educational research and gay and lesbian studies. In W. F. Pinar (Ed.), *Queer theory in education* (pp. 1190–1812). Mahwah, NJ: Lawrence Erlbaum Associates.

Wickens, C. M., & Sandlin, J. A. (2010). Homophobia and heterosexism in a college of education: A culture of fear, a culture of silence. *International Journal of Qualitative Studies in Education*, 23(6), 651–670.

Young, I. M. (1990). Five faces of oppression *Justice and politics of difference* (pp. 39–45). Princeton, NJ: Princeton University Press.

CHAPTER 15

BEYOND TOLERATION—FACING THE OTHER

RICHARD MATTHEWS

Music education is far more ambiguous morally than might be thought. In a culture marked by privilege and oppression, it cannot be otherwise. In systems of oppression, the institutions, practices, character, and lives of all are unjustly distorted. All participants are, as Lisa Tessman (2005) notes, morally damaged (p. 4). In music, generally, this means that, unless they are self-critical, educators, musicians, and producers perpetuate and intensify oppression.

This can take the form of overt violence, as in the use of music to torture through sensory overload and sleep deprivation. It was used in this way in the torture of Abu Zubaydah by the CIA (International Committee of the Red Cross, 2007, p. 15). But the violence in music education is not of this sort. It is subtler, slower, and more covert, though not necessarily less devastating. Such violence is structural rather than intentional (Galtung, 2009, pp. 83–84). It is generated by unfair economics, social norms, prejudices, behaviors, and the habits of populations in their interactions. Music education often plays an important role in structural violence through the marginalization and exploitation of vulnerable populations. The authors of this section on reclaiming difference in music education provide some compelling examples:

- The Eurocentric focus on classical music excludes alternative musical traditions (Bradley, Chapter 12; Kelly-McHale and Abril, Chapter 10)
- The commodification of the traditional New Orleans jazz funeral and marginalization of the living New Orleans tradition (Gould, Chapter 9)
- The marginalization of LGBTQ youth (Bergonzi, Chapter 14)
- The erasure of considerations of ability, class, race, age, and gender (Darrow, Chapter 13; Lamb and Dhokai, Chapter 8).

These are serious problems, since they wreck educational outcomes for vulnerable populations. Yet, the tone of this section is not solely critical. These insightful authors also remind us that music education offers terrific potential as a site of resistance and social transformation. Understanding, navigating, and transforming these tense relations between oppression and opportunity are the fundamental goals of these chapters.

Privilege and Oppression

Privilege and oppression are concerned with socially organized power relations that benefit specific groups while disadvantaging others. The benefits of the privileged and the disadvantages of the oppressed are unearned (McIntosh, 1990). That is, they are not a function of individual choice, genetic variation, or character. They are matters of social and institutional organization that manifest in rules, behaviors, economic practices, and attitudes which produce the relevant advantages and disadvantages, regardless of the specific choices of individuals.

The impacts vary enormously, profoundly shaping the lives of all impacted individuals. They always work to the benefit of privileged groups and to the harm of the oppressed. They impact architecture, as in the ways that ableist building design makes both public and private institutions inaccessible to people with "disabilities." They impact employment, as stigmas concerning class, ability, race, gender, or age both consciously and unconsciously shape hiring and promotion practices. In music, privilege determines whose music gets heard, who gets to create and participate in it, and whose music is excluded. It also determines which traditions count as musical.

Iris Young (1990) famously organized oppression along five lines or "faces." These include (1) exploitation—the transfer of the energies of the oppressed group(s) for the benefit of the privileged; (2) marginalization—where a social or economic system creates classes of people that it simply will not use; (3) powerlessness—in which social institutions assign roles to certain classes of people that drastically diminish or prevent the exercise of creativity and autonomy; (4) cultural imperialism—in which a dominant group seeks to colonize the consciousness of both dominant and subordinate group members so that the behavior of the privileged group supports privilege, and the behavior of the oppressed group supports the privileged; and finally, (5) violence (and, importantly, its terror)—in which group disciplinary techniques ensure subordinate group subservience and guarantee dominant group members' conformity.

These faces mutually influence one another. Cultural imperialism, for example, works to create beliefs in the "legitimacy" of exploitation. This is essential for ensuring that people accept their work, roles, and social positions. For instance, when successful, it justifies, in the minds of both the dominant and the oppressed, the marginalization and powerlessness of people with disabilities or of the homeless. Cultural imperialism, thus, generates "poor bashing" (Swanson, 2001)—the false belief that the homeless lack shelter because of character defects, bad choices, or other individual failings.

Music educators are just as implicated in structural violence as anyone else, for it resides in their prejudices, in the way in which they see the world, and in the classifications that they impose on their students. This presents difficult challenges of which educators may be wholly unaware. It is conceptually easier for an educator to react to an overt act of violence. The teacher can theoretically intervene and stop it. But the structural violence of oppression is typically invisible. It is rooted in the tacit violence and the social psychology of groups. For social justice–oriented music educators, the real challenge is to locate one's own violence and aggression, to identify and transform the often hidden prejudices that arise from what Judith Butler calls "the violence of our own identity formation" (Butler, 2009, p. 172). We choose neither the processes that shape our identities nor our prejudices. These are formed in early childhood and we have no say. They contain all of the seeds of aggression—racist, sexist, ageist, ableist, heterosexist, and classist—that generate the violence we recognize. The creation of an inclusive music classroom requires that music educators critically engage with their prejudices. It is thus a matter of reflexivity.

Reflexivity, generally speaking, is "a turning back on oneself, a form of self-awareness" (Lawson, 1985, p. 9). It is particularly pressing in moral and political philosophy and in its social justice implications. In this political sense, reflexivity requires agents to examine the social, political, and economic conditions of knowledge and choice to determine how these impact and distort important moral life and goals. Using Michael Lynch's (2000, p. 31) classification, this is a form of "standpoint reflexivity," in which agents apply moral and political critique to themselves and their practices.

Privilege and Oppression in Music Education

The failure to be self-critical has profound, direct, and harsh consequences. As these authors show, how educators understand their world profoundly shapes the classroom. Where they have internalized privilege, they harm the oppressed among their students. The failure to reflexively explore questions of privilege and oppression guarantees its perpetuation. If we fail to engage the violence in ourselves, we perpetuate that violence in others. If I, as an educator, do not attend to my own sexism, I will act in sexist ways and thereby disadvantage my female students. Often I will do so while believing that I act for the best. The same goes for any prejudices I bear with respect to ability, race, age, sexuality, and class.

Ableism in Music Education

Alice-Ann Darrow's Chapter 13 on ableism is the appropriate place to begin a consideration of privilege and oppression in music education for at least two reasons. First, as disability studies scholar Gregor Wolbring (2008) argues, ableism is in fact the umbrella term for all oppression (p. 253). He notes that the dominance of privileged groups is invariably defended on grounds of alleged ability—for example, middle-class and wealthy individuals are held to be smarter and have superior character to the "lazy" and "conniving" poor, the elderly are held to be incompetent, racial others are allegedly less intelligent, women are too emotional, and so on. The second reason is that those whom we classically designate as "disabled"—the mentally ill, those with specific physical challenges such as cerebral palsy, or other conditions—are the most marginalized. They have the highest poverty rates, experience greater amounts of homelessness, are the most exposed to violence, and are the most forgotten about in civic planning, such as in disaster relief. In music education they are the least likely to be included or considered in performance or classroom.

As Darrow notes, ableism is the tendency of able-bodied people to privilege themselves and disadvantage the disabled. In ableist practice, the institutions that ground social practice advantage those with a preferred ability set. It stigmatizes other abilities as deficient and ultimately generates marginalization, along with physical and psychological abuse.

Ableism manifests itself in music education in many ways. Disabled students are at much higher risk of physical and psychological bullying. "Abled" people are more likely to maintain greater distance and to conduct abbreviated conversations with those whom they perceive to be disabled. This results in reduced opportunities for socialization, friendship, and group activities. Policymakers often segregate disabled students. Buildings and programs are often inaccessible, and disability stigmas lead to significantly reduced cultural, recreational, and employment opportunities. The consequences of these prejudices in students' lives are enormous and include poor academic performance, depression, absenteeism, anxiety, and suicide.

As Darrow powerfully shows, this is publicly supported marginalization. Educators routinely justify the diversion of resources to abled students on grounds of cost-effectiveness. They believe that more people benefit and higher educational outcomes will be achieved if limited resources are directed to the able-bodied. Yet, this is precisely the justification for their marginalization. It ignores the uniqueness and individuality of students and denies them opportunity on the basis of cultural stigma about their alleged incapacities. They thereby lose access to core conditions of a decent life: friendship, other social opportunities, and participation in vital aesthetic activities.

Gender Oppression in Music Education

Female musicians and music educators are routinely stigmatized in ways that support Wolbring's analysis of disability. In the case of women, the stigmas have a long historical grounding in the alleged emotionality and irrationality of women. Women, the stigma supposes, are physically and cognitively weaker than men. Although this is biological nonsense, in Chapter 8, Roberta Lamb and Niyati Dhokai note its considerable impacts.

For example, female music education scholars are routinely forgotten and their research contributions overlooked or ignored. As a result, female scholars are commonly ignored in scholarly books and journals. Lamb and Dhokai maintain that feminist music scholars as recent as the mid-1990s were not discussed or taught in music education. Their work tends to be forgotten and ignored, and the opportunity to use their insights to transform gender oppression in music education is lost. Wasted effort and marginalization are the results.

Violence, in the form of overt and tacit threats, plays a prominent role in the marginalization of feminist music scholars. Lamb describes how feminist music education scholars were warned that they would be unable to succeed if they pursued a feminist research focus. Stigmas about feminist research meant that articles were not accepted in elite music education journals. This, in turn, created the illusion that their work was insignificant. Male music educators received correspondingly greater attention, and the work of feminists was minimized. The result was that the threats were carried out: feminist scholars were denied access to tenure and promotion. Significantly, the same cost-benefit arguments that marginalize the "disabled" are used to justify diversion of limited financial, institutional, and logistical resources away from feminist music education research. As a result, talented scholars either lose their jobs or never get hired in the first place.

This exclusion profoundly contributes to oppression by eliminating socially critical voices from music education. Policymakers and educators lose access to crucial institutional and moral insights. As a result, they perpetuate male privilege. One set of consequences that Lamb and Dhokai show is weak, ineffectual, or nonexistent policies on sexual harassment and gender violence. This increases the risk of exposure of female students to violence at the hands of both music educators and other students.

The impacts extend beyond the music education classroom. Masculinist bias in music education contributes strongly to the exclusion of women from professional music environments—for example, the absence of female conductors of orchestras and major international bands. Tellingly, Lamb and Dhokai cite the conductor of the Oslo Philharmonic Orchestra, who said that women are "too emotional" and that their sexuality would adversely impact the discipline of the orchestra. It did not seem to occur to him that, as a privileged male, the obligation lies with him and his sexist colleagues to transform their misogynist behavior. He did not get those beliefs from nowhere; he acquired them as a result of both formal and informal education in a misogynist music culture. Such male bias is a major reason that women are rarely taken seriously for such empowered musical roles.

Racism in Music Education

While racism takes many forms and can be directed at diverse groups that share little culturally or historically, the dominant privileged group is the "White" population. As Deborah Bradley notes in Chapter 12, race is not a biological category and has no meaningful genetic or other scientific foundation. Rather, it is a social identity assigned to privileged and oppressed group members along ethnic or other lines. "Whiteness" and the various stigmatized designations assigned to oppressed groups are social classifications aimed at producing benefits for a dominant group through the exploitation of oppressed groups. They are performative categories whose success depends on both the privileged and oppressed internalizing the relevant norms and beliefs.

The maintenance of privilege and oppression depends upon complex and often violent forms of in-group and out-group disciplining. Where privilege is really effective, violence is only occasionally employed. The greatest successes come from the successful spreading of Foucauldian disciplinary strategies, which shape the self-understandings of privileged members so that their beliefs work to their advantage and where the self-understanding of oppressed group members also benefits the privileged. As Marilyn Frye (1983) argues, this creates a double bind for oppressed group members in which disadvantages obtain no matter their choices or character. Simultaneously, it ensures that the privileged always benefit, again no matter their choices or character.

A powerful way in which White privilege manifests itself is in ignorance about the lives and musical traditions of non-White populations. Bradley notes that privileged groups tend to see their lives as normative. Unless they make considerable effort, they fail to see the very different lives experienced by others and do not see how their privilege is dependent on the oppression of others. The privileged can, if they wish, avoid exposure to the realities of the oppressed. For the oppressed, this is not true. So White privileged music educators can expose themselves only to their preferred musical traditions and can comfortably teach them, while knowing that they will be socially, economically, and institutionally supported. White privileged music students also gain these benefits. But, as Gould and Kelly-McHale and Abril remind us, this is not true for African-American or Latino educators and students. If they wish to explore music in educational institutions, they have no choice but to work with the dominant traditions and routinely have little or no institutional access to the richness and resources of their own traditions.

Unreflective music educators privilege their musical traditions, believing them to be universal and transcendent. Yet musical traditions are historically specific evolutionary phenomena, and different cultures have generated unique musical experiments. In privileging Eurocentric music, educators and scholars either assimilate other musical traditions as subordinate forms of the dominant tradition or denigrate them outright. When this happens, music education becomes a vehicle for Anglo-European cultural hegemony and musical dominance.

The impacts of privilege on music education extend beyond the classroom and into economic life. Commodification in music involves transforming music from a living and vital expression of the cultural life of a specific community and turning it into a thing that, as Marx (1867) describes it, has only an exchange value. It becomes something to be possessed, bought, and sold by those who can afford it (p. 59). The artists who produce it do so, not because of its relationship to a living cultural tradition, but because of their subordination to dominant elites who desire their products. Its value comes to be defined by the willingness of a purchaser to buy it, rather than because of any intrinsic value for a given cultural group. The market determines both what is produced and its mode of production. The music's value is leveled, defined in terms of anything that might be given in exchange for it. And, since the market is dominated by the economically privileged, class interests determine what gets rewarded, recognized, and promoted.

Elizabeth Gould explores this in detail in Chapter 9, arguing that when we consider that the purchasers of commodified music do not visit with, get to know, or otherwise engage with the oppressed communities who produce the music, the extent of the exploitation becomes clearer. The artists are alienated labor whose primary purpose is to produce for the pleasure of privileged elites. Musical traditions are raw materials for transformation and consumption, not living embodiments of human resilience and spirit. Gould's example of the traditional New Orleans jazz band is particularly valuable in this regard. She argues that they disappeared 40 years ago because they had become irrelevant and audiences had decreased. Nonetheless, the traditional jazz funeral is propped up and kept alive by documentarians, ethnomusicologists, and tourists. They exploit the locals, as class-oppressed individuals participate in commodified practices in order to earn some cash and alleviate some of the extreme racism and poverty that they experience. Gould's assessment of the behavior of ethnomusicologists is particularly pertinent here. In studying the jazz funeral tradition, she maintains that they typically refuse to visit and engage with the African-American communities upon whom they depend for their careers and benefits. They miss the opportunity to promote greater interaction and mutual group understanding and, instead, entrench social distance, privilege, and ignorance of the musical strength and vitality of those communities.

LGBTQ Oppression in Music Education

While they share many problems in common with the aforementioned oppressed groups, LGBTQ educators and students face a unique set of barriers. In Chapter 14, Louis Bergonzi outlines four specific misconceptions that generate oppression for the LGBTQ community.

One common error is to understand the complexity of LGBTQ experience in terms of male same-sex relationships. While there is no question that homosexual males experience a wide range of gender disadvantages, their situations are quite different from the oppression experienced by lesbians, bisexuals, male-to-female transsexuals, female-to-male transsexuals, and other queer identities. Indeed, each identity is unique, and the stigma and harms assigned to it by heteronormatively dominant groups vary. Music educators have to appreciate this uniqueness or be complicit in their oppression. So to classify LGBTQ in terms of homosexuality oppression is, ironically, to impose a subtle male privilege on a range of cultural groups who do not fit that identity and thus further intensifies their oppression.

Second, the widespread prejudice that educators do not need to learn about LGBTQ issues promotes LGBTQ oppression by ensuring that educators fail to confront and transform their prejudices. They are therefore denied the opportunity to identify and understand their prejudices toward LGBTQ individuals and thus are not able to see how sometimes tacit beliefs harmfully shape their interactions with their students and colleagues. At best, they are insensitive to the unique needs and situations of LGBTQ individuals, and, at worst, they actively stigmatize and harm them. Either way, the educator promotes LGBTQ oppression in the classroom.

Third is the belief that LGBTQ education should not be taught in schools because it is perceived to be too harmful or too controversial. Violence and damage are unavoidable here because what children are supposed to be protected from is the identity, and hence the very being, of LGBTQ persons. They are understood to be harmful by nature. In perceiving the LGBTQ community as a threat, a core condition for violence against them is satisfied. This marginalizes LGBTQ students and excludes LGBTQ role models from the classroom, in spite of the many ways in which such individuals have importantly influenced music. It also violates the alternative developing sexualities of LGBTQ children by denying them the opportunity to explore and understand their unique human natures.

Finally, Bergonzi identifies the belief that LGBTQ music education is offensive to specific religious or cultural beliefs. This is also a fear-driven response and ensures the infliction of harm. Given the extremity of the oppression of LGBTQ individuals and their exclusion from a wide variety of cultural spaces including, for example, washrooms and sporting events, the choice to exclude the LGBTQ community has considerable impact.

CONSEQUENCES OF OPPRESSION

If educators fail to consider privilege, the following are probable consequences:

- The exclusion and marginalization of students from oppressed groups. For instance, with racialized groups, their music is not represented and their interests are left unexplored in the classroom. One consequences is significantly reduced participation due to boredom and the irrelevance of the subject matter.
- Where students stay, they may develop a specific colonized consciousness, in this case the development of beliefs about the normativity and superiority of Eurocentric music. This carries with it negative evaluations of their musical traditions.

Jacqueline Kelly-McHale and Carlos Abril, in Chapter 10, note additional consequences. For example, alternative music programs have a much more difficult time getting the necessary financial and logistical resources. Fewer teachers emerge from oppressed groups, with the resulting absence of positive role models further reducing student participation. Furthermore, when privileged educators and students stigmatize out-group members, they judge these to be less able, thereby further harming the music education environment. Specific physiological and psychological harms ensue.

CRITICAL REFLECTIONS

Discussions of privilege commonly generate defensiveness among listeners, in part because of the failure to understand the difference between systemic and individual violence. A standard position is that violence should only be understood in terms of the interpersonal acts of force that produce some physical injury (Coady, 2009, p. 245). This makes individual intentions central to the moral evaluation of behavior. Defensiveness then arises when educators note their lack of intention to harm. Indeed, they will often honestly (if un-self-critically) point to their good intentions in order to deny their complicity. While intentions matter in some contexts, overemphasis on intention and choice conceals the ways in which unexamined prejudices and harmful institutional and social conditions make violence possible. For systemic violence concerns how groups organize themselves in relation to others, and this is not identical to individual acts of violence, however much the two levels interplay. Most violence occurs as a consequence of the internalization of prejudices, stigmas, and stereotypes. In-groups construct institutions, norms, and practices in ways that advantage some groups and disadvantage others. These disadvantages concretely damage the lives of others.

Oppression and privilege are modes of organization of systemic violence, and they profoundly shape human possibility. If the goal of education is to empower students, to help them achieve their potential as human beings, and to support their flourishing, then the presence of oppression is proof, among others things, of massive educational failure. The failure is rooted in the hearts and minds of the educator and the dominant culture. If the goal of music education is to produce an inclusive classroom, then the non-reflexive behavior of the decent educator is a significant obstacle. Well-meaning and skilled music educators undermine their goals through their failure to understand their prejudices and institutional biases. As an example, the segregation of music classes for children and students with disabilities will reduce, if not eliminate, the dialogical interaction between groups. This in turn damages the essential empathic relationships necessary for decent social relations and ensures the development of stigma.

In order to produce an inclusive classroom, the educator must attend to oppression. The challenges are intensified when we realize that the lives of educators and students are marked by multiple privilege and oppression markers. Most people get some privilege and some oppression. A female Latin-American music student may be marked by disability oppression. Here she suffers from female, race, and ability disadvantage. Yet she may also come from a middle-class or wealthy background, and, to that extent, experiences class privilege. An economically oppressed male, homosexual, African-American student gets some of the benefits of male privilege and yet suffers from class, LGBTQ, and race oppression. To help such students to flourish, educators need to recognize the unique particularities that characterize individual life—a complicated task.

Mab Segrest (2012) reminds us that intersectionality matters for resistance as well, since oppressed group members internalize many of the same violent beliefs and assumptions. They are just as capable of being racist, sexist, heteronormative, or of bearing any other stigmatizing prejudice. This creates divisions among oppressed groups, which undermines effective resistance. Indeed, the consequences can be fatal (p. 216). For example, LGBTQ individuals may be racist, and racialized others may be heteronormative. This generates violence and suffering, as gay bashing and murder, along with other violence, follow quickly. Intersectionality matters for resistance within oppressed groups, as well as for effective socially just interactions between privileged and oppressed group members.

To reduce privilege in music education, decentering of the classical music tradition is necessary. Decentering, however, is not the denial of its beauty and extraordinary creativity. The point is to provide educators and students with the opportunity and the courage to explore multiple musical traditions and to promote the love, curiosity, and celebration of the diversity of music. What is wonderful here is that everyone benefits. The oppressed are not the only winners of reflexive musical education. For example, in unreflexive classrooms, privileged music educators and students fail to encounter the richness and extraordinary diversity of musical traditions and thus experience diminished personal growth and an impoverished education—all masked ironically by the false belief that they are receiving the best education.

Of course, as these authors indicate, there are risks. The privileged educator may commodify the music of others or misrepresent it. There are also risks of error and of inadvertent cultural appropriation. The music educator may be exposed to public criticism, ridicule, embarrassment, and other disciplinary tactics. But it is worse to refuse to dialogically explore the different musical traditions. The risks need to be taken. Refusal guarantees that music educators perpetuate oppression in music. Risk taking is necessary, and carries with it a burden powerfully articulated by Cornel West (2012)　the necessity of suffering to transform socially unjust structures. This need for risk taking is evident in the chapters of this section—for example, in Bradley's critique in Chapter 12 of educators' fears of being seen as "inauthentic" in their presentation of other musical traditions.

Finally, we are not condemned to oppression. Privilege systems are sets of human socioeconomic and cultural possibilities, but they can and do change when intelligent and passionate risk takers commit to doing so. It is here that Kathryn Marsh's Chapter 11 deserves special regard. She provides an example of the powerful role that music can play in transforming oppression while reminding us of the resilience of her subject community. Marsh's essay is an excellent account of one impressive experiment in resistance against privilege—the struggle to help West African refugees to integrate and flourish in Sydney, Australia. It displays many of the virtues described elsewhere in this section: for example, the importance of paying attention to the cultural differences in dance style displayed through "Sia's" improvisations and the choreography of the Sensational Sisters. Marsh is careful to attend to the physiological and psychological trauma that commonly influences the life experiences of refugees and to ensure that her research does not negatively impact them. Her research methodology is dialogical rather than authoritarian, prioritizing the subjectivity of her group.

Music and dance have had profoundly positive effects in this particular case, including, among others, improved self-esteem, the capacity to plan and look forward to a healthy and better life, community, creativity and individual courage, the capacity to work together and share labor, and independence. It has also fostered cultural interaction among discrete African groups and reminds us that every music education environment offers genuine opportunities for important social transformation.

Marsh's work reminds us of a particularly important section from Gould's chapter. As noted, oppression stigmas typically characterize subordinated groups in terms of their weakness and incapacity. Yet careful observation and interaction with oppressed group members show extraordinary resilience, not incapacity. For resistance is omnipresent in all oppression. Gould describes how the locals at New Orleans musical funerals carefully restrict what is shown to outsiders and practice their living musical traditions away from the gaze of privileged elites. The jazz funeral tradition has evolved and remains vibrant but is very different from the commodified displays available to tourists and most ethnomusicographers. It fuses the older funk-brass musical traditions with hip-hop and other more modern and youth-relevant musical developments. The second line brass band funeral is a musical appropriation of public space and thus an act of resistance and occupation of place that, under other circumstances, might be denied the participants. In particular, these funerals are often "expressions of communal outrage" over the men and women who die from violence in drug wars and thus are a direct response to oppression. They make explicit reference to the socioeconomic and racial context in which the murders and violent deaths take place and thus contribute to national (and international) understanding of, and resistance to, race oppression. There is love, creativity, courage, and genius at work here, not incapacity.

Music education is not condemned to replicating oppression, but is in a powerful position to aid in the promotion of socially just states of affairs. This takes work and courage on the part of music educators, but it is perfectly achievable.

References

Butler, J. (2009). The claim of nonviolence. In J. Butler (Ed.), *Frames of war: When is life grievable?* (pp. 165–184). London: Verso.

Coady, C. A. J. (2009). The idea of violence. In V. Buffachi (Ed.), *Violence: A philosophical anthology* (pp. 244–266). London: Palgrave MacMillan.

Frye, M. (1983). *The politics of reality: Essays in feminist theory.* Trumansburg, NY: Crossing Press.

Galtung, J. (2009). Violence, peace and peace research. In V. Buffachi (Ed.), *Violence: A philosophical anthology* (pp. 78–111). London: Palgrave MacMillan.

International Committee of the Red Cross. (2007). *ICRC Report on the treatment of fourteen "high value detainees" in CIA custody.* Washington, DC: International Committee of the Red Cross.

Lawson, H. (1985). *Reflexivity: The postmodern predicament.* London: Hutchinson.

Lynch, M. (2000). Against reflexivity as an academic virtue and source of privileged insight. *Theory, Culture and Society, 17*(3), 26–54.

Marx, K. (1867). *Capital: A critique of political economy*, Volume 1. Translated by Samuel Moore and Edward Aveling. Moscow: Progress Publishers. http://www.marxists.org/archive/marx/works/1867-c1/ch01.htm.

McIntosh, P. (1990). White privilege: Unpacking the invisible knapsack. *Independent School, 49*(2), 31–36.

Segrest, M. (2012). On being white and other lies: A history of racism in the United States. In E. B. Martinez, M. Meyer, & M. Carter (Eds.), *We have not been moved: Resisting racism and militarism in 21st century America* (pp. 214–225). Oakland, CA: PM Press.

Swanson, J. (2001). *Poor-bashing: The politics of exclusion*. Toronto: Between the Lines.

Tessman, L. (2005). *Burdened virtues: Ethics for liberatory struggles*. Oxford: Oxford University Press.

West, C. (2012). King's truth: Revolution and America's crossroads. In E. B. Martinez, M. Meyer, & M. Carter (Eds.), *We have not been moved: Resisting racism and militarism in 21st century America* (p. xvii). Oakland, CA: PM Press.

Wolbring, G. (2008). The politics of ableism. *Development, 51*, 252–258.

Young, I. (1990). *Justice and the politics of difference*. Princeton, NJ: Princeton University Press.

SECTION III

EPISTEMOLOGICAL SHIFTS AND JUST PRACTICES

INTRODUCTION

Socializing the Value of Equity

PATRICK SCHMIDT, SECTION EDITOR

WHEN considering the notion of epistemology, we reflect upon all that surrounds what we have come to understand as knowledge. Epistemology, in simple terms, has to do with how and why we think what we think, and consequently, with the lenses we use, or are given, to see the world. Considering social justice from an epistemological stance is essential then, for even in the act of naming the term we are immediately and already "loading" it with particular assumptions, populating it with experiences, and naturally, excluding possible visions. As we also know well, unspoken ideas and undisputed concepts tend to fade or are co-opted and made commonsensical. Thus, a more complex understanding of social justice within the field of music education requires that we pause and contemplate epistemological positions and challenges imbued within social justice framings. This goal is central to the subsequent 10 chapters that the reader will encounter here.

This section of the *Handbook for Social Justice in Music Education* then emphasizes the ways in which we come to make sense of social justice, as well as how "common senses" can vary according to standpoint and can change over time. Furthermore, the chapters in this section investigate epistemological shifts, emphasizing their practical as well as conceptual manifestations, and thus helping the reader to arrive at his or her own evaluation—and perhaps a new valuation—of this ideal.

In Chapter 16, Cathy Benedict challenges us to consider that social justice in music education should not be simply strategized or "taught" in a direct and didactic way. Using the work of Hannah Arendt to support her claims, she proposes that social justice starts and exists in "a space of appearance," that is, those unplanned moments where we interact with others—and *the* Other. These are the moments when our actions are *not* led by preconceived strategies, but rather are guided by careful listening. The parallels to music are many, from improvisation to active listening to spontaneous musical learning spaces, but the implications go beyond change in pedagogy. To be sure, valuing open moments of interaction where we are challenged to personally and musically acknowledge and engage with others is a much-needed area of exploration, particularly at a time of global conservative encroachment in education. Further, the possibility of finding social justice in the near poetic moment of interaction—rather than in rhetorical replication of platitudes determined by political correctness or polite interaction—is a humanist endeavor that continues to challenge all of us.

Chapter 17, written by Patricia S. Campbell and Christopher Roberts, explores the historical and curricular relations between *multiculturalism* and social justice. Focusing on a North American view, the authors trace several of the overlapping epistemological and political roots between these two areas. Their chapter uses the work of pioneering educationist James Banks—particularly his levels of curriculum reform model—to provide insight on the formation of "more equitable classroom environments." Gary Spruce, one of the co-editors of this Handbook, also combines traditions, exploring social justice from the standpoint of *student voice* in Chapter 18. His epistemological framing brings attention to the rather underdeveloped focus that music education scholarship has placed on student voice. Spruce makes a particularly important distinction by pressing the need for an education in and through music that is not simply open for "participation," but most significantly, accounts for student voice to be included in systematic processes of "construction of musical knowledge, understanding and value." Inclusion is not, however, all that Spruce has in mind, as his framing posits that the potential in student voice—as a practice and manifestation of social justice—is that it can be the venue for possible disruption to powerful hegemonies, impacting the formation of more democratic spaces that "remain largely unfulfilled."

In Chapter 19, Lucy Green and Flávia Narita place the issue of informality in relationship to social justice. They use the work of Nancy Fraser to establish the need for educational politics that attend to both *redistribution* and *recognition,* which can only be achieved, they suggest, by establishing a "parity of participation" where "members of a social context interact with each other as peers." They explore the practical implications of such ideas by highlighting cases collected from an empirical study developed in Brazil. Here, we can see epistemological echoes of similar concerns to those expressed by all the authors mentioned earlier. Green and Narita push forward by focusing on the dialogical aspects of this process and their manifestations through *informal learning approaches.*

Subsequent chapters are quite unique in their approach, as they cleverly and profoundly trouble two important traditions in music education. The authors provide new ways of looking at them, while keeping their focus on socially justice practices. Panagiotis Kanellopoulos, in Chapter 20, addresses the issue of "children's creative acts," while Sidsel Karlsen and Heidi Westerlund, in Chapter 23, argue that multiculturality as the cultivation of "historically justified, authentic musical practices in the classroom is inadequate as the single guiding approach to teaching music today." Kanelopoulos is concerned with the reach of modernist ideals within music education and the co-optation of creativity into a tool for conformity and linearity—what he calls "borrowing from Ranciere," *the police.* Karlsen and Westerlund use Bauman to present the idea that the multiculturality of twenty-first-century youth is *fluid,* and not constituted through geographic boundaries. They join Bauman in proposing that the past century's fight for cultural space—which often constructed ideas of social justice—is being rapidly replaced by a concern with multiple identities, which, they argue, are constantly shifting via personal and mostly virtual interaction. Both epistemological approaches are fresh, and both challenge directly a significant part of the music education literature of the last 40 years.

Ruth Wright, in Chapter 21, uses Pierre Bourdieu to explore social reproduction and inequality, suggesting that "providing students with opportunities to engage in more democratic forms of music pedagogy might help develop cultural resources more evenly across student populations, resulting in wider social inclusion in music and applying a small point of pressure for larger social change." In Chapter 22, Pamela Burnard and her cowritters, Laura Hassler, Lis Murphy, and Otto de Jong, approach the issue of social justice from the lens of interculturality, while using the very practical realities developed by Musicians without Borders as a central point of pragmatic reference. They do so with the intent to show the need to adapt what we currently consider—and at times take for granted—to be creative practices in music education. They suggest that we must mobilize and manipulate diverse creativities as "a means to create a mutual reciprocity of needs and respect." Susan O'Neill, in Chapter 24, also cautions against established and uncritical stances and practices, and how they may, and do, act as "inflections of power" that "reproduce cycles of subordination." Particularly challenging is the fact, she argues, that "controlling and manipulative educational environments have a negative impact on young people's motivation to learn and engagement during learning." What to do then? What she offers is a substantially epistemological approach where "through appreciative and dialogical inquiry, young people are encouraged to *see things differently*. In doing so, they become capable of gaining new insights, overcoming challenges and constraints, and taking positive actions to bring about personal and social transformation."

Last, but certainly not least, is Chapter 25, which closes this section. Gloria Ladson-Billings is a staple of the social justice literature in education in the United States as well as in the world. Her work and research on inequality and race are not only pioneering but also exemplary. It is then a pleasure to have Ladson-Billings as part of this collection, speaking of music, in specific hip-hop, and its historical groundings on social justice issues. Her analysis leads us into the well-known notion of *culturally relevant pedagogies*, but does so by inviting us to consider how the interactive-heavy structure of hip-hop can teach us about educative and musical pedagogical practices that may be pertinent to all learning environments.

I end as I began, pondering not simply on the origin and trajectory of what we know—or *think we know*, to borrow from Benedict's title—about social justice and music education, but also about the epistemological spaces that seem to be most meaningful or most clearly available for our practices today. In this process I find myself puzzled by the fact that, in one way or another, all 10 chapters, written by diverse authors practicing in different corners of the world, seem to value the pressing need of interaction as a central piece for learning social justice, learning through socially just practices, and learning in and by enacting socially just environs. The encounters that emerge within and between these chapters not only provide a wealth of epistemological views on social justice but also seem to offer a concerted direction that might be a new frontier for music education work. The ideas and propositions therein re-establish a balance between a positivist educational structure overly concerned with content, delivery, and management, and humanistic ideals where interaction and voice can lead us to understand ourselves, music, and the Other in more compelling and profound ways.

CHAPTER 16

WHAT DO WE *THINK* WE KNOW?

CATHY BENEDICT

To preserve the world against the mortality of its creators and inhabitants it must be constantly set right anew. The problem is simply to educate in such a way that a setting-right remains actually possible, even though it can, of course, never be assured. Our hope always hangs in the new that every generation brings; but precisely because we can base our hope only on this, we destroy everything if we so try to control the new that we, the old, can dictate how it will look. Exactly for the sake of what is new and revolutionary in every child, education must be conservative; it must preserve this newness and introduce it as a new thing into an old world, which, however revolutionary its actions may be, is always, from the standpoint of the next generation, superannuated and close to destruction. (Arendt, 1958, pp. 192–193)

IN the above passage, from *Crisis in Education,* Hannah Arendt urges us to recognize our responsibility as teachers to set the world anew. This is a complicated passage. It may seem that Arendt is asking us to conserve the past, to insert the child in ways that preserve all that has come before. It might even seem that Arendt is asking us to be "conservative" teachers. Indeed, as one "reads" Arendt, it is all these things and none of these things. In this instance, though, it is the newness we each bring into the world that must be conserved if the world is to be set anew. Any attempt to control action then, or any appearance of a space where each of us retains our distinctness so that we may "communicate" ourselves (p. 176), destroys the very possibility of newness.

Arendt believes that we distinguish ourselves, our distinctness, through speech and action. We can only do this with others, in the plurality of all others, and in doing so our distinctness changes. Plurality, for Arendt, is "*the* condition" (1958, p. 7, italics in original) for action to take place. To control is to mediate and disrupt plurality, to close the space for miracles of "startling unexpectedness" (p. 178), or acts we cannot predict. To control is to assume we know or have met before the person in front of us, eradicating all possibilities of the new entering the world. And if we do this, as Levinson (1997) warns, these assumptions we make with strangers "render[s] . . . this 'other,' much less other" (p. 440). In other words, we have had experiences with this "type" of person before, we don't need to bother, we already know.

For Arendt, and her conception of the human condition, action, then, is the space of freedom. There is no ends-means articulation; there is no preparation or developmental path to some moment in the future. In order to make something new together, without foregone conclusions and expectations, freedom is the condition of "acting out together" (Arendt, 1958, p. 198) without the interruption or mediation of things. Action, however, is only part of the human condition; our human activities also constitute labor and work. Labor is the production and consumption of that which satisfies our biological needs; there is no definable beginning or end, as labor is connected to life-sustaining processes. Work, on the other hand, has a predictable beginning and end; it is that which gives durability to the world. What is fashioned by work can be consumed; products "become means again" (p. 143), dictated by purposeful and objective ends. It is this instrumentality of both work and labor, in which "aims and ends . . . are external to the activity" (Biesta, 2010a, p. 559) that underscores the problematics of the preparation or production of socially just citizens. The educational question for this chapter, then, is *not* how to best prepare or produce a student to be socially just; rather, through a pedagogy of recognition, how can we facilitate moments of being with others so that we are subjects in action?

As the reader will see in the following sections, the ethic of how we act and live with others informs my thinking about pedagogy. More to the point, I am concerned about those ways in which our words as teachers are too often used to "veil intentions [rather than] to disclose realities," and our engagements with students too often used to "violate and destroy [rather than] to establish relations and create new realities" (Arendt, 1958, p. 200). This is a fairly harsh indictment, particularly when many of us believe our goal-directed actions and the spaces we facilitate engender socially just citizens.

It may seem from these words that I do not believe that our engagements with others can generate socially just actions. In actuality, the central aim and premise of this chapter is that, as Arendt does, I too recognize both the necessity and fragility of the/a space where I "appear to others as others appear to me" (p. 198). This is a space in which the words we speak as teachers must not assume to predict or even envision a predetermined end or goal. Such an open, transient, and adaptable space cannot always exist, and as Arendt acknowledges, "no man, moreover, can live in it all the time" (p. 199).[1] This does not suggest, however, that we should not attempt the facilitation of this space. To not do so, in Arendt's thinking, is "to be deprived of reality" (p. 199), which means to be deprived of freedom and identity.

To "Think What We Are Doing"

In the opening pages of *The Human Condition*, Arendt (1958) raises the issue of world alienation. This is a very particular framing of alienation, one in which the human intention to both master and escape the world,[2] as well as our "desire for production, not people" (p. 209), leads to isolation and loneliness. As we think through those ways in which social justice is addressed and presented throughout this Handbook, isolation and loneliness may seem benign concerns. However, far from simple states of mind, Arendt believes that both are product and effect of the "banality evil" ([1963]1977). Arendt (1958), then, in asking us to do "nothing more than to think what we are doing" (p. 5), warns us of how precarious, indeed "fragile," are the conditions under which subjectivity and judgment are possible and how easy (and dangerous) it is to dismiss the conditions necessary for new beginning (natality). Arendt saw this process of world alienation as one in which public spaces that should be the domain of "infinite improbablit[ies]" (1958, p. 178) were replaced and subsumed by the "rise of the social" (p. 38), in which unending production and consumption erase plurality, public life, and freedom, "leav[ing] nothing behind" (p. 87).

The idea that nothing is being left behind should be particularly troubling in that it suggests that none of us is seen, none of us is known; we are all "caught up in the smooth functioning of a never-ending process" (p. 135), stripped of our distinctness and the impossibility to be found in encounters that realize, what Arendt calls, new beginnings. While there are many ways to approach inequalities, injustices, human rights, and even freedom, in an educative system in which world alienation takes on many guises, the "struggle for a life that is fully human" (Nussbaum, 2009, p. 211) is shared by all of us, music teacher/student, parent, principal, board of education member. In this chapter, then, rather than view social justice or even socially just practices through the lens of particular groups of people, I choose to think through those ways *all of us* must "struggle for life that is fully human" in order to combat what Maistry (2012) calls an "alienating culture and discourse" (p. 524). I examine and trouble particular concepts and constructs we take for granted and question whether we "think what we are doing" (Arendt, 1958) as we encounter others. I do this so that we might consider that social justice or socially just actions can neither be the reproduction of an existing discourse nor preparation for future goal-oriented behaviors.

At the time Arendt was writing, the terms "neoliberalism" and "global capitalism" had not yet become embedded in our world consciousness. However, while not exact corollaries to Arendt's framing of world alienation, neoliberalism and global capitalism share many of the ideological trappings that concerned her. Throughout this chapter I posit that this discourse is so pervasive, insidious, and menacing that its rhetoric maneuvers its way in and shapes the very words that come out of our mouths, even in our most aware moments. "One must have classroom rules and management," one should "reward good behavior," one must "focus on each child's dispositions/habits," and competition is "an acceptable, moral characteristic and value" (Maistry, 2012, p. 520); these are but a few of the "common-sense" phrases and axioms that frame our teaching. Throughout the chapter I challenge these common-sense practices and posit that we need to better figure out how those seemingly innocuous phrases prevent and hinder what Arendt (1958) calls "the space of appearance." The task, if we accept this proposition, is not just to consider the educative process as one that prepares for or addresses a specific need—social justice—but rather one in which our encounters with others creates new beginnings, the conditions for freedom, or the "potential space of appearance" (p. 200).

MUSIC EDUCATORS AND ARENDT

The beauty and power to be found in the thinking of Hannah Arendt has not gone undiscovered by music education scholars. We do, however, face a different set of issues as we think through what it would mean to create the conditions for an Arendtian framing of action in music education environments. And indeed, scholars have engaged with Arendt in order to address music and educational concerns through multiple lines of thought. For instance, Pio and Varkøy (2012) use widely varied examples such as Wagner, Hendrix, Lennon, and Fluke to point out that music has always provided the affordance of "entering the world anew" (p. 114)—an argument hard to dispute. At the same time, Pio and Varkøy also share the concern of many in our field that non-musical or extra-musical values are being used to justify music education within the curriculum. As such, they use Arendt to "uncover and safeguard the fundamental importance of musical experience in human life" (p. 100). As I see it, the challenge is to incorporate Arendt in a way that provides at the same time a philosophy for supporting musicing *and* a guide as to how these experiences can be framed and organized in a music education context.

One also certainly recognizes the recent rise of social media and its power and potentiality. Thorgersen-Ferm and Georgii-Hemming (2012) do so as they uncover "virtual and non-virtual social settings [that can] be used for musical learning and communication" (p. 161). Using an Arendtian framework, they looked at "composers, musicians and listeners [engaged in] innovative musical learning . . . constituted by digital existence, intentionality . . . in virtual and non-virtual communities" (p. 163) and describe the development of a project called "Fair Opera," in which students from all over the world composed music, wrote lyrics, and choreographed movement and then shared this with "professional composers, librettists, musicians and dancers" (p. 169). They discovered that the plurality provided by the virtual environment allowed students to bring their own "prerequisites" to the creative process, but they also discovered that the pedagogical challenge in these settings hinges upon how and what strategies and mechanisms can be incorporated so that all can be included in the process.

Ferm (n.d.) has also drawn on Arendt to examine and analyze Swedish national curricula and those ways in which it potentially "enlightens democratic values, equality and uniqueness in relation to varied forms of expression" (p. 1). We are offered a "view of the music classroom as a local place and a public space" as she thinks through musicing and music activities in Swedish public schools. Her guiding question centers on what it would mean to "create a space where children can encounter the other and where they can start the quest to find out what this encounter means" (p. 7).

Kanellopoulos (2007) has thought extensively about action and plurality and the ways in which improvisational engagements open spaces of "freedom and equity" (p. 116). He sees great potential in those ways that improvisation can "[transform] music classrooms from places where knowledge is transmitted to open contexts for acting and thinking" (p. 98). Again, using an Arendtian perspective, Kanellopoulos guides us through the idea that acting with others is only free when not mediated by something else; the end is the action, there is no developmental engagement that leads us to a subsequent or sequential meaningful end. Thus, free improvisation provides a space where students engage in musicing that does not depend on skill-based techniques, but rather solely on listening and responding in the moment. Kanellopoulos sees this space as a way in which the "pursuit of freedom, equity, and plurality" (p. 98) may be forwarded precisely because one cannot know in advance who one is, nor can one assume to know the other. Improvisation, then, is not an instrumental "tool for creativity" (p. 100), but rather moments "free from motive on one side, from its intended goals as a predictable effect on the other" (Arendt, 1968, p. 151).

Clearly, Arendt helps us think through the possibilities of realizing musicing as sites of plurality and thus action and new beginnings. As the above authors also note, however, this plurality and action are at least partially dependent upon on how we interact with each other, and thus on our language. Consequently, we also need to address those verbal pedagogical moments, those words we utter, and how they may help or hinder our students to meet themselves and each other without predetermined expectations. Ferm (n.d.) leaves us with questions to which, through the lens of Arendt, I will later return, that help shape an understanding of these very issues:

- How do we make students understand that all voices are expected to be heard?
- How can we convince all students that they are seen as possible participants? (p. 9)?

Kanellopoulos (2007), too, underscores this very concern, exhorting us to let go of our need to be the "instructor" and to become, rather, a "co-musician," one who can "follow the students' intentions and [preserve] openness, both in musical actions and discussions" (p. 100).

What exactly, then, does this teaching look and sound like within our educative musicing spaces, if the goal were to foster environments in which freedom is experienced, even under the most draconian of accountability expectations? In the following sections, in order to think anew the possibilities of preexisting, sanctioned, alienating pedagogical policies, I examine the pervasive and insidious discourse of neoliberalism and those ways in which a pedagogy of pride precludes the space of appearance; I challenge the widespread acceptance of classroom rules, and problematize (and shift) the common pedagogical strategy of building on what "students know."

PEDAGOGIES OF WORLD ALIENATION

Pride and the Contested Terrain of Neoliberalism

> I am left wondering what strategies redress, or make the best use of, an increasingly pervasive neoliberalism. (Weiss, 2008, p. 97)

We have all been witness and responded to the plea, "Teacher, are you proud of me?" The conundrum this utterance incites is troubling. Not responding to these demands leaves a pedagogical space begging to be filled. By responding to the plea, we become central to the external construction of "learner" and effectively establish authority and control in the classroom. It may seem that the solution to this would be to reposition pride internally by facilitating discussions as to why both the students' need for validation and a teacher's manipulation of that need are problematic. However, "telling" students they should be proud of and find pride in whatever it is they are doing only placates or deflects the quite real need for students to be seen, heard, known to oneself, and to others.

Arendt (1951) differentiates between solitude and loneliness, and this is significant because pedagogy of pride—of leveraging the need for recognition—might be located in the misunderstanding of what lies between these two terms. Solitude is the condition in which we are with ourselves thinking, but not isolated per se, as we not only think based on what we experience with others, but we also talk with ourselves. The condition of loneliness, on the other hand, is possible even when surrounded by others. Morrow (2014) uses the phrase "estranged state of mind" (para. 6) as an analogue to loneliness, arguing that this state of mind can be brought on by exposure to patterns particular to a world in which hyper-individualization calls for self-removal from community. Much like Arendt, it is the loss of one's own self that is most destructive to the possibility of plurality and one's identity, warning us how "the confirmation of my identity, [can depend] entirely upon other people" (Arendt, 1951, p. 476). Morrow further warns of the self-selection of individuals into groups where they are more willing to "expose themselves only to opinions likely to match their own, limit[ing] the chances of encountering checks or dissensions from one's judgments that could effectively alter one's beliefs, or expose a gap between conviction and action" (para. 6). This disheartening notion resonates with Arendt, who argues that external validation, which I see as the basis for a pedagogy of pride, "is the great saving grace of companionship for solitary men [in] that it makes them 'whole' again . . ." (p. 476).

I am suggesting that this self-selection through hyper-individualization is often brought on by the discourse of pride. I also submit that an unexamined acceptance, utilization, and reliance on a pedagogy of pride can be conceived of as a capitalistic productive strategy. The justification and use of pride in the classroom reproduces in language and in deed "a neoliberal relationship between individual class privilege and freedom" (Weiss, 2008, p. 96). In other words, the rhetoric and rationality that underlie both the message and ensuing policies (i.e., acceptable forms of "teaching") do not celebrate plurality and the construction of identity through difference, but rather rely on the construction of private space championed by neoliberal policies. Coté and de Peuter (2007) pose the question: "How do educational practices figure into [an] emerging neoliberal social order?" (p. 13). For this chapter, a certainly more apt question would be to consider what function a pedagogy of pride performs in preventing miracles and the possibility of new beginnings, or that which "cannot be foreseen and calculated as a possibility but literally takes us by surprise" (Biesta, 1998, p. 500). Can pride then be a capitalistic productive strategy?

Neoliberalism and Pride

Hardly just a current "catchphrase" (Boas & Gans-Morse, 2009, p. 138), neoliberalism and neoliberal policies/politics are contested terms and terrains. They are never neutral and often are deliberately positioned as either/or concepts. As a "globalization discourse" (Hursh, 2007, p. 497), many think of neoliberalism as a deterministic force in which we have no option but to accept this inevitable progress, or that it holds the answers to all our needs. There are those who believe that the term is used too often as a pejorative and "characterize[s] an excessively broad variety of phenomena" (Boas & Gans-Morse, 2009, p. 137). Some even see this as an umbrella under which multiple and diverse groups meet in the "church of anti-neoliberalism" (Hursh, 2007, p. 4). Those who support it—or benefit from it—further an understanding of neoliberalism as promoting "personal responsibility through individual choice within markets. [One in which] the individual is conceived as an autonomous entrepreneur who can always take care of his or her own needs" (Hursh, 2007, p. 496). As impossible as it may be to definitively articulate neoliberal engagements, the literature certainly suggests that there seem to be particular ways of engaging in and with the world that forward a neoliberal agenda, rather than facilitating "equitable, active, widespread and fully informed participation" (Apple, 2011, p. 21).

Neoliberalism is significant to the point of this chapter—and the overall discussion of social justice within which it situated—for in many ways it challenges the idea that participation is an unquestionable value of any educational setting. In more ways than one, it dismisses the notion that the contestation over the aims of the educative process, while too often filled with despair, should be the product of a healthy and public democratic process. Today, however, it is not challenging for most of us to recognize how draconian forms of assessment and accountability, as Hursh (2007) writes, "reflect the rise and dominance of neoliberal and neoconservative police discourses over social democratic policy discourses" (p. 494). Schools, rather than spaces into which each of us can "insert ourselves in word and deed" (Arendt, 1968, p. 148) are quite possibly becoming just another space where, as Hardt (1999) suggests, "humanity and its soul are produced in the very processes of economic production" (p. 91).

Pride, I argue, can function as a personal representation of trade, or a personal economy of exchange. Thus pride can push forward and reify arguments of freedom from the state, private property, competition, and superiority. It does so particularly when "good" pride, as an internal source of worth, shifts to "bad" pride. Thomas Aquinas makes the distinction between good and bad pride, delineating both narrow and broad conceptions of pride. In short, good pride "underlies the pursuit of difficult but obtainable goals; it manifests itself in that tempered sense of both abilities and valuable states necessary to the undertaking of significant projects" (Yearly, 2004, p. 317). Good pride is the feeling of self-awareness and reflexivity to which thoughtful pedagogy is aligned.

Bad pride, on the other hand, is more nuanced and stealth-like in its character. Bad pride is excessive in nature; it is without merit. It thrives, for instance, in engagements where empty and false praise is given. It prevents us from engaging in acts in which we feel we may fail and is made manifest as false judgments about what one can do. Narrowly conceived, bad pride refers to the obvious—to those moments we recognize as domination, born too often through competition and the desire to be superior.

Deborah Gould (2009) asks us to consider the power of "forming collectives without squashing difference" (p. 223)—what Arendt would call distinction. A pedagogy of recognition cannot be situated in producing subjugated positions and relationships. It must facilitate the creation of new beginnings so that we are all seen "as a distinct and unique being among equals" (Arendt, 1958, p. 178). To trouble the concept of pride, then, is not to dismiss or suppress, but rather to recognize the human desire and longing to be seen and heard, to know and to be known. To trouble pride is to recognize, as Sedgwick (2009) does, that shame (isolation and loneliness for Arendt) occurs in moments in which we are not or no longer recognized for our distinctness. To trouble the multiple ways in which the neoliberal discourse works on and through us is to question self-doubt, feelings of inadequacy, and teaching traditions rooted in common sense.

Pedagogical engagements that disconnect us from acts of humanity and grace and the development of self fuel ideological aims that ensure competition, domination, and superiority. To be sure, this also suggests an interrogation of pedagogical engagements that have been, as Arendt (1998) suggests, "uncritically and slavishly accepted" (p. 179). I have suggested elsewhere that progressive tenets such as "student-centered learning" can also serve to cloak instructional strategies that in actuality control and isolate the learner from the development of self by denying plurality and the space of appearance. It seems a rather fine line that separates student-centered learning from the furthering of privileged individual freedoms.[3]

"Everyone" knows appropriate behavior makes a positive classroom.

> Education is the point at which we decide whether we love the world enough to
> assume responsibility for it and by the same token save it from that ruin which,

except for renewal, except for the coming of the new and young, would be inevitable. (Arendt, 1968, p. 196)

There are "time-honored" phrases (of which we no longer seem to be consciously aware) that have become embedded in our "what works" vocabulary. "Works at what" rarely seems to be considered and indeed the phases function as a way to "veil intentions" and "violate and destroy" (Arendt, 1958, p. 200). Just as they are now, these phrases, often based on hundreds of years of philosophical contemplation and psychological theories, were part of our own education growing up. Consider the following:

- Raise your hand before speaking.
- I'm only calling on those of you who are sitting up nice and tall.
- Respect others.
- No talking [playing] out of turn.
- Listen and follow [my] directions.
- If everyone behaves we will have a pizza party!

Even for those who recognize the locus of control in these statements, there are further discursive practices hidden within. Consider that for both teachers and students there is predictability and thus routine to be found in the previous statements. For teachers, these are sanctioned and even required practices. For students, they are recognizable statements that enter their lives from the beginnings of schooling.[4] Consider also, teachers and students "use" these rules for multiple purposes. Control and safety are the most immediate; however, "respect for others" is often a classroom mandate. Students, then, may rely on these statements to protect themselves against perceived acts of injustice from others, but they may also just as easily ignore them when they might not work to their benefit.

Furthermore, students quickly figure out that the teacher uses these phrases in the same capricious way. Teachers are never ones for consistency; manipulating teachers to change the rules is simply a constituent of the hidden curriculum. Indeed, while Arendt never spoke of a hidden curriculum, it would hardly be a stretch of one's intellectual imagination to see that what Vallance (1973) refers to as "the inculcation of values, political socialization, training in obedience and docility, the perpetuation of traditional class structure-functions that may be characterized generally as social control" (p. 5) is similar to Arendt's concern over actions that attempt to control by disrupting and mediating plurality. "Doing school" is the ability to recognize from teacher to teacher, and moment to moment, what will and won't "work," and who does "it" the best. This ability to scheme and finesse is what raised us out of the fray of the multitude and obscurity. Everyone recognized that the power of these statements lay only in one's ability (and even responsibility) to work them to one's own best advantage.

One might point out that these phrases are intended to forward equitable and respectful spaces, providing for voice and creativity—that these are phrases that will develop dispositions so that students become democratic citizens. Clearly, however, this isn't the form of responsibility Arendt has in mind when she references our duty to take responsibility for a world we may not have created—to take on the authority of one who must when others will not.

All classrooms contain social, economical, class, cultural, ethical, and other diversities, indeed, plurality. The challenge is to figure out "what makes it bearable for us to live with other people, strangers, forever, in the same world, and makes it possible for them to bear with us" (Arendt, 1994, p. 322). Teachers do this constantly by making predictions and decisions for the common good of the classroom. Rules simply seem an extension of common sense. Britzman (1991) reminds us, however, that as a discourse, "common sense depends upon what is already known—the obvious—and hence resists explanations about the complications we live" (p. 7). Rules are the epitome of what is obvious and known. Unfortunately, they not only resist explanations but cut short "possibilities and infinite improbabilit[ies]" (Arendt, 1958, p. 178).

Arendt leaves the "particulars" of teaching to the "experts and pedagogues" (p. 196), but as she demands us to take responsibility for the world and how it came to be, as well as to afford space for new beginnings, one quickly understands what little established rules do to further the appearance of self and others. What if, however, one engages students in creating the rules together as a class community? Indeed, this oft-cited suggestion, mythical in proportions, sponsors the idea that a "good" teacher creates the rules *with* the students so that there will be "buy-in" to disciplinary action. Surely in this case the teacher is allowing students the freedom to choose rules and consequences? Isn't consensus, after all, one way to ensure that behaviors are just?

Rules may provide the semblance of co-constructed directives, but policies of self-surveillance, false choice, particular ways of knowing and being, and rewards and punishments stabilize the narrative of the status quo. If instead, the distinctness of students is encouraged, nourished, and respected, classrooms can become a forum for a kind of listening and responding—a discourse of uncommon sense—that paves the way for thinking anew and renewal. The aim is not to produce just citizens, but rather to ask, as Biesta (2007) does, how our classes can be spaces "where [students] can bring their beginnings into a world of plurality and difference in such a way that their beginnings do not obstruct the opportunities for others to bring their beginning into this world as well" (p. 760).

THE SPACE OF APPEARANCE: WHAT DO WE THINK WE KNOW?

> The only thing that is needed, therefore, is to remind people that they can see and think for themselves and are not dependent upon others who claim that they can see and think for them. (Biesta, 2010b, p. 544)

Teachers are quite fond of explaining. We are fond of telling, instructing, informing, illuminating, even guiding "from the side." I would say we are motivated to do so from a most kind and generous perspective. We don't want our students to fail. So we explain before the doing, teach before the learning. We prepare and anticipate. We ask questions for which, if there are no immediate answers, we simply supply the answer, or worse, look around for the "right" answer. We break everything down into manageable steps and execute with step-by-step efficiency. They need us, they are not yet ready. As such, we continue to look for that "'secret formula' so that education can be made into a technique with a predictable, positive outcome" (Biesta, 1998, p. 503).

Granted (and I recognize that this may seem like a very large "granted"), it may seem that accountability structures and parameters do not allow for any engagement that does not lead to the assessed endpoint. We are motivated in more ways than one to get our students where they need to be in order for them to get to the next place they need to be. However, if we use Arendt to challenge accountability and what we presume can and cannot be done, it is possible to take on strategies that look to find those spaces that allow for the new.

Building on what is known is a both a pedagogical strategy and a way to shape and direct curriculum. To that end, teachers often incorporate KWL processes (a chart intended to be filled out) as motivation and as a way for students to "[develop] a personal commitment" (Ogle, 1986, p. 567). These quick and easy steps are seen as ways to activate prior knowledge and build interest. Under the K column, students brainstorm everything they already *know*; they then proceed to record what it is they *want* to know in the W column; and finally, after the learning task, they write everything they *learned* under the L column. "What do we know about the blues, boys and girls?" may be one way to interest students in "learning about" the blues and even historic framings, including colonialism and slavery. The leap of faith occurs when we expect students to conjecture out loud with their classmates and announce with certainty what it is they know. It is a question that depends on how safe and confident they feel their certitude will be honored and also a question that reifies what it is they already think they know. The problem is not just that we begin from the pedagogical space of knowing. The problem is the epistemological space that is created when we are asked to speak to what it is we definitely know, whether we know it or not. Without a second thought, we place students in positions to pretend, to come up with a "right" answer, to even lie, and to rely on those they "know will know." Irrespective of how they came to know it and even what it means to know, the pronouncements are uttered and hang there for all to recognize as "known."

If, on the other hand, we shift the construction of that entry point from what we know to "what is it we *think* we know," a different epistemological space opens, one in which the possibility of new beginnings of "startling unexpectedness" (Arendt, 1958, p. 178) can occur. With this shift in language, students are forgiven before they even speak, they are "released from the consequences" (Arendt, 1958, p. 207) of what it is we don't know or can't do. In essence, when we ask what we *think* we know, we promise a space in which there will be freedom to speak that is not predicted on certainly or an identity that we, or society, expect. Of course, as Arendt points out, and which seems patently obvious, we can't predict what will be said or where it will go. Arendt reminds us that this is the price we pay for being human and thus for freedom. The inability to control and not know what the consequences might be regarding how others will react and engage with us is the "price we pay for the joy of inhabiting together with others a world whose reality is guaranteed for each by the presence of all" (p. 245).

Biesta (2010a) makes a distinction between "learn[ing] *for* political existence" and "learn[ing] *from* it" (p. 571). What is it we learn from these moments shared and created in plurality that moves us to think and respond differently as we discuss and music with others? It is not so much that we can "make the pupils understand that all voices are expected to be heard," or even "convince all pupils that they are seen as a possible participants" (Ferm, n.d., p. 9). It is really only to engage in ways in which this being happens. We aren't going to "get away with" not having rules in the classroom. And it's not enough simply to explain to students that you aren't going to post rules for ethical reasons. What we can do is brainstorm rules with students and help them to see that the rules they come up with for the most part are focused on individual behaviors and do not, for instance, demonstrate care for each other. In doing so, the subject matter shifts from "rules" to community building and the space becomes one in which students move beyond the responses to which they have been conditioned (Duckworth, 2005, 2009). Asking students to think first of building a "caring community" (Noddings, 1986, p. 499), rather than individual gain, reinforces new beginnings based on promise and forgiveness.

Naturally, these ideals have direct musical-pedagogical references as well. Providing students with small ensemble experiences within large ensembles (Larson, 2010), as well as asking musicians to engage in popular music learning strategies (Allsup, 2011), or thinking in terms of "applying participatory culture and emerging musical practices" (Tobias, 2013, p. 31) in classrooms encourages students to negotiate meaning, allowing them to learn from the political experience of plurality. Thinking through the "welcome" and "unconditional hospitality," as Higgins (2012, pp. 137–140) does so beautifully in the spaces of community music, also opens possibilities for the space of freedom to be found in moments, rather than something that can be worked toward.

Conclusion

In this chapter I have argued for a pedagogy of recognition and against a simplistic, didactic educative stance of "preparing students for social justice" by suggesting that we "think what we are doing" (Arendt, 1958) in word and in deed. Common-sense pedagogies such as furthering individual pride, creating and posting class rules, and building upon "what is known" are only three problematic engagements that prevent the appearance of a space where we retain our distinctness. These are neither small nor insignificant moments.

I have argued that justice cannot be thought of as a movement, as a "movement describes a mass of people collectively moving towards a definite goal" (Berger, 2007,

p. 8). We cannot predict a definitive goal, but what we can do is believe in Arendt's conception of freedom that is to be found in moments. However, this means our conception of progress and even transformation on any grand scale must shift to accommodate and attend to what Levinson (1997) refers to as the "snail's pace of change" (p. 451). We need remind ourselves that very small shifts in both word and deed have the power to disrupt pedagogies that serve as "mechanism[s] of social control" (Giroux, 1981, p. 37) and bring about, as well as conserve, newness. Believing, as Arendt does, that profound forgiveness and deep promise can be found within and for all of us helps us to find our humanity as we "think what we are doing."

NOTES

1. In a book dedicated to the topic of social justice, it is necessary to respond to any criticisms that may arise with the use of male pronouns. The constraints of this chapter do not allow for an in-depth examination of Arendt and "the woman question" (Benhabib). However, see, for instance, discussions that work toward a "feminist reading of Arendt" (Higgins, 2012, p. 411): Benhabib, S. (2003), *The reluctant modernism of Hannah Arendt* (Lanham, MD: Rowman & Littlefield Publishers; Honig, B. (Ed.), (2010), *Feminist Interpretations of Hannah Arendt* (University Park: Pennsylvania State University Press); and Maslin, K. (2013), The gender-neutral feminism of Hannah Arendt, *Hypatia, 28*(3), 585–601.

2. At the time Arendt wrote *The Human Condition*, the Soviets had just launched Sputnik I. While many saw this as a "great propaganda feat," "nothing to worry us," and "something to tell us to keep on our toes," others spoke of respect, awe, and "terror caused by the discovery of Russian scientific supremacy" (National Aeronautics and Space Administration, 1963). Arendt viewed this newest experience and recent moment of fear as proof of man's desire to escape "imprisonment to the earth" (1958, p. 1).

3. I have troubled the concept of "child-centered" engagements and pedagogy that turns up in both progressive objectives that are made manifest in the profit garnered from polished performances (free from mistakes) that yield "excellent" accolades from key stakeholders and efficiency of learning models from the scientific management systems of Taylor and Bobbitt. See C. Benedict (2015), Reading methods. In C. R. Abril & B. M. Gault (Eds.), *New approaches to teaching classroom music: Methods, issues, and viewpoints.* New York: Oxford University Press.

4. Unpublished research conducted in four different countries by Marja Heimonen, Helsinki, Finland; Cecilia Ferm, Stockholm, Sweden; Panagiotis A. Kanellopoulos, Volos, Greece; and myself in the United States suggests that students in all four settings, as early as first years of schooling, recognize that rules are "something concrete," they are often "written down as a set," "are numerous," are created mainly from "above," and are "there to obey."

REFERENCES

Allsup, R. E. (2011). Popular music and classical musicians strategies and perspectives. *Music Educators Journal, 97*(3), 30–34.

Apple, M. (March 2011). Democratic education in neoliberal and neoconservative times. *International Studies in Sociology of Education*, 21(1), pp. 21–31.

Arendt, H. ([1951]1968). *The origins of totalitarianism*. New York: Meridian Books.

Arendt, H. ([1958]1998). *The human condition*. Chicago: The University of Chicago Press.

Arendt, H. ([1963]1977). *Eichmann in Jerusalem: A report on the banality of evil*. New York: Penguin Books.

Arendt, H. (1968). *Between past and future: Eight exercises in political thought*. New York: Penguin Books.

Arendt, H. (1994). Understanding and politics (the difficulties of understanding). In H. Arendt & J. Kohn (Eds.), *Essays in understanding 1930–1954*. New York: Harcourt, Brace.

Berger, J. (2007). *Hold everything dear: Dispatches on survival and resistance*. New York: Pantheon Books.

Biesta, G. J. (1998). Say you want a revolution . . . Suggestions for the impossible future of critical pedagogy. *Educational Theory*, 48(4), 499–510.

Biesta, G. (2007). Education and the democratic person: Towards a political conception of democratic education. *The Teachers College Record*, 109(3), 740–769.

Biesta, G. (2010a). How to exist politically and learn from it: Hannah Arendt and the problem of democratic education. *The Teachers College Record*, 112(2), 556–575.

Biesta, G. (2010b). Learner, student, speaker: Why it matters how we call those we teach. *Educational Philosophy and Theory*, 42(5–6), 540–552.

Boas, T. C., & Gans-Morse, J. (2009). Neoliberalism: From new liberal philosophy to anti-liberal slogan. *Studies in Comparative International Development*, 44(2), 137–161.

Britzman, D. (1991). *Practice makes practice: A critical study of learning to teach*. Albany: State University of New York Press.

Coté, M., Day R., de Peuter, G. (2007). *Utopian pedagogy: Radical experiments against neoliberal globalization*. Toronto: University of Toronto Press.

Duckworth, E. (2005). Critical exploration in the classroom. *The New Educator*, 1(4), 257–272.

Duckworth, E. (2009). Helping students get to where ideas can find them. *The New Educator*, 5(3), 185–188.

Ferm, C. (n.d.). *The music classroom—a local place and a public space; Hannah Arendt's thinking about democracy as a fundament for educational activities that offer music as a language of us all*. Unpublished manuscript, Luleå University of Technology, Piteå Sweeden.

Giroux, H. (1981). *Ideology, culture, and the process of schooling*. Philadelphia: Temple University Press.

Gould, D. (2009). The shame of gay pride in early AIDS activism. In D. Halperin & V. Traub (Eds.), *Gay Shame*. Chicago: University of Chicago Press.

Hardt, M. (Summer 1999). Affective labor. *Boundary*, 26(2), 89–100.

Higgins, L. (2012). *Community music: In theory and in practice*. Oxford: Oxford University Press.

Hursh, D. (2007, September). "No Child Left Behind" and the rise of neoliberal education policies. *American Educational Research Journal*, 44(3), 493–518.

Kanellopoulos, P. (2007). Musical improvisation as action: An Arendtian perspective. *Action, Criticism, and Theory for Music Education*, 6(3), 97–127.

Larson, D. (2010). *The effects of chamber music experience on music performance achievement, motivation, and attitudes among high school band students* (Doctoral dissertation). ProQuest, UMI Dissertations Publishing, 2010. 3410633.

Levinson, N. (1997). Teaching in the midst of belatedness: The paradox of natality in Hannah Arendt's educational thought. *Educational Theory, 47*(4), 435–451.

Maistry, S. M. (2012). Confronting the neo-liberal brute: Reflections of a higher education middle-level manager. *South African Journal of Higher Education, 26*(3), 515 528.

Morrow, P. (2014, May 27). The emperor's new clothes and pluralist engagements. [Hannah Arendt Center, Quote of the week]. Retrieved from http://www.hannaharendtcenter. org/?p=13216.

National Aeronautics and Space Administration. (1957, October 4). *NASA historical note no. 22. The impact of Sputnik I: Case-study of American public opinion, at the break of the space age.* Retrieved from http://74.125.47.132/search?q=cache/w8oofFyWOtUJ:history.spacebusiness. com spunik/files/sputnik65.pdf+Sputnik+sentor+wiley&cd=7&hl=en&ct=clnk&gl=u&cli e=safari.

Noddings, N. (1986). Fidelity in teaching, teacher education, and research for teaching. *Harvard Educational Review, 56*(4), 496–511.

Nussbaum, M. C. (2009). Creating capabilities: The human development approach and its implementation. *Hypatia, 24*(3), 211–215.

Ogle, D. M. (1986). KWL: A teaching model that develops active reading of expository text. *The Reading Teacher, 39*(6), 564–570.

Pio, F., & Varkøy, Ø. (2012). A reflection on musical experience as existential experience: An ontological turn. *Philosophy of Music Education Review, 20*(2), 99–116.

Sedgwick, E. K. (2009). Shame, theatricality, and queer performativity: Henry James's the art of the novel. In D. Halperin & V. Traub (Eds.), *Gay shame.* Chicago, IL: University of Chicago Press.

Thorgersen, C. F., & Georgii-Hemming, E. (2012). Social networking and democratic practices as spheres for innovative musical learning. In C. Benedict & P. Schmidt (Eds.), *Yearbook of the National Society for the Study of Education, 111*(1), 160–176.

Tobias, E. S. (2013). Toward convergence adapting music education to contemporary society and participatory culture. *Music Educators Journal, 99*(4), 29–36.

Vallance, E. (1973). Hiding the hidden curriculum: An interpretation of the language of justification in nineteenth-century educational reform. *Curriculum Theory Network, 4*(1), 5–21.

Weiss, M. D. (2008). Gay shame and BDSM pride: Neoliberalism, privacy, and sexual politics. *Radical History Review, 100,* 87–101.

Yearly, L. (June 2004). Genre and the attempt to render pride: Dante and Aquinas. *Journal of the American Academy of Religion, 72*(2), 313–339.

CHAPTER 17

MULTICULTURALISM AND SOCIAL JUSTICE

Complementary Movements for Education in and Through Music

J. CHRISTOPHER ROBERTS
AND PATRICIA SHEHAN CAMPBELL

THE move toward educational experiences that are characterized by social justice has gained traction in recent years, both in the fields of education broadly and music education specifically, as articles, books, and scholarly conferences devoted to the topic grow more common (see, for example, *Music Education Research,* 9(2), 2007, and *Music Educator's Journal,* June 2012). Yet as a concept, social justice can be said to remain ambiguous and often unclearly defined (Cochran-Smith, Shakman, Jong, Terrell, Barnatt, & McQuillan, 2009; North, 2006; Reisch, 2007). Scholars who employ the term "social justice" overwhelmingly emphasize the issue of equity as it applies across a variety of contexts and situations, and incorporate action components in which one works to challenge existing inequities (Cochran-Smith, et al., 2009; Sensoy & DiAngelo, 2012). As such, the term is rooted in a critical concern with the complexities of race, ethnicity, and social class in the design and delivery of curriculum.

While not identical, social justice and multiculturalism bear many commonalities that warrant exploration. Equity, for example, is a core construct of both concepts. In a survey of conceptions of multiculturalism, Nieto (2009) notes that multicultural ideals include "advocating for equitable education for students of all backgrounds, and that it goes beyond the classroom walls to implicate societal change as a fundamental goal" (p. 82). This characterization of multiculturalism resembles Reilly Carlisle, Jackson, and George's (2006) definition of socially just education as a "conscious and reflexive blend of content and process intended to enhance equity across multiple social identity groups (e.g. race, class, gender, sexual orientation, ability), foster critical perspectives, and promote social action" (p. 57).

We seek to present the aims and practices of the two named educational movements that in fact parallel, overlap, and enrich one another in educational practice. We accept that there are confirmable connections between the philosophical principles of multiculturalism and social justice, and we will illustrate their presence in music education curricular practice. We will examine the framework of pioneering educationist James Banks, using his levels of curriculum reform (2013a) as a lens through which to view the practical realities of encouraging teachers to work toward more equitable classroom environments. These realities may occur by creating curriculum in graduated steps that progress from contributive "material" to deep structural change. Our focus of consideration is US-based, in that illustrations are drawn from settings and situations of our contextual experience, even while we also recognize the plausibility for global transfer of the theoretical tenets we describe.

In sum, the chapter offers a pathway for teachers in K–12 and university music settings to confront issues of multiculturalism and social justice and to incorporate curricular events into their classes in ways that can penetrate and convert current thought and behavior to an other-directed sensibility.

Ensuring Equity Through Multicultural Education

Multicultural education is more than a social movement: it is a field of study that emerged out of political expediency (Banks, 2013a), whose intent it is to foster equitable learning opportunities for all students. It advocates the design and delivery of a comprehensive and culturally responsive education from kindergarten through secondary school (Banks, 2013a; Grant & Sleeter, 2013). Multiculturally attuned educators are intent on embracing the needs and interests of students from diverse racial, ethnic, social-class, and cultural communities. Consistent with the principles of a democratic society, multicultural education is aimed at facilitating and championing access for all, rather than merely the elite and advantaged few. It seeks to embrace the means for developing logic and intellectual acumen, humanistic understandings, and aesthetic experiences for learners of every social circumstance and need (Banks, 2013b).

The struggle for equal rights in the United States is long and historic, and its schooling system has mirrored, in policy and practice, the overriding perspectives that have directed the societal movement toward greater equality for all citizens (Banks & Banks, 2013). Multicultural education rose out of the civil rights movement of the 1960s and 1970s, and embraces changes in the curriculum, the instructional delivery system, the teaching-learning textbooks, materials, and tests so as to address the needs of learners from all communities. Compelled by many, including multiculturalists (Banks, 2007, 2013a), schooling has been reshaped to attend to the integration of a wide array of cultural sensibilities, and to develop experiences that lead to the validation and empowerment of students from every community.[1]

In over a half-century of attention to changes in school policy and practice, the field of multicultural education has helped to crack open the question of equity that leads to creating a more democratic society through schooling. Not without its ebbs and flows, the field remains fraught with the challenges of turning theoretical analysis and pronouncements of curriculum reform into full-fledged action. Teachers with every intent to be democratic, inclusive, and tuned to the individual needs of all students continue to confront the daily realities of time, energy, and expertise necessary to meet multicultural goals.

Aims and Accomplishments of Multicultural Music Education

Alongside the civil rights movement in the United States and globally, rapid developments in communications and transportation brought an awareness of the musical expressions of local and global communities not previously featured in curricular programs in music. Music teachers gradually awakened to the prospects of teaching music from multicultural perspectives, and then interpreted this to fit the scope of their own education and training. By the 1970s, African-American genres and West African "roots" and rhythmic schemas were featured in textbooks and occasional workshops as demonstration of the broader view of musical practices worldwide (Schippers & Campbell, 2012; Standifer & Lundquist, 1972; Volk, 1998). Particularly in urban areas, teachers were attempting to draw students of color into elective classes of music through genres that might be viewed as relevant, and even familiar, to them (Lundquist, 1985). Activist-educators were delivering songs, dances, and listening experiences in their classrooms, and in-service clinical presentations brought about the canonization of particular "music cultures" and genres that could be taught, learned, and performed at elementary school assemblies (and later, in secondary school choral festivals). By the 1980s, general music and vocal music teachers had become curious of "the musical other," fueled at least in part by the collaborative efforts of ethnomusicologists and educators to provide pedagogical materials for music cultures outside the West (Campbell, 2013). They were then eager to meet the multicultural mandates of their school districts, even while instrumental ensembles continued the skill-building that led to performances of bands and orchestras in school, at contests, and for athletic events. Internationally, too, music educators worldwide were turning toward curricular content that was intercultural.

The tenor of music education shifted, so that by the 1990s it was not unusual for schools to celebrate multiple musical cultures worldwide in evening PTA performances, at district-wide arts festivals, and in student-centered oral histories that encouraged their own investigations of songs, stories, and musical instruments in their family histories. "World music pedagogy" and "cultural diversity in music education" were banners for emerging movements, even as the post–9/11 period triggered in US populations a regression from the global musical expanse to a more insular view of music that was sounding in local communities (Campbell, 2004; Schippers & Campbell, 2012)—regardless of the reality that some school music programs had become more vibrant through the development of in-school or after-school ensembles of "African drumming" ensembles, steel bands of the Caribbean, Mexican-style mariachis, or marimba ensembles featuring Shona-style music of Zimbabwe (Campbell, 2004). By the turn into the twenty-first century, "multicultural music education" was reduced by many to the notion of "multicultural music materials," that is, a South African freedom song for a choral group, an arrangement of a Korean or Japanese traditional song for band, and a set of songs from Brazil or Bulgaria, Puerto Rico or Ghana, were quite likely to suffice for meeting the multicultural mandates (Schippers & Campbell, 2012; Volk, 1998).

Due to the restrictions of tight teaching schedules, teachers have only rarely introduced comprehensive units of music and musicians that realize the potential for cultural understanding. The full extent of the tenets of multicultural education has gone untapped in music programs. Consequently, while the goals of equity and social action are articulated philosophically and in policy documents, they are not at the forefront of the work of most music educators (Campbell, 2013).

SOCIAL JUSTICE AND EDUCATION

Issues of equity and fairness stand at the center of most definitions and applications of social justice in education, including but not limited to concerns over curriculum (e.g., Bell, 2007), pedagogical approaches (e.g., Wade, 2007), and community relationships (e.g., Reilly Carlisle, Jackson, & George, 2006). In educational contexts, social justice recognizes that the inequalities that exist—both in school and in society—should stand at the center of the educative enterprise. Curricularly, this translates into learning activities that explicitly address issues of unfairness, asking students to critically engage to create and execute strategies to help resolve the injustices they identify. The curriculum also recognizes that knowledge is not absolute but culturally defined, and therefore is specifically cognizant of the many peoples that comprise the world's community. The focus on naming and redressing inequities does not come at the expense of content-area knowledge, but supplements and deepens growth in specific subject areas (Adams, 2007; Cochran-Smith et al., 2009; Reilly Carlisle, Jackson, & George, 2006; Sensoy & DiAngelo, 2012).

Pedagogically, educators teaching from a perspective of social justice recognize the importance of students' voices, value multiple perspectives, and emphasize the importance of reflective practice on the part of teachers and students alike. Bell (2007) notes that the process of a socially just education includes interactions between teacher and students that are "democratic and participatory," in which the teacher perceives herself as one who holds "power with" the students, not "power over" them (p. 2). Collaboration among students is common, and student choice often characterizes learning experiences. Peer relationships are valued, with an emphasis on a democratic classroom climate that honors the differences between students' experiences and perspectives, while also working to ensure that students work together harmoniously (Cochran-Smith, et al., 2009; Reilly Carlisle, Jackson, & George, 2006; Wade, 2007).

Listening to the perspectives of the community is also central to many conceptions of social justice in education (Cochran-Smith et al., 2009; Reilly Carlisle, Jackson, & George, 2006). Family involvement contributes to academic success, and facilitating the involvement of families in schools contributes to a socially just experience. Community communication is particularly important when the student body and their parents represent diversities (such as class and ethnicity) that differ from that of the teaching staff and administration.

SOCIAL JUSTICE AND MUSIC EDUCATION

We have identified three major themes that, over time, have emerged from the scholarship of social justice in education, making their way into music education literature and practice: equity of resources (e.g., Freierson-Campbell, 2007; Jorgensen, 2007), equity of pedagogical practices (e.g., Baxter, 2007; Peters, 2009), and equity within the curriculum (e.g., Allsup & Shieh, 2012; Griffin, 2011).

A distributive theory of social justice, in which resources are allocated proportionally, has arisen as an issue in music education. Music educators have condemned the disparity in arts funding, noting that resources have been found to be less prevalent for students of color and those with higher rates of poverty; such inequities in music and arts education have been observed for decades (Abril & Gault, 2008; Anderson, 1991; Campbell, 1985, 1992, 1994, 2013; Hicks, Standifer, & Carter, 1983; Lundquist, 1985; Schippers & Campbell, 2012; Standifer & Lundquist, 1972; Volk, 1998). Such funding discrepancy manifests itself in the number of course offerings, which are likely to be more sizable in large secondary schools than in rural schools, in areas of high poverty, and in schools in which the majority of the student body is non-White (Abril & Gault, 2008). Similarly, music classes at the elementary level are less often taught in dedicated music rooms in schools where the student body comes from lower social economic status or is primarily constituted by students of color (Freierson-Campbell, 2007). Music educators have also noted that the expense of instruments privileges the financially able (Jorgensen, 2007; Younker & Hickey, 2007). In a variety of ways, then, issues of equity play out in terms of the resources that exist for various populations, and proponents of social justice (as well as multiculturalists) have not only recognized the inequities but have also suggested means of adjustments for these imbalances (Campbell, 2013; Howard, Swanson, & Campbell, 2013).

At the classroom level, scholars have also addressed the power inequities that occur as a part of teacher-student relationships in which the instructors control the content and quality of delivery (Benedict & Schmidt, 2007; Peters, 2009). Interactive styles of pedagogy have been seen as being more socially just (Mayhew & Fernandez, 2007), and music educators have documented their efforts to divest themselves of power. For example, in higher education, Baxter (2007) provided an environment in which preservice students crafted their own definitions of social justice, then created units for K–12 students that incorporated their interpretations. Such democratization of student-teacher power relations is seen as more challenging for traditional secondary ensembles such as band and choir, in which the power typically resides with the conductor (Richardson, 2007; Younker & Hickey, 2007). At the elementary level, compositional practices in which teachers cede to the children much of the control over the decision-making process also serve as meaningful examples of socially just practices (Younker & Hickey, 2007). Throughout, the focus is on increased balance in power relations, providing students with greater autonomy and choice.

Finally, and most central to the decades of efforts in the name of multicultural music education (Anderson, 1991; Campbell, 1994, 2013; Volk, 1998), is the attention paid by proponents of social justice to specific curricular content. Scholars inspired by issues of social justice have advocated diversifying the musical content of the curriculum in order to more adequately represent the ethnic and cultural composition of the country and the world. Calls for more varied repertoire have been made for university-level schools of music (Bowman, 2007; Campbell, 2004), music education teacher education programs (Kindall-Smith, 2013; Standifer & Lundquist, 1972), and in K–12 settings (Campbell, 1985; Griffin, 2011). For example, Bowman (2007) urged not only diversifying the array of musical traditions included in the canon at the university level, but also maintained that study of the sociopolitical dimensions of the music should be included along with attention to its musical qualities. Beyond diversifying the musical repertoire, curricular implications of social justice ideals in music education have led to units that target specific injustices named by students (Allsup & Shieh, 2012). To date, examples of such curricular units are rare in music education publications.

CONNECTIONS BETWEEN MULTICULTURALISM AND SOCIAL JUSTICE

Most multicultural education theorists today maintain that multicultural principles apply not only to race and ethnicity, but also to issues such as gender, class, exceptionality, religion, sexuality, and language (e.g., Banks & Banks, 2013b). They acknowledge the complexities of individual students in terms of the varied experiences they bring to schools, and observe that learning is complicated by many family- and community-based circumstances. They recognize that values of home and school are not always resonant with one another, and that sensitivity and respect are critical to the educational enterprise (but that biases are amenable to change, too). Those who espouse social justice in their multicultural approaches to schooling note that while school is the context in which equity pedagogy can be practiced, an educational plan can be put into practice that is responsive to the restrictions of limited school schedules, and that considers sites outside the school building and in the community as important places of learning (Banks, 2007). Moreover, the terms "multicultural education" and "social justice" have often been linked together. Grant and Sleeter (2013), for example, describe "multicultural social justice education" as an approach that "deals . . . directly with oppression and social structural inequality based on race, social class, gender, and disability" (p. 50).

Banks's Levels of Curriculum Reform

The theoretical dimensions of James Banks (2013b) are a particularly illuminating way toward a more equitable curriculum that might also lead to deepened levels of commitment and involvement. Banks's five dimensions of multicultural education can be most helpful to music educators, as they reflect social justice principles and offer an effective framework for understanding the issues. The five dimensions consist of content integration, knowledge construction, prejudice reduction, equity pedagogy, and an empowering school culture.

Content integration refers to "the extent to which teachers use examples and content from a variety of cultures and groups to illustrate key concepts, principles, generalizations, and theories in their subject area or discipline" (Banks, 2013b, p. 16). Traditionally, content across subjects is viewed through the lens of the European-American experience (in the context of the United States), and the incorporation of examples from other cultures is one way to move toward a more multicultural curriculum.

The *knowledge construction process* describes the ways in which ideas and expectations are formed, noting that implicit cultural assumptions characterize interactions between (mostly White, middle-class) teachers and their students, regardless of race, ethnicity, or other group membership status. Banks points out that ideas about what constitutes knowledge always reflects ideology, human interests, values, and perspectives, and that teachers must recognize the vantage point from which they come. Students and educators should learn to "understand, investigate, and determine how the implicit cultural assumptions, frames of reference, perspectives, and biases within a discipline influence the ways in which knowledge is constructed" (Banks, 2013b, p. 19).

A third dimension of multicultural education consists of *prejudice reduction*, the lessons and activities that explicitly address issues of prejudice. Stereotypes about specific minority groups continue to characterize young learners (Aboud, 2009, cited in Banks, 2013b). Learning activities designed to understand the prejudice that continues to exist in specific situations and that work to lessen it are seen as essential parts of multiculturalism.

The fourth of Banks's dimensions of multicultural education is *equity pedagogy*. Equity pedagogy refers to the process in which educators "modify their teaching in ways that will facilitate the academic achievement of students from diverse . . . groups" (p. 19). This consists of incorporating an understanding of the learning styles that characterize many members of particular ethnic, cultural, or social class groups, while not essentializing individual students into a manifestation of their group status; each student is also seen as an individual.

Finally, creating an *empowering school culture* comprises an ultimate goal of multicultural education that encompasses the entire community of students, teachers, and professional staff. To Banks, access to a variety of experiences within the school setting is important. The degrees to which the various groups in a school setting participate in a variety of school experiences, such as differently leveled classes, sports participation, club participation, and levels of academic achievement, should be investigated, with any disproportionality studied to determine the reasons behind it. In an empowered school culture, a student's group status has negligent impact on his or her ability to become involved or to participate successfully in any academic or extracurricular activity.

For teachers with minimal education and experience with these concepts, the prospect of incorporating them into curriculum can seem overwhelming. In an attempt to demystify the process, Banks reconfigured the dimensions into a specific, tiered system of educational application, which he named "levels of multicultural curriculum reform" (Banks, 2013a), consisting of (a) contributions, (b) additive, (c) transformation, and (d) social action. These levels of educational application are meant as a sequential and manageable series of steps that can be taken to move multicultural principles into teaching-learning experiences. The levels clarify curricular design and instructional delivery, thereby rendering the achievement of the overall goals as less daunting.

APPLICATIONS: MULTICULTURAL SOCIAL ACTION AND SOCIAL JUSTICE IN MUSIC EDUCATION

The tiers of practice delineated above establish increasing commitment across the four levels—from "contributions" to "social action"—toward a conversion of music education to the achievement of goals in music and through music, such that all students may benefit from knowing music (and culture) broadly and deeply as performance, listening analysis, creative composition and improvisation.

In the *contributions approach*, the experiences of diverse groups are incorporated into learning experiences as a supplement to the typical, mainstream-centered curriculum. Sometimes referred to as the "heroes-and-holidays" approach, discrete aspects related to specific groups are incorporated at particular times during the year. The curriculum remains unchanged, with educational experiences serving as add-on experiences that often have little relation to the rest of the learning that occurs. Banks notes that this can result in "the trivialization of ethnic cultures, the study of their strange and exotic characteristics, and the reinforcement of stereotypes and misconceptions" (p. 186), leading to a learning environment in which ethnic issues accessorize the dominant Eurocentric paradigm. For teachers with little knowledge or comfort level with teaching concepts of other cultures, lessons within the contributions level serve as an initial first step into multicultural education, however limited it may be.

At the elementary music level, learning experiences in which children sing a song about the United States civil rights leader Martin Luther King in the days around the January holiday are a contributive activity. In a secondary band class, a learning experience with the mariachi tradition can be contributive, if a piece of music from the tradition is learned through a musical score employing conventional Western musical notation rather than the aural/oral model that is typical of mariachi music. In a college music history survey course, students could hear a recording of *Machu Picchu Concerto for Kena and Orchestra*, by Nayo Ulloa, a piece of music that incorporates the kena (a traditional flute from the Andean mountains of Peru) along with a Western-style orchestra; pictures of the instrument might be viewed, but with no further exploration of Peruvian musical culture, the experience stands as contributive. In all of these learning experiences, the music ornaments the traditional curriculum, providing a snapshot view of an alternative music that operates within the dominant musical standard. Music educators have often employed this approach to teaching in the name of multiculturalism (see basal series texts dating back to the mid-twentieth century), and while it is an important first step (particularly for music educators whose comfort level or experience with non-Western musics are limited), the educational outcomes are limited, and could reify tokenism, possibly sustaining rather than mitigating inequalities.

The second level of Banks's multicultural curriculum reform is the *additive approach*. Lessons at this level address issues with more depth than the contributions approach, with content, themes, and concepts incorporated into a variety of activities and understandings. The additional material is more extensive, and allows a greater range of diverse material without changing the basic structure of the curriculum. While relatively easy for teachers to incorporate, ethnic content is still viewed from a mainstream or privileged perspective. In addition, the learning related to the culture often stands as a separate entity, with connections between the minority group and the dominant one not made explicit. For example, a social studies class that studies the westward migration of European settlers across the United States in the 1800s may include the experiences of a particular Native American culture group, but the entire unit is viewed through the experience of the settlers. In addition, the complexities of interconnections between the dominant culture and the minority group are, at best, skimmed over.

In an elementary music classroom, a multi-session unit addressing music from Turkey would allow for more extensive learning experiences with an unfamiliar musical tradition, with the multiple experiences with the unfamiliar musical culture making it more extensive than a contributions lesson. Similarly, a secondary choral setting in which repertoire from multiple African-American spirituals are used in the context of the established class structure—as critical listening experiences, sight-reading exercises, and as a set of pieces in a performance—comprises a multicultural learning experience in the additive realm. At the university level, a world music survey class is classified as an additive experience when the class structure resembles other music history classes, with drop-the-needle tests, lecture classes, and minimal music making, classes in which connections between the new musical cultures and the dominant one remain minimal. In these more extensive units, the fact that the musical material is still viewed through a Western prism renders them additive; for example, in the Turkey unit, students might be exposed to music traditionally performed on instruments common in Turkey (e.g., the oud), but perform them on classroom instruments (e.g., xylophones), with no attention paid to the difference in timbre. Music educators engage in these experiences with less regularity than contributive ones, for they take more organization and planning, but for teachers intent on teaching with a multicultural focus, the lessons are a further step along the continuum.

The *transformation approach* takes an issue and views it from the perspective of different groups. In history, for example, the movement of Europeans to the American continent in the seventeenth century can be examined from the viewpoints of the Europeans, Africans, and Native Americans. Through these experiences, students begin to understand that knowledge is socially constructed, and are asked to consider that diverse groups contribute in a variety of ways to a subject. In order to accomplish this, the typical curriculum must often be revised, which can be time-intensive.

In music education practice, transformation occurs as musical expressions are compared for their sonic structures, their uses and functions within cultures, their symbologies, and their cultural meaning and values. Examples of teaching with transformation in mind are found in Wade (2004) and Campbell (2004), who suggest that musical instruments, pitch, time, and structure can be explored across as many cultures as are available, "live" in person or through access to media and technology. For students in elementary music programs, the transformation approach can happen in a comparison of fiddles (or flutes, or other instruments) across multiple cultures. Different but equally logical ways can be examined of the construction of fiddles (body shapes, size of tuning pegs, number of strings), or of positioning them in the hands of a player, or of tuning the two, three, four or more strings. Secondary school students can sing or play various examples of music for weddings, or for funerals, for purposes of expressing cultural or national identity. University students can be led through an exploration of various solfège systems (in theory and musicianship classes), various Western and world events for which musical works were composed (in music history and culture classes), and various approaches to teaching and learning (in pedagogy and education classes). For students in preparation for careers in music education, projects that encourage the design and delivery of lessons and units on particular musical and cultural themes can lead to a way of conceiving music instruction that allows school-age students an understanding of music from multiple perspectives.

Finally, the *social action approach* begins with learning experiences from a transformative background, but then requires students to "make decisions and take actions related to a concept, issue, or problem" that was studied in the unit (Banks, 2013a, p. 13). Not satisfied with solely identifying issues that exist within the status quo, teachers and students move to the level of social action as they make specific plans that will rectify inequities within society that they have identified. For example, a literature class may write a letter to the editor, or a blog-piece, with suggestions for ways to demonstrate greater sensitivity and fair treatment within situations in which specific racial and ethnic communities are described (or neglected) in the media. This approach enables students to improve their critical thinking skills, articulate their values, and develop a sense that they are powerful, empowering them to contribute to making the world a more equitable and culturally sensitive place. The unit may be more intensive than a typical in-school experience, as activities that transpire out in the community beyond school typically require not only time and energy but efforts to safeguard the off-campus safety of students, as well as even a monetary commitment (for bus rental and meals or snacks).

Social action approaches are fairly rare in music education, in part due to the problems articulated earlier. Not all music teachers are convinced, either, of the need to go beyond repertoire and pedagogical processes within their classrooms in meeting the goals of multicultural education and social justice. To many who view a social action approach as an extra off-campus field trip, the logistics are mind-boggling and the alternative of staying put in the classroom seems entirely within the realm of reason in meeting the call for teaching from a multicultural perspective and with social justice in mind. Still, there are exemplary social action approaches in evidence, where teachers work with students who prepare a repertoire of vocal and instrumental pieces for audiences in their school and at annual festivals and competitions. Such performances can easily encompass wider audiences of senior citizens, disabled populations, and people of diverse neighborhoods, all of whom may be transported to the school or may be visited by students at their residential centers, churches, shopping centers, and community gathering places. Taking a further step forward, teachers facilitate possibilities for their students to visit with their audiences, to use music as an opening to conversations with them, following the performances.

Student ensembles may find themselves invited to community events to perform at civic rallies and political assemblies connected to national holidays or local festivals on a theme (e.g., Memorial Day parades or Martin Luther King commemorations). Music teachers are in a position to organize students for participation as singers or players at community gatherings that call attention to support (or not support) fair trade, the military service, gun control, and civil rights. Students become further attuned to the reasoning behind the issues, and to an understanding of the democratic right to stake a claim on them, through their participation in these musical events; they may read of the issues in advance or following the event, and they may gain further insight through exchanges with others present.

At the university level, many possibilities exist for the involvement of students in social action. *Music Alive! in the Yakima Valley!* (Soto, Lum, & Campbell, 2009) is one such program that drew music education students from their university to a Native American tribal school and to students of 98 percent Mexican-American community schools. Through residencies ranging from multiple one-day visits to a week at a time, students gained perspectives on music, teaching, and social communities far removed from their urban campus life (and earlier suburban school experiences), as they sang, played, and danced the music of their training as well as the music of the students and their families, whom they came to know. With glimpses of life in these rural and remote low-income communities, each of which nonetheless proudly welcomed students into their homes and schools, university students accrued firsthand experiences in the meanings of cultural diversity in education. For some, this social action enlightened them to the extent that they later sought (and found) positions in rural, remote, and impoverished communities across the state.

The impact of the Community Music movement has been felt in curricular reform involving music, multiculturalism, social action, and social justice music education through a greater recognition of how music education can transpire in and outside school (Higgins, 2012). Community Music has helped to bring about the linkages of universities with communities that surround the school, as well as those that may live some distance apart (Schippers & Campbell, 2012). Opportunities have emerged for music major students to become involved in community engagement activities—teaching music to young students in an after-school program, for example. For course credit, for "service learning" requirements, or as internships that develop into employment opportunities, social action projects for university music students have included working with children, youth, and adults in not only applied music lessons but also the development of drumming ensembles, singing groups, rock bands, song-writing classes, and social dance circumstances. In these ways, music educators are at the forefront of this fourth level of curricular reform, social action, and indeed social justice as well, facilitating musical experiences to the communities that request them.

THE WAY FORWARD

The diversity of the United States continues to grow at an astonishing rate; 92 percent of the population growth between 2000 and 2010 was comprised by ethnic minorities (Banks & Banks, 2013), a trend that shows no sign of stopping. Given that our schools will hold children from an increasingly broad array of cultures, multicultural ideals must necessarily stand at the core of conceptions of social justice: an equitable musical curriculum must incorporate a range of musical cultures in meaningful and equitable fashion.

Banks's (2013a) levels of curriculum reform provide a road map for teachers and teacher educators searching for a framework under which curricular change can occur. From the earliest dipping of toes through a contributions lesson to an in-depth social action experience, the levels offer a sequential means by which to guide music educators—even those with minimal experience (and maximal anxiety) about issues of multiculturalism—to alter their teaching to create just learning environments in which all students are seen, heard, and honored.

We build upon the thoughts and endeavors of earlier generations, and the rise of social justice is, to us, deeply entwined within the aims and actions of nations and peoples earnestly committed to equitable treatment of citizens in society and its schools. The realization of social justice by thoughtful music educators is in step with the works of teachers devoted to the ideals of multicultural education who, as early as the Civil Rights movement of the 1960s, were eager to reach all children and youth through school music programs, to offer relevant musical education that was resonant with their local community experiences, and to provide the means for their success as citizens of a mainstream society.

Situated at the nexus of the movements for multiculturalism and social justice, issues of equity and social action are impressively evident in schools, such that these complementary movements are contributing to the education of students in music and through music toward the socially responsible citizens they will become.

NOTE

1. While African Americans led the movement for educational reform, and the works of James A. Banks, Geneva Gay, and Carl A. Grant are early and continuing influences on the development of theory and practice, the evolution of multicultural education includes also specialists in the learning processes of students of various races and ethnicities, such as Carlos E. Cortes, Jack D. Forbes, Eugene E. Garcia, K. Tsianina Lomawaima, Sonia Nieto, and Derald W. Sue.

REFERENCES

Abril, C. R., & Gault, B. M. (2008). The state of music in secondary schools: The principal's perspective. *Journal of Research in Music Education, 56*, 68–81.

Adams, M. (2007). Pedagogical frameworks for social justice education. In M. Adams, L. A. Bell, & P. Griffin (Eds.), *Teaching for diversity and social justice* (pp. 15–33). New York: Routledge.

Allsup, R., & Shieh, E. (2012). Social justice and music education: The call for public pedagogy. *Music Educators Journal, 98*(4), 47–51.

Anderson, W. M. (Ed.) (1991). *Teaching music with a multicultural approach*. Reston, VA: Music Educators National Conference.

Banks, J. A. (2007). *Educating citizens in a multicultural society*. New York: Teachers College Press.

Banks, J. A. (2013a). Approaches to multicultural curriculum reform. In J. A. Banks & C. A. McGee Banks (Eds.), *Multicultural education: Issues and perspectives* (8th ed., pp. 181–199). Hoboken, NJ: Wiley.

Banks, J. A. (2013b). Multicultural education: Characteristics and goals. In J. A. Banks & C. A. McGee Banks (Eds.), *Multicultural education: Issues and perspectives* (8th ed., pp. 3–23). Hoboken, NJ: Wiley.

Banks, J. A., & Banks, C. A. (Eds.). (2013). Preface. In J. A. Banks & C. A. McGee Banks (Eds.), *Multicultural education: Issues and perspectives* (8th ed., pp. iii–v). Hoboken, NJ: Wiley.

Baxter, M. (2007). Global music making a difference: Themes of exploration, action, and justice. *Music Education Research*, 9(2), 267–279.

Bell, L. A. (2007). Theoretical foundations for social justice education. In M. Adams, L. A. Bell, & P. Griffin (Eds.), *Teaching for diversity and social justice* (pp. 1–14). New York: Routledge.

Benedict, C., & Schmidt, P. (2007). From whence justice? Interrogating the improbable in music education. *Action, Criticism, and Theory for Music Education*, 6(4), 21–42.

Bowman, W. (2007). Who is the "we?" Rethinking professionalism in music education. *Action, Criticism, and Theory for Music Education*, 6(4), 109–131.

Campbell, P. S. (1985). A recommitment to multicultural arts education. *Design for Arts in Education*, 86(4), 43–44.

Campbell, P. S. (1992). Cultural consciousness in teaching general music. *Music Educators Journal*, 78(9), 38–46.

Campbell, P. S. (1994). Music, teachers and children: Research in a time of sociocultural transformation. *General Music Today*, 7(2), 19–26.

Campbell, P. S. (2004). *Teaching music globally*. New York: Oxford University Press.

Campbell, P. S. (2013). Children, teachers and ethnomusicologists: Traditions and transformation of music in school. In B. Alge (Ed.), *Beyond borders: Welt-musik-padagogik*. Augsburg: Wissner.

Cochran-Smith, M., Shakman, K., Jong, C., Terrell, D. G., Barnatt, J., & McQuillan, P. (2009). Good and just teaching: The case for social justice in teacher education. *American Journal of Education*, 115(3), 347–377.

Freierson-Campbell, C. (2007). Without the 'ism: Thoughts about equity and social justice in music education. *Music Education Research*, 9(2), 255–265.

Grant, C. A., & Sleeter, C. E. (2013). Race, class, gender, and disability in the classroom. In J. A. Banks & C. A. McGee Banks (Eds.), *Multicultural education: Issues and perspectives* (8th ed., pp. 43–60). Hoboken, NJ: Wiley.

Griffin, S. M. (2011). Reflection on the social justice behind children's tales of in- and out-of-school experiences. *Bulletin of the Council for Research in Music Education*, 188, 77–92.

Hicks, C. E., Standifer, J. A., & Carter, W. L. (1983). *Methods and perspectives in urban music education*. Washington, DC: University Press of America.

Higgins, L. (2012). *Community music: In theory and practice*. New York: Oxford University Press.

Howard, K., Swanson, M., & Campbell, P. S. (2013). The diversification of music teacher education: Six cases from a movement in progress. *Journal of Music Teacher Education*, 24, 26–27.

Jorgensen, E. (2007). Concerning justice and music education. *Music Education Research*, 9(2), 169–189.

Kindall-Smith, M. (2013). What a difference in 3 years! Risking social justice content in required undergraduate music education curricula. *Journal of Music Teacher Education*, 22(2), 34–50.

Lundquist, B. R. (1985). Music education in a multicultural society: The United States of America. *International Journal of Music Education*, 5(2), 49–53.

Mayhew, M. J., & Fernández, S. D. (2007). Pedagogical practices that contribute to social justice outcomes. *The Review of Higher Education*, 31(1), 55–80.

Nieto, S. (2009). Multicultural education in the United States: Historical realities, ongoing challenges, and transformative possibilities. In J. A. Banks (Ed.), *The Routledge international companion to multicultural education* (pp. 79–96). New York: Routledge.

North, C. (2006). More than words? Delving into the substantive meaning(s) of "social justice" in education. *Review of Educational Research, 76*(4), 507–535.

Peters, V. (2009). Youth identity construction through music education: Nurturing a sense of belonging in multi-ethnic communities. In E. Gould, J. Countryman, C. Morton, & L. S. Rose (Eds.), *Exploring social justice: How music education might matter* (pp. 199–211). Toronto: Canadian Music Educators' Association.

Reilly Carlisle, L., Jackson, B. W., & George, A. (2006). Principles of social justice education: The social justice education in schools project. *Equity & Excellence in Education, 39*, 55–64.

Reisch, M. (2007). Social justice and multiculturalism: Persistent tensions in the history of US social welfare and social work. *Studies in Social Justice, 1*(1), 67–92.

Richardson, C. P. (2007). Engaging the world: Music education and the big ideas. *Music Education Research, 9*(2), 205–214.

Schippers, H., & Campbell, P. S. (2012). Cultural diversity: Beyond "songs from many lands." In G. McPherson & G. Welch (Eds.), *Oxford handbook of music education* (pp. 87–104). New York: Oxford.

Sensoy, Ö., & DiAngelo, R. (2012). *Is everyone really equal? An introduction to key concepts in social justice education.* New York: Teachers College Press.

Soto, A. C., Lum, C.-H., & Campbell, P. S. (2009). A university-school partnership for music education students within a culturally distinctive community. *Journal of Research in Music Education, 6*(4), 338–356.

Standifer, J. A., & Lundquist, B. R. (1972). *Source book of African and Afro-American materials for music educators.* Reston, VA: Music Educators National Conference.

Volk, T. M. (1998). *Music, education and multiculturalism: Foundations and principles.* New York: Oxford University Press.

Wade, B. C. (2004). *Thinking musically.* New York: Oxford University Press.

Wade, R. C. (2007). *Social studies for social justice: Teaching strategies for the elementary classroom.* New York: Teachers College Press.

Younker, B. A., & Hickey, M. (2007). Examining the profession through the lens of social justice: Two music educators' stories and their stark realizations. *Music Education Research, 9*(2), 215–227.

CHAPTER 18

MUSIC EDUCATION, SOCIAL JUSTICE, AND THE "STUDENT VOICE"

Addressing Student Alienation Through a Dialogical Conception of Music Education

GARY SPRUCE

INTRODUCTION

THE body of literature around music education and student voice is a relatively small one. Finney (2011), in his study of the child-centered progressive tradition within music education in England since 1950, devotes a chapter to student voice, considering it in relation to pupil autonomy and children as musical leaders. Finney is also the co-editor of, and contributor to, a valuable multi-authored volume on student voice and music education produced by the English National Association of Music Education (Finney and Harrison, 2010). There are also a number of scholarly articles (e.g., Lamont et al., 2003) and research reports (e.g., Harland et al., 2000) that draw on "student voice" in order to explore young people's perceptions of, and attitudes toward, their music education and music making in and outside school. Perhaps inevitably in a market-driven educational context, a large number of "evaluation reports" commissioned by music education organizations draw on the voice of the student as one way of demonstrating that what they have to offer delivers the greatest benefits to children's musical learning and/or social and cognitive development. These, in their different ways, draw on the student voice as the voice of a consumer of music education. This chapter resonates most strongly, however, with the literature around critical pedagogy and musical education (e.g., Abrahams, 2005; Allsup, 2003; Finney, 2010; Spruce, 2012) in that it seeks to explore ways in which the "student voice" might be elicited in pursuit of a more socially just approach to music education in schools in order to address the alienation of many young people from music in the school curriculum.

The concept of social justice is multi-faceted and multi-defined. However, following Spruce (2013), for the purposes of this chapter one of the defining characteristics of a socially just approach to music education is taken to be the opportunity for students not only to "participate" in music education, but also to be "included" in it as their voices being heard in decisions about curriculum and pedagogy and in the construction of musical knowledge, understanding, and *value*.

The chapter is structured in three main sections. The first looks at the background to the rise in interest in the "student voice" and identifies some of the concepts, issues, and challenges associated with it. The second takes English music education over the last 40 years as a "case study" of how initiatives that have as their primary intention increasing the "participation" and "inclusion" of young people in school music education can be subverted by dominant musical ideologies, resulting in the silencing of the voices of many students and their subsequent disengagement from the school music curriculum. The final section posits a dialogical approach to music education as one means by which music classrooms might become democratic spaces within which student voices (musical and otherwise) are heard and enacted and issues of student alienation and disengagement are addressed.

The chapter begins by setting out the background to the rise in interest in student voice over the past 40 years. This is followed by a survey of the literature that seeks to identify the main generic issues, debates, and challenges associated with the promotion and elicitation of student voice initiatives in the classroom. The argument will be made that an unproblematized account of "student voice" typically projected within official documents and realized within schools has served to mask its political and ideological dimensions, laying it open to being appropriated in support of management and performativity agendas—performativity agendas that typically seek to translate "complex social processes and events into simple figures or categories of judgements" (Ball, 2003, p. 217). Consequently, the potential of student voice to disrupt powerful hegemonies and create more democratic spaces remains largely unfulfilled.

Drawing then on the work of Arnot and Reay (2007) and, *inter alia*, the English sociologist Basil Bernstein (2000), the suggestion will be made that the "student voice" cannot be understood as an independent variable, aloof from the context in which it is developed and enacted, but rather that the messages it articulates, and which teachers hear, emerge from the pedagogical contexts that students encounter. It therefore follows that in order to disrupt the power and hierarchical relationships that work against the furtherance of social justice within education, the elicitation of the student voice is not sufficient in itself. Rather, one needs to interrogate the pedagogical values and ideologies that construct the voice and which privilege certain voices and messages while rendering others unheard.

This then sets the context for the second section of the chapter where, picking up on the need for this interrogations of pedagogies, developments and initiatives in music education in England over the last 40 years are analyzed in terms of the extent to which they have allowed for the creation of music classrooms as democratic spaces within which the student voice might be heard. The case is made that, despite the focus of many of these developments and initiatives on addressing the disengagement of young people from school music education, the continuing hegemony of the values and practices of Western art music within the formal curriculum has resulted in the creation of a "monological discourse," which has had the effect of silencing the voices of many young people, thus alienating them from music in school.

The third and final section argues for a dialogical approach to music education in order to counter the monological discourses that have been instrumental in sustaining dominant musical ideologies. The notion of the student voice as "singular" and as existing autonomously will be challenged and the argument made that the voice of the student can *only* be heard in relation to other voices—both temporal and historical. Drawing particularly on the work of Wegerif (2011) and, *inter alia*, the ideas of the Russian philosopher Mikhail Bakhtin, key themes and ideas underpinning a dialogical approach to education will be outlined, along with suggestions of how a dialogic approach to music education might allow for the voice of the student to be heard and student agency to be exercised. A key idea underpinning both a socially just approach to music education (as defined earlier) and a dialogical approach to music education is a recognition that there are "multiple ways of knowing" music and that "musical learning in its widest sense is a lifelong, continuing and always incomplete endeavour" (Spruce, 2013, p. 25).

Although the English educational system is the locus of most of the examples drawn upon, the ideas explored here hopefully have relevance for other settings. "Student voice" (singular) will be adopted throughout the chapter, as indeed it is in much of the literature and policy documents where it is discussed. However, it is recognized that the voice of the learner it is neither singular nor homogenous. Rather, it is as diverse and multiple as the contexts in which is enacted and the purposes to which it is put (Flutter, 2010).

BACKGROUND AND CONTEXT, CHALLENGES, AND PROBLEMATIZATIONS

Rudduck and Fielding (2006) point out how the concept of "student voice" is not a recent one. They note a 1978 "special" issue of *Educational Review* devoted to "student voice" and go on to describe three schools from the 1890s, 1920s, and 1940s where "commitment to participation and voice was central" (Rudduck & Fielding, 2006, p. 221). Similarly, Finney (2011) draws attention to the Schools Council "Arts and the Adolescent" project undertaken in the late 1960s and early 1970s, where almost 4,000 students were consulted about their experiences of school and what they believed should be included in an arts curriculum. However, as Cook-Sather (2006) says, it is only since the beginning of this century that the idea of student voice has taken root in the wider educational discourse and has begun to have an impact on schools and educational policy and practice.

Flutter (2010) argues that the impulses for the recent implementation of student voice strategies have their origins in one or more of the following:

- The requirements of international legislation;
- As a tool for raising educational standards;
- As a means of developing more personalized approaches to learning;
- As a means for promoting citizenship and democracy.

These form what Flutter describes as a "nexus of ideas" that have as a common theme "giving children and young people a more active, participative role in their learning and schools" (Flutter, 2010, p. 17) and the belief that "through listening to what pupils say about their experience as learners, teachers are able to gain new insights into the factors that make a difference to pupils learning and progress" (Flutter, 2007, p. 352).

Although the work of all the authors thus cited (and others) has served to raise the awareness of the concept of "student voice" in schools, the problematized and subtle accounts that they provide have not generally permeated in any significant way into education policy or the implementation of student voice approaches within the classroom. Rather, under-theorized, unproblematized accounts of student voice have taken root, resulting from what Flutter (2007) describes as the "confidence and prescriptiveness" of the language of official guidelines and documentation and a proliferation of "manuals and 'how to guides', yielding a limited conceptual understanding of the nature of 'student voice' and 'a picture of pupils' views that is partial" (p. 342). Limited conceptual understanding has led to perhaps somewhat crude understandings of student voice, including that it is

- simply "out there," " 'waiting to be discovered" ' and once discovered will, *ipso facto*, result in more " 'authentic' relations between teachers and students" and thence to students becoming "better citizens and more active learners, and schools to become better places" (Bragg, 2007, p. 344);
- a homogenous concept that can "speak" as the unison utterance of a particular individual, social, or cultural group;
- either independently constructed (i.e., unaffected by its context) and/or the product of individual consciousness.

Undertheorized accounts of student voice have also led to it acquiring a portmanteau function in schools where, *as a term*, it is drawn upon to describe a wide range of student voice engagements and manifestations. Sabia (2012) conceptualizes these as being on a kind of democratic continuum. At one end, students' views are sought simply as data sets to be analyzed and drawn upon as required (often only required when they support dominant discourses or managerial agendas), moving through consultations with pupils as members of school councils on issues that focus on the pastoral and environmental aspects of the school, and finally to "more egalitarian and participatory" approaches around student-teacher collaboration and core educational issues (Sabia, 2012, p. 382).

Hart (1992), in his oft-cited "Ladder of Participation," also suggests that certain kinds of student voice elicitations within schools provide a veneer of democratic legitimacy in support of managerial and performativity agendas. Similarly, Bragg, Fielding, and Flutter have all, over a number of years, drawn attention to how under-theorized conceptions of "student voice" have laid it open to being appropriated as a means of sustaining dominant discourses, thus undermining its potential to disrupt the power relationships that work against the creation of more democratic and equitable sites of learning. Fielding goes further, warning that the lack of theoretical attention to student voice can result in it being drawn upon to sanction "intellectual assumptions and energetic developments that serve to secure us more comfortably to purposes we abhor and practices we may come to regret" (Fielding, 2008, p. 58).

Fielding has drawn particular attention to how "student voice" has been yoked to a "personalisation" agenda that lacks any "convincing account of the common good" (Fielding, 2004, p. 205) and which serves to promote a key tenet of neo-liberal philosophy by privileging "self" over "community." Personalization is then promoted as being synonymous with freedom. However, as Greene points out, this is a form of freedom characterized by "self-dependence rather than relationship; self-regarding and self-regulated behaviour rather than involvement with others" (Greene, 1988, p. 7). Fielding further argues that, far from being a mechanism for liberating the individual, personalization, along with its handmaiden, "choice," typically provides a range of pre-ordained options which are limited to those that serve to sustain dominant discourses and power relationships.

Personalization is one means by which the student voice is delimited. Another is through mechanisms that determine which voices are heard and which are not. According to Bernstein (2000), it is often only those students who are able to articulate the sanctioned or "legitimate text" that are heard within the "acoustic" of school. Because these students have command of the legitimated text and their voices appear to be (and are) the more articulate, they are more able to engage within the discourse of the school and are therefore more easily heard. Those students who do not, cannot, or will not articulate the sanctioned text are effectively muted. Elena Silva (2001), for example, notes that when consultation takes place primarily through student councils, it is important to consider "which students are representing the 'student voice' of their school? And, in the context of reform, can those students who are best-served by the current setup of their school possibly serve the interests of those students who are least served?" (Silva, 2001, p. 98). Cremin, reporting on interviews with minority ethnic pupils, describes how one felt that his voice was not heard and that the "sanctioned" voice of the student council was "just as alien to his world as the headteacher" (Cremin et al., 2011, p. 599). However, through privileging those voices that articulate the sanctioned messages, the school is able to present itself as promoting discourse, dialogue, and democratic engagement and, by implication, a social justice agenda, without risk to the dominant structures and power relationships that ensure the maintenance of the status quo. These dominant discourses will include pedagogical messages but also management messages about "what makes a good lesson" or a "good teacher." In such ways, the student voice is appropriated as a managerial tool with the potential to constrain individual teachers' pedagogies within the framework of a "school view." Student voice in this case is used as the means of "rearticulating the largely predictable list of what makes a good teacher, a good lesson or a good school" de facto transforming students into "unwitting agents of government control" (Fielding, 2004, p. 205).

Arnot and Reay (2003) draw on the work of Basil Bernstein to argue that when considering the "student voice" a distinction needs to be made between "voice" and "message." They suggest that the student voice is constructed from particular pedagogical contexts. Citing Diaz (2011), they describe these pedagogical contexts as "fields of meanings and practices" that evolve from power relationships based around the concepts of "classification" (who has the power to teach what to whom and the extent to which things are kept apart or brought together) and "framing" (how knowledge is acquired and constructed and the extent to which the learner has power over those aspects). These pedagogical contexts produce what Bernstein calls the "voice of pedagogy" or "pedagogical voice" (Arnot and Reay, p. 316). What is then "heard" is not "the voice" but "the message"—a message that reflects and sustains the power relationships of the pedagogical context within which the voice is formed. As Arnot and Reay (2007) say elsewhere, "the student voices heard in [the] process of consultation are not in fact independently constructed 'voices' rather they are 'the messages' created by particular pedagogical contexts" (p. 317).

Bernstein argues that in order to be heard—to be a "communicant"—it is necessary to understand both the rules of the pedagogical context and the rules "which govern the realisation of such competence" (Arnot & Reay, 2003, p. 317). Bernstein's proposition is that "voice" represents recognition of the pedagogical rules while "the message" is the *realization* of these rules in particular contexts. Some children may possess "the recognition rule (they can recognise power relations and their own position in them) but they do not possess the realisation rules. Hence they cannot speak the expected legitimate text or produce the 'legitimate communication'" (Arnot & Reay, 2007, p. 320).

Consequently, for some children, their experience of school is one in which they are aware of the power relationships and frameworks within which they find themselves, though they are unable to articulate the expected or required messages that enable them to be heard—they are in effect muted, marginalized, and potentially alienated. But this muting, marginalization, and alienation are masked by the illusion that consultation and the elicitation of the student voice inevitably realize and release principles and frameworks of equity, democratic engagement, and social justice. However, in Bernstein's view, the messages that are heard in schools (particularly within strongly framed and classified pedagogical contexts) are from those voices that have been successfully enculturated into the dominant discourses. Thus the potential for the student voice to disrupt hierarchies and power relationships through democratic engagement with the processes of music education is negated, as the messages that are heard are only those that project the school's legitimated text.

MUSIC EDUCATION, ALIENATION AND STUDENT VOICE: A CASE STUDY FROM ENGLISH MUSIC EDUCATION

If, as Bernstein suggests, student voices and the messages they articulate emerge from, and are constructed by, particular pedagogical contexts, and if some pedagogies silence certain voices, then it is to pedagogy and sites of pedagogy that we must turn to understand why many young people disengage from the music curriculum in schools.

The long-term and continuing dissatisfaction of young people in England with classroom music education is well-documented (e.g., Evans, 2012; Harland, Kinder, & Hartley, 1995; Harland et al., 2000; Lamont & Maton. 2008; Ross, 1995; Schools Council Enquiry, 1968; Swanwick, 1988). This dissatisfaction is somewhat ironic, given that many (and perhaps most) initiatives and developments in music education in England over the last 40 years—from the Schools Council Music Project under John Paynter in the late 1960s and early 1970s to the Music National Strategy of 2006–2007 (DfES, 2006)—have been directed toward engaging the interest of more young people in the school music curriculum. Approaches have tended to focus on increasing the diversity of musical styles and traditions included within the curriculum—particularly the greater inclusion of "pop" music—as well as adopting a more participatory approach to music lessons through providing opportunities for young people to make music as performers and composers; these remain, today, the primary strategies employed by teachers as they look to engage students' interest in the school music curriculum. However, as Green (2003), Spruce (2007), and Philpott (2010), among others, have pointed out, whereas the school music curriculum might now include a broader repertoire of music than previously, the paradigm of musical and knowledge-teacher-learner relationships within which young people are required to work has remained the same: primarily those promoted by the Western music aesthetic.

The Western music aesthetic is underpinned by the dual ideology of musical reification and musical autonomy. Musical reification is the process by which music comes to be thought of not as an abstract concept but as an object. This process of reification is underpinned by the ideology of musical autonomy that sees musical meaning as constructed by the relationship between sonic materials and contained within "musical structures"—the object. The ideology of musical autonomy and reification, with the consequent perception of music as an object, is reinforced in a number of ways. The most obvious is through the notion that "music" and "the score" (its literary/scripted and most obviously objectified form) are virtually synonymous. Spruce (2007, pp. 19–20) describes how the language that is typically used to talk about music—for example, "pieces of music" and "don't forget to bring your music to rehearsal"—reinforces this idea of music-as-object. Similarly, phrases such as, "look at the music" have both the effect of distancing a person from the music as sound and the "potential to instill the notion that the written score is more real than the music" (Louth, 2013, p. 77). This all leads to what Cook describes as the basic premise of the Western "art" tradition being "the extraordinary illusion—for that is what it is—that there is such a thing as music, rather than simply acts of making and receiving it" (Cook, 2003, p. 208).

Louth (2013), citing Erikson (1995), suggests not only that metaphors commonly used when talking about music reinforce the ideologies of reification and musical autonomy, but also that the means by which these metaphors come into being themselves provide examples of the process of reification, in which something comes to be seen as self-evident and always to have been so. Louth argues that over time these metaphors "congeal into apparently objectified forms that critical theorists 'call second nature'" (p. 67). He describes these as "frozen metaphors." Frozen metaphors valorize those aspects of music that are particular important in Western music—structure, pitch, and harmony—while ignoring aspects such as timbre, texture, and color, which are not. This then sets up a discourse that implicitly devalues those musics that lie outside the "Western European mainstream" (p. 67); and by implication those who make music within those practices. This is then reflected in and through the school curricular in terms of its predetermined content, the musical values it promotes, and the criteria by which musical achievement is evaluated and assessed.

Louth (2013) describes how the perception of music as an object results in the "conduit metaphor" where "much like the word 'poem' is thought of as a container of thoughts and ideas . . . the word 'music' connotes a container of sonic content, which travels along a conduit of sound waves from person to person" (p. 74). This reinforces then the "static and reproductive view of music at the expense of a dynamic, albeit less stable view" resulting in the common tendency to "focus on performance as the conveyance of the work's meaning rather than consider the context of its creation and reception as sites for constructing new meanings" (p. 74). A consequence of this is that the core musical roles of "composer," "performer" and "listener" are highly differentiated and, in Bersteinian terms, strongly framed and insulated. The function of the composer within this paradigm is to create the musical object and imbue it with meaning through the way in which the sonic materials are organized. The performer, in turn, communicates that meaning through accurate and sympathetic realization of the music's scripted form (a "conduit"), while the listener's role is to listen attentively so as to "understand" the message that is being communicated (that is enshrined within the musical object). The role of the listener is, then, "simply to contemplate the work, to try and understand and respond to it, but that she or he has nothing to contribute to its meaning. That is the composer's business" (Small, 1998, p. 6). The roles of performance and listener are thus rendered essentially passive, or at least limited in their potential to engage in the creation or construction of musical meaning.

Cook (2003) describes how educational institutions have "naturalized" this way of thinking such that it appears self-evident and the only way of engaging with music, resulting in pedagogies and curricular content and structure that simultaneously reflect and sustain the dominant musical paradigm and the values, practices, and discourses which it promotes and valorizes. Curriculum and assessment reinforce, in Bernstein's terms, the strong framing of the roles of "composer," "performer" and "listener" that are consequently taught and assessed as discrete and separate fields of musical learning. The belief that musical meaning is contained within the organization of the sonic materials of music is realized, pedagogically, in a concentration on the "elements" of music as the preeminent curricular and pedagogical focus of attention. Rose and Countryman (2013) point to the ubiquity of "the elements" in music curricula and, echoing Elliot (1995), argue that they have become "verbalizable objects of knowledge, decoupled from a vision of music education as a search for personal meaning in music" (Rose & Countryman, 2013, p. 47).

The lack of opportunity for the personal construction of musical meaning is also inherent within the idea of meaning as fixed within a musical object such that meaning is understood to exist independently of any knower. This then "controls teachers, framing them as deliverers of non-negotiable truths," a role that "denies that students are already musickers capable of constructing their own understanding, framing their own questions and collectively shaping language to communicate these understandings and questions" (Rose & Countryman, 2013, p. 47). As Philpott says, because control of school knowledge is situated firmly with the teacher, young people act simply as "curriculum consumers" rather than "curriculum makers" (Philpott 2010, p. 84). Thus are created pedagogical contexts and curriculum structures that both reflect and sustain the musical values and relationships of Western art music and within which the student voice is constructed and the sanctioned messages heard.

The extent to which students are "heard" is dependent on them being able to articulate what Lamont and Maton (2008), drawing on Bernstein, refer to as the "languages of legitimation." These "languages of legitimation" are underpinned by "legitimation codes," such as "knowledge codes" that encode the legitimated and sanctioned (specialist) knowledge of a particular field, and "knower codes" that refer to "one's sensibilities and dispositions or 'what kind of knower you are'" (p. 270). The "knowledge codes" within the music curriculum tend toward the encoding of the processes, procedures, and underpinning "theoretical" knowledge associated with Western art music. Similarly, the "knower codes"—the dispositions—are those of the "practitioners" of Western music, characterized by the specialized and highly insulated roles of composer, performer, and listener.

For those who are able to articulate the messages that demonstrate possession of legitimated and sanctioned knowledge and knower codes, their voices are heard as they project a musical identity that resonates with the acoustic of the school; though the extent to which they are in sympathy with that acoustic as "musicians" and whether or not they choose to sustain this identity beyond the school is a moot point. Those whose voices do not, cannot, or will not articulate the messages of the sanctioned knowledge and knower codes are likely then, as Lamont and Maton (2008) say, to disengage from school music. Disengagement from school music, or being unable to construct a voice that is accepted and heard within the school, is not, however, necessarily a symptom or consequence of any lack of "musical ability" or interest in music. Rather, it is often the result of a disjuncture between how music is experienced and engaged with outside school and the paradigm of musical engagement required by a "socially mediated school music curriculum" (Philpott, 2010, p. 83).

As an example of this "disjuncture," Rose and Countryman (2013) argue that young people often find the sanctioned discourse of the school music curriculum (which seeks to describe music and musical experience in the atomized terms of the elements) insufficient for their needs in that it fails to adequately describe the richness of their musical understanding and experience.

> The recurring musical components that our students noticed and described were never simple identifications of, for example, duple and triple feel or disjunct or conjunct melodies. Rather, students addressed complexities of musical relationships. Where *the elements* seek to simplify, to discriminate and categorize, our students seek to relate, create, play, and celebrate. (p. 55)

Greene (1988) writes that knowing that one has something to say which one is not allowed to say (or, one might add, not being allowed to say it in the way one wants, or being forced to say something one does not wish to) offends one's awareness of freedom and sense of social justice:

> Desiring to speak and write their own words they experience the controls of the dictatorship as concrete barriers to their very beings. They take the obstruction personally; it is the way in which their living situations speak to them. To be something other than an object, a cipher, a thing such a person must reach out to create an opening; he/she must engage directly with what stands against him/her, no matter what the risks. (p. 11)

It is perhaps this offense to their awareness of their freedom and their sense of social justice—resulting from their lack of inclusion in the discourse of curriculum and pedagogy and questions of musical knowledge and value—that causes the alienation of many young people from the school music curriculum.

From Monological to Dialogical Discourses of Music Education

In this final section, the argument will be made that the continuing hegemony of the Western art music aesthetic, which allows for only "legitimated texts" to be heard, has resulted in many instances in a "monological discourse" of music education. A monological discourse is characterized by Robinson (2011) as being

[m]ade up of objects, integrated through a single consciousness. Since other subjects have value only in relation to the transcendent perspective, they are reduced to the status of objects. They are not recognised as 'another consciousness' or as having rights. Monologism is taken to close down the world it represents, by pretending to be the ultimate word. In monologism, 'truth', constructed abstractly and systematically from the dominant perspective, is allowed to remove the rights of consciousness. Each subject's ability to produce autonomous meaning is denied. This performs a kind of discursive 'death' of the other, who, as unheard and unrecognised, is in a state of non-being. (Robinson 2011: http://ceasefiremagazine.co.uk/in-theory-bakhtin-1/)

The ideologies underpinning the Western art music aesthetic are clearly evident in Robinson's description of monological discourses as being "made up of objects, integrated through a single consciousness." A monological discourse promotes the centrality of the object (reification) with meaning contained exclusively within it (autonomy), and the Western art aesthetic as the transcendent "ultimate word" by which all other musics must be judged, with the consequent closing down of spaces for alternative meanings or understandings. Monological discourses project knowledge as fixed and static, silencing the voice of the "other"—in this instance, "the students"—through denying them the opportunity to produce autonomous or alternative meanings. The monological discourse presents the voice of the teacher as preeminent—as the "authoritative voice" that, from the perspective of the student, "remains outside of me and orders me to do something in a way that forces me to accept or reject it without engaging with it" (to be, as Greene suggests above, simply a cipher) rather than the "persuasive voice" which "[enters] into the realm of my own words and changes them from within" (Bahktin, cited in Wegerif, 2011, p. 181).

Wegerif maintains that "[e]ducation, as opposed to training . . . always requires [the] persuasive or dialogic voice that speaks to the student from the inside" (p. 181). Arguing against conventional understandings of dialogues as simply occurring between (usually) two people within a particular time and space and with the "meaning" of a dialogue embedded within the utterances and responses of those participants, he posits a much richer conception in which the meanings of dialogues are not "reducible to the intentions of the speaker or to the response of the addressee but emerges between these two in 'dialogical spaces' " (Wegerif, 2008, p. 349). Within these dialogical spaces there is a "dynamic continuous emergence of meaning" from the "interplay of two or more perspectives" (Wegerif, 2011, p. 180). These perspectives include not only the embodied voices of the immediate participants but also the voices of those that have used the words and phrases previously and who have also embedded meanings in them. Moreover, the voices present are not only—or not even—just embodied voices (either those present or those distanced by time or space) but also historical or cultural voices, voices of events past and future, the voices of political, philosophical, or ideological movements or works or events of literature or music. In all cases, each utterance—each word, phrase, novel, musical event—informs subsequent utterances and is similarly informed by the new utterances; the dialogue extends in both directions. Consequently, these voices/

events/prior utterances not only bestow meaning on a particular dialogue, but they in turn receive meaning from it.

Before moving on to consider what dialogical discourse might look like in the context of music education, it might be useful to begin with a purely musical example. In 1910 the English composer Ralph Vaughan Williams's (1872–1958) *Fantasia on a Theme of Thomas Tallis* was premiered in Gloucester Cathedral. The work is based around Tallis's Third *Mode Melody* written for Archbishop Parkers Psalter (1567), which Vaughan Williams had encountered through his editorship of the English Hymnal. Much has been written about this work, it being one of the most popular in the English repertoire, but its importance from a dialogical perspective is that the work does not seek to subsume Tallis's musical utterance, but to engage dialogically with it. This dialogue is not just with Tallis's musical material but also with his musical world. Frogley (2013) writes that the work juxtaposes "unadorned ... triads riven by false relations that evoke sixteenth and seventeenth-century English music" (Frogley, 2013, p. 91). On hearing the first performance, a critic wrote that "one is never quite sure whether one is listening to something very old or very new" (Thompson, 2013, p. 65). The "greatness" of the work can be expressed—as it often is—in terms of the organization of its musical materials (as an autonomous object). Equally, however, its greatness can be understood in terms of how each performance instigates a dialogical space within which the voices of those present and those long dead, the sonic voice of the music and the "voices" of events historical and contemporary, reanimate and change the meanings of both works.

Imagine now what a musical classroom might be like where musical knowledge, meanings, and understandings emerge and are constructed from the multiplicity of voices—embodied, cultural, and historical, but most especially musical—that are present within any particular musical-dialogical encounter. Each musical encounter and educational interaction is unique, as the voices present and the circumstance within which a musical encounter occurs will be uniquely differentiated by repertoire (with its associated praxes)—the culture and lived experiences and histories of those participating and of those who have encountered and experienced the music on previous occasions. For example, students from a school with a multicultural and ethnic intake are working on a "cover" version of Bob Marley's *Exodus*. They discuss the political message behind the lyrics, considering what these meant at the time of its composition and the resonances that these have in contemporary society. They draw parallels with what they consider to be the growing oppression of the Muslim communities within the United Kingdom and decide to communicate this "resonance" through incorporating digitalized sounds of traditional instruments associated with Muslim communities into their version of *Exodus*. Over the course of three lessons and a subsequent performance, they engage in a dialogical discourse in which not only their voices are present but also the voices of those attending the "event" as well as the voices of previous performers of this music and the voices and events "represented" both by Marley's original composition and those of their "cover" version. The lessons become occasions for rethinking the musical characteristics/knowledge of "Reggae" so that this knowledge is not treated as fixed but dynamic and at the service of this particular and unique musical encounter.

If each musical and educational encounter is unique, then the musical knowledge, understandings, meanings, and experiences that emerge from those dialogical spaces are also unique. As in this example above, dialogical educational encounters cannot by definition provide sites for "closure"—for concepts, ideas, and propositions having been noted as finally understood and learned. Students can no longer look to educational encounters to enable them to say, "now I know the truth, I can stop thinking," but rather to ask, "how has this musical interaction or encounter changed my perception and understanding of my musical world, and how might this understanding of my world have changed the understandings and experiences of others?" This then demands a radical reconceptualization of the traditional relationship between knowledge, learner, and teacher from that based around a "monological discourse" in which the teacher, as the "authoritative voice," transmits static, closed bodies of musical knowledge and meaning to an essentially passive and disempowered learner.

A dialogical approach to music education requires dispositions of both teacher and student that eschew the possibility of "one single true perspective" inherent in the concept of monological discourse. This is displaced in favor of a willingness to enter into the world of other voices (of those present within the immediate time and space and those not) and to see and hear things—to see potential meanings—from the perspectives of those other voices, to consider these perspectives and to entertain fully the possibility of changing one's own beliefs and understandings in the light of entering into those worlds. Participants within a dialogic space are asked to reflect on what has been said—verbally or musically—by themselves and other voices and to rethink their own thoughts and utterances in the light of this reflection, leading to a growing understanding rooted in an increasing awareness of the multiple perspectives that can be brought to bear upon a particular idea, concept, or proposition (Wegerif, 2011).

Thinking about music in these dialogical terms reveals a rich and fertile ground for the creation of a musical pedagogy that seeks to engage the voice of the learner—both musically and verbally—not as an individualized, "personalized self," but as existing always in relation to an "other." For as Bakhtin, writes, "the basis of being human is not self-identity but the opening of a dialogue, an opening which always implies the simultaneous inter-animation of more than one voice." (Sidorkin, cited in Wegerif, 2008, p. 350). Dialogical education and critical pedagogy thus come together in the process of raising students "conscientization"—their awareness—of the power relationships that impact their lives and those of others; for, as Wegerif puts it, "It is within dialogues that people come to define and know their situations and interpret them" (Wegerif, 2011, p. 181). A dialogical music education focuses not on the (re) production of musical objects or their disinterested study, but on the engagement of young people's voices as reflective, thinking musicians and as equal participants in the construction of pedagogy and curriculum and the revealing and creation of music meaning.

References

Abrahams, F. (2005). Transforming classroom music instruction with ideas from critical pedagogy. *Music Educators Journal, 92*(1), 62–67.

Allsup, R. E. (2003). Transformational education and critical music pedagogy: examining the link between culture and learning. *Music Education Research, 5*(1), 5–13.

Arnot, M., & Reay, D. (2007). A sociology of pedagogic voice: power, inequality and pupil consultation. *Discourse: Studies in the Cultural Politics of Education, 28*(3), 311–325.

Ball, S. (2003). The teacher's soul and the terrors of performativity. *Journal of Education Policy, 18*(2), 215–228.

Bernstein, B. (2000). *Pedagogy, symbolic control and identity. Theory, research, critique.* Oxford: Rowman and Littlefield.

Bragg, S. (2007). "Student voice" and governmentality: The production of enterprising subjects? *Discourse: Studies in the Cultural Politics of Education, 28*(3), 343–358.

Cook, N. (2003). Music as performance. In M. Clayton, T. Herbert, & R. Middleton (Eds.), *The cultural study of music* (pp. 204–214). London: Routledge.

Cook-Sather, A. (2006). Sound, presence and power: "Student voice" in educational research and reform. *Curriculum Enquiry, 46*(4), 359–390.

Cremin, H., Mason, C., & Busher, H. (2011). Problematising pupil voice using visual methods: findings from a study of engaged and disaffected pupils in an urban secondary school. *British Educational Research Journal, 37*(4), 585–603.

Department for Education and Science (DfES). (2006). *National strategy for music programme foundation subjects: Key stage 3 music.* London: Crown Copyright.

Evans, K. (2012). Music 14–19: Choices, challenges, and opportunities. In C. Philpott & G. Spruce (Eds.), *Debates in music teaching* (pp. 197–208). Abingdon, UK: Routledge.

Fielding, M. (2008). Personalisation, education and the market. *Soundings, 38,* 55–69.

Fielding, M. (2004). "New wave" student voice and the renewal of civic society. *London Review of Education, 2*(3), 187–217.

Finney, J. (2011). *Music education in England 1950–2010: The child-centred progressive tradition.* Farnham, UK: Ashgate Press.

Flutter, J. (2010). International perspectives on the students' voice movement: Sonorities in a changing world. In J. Finney & C. Harrison (Eds.), *Whose music education is it? The role of the student voice* (pp. 16–23). Solihull, UK: National Association of Music Educators.

Flutter, J. (2007). Teacher development and pupil voice. *The Curriculum Journal, 18*(3), 342–354.

Frogley, A. (2013). History and geography: The early orchestral works and the first three symphonies. In A. Frogley & A. J. Thompson (Eds.). *The Cambridge companion to Vaughan Williams* (pp. 81–105). Cambridge: Cambridge University Press.

Green, L. (2003). Music education, cultural capital and social group identity. In M. Clayton, T. Herbert, & R. Middleton (Eds.), *The cultural study of music* (pp. 263–274). London: Routledge.

Greene, M. (1988). *The dialectic of freedom.* New York: Teachers College Press.

Harland, K., Kinder, K., & Hartley, K. (1995). *Arts in view: A study of youth participation in the arts.* Slough: National Federation for Educational Research.

Harland, J., Kinder, K., Lord, P., Stott, A., Schagen, I., & Haynes, J. (2000). *Arts Education in Secondary Schools: Effects and Effectiveness.* Slough, UK: National Federation for Education Research.

Hart, R. A. (1992). *Children's participation: From tokenism to citizenship*. Innocenti Essays. Florence: UNICEF International Child Development Centre.

Lamont, A., Hargreaves, D. J., Marshall, N. A., & Tarrant, M. (2003). Young people's music in and out of school. *British Journal of Music Education, 20*(3), 229–241.

Lamont, A., & Maton, K. (2008). Choosing music: Exploratory studies into the low uptake of Music GCSE. *British Journal of Music Education, 25*(3), 367–382.

Louth, P. (2013). Frozen metaphors, ideology and the language of musical instruction. *Action, Criticism & Theory for Music Education, 12*(3), 65–91.

Philpott, C. (2010). The sociological critique of curriculum music. In R. Wright (Ed.), *Sociology and music education*. Farnham, UK: Ashgate Press.

Robinson, A. (2011). In theory Bakhtin: Dialogism, polyphony and heteroglossia. *Ceasefire*, http://ceasefiremagazine.co.uk/in-theory-bakhtin-1/, accessed March 2, 2014.

Rose, L. S., & Countryman, J. (2013) Repositioning "The Elements": How students talk about music. *Action, Criticism & Theory for Music Education, 12*(3), 44–64.

Ross, M. (1995). What's wrong with school music? *British Journal of Music Education, 12*(3), 185–120.

Rudduck, J., & Fielding, M. (2006). Student voice and the perils of popularity. *Educational Review, 56*(2), 219–231.

Sabia, D. (2012). Democratic/utopian education. *Utopian Studies, 23*(2), 374–405.

Schools Council Enquiry 1. (1968). *Young School Leavers*. London: HMSO.

Sidorkin, A. M. (1999). *Beyond discourse: Education, the self and dialogue*. Albany: State University of New York Press.

Silva. E. (2001). "Squeaky wheels and flat tires": A case study of students as reform participants. *Forum, 43*(2), 95–99.

Small, C. (1998). *Musicking: The meanings of performing and listening*. Middletown, CT: Wesleyan University Press.

Spruce, G. (2007). Culture, society and musical learning. In C. Philpott & G. Spruce (Eds.), *Learning to teach music in the secondary school: A companion to school experience* (pp. 16–27). Abingdon, UK: Routledge.

Spruce, G. (2012). Musical knowledge, critical consciousness and critical thinking. In C. Philpott & G. Spruce (Eds.), *Debates in music teaching* (pp. 185–196). Abingdon, UK: Routledge.

Spruce, G. (2013). Participation, inclusion, diversity and the policy of English music education. In C. Harrison & P. Mullen (Eds.), *Reaching out: Music education with "hard to reach" children and young people* (pp. 23–31). Salisbury: The United Kingdom Association for Music Education-Music Mark.

Swanwick, K. (1988). *Music, mind and education*. London: Routledge.

Thompson, A. J. (2013). Becoming a national composer: Critical reception to c. 1925. In A. Frogley & A. J. Thompson (Eds.), *The Cambridge Companion to Vaughan Williams* (pp. 56–78). Cambridge: Cambridge University Press.

Wegerif, R. (2008). Dialogic or dialectic? The significance of ontological assumptions in research on educational dialogue. *British Educational Research Journal, 24*(3), 347–361.

Wegerif, R. (2011). Towards a dialogic theory of how children learn to think. *Thinking Skills and Creativity, 6*, 179–190.

CHAPTER 19

INFORMAL LEARNING AS A CATALYST FOR SOCIAL JUSTICE IN MUSIC EDUCATION

FLÁVIA M. NARITA AND LUCY GREEN

INTRODUCTION

SOCIAL justice is a term that has been understood in different ways and, consequently, its application has also been diverse (Fraser, 1995, 2001, 2005, 2008; Gould, 2007; Jorgensen, 2007; Sands, 2007). Jorgensen (2007) suggests the broader term "justice" instead of social justice because "the notion of social justice may . . . turn out to be limiting and exclusive in bypassing individual interests and perspectives in favor of emphasizing social considerations or the groups to which these individuals belong" (p. 176). In a way, Jorgensen alerts us to the dominance of a group and the silencing of minorities, as she also points out in the opening chapter of this Handbook. Also questioning the subjugation of minorities by a dominant group, Gould (2007, p. 237) criticizes the liberal discourse of social justice that erases differences as a "façade of equality." This tension between individual and group interests is reflected in the "decoupling of cultural politics from social politics, of the politics of difference from the politics of equality" (Fraser, 2001, p. 21).

On one hand, according to Fraser (1995, 2001), socioeconomic inequities have compelled those who understand social justice as a more just allocation of resources to see the redistribution of those resources as a remedy for injustice. On the other hand, those seeking an affirmation of specific cultural value need the recognition and the differentiation of that value to remedy injustice. These different views of injustice and of its remedies (justice) become problematic when they work against each other, as Jorgensen (2007) and Gould (2007) alerted.

In order to address such a contention, Fraser (2001, 2005) proposes a framework that accommodates both redistribution and recognition by treating "recognition as a question of *social status*," not as a question of identity. Therefore, "what requires recognition is not group-specific identity but rather the status of group members as full partners in social interaction" (Fraser, 2001, p. 24, emphasis in original). She extends this notion of full partners in social interactions or of "parity of participation" to issues of redistribution, defending that "the distribution of material resources must be such as to ensure participants' independence and voice" (Fraser, 2001, p. 29). Later, she includes the political dimension of representation in her framework, arguing that by

> ... [e]stablishing criteria of social belonging, and thus determining who counts as a member, the political dimension of justice specifies the reach of those other dimensions: it tells us who is included, and who excluded, from the circle of those entitled to a just distribution and reciprocal recognition. (Fraser, 2005, p. 6)

Adopting Fraser's (2001, 2005, 2008) framework to understand social justice as involving "parity of participation," in which members of a social context interact with each other as peers, we argue that informal learning approaches within music education may offer grounds for such participatory parity through dialogical interactions between teachers and learners and among learners themselves. These "dialogues" require a role and attitude from both teachers and learners that challenge many formal educational assumptions, as teachers and learners are expected to contribute equally, but differently, in the learning process.

This attitude is also emphasized in the critical pedagogy of Paulo Freire (1974, [1970]2000), as the starting point of a process that reminds us that teachers can be agents of resistance against unjust and oppressive educational situations that may overlook the knowledge and interests brought to the learning experience by the learners. Freire summons teachers to work together with learners through a dialogical and problem-posing approach, within what should be a liberating education. This involves questioning and attempting to understand the world we inhabit, in relation to the transformations that are needed to ensure the right of being active subjects in control of our choices. In contrast to this approach, Freire criticizes what he calls the "banking model" of education, which reduces learners to the status of objects that passively receive knowledge "deposited" by teachers, as if depositing money in a bank, within a domesticating and oppressive education system.

A range of what may be termed "informal music learning practices" can, we argue, operate as a form of resistance to that banking model of education and, thus, contribute to a more just participation of the different members in the educational context. We also relate these practices to what Fraser (1995) calls "transformative measures," in contrast with affirmative ones. While the latter corrects "inequitable outcomes of social arrangements without disturbing the underlying framework that generates them," the former corrects "inequitable outcomes precisely by restructuring the underlying generative framework" (p. 82).

In the first section of this chapter, we bring Fraser's framework of social justice to the educational context and discuss the potential of informal learning in music education to promote parity of participation in musical practices. Besides acting to remove the barriers that might impede that participatory parity, we revisit Green's ([1988]2008a) theory of musical meaning to explain how our understanding of the sonic materials and of their interrelations, allied to extra-musical values, can offer an opportunity to deepen students', as well as teachers', understanding of those sonic materials in relation to rethinking their extra-musical values, which may transform our musical experiences. In this sense, our musical understanding can potentially incorporate a more critical response to music, which helps us understand our own and other people's musical worlds. This is paralleled to Freire's idea that, as conscious beings, we "are not only *in* the world, but *with* the world," (1970, p. 452, emphasis in original) in such a way that we can reflect, question, and transform ourselves and our worlds, with the potential to free ourselves from unjust or oppressive relations.

In the second section of this chapter, we discuss how some informal music learning practices were "translated" into pedagogical practices by student teachers participating in a module delivered as part of a distance education program in Brazil aimed at music teacher education. We address examples of three distinct teaching approaches adopted by the teachers, and consider them in relation to the discussion noted earlier. The program (Open University of Brazil) is part of a broader Brazilian educational policy aimed at expanding access to free higher education. As an example of a redistributive measure, distance education in Brazil is an attempt to raise the low rates of 14.4% (net) of youngsters aged 18–24 enrolled in higher education (INEP, 2012, p. 36).

The reasons for exclusion from higher education in Brazil are varied and complex, and we do not deal with them here. Moreover, we are aware that the creation of more places via distance education and other educational policies, per se, will not ensure parity of participation in the socioeconomic, cultural, and political spheres of any society. However, although distance education may be only a palliative measure to deal with inequitable access to higher education in Brazil, the fact is that programs currently in operation (since 2007 at the University of Brasilia) have been offered in two distinct modes: the traditional on-campus, face-to-face mode, and through distance education.

INFORMAL MUSIC PEDAGOGY: PARTICIPATORY PARITY LEADING TO A POTENTIALLY LIBERATING EDUCATIONAL EXPERIENCE

Informal music pedagogy does not refer to "an" approach but to the blossoming of a range of approaches over the last decade or two. In general these approaches tend to adapt different informal learning practices of various musicians outside the education system, bringing them, to differing degrees and in different ways, into formal settings.[1] Our own research has spanned the informal learning model in what is known as the Musical Futures movement (Green 2008a, 2014; www.musicalfutures.org; Hallam, Creech, & McQueen, 2011; Jeanneret, McLennan, & Stevens-Ballenger, 2011; Wright 2012) and a project bringing informal learning into teacher-education at the Open University of Brazil, offered by the University of Brasília (Narita, 2012).

Across these projects, among other things, we have brought to the formal context of education five main learning practices of popular musicians (see Green, 2001, 2008a), and have applied them more or less directly to what the students are asked to undertake in the classroom. These are the following: choosing their own repertoire; copying the music by ear from a recording; learning in friendship groups through conscious and unconscious sharing of knowledge and skills; approaching whole "real-world" pieces of music, involving finding their own way through the learning, rather than using music that has been simplified and structured progressively; and integrating the practices of listening, performing, and composing, with an emphasis on creativity. While the role of teachers is crucial (see Green, 2014, for detailed examples), it differs from authoritarian models, since teachers take a more responsive and less instructional position. Hence, learners in this pedagogy take an active role in controlling their own musical practices and learning processes, which can lead to a deep understanding of their potential, needs, and the strategies they themselves develop to improve their learning.

In this chapter, we wish to focus on the dialogical relation between teachers and learners and between learners themselves that this kind of approach can engender. We assume that "there is no complete knowledge possessed by the educator, but a knowable object which mediates educator and educatee as subjects in the knowing process" (Freire, 1971, p. 7). Hence, this dialogical knowing process involves collaborative teaching, in which teachers become "educator-educatee" and learners become "educatee-educators" (Freire, 1974, p. 127). Grounded in the lived experiences of the learners and showing respect for the knowledge and skills that they already possess, the teachers, while learning along with the learners, instigate the development of learners' abilities, acting with them and not upon them. The role and relationship between teacher and taught promoted in the informal learning model is also related to Freirean critical pedagogy by Wright and Kanellopoulos (2010, p. 74), who highlight its "more egalitarian and dialogic relationship." It is worth mentioning that neither informal learning practices nor Freire's pedagogy implies that the roles of teachers and learners are equal. In a dialogue with Gadotti and Guimarães, Freire clarifies:

> The educator is different from the pupil. But this difference, from the point of view of the revolution, must not be antagonistic. The difference becomes antagonistic when the authority of the educator, different from the freedom of the pupil, is transformed into authoritarianism. (cited in Gadotti, 1994, pp. 56–57)

Hence, without denying the teacher's authority, informal learning in music proposes that learners' knowledge and voices are manifested and represented in the educational context. It also involves collaborative learning, as peers find ways to organize themselves in groups, with the consequent emergence of group leaders and the development of new group cooperation strategies. Although we are aware of the various subjectivities that are involved in an educational scenario, and of the potential unequal power and participation that may lead to struggles of identity recognition, when subscribing to Fraser's (2001) status model of social justice we do not aim at the recognition of a specific (group) identity; rather, "claims for recognition in the status model seek to establish the subordinated party as a full partner in social life, able to interact with others as a peer" (p. 25).

For example, to balance an educational situation in which learners able to read musical notation are considered "brighter" or "more musical" than those who do not read music, we need to promote parity of participation. We can do this by supporting those who do not read music to participate, not necessarily in the same way, but in ways that are equally fulfilling and equally recognized. Informal learning practices, with an emphasis on oral-aural learning, can counterbalance the dominance and the importance of musical notation skills, allowing the participation of non-musical readers on a par with readers (Green, 2008a). By this, we mean that the practices proposed did not require a specific musical ability that would prevent some who did not possess such an ability from participating and, in this sense, both readers and non-readers stood on an equal footing. It does not mean, however, that every learner will achieve the same result.

> . . . the task involved what is known as 'differentiation by outcome'. In other words, all pupils were set the same task, but it was adaptable to the differing abilities of individuals, not by virtue of being divided up into separate, progressive levels of difficulty, but according to what each individual produced as the outcome. (Green, 2008b, p. 187)

This adaptation to the various abilities of participants aided in making the informal learning practices accessible, inclusive, and potentially ensuring parity of participation of every learner. We say potentially because once in a group, participants' values, knowledge, abilities, and status are renegotiated, and other inequalities may arise. However, insofar as inclusion in musical practices is concerned, the proposed task, (involving self-chosen music and group-directed learning, as outlined earlier) met a first level of parity of participation.

This inclusion "should not be at the expense of academic rigour" because "academic achievement is crucial to pursuing economic justice, to fostering students' future access to the material benefits of society" (Keddie, 2012, p. 33) and to expanding their worlds so that they can make informed choices. Therefore, participation of learners in the proposed musical practices is not a "concession," but an educational act and, as such, should enable learners to go beyond what they already know, expanding their musical and general worlds, (re)constructing and revaluing the meanings attributed to their musical experiences, as a transformative practice.

MUSICAL MEANING AND THE CLASSROOM

We wish to offer an understanding of students' musical experiences through a lens developed specifically with the classroom context in mind. According to Green's ([1988]2008a) theory, musical meaning can usefully be conceived as a dialectical relation between two meaning-making processes that coexist and interrelate in every musical experience. One is what we will refer to as "inter-sonic" meaning[2] (Green, 2008a), which refers to the recognition and understanding of interrelationships between musical materials such as intervals, chords, phrases, and cadences. This is a learned, historically specific category that depends as much on the listener's prior experience as any other construction of meaning must do. That is, the level of listeners' familiarity and competence with a certain style of music correspondingly affects their ability to understand the interrelationships of sonic materials within that style and to attribute some meaning to those materials. The other is called "delineated" meaning, referring to the relation of sonic materials to implicit or explicit extra-musical associations lying beyond the musical materials, such as ethnic, religious, or political connotations, which can be at a collective and/or an individual level (Green, 2005, 2006, 2008a).

In this formulation, one type of relationship to both meanings can be established when (a) we are familiar or competent with a musical style so that we can correspondingly understand and attribute meaning to its inter-sonic materials and in this sense, we "know" the music and have "open ears"; and (b) we can relate the music's delineations with something we agree with, identify with, or have good feelings about. This combination of such responses to both types of musical meaning would lead to musical "celebration." It is important to mention that such celebration is not necessarily a desirable outcome of all music education all the time, since there are many cases where, rather than being celebrated, students could take a more critical stance to music. The other extreme of a musical experience would be musical "alienation"—which represents a state that, as with the alienation of the worker in classic Marxist theory, requires critical engagement in order to be thrown off. This would occur as a result of a lack of drawn relations to both inter-sonic and delineated meanings, in such a way that unfamiliarity with a musical style would prevent us from making sense of the sonic relationships, on one hand, and we would not relate to this style's delineations at all, on the other hand (Green, 2006, p. 103).

In this model, musical experience can also be "ambiguous" if our responses to inter-sonic meaning do not correspond with our responses to delineated meaning. In other words, on the one hand, we may be positive toward a certain musical style that is familiar, and in which we are able to finely decipher the inter-sonic arrangement and use of musical materials; but on the other hand, we may be negative toward that same music's delineations—for example, we may not identify or agree with the political use of this music, or we may relate it to an unpleasant experience. In such a case, we would be responding to inter-sonic meanings with a sense that, to us, involves familiarity and understanding, or other such generally welcoming frames of mind; but we would be responding to delineated meanings with a sense of dislike, being "thrown off," or other such generally unpleasant states. The opposite situation can occur, where we may have a response to inter-sonic meanings that involves unfamiliarity, bewilderment, boredom, or other similar states, but a response to delineated meanings that involves liking, belonging, a sense of the music supporting our identity, or other such generally pleasant states. This type of response would also lead to ambiguity, but of a different quality.

Using this theory to interpret musical experiences, we suggest that students stand a greater chance of engaging critically with music when their responses to its inter-sonic meanings are competent and knowing. This puts them in the position of a listener with "open ears" who can come to know the music from the inside. Additionally, a student who might otherwise dismiss certain music through an alienated experience can be brought to question the nature of his or her experience through becoming competent with deciphering its inter-sonic relationships. In Marxist and Freirean theory, the oppressed person ceases to be alienated, not only through the material throwing off of the oppressive conditions that alienate him or her, but initially through the throwing off of the "false consciousness" that is involved in the acceptance of the alienation in the first place. When the person becomes more able to understand the processes that are causing the alienation, they have taken the first steps toward what is needed materially to throw off the alienation. This involves a dialectical process between knowledge, or what here is referred to as musical "competence," and alienation. Such an understanding is consonant with Freire's interpretation of the power of education, knowledge, and understanding to challenge alienation. Furthermore, greater competence with responding to inter-sonic meanings involves coming to understand that what we previously took to be immutable and unchangeable is actually socially and historically constructed, which is another vital aspect in the path toward throwing off alienation. For through such paths, students can come to understand that musical meanings are socially and historically constructed at not only the delineated but also the inter-sonic levels (see also Green, 2005).

Many music educators would agree that students' responses and attention to what we are here calling inter-sonic meanings can be enhanced when they are engaged in music making itself (see Elliott, 1995). An engagement that, we have argued, is particularly inclusive and particularly direct occurs within the proposed practices based on informal learning. Furthermore, we do not assume that in being allowed to choose their own music to work on, students are necessarily free from a range of influences, including delineations directed by the media. However, their direct engagement with the inter-sonic materials of music has led students to question the delineations imposed on certain music by the mass media, which they had previously not questioned:

> ... pupils' engagement with inter-sonic musical meanings enables them to recognize the *arbitrariness* of delineations; or in other words, the notion that delineations are not fixed entities belonging to sonic musical properties and their inter-relationships, but are socially constructed associations that arise from the ways music is *used* in different cultural contexts. (Green, 2008a, p. 91, emphasis in original)

Being aware of the arbitrariness of musical delineations and alert to the uses of music in different contexts are examples of a more critical engagement with music that might help students realize that, as Freire (1970) would remind us, we are both "*in* and *with* the world" (p. 452, emphasis in original)—that is, because we engage with the world, including the musical world, and reflect upon the world and upon that engagement, we are potentially able to transform both the world and ourselves, being conscious of and responsible for our choices and decisions. Informal music learning practices, in this sense, can be a critical and also potentially a liberating musical experience.

INFORMAL MUSIC PEDAGOGY IN A TEACHER EDUCATION DISTANCE LEARNING MODULE

This section illustrates our discussion with contrasting examples of informal learning practices taken from an eight-week module offered three times as an action-research project within the context of the Open University of Brazil/University of Brasília. The module was part of a distance education program that offers initial music teacher education (Narita, 2010, 2012).[3] The practices are discussed in relation to the original project carried out within secondary school music classrooms in the United Kingdom (Green, 2008a, 2014).

According to Zeichner and Flessner (2009, p. 25), "social justice teacher education" is a term loosely used when there is an intention to educate teachers who embrace a progressive agenda. Despite its loose use, the authors point to some practices that drive social justice teacher education: they go beyond a celebration of diversity; they encourage teachers' agency; and they "give prospective teachers the practical tools that they need to transform their good intentions into effective actions" (Zeichner & Flessner, 2009, p. 27).

In order to give prospective teachers such practical tools, teacher education needs to provide opportunities for student teachers to enact and live the notions of social justice to which they may already subscribe, or which they are being asked to consider subscribing to. In the informal music learning module offered by the Open University of Brazil/ University of Brasília, as with the Musical Futures teacher training programs, student teachers were asked to enact what their school students would later be asked to do: get into groups, copy a song by ear, and play the music as a band. Narita, as a researcher and a supervisor teacher, together with the associate tutors (who assist, interact, and assess the student teachers via online activities) and the local tutors (who assist and organize the face-to-face activities), observed them, allowed them to negotiate their ideas among their peers, and, only later, intervened with guidance, suggestions, modeling, and other practices. Next we discuss how these musical practices were taken into schools by the student teachers in this program.

Musical Practice as Teaching Practice

This module had musical practices geared toward training for the students' teaching practices. These were organized and structured with the intention of facilitating first-hand informal learning practices for the student teachers, while helping them design pedagogical materials to be used with their school students. The materials consisted of audio tracks of a chosen song broken into layers or riffs and, sometimes, some form of notation to support the practice: indication of chords, some rhythmic patterns, and lyrics. The preparation of such materials required both musical and pedagogical skills since the student teachers needed to think about their school students' musical abilities and the appropriateness of each riff or musical line to be learned by ear (avoiding very long musical phrases and big interval leaps, for instance).

In this sense, the entire process of devising the pedagogical materials required student teachers to think about their school students' musical worlds. This process of devising the pedagogical materials required what Shulman (1987) calls "forms of transformation," in which the teacher "moves from personal comprehension to preparing for the comprehension of others" (p. 16). The creation of a musical arrangement, specifically breaking the song into layers accessible for their school students, was mentioned by some student teachers as one of the learning outcomes. In Ari's[4] words:

> I think we have to be more observant and put ourselves in learners' shoes, analyzing more carefully the stages of their development. When devising these materials, you have to forget what you already know and think: "If I was starting now how to learn this piece of music, what would the best way be? What would help me in this moment?" So, that's the reflection I got from this [module]; I think it gave us more structure to our pedagogical practice: [we had to] reflect on which material we would use, how it would be presented, the space, a better systematization. And you're even more prepared for improvisations, for the things that happen during the lesson.
>
> (group interview: first offer, September 23, 2011)

The musical practices of devising the pedagogical materials also provided student teachers with opportunities to deepen their understandings of the inter-sonic meanings of the chosen song, allowing student teachers to better tailor the materials for their school students, ensuring that the materials themselves would be accessible and inclusive. Thus, before informal learning practices were taken into classrooms, participatory parity had to be considered and planned in a way that the materials would not privilege certain groups of students with a specific ability, thus restricting the participation of others. Rather, the materials should allow room for the negotiation of abilities and the inclusion of every participant in the musical practice, with each one working at his or her own level, according to prior experiences and needs.

Once the pedagogical materials were approved, student teachers went into schools. The teaching practice with their school students was based not so much on the fullest informal learning, but on Green's (2008a) Stage 2, that is, rather than choosing the songs themselves and working on whole, "real-world" songs, the school students received the materials, got into their friendship groups, tried to play the song using the available resources, and made their own versions of the song. Although they did not choose their song, when they were asked to make their own versions of the given song, the school students could still voice their musical worlds and affirm their musical identities. Both the first author and the tutors who assisted her wanted to make clear to the student teachers that music teaching should provide learners with a direct contact with music making.

The view of musical practice as a teaching practice was seen by a respondent from the third offer of the module as "an attractive way to effectively involve learners with music," and can be summarized by the following statement:

> The musical practice is the moment in which we put into practice everything we have studied, based on theoretical and pedagogical underpinnings. In the moment of the practice, the teacher must be confident about its content and prepared for any change during the lesson.
>
> (anonymous online module evaluation questionnaire: third offer, October 2012)

By observing the school students' musical practice, it was possible to analyze the student teachers' approaches to teaching. In the third offer of the module, teaching practices were assessed by video snippets of around 20 minutes. While it could be argued that the snippets do not represent what "really" happened, they do represent what the student teachers wanted to show. In that sense, they were potentially biased; but in a different sense, they were authentic replications of idealized identities and outcomes from the student teachers' perspectives.

Although the student teachers were advised to stand back and, first, observe what the school students were attempting, and only then start to make intervention as musical models, some could not do this. Thus, their school students' musical practice reflected the student teachers' pedagogical choices. In contrast to what had been proposed, some student teachers adopted controlled and instructional practices that resembled the "banking model of education," in which the teacher is the "owner" of the knowledge to be deposited into learners' heads (Freire, [1970]2000).

In Nando's lesson, he was in control of his group all the time: he distributed the lyrics of the song and played the CD; then he asked questions about the musical style and its structure, and played track by track of his prepared material, asking the school students which instrument they could hear. He asked his students to clap some of the rhythmic patterns and, only after that, allowed them to get the instruments. In his reflections, he wrote:

> After listening to all the tracks, I asked them to reproduce the rhythm they had just heard, the way they wanted, without my help, whilst I was only an observer. The text [we read] mentions the initiative of the students to organize, to suggest, to be a spontaneous leader, which didn't happen in my group. So, each one played their own way, without pulse, tempo, . . . I had to intervene because in spite of having percussion

lessons for a year, the students didn't have the minimum basic knowledge to do this task by themselves.

(Nando's reflections 1: third offer, October 4, 2012)

Nando's account demonstrates that he used this approach as an aural-skill test rather than a holistic musical practice. It also suggests that, as with many of the highly experienced teachers using this approach for the first time in Green's research (2008a), he had a view of his students as being "incapable" rather than "capable." Teachers in Green's research repeatedly stated how this activity had made them aware that they had previously expected too little of their students, and that their students were more capable than they had realized. Nando's attitude toward testing his students and considering that they "didn't have the minimum basic knowledge" also corresponds to Freire's banking education, in which the teacher deposits knowledge into learners' minds as if they were empty vessels to be filled with the knowledge brought by the teacher. In terms of that student teacher's use of his authority, we could say that his controlled actions prevailed over school students' choices, there was misrecognition of students' knowledge, and the musical practice represented the student teacher's values.

Another teaching approach adopted by some other student teachers was termed "laissez-faire." In those cases, there was no intervention of the student teachers and their school students were left to do whatever they wanted. As Freire would remind us, "Teachers . . . have an ethical obligation to be 'biased,' that is, to direct their teaching towards the construction of a just and humane society" (cited in McCowan, 2006, p. 68). Thus, student teachers' over-exaggerated lack of intervention in the laissez-faire approach contributes to a domesticating practice in which they neutralize school students' initiatives by not establishing a dialogical relation with them. In fact, these two apparently opposite approaches—that of Nando and that of the laissez-faire students—both lead to domestication exactly because of the lack of dialogue between the participants in the learning process.

The liberating practices identified in other student teachers' actions across the three offers of the module did contain evidence of a dialogical relation among the participants, student teachers' intervention as musical models, and the recognition and representation of the musical values and identities of both student teachers and school students. Student teachers such as Priscila supported the exploration of the musical instruments while also making interventions, suggesting ways of putting the song together and, thus, establishing a dialogical interaction with her students. By giving her students opportunities to find out and develop their own capabilities, Priscila began to value the process of learning and teaching, instead of focusing only on the musical performance as a final product of her lessons.

> If creativity and self-knowledge are important capabilities to be developed in school, there's nothing more interesting than allowing students to discover their capabilities. I was lucky to introduce a song that called their attention and I was surprised with one of the groups because they really committed themselves: they changed the

rhythm of the song, used elements of funk, and even choreographed their singing and playing. I was very anxious and worried about the outcomes, but I realised that the group work, the sharing of experiences and the value of self-knowledge were more valid than the final presentation.

(Priscila's reflections 2: third offer—October 7, 2012)

It is worth remembering that we do not assume that the musical choices of school-age students are exempt from influences of the media. As Woodford (2005) warns, "The commodification of popular music and culture serves the interests of corporations and not children" (p. 68). Thus, students' choices cannot be taken to be some expression of "freedom" but rather are a rich starting point for the Freirean idea of problem-posing, or problematization. According to Freire (1974), "The process of problematization is basically someone's reflection on a content which results from an act, or reflection on the act itself in order to act better together with others within the framework of reality" (p. 154). In his view, the problematization, in conjunction with a dialogical relationship, would allow the development of critical consciousness ("conscientization") to liberate people to fulfill their roles as learners, educators, citizens and, mainly, as human beings in the fullest sense of the term. This also corresponds with our earlier argument that direct engagement with musical materials, leading to a positive experience of inter-sonic meanings, can underpin a more critical engagement with music, since students' ears are "opened" and they are therefore in a better position to "know" what they are listening to.

SOME REFLECTIONS

We have argued that teaching for social justice in the music classroom and in teacher-education requires awareness of the various musical values, knowledge, and identities that both learners and teachers bring to a learning situation and that need to be (re)negotiated to allow parity of participation. We have also advocated a dialogical relation to enable this (re)negotiation. However, it is worth remembering that dialogical approaches do not ensure an "automatic" conscientization resulting in liberating people and achieving social justice. Freire (1974) alerts us that there is a stage of "naïve transitivity," when "the developing capacity for dialogue is still fragile and capable of distortion" (p. 18). Conscientization, or critical transitive consciousness, can be achieved through a critical engagement with the worlds we inhabit, aiming for personal transformation that empowers us to be "beings for ourselves" instead of "beings for others" (Freire, [1970]2000, p. 74).

A critical engagement with musical worlds may be achieved when we understand musical meanings and are thus capable of making informed choices in relation to our musical experiences. Transformative actions, such as informal learning practices, can produce ways of engagement with music making that are not in themselves new, but that have been overlooked in many formal music education settings until recently and that can be a potential means of enhancing critical musical engagement. Accompanying such transformative actions, we have highlighted the importance of problematizing and critically analyzing our actions and those of our student teachers and school students, so that we do not forget that cultural, historical, economical, political, and ideological contexts are implicit in our own choices and assumptions.

Going beyond the reflection on our practices, Moore (2012, pp. 124–125) reminds us to question not only our actions, but also the motives we had that led to those actions, in an attitude of reflexivity.

> Through a closer examination of one's responses in the context of one personal history and its interface with life in the classroom, reflexivity seeks to explain and critique not just classroom situations but the ways in which we are constrained to experience and respond to them. Reflexivity directs the practitioner to acknowledge the complex nature of *the self* and the way in which selves are constructed through experience and through social structures. (Moore, 2012, p. 136, emphasis in original)

Therefore, through reflective and reflexive attitudes, both teachers and learners at all levels can examine our actions, and potentially better understand ourselves, empowering us to renegotiate and transform our values and ideals.

Notes

1. For a few of the most recent examples of classroom action in schools and teacher education, out of many possible ones, see Chua (2013a, 2013b); Chua & Ho (2013a, 2013b); Costes-Onish (2013); Feichas (2010); Finney and Philpott (2010); Gower (2012); Ho (2013a, 2013b); Karlsen (2010); McPhail (2012, 2013); O'Neill & Bespflug (2012); Vakeva (2010); Wright & Kanellopoulos (2010).
2. Originally referred to as "inherent" meaning; Green has occasionally changed the term (e.g., 2005, 2008a) as it had led some readers to assume this meaning was regarded as "essential," although clearly no meaning can logically be essential since all meaning must be interpreted in a mind. Rather, the term "inherent" referred to the notion that both signifier and referent were inherent in the musical materials. However, the term "inter-sonic" is newer and, we hope, clearer.
3. The empirical research was carried out by Flávia Narita as part of a PhD program at the Institute of Education, University of London (UK), with the collaboration of the Open University of Brazil/University of Brasília, funded by the Capes Foundation, Ministry of Education of Brazil.
4. The names used here are pseudonyms.

References

Chua, S. L. (2013a). Informal learning for song writing. In S. L. Chua & H. P. Ho (Eds.), *Connecting the stars: Essays on student-centric music education* (pp. 87–97). Singapore:

Singapore Teachers' Academy for the aRts, (STAR) Ministry of Education. http://www.star. moe.edu.sg/resources/star-research-repository.

Chua, S. L. (2013b). STOMPing up musical engagement the non-formal and informal way. In S. L. Chua & H. P. Ho (Eds.), *Connecting the stars: Essays on student-centric music education* (pp. 127–142). Singapore: Singapore Teachers' Academy for the aRts, Ministry of Education. http://www.star.moe.edu.sg/resources/star-research-repository.

Chua, S. L., & Ho, H. P. (2013a). Piloting informal and non-formal approaches for music teaching in five secondary schools in Singapore: An introduction. In S. L. Chua & H. P. Ho (Eds.), *Connecting the stars: Essays on student-centric music education* (pp. 52–65). Singapore: Singapore Teachers' Academy for the aRts, Ministry of Education. http://www. star.moe.edu.sg/resources/star-research-repository.

Chua, S. L., & Ho, H. P. (2013b). Connecting findings, reflections and insights: Student-centricity musically, creatively. In S. L. Chua & H. P. Ho (Eds.), *Connecting the stars: Essays on student-centric music education* (pp. 143–154). Singapore: Singapore Teachers' Academy for the aRts, Ministry of Education. http://www.star.moe.edu.sg/resources/star-research-repository.

Costes-Onish, P. (2013). Negotiating the boundaries of formal and informal learning. In S. L. Chua & H. P. Ho (Eds.), *Connecting the stars: Essays on student-centric music education* (pp. 98–109). Singapore: Singapore Teachers' Academy for the aRts, Ministry of Education. http://www.star.moe.edu.sg/resources/star-research-repository.

Elliott, D. J. (1995). *Music matters: A new philosophy of music education.* New York: Oxford University Press.

Feichas, H. (2010). Informal music learning practices as a pedagogy of integration in Brazilian higher education. *British Journal of Music Education, 27*(1), 47–58.

Finney, J., & Philpott, C. (2010). Student teachers appropriating informal pedagogy. *British Journal of Music Education, 27*(1), 7–19.

Fraser, N. (1995). From redistribution to recognition? Dilemmas of justice in a "post-socialist" age. *New Left Review, I/212* (Jul–Aug), 68–93.

Fraser, N. (2001). Recognition without ethics? *Theory, Culture & Society, 18*, 21–42.

Fraser, N. (2005). Reframing justice. *New Left Review, 36* (Nov–Dec), 1–19.

Fraser, N. (2008). Abnormal Justice. *Critical Inquiry, 34*(3), 393–422.

Freire, P. (1970). Cultural action and conscientization. *Harvard Educational Review, 40*(3), 452–478.

Freire, P. (1971). *Unusual ideas about education.* Series B: Opinions, no. 36, International Commission on the Development of Education. UNESCO. http://unesdoc.unesco.org/ images/0022/002218/221865eo.pdf.

Freire, P. (1974). *Education for critical consciousness.* Originally published as *Educação como prática da liberdade*, Editora Paz e Terra, Rio de Janeiro, 1967, and *Extensión y Comunicación*, Institute for Agricultural Reform, Santiago (Chile), 1969. London: Sheed and Ward.

Freire, P. ([1970]2000). *Pedagogy of the oppressed.* 30th anniversary edition. London: Continuum.

Gadotti, M. (1994). *Reading Paulo Freire: His life and work.* New York: State University of New York Press.

Gould, E. (2007). Social justice in music education: The problematic of democracy. *Music Education Research, 9*(2), 229–240. doi: 10.1080/14613800701384359.

Gower, A. (2012). Integrating informal learning approaches into the formal learning environment of mainstream secondary schools in England. *British Journal of Music Education, 29*(1), 13–18.

Green, L. (1988). *Music on deaf ears: Musical meaning, ideology, education.* Manchester: Manchester University Press.

Green, L. (2001). *How popular musicians learn: A way ahead for music education.* Aldershot, UK: Ashgate.

Green, L. (2005). *Meaning, autonomy and authenticity in the music classroom.* Professorial Lecture. Institute of Education, University of London.

Green, L. (2006). Popular music education in and for itself, and for "other" music: Current research in the classroom. *International Journal of Music Education, 24*(2), 101–118.

Green, L. (2008a). *Music, informal learning and the school: A new classroom pedagogy.* Aldershot, UK: Ashgate.

Green, L. (2008b). Group cooperation, inclusion and disaffected pupils: Some responses to informal learning in the music classroom. Presented at the RIME Conference 2007, Exeter, UK. *Music Education Research, 10*(2), 177–192. doi: 10.1080/14613800802079049.

Green, L. (2014). *Hear, listen, play! How to free your students' aural, improvisation and performance skills.* New York: Oxford University Press.

Hallam, S., Creech, A., & McQueen, H. (2011). *Musical futures: A case study investigation.* Final report from Institute of Education University of London for the Paul Hamlyn Foundation. https://www.musicalfutures.org/resource/27646/title/instituteofeducationlongitudinal-studyofmusicalfutures, accessed August 9, 2013.

Ho, H. P. (2013a). Rollin' in at the deep end: Choice, collaboration and confidence through informal learning with the guitar. In S. L. Chua & H. P. Ho (Eds.), *Connecting the stars: Essays on student-centric music education* (pp. 66–85). Singapore: Singapore Teachers' Academy for the aRts, Ministry of Education. http://www.star.moe.edu.sg/resources/star-research-repository.

Ho, H. P. (2013b). Connecting the curricular and co-curricular through formal and non-formal teaching. In S. L. Chua & H. P. Ho (Eds.), *Connecting the stars: Essays on student-centric music education* (pp. 110–126). Singapore: Singapore Teachers' Academy for the aRts, Ministry of Education. http://www.star.moe.edu.sg/resources/star-research-repository.

INEP. (2012). *Censo da Educação Superior de 2010.* Brasília: INEP.

Jeanneret, N., McLennan, R., & Stevens-Ballenger, J. (2011). *Musical futures: An Australian perspective.* Findings from a Victorian Pilot Study. https://www.musicalfutures.org/resource/27551/title/mfozevaluationofpilots, accessed August 9, 2013.

Jorgensen, E. R. (2007). Concerning justice and music education. *Music Education Research, 9*(2), 169–189. doi: 10.1080/14613800701411731.

Karlsen, S. (2010). BoomTown music education/authenticity: Informal music learning in Swedish post-compulsory music education. *British Journal of Music Education, 27*(1), 35–46.

Keddie, A. (2012). *Educating for diversity and social justice.* Routledge Research in Education 71. Oxon: Routledge.

McCowan, T. (2006). Approaching the political in citizenship education: The perspectives of Paulo Freire and Bernard Crick. *Educate, 6*(1), 57–70.

McPhail, G. (2012). Knowledge and the curriculum: Music as a case study in educational futures. *New Zealand Journal of Educational Studies, 47*(1), 33–45.

McPhail, G. (2013). Developing student autonomy in the one-to-one music lesson. *International Journal of Music Education, 31*(2), 160–172.

Moore, A. (2012). *Teaching and learning: Pedagogy, curriculum and culture* (2nd ed.). Oxon: Routledge.

Narita, F. (2010). Music teacher education: Teachers' knowledge and collaboration in distance learning. *Proceedings of the 29th World Conference of the International Society for Music Education* (pp. 162–165), Beijing, China.

Narita, F. (2012). Music education in the Open University of Brazil: Informal learning practices. *ICT in Musical Field,* 3(2), 43–48.

O'Neill, S., & Bespflug, K. (2012). Musical futures comes to Canada: Engaging Students in real-world music learning. *Canadian Music Educator,* 53(2), 25–34.

Sands, R. (2007). Social justice and equity: Doing the right thing in the music teacher education program. *Action, Criticism, and Theory for Music Education,* 6(4), 43–59. http://act.maydaygroup.org/articles/Sands6_4.pdf.

Shulman, L. S. (1987). Knowledge and teaching: Foundations of the new reform. *Harvard Educational Review,* 57(1), 1–22.

Vakeva, L. (2010). Garageband or GarageBand? Remixing musical futures. *British Journal of Music Education,* 27(1), 59–70.

Woodford, P. (2005). *Democracy and music education: Liberalism, ethics, and the politics of practice.* Bloomington: Indiana University Press.

Wright, R. (2012). Tuning into the future: Sharing initial insights about the 2012 Musical Futures Pilot Project in Ontario. *Canadian Music Educator,* 53(4), 14–18.

Wright, R., & Kanellopoulos, P. (2010). Informal music learning, improvisation and teacher education. *British Journal of Music Education,* 27(1), 71–87. doi: 10.1017/S0265051709990210.

Zeichner, K., & Flessner, R. (2009). Educating teachers for social justice. In K. Zeichner (Ed.), *Teacher education and the struggle for social justice* (pp. 24–43). Oxon: Routledge.

....

CHAPTER 20

MUSICAL CREATIVITY AND "THE POLICE"

Troubling Core Music Education Certainties

....

PANAGIOTIS A. KANELLOPOULOS

INTRODUCTION

....

SINCE Satis N. Coleman's groundbreaking *Creative Music for Children* (1922), music education practice and research have increasingly focused on the study and development of children's musical creativity. Various music pedagogies began to acknowledge the primacy of direct creative engagement with sound—what is traditionally called the "sound before sign" principle (see McPherson & Gabrielsson, 2002, p. 101). Music educators' passionate efforts to develop children's "creative acts" (Canfield, 1935, p. 238) became the cornerstone of child-centered music pedagogies that sought to liberate teaching and learning, based on the belief that "the child's insights derived from their lived experience could yield to the authority of conventions and formal devices found in the work of other artists" (Finney, 2011a, p. 16). Such pedagogies assumed a direct link between creativity and natural learning processes,[1] active engagement and self-realization, as well between openness, inclusiveness, and personal and societal freedom (Benedict & Schmidt, 2011). As a result, music educators entered a lifelong, life-enriching, and life-changing adventure that aimed at nurturing these ideals, which are vividly expressed it the following words of Christopher Small:

> By allowing our pupils the opportunity to make music in the present tense, we can introduce into the school [. . .] a concept that can overthrow the future-oriented, instrumental ethos of the school, [. . .] [I]f we acknowledge the creative power of children in art, we must also recognize their ability to create other forms of knowledge (since art is a form of knowledge, [. . .]), and to ask their own questions. ([1977]1996, p. 216)

The roots of such approaches are to be found in the constitutional principles of the modernist notions of human subjectivity: in, for example, Rousseau's "insistence on originality, authenticity, and self-expression uncorrupted by social pressures and constraints, alongside of a championing of greater social and political equality and justice" (Simon, 2011, p. 317); and also in ideas about artistic creativity as a quest for authenticity, wholeness, and freedom to create playful relationships with meaning and form that can be traced back to Schiller.[2] Increasingly, music education developed firm links with modernist notions of school as a site for nurturing forms of creative music making that would foster democratic ideals: "The development of a divergent attitude of mind through creative activity is likely to act more effectively as a corrective to a basically convergent society" (Payne, 1976, p. vii).

However, modernist ideals of education as a means of progression, authentic expression, openness, questioning the given, and individual freedom are currently being re-contextualized in an educational climate dominated by neoliberal ideals that promote a highly individualist vision of humans as flexible, competitive entrepreneurs who are always in a position to invest in creativity so as to experiment with unpredictable situations, creatively exploiting uncertainty in profitable nonlinear ways. Thus, notions of musical creativity as a natural resource of personal fulfillment, as an integral part of a musical education that sees art as "a way of understanding ourselves and the modern *condition humaine*" (Dissanayake, 1988, xi, in Reimer, 2012, p. 120), are being re-appropriated in educational situations that seem to enforce a neoliberal rationale for creativity, based, for example, on theories such as Sternberg and Lubart's (1991) *investment theory of creativity*. Notions of creativity that "expect children to create music in response to things about which they felt deeply, about matters that engaged their imaginations" (Finney, 2011a, p. 19) seem to be overthrown by a "buying low and selling high" (Lubart & Sternberg, 1995, p. 271) approach. As a consequence, the way is paved for the institutionalization of "(self-) exploitation" (Raunig, 2013, p. 106), masked by a rhetoric of "personalization of goals" and preparation "of young people and their future entrepreneurial character as citizens" (Finney, 2011b, p. 139).

In what follows, it is argued that neoliberal discourse on creativity subverts the potential of creative music education to function as a site of engagement with social justice. It does so by way of introducing an imperceptible shift of the notion of inclusion, from a notion that relates to welcoming difference as a means for cultivating personal freedom and democratic participation, to a notion that designates readiness to be considered as a legitimate "player" in the ruthless competitive struggle for "creative work." Whereas "modernist" creativity discourse in music education emphasized the creative abilities of all students and the value of creative engagement as a means for opening up to new ideas and sensibilities, neoliberal discourse of "[i]nclusion mainly concerns one's participation in the antagonistic terrain of neoliberal society" (Mylonas, 2012, p. 1).

This chapter offers "a cautionary tale about the institutionalization of creative practices" (Benedict & Schmidt, 2011, p. 134) in contemporary educational contexts, examining current understandings of musical creativity and its educational value as they emerge in certain prominent research perspectives and policy-informing documents.

It thus questions the widely held view that emphasis on musical creativity de facto counterbalances the curriculum's excessive cognitive orientation or overemphasis on the measuring and constant monitoring of performance. Drawing on Raunig's (2013) *Industries of Creativity* and Rancière's (1999) distinction between *politics* and *the police*, this chapter aims at theorizing how notions of music education creativity acquire new and particularly problematic meanings in the context of currently dominant entrepreneurial neoliberal visions of schooling.

The chapter's argument unfolds in five sections. The first section provides a framework for understanding the entrepreneurial turn in education and the unprecedented emphasis on education as a vehicle for preparing young people for the twenty-first-century knowledge economy. The second section sketches the new socioeconomic and cultural context that has enabled the emergence of the new role that creativity has been called to play within the current socioeconomic situation and how the rationale on which this is based has led to the re-appropriation of modernist conceptions of creativity. In the light of these, the third section offers a way of understanding the recent renewed interest of the role of creativity in education. Following on from that, the chapter elaborates on how music education discourse on creativity is gradually being re-contextualized within a performativity-oriented education. The final part inquires into music education's ability to counter this situation. It is argued that music education may still be able to advance a vision of creative engagement that addresses issues of social justice in forms of *prefigurative pedagogies* (after Miner, 2013; see also Breines, 1989; Del Gandio, 2008) of an activist orientation.

The Entrepreneurial Turn in Education

Ever since the 1990s we have witnessed a profound change in dominant educational policy thinking, namely, what in this chapter it is called *the entrepreneurial turn*. The progressive modernist vision of education (Reese, 2001; Salazar, 2013; Thayer-Bacon, 2012; Wyatt, 1979; on music education and progressivism, see Finney, 2011b; Kelly, 2012; Woodford, 2012), despite its limitations (see Burman 2007; Walkerdine, 1986), promoted a deeply humanistic educational vision. This vision delineated a view of education as (a) a process of educating the "universal" child informed by developmental psychology, (b) induction to "higher" cultural values, coupled with the cultivation of critical democratic citizenship, (c) development of a rounded self, capable of self-expression and self-actualization, and (d) a means for reducing inequalities. We contend that this has currently been abandoned in favor of a view of education as a vehicle for survival within twenty-first-century knowledge economies. As Peters, Liu, and Ondercin note, "[t]he knowledge economy recognizes knowledge as the basis of innovations that support economic growth" (2012, p. 4). Consequently, producing lifelong learners, equipped with flexible skills relevant to the rapid changes in the knowledge economy, coupled with the cultivation of an entrepreneurial attitude to life as a whole has been recognized as a core task of contemporary education.[3] A recent report (EESC, 2006) has openly admitted that this concerns education in its totality: "Achieving an entrepreneurial mindset is a lifelong learning process, which needs to *start at an early age* and which should run like a *'red thread'* throughout the whole education system" (p. 111, emphasis added). In this forcefully emerging vision of schooling, "'learning,' 'reflection' or 'development' [. . .] often implicitly [. . .] reproduce the neoliberal values of individualism, success and competition" (Kontopodis, 2012, p. 5).

That education produces competitive individuals must be assured by "putting schools under new kinds of economic and managerial surveillance and control" (Dimitriadis, 2008, p. 6). As Ball argues, "the new technologies of reform play an important part in aligning public sector organizations with the methods, culture and ethical system of the private sector" (Ball, 2003, p. 216). One of the most pervading means of this alignment is the culture of performativity that is currently imposing a complex array of technologies of monitoring output through high-stakes testing, managerial approaches of accountability, and privatization of a variety of services (Hursh, 2008). Such a context induces a repositioning of notions of the *personal* and the *communal* in ways that appear somewhat paradoxical. Personal perspectives are valued *as long as* they produce tangible and measured outcomes relevant to the market (Ball, 2004). And collaborative efforts are highly "valued, but primarily for instrumental purposes within the context of the market place" (Fielding, 2003, p. 10, in Ball, 2004).

CREATIVITY
RE-CONTEXTUALIZED: PERFORMING
ENTREPRENEURSHIP

At the same time, in recent years we have witnessed an increasing use of creativity discourse in the context of entrepreneurial economy. A basic precondition of this has been the reappropriation of the significant shift from the traditional conception of creativity as an attribute of *artistic* genius to the "new" concept (Elliott, 1971) that sees creativity as "the activity of every human mind" (Williams, 1961, p. 33; see also Lehrer, 2012). Knowledge economy does not rely solely on the accumulation of traditional forms of capital but sees the link between creativity and economy as a source of new forms of immaterial capital (Rosanvallon, 2013). Michael Peters refers to media entrepreneur John Howkins's (2002) thesis that "it is ideas, people and things rather than land, labor and capital that have become the most important factors of production in the leading-edge liberal-capitalist economies" (Peters, 2009, p. 41).

In recent years there has been a growing emphasis on the so-called creative or cultural industries (and its agents, "the creatives") as a thriving part of the knowledge economy.[4] Raunig (2013) notes that today's "creative industries are no longer structured in the form of huge media corporations, but mainly as micro-enterprises of self-employed cultural entrepreneurs in the fields of new media, fashion, graphics, design, pop, etc." (p. 101). The age-old Frankfurt school complaint about contemporary art's loss of autonomy and its unconditional surrender to the laws of cultural industry has been turned on its head: in the contemporary world of cultural/creative industries, it is considered that "the creatives are released into a specific sphere of freedom, of independence and self-government" (p. 102) exactly because of their entrepreneurial spirit. Ross (2008) put the matter succinctly: "In the business world, creativity is viewed as a wonderstuff for transforming workplaces into powerhouses of value, while intellectual property—the lucrative prize of creative endeavor—is increasingly regarded as the 'oil of the 21st century'" (p. 32).

This promise of salvation stems from the alleged potential of particular characteristics of creative industries: establishment of small-scale project-based institutions; emphasis on self-employment as a means of achieving flexibility; extensive use of informal production modes and of a wide array of skills that are the result of informal learning; celebration of self-determination; immediate response to unexpected opportunities; creative adaptation to new challenges; learning to detect the potential of ideas that at certain points seemed unrealistic or marginal; and striving for innovation. All these create a sense of opening up a world of real opportunities available to anyone who is "included" in the game. At the same time, these very characteristics result in "precarization and insecurity" (Raunig, 2013, p. 101), stress, and ruthless competition at all levels, valorizing old and creating new hierarchies through "the marketizing of 'equality'" (Littler, 2013, p. 52; see also Gilroy, 2013)—and it is even more astonishing that these conditions are being viewed as *productive* (Lorey, 2010). It is of particular significance that these developments proceed against the backdrop of an increasing (exchange) value measurement and continuous monitoring of progress: "Together with the praise of an independent, entrepreneurial artist life for as many as possible, a system of measuring and striating is introduced in all areas of art production" (Raunig, 2013, p. 106).

How could it be that the egalitarian ideals that informed so many artistic and educational projects that forcefully fought elitist canonic impositions, and that marched in favor of the dictum that everyone is an artist and problematized hierarchies both in art and art education, could be so extensively co-opted by neoliberalism? How could informality, marginality, freedom, adventurousness, innovation, risk—concepts long associated with artistic practices that were beyond "the reach of social systems' control— [become] nowadays a vital part of late capitalist mode of value production, consumption and reproduction of capital" (Mylonas, 2012, p. 5; also Wade, 2014)? Raunig ironically observes that core ideals of radical modernist cultural programs and artistic movements of the twentieth century

> surprisingly seem to be increasingly realized, but in a completely inverse form. 'Culture for all' implies the culture-political obligation of art institutions to push quantity and marketing in a populist spectacular way, and in its perverted form, 'culture from all' indicates an all-encompassing (self-) obligation to be creative. (2013, p. 114)

The concurrent transformation of cultural institutions into players in the business sector, and of creativity into a "tool" integral in the redefinition of "work" (Rosanvallon, 2013) have created a rather peculiar context, which significantly affects the place of creativity in education. It is to this issue we must now turn.

CREATIVITY IN TIMES OF PERFORMATIVITY-ORIENTED EDUCATION

The recent interest of important educational stakeholders and policy designers toward creativity in education should be seen in the general context outlined in the preceding two sections. Pascal Gielen (2013) offers a timely critique of "[a]rt education's embrace of artistic and cultural entrepreneurship" (p. 68), commenting that the (at first glance) curious coexistence of a neoliberalist rhetoric of creativity with processes of striation is based on neoliberalism's redefinition of "the social field as a productive space where one lives and learns in an investing, calculating manner" (p. 69).[5] This chapter presents a counter-argument to the commonly held belief that "commitment to creativity in education from the highest governmental levels" (Brundrett, 2004, p. 72) constitutes an acknowledgment of the need for a balanced education (see Turner-Bisset, 2007). It is argued that creativity discourse in education does *not* aim at counterbalancing performativity-centered educational policies but is (a) a response to the emergent entrepreneurial turn in education, and (b) a sign of recognition of the importance of the developing industries of creativity for economic growth along the lines of neoliberalism (see also Jones, 2011). Exactly because the contemporary celebration of artistic independence, creativity, flexibility, and risk-taking is currently coupled by a "measuring and striating" system "in all areas of art production" (Raunig, 2013, p. 106), the current celebration of creativity in education does not aim at countering exam-based teaching practices. Rather, and paradoxically, both constitute two sides of the same coin. In neoliberal educational contexts, creativity emerges as an indispensable supplement to "the culture of checking, auditing and general surveillance" (Finney, 2011b, p. 125).

The renewed interest in "including" creativity as an integral aspect of education is characterized by an urgency to show its usefulness, first as a "tool" for boosting children's learning, and second as "a desirable 'thinking style'" (Odena & Welsh, 2009, p. 418), necessary for all in the emerging societal and economic conditions. This seems to be based on a clear rationale that relates creativity to economic growth. For example, the *Leading the Creative School* (NCSL, 2002) initiative in Britain promotes creativity as a key element for achieving "continuous improvement and renewal" (Bentley, 2003, p. 2, in Brundrett, 2004, p. 73), in an increasingly competitive global economy. Seltzer and Bentley (1999, in Craft, 2005, p. 105), in their eloquently titled book, *The Creative Age: Knowledge and Skills for the New Economy*, argue that teaching for creativity is a means for creating the potential for immaterial capital, developing the "creative potential of all citizens" with the aim "to boost competitiveness" (p. 9; see also the critique by Gibson, 2005). In a similar vein, the *All Our Futures* report (NACCCE, 1999) adopts a clear managerial approach to creativity, making a strong case for its value as "the foundation of a new generation of high-tech, high-skills industries. Ideas are the building blocks of innovation and innovation builds industries" (British MP Chris Smith in NACCCE, 1999, p. 19). Such polished words mask the basic features of an emergent socioeconomic situation where "creativity becomes the imperative, flexibility becomes a despotic norm, the precarization of work becomes the rule" (Raunig, 2013, p. 102). From the moment that "[i]ncreasingly, employment criteria include a creativity requirement" (McArdle & Grieshaber, 2012, p. 144) the latter becomes a new, strong, albeit quite fleeting tool to be used by individuals in their calculated effort (that for some turns to be a daunting task) to be included as competitive candidates;[6] and, from a means of exploring personal freedom, the struggle for creativity becomes an act of "symbolic violence resulting from the exploitation of this new axis of economical and social competition" (Darras, 2011, p. 91).

It is ironic, then, that the discourse that emerged out of decades of research in the fields of developmental psychology, childhood studies, and arts education seeking to counter the traditional paradigm that presented young children only in terms of what they lacked, and focusing instead on children as culture-makers and active creators of meaning (Campbell, 1998; Christensen & James 2000; Cobb, 1977; Hardman, 1973; Kanellopoulos 2007; Matthews, 1978; Read, 1943; Silvers, 1983; Tobin, 2000), is currently being used to prop up neoliberal educational policies that aim at "producing creative thinkers who will eventually become competent adults" (McArdle & Grieshaber, 2012, p. 144). Nominalist accounts of children's development that emphasized children's neglected creative agency and critiqued the excessively normative and adult-centric conceptions of developmental psychology of the past are being re-contextualized, becoming the basis for the creation of a vision of the young child as a "superchild" destined to exceed the expected norms (see Kascak & Pupala, 2013). Teaching for uniqueness, distinction, risk, and exceptionality within the context a competence-oriented educational practice informed by the larger vision of the child as entrepreneur creates "a new normalising discourse" where "[n]orms have been replaced by a consideration of uniqueness and include an emphasis on the potential to exceed norms" (Kascak & Pupala, 2013, p. 324; see also Hultqvist, 1998; Nadesan, 2002).

"POLICING" MUSIC EDUCATION CREATIVITY

Where does music education stand in relation to these developments that have created a new set of relationships between perfomativity-oriented practices of control, construction of entrepreneurial mindsets, and use-value notions of creativity? It seems that music education has had serious difficulties in accommodating its practices and rationales to the new educational climate. An example can be seen in the problems that arise as emancipatory music education projects of the postwar period are forced to live in a context of checklists for creativity development. In one of his latest writings, John Paynter put the matter succinctly:

> there is pressure upon teachers to produce verifiable evidence of progress. If, to do that, it becomes necessary to compromise by making important whatever is easi- est to assess/evaluate rather than assessing/evaluating those things which are truly important to a subject, then students' achievements may be trivialised. (2000, p. 5; see also Kushner, 1999, 2010; Salaman, 2008)

It seems plausible to conjecture that music education, in its struggle to justify its place in the curriculum, looks for help in those strands of music education creativ- ity research whose excessive individualism, psychologism,[7] and scientism (Regelski, 1996) renders them useful in this process of institutionalizing creativity. Such forms of music creativity discourse favor analytical observation of individual and group dif- ferences (e.g., Kiehn, 2003; Schmidt & Sinor, 1986), close examination of different cre- ativity contexts, measurement of their effectiveness (e.g., Fung, 1997), and emphasis on prediction (e.g., Priest, 2001). A large number of musical creativity measurement stud- ies exist that center around notions of *fluency, flexibility, originality*, and *elaboration* that have been based on Guilford (1950) and the widely used *Torrance Tests of Creative Thinking* (Torrance, 1974). Examples of such approaches include Gorder's (1980) *Measures of Musical Divergent Production (MMDP)* that centered around notions of fluency, flexibility, elaboration, and originality; Webster's *Measure of Creative Thinking in Music (MCTM)* (Hickey & Webster, 1995), which uses the criteria of "extensive- ness, flexibility, originality, and syntax, as well as overall musical creativity" (Hickey & Lipscomb, 2006, p. 98). It is also notable that studies of improvisational and composi- tional creativity often create hierarchies (Hickey, 2001a), assess improvisational skills and their development as measurable competencies "clean" of all social influences (Kiehn, 2007; Paananen, 2006), and treat person, process, product, and place as vari- ables influencing the creative process. Moreover, these perspectives fail to consider the stylistic particularities and the aesthetic intentions that might lead to variable inter- pretations of what constitutes a creative response to music (consensual assessment as a remedy to this problem may be regarded as only of partial success; see Amabile, 1982; Hickey, 2001b).

I argue that such approaches are creating a normalizing discourse that assists processes of striation and provides the basis for forms of argumentation that aim at communicat- ing the value of musical creativity for boosting creativity and learning potential in gen- eral (see Hallam, 2010; Mas & Gomez, 2012). And this is what makes them susceptible to co-option by neoliberal educational discourses. It might therefore be said that tradi- tional reductionist music education epistemologies have paved the way for the currently dominant institutionalization of musical creativity. But a further tendency has arisen—a tendency that I think constitutes a characteristic example of "the inversion of thoughts of subversion to the advantage of order" (Rancière, 2012, p. 12, in Fraisse, 2013, p. 48).

An extensive literature of sociocultural creativity studies rooted in a constructivist epistemology and influenced by neo-Vygotskian studies of distributed intelligence and situated cognition are key here (see Matusov & St. Julien, 2004; Sawyer, 2006, 2012; Shotter & Billig, 1998). Such sociocultural studies of children's musical practices in a variety of formal and informal settings emphasize the collaborative nature of children's creativity (Barrett, 2003; Burnard 2006; Marsh, 2008). As Rogoff (1990) puts it, "children advance their ideas in the process of participation. It is not a matter of bringing to the internal plane a product that was produced externally. It is a matter of *social engagement* that leaves the individual *changed*" (p. 196, italics added). Such research perspectives also give special emphasis to the value of reflection, both on an individual and on a shared level. For example, Balkin argues that "[t]he creative person must continually rethink, reconsider, replace, refine, redo, reaffirm, reprocess, rewrite, and reconceptualize" (Balkin 1990, p. 32, in Marsh, 2008, p. 28). This emphasis on relational, distributed, sociocultural conceptions of musical creativity has led to the acknowledgment of children's creative musical agency in a wide spectrum of children-led informal music learning settings (e.g., Marsh, 2008), as well as to research perspectives that document and theorize children's deep concern for meaningful reflection on their music-making processes (Kanellopoulos, 1999, 2007).

In an act of inversion of thoughts of subversion, the above-mentioned imperatives have been twisted so as to suit the ethos of a neoliberal educational context that promotes an entrepreneurial view of creativity against the backdrop of a performativity culture that pervades every aspect of education. Within this context, notions of *agency, flexibility, originality, adaptability, responsiveness reflection of the possibilities at hand, collaboration*, and *self-evaluation* are stripped of their emancipatory potential and are being linked to wider "features" of neoliberal subjectivities. As such, music creativity discourse has been forced to function as a part of a larger process of production of a new form of subjectivity, namely the creative and cultural entrepreneur. Thus, Susan Young feels the need to connect creative music education to this wider project, arguing that "concern that education for an uncertain future requires adults who are *flexible* and able to make *independent* decisions [. . .] [leading] to a new emphasis on creativity" (2007, p. 23, emphasis added). Augusto Monk (2013) proposes a set of strategies for teaching improvisation, based on a neutralized and neutralizing view of "improvisation as a form of interaction" (p. 76), aligning his approach to a broader effort to develop "collaboration and communication," thought of as "[t]wo of the '21st century skills'" (p. 77). And recent views that celebrate the multiplicity of music-making processes are beginning to create links between musicali*ties* and notions of the artist-as-entrepreneur and the entrepreneur-as-artist:[8] "For music educators nurturing creativity, Steve Jobs may be a useful role model" (Bolden, 2012, p. 3).

Therefore, the claim that music education can continue "business as usual" simply will not do. "[A]rt [and music] teachers can no longer ignore politics when ideologically driven principles and practices colonise their classrooms" (Adams, 2013, p. 273, based on Wild, 2013). Openness, diversity, novelty, flexibility, adaptability, collaboration, independence, and reflection-for-effectiveness within a competitive culture of entrepreneurship and accountability cannot just be viewed as positive keywords[9] signaling individual "readiness" to contribute to societal progress. Rather, they may function as indicators of particular competencies and, despite egalitarian declarations such as that "[c]reativity is for all!" (Fautley & Savage, 2007, p. 97), or, that "[f]ostering creativity is an integral part of education and should be a guiding principle for teaching all children" (Cropley, 2001, p. 151, in Compton, 2007, p. 114), they might end up facilitating notions of inclusiveness that relate to the neoliberal dictum that one should always be able to remain "part of the game" (not being *excluded* from the game), instead of meaning that everyone should be able to develop a creative relationship to music that is "autonomous" and is not part of an "accumulation of knowledge capital" project. Thus, Hickey and Lipscomb's (2006) assertion that "[i]f as teachers we want to *encourage* creativity, then we should support and promote that which might be perceived as 'different'" (p. 108) might lead to very different educational approaches depending on whether this "encouragement" functions in the context of entrepreneurial visions or not.

We seem to be at a crucial moment when the modernist vision of creativity as authentic self-expression and as a means for critical encounter with the tradition seems to have lost its radical character. We seem to be at a time when music education's practices that once exhibited a sense of wonder, experimentation, hope, and unashamed belief in every child's flights of musical imagination (see Finney, 2011a, 2011b; Kanellopoulos, 2011; Kennedy, 2000; Murray-Schafer, 1986; Pond, 1981; Stumme, 1973) are now being re-thought and re-contextualized so that they can fit the new educational agenda. As such, they have ceased holding the potential for acting as *political interventions*, and have instead become part of what Rancière (1999) calls "the police": "an order of bodies that defines the allocation of ways of doing, ways of being, and ways of saying, and sees that those bodies are assigned by name to a particular place and task" (p. 29).

What once was a move that created a crack in the partition of the sensible (*partage du sensible*) (which for Rancière is the precondition for politics; see Rancière, 2004), what once was an act of giving a (musical) voice to those who were seen and taught but were never heard, is now part of the police order.[10] Consequently, the subversive potential of creating a context for students' search for their own voice through critically encountering various dominant musical practices has come to be regarded as a non-profitable waste of time and effort, giving its place to students' struggle to pile up promising portfolios and make "smart" "educational choices." Flexibility, originality (authenticity), adaptability, and autonomy are now qualities that are *demanded* by powerful educational policy agents; and creativity is the key process that ensures that such qualities are developed.

MUSICAL CREATIVITY AND THE ADVANCEMENT OF NEW POTENTIAL FOR RESISTANCE

Understanding the current processes of institutionalization of creativity discourse through Rancière's notion of the "police" is, it is argued, particularly helpful, for it enables one to conceive of counter-strategies that create cracks in the existing order. This is possible because, for Rancière, the police order is always "attacked" by activities that create cracks in the existing partition of the sensible through modes of thought and practice that antagonize the hierarchies of the police; it is for these activities that Rancière (1999) reserves the term "politics" (*la politique*):

> Political activity is always a mode of expression that undoes the perceptible divisions of the police order by implementing a basically heterogeneous assumption, that of a part of those who have no part, an assumption that, at the end of the day, itself demonstrates the sheer contingency of the order, the equality of any speaking being with any other speaking being. (p. 30)

In this way, politics might be understood as constituting modes of local action that bring the issues of exclusion and inclusion to the fore. In turn, this leads to the establishment of a strong link between politics and social justice. As Wayne Bowman has argued, "concerns about social justice in music education cannot be resolved without acknowledging this linkage and exploring the complexity of the ways these inclusive/exclusive moves interrelate" (2007, p. 110). Awareness of the sociopolitical situatedness of how we think about creativity in music education must not be seen as impeding or dismissing the potential of musical creativity as a window toward more socially just practices. On the contrary, it permits us to concentrate on the very workings of making music with children, for in these workings lies the function of music as a tool for social justice. In these workings, music creates for itself the potential to produce small cracks in the police order, thus becoming part of a larger project of creating a culture that addresses issues of justice through local, everyday interventions.

Thus, against the overwhelming deluge of "profitable" creativity, one could begin formulating forms of resistance by *politicizing* musical creativity. The first step toward this politicization is to expose the uses of creativity in neoliberal educational policies, its appropriation for shaping forms of subjectivity that seem suited to the entrepreneurial regimes of knowledge economy and creative industries. A second step is to critique superficial and automatic equation of creative practices with inclusive practices, as well as totalizing accounts of creativity research. For notions of creativity are far from neutral and cannot be a priori equated with openness, open-mindedness, and sensitivity to difference, and therefore cannot be regarded as a simple "key" for engaging students with issues of social justice.

How then might creative music education practices address issues of social justice? It is suggested that our guiding vision could be "to use pedagogy to *explore cultural dissonances* between adult and youngster, provoking musical expression which *precedes* understanding by both child and teacher and which turns the pedagogical act into one of research and *experimentation*, seeking meaning *on the young person's terms*" (Kushner, 2010, p. 9, emphasis added). I contend that understanding classrooms and other learning contexts as sites of experimentation that are not restricted to a logic of accumulating usable creative skills is imperative for a creative music pedagogy that is concerned with inclusiveness and therefore actively confronts issues of social justice. In this view, inclusiveness does not entail "learning to remain part of the game" but constitutes an invitation to create forms of music making that explore what is *not* known in advance and therefore bring to the fore cultural dissonances that are the result of various perspectives that are put forward by both students and teacher(s). Learning to be "included" as a viable competitor is indeed quite different from a notion of inclusiveness that delineates the welcoming of difference within a larger context of understanding music education encounter as an event "where pupil impulse to create music and find aesthetic significance could be shaped and refined through the making process" (Finney, 2011b, p. 127).

In this way, thinking-discussing-reflecting-problematizing *what is creativity* (but also what it means for individuals or groups to think of their engagement as creative) appears imperative. Kushner (2010) argues that "[m]usic-making as an enquiry site is both rich and transparent with key issues in the struggle for independence such as ownership, authority, chance-versus-order, judgment and control" (p. 9). What I'm arguing for is an educational encounter based on reflective and responsive music making that is actively concerned with making issues of social justice visible, and is determined to work on these issues. And it does so by creating local practices that enable us to ponder issues such as the following:

- Ownership: How is creative space formed and negotiated? What does it mean that an idea "belongs" to someone? How do ideas travel and change between minds and across time? How do different music-creative practices (e.g., composing individually, group composition, collective free improvisation) induce different conceptions of ownership? When is expression "authentic"?

- Authority: Who decides, when and why? Is the teacher the ultimate authority in the class? Who controls which aspect of the process of creating, and what is the rationale behind such decisions? What is the role of doubt? How does one build a sense of admiration, wonder, and passion for deep search for socio-musical past and present achievements while doing away with authoritative transmission?

- Inclusion: How are different viewpoints encouraged and pursued? How do children's discoveries within and outside a specific learning context feed back to it? Does the created context permit agonistic struggles for shaping practices and ideas, or is it just based on apolitical views of tolerance (see Benedict & Schmidt, 2011)? How do we ensure that informality retains its radical aspects without surrendering to the rules of the market?

- Difference: How is exploration of the unknown pursued? How does one cultivate a continuous trust to the power of spontaneity? How can one develop an everyday music education culture in which "finding time to make mistakes" (Adams, 2014, p. 2) is an integral aspect of the work? How are issues of difference and identity discussed?

Developing a mode of working that centers on creating music while at the same time problematizing issues of musical creativity might be linked to examples of socio-musical movements that insist on "the nonneutrality of the musical act" (Allsup & Shieh, 2012, p. 51). Allsup and Shieh use the example of the musical and pedagogical practice of the American Association of Creative Musicians (AACM), for whom "composition and improvisation are taught as inseparable from political and economic response" (p. 51). John Finney (2011b, pp. 75–86) documents the informal-learning-based teenage group *Cell I*, whose practice constitutes a critique of what counts as child-centered pedagogy. For Finney, *Cell I* created a "musical world, [that] in its imaginal roots and value orientation, attempts to embrace the whole of life and thus [enabled them to think of] being musical [. . .] as embracing the whole of life" (Finney, 2011b, p. 86). Stefanou (2011, p. 6) refers to the *6daEXIt*, a Thessaloniki-based free improvisation collective whose mixed-media performances around 2010–2011 exemplify "Ben Watson's idea of free improvisation as an act that 'shrieks protest' at the 'business-as-usual' modes of promoting artistic communication as an official, formally framed and institutionally approved activity (Watson, 2004, p. 256)." Lapidaki, de Groot, and Stagkos (2012) document C.A.L.M. project, an Aristotle University of Thessaloniki initiative that fosters "responsible pedagogical action through music creativity" (p. 381), inducing "inclusive pedagogical practices in a association (a 'collectivity') formed between students at university and students at 'high risk' schools" (p. 371).

Other recent examples might include the London-based experimental music group *Cardboard Citizens New Music Ensemble*[11] led by composer Raynaldo Young, whose members have been homeless (or at risk of becoming homeless) people, and the University of Thessaly–based "The scandal of (musical) democracy" research project.[12] This latter project documents and researches the ways in which preschool student teachers, traditionally identified as "non-musicians," develop their identity as music makers through a sustained effort to create, discuss, and record their own music, creating a window through which everyday cultural and educational realities can be critiqued.

Such moves for politicizing musical creativity create small but not insignificant cracks to the perceived ways of thinking about creativity. Each one on them could be understood as "implementing a basically heterogeneous assumption" (Rancière, 1999, p. 30) that results in giving a voice to those who, up to that moment, could not be heard. Such instances could therefore be understood as forms of what Miner (2013) calls prefigurative[13] pedagogies, pedagogical practices that are based on anti-hierarchical music-creative practices that work on the basis of equality (Rancière, 1991). Prefigurative pedagogies aim at creating "alternative universes within the educational setting" (Miner, 2013, p. 13), enacting a vision of public school as a space "of *suspension* and *profanation* regarding time, space and matter" (Masschelein & Simons, 2011, p. 158). Contrary to the current overemphasis on linking school to the needs of the market, musical creative practices that do not operate as forms of legitimation of entrepreneurship might be able to create micro-worlds that envision a different understanding of what it means to create music, suspending dominant policies and ideologies: "Suspension here could be regarded as an act of de-privatization, de-socialization or de-appropriation; it sets something free" (Masschelein & Simons, 2011, p. 158). Masschelein and Simons emphasize that suspension should be taken to mean not "free from" but "free to": free to create a musical micro-world "where things are not a property and to be used according to familiar guidelines, where acts and movements are not yet habits of a culture, where thinking is not yet a system of thought" (p. 158). Profanation is a term that Masschelein and Simons borrow from Giorgio Agamben in order to sketch a view of school as a public space where things are freed from their sacred heritage and are, instead, offered for playful engagement, as common objects "at everyone's disposal for 'free use'" (p. 159). In this perspective, setting musical imagination free induces the development of a music education culture that re-inserts into play "the fundamental condition for achieving both good art and craft—namely, *dismeasure*" (Gielen, 2013, p. 70). This might lead to the creation of small cracks to imposed conceptions of talent, efficiency, productivity, and value, thus reclaiming the notion of creativity, taking it away from the realm of the police and placing it back into the realm of politics.

Based on the belief that "criticism (and radical criticism) is utterly indispensable for any transformation" (Foucault, 2000, p. 456), this chapter has tried to suggest a framework for understanding the emerging links between the contemporary entrepreneurial turn in education, the process of striating the pedagogical encounter based on notions of accountability and performativity, and the new roles that creativity is called to play in twenty-first-century global economies. It has been argued that in this paradoxical and often contradictory context, familiar terms and ideas long associated with creativity begin to acquire new meanings; and that, therefore, music education's role in facilitating musical creativity has to be reconsidered, so that we can reclaim its radical aspects. It has been suggested that music educators' answer to this situation might be the explicit politicization of musical creativity. Politicizing musical creativity would mean that we are prepared to work, reflect, invent, and experiment with music on the basis of equality. In this respect, "the classroom can be seen as a battleground for democracy, a daily struggle between the neoliberal discourses of education and the lived lives of the plurality of staff and students" (Wild, 2013, p. 294); and our work can be seen as an encounter with what Derrida calls the *aporetic* experience of justice:

> [A]poretic experiences are the experiences, as improbable as they are necessary, of justice, that is to say of moments in which the decision between just and unjust is never insured by a rule. (Derrida, 1990, p. 947, in Friedrich, Jaastad, & Popkewitz, 2011, p. 71)

For music creativity to retain its humanness, enabling us to search for its possible non-marketable value for our lives, it *has to* remain an aporetic experience.

ACKNOWLEDGMENTS

Thanks to Patrick Schmidt and the two anonymous reviewers, whose at once gentle and sharp criticisms led to significant improvements of the text. Also to Ruth W. Wright,

Danae Stefanou, and Yiannis Pechtelidis for their generous help at various stages of this work. The final responsibility of all shortcomings of this effort lies of course with the author.

NOTES

1. The link between creativity and children's "natural" developmental trajectory has a long history. The reader is reminded of the following assertion by Coleman: "[T]he child who begins in the earliest stages of his musical development to improvise songs and dances and instrumental melodies, will grow naturally into it as flowers turn to the sun, for the joy he takes in original work is all the stimulation he needs. And it is not difficult when one begins at the natural beginning" (1922, p. 176).

2. See Ken Jones's (2011) illuminative discussion of the "radical Enlightenment tradition" (p. 16), a tradition that induced an "artistic critique of capitalism (and of modernity more generally)", and its connections with "major strands of educational thinking about creativity" (p. 20).

3. This has its roots in the "individualistic conception of human selfhood" that characterizes neoliberalism and, more importantly, in the subsequent belief that the individual is both "the ideal locus of sovereignty and [. . .] the site of governmental intervention" (Gilbert, 2013, p. 11).

4. For a characteristic example of the emerging forms of discourse that are used by such approaches, see Fletcher's (2008) article on the professional identity of the "artist-entrepreneur" for whom "the song is not the artwork, the festival is. The canvas is not the artwork, the gallery is" (p. 145); for an example from the contemporary popular music scene, see Wade (2014); for an argument in favor of the creatives' emerging opportunities for "reaching out to help teach creative process in fields currently regarded in Western societies as non-creative—fields such as business, law or medicine" see Gustina and Sweet (2014, p. 47). For a historical overview of the emerging links between the arts and creative industries, see O'Connor (2011).

5. As Gielen characteristically says, "even more fascinating is the manner in which increased bureaucracy and neoliberalism mesh with each other, influence each other, and in an even more subtle way disturb the relation between theory and practice within education" (Gielen, 2013, p. 69).

6. This has been the result of a significant shift of emphasis from the notion of *relevant qualifications* to that of *competencies* (Rosanvallon, 2013). In the emerging context of what Rosanvallon calls *"the individualism of singularity"* (p. 226, emphasis added), creativity and the ability of the individual to respond to unforeseen situations figure prominently in the list of desirable competencies (Segrestin, 2004, in Rosanvallon, 2013).

7. Following Gur and Wiley (2009), psychologism "refer[s] to those psychological approaches that, using a narrower positivistic and epistemological language, do not seriously deal with cultural, political, and ethical issues in education" (p. 308).

8. See Burnard (2012), as well as the conference *Creativities, Musicalities, Entrepreneurships Conference on Arts, Management, Business, Creativity, Education* (September 2014, see http://icmp. co.uk/events/cmeconference).

9. O'Neill's (2013) notion of "transformative musical engagement" (p. 179) that is based on identifying and building on learners' competencies constitutes a characteristic example of

how currently dominant learning discourse gradually enters music education scholarship; for an excellent critique of the supposed neutrality of such approaches, see Biesta's *Learner, Student, Speaker: Why It Matters How We Call Those We Teach* (2011), as well as Straume (2011).

10. Rancière has offered the following cautionary observation: "The category of 'the police,' as I intend it, is neither a repressive instrument nor the idea of a 'control on life' theorized by Foucault. The essence of the police is the principle of saturation; it is a mode of the partition of the sensible that recognizes neither lack nor supplement. As conceived by 'the police,' society is a totality comprised of groups performing specific functions and occupying determined spaces" (Rancière & Panagia, 2000, p. 124).

11. https://myspace.com/ccitznme/music/songs. See also http://en.wikipedia.org/wiki/Cardboard_Citizens_New_Music_Ensemble.

12. http://lecad.arch.uth.gr/en/nodes/show/1.

13. As Miner (2013) notes, the roots of the notion of prefigurative pedagogies are to be found in Winifred Breines's (1989) notion of prefigurative politics.

References

Adams, J. (2013). Editorial. Creativity and democracy: *iJADE* Conference Issue. *International Journal of Art and Design in Education, 32*(3), 272–274.

Adams, J. (2014). Editorial. Finding time to make mistakes. *International Journal of Art and Design in Education, 33*(1), 2–5.

Allsup, R. E., & Shieh, E. (2012) Social justice and music education: The call for a public pedagogy. *Music Educators Journal, 98*, 47–51.

Amabile, T. M. (1982). Social psychology of creativity: A consensual assessment technique. *Journal of Personality and Social Psychology, 43*(5), 997–1013.

Balkin, A. (1990). What is creativity? What is it not? *Music Educators Journal, 76*(9), 29–32.

Ball, S. J. (2003). The teacher's soul and the terrors of performativity. *Journal of Education Policy, 18*(2), 215–228.

Ball, S. J. (2004). *Education for sale! The commodification of everything?* King's Annual Education Lecture, University of London. Retrieved February 8, 2014, from: http://nepc.colorado.edu/publication/education-sale-the-commodification-everything.

Barrett, M. (2003). Freedoms and constraints: Constructing musical worlds through the dialogue of composition. In M. Hickey (Ed.), *Why and how to teach music composition: A new horizon for music education* (pp. 3–27). Reston, VA: Music Educators National Conference.

Benedict, C., & Schmidt P. (2011). The politics of not knowing: The disappearing act of an education in music. *Journal of Curriculum Theorizing, 27*(3), 134–148.

Bentley, T. (2003) *Distributed intelligence: Leadership and learning.* Nottingham, UK: National College for School Leadership.

Biesta, G. (2011). Learner, student, speaker: Why it matters how we call those we teach. In M. Simons & J. Masschellein (Eds.), *Ranciére, public education and the taming of democracy* (pp. 31–42). Chichester, West Sussex, UK: Wiley-Blackwell.

Bolden, B. (2012). Editorial: The residue of wasted time. *Canadian Music Educator/Musicien Éducateur Au Canada, 53*(4), 2–3. Retrieved May 25, 2013, from http://benjaminbolden.ca/wp-content/uploads/2011/06/CME-editorial-53-4-the-residue-of-wasted-time.pdf.

Bowman, W. (2007). Who is the "We"? Rethinking professionalism in music education. *Action, Criticism, and Theory for Music Education, 6*(4), 109–131. Retrieved December 15, 2007, from http://act.maydaygroup.org/articles/Bowman6_4.pdf.

Breines, W. (1989). *Community and organization in the New Left, 1962–1968: The great refusal.* New Brunswick, NJ: Rutgers University Press.

Brundrett, M. (2004). Leadership and creativity. *Education 3–13: International Journal of Primary, Elementary and Early Years Education, 32*(1), 72–76.

Burman, E. (2007). *Developments: Child, image, nation.* London: Routledge.

Burnard, P. (2012). *Musical creativities in practice.* Oxford: Oxford University Press.

Burnard, P. (2006). The individual and social worlds of children's musical creativity. In G. McPherson (Ed.), *The child as musician: A handbook of musical development* (pp. 353–374). Oxford: Oxford University Press.

Campbell, P. S. (1998). *Songs in their heads: Music and its meaning in children's lives.* New York: Oxford University Press.

Canfield, S. T. (1935). Research applied to creative music, and to power with rhythm and rhythm notation. *Yearbook of the Music Educators National Conference* (pp. 238–242). Chicago: The Music Educators National Conference.

Christensen, P., & James, A. (Eds.) (2000). *Research with children: Perspectives and practices.* London: Falmer.

Cobb, E. (1977). *The ecology of imagination in childhood.* London: Routledge & Kegan Paul.

Coleman S. N. (1922). *Creative music for children: A plan of training based on the natural evolution of music, including the making and playing of instruments, dancing, singing, poetry.* New York: G. P. Putnam's Sons.

Compton A. (2007). What does creativity mean in English education? *Education 3–13: International Journal of Primary, Elementary and Early Years Education, 35*(2), 109–116.

Craft, A. (2005). *Creativity in schools: Tensions and dilemmas.* New York: Routledge/Falmer.

Cropley, A. J. (2001). *Creativity in education and learning: A guide for teachers and educators.* London: Kogan Page.

Darras, B. (2011). Creativity, creative class, smart power, social reproduction and symbolic violence. In J. Sefton-Green, P. Thomson, K. Jones, & L. Bresler (Eds.), *The Routledge international handbook of creative learning* (pp. 90–98). London: Routledge.

Del Gandio. J. (2008). Global justice rhetoric: Observations and suggestions. *Ephemera, 8*(2), 182–203.

Derrida, J. (1990). Force of law: The mystical foundation of authority. *Cardozo Law Review, 11*(5–6), 920–1045.

Dimitriadis, G. (2008) Revisiting the question of evidence. *Cultural Studies-Critical Methodologies, 8*(1), 3–14.

Dissanayake, E. (1988). *What is art for?* Seattle: University of Washington Press.

EESC. (2006). Opinion of the European Economic and Social Committee on the Communication from the Commission to the Council, the European Parliament, the European Economic and Social Committee and the Committee of the Regions Implementing the Community Lisbon Programme: *Fostering entrepreneurial mindsets through education and learning COM (2006) 33 final* (2006/C 309/23). Brussels: Official Journal of the European Union. Retrieved September 20, 2013, from http://eurlex.europa.eu/LexUriServ/LexUriServ.do?uri=OJ:C:2006:309:0110:0114:EN:PDF.

Elliott, R. K. (1971). Versions of creativity. *Proceedings of Philosophy of Education of Gt. Britain, 5*(2), 139–152.

Fautley, M., & Savage, J. (2007). *Creativity in secondary education*. Exeter: Learning Matters.

Fielding, M. (2003). *Working the soul: The earnest betrayal of high performance schooling. Challenging the orthodoxy of school leadership*. Falmer: University of Sussex.

Finney, J. (2011a). John Paynter, music education and the creativity of coincidence. *British Journal of Music Education, 28*(1), 11–26.

Finney, J. (2011b). *Music Education in England, 1950–2010*. London: Ashgate.

Fletcher, R. (2008). The artist-entrepreneur in the new creative economy. *Aesthesis: International Journal of Art and Aesthetics in Management and Organizational Life, 2*(3), 144–150. Retrieved May 25, 2014, from http://digitalcommons.wpi.edu/aesthesis/27.

Foucault, M. (2000). So is it important to think? In J. D. Faubion (Ed.), *Power: The essential works of Michel* Foucault, vol. III (pp. 454–458). New York: New Press.

Fraisse, G. (2013). Emancipation versus domination. In O. Davis (Ed.), *Rancière now: Current perspectives on Jacques Rancière* (pp. 47–65). Cambridge: Polity.

Friedrich, D., Jaastad, B., & Popkewitz, T. S. (2011). Democratic education: An (im)possiblity that yet remains to come. In J. Masschellein & M. Simons (Eds.), *Rancière, public education and the taming of democracy* (pp. 60–75). Chichester, West Sussex, UK: Wiley-Blackwell.

Fung, V. C. (1997). Effect of a sound exploration program on children's creative thinking in music. *Research Studies in Music Education, 9*(1), 13–19.

Gielen, P. (2013). Artistic praxis and the neoliberalization of the educational space. *The Journal of Aesthetic Education, 47*(1), 58–71.

Gilbert, J. (2013). What kind of thing is "neoliberalism"? *New Formations, 80–81*, 7–22.

Gilroy, P. (2013). ". . . We got to get over before we go under . . .": Fragments for a history of Black vernacular neoliberalism. *New Formations, 80–81*, 23–38.

Gorder, W. D. (1980). Divergent production abilities as constructs of musical creativity. *Journal of Research in Music Education, 28*(1), 34–42.

Guilford, J. P. (1950). Creativity. *American Psychologist, 5*(9), 444–454.

Gur, B. S., & Wiley, D. A. (2009). Psychologism and instructional technology. *Educational Philosophy and Theory, 41*(3), 307–331.

Gustina, C., & Sweet, R. (2014). Creatives teaching creativity. *International Journal of Art and Design in Education, 33*(1), 46–54.

Hallam, S. (2010). The power of music: Its impact on the intellectual, social and personal development of children and young people. *International Journal of Music Education, 28*(3), 269–289.

Hardman, C. (1973). Can there be an anthropology of children? *Journal of the Anthropological Society of Oxford, 4*(2), 85–99.

Hickey, M. (2001a). *More or less creative? A comparison of the composition processes and products of "highly-creative" and "less-creative" children composers*. Paper presented at the Second International Research in Music Education Conference, April 3–7, 2001, University of Exeter School of Education, UK.

Hickey, M. (2001b). An application of Amabile's consensual assessment technique for rating the creativity of children's musical compositions. *Journal of Research in Music Education, 49*(3), 234–244.

Hickey, M., & Lipscomb, S. D. (2006). How different is good? How good is different? The assessment of children's creative musical thinking. In I. Deliége & G. A. Wiggins (Eds.), *Musical creativity: Multidisciplinary research in theory and practice* (pp. 97–110). New York: Psychology Press.

Hickey, M., & Webster, P. (1995). Rating scales and their use in assessing children's composi-tions. *The Quarterly Journal of Music Teaching and Learning, 6*(4), 28–44.

Howkins, J. (2002). *The creative economy.* Harmondsworth, UK: Penguin.

Hultqvist, K. (1998). A history of the present on children's welfare in Sweden: From Fröbel to present-day decentralization projects. In T. S. Popkewitz & M. Brennan (Eds.). *Foucault's challenge: Discourse, knowledge, and power in education* (pp. 91–116). New York: Teachers College.

Hursh, D. (2008). *High-stakes testing and the decline of teaching and learning: The real crisis in education.* Plymouth, UK: Rowman & Littlefield.

Jones, K. (2011). Capitalism, creativity and learning: Some chapters in a relationship. In J. Sefton-Green, P. Thomson, K. Jones, & L. Bresler (Eds.), *The Routledge international hand-book of creative learning* (pp. 15–26). London: Routledge.

Kanellopoulos, P. A. (2011). Cage's short visit to the classroom: Experimental music in music education—A sociological view on a radical move. In J. O'Flynn (Ed.), *Proceedings of the 6th International Symposium on the Sociology of Music Education, held at Mary Immaculate College, University of Limerick, Ireland (5th–9th July 2009).*

Kanellopoulos, P. A. (2007). Children's early reflections on improvised music making as the wellspring of musico-philosophical thinking. *Philosophy of Music Education Review, 15*(2), 119–141.

Kanellopoulos, P. A. (1999). Children's conception and practice of musical improvisation. *Psychology of Music, 27*(2), 175–191.

Kascak, O., & Pupala, B. (2013). Buttoning up the gold collar: The child in neo-liberal visions of early education and care. *Human Affairs, 23,* 319–337.

Kelly, S. N. (2012). John Dewey and James Mursell: Progressive educators for contemporary music education. *Visions of Research in Music Education, 21.* Retrieved September 22, 2013, from http://www.rider.edu/~vrme.

Kennedy, M. A. (2000). Creative music making since the time of the singing schools: Fringe benefits. *Journal of Historical Research in Music Education, 21*(2), 132–148.

Kiehn, M. T. (2003). Development of music creativity among elementary school students. *Journal of Research in Music Education, 51*(4), 278–288.

Kiehn, M. T. (2007). Creative thinking: Music improvisational skills development among elementary school students. *Journal of Education and Human Development, 1*(2). Retrieved February 13, 2009, from http://www.scientificjournals.org/journals2007/j_of_edu2.htm.

Kontopodis, M. (2012). *Neoliberalism, pedagogy and human development: Exploring time, mediation and collectivity in contemporary schools.* London: Routledge/Taylor & Francis.

Kushner, S. (1999). Fringe benefits: Music education out of the National Curriculum. *Music Education Research, 1*(2), 209–218.

Kushner, S. (2010). Falsifying (music) education: Surrealism and curriculum. *Critical Education, 1*(4). Retrieved August 15, 2012, from http://m1.cust.educ.ubc.ca/journal/index.php/criticaled/issue/view/61.

Lapidaki, E., de Groot, R., & Stagkos, P. (2012). Communal creativity as sociomusical practice. In G. E. McPherson & G. F. Welch (Eds.), *The Oxford handbook of music education* (Vol. 2, pp. 371–388). New York: Oxford University Press.

Lehrer, J. (2012). *Imagine: How creativity works.* New York: Houghton Mifflin Harcourt.

Littler, J. (2013). Meritocracy as plutocracy: The marketising of "equality" under neoliberalism. *New Formations, 80–81,* 52–72.

Lorey, I. (2010). Becoming common: Precarization as political constituting. *Flux Journal*, *17*. Retrieved July 15, 2012, from http://www.e-flux.com/journal/becoming-common-precarization-as-political-constituting/.

Lubart, T. I., & Sternberg, R. J. (1995). An investment approach to creativity: Theory and data. In S. M. Smith, T. B. Ward, & R. A. Finke (Eds.), *The creative cognition approach* (pp. 271–302). Cambridge, MA: MIT.

Marsh, K. (2008). *The musical playground: Global tradition and change in children's songs and games*. New York: Oxford University Press.

Mas, A. C., & Gómez, M. D. (2012). Music making: A bridge joint of students' cultural and musical diversity. *Procedia—Social and Behavioral Sciences, 46*, 2215–2219.

Masschellein, J., & Simons, M. (2011). The hatred of public schooling: The school as the mark of democracy. In J. Masschellein & M. Simons (Eds.), *Rancière, public education and the taming of democracy* (pp. 150–165). Chichester, West Sussex, UK: Wiley-Blackwell.

Matthews, G. B. (1978). The child as natural philosopher. In M. Lipman & A. M. Sharp (Eds.), *Growing up with philosophy* (pp. 63–77). Philadelphia: Temple University Press.

Matusov, E., & St. Julien, J. (2004) Print literacy as oppression: Cases of bureaucratic, colonial, totalitarian literacies and their implications for schooling. *TEXT International Journal, 24*(2), 197–244.

McArdle, F., & Grieshaber, S. (2012). The creative dis-ease. In O. Saracho (Ed.), *Contemporary perspectives on research in creativity in early childhood education* (pp. 135–160). Scottsdale, AZ: Information Age Publishing.

McPherson, G. E., & Gabrielsson, A. (2002). From sound to sign. In R. Parncutt & G. E. McPherson (Eds.), *The science and psychology of music performance: Creative strategies for teaching and learning* (pp. 99–115). Oxford: Oxford University Press.

Miner, D. A. T. (2013). Teaching "art as social justice:" Developing prefigurative pedagogies in the (liberal) art studio. *International Journal of Education & the Arts, 14*(SI 2.2). Retrieved October 1, 2013, from http://www.ijea.org/v14si2/.

Monk, A. (2013). Symbolic interactionism in music education: Eight strategies for collaborative improvisation. *Music Educators Journal, 99*, 76–81.

Murray-Schafer, R. (1986). *The thinking ear*. Toronto: Arcana.

Mylonas, Y. (2012). Amateur creation and entrepreneurialism: A critical study of artistic production in post-Fordist structures. *tripleC, 10*(1): 1–11. Retrieved October 3, 2013, from http://www.triple-c.at/index.php/tripleC/article/view/287.

NACCCE (National Advisory Committee on Creative and Cultural Education Report). (1999). *All our futures: Creativity, culture and education*. London: DfEE Publications.

Nadesan, M. H. (2002). Engineering the entrepreneurial infant: Brain science, infant development toys, and governmentality. *Cultural Studies, 16*(3), 401–432.

NCSL (National College for School Leadership). (2002). *Leading the creative school: A leading edge seminar*. Nottingham, UK: NCSL.

O'Connor, J. (2011). *Arts and creative industries: An Australian conversation*. Australia Council for the Arts, Sydney NSW. Retrieved May 3, 2014, from http://www.australiacouncil.gov.au/__data/assets/pdf_file/0007/98431/Arts_and_creative_industries_FINAL_Feb_2011.pdf.

Odena, O., & Welch, G. (2009). A generative model of teachers' thinking on musical creativity. *Psychology of Music, 37*(4), 416–442.

O'Neill, S. (2012). Becoming a music learner: Towards a theory of transformative musical engagement. In G. E. McPherson & G. F. Welch (Eds.), *The Oxford handbook of music education* (Vol. 1, pp. 163–186). New York: Oxford University Press.

Paananen, P. (2006). The development of rhythm at the age of 6–11 years: Non-pitch rhythmic improvisation. *Music Education Research, 8*(3), 349–368.

Payne, V. (1976). Foreword to George Self, *Make a New Sound*. London: Universal Edition.

Paynter, J. (2000). Making progress with composing. *British Journal of Music Education, 17*(1), 5–31.

Peters, M. A., Liu, T. C., & Ondercin, D. J. (2012). *The pedagogy of the open society: Knowledge and the governance of higher education*. Rotterdam: Sense Publishers.

Peters, M. A. (2009). Education, creativity and the economy of passions: New forms of educational capitalism. *Thesis Eleven, 96*, 40–63.

Pond, D. (1981). A composer's study of young children's innate musicality. *Bulletin of the Council for Research in Music Education, 68*, 1–12.

Priest, T. (2001). Using creativity assessment experience to nurture and predict compositional creativity. *Journal of Research in Music Education, 49*(3), 245–257.

Rancière, J., & Panagia, D. (2000). Dissenting words: A conversation with Jacques Rancière. *Diacritics, 30*(2), 113–126.

Rancière, J. (1991). *The ignorant schoolmaster: Five lessons in intellectual emancipation* (K. Ross, Trans.). Stanford, CA: Stanford University Press.

Rancière, J. (1999). *Disagreement: Politics and philosophy* (J. Rose, Trans.). Minneapolis: University of Minnesota Press.

Rancière, J. (2004). *The politics of aesthetics* (G. Rockhill, Trans.). New York: Continuum.

Rancière, J. (2012). Foreword to the new French edition of *La Lecon d'Althusser*. Paris: La Fabrique.

Raunig, G. (2013). *Factories of knowledge, industries of creativity*. Los Angeles: Semiotext(e).

Read. H. (1943). *Education through art*. London: Faber.

Reese, W. J. (2001). The origins of progressive education. *History of Education Quarterly, 41*(1), vi, 1–24.

Regelski, T. A. (1996). Scientism in experimental music research. *Philosophy of Music Education Review, 4*(1), 3–19.

Reimer, B. (2012). Uncomfortable with immanence: The nature and value of music and music education as singular or supplemental. In W. Bowman & A. L. Frega (Eds.), *The Oxford handbook of philosophy in music education* (pp. 111–128). New York: Oxford University Press.

Rogoff, B. (1990). *Apprenticeship in thinking: Cognitive development in social context*. New York: Oxford University Press.

Rosanvallon, P. (2013). *The society of equals* (A. Goldhammer, Trans.). Cambridge, MA: Harvard University Press.

Ross, A. (2008). The new geography of work: Power to the precarious? *Theory, Culture and Society, 25*(7–8), 31–49.

Salaman, W. (2008). Reflections on progress in musical education. *British Journal of Music Education, 25*(3), 237–243.

Salazar M. C. (2013). A humanizing pedagogy: Reinventing the principles and practice of education as a journey toward liberation. *Review of Research in Education, 37*, 121–148.

Sawyer, R. K. (2006). *Explaining creativity: The science of human innovation*. Oxford: Oxford University Press.

Sawyer, R. K. (2012). Extending sociocultural theory to group creativity. *Vocations and Learning, 5*, 59–75.

Schmidt, C. P., & Sinor, J. (1986). An investigation of the relationships among music audiation, musical creativity, and cognitive style. *Journal of Research in Music Education, 34*(3), 160–172.

Segrestin, D. (2004). *Les chantiers du manager*. Paris: Armand Colin.

Seltzer, K., & Bentley, T. (1999). *The creative age: Knowledge and skills for the new economy*. London: Demos.

Shotter, J., & Billig, M. (1998). A Bakhtinian psychology: From out of the heads of individuals and into the dialogues between them. In M. Mayerfeld Bell & M. Gardiner (Eds.), *Bakhtin and the human sciences: No last words* (pp. 13–29). London: SAGE.

Silvers, R. J. (1983). On the other side of silence. *Human Studies, 6*(1), 91–108.

Simon, J. (2011). Rousseau. In T. Gracyk & A. Kania (Eds.), *The Routledge companion on philosophy and music* (pp. 317–327). London: Routledge.

Small, C. ([1977]1996). *Music, society, education*. Hanover, NH: Wesleyan University Press.

Stefanou, D. (2011). Towards a practical philosophy of collectively improvised space. Online Resource of the *CMPCP Performance Studies Network International Conference*, University of Cambridge, July 14–17, 2011. Retrieved November 11, 2013, from http://www.cmpcp.ac.uk/conferences_PSN2011_Thursday.html.

Sternberg, R. J., & Lubart, T. I. (1991). An investment theory of creativity and its development. *Human Development, 34*(1), 1–31.

Straume, I. S. (2011). "Learning" and signification in neoliberal governance. In I. S. Straume & J. F. Humphrey (Eds.), *Depoliticization: The political imaginary of global capitalism* (pp. 229–259). Malmö: NSU Press.

Stumme, W. (Ed.) (1973). *Über Improvisation*. Mainz: B. Schott.

Thayer-Bacon, B. (2012). Maria Montessori, John Dewey, and William H. Kilpatrick. *Education & Culture, 28*(1), 3–20.

Tobin, J. (2000). *"Good guys don't wear hats": Children's talk about the media*. New York: Teachers College Press.

Torrance, E. P. (1974). *The Torrance tests of creative thinking: Technical-norms manual*. Bensenville, IL: Scholastic Testing Services.

Turner-Bisset, R. (2007). Performativity by stealth: A critique of recent initiatives on creativity. *Education 3–13: International Journal of Primary, Elementary and Early Years Education, 35*(2), 193–203.

Wade, M. J. (2014). Artists as entrepreneurs, fans as workers. *Popular Music and Society, 37*(3), 273–290.

Walkerdine, V. (1986). Progressive pedagogy and political struggle: Valerie Walkerdine looks back at an educational fantasy. *Screen, 27*(5), 54–61.

Watson, B. (2004). *Derek Bailey and the story of free improvisation*. London: Verso.

Wild, C. (2013). Who owns the classroom? Profit, pedagogy, belonging, power. *International Journal of Art and Design in Education, 32*(3), 288–299.

Williams, R. (1961). *The long revolution*. Harmondsworth, Middlesex, UK: Penguin.

Woodford, P. (2012). Dewey's bastards: Mursell, Broudy, McMurray, and the demise of progressive music education. *Visions of Research in Music Education, 21*. Retrieved September 22, 2013, from http://www.rider.edu/~vrme.

Wyatt, J. F. (1979). Hanna Arendt: A political theorist on the theme of renewal in education. *Educational Studies, 5*(1), 7–13.

Young, S. (2007). Early childhood music education in England: Changes, choices, and challenges. *Arts Education Policy Review, 109*(2), 19–26.

CHAPTER 21

MUSIC EDUCATION AND SOCIAL REPRODUCTION

Breaking Cycles of Injustice

RUTH WRIGHT

The social world is accumulated history, and if it is not to be reduced to a discontinuous series of instantaneous mechanical equilibria between agents who are treated as interchangeable particles, one must reintroduce into it the notion of capital and with it, accumulation and all its effects.... the structure of the distribution of the different types and subtypes of capital at a given moment in time represents the immanent structure of the social world, i.e., the set of constraints, inscribed in the very reality of that world, which govern its functioning in a durable way, determining the chances of success for practices. (Bourdieu, 1986, p. 241)

INTRODUCTION

It appears that, despite a number of political and economic strategies more or less purportedly aimed at fairly distributing wealth, or at least some of society's wealth, among members in "developed" countries, the rich become richer and the poor become poorer. The United Kingdom's *Sunday Times* "rich list," released in May 2014, claimed the "total wealth of the richest 1,000 individuals, couples, or families jumped 15% in a year" (BBC, 2014). This contrasted with a report on May 29 that five million UK children face a life of poverty (Independent, 2014). This pattern is repeated in many countries around the world, presenting a clear and practical example of how society reproduces itself to maintain the advantage of those already privileged.

Numerous sociologists have identified the crucial role that education plays in such social reproduction, and key figures have highlighted the role of culture in these cycles of injustice. As Bourdieu (1973, p. 80) so discerningly perceived, "the education system demands of everyone alike that they have what it does not give." He referred here to access to the "code" within which he observed education to operate, a sociolinguistic and behavioral/attitudinal code, a cultural code or set of resources developed during early life, largely within the family, and acquired differentially according to class. He termed these resources "cultural capital" and argued that possession of such capital predisposes one to take advantage of education. The code is never overtly taught during the education process, however. It has to be learned in the home and is not found in all homes. Children of more socially advantaged groups tend to acquire the code, whereas their less advantaged peers do not.

In 2010 (Wright, 2010a, 2010b) I wrote of the role that music education might play in larger societal patterns of injustice such as this. I also suggested that providing students with opportunities to engage in more democratic forms of music pedagogy might help develop cultural resources more evenly across student populations, resulting in wider social inclusion in music and applying a small point of pressure for larger social change. Since then my empirical work with colleagues (Wright et al., 2012) has led me to question the micro interactional processes between students and teachers that might make a difference in changing such patterns of inclusion. I have continued to consider the role of pedagogy in social reproduction and in particular the roles of two forms of cultural capital, which I term "pedagogical" and "musical capital" in these processes (Wright, 2015). I suggest that it is in embracing pedagogies that allow the interruption of pre-formed, rationalized communities of knowledge and that permit accumulation of pedagogical and musical capital by diverse students, irrespective of social group or background, that alternative approaches to music education might act to break cycles of injustice and in whatever small way act to disrupt the social status quo. This may perhaps explain why previous attempts to include more students in music education by attempting to reduce curricular domination by elite cultural content such as Western art music have failed to change patterns of inclusion in music education and why some new approaches are proving more successful.

Music, Culture, Education, and Social Reproduction

Culture is defined as "that complex whole which includes knowledge, belief, art, morals, law, custom, and other capabilities acquired by man as a member of society" (Tylor, 1958, p. 1). Culture also operates at the level of individual societal institutions such as schools, however, when socially determined patterns of preference and value underlay "the way things are." As such, culture often becomes invisible, a "given," when it comes to the workings of social institutions such as schools. The cultural framework within which such institutions operate, however, has immense effects on the outcomes for the students who study within them. Music is an integral element of humanity's culture. We have yet to find a society, no matter how remote, without music. Bannan (2014, p. 105) writes of humanity's "biological-determined musicality," concurring with anthropologists such as Blacking (1973) and Mithen (2006) who suggest that humanity has a deep-rooted need to participate in communal music making—that said need is "embedded in the human genome" or that humans are "hard-wired for music" (Bannan, 2014, p. 1). Many music educators have therefore argued for the needs and rights of young people to an engaging and satisfying experience of music in education, placing it as a human right (Mullen & Harrison, 2013; Wright, 2010a).

As such, music is deeply embedded in human culture, and therefore in cultural issues of power and control, as societies produce and reproduce themselves over time. Education plays a key role in social reproduction, according to Bourdieu (1984, 1986, [1987]1994) The role of music education in social reproduction—implying the reproduction of societal models favoring the cultural interests of currently dominant social groups—should therefore not be underestimated.

Music Education, Social Inequality, and Social Reproduction

We know that social class, wealth, family culture, gender, race, ethnicity, and identity shape, and to some extent predetermine, the extent to which young people benefit from education. Evidence now supports the idea that this is not an accidental correlate of birth, but that parents deliberately engage in "concerted cultivation" (Hofvander Trulsson, 2012; Lareau, 2003), harvesting cultural resources and qualifications such as music, ballet, and athletic examinations and certificates for their children to ensure that sufficient cultural capital is accrued to come out ahead in the education race. Hofvander Trulsson's work also suggests that children of some socially upward aspirational lower class and immigrant families who understand "the rules of the game" also engage in such practices to secure advantage for their children (Hofvander Trulsson, 2012). This lends credence to Lareau and Weininger's (2003) assertion that parental skill in manipulating interactions with education may have a significant role to play in child educational success.

It might be contended that in the case of music education, distributive inequalities are exaggerated to a degree found nowhere else. Class, socioeconomic status, race, ethnicity, sexuality, and gender have all been shown to affect access to music education in ways not experienced in other school subjects (Bates, 2012; Gould, 2012; Gustafson, 2008; Lamont & Maton, 2010; Rabkin, Hedberg, & Arts National Endowment, 2011). While teachers of other subjects have been engaged in long and often government-prompted battles to increase access to and achievement of children across the social spectrum—efforts that have met with varying degrees of success—music education appears until recently to have been left behind in the battle to recruit, retain, and foster positive achievement among diverse student groups. Ontario, Canada, serves as an example, with data indicating that music education serves on average 10%–12% of secondary school students, once they complete compulsory music education at the age of 14 (Bolden, 2012; Veblen, 2012). Yet we know that young people remain passionately attached to music as a force in their day-to-day lives (Herbert, 2012), including the most dispossessed—the homeless (Palzkill Woelfer & Lee, 2012).

Lamont and Maton (2010) use the concept of legitimation codes to describe student understandings of success criteria required in various curriculum subjects. They provide analysis from an empirical study demonstrating that UK students perceive music as an elite code, which requires special knowledge, skills, and special talents, and that this may play a central role in student decisions concerning whether or not to study music. By choosing not to study music for such reasons, I suggest that many students actively position themselves as "non-elite," as lacking the cultural capital required to succeed in music. I would suggest, however, that such self-positioning may result for some students in a larger, albeit unwitting, educational statement about how the student sees herself in relation to the cultural capital required to succeed in education per se. Such statements may speak to enduring issues of self-confidence and "self-imposed" (although societally conditioned) limitations on future educational potential. This is discussed further in the section that follows.

Bourdieu and Reproduction

Pierre Bourdieu developed a theory of social reproduction that helps us to understand how this disadvantageous self-positioning may happen. He asks us to consider how social behavior is regulated if people do not merely follow social rules (Bourdieu, [1987]1994). Attempting to answer this conundrum, he developed a view of social life conceptualized in terms of a "game." Bourdieu (1986) asserted the game to be competitive and its objectives to maintain or advance the player's position on the social field by accumulating various sorts of capital: economic (money assets), cultural (certain types of knowledge, taste, discrimination, cultural preferences, language), social (connections and networks, family, religious and cultural heritage), and symbolic (things that stand for all the other types of capital and can be exchanged in other fields, such as qualifications). The game, he asserted, was not played on a level field, however. In fact, a better analogy might be to say that the site of the game was a steepish hill. Some players begin the game already holding stocks of preferential capital, and this gives them an advantage, placing them further up the hill than others. We saw an example of this earlier in Lamont and Maton's analysis of student decisions concerning whether or not to study music. Students who see themselves as "elite" due to background, family cultural habits, or private music tuition—that is, as special knowers capable of developing, or already holding, the special knowledge required to succeed in music—are positioned higher up the hill than their less fortunate peers. They hold more capital. Moreover, such students are likely to accumulate proportionately more of the capital over time than their peers because of their advantageous start and the advantageous conditions within which they continue to exist.

Players also develop dispositions or behavioral tendencies that are derived from *habitus*, that is, "a way of being, *a habitual state* (especially of the body) and in particular *a predisposition, tendency, propensity or inclination*" (Bourdieu, [1972]1977, p. 214, original italics). This explains why individuals tend to behave in certain patterned ways and why similar patterns of behavior can be observed among people of similar social class. The habitus was structured by one's past social experiences, particularly those within the family and education. It then tended to shape actions, as it established ways of seeing and responding to the world, and generated tastes and values consistent with past experiences and projected futures (Maton, 2012). Such patterns can also extend to how one perceives oneself in relation to education, and particularly in relation to elite knowledge codes such as music education, leading to self-positioning as non-elite by many students.

These three concepts together—habitus, capital, and field—explained individual and collective practice, described by Bourdieu (1986) in the following equation (p. 101):

$$[(habitus)\,(capital)] + field = practice$$

In other words, practice (action/behavior) is the product of the relationship between an individual's dispositions (habitus) and his or her position in a field, defined in terms of the amount of capital held by the individual within that field. Such practices explain why society tends to reproduce in patterns, as habitus is patterned and produces predictable behaviors, and why such reproduction is largely governed by distribution of capital, as capital shapes habitus. It therefore helps us understand how patterns of social exclusion perpetuate and how subjects such as music may form part of a larger pattern of culturally based distributive injustice, perpetuated in and through education.

Bourdieu and Education

For Bourdieu, education played a central role in the distribution of patterns of social advantage, including the reproduction of existing social patterns of inequality. Bourdieu and Passeron (1990) described this educational reproductive power as a type of "symbolic violence" in that it gave education the authority to convey meanings and convey them as fact, while divorcing them from the social power base that had first given them their legitimacy. He describes this as follows:

> Every power to exert symbolic violence, i.e. every power which manages to impose meanings and to impose them as legitimate by concealing the power relations which are the basis of its force, adds its own specifically symbolic force to those power relations. (Bourdieu & Passeron, 1990, p. 4)

An example of this might be seen in the continuing battles about the nature and purpose of music education, curriculum content, and pedagogy. While appearing to be pedagogic discussions, these are in fact social power struggles. The cultural values and philosophies of the socially dominant group frequently become embodied in music curricula or national standards without overtly being revealed as such. They appear as pedagogic innovation, rather than social control.

Moreover, Bourdieu and Passeron (1990) saw culture as occupying a central role in the symbolic violence enacted by education, suggesting that "all Pedagogic Action (PA) is, objectively, symbolic violence insofar as it is the imposition of a cultural arbitrary by an arbitrary power" (p. 5). Furthermore, the choice of cultural values dominant in education was anything but arbitrary, but rather an expression of the cultural values and interests of the socially dominant class. As they argue,

> in any given social formation the cultural arbitrary which the power relations between the groups or classes making up that social formation put into the dominant position within the system of cultural arbitraries is the one which most fully, although always indirectly, expresses the objective interests (material and symbolic) of the dominant groups or classes. (Bourdieu & Passeron, 1990, p. 9)

Bourdieu argued that by this means, education plays a trick on the less advantaged members of society. By wrapping education within a cultural code familiar to those from dominant sectors of society, the children of these dominant social groups are predisposed to understand and benefit from education before their less advantaged peers. Because this process is imperceptible, however, contained in the invisible waters of a culture pervading education without overtly revealing itself, it appears that some children sink and others swim in school due to merit alone, whereas in fact, there are very clear explanations for relative success and failure; all we need to do is to introduce a little dye to allow the cultural waters to be revealed. Moreover, "in nearly all economically advanced countries, schools play a crucial and growing role in the transmission of advantage across generations" (Lareau & Weininger, 2003). I suggest, however, that this trick is no longer covert, as it appeared to be in Bourdieu's analysis of French society. Lamont and Maton's analysis suggests that students are very well aware that certain subjects, such as music, as it is delivered in many traditional pedagogic models, are more accessible to "elite" students. Students who exclude themselves from participation in music because they recognize themselves as "non-elite" are therefore acknowledging that they know the rules of this particular game and recognize that they are unlikely to win it.

Elite Knowers

Within educational research, Bourdieu's cultural theory has had a great impact, becoming a standard topic in education textbooks (Lareau & Weininger, 2003, p. 576). Lareau and Weininger (2003) contend, however, that much of the research conducted on the basis of Bourdieu's cultural theory might be based on a misinterpretation of his concept of cultural capital.

> We argue that a dominant interpretation, resting on two crucial premises, has emerged concerning cultural capital. First, the concept of cultural capital is assumed to denote knowledge of or competence with "highbrow" aesthetic culture (such as fine art and classical music). Second, researchers assume that the effects of cultural capital must be partitioned from those of properly educational "skills," "ability," or "achievement". (p. 567)

According to Lareau and Weininger, the prevailing interpretation of cultural capital in educational research can be attributed in large part to the work of DiMaggio, particularly his 1982 article investigating the association of cultural capital to school achievement. Here Lareau and Weininger assert that DiMaggio sees cultural capital as

> [m]ore completely filling out models of the "status attainment process." [and] ... interprets cultural capital in terms of the Weberian notion of "elite status cultures" ...
>   Cultural capital is thus definitionally yoked to "prestigious" cultural practices, in DiMaggio's interpretation. (2003, p. 568)

For Lareau and Weininger, such assertions may rest on some basic misunderstandings of Bourdieu's concept of cultural capital. They suggest that DiMaggio's assumptions—first, that Bourdieu intended his concept of cultural capital to indicate elite or highbrow culture, and second, that such capital has effects independent of ability or skill—might be questioned.

While Distinction (1984) takes great pains to document lifestyles in France coherent across status groups, and to prove that highbrow culture is part of the "art of living" consistent with the dominant status group, the relationship between familiarity with such highbrow culture and achievement in education is less well supported, nor is the educational process itself by which such advantage might be transmitted closely examined (Lareau & Weininger, 2003, p. 577).

Lareau and Weininger suggest, however, that a closer inspection of this work causes further questioning of the highbrow interpretation:

> For we also find Bourdieu stating here that the educational system's ability to reproduce the social distribution of cultural capital results from "the educational norms of those social classes capable of imposing the ... criteria of evaluation which are the most favorable to their products. (p. 578)

As they go on to state:

> Bourdieu's remarks highlight two important issues. On the one hand, he did see a congruity between the aptitudes rewarded by the school and the styles and tastes that

engender status group inclusion among members of the dominant class: the "subtle modalities in the relationship to culture" that he names do indeed recall the cultural attributes of the dominant class as described in Distinction. On the other hand, Bourdieu also indicates that this concept of cultural capital was intended to reflect the peculiarities of the French context that was being analyzed. Thus, the question arises whether Bourdieu considered congruity between educational norms and status practices to be essential to the concept of cultural capital, and, if so, whether they necessarily take a "highbrow" aesthetic form. (p. 579)

Lareau and Weininger show that other interpretations have been adopted, however. They cite Sullivan's study of final year English students that took a broad variety of indicators of cultural capital to attempt to determine which might be determined capital. Findings suggested that reading was more significant than arts participation as providing "intellectual resources which help pupils at school" (p. 579). These intellectual resources of "cultural knowledge" and "vocabulary" begin to dissolve DiMaggio's sharp distinction between a status culture, which revolves around prestige, and "ability," which revolves around technical skill and knowledge. They conclude by providing an alternative definition of cultural capital that does not restrict its scope exclusively to "elite status cultures," and that does not attempt to partition it analytically or empirically from "human capital" or "technical" skill." Their approach "stresses the importance of examining micro-interactional processes whereby individuals' strategic use of knowledge, skills, and competence come into contact with institutionalized standards of evaluation" (p. 560)

To summarize this argument, therefore, Lareau and Weininger adopt a definition of cultural capital that accords very closely with Lamont and Maton's (2010) description of knowledge legitimation codes. Not only do the social-cultural origins and affiliations of curriculum content have a role to play in whether diverse students feel able to succeed in particular subjects, but so too do the types of intellectual resources, cultural knowledge, and vocabulary required to succeed and the extent to which these are available solely within the educational context.

If music education is based in an elite knowledge code formed from a status culture that is foreign to students and that requires elite knowers (possessed of pedagogical and musical skills and understandings not available to them solely, or at least largely, within the classroom), many students will be excluded or will choose to self-exclude. By determining that success in music requires elite knowledge and an elite knower and by deciding that she is not such an elite student, a young person may position herself as "non-elite." While being hesitant to overstate the effects of such decisions, it may be possible, especially within the context of the importance of music in the lives of young people, that such positioning begins or contributes to a sense of lower self-worth or potential educational ability in comparison to those peers positioned as "elite" in the eyes of the student. Thus existing patterns of social reproduction recur, and cultural hegemony is perpetuated.

Disrupting patterns of social reproduction—the role of music pedagogy—educational philosopher Gert Biesta (2010) suggests that one of the problems with the subject-based nature of education is that it frequently serves only to permit students to speak as agents of particular knowledge communities, already formed by a consensus in which the student had no part. In this way, education may function as a way of inducting students into previously formed rational communities. By predefining what we take the subject "music" to be, what being "musical" or "making music" means, we close off to our students the possibilities inherent in engaging with music as "other" and discovering their own unique way of being musical. In this way, we create self-replicating loops with all their attendant hegemonic practices and effects.

It is here I suggest that alternative music pedagogies may offer potential in disrupting previously established patterns of social reproduction. The comparatively late focus on pedagogy and its role in this respect may indeed provide further explanation as to why previous attempts to move away from music education dominated by elite cultural content such as Western art music have failed to change patterns of inclusion in music education and why some new approaches are proving more successful.

In schools in the United Kingdom where an "informal learning music pedagogy" developed by Green (2008) from her observations of the practices of popular musicians has been implemented, uptake of elective music education has risen to up to 40 percent of the cohort, with high reported levels of enthusiasm, motivation, and engagement in school music (Hallam, Creech, Rinta, & Shave, 2008). Similar results are also observed in Australia and Canada, where projects founded on Green's work have been initiated.

This is an example of "alternative" music pedagogy that appears to make a difference in young people's engagement with music in schools. Yet, as Lareau and Weininger assert, our understanding of how pedagogy is effective may be aided by close examination of the micro interactional processes that allow students to develop understanding of the strategic "use of knowledge, skills, and competence" and ways in which such abilities may come into contact with institutionalized standards of evaluation that receive them positively.

PEDAGOGICAL AND MUSICAL CAPITAL

Within the music education classroom, I would suggest that two specific forms of cultural capital may be identified: pedagogical capital and musical capital. Pedagogical capital is composed of skills, knowledge, and understanding related to learning and teaching; moreover, it concerns ownership of pedagogical decision-making. Musical capital relates to skills, knowledge, and understanding relating to music but also importantly to self-perceptions of musicality and musical potential (Wright, 2015).

Bourdieu used economic and cultural capital as axes against which to plot positions within the dominant field of power. I would suggest (Wright, in press) that within the field of classroom music education, useful determinants of position might be relative possession of musical and pedagogical capital. What follows below derives from an empirical study and serves to illustrate the concepts articulated thus far. In particular, I wish to look at what occurs within these learning situations in terms of accumulation and relative possession of pedagogical capital and musical capital and the ways in which possession of varying amounts of these capitals allocate agents to different positions within the field of music education.

An Example

The study took place in two schools in Southern Ontario, Canada, in 2012 (Wright, Beynon, Younker, Linton, & Hutchison, 2012) involving the introduction of informal music pedagogy (IMP) based on the work of Green (2008) to two Ontario schools, one secondary and one elementary. Participants were 74 rural elementary students in grades 7 and 8 (aged 12–14) and 37 urban secondary school students in grades 9 and 10 (aged 15–16). The lessons followed a similar form to those of Green's (2008) Musical Futures pilot study in that

- students moved through a number of activities based on principles of informal learning;
- they were encouraged to work in groups with friends;
- each group learned music chosen by the group, mainly popular music;
- they learned the music by purposive listening to recordings and copying;
- they had control of their learning sequence and this was directed by their musical goals, not by a hierarchical curriculum;
- they improvised, composed, and performed in a holistically integrated way; and
- teachers were encouraged to watch, listen, and empathize with students' learning goals first of all, and then to work as mentors, coaches, and co-musicians to help students achieve their goals.

Pedagogical Capital

Student comments from the informal learning project data appeared to indicate that perceptions of their holdings of pedagogical capital changed during the project. Students' initial interview comments at the beginning of the project indicated that they viewed themselves as holding little pedagogical capital. The teachers were the pedagogic experts in the classrooms, planning content and learning for students, making decisions concerning sequence, pacing, and acquisition of content, and directing the learning process. All teaching was the domain of the teacher. Elementary students indicated this when describing previous music lessons:

ANNA: Regular music lessons we would usually just sing from a book . . . [with] Mrs. D just playing on her own keyboard.

Secondary students said:

> STRIKER: So there's like, she'll take different songs [scales] and we practice with
> them. B flat, B flat concert down or something.

Comments about lessons later in the project indicated an increased sense of autonomy within the learning and teaching situation, of having a voice in what happened and how it happened in their classes.

> SHANNON: Well I like learning this way because it's almost like you're figuring out
> like you're teaching yourself so you almost have that sense of pride that you're
> doing this all yourself and it's a cool experience doing that.

This led to feelings of independence and responsibility:

> JASON: It's made me feel independent without the teacher here teaching you. It just
> gives you a sense of responsibility like *I* get to do this. . . .

These students appeared to see themselves as being a true part of the pedagogic process, as holding more of the pedagogical capital that was circulating. Students then perceived themselves as teachers of others and of themselves. They began to recognize themselves, albeit implicitly, as co-owning the pedagogical interactions:

> SARAH: . . . we do learn but not from a teacher sometimes. We learn from friends and
> what they know and we learn by ourselves, not all from the teacher.

The change in distribution of pedagogical capital was also noticed by the teacher, as this comment indicated:

> S: So yeah, it's just the classical training and then switching over to the oral learning
> [that are difficult] but you just have to think of it like you're learning everyday too
> and you learn along with your students and that's what makes it probably the most
> rewarding.

No longer was she the owner of all the knowledge, charged with transmitting it to her students, now she was a co-learner alongside them.

Assessment also played an important role in the accumulation of pedagogical capital. The role of the teacher in non-formal teaching required a change in assessment practices away from the previous testing model. Now students were assessed through observation of group practice both formatively and summatively. Students reported that this affected their self-perceptions:

> PETE: It made me feel happier and I feel smarter because there's no tests. You don't
> have to worry about your marks.

JASON: It just gives you a sense of responsibility like I get to do this and not have to like
be playing the perfect notes for the teacher because I can't, sometimes when I mess
up I feel like oh no, I'm not going to get in trouble for it.

The new evaluation processes allowed this student and others to feel smarter, to accumulate pedagogical capital in terms of self-recognition as a competent learner. In this
sense, students' development of skills, knowledge, and abilities were meeting evaluation criteria that allowed them to be successful, to demonstrate what they could do
within musical genres that did not previously permit positive evaluation. This required
a shift from assessment criteria formed from a dominant culture (academic music)
perspective toward those based on more pragmatic and flexible criteria.

The changes indicated by these students illustrated a changing situation in which
students appeared to accrue pedagogical capital, with more ownership and autonomy
over musical content and learning and teaching. In Bourdieu's terms, we might say
that the students had moved to occupy more advantageous positions within the field
of music education. If pedagogical capital were to be used as the vertical axis against
which to plot student positions within the field of music education, a graph would show
a rising line depicting the increasing amount of pedagogical capital held by students.
If field positions were to be indicated by the student's position within the graph area
against the vertical axis, students would now be positioned higher than previously in
the area or field. Their position would have advanced. In Lareau and Weininger's (2003)
definition of cultural capital, students acquired strategic use of knowledge, skills, and
competence that came into contact with institutionalized standards of evaluation that
accommodated them positively. In Biesta's (2010) terms, we might say that rationalized
communities had been disrupted and that students experienced a pedagogy of interruption in which they could form alternative music discourses. Students were placed
in situations where many more of them could accumulate pedagogical capital as they
gained a deeper understanding of what it means to learn and teach music, and as they
gained confidence in themselves as music learners and teachers. Moreover, they were
constructing what the subject "music" was and could therefore construct it to recognize their own abilities and skills. A more socially just distribution of pedagogical capital occurred, as capital was available to more students on the basis of classroom music
instruction and its acquisition was less dependent upon knowledge acquired in other
social contexts.

Musical Capital

Students' initial self-perceptions of musicality and musical potential were largely
negative prior to the informal learning project. Common statements from students
included:

I never knew I'd be able to play what I'm playing today.
Most of us were thinking before that we're not going to be able to play anything, it's
so hard.

This concurs with Lamont and Maton's (2010) thesis that students believe music to be an elite knowledge code that requires special abilities and knowledge. It could be asserted, therefore, that at the commencement of the IMP project, these students, like many perhaps, exhibited a weak sense of their own musicianship and their musical ability. They saw themselves as unlikely to be able to play anything, and that playing instruments was hard. They could therefore be said to have held (or perceived themselves to hold) only a small amount of musical capital. When students were questioned about their experiences in the informal learning program, different self-perceptions began to emerge, however:

> SEXTER: I feel a lot more confident playing the guitar because I always used to think I can't do it and I would never be able to play it.
> BRIAN: We feel like a supported group of independent musicians.

This was confirmed by a comment from a student, recorded in field notes at the end of a session: "you know, now we're the musicians not just the teacher." For students this appeared to result in feelings of legitimacy or authenticity in their music making:

> JASON: Because it's like, I don't know it just feels like we're actually uh, like we're actually like legit.

I have defined musical capital as relating to skills, knowledge, and understanding in and of music and also to self-perceptions of musicality and musical potential. These students' comments (supported by numerous others) indicated increases in student self-perceptions of holdings of musical capital after the informal learning projects. The self-perception of legitimacy is a particularly important one in relation to musical capital, and I believe indicates a significant change in student field positioning; students who had initially perceived themselves as not musicians (and not musical) now identified themselves with the label "musician."

If we plotted students' possession of musical capital on a similar graph to the one used to measure pedagogical capital, we would again see a rising line and a gain in vertical position within the area of the graph. Student perceptions of knowledge and knower codes were again altered, and more diverse students were included within the music education experience. I would suggest that as more students recognized themselves as holding musical capital, they moved away from self-positioning as non-elite, as "not the type of student who could succeed in music." The implications for social justice result from the consequent self-positioning of fewer students as non-elite and the self-recognition of more students as being the type of knower who can succeed in music in school and life, with possible wider applications of this self-knowledge to other educational and existential arenas.

These brief illustrations indicate the ways in which concepts of pedagogical and musical capital might be used to analyze music learning situations through a lens of social justice. By evaluating the distribution of two specific types of cultural capital, pedagogical and musical capital, within a pedagogic situation that appears to allow such capitals to be more equitably acquired across a diverse group of students, we may better arrive at an understanding of how alternative pedagogies such as informal learning act to further social justice and broaden inclusion within music education. The illustrations are also intended to provide a brief example of one way in which Lareau and Weininger's (2003) reconceptualization of cultural capital in education might be operationalized in the music education concept. I believe they provide some interesting insights into the music learning situation using informal learning but could be equally applied to other pedagogical models.

Conclusion

In this chapter, I have attempted to situate music education within the "big picture" issues of social injustice and inequality deriving from large-scale hegemonic cycles of social reproduction. I have outlined some sociological theory investigating the role of education in these processes that may be brought to bear upon examination of such issues, with particular reference to the work of Pierre Bourdieu. I have looked at issues of cultural capital and Lareau and Weininger's (2003) expansion of this term in the educational context to include "micro-interactional processes whereby individuals' strategic use of knowledge, skills, and competence come into contact with institutionalized standards of evaluation" (p. 560). I have suggested using the forms of cultural capital that I term "pedagogical capital" and "musical capital" as ways to measure student position within the field of music education and have illustrated their use with examples from an informal music learning project conducted with colleagues in Canada. I have also posited that the introduction of what Biesta (2010) terms "pedagogies of interruption" within which such forms of capital may be advantageously accrued by students may lead to more equitable field positioning for more students.

I will conclude by venturing to suggest some tentative precepts drawn from the preceding material that might permit alternative music education pedagogies to make an impact in furthering social justice. First, we must co-define with our students what we take the subject "music" to be, what being "musical" or "making music" means in much more open terms, so that our students have possibilities to engage with music as "other" and to discover their individual, unique way of being musical. This may shift the knowledge legitimation code of music away from its current elite status in the eyes of students and may result in more students being included in music education. It may also result in fewer students positioning themselves as "non-elite" knowers. This is perhaps the starting point from which to break our previous self-replicating loops, with all their attendant hegemonic practices and effects. Second, we need to consciously develop pedagogies of interruption that disrupt traditional hegemonic cycles by providing space for students to speak with their own unique voices, to create their own new knowledge communities (see Wright, 2014). Third, we should plan learning and teaching so that pedagogical and musical capital are more fairly distributed between learner and teacher and between and among students, with the emphasis on the learner accruing ever increasing amounts of capital, to the end that the teacher ultimately becomes a co-learner or facilitator. Fourth, we need to revisit evaluation modes and criteria to ensure that they do not reflect dominant cultural or social paradigms and values but that they permit positive evaluation of "other" modes of musicality and musicianship. If, as the quotation at the beginning of this chapter suggests, the "structure of the distribution of the different types and subtypes of capital at a given moment in time represents the immanent structure of the social world" (Bourdieu, 1986, p. 241), any hope for music education to play even a small role in a more socially just society must lie in changing such structures and distributions of capital.

REFERENCES

Bannan, N. (2014). Music, play and Darwin's children: Pedagogical reflections of and on the ontogeny/phlogeny relaitonship. *International Journal of Music Education*, 32(1), 98–118.

Bates, Vincent C. 2012. Social class and school music. *Music Educators Journal*, 98(4), 33–37.

BBC. (2014, May 18). *Sunday Times Rich List 'wealthier than ever'*. Retrieved May 29, 2014, from BBC News, UK, http://www.bbc.co.uk/news/uk-27459621.

Blacking, J. (1973). *How musical is man?* Seattle: University of Washington Press.

Bourdieu, P. ([1972]1977). Outline of a theory of practice [Esquisse d'une theorie de la pratique: Precede de trois etudes d'ethnologie kabyle (Geneva: Droz)]. (R. Nice, Trans.) Cambridge: Cambridge University Press.

Bourdieu, P. (1973). Cultural reproduction and social reproduction. In R. Brown & R. Brown (Ed.), *Knowledge, education and cultural change* (pp. 71–112). London: Tavistock Publications.

Bourdieu, P. (1984). *Distinction* [Originally published as *La Distinction: Critique sociale du jugement* (Paris: Les Editions de Minuit)]. (R. Nice, Trans.) Cambridge: Polity.

Bourdieu, P. (1986). The forms of capital. In J. Richardson & J. Richardson (Eds.), *Handbook of theory and research for the sociology of education* (pp. 241–258). New York: Greenwood.

Bourdieu, P. ([1987]1994). *In other words: Essays towards a reflexive sociology [Choses dites]*. (R. Nice, Trans.) Cambridge: Polity.

Bourdieu, P., & Passeron, J.-C. (1990). *Reproduction in education society and culture* (2nd ed.). London; Thousand Oaks, CA: SAGE.

DiMaggio, P. (1982). Cultural capital and school success: The impact of status culture participation on the grades of U.S. high school students. *American Sociological Review*, 47(2), 189–201.

Green, L. (2008). *Music, informal learning and the school: A new classroom pedagogy*. Farnham, UK: Ashgate.

Gould, E. (2012). Re-membering bands in North America: Gendered paradoxes and potentialities. In C. Beynon & K. Veblen (Eds.), *Critical perspectives in Canadian music education* (pp. 101–122). Waterloo: Waterloo University Press, p. 109.

Gustafson, R. (2008) Drifters and the Dancing Mad: The public school music curriculum and the fabrication of boundaries for participation. *Curriculum Inquiry*, 38(3), 267–297.

Hallam, S., Creech, A. S., Rinta, T., & Shave, K. (2008). *Survey of musical futures: A report from Institute of Education University of London for the Paul Hamlyn Foundation*. Institute of Education, University of London.

Herbert, R. (2012). Young people's use and subjective experience of music outside school. In E. T. Cambouropoulos (Ed.), *Proceedings of the 12th international conference on music perception and cognition and the 8th triennial conference of the European society for the cognitive sciences of music*, July 23–28, Thessaloniki, Greece. Thessaloniki: ICMPS-ESCOM.

Hofvander Trulsson, Y. (2012). Chasing children's fortunes: Cases of parents' strategies in Sweden, the UK and Korea. In P. Dyndahl (Ed.), *Intersection and interplay: Contributions to the cultural study of music in performance, education, and society*. Malmö Academy of Music Perspectives in Music and Music Education. Malmö: Lund University.

Independent, T. (2014, May 29). *The real cost-of-living-crisis: Five million British children 'sentenced to life of poverty thanks to welfare reforms'*. Retrieved May 29, 2014, from The Independent: http://www.independent.co.uk/news/uk/politics/the-real-costoflivingcrisis-five-million-british-children-face-life-of-poverty-thanks-to-welfare-reforms-9442061.html.

Lamont, A., & Maton, K. (2010). Unpopular music: Beliefs and behaviours towards music in education. In R. Wright (Ed.), *Sociology and music education* (pp. 63–80). Farnham, UK: Ashgate.

Lareau, A. (2003). *Unequal childhoods: Class, race and family life*. Berkely and Los Angeles: University of California Press.

Lareau, A., & Weininger, E. (2003). Cultural capital in educational research: A critical assessment. *Theory and Society, 32*(5–6), 567–606.

Maton, K. (2012). Habitus. In M. Grenfell, & M. Grenfell (Ed.), *Pierre Bourdieu: Key concepts* (pp. 49–65). Durham, UK: Acumen.

Mithen, S. (2006). *The Singing Neanderthals: The origins of music, language, mind, and body*. Cambridge, MA: Harvard University Press.

Mullen, P., & Harrison, C. (Eds.). (2013). *Reaching out: Music education with hard to reach children and young people*. London: UK Association for Music Education—Music Mark.

Palzkill Woelfer, J., & Lee, J. (2012). *The role of music in the lives of homeless young people: A preliminary report*. Retrieved June 1, 2014, from http://dub.washington.edu/djangosite/media/papers/WoelferLee_RoleOfMusicHomelessYoungPeople.pdf.

Rabkin, N., Hedberg, C. E., & National Endowment for the Arts. *National Endowment for Arts Education in America: What the declines mean for arts participation*. Based on the 2008 Survey of Public Participation in the Arts. Research Report #52. Washington, DC: National Endowment for the Arts.

Tylor, E. (1958). *Primitive culture: Researches into the development of mythology, philosophy, religion, art, and custom*. Gloucester, MA: Smith.

Wright, R. (2010a) (Ed.). *Sociology and music education*. Farnham, UK: Ashgate.

Wright, R. (2010b). Democracy, social exclusion and music education: Possibilities for change. In R. Wright (Ed.), *Sociology and music education* (pp. 263–282). Farnham, UK: Ashgate.

Wright, R. (2014). The Fourth Sociology and Music Education: Towards a sociology of integration. *Action, Criticism and Theory, 13*(1), http://act.maydaygroup.org/php/archives_v13.php#13_1.

Wright, R. (2015). Transforming habitus, changing practice in music education: Using Bourdieu's concepts of habitus, capital and field to analyse informal learning in Canadian music education. In P. Burnard, J. Soderman, Y. Hofvander-Trulson, P. Burnard, J.

Soderman, & Y. Hofvander-Trulson (Eds.), *Bourdieu and the sociology of music, music education and research*. Farnham, UK: Ashgate.

Wright, R., & Finney, J. (2010). Culture, society and music education. In R. Wright (Ed.), *Sociology and music education*. Farnham, UK: Ashgate.

Wright, R., Younker, B. A., Hutchison, J., Linton, L., Beynon, S., Davidson, B., et al. (2012, July). Tuning into the future: Sharing initial insights about the 2012 Musical Futures pilot project in Ontario. *Canadian Music Educator*, 53(4), 14–18.

CHAPTER 22

THE IMPERATIVE OF DIVERSE AND DISTINCTIVE MUSICAL CREATIVITIES AS PRACTICES OF SOCIAL JUSTICE

PAMELA BURNARD, LAURA HASSLER,
LIS MURPHY, AND OTTO DE JONG

INTRODUCTION

In a globalized world in which cultural diversity and intercultural dialogue are key levers for strengthening consensus on the universal foundation of human rights, there is a pressing need to engage with what constitutes "interculturality" and "empathy." The term "intercultural" acknowledges the complexity of locations, identities, and modes of expression in a global world, and the desire to facilitate awareness, dialogue, or understanding across contexts. "Interculturality," as with arts practice, resides both in a location—whether geographical, spatial, or corporeal—and also within an in-between space—among and within individuals, milieux, social constructs and cultures (Lauder et al. 2006). Intercultural practice refers to conceptual processes, as well as to processes of making and becoming. Arts practices produce possibilities for intercultural translation.

Researchers have observed how cultures are not self-enclosed or static entities, and yet one of the fundamental obstacles to intercultural dialogue remains our habit of conceiving cultures as fixed, as if fault lines separated them. As Ruitenberg and Philips (2012) remind us, "interculturality" takes place in a dialectic of "resistance and accommodation," which in practice is what Pickering terms "the mangle of practice" (Pickering,

2010, p. 10). Multiple perspectives are consistently engaged (overtly and covertly). The complexity and multidimensionality of interculturality *in* practice requires agreement to privilege a multispectval approach *to* practice. This approach would embrace the diverse ways of knowing that emerge from new perspectives on, and respect for, what intercultural arts practice *is* and *does*. Yet, making visible how the arts translate intercultural creativities and distinct experiences of them remains hugely problematic.

As we will illustrate in this chapter, songwriting can be one of the most intercultural and cooperative of creative sites in social, cultural and geopolitical discourses. The political, social, cultural, and personal construction of songs, as with constructions of space (encompassing components of social, physical, or mental practices) in culture, education, and community (feelings and finding "at-homeness" and belonging) is characterized by social systems of meaning and representation (Bharucha, 2000). Songs transport us. Songs surround us. Songs can embrace the past with their power of story and identity; they can invoke the imagination and allow us to speculate on who we are and can be, or enable us to share with others; their repetitions can open doors into diverse creativities and related practices (Bennett, 2015).

This chapter suggests several ways in which intercultural creative music practices can be adapted to further social justice engagement: (1) by activating diverse creativities as a means of providing and supporting a mutual reciprocity of needs and respect; (2) by promoting the importance of differentiating between intercultural and empathic creativities, which requires a shift of perspective that reinforces a growing realization that the ethics of creativity, like the ethics of care, cannot be divorced from important issues of justice; and (3) by attending to the cultural dimensions in which diverse creativities extend in two or more directions, not just in one (Burnard, 2012).

Concurrently there is a further realization, as identified by Martha Nussbaum (2000), that care-related factors such as love, empathy, collaboration, reflexivity, power, empowerment, and voice, are central human capabilities that practices *of* and *for* social justice need to promote. In a brilliant and insightful book titled *Educational Research for Social Justice*, Morwenna Griffiths (2011) describes collaboration in terms of improving research and collaboration *for* justice in similar terms to our own view of creativities *for* justice. Here, the role of the researcher (or of the arts practitioner) is discussed in the context of achieving social justice in relation to the possibility of collaboration of a sort that can take place at every research (or project) stage *with* those directly involved, getting others' perspectives, speaking in their voices, and working together to empower and implement action. The link with "creativities" and Griffiths's emphasis of empowerment and voice in research related to social justice is clear. Like research, the practice of diverse creativities can refer to something individual and personal, or it can mean something far more collective, social, empathic, or intercultural. When these differences are not made explicit and recognized, opportunities to activate and encourage diverse creativities are lost, as well as opportunities to bring about improvement in social justice in and from distinctive musical creativities as practices of social justice.

The chapter presents an exploration of the empathic and intercultural creativities that emerge in the songwriting practices of Musicians without Borders. Musicians without

Borders (UK) was established as an independent charity in 2010, inspired by the methods and approach of Musicians without Borders based in the Netherlands. The two organizations work in close coordination, developing and implementing projects that use the power of music to bridge divides, connect communities, and heal the wounds of war and conflict. Thus, this chapter puts forth a rationale for authoring diverse creativities as practices of social justice within the context of, and as facilitated through, diverse and distinctive musical creativities, all of which have the potential to enable, empower, and inform social justice. The diversity of creativities elaborated here in narratives on practices by diverse practitioners from Musicians without Borders highlights how specific creativities, along with "affective equality" ("caring"), are inspired and embraced as a manifestation of social justice. How these different conceptions and practices of creativities inspire interpersonal processes and dialogues among peoples, cultures, and contexts, in ways that build participants' capacity for transcendence, openness, empathy, mutuality, and generosity, are elaborated through reflections on practice. In this way, experiences and practices of diverse musical creativities are categorized and positioned in ways that are not removed from lived realities.

ARTICULATING DIVERSE MUSICAL CREATIVITIES

The social and cultural context of *diverse musical creativities*, such as *intercultural creativity* and *empathic creativity*, are significant factors that lead creators to develop and mobilize new creativities. Culturally related meanings are embedded within our life history and act as cultural layers. These layers are interdependent and help us to identify ourselves. Contrary to a Western position, *intercultural creativity* involves non-hierarchical and intersubjective relationships, not grounded in the politics of difference, or the commodification of culture. Interculturality advocates and enables the feeling of "respect," "belonging," or "inclusion." It is linked to indeterminate transitional spaces that lie between cultural certainties and misrepresentations of otherness (Burnard, 2013).

The practice of *intercultural creativity* acknowledges the complexity of locations, identities, and modes of expression. The practice resides both in a location—whether geographical, spatial, or corporeal—and within an in-between space, among and within individuals, milieux, social constructs, and cultures. Intercultural creativities are many. At the intersections of *intercultural creativities*, there is an openness and respect for cultural understandings of time (that is, temporal awareness of event time, cyclical processes rather than chronological time), of identity and diverse readings of our relationships with multiple spaces and pathways made by our own and others' community and ancestors. Intercultural creativities produce possibilities and new arts practices, and therefore entail thinking not only about music practice but also about the role of the artist and memory (within intercultural dialogue, the act of recollection and cultural memory also play a role).

Empathetic creativities are characterized as and promote co-participation, reciprocity, openness, mutuality, intercultural understanding, and "affective alignment" (Cross, Laurence, & Rabinowitch, 2012, p. 341). Empathic creativity is about creating music together in ways that lead to one's own feeling responding to the other's experienced feeling—a kind of symmetry of everyone's relation to one another (Rabinowitch, Cross, & Burnard, 2013). There is a celebration of differences and a symmetry between everyone's relation to one another without polarization. It's a relational, participatory experience in music creation. Songs can serve as a container that stimulates insight into the spaces of feeling, and perhaps the reality of being, accepted, and the presence of unconditional love, which can be described as being held, feeling safe, experiencing a musical sensation of "at-homeness." According to Jourdan (2013), when musicians play with and encounter music from other sound worlds, other cultures and communities, the orientation in this encounter needs to be argued from a perspective of where the "other" is. In other words, the aim is not to encounter it as a primarily stylistic phenomenon, but one into whose face we have looked, whose voice we have heard and whose ethical call we have heeded, rather than for us simply to "come to know," to be enriched by, or to "collect" experiences (p. 208). Empathy is a process in which music can be viewed as a way to promote diverse creativities that enhance intercultural understanding, mutual tolerance, self-identity, and peace-building.

There are other views on musical creativities and creative musical practices that are bound up with, and demonstrated, as the "collective identities" (Bennett, 2001, p. 151) forged by, for example, original bands that reflect the common youth practice of "being in the know"—having insider-group knowledge, which serves as a form of cultural power and the possession of "subcultural capital." As Boden (2004) explains, one might

> [m]ake a distinction between 'psychological' creativity and 'historical' creativity (P-creativity and H-creativity, for short). P-creativity involves coming up with a surprising, valuable idea that's new to the person who comes up with it. It doesn't matter how many people have had that idea before. But if a new idea is H-creative, that means that (so far as we know) no one else has had it before: it has arisen for the first time in human history. (p. 2)

If diverse and differentiated musical creativities inspire, entertain, connect, and engage diverse groups of people, then the educational possibilities of broadening and deepening the relationship between creativities and practice in education could serve as a container that stimulates insight and the potential for social justice in teaching and learning music. Here, then, we explore ways in which the arts and music education sector can address the teaching of diverse and distinctive musical creativities as a practice of social justice by looking at ways to nurture appropriate teaching spaces for diverse musical creativities as practices that creatively connect with key notions of social justice.

Understanding cultural variation in approaches to learning and social justice—that is, how to characterize regularities of individuals' approaches according to their cultural background and how to develop a nuanced understanding of new practices—has been a continuing and complex dilemma in the social sciences. The persistent surge in immigration globally makes understanding these questions more urgent as the intercultural nature of people's everyday lives has increased and members of different cultural communities come into contact with one another with more regularity.

The potential role that diverse creativities play, as powerful vehicles in analyzing social justice translation, both within and across academic and non-academic sectors, is both underestimated and under-theorized. With the unquestionable significance of public concern for the health, well-being, and welfare of society—to which the arts make an essential contribution—there is a pressing need for academic and researcher communities, in partnership with arts and cultural communities, to establish and share how arts translate intercultural experience (Lederach & Lederach, 2010). To this end, collaboratively working together in enacting intercultural dialogue is crucial if we are to help a globalized world grasp that intercultural translations are co-constructed through collaboration.

EXPLORING DIVERSE CREATIVITIES FOR SOCIAL JUSTICE

The 2010 UNESCO World Report 2 foregrounded the importance of "intercultural dialogue," making clear the need for a shift in the politics and positioning of social spaces where cultures meet, clash, and grapple with each other, using dialogue to co-create and communicate symmetrical relations. Negotiating and mediating musical borders through collaborative music making and establishing new musical creativities to translate and explore cultural interfaces emphasize equal opportunity. Developing ways to explore intercultural dialogue in music and the interrelations between musics through intercultural creativity could itself support the idea of intercultural musical creativities as a practice of social justice. This idea remains under-theorized. Time, space, presence, and education are needed for converting theory into practice and policy change (Pavis, 1996).

In spite of the importance of intercultural dialogue for human survival, there is a deep ambivalence in Western society about "the forms and amount of nurturing capital." Being deprived of the capacity to develop supportive "affective relations," or of the experience of engaging in them when one has the capacity, is therefore a serious human deprivation and injustice; it is a form of "affective inequality" (Lynch, Baker, & Lyons, 2007, p. 2). Lynch, Baker, and Lyons (2007) invite a reconceptualization of the dimensions of love, care, and solidarity. Indeed, they argue that equality of condition should not simply be defined in the affective sphere.

Questions of justice inevitably arise from conflicts of interest. Understanding the issue of *translation* is therefore essential when researching the phenomenon of "interculturality." Translation problems arise from the boundary crossing that occurs as people move across the activities and settings of everyday life and encounter different forms of culturally organized practices. As musical creativities foreground conversations and collaborations between artists, in which intercultural dialogue is built into the collaborative arts space where there is an avoidance of exploitation of marginalized cultures or inequalities and a concern for equality of opportunity, status, and power, they have a significant role to play in addressing *translation* concerns. New forms of practice can result in new creativities depending on the histories of the participants in particular cultural communities, with sources of variation arising from and across individual and community practices. How are differences addressed? How do we expose and redress unequal power relationships between cultures? The determination of intercultural meaning and representation in the arts requires academics and non-academics (particularly artists developing new practices) to collaboratively take into account and reconcile the politics of representation and the possibility of disparity in the relationship. All of this may well play out in a highly ambivalent light with broader issues of performance and performativity, and thus we ask a fundamental question: How do music and musicking function as technologies of translation that allow us to understand and conceptualize practices of diverse musical creativities as a (trans)formation of experience, knowledge, and action in the context of manifestations of practices of social justice?

In the plural notion of musical creativities, the major themes that inform ideas about diverse musical creativities concern the complexity and demanding nature of the myriad forms of multiply mediated musical creativities that arise in musical spaces. These are deeply influenced by complex societal factors; different communities of taste; the political economy of music; the way that musical creativities impact on the performance space itself; the open sourcing of recorded sound; the dialectic through which new musical sounds influence the development of taste; the digital technologies that influence the mobility and flexibility of music-making practices; the globalization of the music industry; and local market forces. This all suggests a broadening and deepening of the relationship between creativities and practice (Burnard, 2013, p. 79).

Social injustice and intercultural tensions are often bound up with conflicts that create intolerances: conflicts of memory, conflicts of value, and conflicts of cultural stereotyping, which serve to demarcate one group from the alien "other." Raising awareness through translational research needs to position academics, researchers, non-academics, and arts organizations as collaborative partners for deliberating about and developing intercultural translation; this requires dialogue, exchange, and co-construction.

What forms the core of this chapter then, are findings of ongoing research presented as a layered story, a narrative research technique that can reflect different voices containing fragments of information, reflections, and remembrances of practice and reflexive experiences.

Laura Hassler is the founder and director of Musicians without Borders, an international network organization that uses music to bridge divides, build community, and heal the wounds of war. Musicians without Borders cooperates with local musicians and partners on behalf of people suffering the effects of war and conflict. Its projects include rock music schools for youth in divided Balkan cities, community music training projects in Palestine and Rwanda, rap and samba percussion projects for human rights and social change (Palestine), and the therapeutic application of singing and movement for war-traumatized adults (refugees in the UK, genocide survivors in Bosnia and Rwanda).

Musicians without Borders (MwB) has trained 90 young people as community music workshop leaders in Palestine, where it now brings music to more than 5,000 marginalized children.[1] Strengthening children's resilience and advocating for human rights through music are two of many aims. In 2013 MwB's project initiatives included the following:

- In the ethnically divided city of Mitrovica, Kosovo, the Mitrovica Rock School launched its Ambassador Band program, forming four new ethnically mixed youth rock bands to compose, rehearse, perform, record, and tour together.
- In Bosnia and Herzegovina, the Mostar Rock School ran its first successful year, attracting youth from both sides of the divided city, starting new mixed bands and organizing dozens of concerts and performances.
- In Rwanda, 25 youth leaders completed their training and were certified to lead music activities for HIV+ children. The youth leaders launched their own outreach program, and now bring music to more than 1,500 HIV+ children in Kigali and the surrounding region.
- In Rwanda, MwB brought a full-time music therapist to Kigali and integrated music therapy into its project for HIV+ children and youth.
- In Eastern Bosnia, it trained a team of young musicians and dancers to work in refugee camps with women who lost their men and boys during the genocide at the end of the Bosnian war.
- In Palestine, MwB reached 5,000 marginalized children regularly through music, rap, and samba workshops; in 2013, the project expanded to include music training and activities for hearing-impaired youth and special needs children.
- In Northern Ireland, 10 MwB trainers, teachers, and performers helped launch Singing the Bridge, a new cooperative project using music to bridge the lasting divides of armed conflict.
- In Manchester, UK, MwB has trained four refugee music facilitators, and helped reduce trauma through singing and songwriting with around 800 refugees and asylum seekers, including 60 torture survivors and 100 children.

Musicians without Borders started almost 15 years ago with a new idea: that music could be a powerful tool for reconciliation and healing in the very places where people suffer most from war and conflict. Today, Musicians without Borders is one of the world's pioneers in using the arts for social change and peace-building. It is a growing community of musicians, trainers, local workshop leaders, organizers, project managers, fundraisers, volunteers, and supporters of many kinds. Musicians without Borders has proven that where war has divided, music can connect.

In the following paragraphs, Laura Hassler, founder of Musicians without Borders, reflects on how its practice involves crossing borders and, despite facing barriers to communication, works collaboratively on intercultural projects, negotiating the making and translating of meaning.

Laura Hassler:

Music's capacity to create empathy is at the heart of Musicians without Borders' vision and work. As musicians, we know, from experience, what recent research has begun to explore and explain: that sharing musical experiences reduces aggression, fear, and anxiety, and increases people's ability to connect and to heal. Long-haired youths in a heavy metal garage band, children using sticks to tap rhythms together in a refugee camp kindergarten, old women sitting in a circle, remembering a lost lullaby, or torture survivors writing their stories in songs—all can find connection, comfort, and community in making music together. The music taps into our common human sense of being and allows us to share it with others and feel it radiating back to us.

However, tapping into that space with people who have survived the trauma of war and violent conflict, or who grow up living in its shadow, requires a combination of skills, intuition, and empathy on the part of the practitioners. A fine-tuned empathic capacity, along with highly developed musical, didactical, and communications skills, is an essential quality for every Musicians without Borders' trainer. The capacity for empathy is perhaps difficult to define or measure, but it is easy to recognize. In the context of our work, the capacity for empathy may be recognized in practice by

- *a trainer's ability to honor all participants, whatever their level of musical competence, and to stimulate and value musical progress—both of the group and its individual members—based not on arbitrary standards, but on the group or individual's willingness to enter the shared musical space and move creatively within it;*
- *a trainer's sensitivity to the overlapping dynamics of the participants' context—such as traumatic past experiences, physical or psychological health issues, domestic or community problems, stress or depression—that may influence participants' ability to engage in the process. Trainers must be prepared for complications and must be able to navigate the complexities they encounter (or intuit when not completely known or understood). This requires a high degree of flexibility and improvisational talent on the part of the trainer;*
- *a trainer's sense for the right moment to "step back and let them shine their own light"; the ability to be a leader who encourages leadership and guides the process of empowerment, whose ego is sufficiently satisfied by the success of his or her teaching, rather than needing to be the central point of attention.*

For Musicians without Borders, empathic sensitivity is also critical to the organizational and management functions behind the actual music making, as reflected, for example, in

- *a manager's ability to develop working relationships with local counterparts, based on mutual respect, taking into account differences in styles of leadership, communication, and organization;*

- *a manager's ability to listen attentively, to hear and understand the interests and wishes of the partner(s), and to (help) articulate the common ground of both/all partners, thus making visible the added value for all in a collaboration while at the same time assuring that projects remain "on mission";*
- *the ability of all MwB staff, managers, and trainers to communicate and cooperate within a nonlinear organizational structure, with function and responsibility based on competences and collaboration; ideally, this allows MwB simultaneously to function as an organization, a community, and a network.*

While we often work in places that have been divided along "ethnic" or "cultural" lines, "intercultural dialogue," as it is usually understood, is not part of the practice of MwB. The idea of "intercultural dialogue" assumes and implies that the problems of postwar communities have their roots in cultural differences and can be addressed by bringing representatives of the different "cultures" into contact and engaging them in dialogue—conversation—with each other. Musicians without Borders grounds its approach to peace-building in the conviction that, while cultural differences often come to play a role in war and armed conflict, they are more often the tools of political or economic forces than the real root of the conflict. Local and/or global political and economic interests are almost always involved, and hidden agendas frequently manipulate both the real and contrived differences between people to incite the wars that lead to power or land grabs, at the expense of ordinary people of any and all cultural backgrounds.

In most regions where MwB works, people of different cultural backgrounds have, throughout most of their history, devised mechanisms to deal with those differences and have lived, more or less peacefully, as neighbors on shared space. A war that becomes defined along ethnic or cultural lines means that people of mixed families are forced either to choose one "ethnicity" or to flee; that geographical territory once shared becomes divided into pieces identified with one or the other group, forcing members of the minority group to leave their homes and move to "the other side"; and that those in the society who never saw themselves as members of one particular "ethnic group" lose their voices within the society.

By the time the violence ends, of course, most people have become divided along those "cultural" lines, whether they chose to be or not. So finding ways to reconnect across those divides is essential to any long-term peace-building process. But, for it to be meaningful, that process of reconnection must also address common needs, such as breaking out of postwar isolation, making up for lost time in skills learning and education, and providing handles for professional development and career aspirations.

To support processes of reconnection without identifying people by ethnic or cultural labels, MwB works to create a neutral musical space in which participants can both identify (themselves) and relate (to each other) primarily as musicians. We take their talents, passions, and potentials seriously and offer them real chances for musical growth and creative development, contact and connection to other young musicians (often through the social media) and, where possible, a path to employment. We then trust the music to do its work and leave it to them to choose whether, and how, to meet the "other" outside the musical space. What we invariably see is friendships emerging, along with empowerment and a feeling of relief at not being primarily defined by ethnicity or culture. In fact, these same principles apply to our projects that do not bring people of different backgrounds together, but rather work to build

resilience and a culture of nonviolence and participation for youth and children suf-
fering from the effects of conflict in their own "monocultural" communities, for exam-
ple in Palestine.

It is this fine line of balancing between the real divides that have been created or
greatly exacerbated by war, and the ability to tap into shared passions and creativities
that is definitive of Musicians without Borders' vision and program. That music can
provide the space on which this fine line can be navigated has everything to do with its
quality of creating a place of empathy.

The initiatives and approaches explored in this chapter are based upon the same ideals articulated by Hassler and were developed by a team of practitioners. One member
of the team is Lis Murphy, a music facilitator, trainer, and UK director of Musicians
without Borders, UK. She spent two years in Mostar, Bosnia-Herzegovina, in the
first decade of the 2000s, running an outreach music program for traumatized children, for Warchild and the Pavarotti Music Centre. Last April, she visited Palestine,
where she worked with MwB project manager Fabienne van Eck, delivering training
with Palestinian women in isolated villages in South Hebron. This summer, she was
one of two trainers to set up a music and dance program in Bosnia-Herzegovina for
women survivors of the 1995 genocide in Srebrenica. Lis established Musicians without
Borders in Manchester, supporting refugee/asylum-seeker adults and young people
through creative music projects to reduce trauma and isolation. In partnership with
Freedom from Torture NW, Musicians without Borders has created a groundbreaking
music project, Stone Flowers, in which music facilitators work with torture survivors
to write poems, song lyrics and melodies, to learn new instruments, and to sing and
perform in each other's languages.

Lis Murphy:

It has always amazed me that a human expression of love, anger, fear, or hope that was
expressed by someone we have never met, who doesn't speak the same language, or who
lived hundreds of years ago, can still make us want to dance, make us laugh, move us to
tears, and reach our souls. The work I do and the music I play is never intercultural art for
its own sake; it has become a natural consequence of being passionate about how human
beings communicate and respond to music, as well as working with people from many dif-
ferent cultural backgrounds affected by war. I trained as a classical musician, and growing
up in Manchester was inspired by the vibrant music scene there, playing in Irish, rock, funk
and Indy bands. After hearing the beautiful folk music of Bosnia-Herzegovina (Sevdah),
I was inspired to move there.

The approach to music making I experienced there was about removing the barrier
between the elitist performer and silent audience, creating a completely inclusive environ-
ment where it doesn't matter how good you are, or whether you can sing in tune; the most
important thing is that you're there in that moment with those people, expressing your emo-
tions, nobody is judging, everyone just wants you to be part of that energy, of solidarity. You

sing because it feels good and because you need to. My work since then has developed from a combination of the different approaches to music I have experienced, while still allowing an open space for new approaches.

My aim is that anyone who comes to music sessions can begin by feeling that uplifting, collective experience. Through the next phase of sharing songs, improvising and collaboratively creating new material to express and communicate emotions and personal stories, the incentive develops to want to give those expressions the best chance of being effectively communicated to audiences. The desire to rehearse, to craft skills, and to develop performance technique is therefore driven by the need to realize the creative potential to its highest level, to share the energy and message with the audience through the music, creating empathy and connection with the listener.

Stone Flowers is a project created in response to the use of music as a form of torture around the world. In partnership with Freedom from Torture, Stone Flowers delivers weekly music sessions for refugee/asylum seekers and torture survivors now living in the United Kingdom who have been subjected to unbearable extremes of physical and psychological pain, or have sustained serious injuries. Stone Flowers' members write and perform songs in English, Lingala, Farsi, Kurdish, French, Swahili, Tamil, and Kikongo, blending traditional and modern instruments with musical influences ranging from folk, jazz, classical, spoken word, roots, and hip-hop.

Lis reflects on her practice and describes instances of her own practice:

> *Inclusive, creative music making starts with exploring the interest, taste, and musical experience of the individuals in the group. In this way, meaningful contribution to the content and development of the group sessions is given to the group members, who as a result invest more of themselves, as they understand that their individual contribution influences the end group result. In Stone Flowers, the participants do not begin the process as a group, but as individuals from completely different social, cultural, educational, religious and musical backgrounds, who have the traumatic experience of torture in common.*
>
> *The unique structure, facilitation and management in place is key to making the project work. The facilitation team is made up of specialized musicians—half of whom are themselves refugees and/or torture survivors, and a clinical psychologist musician. The facilitation team collectively leads the process and begins by creating a safe environment, where endorsing respect and recognition informs and equalizes trusting relations. The importance placed on equal leadership roles of musicians from different cultural, language, and musical backgrounds immediately reinforces the aims of the project and enables a deeper, more informed process of exploring the music being produced, alongside a considered approach, influenced by personal understanding within the team of the trauma experienced by the survivors.*
>
> *The facilitators' role is literally that: to use their own skills and experiences to collectively facilitate the participants in creating their own music to the highest level, as they want to say it, and to guide the collaborative process to ensure that each individual is*

cared for, that their voice is heard, and that they contribute and realize their own poten-
tial, within the space they feel comfortable with. The emphasis on individuals' own
experiences, language, and musical influences creates a situation in which participants
become group leaders, as they teach and share with the group, as they become more
experienced in their own language, musical approach, and personal experience. The
leaders within the group at points become the participants, placing value on the shared
learning and experiences from everyone within the group.

What has developed from the performance aspect of the work is an understanding
from participants, many of whom were persecuted for being activists in their own coun-
try, that the music acts as a vehicle for spreading a message of peace and hope and for
raising awareness about human rights abuses. Group members begin to feel their own
sense of personal responsibility to speak out for others who are in their situation and
who don't have a voice. Many of the songs written by Stone Flowers participants have
now been taught and performed by schoolchildren in Manchester and beyond through
other MwB projects.

Otto de Jong has been a workshop leader, animator, and trainer with Musicians without Borders since the very beginning in 1999; he has worked for MwB in every project
region: the Balkans, the Middle East, and Central Eastern Africa. In his day job(s), he
designs and coordinates music education programs for primary schools on behalf of the
Amsterdam Music School, and he conducts children's choirs and an orchestra. Emerging
organically over time, Otto's understanding, both practical and theoretical, of improvisational and intercultural creativities has taken place between and among his partners,
trainees, and the children they work with, sharing with them in a dynamic, exploratory,
yet safe space. Otto explains how musicking may catalyze specific creativities:

In my practice I always emphasize the importance of nonverbal communication; this is the
creative experience of mutual tuning. That is my speciality. I have many tips and tricks to
create a safe atmosphere for children (and adults). Cooperative music making means that
we connect with each other in expressive ways.

Creativity is a very important part of my practice. I only can give the framework, offering
possibilities in didactics, pedagogical, and methodical ways of working. I use examples of
music that I know; then the trainees need to adapt the techniques, using music from their
own cultures. It's a meeting, giving room for human agency. As a workshop leader, I have to
be creative, because you never know what will happen when you work with children (this
is no different in Rwanda than in the Netherlands or any other country). Sometimes you
are only focused on creating a safe atmosphere and environment: that, in itself, is a very
creative process for the leader.

Improvisation is a method to stimulate certain types of creativity, even on a "micro-level"
(for example: creating a short sound on a drum can in a certain way already be improvisa-
tion). The Russian education theorist Vygotsky says that children learn better when they
are in a safe social situation where they feel free to develop themselves and where there
is space and opportunity to develop self-esteem and expressivity. When children have the

opportunity for creative education and can learn to align musically with each other and play in sync through creativity, this gives us the opportunity to create situations where communication is key, as a way of contributing to positive change. In this process of change, we are moved and feel a sense of flow in the musical interaction.

Here lie huge opportunities for creative communication contributing to peace-building. In any case, what I see is that it makes trainees happier: they come to believe more in themselves as they make many children happy through the music.

Activating Musical Creativities as Tools for Social Justice

This chapter has explored interlocking elements in theory and practice relating to issues of healing, reconciliation, and social justice through music within the context of, and as facilitated through, distinctive forms and diverse arrays of music creativities. Each element addresses how different types of creativities are recognized and communicated in the diverse practices of a particular organization, Musicians without Borders, whose projects work with the power of music to connect communities.

Culture determines which theories and conceptions of creativity are privileged within the practice of social justice through the arts, as it does the roles that participants enact in social settings. Such matters, and the empathic ways they operate, form the backdrop for identifying how we might use the new insights that we acquire through these practices to engage with issues of healing, reconciliation, peace-building, and social justice within and beyond the classroom (Hanley et al., 2013).

Approaches to studying these caring spaces and practices (for different ways of being, for playing with diverse constellations of creativities in the arts, for engaging with counter-hegemonic discourses, and the possibilities made available through solidarity-oriented creativities) have been explored.

In essence, the imperative of articulating the inherent qualities of diverse musical creativities in enhancing social justice in music education has been to explore the potential of what it can reveal and inform (among other things) about how performance creativities evoke a path to constructive dynamics that help us "feel" the spiritual and healing elements of musical communication and the contract between the performer and the audience. This process may involve as much clashing as synthesizing of culturally divergent matter. For artists working on the performance of new music in this realm, as well as educators in school classrooms, embracing an intercultural and empathic creative space could be both an aesthetic and a political choice. If there is to be a second wave of interculturality and empathic performance theory that manages to negotiate the vagaries of the marketplace and educational reform, we believe it will emerge from community artists and educators whose performance practice shapes creativities from the indeterminate, transitional spaces that lie between cultural certainties and that explore the complex relationships between relational and participatory types of social justice musical creativities. The participatory activities of "improvisation," "songwriting" and "singing," "drum circles," and the relational contingencies of space, time, and relationships are vital components of these practices of social justice.

NOTE

1. https://secure.musicianswithoutborders.org/2013/12/a-video-message-from-halimeh-palestine/.

REFERENCES

Bennett, A. (2001). *Cultures of popular music*. Buckingham, UK: Open University Press.

Bennett, J. (2015). Creativities in popular songwriting curricula: Teaching or learning? In P. Burnard & L. Haddon (Eds.) *Activating diverse musical creativities: teaching and learning in higher music education* (pp. 186–199). London: Bloomington.

Bharucha, R. (2000). *The politics of cultural practice*. London: Athlone Press.

Boden, M. (2004). *The creative mind: Myths and mechanisms* (2nd ed.). New York: Routledge.

Burnard, P. (2012). *Musical creativities in practice*. Oxford: Oxford University Press.

Burnard, P. (2013). (Ed) *Developing creativities in higher music education*. London: Routledge.

Cross, I., Laurence, F., and Rabinowitch, T. (2012). Empathy and creativity in group musical practices: Towards a concept of empathic creativity. In G. E. McPherson & G. F. Welch (Eds.), *The Oxford handbook of music education* (Vol. 2, pp. 337–354). Oxford: Oxford University Press

Griffiths, M. (2011) *Educational research for social justice: Getting off the fence*. Buckingham, UK: Open University Press.

Hanley, M. S., Noblit, G. W., Sheppard, G. L., & Barone, T. (2013). *Culturally relevant arts education for social justice*. New York: Routledge.

Jourdan, K. (2013). Making sense of the music of the stranger. In J. Finney & F. Laurence (Eds.), *Masterclass in music education: Transforming teaching and learning* (pp. 201–209). London: Bloomsbury.

Lynch, K., Baker, J., & Lyons, M. (2007). *Affective equality: Love, care and injustice*. New York: Palgrave Macmillan.

Lauder, H., Brown, P., Dillabough, J. & Halsey, A. H. (2006). *Education, globalizaton and social change*. Oxford: Oxford University Press.

Lederach, J. P., & Lederach, A. J. (2010). *When blood and bones cry out: Journeys through the soundscape of healing and reconciliation*. Oxford: Oxford University Press.

Nussbaum, M. (2000). *Women and human development: The capabilities approach*. Cambridge: Cambridge University Press.

Pavis, P. (1996). Introduction: Towards a theory of interculturalism and theatre. In P. Pavis (Ed.), *The international performance reader* (pp. 1–19). London: Routledge.

Pickering, A. (2010). *The mangle of practice: Time, agency and science.* Chicago: University of Chicago Press.

Rabinowitch, T., Cross, I., & Burnard, P. (2013). Long-term musical group interaction has a positive influence on empathy in children. *Psychology of Music, 41*(4), 484–498.

Ruitenberg, C., & Phillips, D. C. (Eds.) (2012). *Education, culture and epistemological diversity: Mapping a disputed terrain.* Dordrecht, Netherlands: Springer.

UNESCO. (2010). World Report 2: Investing in Cultural Diversity and Intercultural Dialogue. http://unesco.org/new/en/culture/themes/dialogue/intercultural-dialogue/.

CHAPTER 23

MUSIC TEACHERS' REPERTOIRE CHOICES AND THE QUEST FOR SOLIDARITY

Opening Arenas for the Art of Living with Difference

SIDSEL KARLSEN AND HEIDI WESTERLUND

INTRODUCTION

DURING the past few decades, the music education academic community has made much effort to explain the diverse nature of the musical world, how to recognize and celebrate this diversity in education, and how to choose and incorporate world musics in the classroom (see, e.g., Campbell, 2004; Elliott, 1989, 1995; Schippers, 2010; Volk, 1998). The primary agenda of this strand of music education scholarship has been to pinpoint cultural diversity within musical phenomena and the richly diverse traditions and their associated pedagogical practices around the world, and thus to do justice in education. This project against the hegemony of Western classical music has constructed its basic epistemological understandings of multicultural music education around and from a specific notion of world music education: the concentration on and preservation of cultural roots and distinctiveness, and the cultivation of historically justified, authentic musical practices in the classroom. As such, this underlining of diversity has been an essential project in a field in which most music teachers were, and in many cases still are, educated within the realm of Western music and its notation-based teaching and learning practices. By pointing out how music learning around the globe happens in a plethora of ways, this project has also contributed to questioning the taken-for-granted position of Western teaching methods at universities (Kodaly, Orff, Dalcroze, and others) where music teachers are educated, even though the change, in many places, may have been more noticeable in the published academic output than in the actual practices of music education.

However, as the single guiding approach to teaching music today, this "world musics project" is inadequate and, as will be argued in this chapter, may not give solutions to the most recent social challenges that need to be addressed within school-based music education in particular. Our experience and recent North European research (see Karlsen, 2012, 2013, 2014; Sæther, 2008) show that musical diversity is self-evident for today's students. This is so even in school environments generally described as fairly mono-cultural, in other words, those that appear as fairly mono-lingual, mono-ethnic, or mono-racial. Overall, due to global media and technological advancements, various cultural materials are now more available, even in contexts that could be called highly traditional (see Kallio & Westerlund, Kallio, A. A., & Westerlund, H. (2015). The ethics of survival: Teaching the traditional arts to disadvantaged children in post-conflic Cambodia. International Journal of Music Education. http://dx.doi.org/10.1177/0255761415584298. As the eminent sociologist Zygmunt Bauman argued already at the end of the 1990s, "motility, non-rootedness and global availability/accessibility of cultural patterns and products is now the 'primary reality' of culture" (Bauman, 1999, p. xiv).

Thus, this reality seems to differ radically from the musical reality depicted within the larger, multicultural world musics project, which is based on the presumption that musical identities primarily develop in historically rooted, distinct cultures, or ethnically defined communities that cultivate unique and authentic forms of music making. Moreover, the main critical angle of this project seems to fit best to the older generation of musicians and music teachers, and the institutionalized (Western) educational structures and practices, as well as the policies created by and within them. Since cultural diversity (including musical diversity) is now experienced and negotiated by students on a daily basis, motility, non-rootedness, and global accessibility also unavoidably penetrate the territories of music education, making it difficult for teachers to conduct any simple interpretations of their students' musical identities.

In this chapter, we offer a critical perspective and a balancing correction of the bias of the dominant approach toward multicultural music education, arguing that instead of making attempts for our presumably mono-cultural students to grasp world musical traditions and, therewith, the pluralistic values of music in human life in general, we could teach music with intercultural lenses, responding both to "the new context of globalization" (MacPherson, 2010, p. 272) and to "local contexts of everyday practices" (Andreouli, Howarth, & Sonn, 2014, p. 16) in diverse societies. Instead of simply trying to cover, illuminate, or relate students' identities to what Bauman calls the *mappa mundi* (in other words, the geography of world musics), this approach would take the local, already ongoing negotiations of musics as a point of departure in order to create new musical negotiations and multiple belongings, as well as to facilitate social bonding in particular (Westerlund, 2001; see also Westerlund, 2002, pp. 210–212; Kallio, Westerlund, & Partti, 2014).

In the following, we will extend some of the basic starting points found in the multicultural music education literature by rereading them against Karlsen's research findings regarding immigrant students' musical agency in Finland, Sweden, and Norway[1]

(Karlsen, 2011, 2012, 2013, 2014) and against Bauman's sociological analysis (1999, 2000, 2008, 2010, 2011). Bauman's theory redefines the ethical and educational meaning of the concept of culture from the perspective of the powerful new forces of globalization and the intermingling of populations within our own neighborhoods. We will show that, if taken seriously, the picture that Bauman draws of current societies requires that music educators take an active part in creating conditions for dealing with diversity in our day-to-day interactions and politics. It is argued that by working together with others, teachers and students could build learning communities in which epistemological horizons are not only brought from *outside* the classroom and school but from *within* its own existences in order to simultaneously work toward solidarity.

Our examples, taken from the data collected from lower secondary schools in the Nordic context, aim to illustrate first how cultural heterogeneization, motility, and global availability/accessibility complicate repertoire choices in school music education. Second, they underline how music education may significantly contribute to the acquisition of knowledge and musical activities that function as a powerful medium for associated social life in schools. The data show numerous examples and stories of how students and teachers drew on and attempted to handle the culturally diverse contexts that surrounded them and of which they were a part.

Dissemination of Musical Diversity and Recognition of Cultural Identity: Two Basic Ideas from the "World Musics Project"

When revisiting the literature on multicultural music education, two commonly held ideas can be identified. The first idea, according to which different musics ought to be presented and disseminated within the frame of school music lessons (e.g., Campbell, 2004; Lundquist & Szego, 1998; Schippers, 2010; Volk, 1998), was powerfully articulated in Elliott's *Music Matters: A New Philosophy of Music Education* (1995). Elliott argues that "if MUSIC consists in a diversity of music cultures, then MUSIC is inherently multicultural. And if MUSIC is inherently multicultural, then music education ought to be multicultural in essence" (p. 207). Furthermore, he holds that children should "learn to understand practices and artefacts (including musical practices and artefacts) of all cultural varieties" (Elliott, 1989, pp. 17–18) and hence be exposed to different ways of "*being* musical" (p. 18, italics in the original). In other words, music teachers' repertoire choices should follow a principle of freeing students from any ideologically biased views in order to understand that music is not something in particular, or singular, but rather something plural. This idea is reiterated and further developed in the second edition of *Music Matters* (Elliott & Silverman, 2015), the authors claiming that students should "examine the musical consequences of the beliefs underlying different musical cultures" (p. 450), as well as develop their abilities "to discriminate the similarities and differences among and between music cultures" (p. 450), and hence achieve "self-understanding through other-understanding" (p. 450).

The second idea concerns principles for the selection of multicultural repertoire, further understood as choosing which specific musical practices should be included in music curricula. Here, it is urged that the music teacher ought to pay attention to the potential that music education carries for the recognition of students' various cultural backgrounds. This idea was articulated in North American music education already in the early twentieth century (see Volk, 1998, p. 41). Following this idea, and by leaning on the philosopher Charles Taylor (1992) and other educational multiculturalists, Elliott (1996, p. 13; 1995, p. 200) for instance asserted in 1995 that recognition is a key tenet of multiculturalism and an important criterion for selecting among musical practices: "[R]ecognition is closely tied to self-identity... [and] the development of personal identity rests on the deliberate and accurate recognition (or affirmation) of people's beliefs and values" (Elliott, 1995, p. 212). Furthermore, Elliott suggests that "people tend to identify themselves with particular Music(s) and that people's Music is, very often, something they are" (p. 212). Consequently, "recognizing the traditional music cultures of one's students and one's community may contribute significantly to [the students'] self-identity" (p. 212). Also, Drummond (2005) argues that such recognition carries promises of providing social justice to music education, since the inclusion of one's culture is considered as "removal of disadvantage" (p. 2) and, conversely, having one's music disregarded in the school environment is thought to create unjust educational paths (see also Ruud, 2007). Recognition of one's identity in content and repertoire choices has indeed been one of the most common arguments for more conscious multicultural strategies in schooling, particularly in North America (see, e.g., Banks, 2010; Gay, 2010).

The crucial questions concern whether students' identities *can* become recognized or whether we *can* know what their musical identities are and what *students wish to become* in this new situation of motility, non-rootedness, and global accessibility. Moreover, this "politically correct," affirmative multicultural position has been criticized for being fundamentally uncritical in its absolute respect for other cultures and its teaching of an uncritical loyalty to one's own culture (see, e.g., Green, 1998), at the same time that its value-relativism does not support stronger political goals and interests (e.g., Papageorgiou, 2010). Furthermore, it does not necessarily pay attention to the creation of such effective cooperative attempts, which could lead to resolving shared problems and in this way democratic practices, transforming the institutions and forces that shape the students' life situations. Indeed, an investigation into students' experienced identity may lead us away from the conception of teaching the *mappa mundi* of the world musics project and away from conventional criteria for defining one's musical identity, and into an understanding of what the purpose of music education in a school context could be and how music could be taught in schools that already are multicultural.

Building Solidarity and Assuming Plurality of Identification: Some Examples from Music Education in Culturally Diverse Schools

The Nordic study on the musical agency of immigrant students that this chapter leans on demonstrates the problems when repertoire choices in music are made according to students' musical identity; in addition, music teachers in already culturally diverse schools may not be satisfied with "labeling" students' musical identities and simply choosing musical material accordingly. Music in such schools may be a key existential means of being different but, importantly, it can also be used to respond to the lack of communal life within school.

Helsinki: The Cosmopolitan Boy and the Girl Who Liked Korean Pop Music

In contrast to the idea that cultural recognition is something inherently good and helpful, students may equally feel that their background is something that should not be revealed, and that school is a place where student or parent backgrounds are not always relevant. Students construct their own future against this social reality, as with the example of a Beijing-born student in a Helsinki classroom who refused to be categorized as "Chinese," choosing instead to pursue a self-defined cosmopolitan identity. Asked to present Chinese music to his classmates by a teacher who wanted to recognize the traditional musical cultures she assumed her student identified with, or perhaps even *was* (to follow Elliott's [1995] terminology), he turned to Scottish music instead, claiming it as a preferred space to anchor himself and learn something new (see Karlsen, 2013).

Unexpected and deep musical identification in the Helsinki classroom was also found with Sari, a Finnish-born girl who had a fixation with Korean popular music—a choice that could be construed as far from her assumed "cultural home." While making explicit that she "hated music class," Sari could always be found with her iPod on and music in her ears, even during music lessons (much to her music teacher's great annoyance). After the puzzling revelation that Korean popular music was Sari's main musical preference—Sari was born in Finland, after all—the researcher followed her classroom activities, uncovering that Sari had an ongoing music-exchange relationship with Ae-cha, a girl of Korean descent who had lived in Finland for some years (see Karlsen, 2013). During an interview, Ae-cha told how this relationship had started, describing how, at that point, Sari was probably more "into" Korean popular music than she was herself:

First I just listened [alone], and then she started to borrow one of my earbuds, and then she asked what country this music came from. She has another friend as well; he used to like Japanese music, but this year he started to listen to Korean music and he downloads stuff for Sari. I think she listens to it more than I do.

As is apparent in this quote, Sari is not the only Finn who was converted to the Korean popular music landscape, and this music thus seems to travel with Ae-cha's social network, and has already spread to other parts of Finland:

My friends just seem to like Korean music, and one girl who moved to [another Finnish city] she listens there as well, and she spreads this music further and then it just moves on somehow.

Seen together, these two Helsinki examples demonstrate that one cannot assume students' acts of cultural-musical identifications to be uncomplicatedly straightforward and something in singular. Rather they must be considered against, and as part of, complex cultural-musical pluralities. Furthermore, the example involving Sari shows a kind of intercultural exchange, which, if picked up and handled wisely by her music teacher, could have provided a fertile point of departure for making the classroom practice more heterogeneous from *within*, and could even lead to fruitful discussions and practices of musical and cultural hybridity. Above all, however, it is important to recognize the difference between assumed identities and those that are freely chosen. The students in the Helsinki classroom resisted imposed identities and rather chose cosmopolitanization, that is, the "pluralism within oneself" (Papageorgiou, 2010, p. 646) through exploring and learning beyond cultural expectations.

Oslo: Enhancing Mutual Respect and Creating a Common Ground

The research in Oslo showed that, despite the apparent diversity of the students, a quite rigorous system for categorizing diversity into manageable uniformity was in place, which, among other things, implied that students themselves were not allowed to be "different"; peer pressure dictated sameness with regard to interests, clothes, and musical taste. Moreover, in the field of music, these codes followed—broadly—the lines of the students' ethnic backgrounds (see Karlsen, 2014). While contemporary R&B was a musical style available to all students, the "white, native Norwegians" listened to rock, and the students with minority population backgrounds listened to hip-hop. Attempts to go outside these quite rigorous musical lines of direction could result in punishments handed out by other students to the transgressing individuals.

The data showed that all the participating teachers in the three Nordic countries were conscious of their role and responsibilities as music teachers in schools where a multiplicity of cultures were represented. Christina, a Norwegian teacher, had perhaps developed the most effective strategies, teaching music in ways that attempted to tackle some of the social difficulties that emerged from this situation. Christina told us about a student with an explicit liking for punk rock—and a fashion sense to match this preference—who was beaten up because of his deviant musical taste. In order to deal with this unfortunate situation, Christina allotted time during her music lessons so that the students could play their own music and present it to their peers. By allowing the students to bring their musical belongings—often in the form of recordings and videos of what they preferred and listened to—into the classroom, she hoped to be able to start from the already existing diversity of the class and enhance the mutual respect and understanding among her students. Christina also stressed the close connection between identity—who one *is*—and music, and explained why she believed that presenting one's music to others could help ease the school's strained social climate:

> It is crucial to be able to express oneself and who one *is* . . . to be able to explain what *I* like about R&B or what *I* like about rock . . . why I prefer this [way of being in the world]—that is pretty important because then you can make yourself understood and then other people might have opportunities to understand you and to relate to your situation . . . [telling about your music] is simply about telling who you are and how you think.

While Christina did not *disseminate* musical differences in these situations, she instead enabled her students—in musical ways—to *express* and *be respected* for their differences. However, she also stressed the need to create a common ground and a joint experiential platform. She knew that the diversity of her students' backgrounds sometimes caused a lack of shared understandings, even violence, and she consciously used music lessons to facilitate learning situations that would build a sense of community among her students:

> Each and every one of them is allowed to test the drum kit [with the other students sitting around in a circle], I am there to supervise them, and in the beginning they don't want to, but I say "everyone should give it a try," and after a while they cheer each other and tell each other how to think in order to make it right—everybody wants everyone to succeed . . . and I think it is because all of them have been in that situation themselves . . . so then we have a joint [experience]—this is what I consider to be an *existential* experience . . . a joint experience, they have fought *together* to achieve something . . . we have been through this *together*.

Although Christina's solution in this case could, of course, be brought beyond testing in order to facilitate joint music making, her choice of repertoire and musical activities was made in an effort to tackle the school's music-related social challenges stemming from a lack of tolerance of diversity. Her solution was not only to recognize her students' plurality of preferences, but also to build solidarity among them by channeling individual energies into shared projects and joint experiences, to open "safe spaces" (see also MacPherson, 2010). The two angles to the challenges of diverse classrooms, namely offering an environment for self-chosen expressions of diversity and identity, on the one hand, and facilitating the sense of collectivity, on the other hand, are indeed not contradictory to each other but can be mutually supporting. Investigating teachers' collaborative conversations about culture, MacPherson (2010) emphasizes that such "safe spaces" in diverse educational contexts are not simply places to represent one's culture or identity, but spaces in which constant discussions should be encouraged, and where students should be allowed to make mistakes and to practice how to interact or respond (p. 279). In MacPherson's study, the teachers also "opened the door to uncertainty and debate over issues of cultural authenticity" (p. 282). This kind of learning is thus not simply content-driven multicultural education but also effective intercultural teaching and learning.

The Plurality of Selves and Their Multiple Belongings

The research findings of Karlsen's study illustrate how students' musical identities and preferences today may have little to do with their nationality, their ethnic, religious, or racial background, or their earlier formal music studies—as opposed to the idea that identity is something we are born into, something fixed or essential (e.g., Hall, 1992, p. 275), and that there is an authentic connection between this "essence of self" and the musical expressions of an individual's region or nation (e.g., Elliott, 1996, p. 13). Bauman (1999) highlights the liquidity of identity and how identities' continuity is secured in "movement and capacity for change" (p. xlv), not by clinging to once-established forms and contents. For grasping the nature of such cultural identities, he suggests using the image of "the *eddy* rather than the *island*" (p. xlv). The former is connected, among other things, to our present-day patterns of migration and the increasingly apparent fact that we all belong, simultaneously, to various cultural realities.

Reminding us that our most recent pattern of modern migration has led to an age of "*diasporas*: archipelagos of ethnic, religious and linguistic settlements crisscrossing the world" (Bauman, 2010, p. 150), Bauman acknowledges that we all either live "*in* a diaspora" or "*among* diasporas" (p. 151, italics in original), as, for example, the students in the Nordic classrooms. Consequently, we are all continuously in the process of connecting and disconnecting to various social and cultural contexts, which again entails that we develop not one, but several ways of belonging. This again moves the project of forming our selves from "*identity-building* to a lifelong, and for all practical purposes unfinishable, process of *identification*" (Bauman, 2008, p. 86). Elaborating on the topic of self and belonging, Bauman writes: "Hardly, any kind of 'belonging' these days engages 'the whole self,' since each person at any moment of their life is involved in, so to speak, 'multiple belongings'" (p. 86). The empirical examples noted earlier vividly illustrate this phenomenon.

When the "straight line" between one's self and the point of identification has ceased to exist—both because an individual potentially encompasses more selves and can access a seemingly endless number of possible points of identification—the concept of "roots" will, according to Bauman (2010), be displaced by "anchors" as the "primary tools of identification" (p. 151). This has obvious consequences for such multicultural music education approaches, which claim that recognizing students' "traditional music cultures" (ref. Elliott, 1995) strengthen their self- and cultural identity. This Taylorian idea of recognition presupposes "roots" in the sense that the students self-evidently "belong" to an identifiable tradition. However, even if these roots exist, this undermines the importance of the students' potential "multiple belongings" or their possible wishes for "future musical belongings," that is, the phenomenon that students may prefer to temporarily "anchor" themselves in a musical tradition or style that seemingly belongs to someone else, as both the Beijing-born student and Sari did in the previous examples. Moreover, students may prefer their peer group's points of musical identification over that of their parents or ethnic group (e.g., Sæther, 2008).

From Teaching the *Mappa Mundi* of the World's Musics to Learning the "Art of Living with Difference"

Returning to the vision of the multicultural music education project, the most naïve interpretations assume uncomplicated musical geography, or acknowledge mainly ethno-cultural differences (Govaris, 2004), in this way simplifying what are complex musical realities. As with the original *mappae mundi*, which depicted the (known) world in schematic ways, the epistemological aim of the dominant multicultural music education approach is to represent *different principles*. Accordingly, by attending to, illustrating, and even letting the students engage with different musical cultures, music teachers of multiculturalism are assumed to give an overview of distinct musical practices and expressions so that all involved can learn *about* their principles, and consequently acknowledge and even respect the culturally distant other (see, e.g., Anderson & Campbell, 2010). Besides assuming that musical and cultural diversity needs to be disseminated and taught, Bradley (2007), for instance, reminds us that the otherness that students are supposed to acknowledge and respect is often constructed "through and framed by colonialist representations" (p. 150). Identities are identified by using "a basic anthropological framework" (Jenkins, 2008, p. 116; see also van Meijl, 2010), in which a link is drawn between collective categories and groups of people with assumed similarity. It is noteworthy, however, that the medieval maps were never meant to be used as navigational charts; it was obvious that their lack of complexity made them unsuitable for such purposes. Likewise, the visions of the world musics project have apparent shortcomings when it comes to connecting to students' lives and preparing them for navigating culturally and musically complex and pluralistic waters in everyday contexts, similar to those depicted through our empirical examples.

Thus, while recognizing and respecting differences between cultures have often been among the core values of multicultural politics and education, Bauman (2011) identifies the perils of such a political outlook. By drawing on the work of Constant (2000), who holds that the above stance contains two compound premises, namely "that people have the right to be distinct, and that they also have the right to be indifferent to difference" (Bauman, 2011, p. 59), Bauman reminds us that when mutual tolerance is combined with mutual indifference, this makes it very hard for cultural communities in a multicultural world "to gain benefits and enjoyment from their coexistence" (p. 59). So, if social justice in schools is based only on individual rights and not on principles of communal life, social justice means not simply mutual tolerance but also that students have the right *not to be interested in each other*. In a school environment in which the goals are not only each student's cognitive achievements and the enhancement of tolerance, but also the building of mutual solidarity, such an individualistic approach to "rights," freedom, and social justice may simply not suffice. In fact, it may even lead to forms of violence similar to those experienced by Christina in her Oslo school, and toward which her remedy was to create a music-related platform for bonding and sharing. Bauman (2011) writes about it from a more overarching angle:

> When mutual tolerance combines with mutual indifference, cultural communities may live in close proximity but they will rarely speak to one another; and if they do, it will not be via the telephone but via the barrel of gun, since any loud expostulation under these conditions is evidence of a violation of an agreement and a challenge to the status quo. A "multicultural" world allows cultures to coexist, but the politics of "multiculturalism" does not make it easier, indeed possibly makes it more difficult, for these cultures to gain benefits and enjoyment from their coexistence. (p. 59)

Moreover, it is highly difficult for teachers to respect simultaneously "the right of a community to protect its way of life," for instance, restricting young people's musical identities, on the one hand, and "the individual's right of self-defense against community authorities that withhold the right to choose," on the other (p. 64). Consequently, in Bauman's view, the acknowledgment of cultural difference—or the laying out of the musical *mappa mundi*—is "the beginning rather than the end of the matter" (p. 60). Instead of illustrating difference, Bauman (2010) argues, we need to learn "the art of living with difference" (p. 151), and how to navigate in a world in which cultural diversity exists within the borders of locality. The latter requires a willingness of the teacher to " 'move between' cultures" (MacPherson, 2010, p. 272), more so than recognizing or disseminating "historical assumptions of cultural and linguistic hierarchies" (p. 272), and can hence be seen as more related to an intercultural approach to education than the older and more essentialist forms of multiculturalism.

Given that the overarching aim of schooling is to educate students to become active citizens, one is justified in assuming that such navigation could and should be learned already within the borders of the locality of schools and classrooms that, more often than not, have pluralism as one of their strongest and most characteristic features. Instead of aiming to illustrate or experience how music presumably is performed in "distant Africa" or "unknown Asia," to cover the *mappa mundi* of the world musics, teachers could rather lead the students in searching for activities and materials that they themselves find culturally interesting, unusual, or that already belong to their everyday musical lives. Also, teachers could use the power of joint musical activities to build solidarity and common ground, as Christina has, striving to teach music in ways that are geared toward helping her students learn how to live constructively with difference.

In this kind of world music education, it may be more important to search for jointly created harbors; to *co-create* unity within the plurality when a shared musical repertoire no longer exists; to search for shared experiences in the musical eddies—or, hybrids, even ethnic *bricolage*—through joint experiments and inquiries (see also Green, 1998). For such collaborative purposes, repertoire would need to be co-created, more so than teacher-chosen, and diversity would be exercised instead of classified and disseminated. The shift from teaching using the musical *mappa mundi* to teaching using active navigation in the midst of changing waters represents one way to reconnect music with the daily sociocultural and sociopolitical life in which teachers and students are living. In this way, it will be possible to incorporate the ethical issues of today's society into world music education and to deal with issues of social justice in everyday, face-to-face situations.

CONCLUDING REMARKS: SOCIAL JUSTICE AND DEMOCRACY

This chapter argues for the need to revisit the presumptions and justifications of the prevalent world musics project, particularly the grounding premise that musical diversity needs to be *transferred* into the classroom. This project might no longer be relevant in our present societies (including developing countries) given today's motility, non-rootedness, and global accessibility. Rather, as we have argued, and have shown through our empirical examples, in contemporary classrooms, diversity is always already present. This diversity is manifest in a plethora of ways, not only through the most obvious markers, such as ethnic, religious, linguistic, or in-group/out-group identifications, but also through lines of demarcation that may not be immediately detectable or visible, for example, class, gender, and sexuality. Consequently, we have suggested that in present societies we should consider the existing musical negotiations between the students—as Christina did—with their already diverse "musical belongings," which may or may not follow the students' assumed ethno-geographical origins.

This chapter has aimed to illustrate not only how the earlier world musics project, with its intention to make different musics more equal in education, may have contributed to social justice within the school, but also how it may have overlooked the complex dynamics of identity construction and musical life and the related complexity of ethical aspects in the social context of schools and classrooms. As Jorgensen (1998) has argued, "a sort of musical mapping . . . is rightly the province of geography" (p. 78), but what is included will be influenced by many different criteria, including "teachers' personal preferences and ethical, moral, religious, and artistic values" (p. 84). Moreover, the world musics project may even end up reproducing and justifying the essentialist idea of untouchable authentic musics, an idea that, indeed, is foreign not just to youngsters but also to a large number of musicians today. In that case, the order of the sociocultural and political world of musical islands is also fixed; in other words, the anthropology of the music, so to speak, is expected to be transferred to the classroom context and replicated without an analysis of said particular context. However, a shift to choices that are made for enhancing associated social life in schools is not easy given the long tradition of depoliticizing music education—a tradition that advises music teachers *not* to consider "all of the societal issues that will always surround music education" (Reimer, 2009, p. 131), and that is built on a universal hierarchy of purely musical values (see, e.g., Swanwick, 2001, p. 65; and also Reimer, 2009, p. 11), which further guides teachers' repertoire choices and frees them from active involvement with societal change.

Some developments in educational theory support this social shift in music education. Bruner (1996), for instance, emphasizes the importance of jointly produced oeuvres that, according to him, promote a sense of the division of labor and contribute to pride, identity, and a sense of continuity for those who participate in the process (pp. 22–23). A jointly negotiated and achieved experience "becomes an earned experience rather than just thoughtless sharing," as Sennett puts it (2012, p. 13). Again, for Dewey, the key aspect in how schooling can respond to the needs of a pluralist society is the degree to which it promotes the give-and-take experiences: social efficiency includes "all that makes one's own experience more worth while to others, and all that enables one to participate more richly in the worthwhile experiences of others" (Dewey, MW 9, p. 127). Arts and the aesthetic realms of life are no exception in this respect. Looking at school music education from this angle, one might ask if music educators can afford to be non-political and to devalue what for Dewey was the measure of "citizenship" (p. 127). Hence, our suggestion stems from a more profound *ethical* and *political* need to strengthen students' ability to navigate within a societal state of fast change and fluidity (Baumann, 2000, 2010), to teach them how to sail and anchor musically, and how to interact interculturally and ethically in the most local, everyday level of diversity—in other words, to learn "the art of living with difference."

Aiming for an approach to choosing, or rather *creating*, content and repertoire would also align with the principles of culturally responsive teaching. It would certainly require that the teachers are "familiar with their students' prior knowledge and beliefs" (Villegas & Lucas, 2002, p. xiv) and further, that the instruction stretches the students "beyond the familiar" (p. xiv) on a ground built together, by all participants. Furthermore, it would be "respectful of student diversity and [recognize] the central role that individual and cultural differences play in the learning process" (p. xv). As noted earlier, while difference is not to be pinpointed *as* difference, difference still plays an indelible part of the educational processes in the sense that learning to handle it requires intimate knowledge of its various aspects and qualities. Hence, in order for the students to search for joint harbors, they need to know what everyone brings to the process, and to be able to elicit and draw on that in ways that are socially just.

This kind of music education envisions that music in schools has a significant role in processes of developing a socially just society and that this contribution takes place through *participatory processes* and *collaborative inquiry* that may question any stable views of knowledge and prefer "connectedness compatible with innovation" (Green, 1998, p. 436). From the teacher, it requires imagination to break the established social practices that stem from existing musical traditions or school contexts. It also requires tolerance for uncertainty and a drive toward change. Moreover, the teachers may challenge their roles as cultural authorities by having "an inquiry-based approach to the learning of culture" (MacPherson, 2010, p. 282). Thus, for a music teacher, repertoire choices are only a part of the larger process toward what Green (1998) has called "deep democracy": an ongoing process that is based on the belief that "the voluntary activities of individuals in voluntary association with one another is the only basis of democratic institutions" (Dewey, LW 14, p. 92). Indeed, as we have argued in previous writings (see Karlsen & Westerlund, 2010), culturally diverse school contexts, and teachers' choices when operating within them, may form "a healthy test . . . in terms of how democracy is enacted and developed in music education" (p. 226). Through ethical acts toward a deep democracy, the music room could thus constitute an arena for intercultural community-building in which social justice is produced through solidarity practiced "in action."

NOTE

1. Following a multi-sited ethnographic design (Bogdan & Biklen, 2007), three classroom practices were observed over an eight-week period each, and the participating teachers and most of the students were interviewed. The student interviews were aimed toward mapping the students' experiences and ways of engaging with music in a broad sense, both within and outside music lessons, and the teacher interviews focused on what it implied to the teachers to act in and through music, how they facilitated this in their classrooms, and how they considered such music-related actions to be useful or valuable for their students.

REFERENCES

Andreouli, E., Howarth, C. & Sonn, C. (2014) The role of schools in promoting inclusive communities in contexts of diversity. *Journal of Health Psychology, 19*(1), 16–21.

Anderson, W. M., & Campbell, P. S. (Eds.). (2010). *Multicultural perspectives in music education*. Vol. 1. Lanham, MD: Rowman & Littlefield Education.

Andreouli, E., Howarth, C., & Sonn, C. (2014). The role of schools in promoting inclusive communities in contexts of diversity. *Journal of Health Psychology*, *19*(1), 16–21.

Banks, J. A. (2010). Multicultural education: Characteristics and goals. In J. A. Banks & C. A. McGee Banks (Eds.), *Multicultural education. Issues and perspectives* (7th ed.) (pp. 3–30). Hoboken, NJ: Wiley.

Bauman, Z. (1999). *Culture as praxis*. London: Sage.

Bauman, Z. (2000). *Liquid modernity*. Malden, MA: Polity Press.

Bauman, Z. (2008). *The art of life*. Malden, MA: Polity Press.

Bauman, Z. (2010). *44 letters from the liquid modern world*. Malden, MA: Polity Press.

Bauman, Z. (2011). *Culture in a liquid modern world*. Malden, MA: Polity Press.

Bogdan, R. C., & Biklen, S. K. (2007). *Qualitative research for education: An introduction to theories and methods* (5th ed.). Boston, MA: Pearson International Edition.

Bradley, D. (2007). The sounds of silence: Talking race in music education. *Action, Criticism, and Theory for Music Education*, *6*(4), 132–162.

Bruner, J. 1996. *The culture of education*. Cambridge, MA, & London: Harvard University Press.

Campbell, P. S. (2004). *Teaching music globally: Experiencing music, expressing culture*. New York: Oxford University Press.

Constant, F. (2000). *Les multiculturalisme*. Paris: Dominos Flammarion.

Dewey, J. (LW). The later works of John Dewey. In L. Hickman (Ed.). (1996), *The collected works of John Dewey, 1882–1953*, Vol. 14. The electronic edition. Charlottesville, VA: InteLex Past Masters.

Dewey, J. (MW). The middle works of John Dewey. In L. Hickman (Ed.). (1996), *The collected works of John Dewey, 1882–1953*, Vol. 9. The electronic edition. Charlottesville, VA: InteLex Past Masters.

Drummond, J. (2005). Cultural diversity in music education: Why bother? In P. S. Campbell, J. Drummond, P. Dunbar-Hall, K. Howard, H. Schippers & T. Wiggins (Eds.), *Cultural diversity in music education: Directions and challenges for the 21st century* (pp. 1–11). Brisbane: Australian Academic Press.

Elliott, D. J. (1989). Key concepts in multicultural music education. *International Journal of Music Education*, *13*(1), 11–18.

Elliott, D. J. (1995). *Music matters: A new philosophy of music education*. Oxford: Oxford University Press.

Elliott, D. J. (1996). Music education in Finland: A new philosophical view. *Finnish Journal of Music Education*, *1*(1), 6–20.

Elliott, D. J., & Silverman, M. (2015). *Music matters: A philosophy of music education* (2nd ed.). New York: Oxford University Press.

Gay, G. (2010). *Culturally responsive teaching. Theory, research, and practice* (2nd ed.). New York: Teachers College Press.

Govaris, C. (2004) *Introduction to intercultural education*. Athens: Antrapos.

Green, J. M. (1998). Educational multiculturalism, critical pluralism, and deep democracy. In C. Willett (Ed.), *Theorizing multiculturalism. A guide to the current debate* (pp. 422–448). Malden, MA, & Oxford: Blackwell.

Hall, S. (1992). The question of cultural identity. In S. Hall, D. Held, & A. McGrew (Eds.), *Modernity and its futures* (pp. 274–316). Oxford: Polity in association with the Open University.

Jenkins, R. (2008). *Social identity* (3rd ed.). New York: Routledge.

Jorgensen, E. (1998). Musical multiculturalism revisited. *Journal of Aesthetic Education*, 32(2), 77–78.

Kallio, A., & Westerlund, H. (Kallio, A. A., & Westerlund, H. (2015). The ethics of survival: Teaching the traditional arts to disadvantaged children in post-conflic Cambodia. International Journal of Music Education. http://dx.doi.org/10.1177/0255761415584298). The ethics of survival: Teaching the traditional arts to disadvantaged children in post-conflict Cambodia. *International Journal of Music Education*.

Kallio, A., Westerlund, H. & Partti, H. (2014). The quest for authenticity in the music classroom: Sinking or swimming? In S.-E. Holgersen, E. Georgii-Hemming, S. G. Nielsen & L. Väkevä (Eds.), *Nordic research in music education. Yearbook 15* (pp. 205–223). Oslo: Norwegian Academy of Music.

Karlsen, S. (2011). *Music education in multicultural schools: Report from the Nordic research project "Exploring democracy: Conceptions of immigrant students' development of musical agency."* Oslo: Konsis Grafisk.

Karlsen, S. (2012). Multiple repertoires of ways of being and acting in music: Immigrant students' musical agency as an impetus for democracy. *Music Education Research*, 14(2), 131–148.

Karlsen, S. (2013). Immigrant students and the "homeland music": Meanings, negotiations and implications. *Research Studies in Music Education*, 35(2), 158–174.

Karlsen, S. (2014). Exploring democracy: Nordic music teachers' approaches to the development of immigrant students' musical agency. *International Journal of Music Education*, 32(4), 422–436.

Karlsen, S., & Westerlund, H. (2010). Immigrant students' development of musical agency: Exploring democracy in music education. *British Journal of Music Education*, 27(3), 225–239.

Lundquist, B., & Szego, C. K. (1998). *Musics of the world's cultures.* Reading, UK: International Society for Music Education.

MacPherson, S. (2010). Teachers' collaborative conversations about culture: Negotiating decision making in intercultural teaching. *Journal of Teacher Education*, 61(3), 271–286.

Papageorgiou, I. (2010). For an education that makes the most out of globalisation: A critical interculturalist approach. *Current Sociology*, 58(4), 642–660.

Reimer, B. (2009). *Seeking the significance of music education: Essays and reflections.* Plymouth, UK: MENC.

Ruud, E. (2007). Musikk, identitet og kulturell anerkjennelse [Music, identity and cultural recognition]. In E. Georgii-Hemming (Ed.), *Kunskapens konst. Vänbok till Börje Stålhammar* (pp. 273–283). Örebro: Örebro university.

Sæther, E. (2008). When minorities are the majority: Voices from a teacher/researcher project in a multicultural school in Sweden. *Research Studies in Music Education*, 30(1), 25–42.

Schippers, H. (2010). *Facing the music: Shaping music education from a global perspective.* Oxford: Oxford University Press.

Sennett, R. (2012). *Together: The rituals, pleasures and politics of cooperation.* New Haven, CT: Yale University Press.

Swanwick, K. (2001). Response to book review. *Philosophy of Music Education Review*, 9(1), 65.

Taylor, C. (1992). *Multiculturalism and "the politics of recognition."* Princeton, NJ: Princeton University Press.

van Meijl, T. (2010). Anthropological perspectives on identity: From sameness to difference. In M. Wetherell & C. T. Mohanty (Eds.), *The SAGE handbook of identities* (pp. 63–81). London: SAGE Publications.

Villegas, A. M., & Lucas, T. (2002). *Educating culturally responsive teachers: A coherent approach.* Albany: State University of New York Press.

Volk, T. M. (1998). *Music, education, and multiculturalism: Foundations and principles.* Oxford: Oxford University Press.

Westerlund, H. (2001). In dialogue: Boom diddy boom boom: Critical multiculturalism and music education. *Philosophy of Music Education Review, 9*(1), 62–63.

Westerlund, H. (2002). *Bridging experience, action, and culture in music education.* Studia Musica 16. Helsinki: Sibelius Academy.

CHAPTER 24

YOUTH EMPOWERMENT AND TRANSFORMATIVE MUSIC ENGAGEMENT

SUSAN A. O'NEILL

INTRODUCTION

THE pathways along which young people engage in music learning are sometimes found, sometimes forged, and sometimes forced through what might seem to be ordinary educational practices. We may not always recognize the "inflections of power" that reproduce cycles of subordination and systematic oppression (Cammarota & Fine, 2008, p. 3). And yet, oppressive practices continue to operate in educational environments, no matter how much we might deny their existence, ignore them, or negotiate around them. Controlling and manipulative educational environments have a negative impact on young people's motivation to learn and engagement during learning (Boggiano & Katz, 1991; Stipek, 1996, 2002). Frequent experiences of alienation and marginalization at school often result in disconnection and lack of engagement in learning and achievement (Sefa Dei, 2003; Zyngier, 2003). A focus on "high stakes" performance outcomes has negative implications for how learners think and feel about themselves as learners, how they perceive their capacity to learn, and how much energy they have for learning (Harlen & Deakin Crick, 2003). In music education, deficit approaches to solving performance-related problems exacerbate negative outcomes by emphasizing what learners are lacking or need to "fix." They also suppress "worthwhile" or real world educational connections that Freire (2008) argues only emerge through being "re-creators" engaged in "hopeful inquiry [. . .] in the world, with the world, and with each other" (p. 244).

From this perspective, it appears that what is needed is a responsive and learner-centered approach that is capable of guiding young people along music learning pathways where they encounter real world challenges that embrace diversity, foster potential, and enact positive change through collaborative, active, and transformative forms of music engagement (O'Neill, 2006, 2012). This transformative vision seeks to enable and encourage youth empowerment in music learning in ways that strengthen youth voices, wellbeing, and *musical flourishing* (Ansdell & DeNora, 2012). Transformative music engagement (O'Neill, 2012, 2014, in press[a]) approaches encourage youth empowerment—the word *transformative* means having the power to transform—through expansive learning opportunities (Engeström & Sannino, 2010) that begin by involving young people in a reflective process about issues that interest and matter to them. Through appreciative and dialogical inquiry, young people are encouraged to *see things differently*. They are encouraged to *speak back* to the realities of their world and discover that they are capable and ready to effect positive change. In doing so, young music learners become capable of gaining new insights, overcoming challenges and constraints, and taking positive actions to bring about personal and social transformation. It is a way of engaging along a music-learning pathway whereby learners and educators might "reflect simultaneously on themselves and the world without dichotomizing this reflection from action [. . .] to establish an authentic form of thought and action" (Freire, 2008, p. 252). Through this collaborative process, young music learners have the opportunity to develop the self-knowledge, supportive learning relationships, and sense of empowerment necessary for experiencing deep, purposeful, meaningful, and transformative music engagement.

Since music education environments are not immune from the consequences of controlling, manipulative, and oppressive practices and subjugating discourses, there is a need to help young music learners recognize, understand, and overcome challenges and constraints, while at the same time realizing the power of their own efforts to explore untapped potential and create new possibilities. If we do not provide young people with these kinds of learning opportunities, how can we expect them to recognize, question, challenge, and transform unjust practices and generate greater social justice? In this chapter, I consider the concept of *youth empowerment* and how it is encouraged through transformative music engagement. In the latter part of the chapter, I will discuss the conditions that *enable* and *encourage* youth empowerment through transformative music engagement, drawing on Jennings et al.'s (2006) critical youth empowerment framework. Although there is no recipe or formula for empowering youth or bringing about transformative engagement experiences (Sarkissian, Hurford, & Wenman, 2010), the theoretical foundations reviewed in this chapter offer guidance for researchers, educators, and young people engaged in collaborative efforts to enable and encourage youth empowerment and transformative music engagement, and to enact positive change through existing conditions of possibility within music education contexts.

Youth Empowerment

The concept of empowerment can be viewed from different perspectives. Rappaport (1981) describes empowerment as a relational, nonlinear process that increases people's control over access to resources that affect them. Freirian scholars view it as a vehicle for social transformation (Freire, 1973) or a way of resisting oppression and marginalization (Biesta, 2004; Giroux et al., 1996). Gieve and Magalhães (1994) refer to empowerment as learning to value one's own knowledge and potential. Empowerment is considered a necessary endeavor for the sustainability of today's knowledge-based society and information age (Cummins, 2001) and has gained considerable momentum in education in recent decades. Empowerment is thus a key concept in twenty-first-century educational reforms (Itin, 1999; Romanish, 1991) and in emancipatory and critical pedagogies (Kincheloe, 2008), as well as lifelong learning (Longworth, 2013). According to Sarason (1990), "any educational reform that does not explicitly and courageously own up to issues surrounding changing patterns of power relationships is likely to fail" (p. 31). Further, the concept of empowerment cannot be separated into decontextualized accounts of youth experience. Empowerment is a multilevel construct with sociocultural and sociopolitical dimensions and integrated individual and collective processes and outcomes. As such, it is a "complex social action process" (Jennings et al., 2006, p. 33).

Youth empowerment in education is about providing learning opportunities that engage young people in a process that enables them to *speak back* to the reality of today's uncertain and unstable world—a world marked by dissolving boundaries and rapid change (Barnett, 2012). Bauman (2000) describes it as a "liquid world" that signals a "fluid modernity," which requires us to rethink old concepts that bind systemic structures and envision in their place new possibilities "for power to be free to flow" (p. 14). The complexity and turbulence of today's world "[present] individuals with challenges to understand themselves anew and to find a new relationship with the world" (Barnett, 2012, p. 9). These factors are reflected in developmental challenges that young people face in what Larson (2011) refers to as "coming of age in a disorderly world" (p. 330). In schools, educators are described as "full of spurious emotions" (Hargreaves, 2001) as today's learners are more "alienated, resistant and disengaged than ever before" (Zyngier, 2004). When youth empowerment is contemplated in school settings tensions often surface as policies and structures continue to constrain and diminish empowering contexts (Kohfeldt et al., 2011; Langhout & Mitchell, 2008). There is a need within educational environments for educators to learn how to increase "conscious power-shaping" (Jennings et al., 2006) and opportunities for shared critical reflection activities if we are to support the broad goal of youth empowerment in education.

Tan (2009) describes "empowerment of self" as a way of helping learners develop a sense of self-worth by gaining greater knowledge of self. He argues that by gaining self-knowledge, young people develop an awareness of how the suffering and frustration they experience is a result of societal forces outside their control and therefore not their fault. Tan describes how one young female student, who would often break down in class and say how much she hated herself and her life, came to realize that she was not alone in feeling this way. Tan encouraged her to express herself through writing poetry within a safe and caring classroom environment. Her "budding knowledge of self" motivated her to become involved in organizing artistic creations in her own community. In addition to realizing that she could be active in her community "supporting causes that would directly impact on the conditions that frustrated her," she also "learned to express the love she had for her family, home, community, and more importantly, herself" (p. 489). Tan's approach to youth empowerment aims to help learners realize their worth and potential agency by encouraging them to express themselves through an artistic medium. The argument is that such an approach not only affords opportunities for self-knowing, it also helps learners discover that they are capable and "ready for emancipatory action" (p. 489).

Empowerment refers to a process whereby people come to believe in their ability "to act" and this belief "is tied to capable action" (Romanish, 1991, p. 4). Few would argue with this noble aim for education; however, the use of the concept of empowerment in practice has been criticized. For example, Kohfeldt and her colleagues (2011) point out that the concept is often criticized for failing to recognize the "overarching structures" or sociocultural and sociopolitical contexts within which youth empowerment programs are situated and shaped in ways that create both affordances and constraints. Further, when applied to prevention-oriented youth programs, empowerment tends to be associated with solving problem behaviors or is predefined by adults "rather than co-constructed with youth" (Kohfeldt, Chhun, Grace, & Langhout, 2011, p. 28). In music education, the notion of empowerment as enabling is often undermined when it is referred to as something that should be "achieved" (Spruce & Odena, 2012, p. 439) or "promoted" (Davis, 2012, p. 419) by music teachers. Similarly, the idea that music learners become "agents of their own learning" can also be misinterpreted or misunderstood if teachers merely "allow" their students to choose some of their own repertoire or a song to bring into the classroom (Harwood & Marsh, 2012, p. 335). We must recognize that to be "able to act" is tied to the notion of being "enabled" versus "allowed" to act. Merely allowing youth to engage in decisions or choose a learning activity does not equate with empowerment: "To have power in its true sense means there is no need for it to be 'allowed' " (Romanish, 1991, p. 5). "Allowing" youth opportunities to influence and participate in decisions implies that this is a privilege that can also be withdrawn by powerful others. If youth are to be empowered, their equitable engagement needs to be assured, not allowed.

Due to the structure of classroom environments dictating that the teacher is always in a position of authority, it may be viewed that this sort of equitable engagement is limited. Yet, within these spaces, it is possible to provide learning opportunities that lessen the teacher's authority and open up spaces for more equitable dialogical encounters. This requires patterns of interaction to be established that encourage learners and educators to question deliberately and to remain open to new knowledge and insights. For example, if a teacher asks a question and already knows the answer, learners are usually directed toward a particular outcome and are not encouraged to engage in their own explorations. However, if the teacher poses a question without intending to direct the outcome, even if he or she might expect some of the answers, a space is opened up for responses the teacher may not have considered but which are capable of making possible "a more inclusive, discriminating, and integrating perspective" (Mezirow, 1991, p. 167).

Schwarzer and colleagues (2006) view the *encouragement of empowerment* to be a key common element across definitions of empowerment. They also recognize that any young learner is what Cameron et al. (1992) describe as an "intricate mosaic of different power potentials in social relations" (p. 20). What this means in practice is that each learner has "varying levels of power depending on the context" (Schwarzer et al., p. xxvii) and therefore differ in their potential for empowerment to be realized in educational contexts. Jennings and her colleagues (2006) describe the conditions that foster the encouragement of empowerment as welcoming, youth-centered environments. They remind us of the need to take into account the philosophy and values of programs and initiatives, the dynamics of youth-adult relationships within programs, and individual and collective processes of "critical reflection and reflective action" (p. 34).

As with many innovative pedagogical approaches, encouraging youth empowerment draws on a number of strategies that redefine the parameters of what constitutes traditional forms of knowledge and the content of what is taught (Giroux, 1994). Further, rather than view youth empowerment as a mere "tool" for engaging young people, it needs to be viewed as a sociocultural process that is contextually determined, politically reactive, and inherently reflexive. It is situated within real-world understandings that draw on experiential and participatory approaches to learning in a non-judgmental and supportive environment. This, in turn, stimulates opportunities for meaningful and transformative learning and engagement, as well as "knowledge, skill and leadership development, critical reflection on societal forces and power relations, and active community participation" (Jennings et al., 2006, p. 33). Two noteworthy frameworks that recognize the fluidity and entanglements of the hinterland surrounding the encouragement of youth empowerment are discussed in the following sections and related to music education contexts: honoring youth voices and positive youth music engagement as a form of appreciative inquiry.

Honoring Youth Voices

Youth empowerment is based on the assumptions that youth should have a voice in issues that interest or matter to them and concern them, and that they should be part of the decisions that affect them. According to Turley (1994), "listening to the voices of students validates them as partners in the education process" (p. 4). Honoring youth voices is often equated with listening to youth, particularly those who have been marginalized or silenced. However, Freire (2008) reminds us that those who have been silenced may not be able to speak with their own authentic voice. Instead, they may "reflect or echo the voice of the dominant culture" (Schwarzer et al., 2006). As Ellsworth (1989) suggests, attempts to please or submit to a person in authority may also suppress authentic voice. She also advocates for the use of the term "voices" rather than "voice" to acknowledge the multiple authentic voices that result from having different sociocultural and political backgrounds. Rather than seek consensus in the form of expressing multiple voices at once or as a singular voice, it is important to provide spaces for the expression of multiple and diverse voices. Further, listening to and honoring youth voices is not necessarily a dynamic means of empowerment if their voices are not responded to through some kind of deliberate, positive action. Arnot and Reay (2007) argue for caution in assuming that power relations can be changed through the notion of "student voice" as "pedagogies construct the voice/message which teachers and researchers hear" (p. 311).

In considering the role of "student voice" in music education, Finney and Harrison (2010) recognize the need to "preserve the integrity of student and teacher" (p. 15) in taking actions to listen to youth voices in music learning contexts "to ensure a jointly made journey of learning" (p. 15). In the same book, Flutter's (2010) informative and succinct chapter points out the many concepts "entwined" within the notion of student voices, including "respect, reciprocity, engagement, autonomy, empowerment, community, democracy and dialogue" (p. 17). Flutter argues that by adopting a "students' voices approach," an educator is capable of bridging the gap that often exists between young people's musical interests outside school and music that takes place at school. One approach is to recognize young people's musical lives as "situated perspectives" that are used to navigate musical boundaries (O'Neill, in press[b]). Helping music learners acquire a new power of navigation can make all the difference by opening up possibilities for imagining new destinations and for negotiating the various pathways they might encounter on the way (O'Neill, 2012). However, "situated perspectives" can also become bounded expectations of music learners, which are resistant to change and disconfirmation (O'Neill & Senyshyn, 2011). Overcoming these bounded conceptualizations requires an approach that recognizes and scrutinizes the ways in which particular epistemologies have become *ideologies of power* that indoctrinate us into the beliefs, values, and images that construct our sense of music learners in particular ways.

Listening to and honoring youth voices requires a constant critical and reflective exploration of the specific contexts and relationships in which learning activities take place (Kincheloe, 2008). Research has identified the main challenges and pitfalls of having to alter traditional structures, practices, beliefs, and values to enable youth voices to flourish (McQuillan, 2005). Youth or learner voices approaches are most effective at increasing learning engagement when educators strive to

1. Ensure that learner voices activity is not reduced to a mere token gesture by coordinating a clear set of objectives, roles, responsibilities, and resources, as well as opportunities for learning from youth (Fielding, 2004). This requires shifting the role from information deliverer to a "knowledge-producing professional" (Kincheloe, 2008, p. 29). It also requires efforts to ensure that the inclusion of all voices is being achieved (Rudduck, 2007).

2. Become comfortable with not having all the answers and cultivate instead a climate of "respectful disagreement" between learners and between learners and the teacher (Denner, Meyer, & Bean, 2005). Help learners recognize that there is much to be learned in the space between different positions. Rather than seeking consensus or a unified position, there is great potential and possibility in the process of listening to and learning from the ideas of others (O'Neill, 2012).

3. Recognize "surface compliance" on the part of learners (Rudduck & Fielding, 2006) as potentially part of the initial engagement process or even part of the ebb and flow of engagement over time.

4. Understand that change is a process and that setbacks and challenges such as lack of time, lack of administrative support, concerns over losing control or discipline in the classroom, and concerns over the authenticity of the learning are not insurmountable problems if approached with patience, resolve, and perseverance (Toshalis & Nakkula, 2012).

Positive Youth Music Engagement as a Form of Appreciative Inquiry

In a past publication on positive youth music engagement (O'Neill, 2006), I explored positive youth development frameworks for understanding initiatives in adolescent development that promote, build on, and strengthen the competencies and social contexts that foster young people's resiliency or ability to thrive in the face of adversity (Lerner, Brentano, Dowling, & Anderson, 2002; Villarruel, Perkins, Borden, & Keith, 2003). The main premise of this work is that *all* young people have the *potential* and *capacity* for healthy growth and development. In terms of music, this translates into the notion that every young person has the potential and capacity for positive musical development, or more specifically, that engagement in musical activities should be associated with positive or healthy outcomes for all young people. No longer are musical skills and knowledge viewed as the domain of a few talented individuals, and no longer are distinctions made in terms of the relative merits of formal or informal musical activities or teaching and learning practices. Rather, the focus shifts to the development of musical strengths and competencies that are present within *all young people* in *all contexts* in which their development occurs.

Indeed, in the twenty-first century, young people have become "lifewide" learners (Barnett, 2012, p. 12) and their learning has become "unbundled" (Sefton-Green, 2008) and "freed from the boundaries of educational institutions" (Coleman, 2012, p. 2). Music learning is taking place across physical and virtual life spaces within home, school, local and online communities, and (mostly through the Internet) the wider world. Distinctions between formal and informal learning now seem "crude and misleading" (Furlong & Davies, 2012, p. 52) as elements of both formality and informality occur in the classroom, home, and other places in the community. Instead of viewing formal and informal as two separate worlds, Erstad (2012) suggests that we take a *learning lives approach* "to find ways of understanding the interconnections between these two worlds as experienced by young people" (p. 25) and "to reorient our research" and "move beyond conceptions of formal and informal learning" (p. 40). A further insight from Furlong and Davies, who draw on Bernstein's (1971) notion of *framing*, suggests that we should consider the degree of control and responsibility that a teacher or external person has over the content and direction of learning, which may be strong or weak and might even fluctuate along a continuum depending on the learning situation.

Regardless of the location, for young people to become fully engaged in active learning in today's technologically evolving world, the activities they are involved in should occur in a context that provides opportunities for self-expression and self-direction (Kleiber, 1999). Such contexts promote the bioecological developmental space necessary for youth to function as both indirect producers (e.g., self-directed learners) and as products of their own music engagement (e.g., the emotional and creative expressions of musical outcomes). According to Pittman (1992), a leading youth advocate, identifying (and even solving) young people's problems in terms of providing adequate opportunities does not necessarily prepare them for the future. And preparing youth in terms of acquiring specific skills and knowledge does not necessarily mean they will be fully engaged in active learning or active agents in their own development. Rather, "effectively preparing young people to meet challenges requires providing them with the foundation to make decisions that will promote their own positive development" (Perkins, Borden, Keith, Hoppe-Rooney, & Villarruel, 2003, p. 2). This has important implications for musical development since the vast majority of young people have a great deal of autonomy in the way they engage with musical activities as both consumers and performers. As such, they are already active agents and constructors of their own musical skills and knowledge (O'Neill, 2005). This suggests a need for collaborative engagement on the part of all individuals and institutions within a community in promoting youth involvement in music activities. Such an approach has much to offer in terms of developing young people's sense of self, self-responsibility, interest, and motivation in relation to their own musical development (O'Neill, 1999; O'Neill & McPherson, 2002).

In considering a range of initiatives that might best support positive youth music engagement, I believe that the concept of *appreciative inquiry* offers great potential for realizing this intention. Appreciative inquiry (AI) is a generative and transformative approach developed by David Cooperrider and his colleagues in the 1980s with the aim of transforming the capacity of individuals to enact positive change "by deliberating focusing on positive experiences and hopeful futures" (pp. 54–55). As such, Gergen, Gergen, and Barrett (2004) describe AI as a "highly effective transformative practice" (p. 54). The goal of AI is to encourage people to "develop an appreciative eye" and to recognize that no matter how dysfunctional or conflictual a human environment or system might be, it will have elements of beauty, goodness, and value that can become "alive with infinite imagination" and that "guide attention toward peak experiences and strengths" (Cooperrider & Barrett, 2002, p. 236). Gergen and his colleagues (2004) argue that action research in the past has tended to focus on problems and deficits "in which participants are encouraged to notice and talk about breakdowns and plan action around solutions that address these problems (p. 55). In contrast, AI focuses on strengths and what brings out the very best in systems and organizations; it is therefore more likely to lead to deep engagement in personal and social transformations as individuals strive to ask questions and deliberately focus on factors that contribute to the co-creation of new worlds or "designing new futures" (p. 56).

When young people learn to work together to share, reflect, question, refine, elaborate, expand, and represent their knowledge and understanding of their own and others' progress and sense of wellbeing, they become deeply engaged in learning, which helps them reach a deeper level of understanding (Meyer, Land, & Baillie, 2010). An example that might serve as a catalyst to understanding this in practice within music learning is when a young person encounters deeply challenging material or ideas, such as understanding a difficult passage or how music is played within a different cultural tradition, and then proceeds to unpack these ideas with his or her peers. The discussions, reflections, and ways of forming and presenting their views to their peers then becomes an interconnected way of mapping students' understanding of the issue, while through their journey with other young people, they are able to reach a deeper level of empathy, learning, and engagement. The challenge, however, is to guide these efforts toward positive and self-affirming explorations of attitudes, peak experiences, strengths, and resilience. One step toward achieving this is to involve learners in asking questions that move beyond "What do we know or need to know?" toward questions concerning values and generative actions, such as "What are we interested in and what matters to us and others?" "How can we share our knowledge/abilities to help strengthen each other?" and "What actions can we take for positive change?" Rather than focus on deficit orientations (e.g., "I am not good at this difficult passage or I am not interested in learning about a different cultural music tradition") that reinforce negative and self-defeating thoughts and actions, the aim is to adopt what Buber (1958) describes as *confirming the other* by accepting the whole potentiality of others (e.g., "I wonder if the same things that interest and matter to me are of interest to others and how they might view these things differently or in ways that help them"). Youth then become engaged in planning and taking actions that build on and expand their own strengths to help realize their own and others' potential. In doing so, young people not only learn to appreciate the positive contributions of others, they learn to appreciate their own ability to gain a new insight and/or contribute to positive change (e.g., "I recognize new ways that I might engage with others musically that I did not see before").

When appreciative inquiry is combined with dynamic youth empowerment, learners develop a critical and collective social justice orientation (Schwarzer, Bloom, & Shono, 2006). In music education, this form of generative or transformative engagement occurs when learners reflect critically on their values and music learning contexts and make conscious efforts to plan and implement actions that bring about new ways of transforming themselves, others, and their community within the context of their learning activities and relationships. Transformative music engagement (O'Neill, 2012) operates within an appreciative inquiry framework that encourages youth and educators to work deliberately and collaboratively on creating the best conditions possible within their own educational contexts for promoting positive change.

CREATING THE CONDITIONS FOR YOUTH EMPOWERMENT WITHIN TRANSFORMATIVE MUSIC ENGAGEMENT

A key aspect of fostering youth empowerment is to provide opportunities to learn leadership and life skills and to apply these skills to making a difference with others. This requires shifting the focus from merely instructing and supporting learners to fostering the empowerment and resiliency necessary for sustaining music engagement and overcoming negative constraints on learning (O'Neill, 2011; Wang, Haertel, & Walberg, 1997). Within music education, the aim is to create expansive music learning opportunities within a social justice orientation that guide youth toward developing their distinctive voice and the capacity to envision and express what interests and matters to them in ways that enact positive change through existing conditions of possibility.

Jennings et al. (2006) describes the conditions of possibility for critical youth empowerment through the dynamic, integrated nature of six dimensions:

1. *A welcoming and safe environment.* The learning environment, in addition to being welcoming and safe, should be perceived by youth as supportive, fun, caring, and challenging. Youth within these environments have a "sense of ownership and yet are challenged and supported to move beyond their usual comfort zone" (p. 41). A key feature of these environments is that they are co-created by youth and adults and provide opportunities for youth and adults to interact as co-learners (Wallerstein et al., 2005). Jennings et al. (2006) also point out that a welcoming and safe environment should involve "creative spaces" that encourage youth to take risks "explore and try out new skills, build personal and collective capacities, experiences success or make mistakes" (p. 42).

2. *Meaningful participation and engagement.* This involves providing opportunities for youth to develop capacities through meaningful and real-world learning that encourages youth responsibility and decision-making.

3. *Equitable power sharing between youth and adults.* It is important that power is shared and that spaces are created that lessen the authority of the teacher in educational contexts. There should be opportunities for an incremental transfer of power to youth as they gain capacity. Youth empowerment and youth-empowered leadership roles are associated with significant adult support. When youth and adults work together in creative, collaborative partnerships, possibilities for bringing about social change are greatly increased. According to Blanchet-Cohen et al. (2013), youth-adult partnership based on equitable and respectful practices "opens up possibilities for personal, organizational, and societal changes" (p. 325). They describe the meeting place of youth and adults as an "ecotone"—an ethical space where "two different world views encounter one another" and then "overlap

and transition into one another" (p. 326). When youth are engaged in this way with adults, they begin to see viable alternatives for leading a meaningful life, regardless of the challenges they have experienced in their own lives.

4. *Engagement in critical reflection on interpersonal and sociopolitical processes.* There needs to be recognition that individual and collective empowerment are interwoven.

5. *Participation in sociopolitical processes to effect change.* Programs should emphasize societal analysis and encourage social change goals.

6. *Integrated individual- and community-level empowerment.* Critical reflection is integral through varied youth-based approaches.

In a recent exploratory study with young people, educators, and researchers, we used youth-led participatory action research (YPAR) frameworks (Cahill, 2007; Ozer, Ritterman, & Wanis, 2010) to create the conditions of possibility for critical youth empowerment through the dynamic, integrated nature of the above six dimensions. Our aim was to engage music learners in deep explorations about why music matters to them and their school community (Erickson, O'Neill, & Senyshyn, 2012, 2013). We were interested in how young people might make vital contributions to understanding the ways that youth value music learning in a school environment and how this might both empower music learners and foster transformative music engagement. YPAR involves asking learners to identify a problem or burning question, devise and research the problem or question, and propose a solution and/or a way of representing their new understanding. The YPAR process also increases young people's capacity for critical reflection and analysis, which are crucial for participating in social change. It provides them with the opportunity to explore issues in ways that incorporate their own lived experiences/ geographies (Cahill, 2007). It also involves a braiding of traditional and innovative methods that speak to local conditions (Cammarota & Fine, 2008). YPAR has become an increasing part of school curricula designed to promote sustainable school and community improvements (Barton, 2001; Hughes, 2003; McIntyre, 2000).

This research (see also O'Neill, in press[a]) involved an interrelated program and study component with 12 middle school learners during weekly 90-minute sessions over a 12-week period. The learners engaged in reflections, inquiry, and actions related to why they valued participation in music. Four youth-led inquiry projects were worked on collaboratively with each other, a teacher, and two researchers. We asked our young participants to *think* about their musical world and all the music activities they are involved in, what matters to them and why, what got them started and keeps them interested, what benefits they get out of being involved in music, and their struggles and passions. They were asked to *identify* and choose one thing to focus on, such as an issue/problem/question that might help music learners feel one or more of the following: connected, valued, better prepared, successful, motivated, inspired, and treated equally. In the second stage, the learners were asked to *research* their focus area by locating, selecting, and gathering information and evidence. In the third stage, the learners processed the information and evidence through analysis, evaluation, testing, sorting, and synthesizing. And in the last stage, they were asked to revise, present, reflect, and transfer their findings to others by disseminating their new understandings. And ultimately, they were asked to *advocate* their main findings by selecting a key message and devising and executing a plan for getting the message out to those they felt needed to hear it if they were to promote positive change.

We videotaped each session and examined the processes the learners engaged in over the course of each project. Each project was unique and is briefly summarized here (see also Erickson, 2012). *Project A*: This group decided to deliver a motivational/ inspirational message to other music students at their school by performing and creating their own original choreography to the song "Don't Stop Believing." *Project B*: This group consisted of soundtrack recording musicians who performed and recorded the title sound track for the mini-documentary that the full group of participants later produced. *Project C*: This group designed questions and interviewed members of a local rock band about how these musicians were inspired to write music and how they managed to keep their band working together. *Project D*: This group recorded the responses of teachers, staff, and students at the school to the question: "Why does music matter to you?" The final result from these four projects was the collaborative creation of a mini-documentary and music advocacy video.

This short film led to an unexpected and dramatic outcome. Shortly after the study had been concluded, the authorities at this school decided to close down the popular music program, which was a favorite music program among many of our young participants. As is frequently the case, the administration was trying to save money and did not consider the impact this decision would have on students at the school. The music teacher told us that some of the learners were traumatized by this unforeseen and highly regrettable incident. On their own initiative, our young participants decided to post an edited version of their mini-documentary on YouTube, which they called "Music Matters." This video was watched by a number of people from the local community who were aware of and outraged by the decision of school officials to close down the popular music program. Eventually, our participants' youth-led music advocacy drew local media attention. As a result, the administrators involved in closing down the program invited the young participants in our research to visit the local school district office and present their case for keeping the popular music program, which was soon after reinstated.

The impact these projects had on the young people involved is reflected in one student's reflection at the end of the program: "Thank you for giving me the chance to make a difference." Erickson (2012), the teacher-researcher on this project, summed up the students' experiences as follows:

> The sense of empowerment conveyed by this "gift of chance" is the kind of "problem-posing" education to which Paolo Freire ([1970]2008) refers, "responding to the essence of consciousness—*intentionality*" (p. 79). By this student "being *conscious of*" her actions as making a difference in her own life and in the lives of others, this serves as a gently understated example of Freire's goal of "liberating education"

and how both teacher and student "become jointly responsible for a process in which all grow. (p. 80)

In a follow-up study of the learners in this program a year later, they identified the following features as important for helping them gain deep, meaningful, and transformative experiences from their engagement in the program:

1. Consistency of the program over time;
2. Being given time to reflect on what mattered to them;
3. Being interviewed about something they loved to do;
4. Having older, experienced musical mentors responding to their interests;
5. Meeting others who were new and different from themselves, from both inside and outside the school community, who were united by a common interest in the music; and
6. Having the opportunity to do something that made a positive impact in the real world.

According to their teacher-researcher,

the project succeeded partly because it was able to engage students whose musical identities did not reside solely in "school music," yet these "outside" passions somehow found a way "inside." The students' positive perceptions of their engagement in the project emphasizes the notion that music programs designed to "engage the individual interests of our students, while findings ways to connect these "selves" to a greater community that helps them become who they are, should be a presiding goal for music education. In this way, music can truly *matter*. (Erickson, 2012, p. 148)

CONCLUSION

Youth empowerment is based on the assumption that youth should have a voice in issues that interest or matter to them and concern them, and they should be part of the decisions that affect them. Realizing the potential of youth empowerment through transformative music engagement requires a continual process of conceptualizing how we might create expansive music learning opportunities within a social justice orientation that guide youth toward developing their self-knowledge, supportive learning relationships, distinctive voices, and the capacity to express and redefine what interests and matters to them "as actions in pursuit of social justice" (Cammarota & Fine, 2008, p. 6). The affordances of transformative music engagement inform and support each other and are united through a theoretical orientation that focuses on agentive and integrated actions or dialogical encounters within multiple learning spaces and places, with the aim of optimizing youth voices, wellbeing, and musical flourishing. It requires a consideration of what is needed for young musicians to become deeply, purposefully, and meaningfully engaged in the process of music learning by aligning the strengths or potentials for positive change of individuals and contexts. It does this through a process of experiential, learner-centered, emergent, and lived curricula and transformative pedagogies that enable and encourage youth empowerment whereby young people are guided to undertake their own engaged praxis through reflection, dialogue, appreciative inquiry, and action (O'Neill, 2012). In this way we provide young people with the kinds of learning opportunities that are capable of helping them to recognize, question, challenge, and transform unjust practices and generate greater social justice. As Schwarzer, Bloom, and Shono (2006) point out, we "cannot directly empower others," but we can provide opportunities for fostering "self-empowerment" or "social empowerment" by "freeing individuals from directives and inviting them to take control" (p. xxviii). Transformative music engagement is a dynamic and interactive approach to providing music learning opportunities for youth to recognize, understand, and overcome some of the challenges and constraints within their own musical and personal lives, and to invite them to take control and realize the power of their own efforts to explore untapped potential and enact positive change through existing conditions of possibility along their music learning pathways.

REFERENCES

Ansdell, G., & DeNora, T. (2012). Musical flourishing: Community music therapy, controversy, and the cultivation of wellbeing. In R. A. R. MacDonald, G. Kreutz, & L. Mitchell (Eds.), *Music, health, and wellbeing* (pp. 97–112). New York: Oxford University Press.

Arnot, M., & Reay, D. (2007). A sociology of pedagogic voice: Power, inequality and pupil consultation. *Discourse: Studies in the Cultural Politics of Education, 28*(3), 311–325.

Barnett, R. (2012). The coming of the ecological learner. In P. Tynjälä, M-L. Stenström, & M. Saarnivaara (Eds.), *Transitions and transformations in learning and education* (pp. 9–20). New York: Springer. doi: 10.1007/978-94-007-2312-2_2.

Barton, A. C. (2001). Science education in urban settings: Seeking new ways of praxis through critical ethnography. *Journal of Research in Science Teaching, 38*(8), 899–917.

Bauman, Z. (2000). *Liquid modernity.* Cambridge, MA: Polity Press.

Bernstein, B. (1971). *Class, codes and control: Theoretical studies towards a sociology of language.* London: Routledge & Kegan Paul.

Biesta, G. (2004). The community of those who have nothing in common: Education and the language of responsibility. *Interchange, 35*(3), 307–324.

Blanchet-Cohen, N., Linds, W., Mann-Feder, V., & Yuen, F. (2013). Introduction to the special issue on transforming practices: Emancipatory approaches to youth engagement. *International Journal of Child, Youth and Family Studies, 3,* 320–327.

Boggiano, A. K., & Katz, P. (1991). Maladaptive achievement patterns in students: The role teachers' controlling strategies. *Journal of Social Issues, 47*(4), 35–51.

Buber, M. (1958). *I and thou* (R. G. Smith, trans.). New York: Charles Scribner's Sons.

Cahill, C. (2007). Doing research with young people: Participatory research and the rituals of collective work. *Children's Geographies, 5*(3), 297–312.

Cameron, D., Frazer, E., Harvey, P., Rampton B., & Richardson K. (1992). *Researching language: Issues of power and method.* London: Routledge.

Cammarota, J., & Fine, M. (2008). *Revolutionizing education: Youth participatory action research in motion.* New York & London: Routledge.

Coleman, J. (2012). Introduction: Digital technologies in the lives of young people. *Oxford Review of Education, 38*(1), 1–8. doi: 10.1080/03054985.2011.577937.

Cummins, J. (2001). *Negotiating identities: Education for empowerment in a diverse society.* Los Angeles: California Association for Bilingual Education.

Davis, S. G. (2012). Instrumental ensemble learning and performance in primary and elementary schools. In G. E. McPherson & G. Welch (Eds.), *The Oxford handbook of music education* (Vol. 1, pp. 417–434). New York: Oxford University Press.

Denner, J., Meyer, B., & Bean, S. (2005). Young women's leadership alliance: Youth-adult partnerships in an all-female after-school program. *Journal of Community Psychology, 33*(1), 87–100.

Ellsworth, E. (1989). Why doesn't this feel empowering? Working through the repressive myths of critical pedagogy. *Harvard Educational Review, 59*(3), 297–324.

Engeström, Y., & Sannino, A. (2010). Studies of expansive learning: Foundations, findings and future challenges. *Educational Research Review, 5*(1), 1–24.

Erickson, D. (2012). Music that matters: Reconceptualizing curriculum for the enhancement of self and others through personalized learning and youth participatory action research. In S. A. O'Neill (Series Ed. & Vol. Ed.), *Research to practice,* Vol. 5: *Personhood and music learning: Connecting perspectives and narratives* (pp. 135–152). Waterloo, ON: Canadian Music Educators' Association.

Erickson, D., O'Neill, S. A., & Senyshyn, Y. (2012). *Youth-led participatory action research: Building purpose through personalized music learning.* Paper presented to the Conference on Music Learning: Benefits for the 21st Century Learner, Laval University, Québec, Canada.

Erickson, D., O'Neill, S. A., & Senyshyn, Y. (2013). *Beyond Music Matters: A follow-up study of secondary school students' experiences of transformative music learning during middle school.* Poster presented at the Annual Conference of the Canadian Society for the Study of Education (CSSE), University of Victoria, Victoria, British Columbia, Canada.

Erstad, O. (2012). The learning lives of digital youth: Beyond the formal and informal. *Oxford Review of Education, 38*(1), 25–43. doi: 10.1080/03054985.2011.577940.

Fielding, M. (2004). Transformative approaches to student voice: Theoretical underpinnings, recalcitrant realities. *British Educational Research Journal, 30*(2), 295–311.

Finney, J., & Harrison, C. (2010). *Whose music education is it? The role of the student voice.* Solihull, West Midlands, UK: National Association of Music Educators.

Flutter, J. (2010). International perspectives on the students' voices movement: Sonorities in a changing world. In J. Finney & C. Harrison (eds.), *Whose music education is it? The role of the student voice* (pp. 16–23). Solihull, West Midlands, UK: National Association of Music Educators.

Freire, P. (1970). *Pedagogy of the oppressed.* New York: Continuum.

Freire, P. (1973). *Education for critical consciousness.* New York: Seabury Press.

Freire, P. (2008). The "banking" concept of education. In D. Bartholomae & A. Petrosky (Eds.), *Ways of reading* (8th ed., pp. 242–254). Boston: Bedford-St. Martins.

Furlong, J., & Davies, C. (2012). Young people, new technologies and learning at home: Taking context seriously. *Oxford Review of Education, 31*(1), 45–62. doi: 10.1080/03054985.2011.577944.

Gergen, K. J., Gergen, M. M., & Barrett, F. J. (2004). Dialogue: Life and death of the organization. In D. Grant, C. Hardy, C. Oswick & L. Putnam (Eds.), *The SAGE handbook of organizational discourse* (pp. 39–60). London: SAGE.

Gieve, S., & Magalhães, I. (1994). On empowerment. In S. Gieve & I. Magalhães (Eds.), *Occasional Report 6: Power, Ethics and Validity* (pp. 121–145). Lancaster: Centre for Research in Language Education.

Giroux, H. A. (1994). *Disturbing pleasures: Learning popular culture.* New York: Routledge.

Giroux, H. A., Lankshear, C., McLaren, P., & Peters, M. (1996). *Counternarratives: Cultural studies and critical pedagogies in postmodern spaces.* New York: Routledge.

Hargreaves, A. (2001). Emotional geographies of teaching. *Teachers College Record, 103*(6), 1056–1080.

Harlen, W., & Deakin Crick, R. (2003). Testing and motivation for learning. *Assessment in Education, 10*(2), 169–208.

Harwood, E., & Marsh, K. (2012). Children's ways of learning inside and outside the classroom. In G. E. McPherson & G. Welch (Eds.), *The Oxford handbook of music education* (Vol. 1, pp. 163–186). New York: Oxford University Press.

Hughes, J. N. (2003). Commentary: Participatory action research leads to sustainable school and community improvement. *School Psychology Review, 32*(1), 38–43.

Itin, C. M. (1999). Reasserting the philosophy of experiential education as a vehicle for change in the 21st century. *Journal of Experiential Education, 22*(2), 91–98. doi: 10.1177/105382599902200206.

Jennings, L. B., Parra-Medina, D. M., Hilfinger Messias, D. K., & McLoughlin, K. (2006). Toward a critical social theory of youth empowerment. *Journal of Community Practice, 14*(1/2), 31–55.

Kincheloe, J. L. (2008). *Critical pedagogy primer* (2nd ed.). New York: Peter Lang.

Kleiber, D. (1999). *A dialectical interpretations: Leisure experience and human development.* New York: Basic Books.

Kohfeldt, D., Chhun L., Grace, S., & Langhout, R. D. (2011). Youth empowerment in context: Exploring tensions in school-based yPAR. *American Journal of Community Psychology, 47*, 28–45. doi 10.1007/s10464-010-9376-z.

Langhout, R. D., & Mitchell, C. A. (2008). Engaging contexts: Drawing the link between student and teacher experiences of the hidden curriculum. *Journal of Community and Applied Social Psychology, 18*, 593–614.

Larson, R. W. (2011). Positive development in a disorderly world. *Journal of Research on Adolescence, 21*(2), 317–334.

Lerner, R. M., Brentano, C., Dowling, E. M., & Anderson, P. M. (2002). Positive youth development: Thriving as a basis of personhood and civil society. *New Directions for Youth Development, 95*, 11–33.

Longworth, N. (2013). *Lifelong learning in action: Transforming education in the 21st century.* New York: Routledge.

McIntyre, A. (2000). Constructing meaning about violence, school, and community: Participatory action research with Urban Youth. *Urban Review, 32*(2), 123–154.

McQuillan, P. J. (2005). Possibilities and pitfalls: A comparative analysis of student empowerment. *American Educational Research Journal, 42*(4), 639–670.

Meyer, J. H. F., Land, R., & Baillie, C. (2010). *Threshold concepts and transformational learning.* Rotterdam, The Netherlands: Sense Publishers.

Mezirow, J. (1991). *Transformative dimensions of adult learning.* San Francisco: Jossey-Bass.

O'Neill, S. A. (1999). Flow theory and the development of musical performance skills. *Bulletin of the Council for Research in Music Education, 141*, 129–134.

O'Neill, S. A. (2005). Youth music engagement in diverse contexts. In J. L. Mahoney, R. W. Larson, & J. S. Eccles (Eds.), *Organized activities as contexts of development: Extracurricular activities, after-school and community programs* (pp. 255–273). Mahwah, NJ: Lawrence Erlbaum Associates.

O'Neill, S. A. (2006). Positive youth musical engagement. In G. McPherson (Ed.), *The child as musician: A handbook of musical development* (pp. 461–474). Oxford: Oxford University Press.

O'Neill, S. A. (2011). Developing a young musician's growth mindset: The role of motivation, self-theories and resiliency. In I. Deliège & J. Davidson (Eds.), *Music and the mind: Essays in honour of John Sloboda* (pp. 31–46). Oxford: Oxford University Press.

O'Neill, S. A. (2012). Becoming a music learner: Towards a theory of transformative music engagement. In G. E. McPherson & G. Welch (Eds.), *The Oxford handbook of music education* (Vol. 1, pp. 163–186). New York: Oxford University Press.

O'Neill, S. A. (in press[a]). Transformative music engagement and musical flourishing. In G. E. McPherson (Ed.), *The child as musician* (2nd ed.). New York: Oxford University Press.

O'Neill, S. A. (in press[b]). Young people's musical lives: Identities, learning ecologies and connectedness. In R. A. R. MacDonald, D. J. Hargreaves, & D. Meill (Eds.), *Oxford handbook of musical identities*. Oxford: Oxford University Press.

O'Neill, S. A., & McPherson, G. E. (2002). Motivation. In R. Parncutt & G. E. McPherson (eds), *The science and psychology of music performance: Creative strategies for teaching and learning* (pp. 31–46). Oxford: Oxford University Press.

O'Neill, S. A., & Senyshyn, Y. (2011). How learning theories shape our understanding of music learners. In R. Colwell & P. Webster (Eds.), *MENC handbook of research in music learning, Vol. 1: Strategies* (pp. 3–34). New York: Oxford University Press.

O'Neill, S. A. (2014). Mind the gap: Transforming music engagement through learner-centred informal music learning. *The Recorder: Journal of the Ontario Music Educators' Association, 56*(2), 18–22.

Ozer, E. J., Ritterman, M. L., & Wanis, M. G. (2010). Participatory action research (PAR) in middle school: Opportunities, constraints, and key processes. *American Journal of Community Psychology, 46*, 152–166. doi: 10.1007/s10464-010-9335-8.

Perkins, D. F., Borden, L. M., Keith, J. G., Hoppe-Rooney, T. L., & Villarruel, F. A. (2003). Community youth development: Partnership creating a positive world. In F. A. Villarruel, D. F. Perkins, L. M. Borden, & J. G. Keith, (Eds.), *Community youth development: programs, policies, and practices* (pp. 1–24). London: SAGE.

Pittman, K. J. (1992). *Defining the fourth R: Promoting youth development*. Washington, DC: Center for Youth Development and Policy Research.

Rappaport, J. (1981). In praise of paradox: A social policy of empowerment over prevention. *American Journal of Community Psychology, 9*(1), 1–25.

Romanish, B. (1991). *Empowering teachers: Restructuring schools for the 21st century*. Lanham, MD: University Press of America.

Rudduck, J. (2007). Student voice, student engagement, and school reform. In D. Thiessen & A. Cook-Sather (Eds.), *International handbook of student experience in elementary and secondary school* (pp. 587–610). Dordrecht, The Netherlands: Springer.

Rudduck, J., & Fielding, M. (2006). Student voice and the perils of popularity. *Educational Review, 58*(2), 171–181.

Sarason, S. B. (1990). *The predictable failure of educational reform*. San Francisco, CA: Jossey-Bass.

Sarkissian, W., Hurford, D., & Wenman, C. (2010). Transformative engagement methods for working at the edge. London & Washington, DC: Earthscan.

Sefton-Green J. (2008). Informal learning; a solution in search of a problem. In K. Drotner, H. S. Jensen, & K. C. Schroder (Eds.), *Informal learning and digital media* (pp. 238–255). Newcastle, UK: Cambridge Scholars Press.

Schwarzer, D., Bloom, M., & Shono, S. (2006). *Research as a tool for empowerment: Theory informing practice*. Charlotte, NC: Information Age Publishing.

Sefa Dei, G. J. (2003). Schooling and the dilemma of youth disengagement. *McGill Journal of Education, 38*(2), 241–256.

Spruce, G., & Odena, O. (2012). Music learning and teaching during adolescence: Ages 12–18. In G. E. McPherson & G. Welch (Eds.), *The Oxford handbook of music education, Vol. 1* (pp. 437–440). New York: Oxford University Press.

Stipek, D. (2002). Good instruction is motivating. In A. Wigfield & J. Eccles (Eds.), *Development of achievement motivation* (pp. 309–332). San Diego, CA: Academic Press.

Tan. L. (2009). The 5 E's of emancipatory pedagogy: The rehumanizing approach to teaching and learning with inner-city youth. In W. Ayers, R. Quinn & S. David (Eds.), *Handbook of social justice in education*. New York: Routledge.

Toshalis, E., & Nakkula, M. J. (2012). *Motivation, engagement, and student voice: The students at the center series*. Boston, MA: Jobs for the Future.

Turley, S. (1994). *"The way teachers teach is, like, totally whacked": The student voice on classroom practice*. Paper presented at the Annual Meeting of the American Educational Research Association, New Orleans, LA.

Villarruel, F. A., Perkins, D. F., Borden, L. M., & Keith, J. G. (Eds.) (2003). *Community youth development: Programs, policies, and practices*. London: Sage.

Wallerstein, N., Sanchez-Merki, V., & Verlade, L. (2005). Freirian praxis in health education and community organizing: A case study of an adolescent prevention program. In M. Minkler (Ed.), *Community organizing and community building for health* (2nd ed.). New Brunswick, NJ: Rutgers University Press.

Wang, M. C., Haertel, G. D., & Walberg, H. J. (1997). Fostering educational resilience in inner-city schools. *Children and Youth, 7*, 119–140.

Zyngier, D. (2003). Connectedness—isn't it time that education came out from behind the classroom door and rediscovered social justice. *Social Alternatives, 22*(3), 41–49.

Zyngier, D. (2004). *Doing education not doing time: Engaging pedagogies and pedagogues—what does student engagement look like?* Paper presented at the International Education Research Conference, Melbourne.

CHAPTER 25

YOU GOTTA FIGHT THE POWER

The Place of Music in Social Justice Education

GLORIA LADSON-BILLINGS

INTRODUCTION

I begin this chapter with a caveat—indeed, several caveats. I am not a music educator, music historian, or ethnomusicologist. I am a former history teacher with a specialization in the history of African Americans and a love for music. I have never taught a class where music was not a significant part of its conception and development. My road to this particular chapter is less about my credentials as a musician than it is about my understanding of how music has been pivotal in telling the history of a people who have suffered profound oppression and exclusion. This chapter looks specifically at the role of hip-hop culture in social justice education and its potential for improving urban education. I make this argument by demonstrating how hip-hop finds its origins in community struggle and protest, rather than the glamorization and valorization of antisocial and hyper-capitalist behaviors that demean and denigrate women, LGBT community members, and peaceful solutions to social and community conflict.

This chapter addresses the ways that youth culture, specifically hip-hop, can be used as a rubric for what we identify in the literature as culturally relevant pedagogy (Ladson-Billings, 2014) by taking a brief look at the history of Black music, the epistemic rupture that occurred in youth culture, hip-hop as social justice praxis, and hip-hop as a form of culturally relevant pedagogy.

A NECESSARILY BRIEF HISTORY
OF BLACK MUSIC

What follows is a necessarily brief discussion of the relationship between the African American struggle for liberation and the music that emerged because of and alongside that struggle. The story of African Americans and liberation movements is long and impressive. From their initial capture on the continent of Africa to the remarkable accomplishment of governing the nation, African American culture writ large has found a way to use music to advance important and life-affirming causes. Social justice was rarely an afterthought. There are well-documented examples of songs, chants, and drumming as a way to communicate the pain, pathos, and plans of the enslaved African as she or he worked for freedom and liberation (). Songs like "Wade in the Water," "Swing Low Sweet Chariot," or "Follow the Drinking Gourd" signaled multiple meanings and alerted enslaved communities about various liberation activities.

In a concise history of rock 'n' roll, Michael Ventura (1985) describes the activities of enslaved Africans in New Orleans as they gathered on Sundays at Congo Square to express themselves culturally and to encourage each other to continue to strive for liberation and real freedom—either in this world or the next. Ritual and music from Africa survived throughout the Caribbean and South Africa where Blacks made and played drums. However, in the United States (with the exception of New Orleans) the African drum was banned. The captors did not understand the drum signals, but they did recognize the drum as subversive and central to an underground communication. In New Orleans, slave owners felt it harmless to allow the slaves to "blow off steam" via their drumming and dancing. That little African "survival" proved to be a powerful weapon for both advancing the artistic culture *and* promoting liberation.

Despite the attempt to disconnect enslaved Africans from their culture and traditions, the Africans found ways to transpose and appropriate what White society gave them—a new religion—into a form of resistance through music. It would be incorrect to assume that the music forms made in the Americas were the only forms enslaved Africans knew. Prior to enslavement, the sounds and rhythms of the African continent suffused the lives of the initial captives, and they passed on their musical traditions ("Fisk Jubilee Singers," digital history, retrieved June 6, 2014, from http://www.digitalhistory.uh.edu/index.cfm).

The work songs of plantation workers and African Americans searching for God created a song form that both explored their condition and sought relief in the hope of a world beyond this one. But plantation work songs and spirituals were not merely songs about the present pain or a pie-in-the-sky hopefulness. Those songs were also songs of liberation and escape (Lawrence-McIntyre, 1987). Songs such as "Follow the Drinking Gourd," "Swing Low, Sweet Chariot," or "Steal Away" held dual meanings and were regularly used to aid in escape from slavery. These songs predate both the blues and gospel genres of African American music. In their own way they laid the foundation for

African American music as a form of social protest and social justice (Thomas, 2001). By the time the *maafa* (the word for the Black holocaust of enslavement) ended, by way of a bloody Civil War, spirituals were a regular form of worship music closely associated with the African American experience.

From the spirituals of enslaved Africans came another music form known as blues music.[1] Like the spirituals before them, the blues was often associated with hard labor and struggle. After Emancipation, the newly freed former slaves found themselves without the proper economic and social infrastructure to prosper in a nation that was reaping the fruits of the Industrial Revolution. Without education, capital, or societal support, the only option for many of the formerly enslaved was the sharecropping system. This system relied on keeping African Americans ignorant and bolstering the power of White supremacy to compel African Americans to remain in subservient roles. Even though they were nominally "free" according to the federal laws, many of the former slaves of the South found themselves working the same plantations they worked before the Civil War, and for little or no money. This system was a perfect environment for the growth of the music form known as the blues (Oakley, 1997). The blues emerges from spirituals, works songs, field hollers, and chants, and is famous for its 12-bar chord progressions and minor third to major third flattening or bending of notes. However, more significant than its technical form is the meaning and substance associated with the genre.

Despite the birth of the blues in the Deep South, in places like the Mississippi Delta, the Great Migration that coincided with the United States' entrance into World War I brought the blues to cities like St. Louis, Kansas City, and Chicago. Singers like Ma Rainey and Bessie Smith worked the Black vaudeville circuit of Northern cities in the 1920s (Oakley, 1997; Hazzard-Gordon, 1990), but this music, unlike the spirituals that preceded it, was more about individual pain and suffering. The spirituals almost always spoke to the collective suffering of the people. The blues seemed to turn more inward to the personal and individualistic longings of a people who could see the American Dream but could not really touch it.

Out of the blues came a music form we think of as "rhythm and blues" (R&B), or "soul" music, along with jazz. The term was originally used to describe the music that recording companies intended to market to African American audiences in cities. Because African Americans were quickly migrating to urban industrial centers like Chicago, Detroit, New York, Philadelphia, and Los Angeles in the 1920s and 1930s, a new market emerged for blues and jazz. The invention and wide dissemination of radio brought music into the average person's household; but it was clear that the music itself was segregated on the radio dial. Black music, or what was then known as "race music," lived at the weaker higher frequencies on stations that catered to the Black community. Soul singers like Sam Cooke, Lloyd Price, Hank Ballard, Etta James, and eventually James Brown reached their audiences via "Black" radio during the 1950s and 1960s.

By the 1960s, music entrepreneur Berry Gordon created a new sound that merged the grittiness of Detroit's union sensibilities and a "smoother," more "palatable" sound that allowed Black performers to "cross over" and reach White audiences. Acts like the Supremes, Martha and the Vandellas, the Miracles, and the Temptations fused a steady blues backbeat with lush orchestral arrangements. Their popularity transcended Black audiences as they received airplay on "Top 40" stations. However, despite the growing popularity of "the Motown Sound," there was another parallel strain of Black music that was emerging along with the changing and volatile times of the 1960s.

THE EPISTEMIC RUPTURE

A tool of the historian is something called "periodization." Through it, historians examine patterns and themes to determine how seemingly disjoint people, places, and events may cohere in order to tell a compelling narrative. For instance, from 1492 to the early 1600s in the Americas we talk about the "Age of Exploration." The late 1600s to the end of the American Revolution is known as the "Colonial Period," and the decade before the Great Depression is called the "Roaring Twenties." Although familiar to most educated people, these are terms crafted by historians. People living during these time periods did not identify with these labels. One such period in more recent history is the 1960s, or what some call the "Antiwar Era," the "Civil Rights Era," or the "Era of Social Unrest." Having grown up in that time period, I am certain no one said, "We are in the Civil Rights Era."

One of the ways that historical periods or eras emerge is through a cataclysmic event or a decidedly new way of thinking. Kuhn (1996) argues that these new ways of thinking (that are always challenging to an established order) are what lead to scientific revolutions. Wynter (1984) calls these shifts "epistemic ruptures."

In modern contexts, epistemic ruptures have occurred with the invention of the television or the advent of space flight. Both caused us to think differently about who we are and how we would function on the planet. From a different perspective, the emergence of HIV/AIDS in the 1980s forced us to see a population in a qualitatively different way and to ask questions about who we would include in the human family. In the 1960s we experienced epistemic ruptures on a variety of fronts—race, class, and gender. The development of the birth control pill forced a fundamental shift in the way women thought about their sexuality and the possibility of reproductive freedom. The entire 1960s era was seen as a time of rebellion and challenge to established rules and social mores. Songs of rebellion and challenge were on the radio airways.

For White audiences, songs like Don McLean's "Bye Bye Miss American Pie" and "Abraham, Martin, and John," spoke to their antiwar sentiments. Black people, however, were deeply entrenched in a civil rights struggle that found little legitimacy among a White mainstream. Activists like Vernon Johns, Martin Luther King, Jr., Fred Shuttlesworth, C. T. Vivien, Wyatt Tee Walker, Ella Baker, Daisy Bates, Septima Clark, and Rosa Parks were mature, "respectable adults," not a bunch of college kids. They needed a different kind of music to reach their masses and they used the music they knew best—the music of the church.

Before each mass meeting in Southern churches, a group of young singers would emerge to prepare the crowd. People like the young Bernice Reagon (later of Sweet Honey and the Rock) would take a familiar gospel song and give it a civil rights lyric, creating a new genre that we now call "Freedom Songs." For example, the song, "Ain't Gonna Let Nobody Turn Me Round" was initially a song that spoke to marching up to heaven. However, in the midst of the movement, the singers had the masses marching up to "freedom land!" Or, the anthem of the movement, "We Shall Overcome," had already come out of the church as a part of a garment workers strike (Adams, 2013); instead of overcoming the present world on a journey to heaven, people sang of overcoming the injustices of this world. The people who were used to singing, "I woke up this morning with my mind stayed on Jesus" were now singing, "I woke up this morning with my mind stayed on freedom." The melodies were the same and most of the words were the same, and the slight changes in lyrics gave the Civil Rights movement the veneer of a holy war.

It would be wrong to presume that Black popular music did not pick up on the changing tenor of the times. Even though Motown had created a broadly popular sound that continued to sing happy love songs ("Can't Hurry Love," "Baby Love," "Dancing in the Streets," etc.), there were artists who were beginning to weave songs of protest, civil rights, antiwar, Black Power, and Black pride. Curtis Mayfield and the Impressions sang "Keep on Pushing" and "People Get Ready" to signal the need for forward movement and racial uplift. James Brown declared that Black people should "Say it Loud, I'm Black and I'm Proud." Irwin Starr brought the community "War . . . What Is It Good For?" and later (1971) Marvin Gaye would challenge the Motown brand by releasing "What's Going On?" an album that spoke to antiwar, poverty, drug use, and ecology. While the 1980s saw Donna Summers, The Jackson 5, and others focus on dancing and away from social concerns, at this same time there was a nascent group of organic music makers emerging in the housing projects of the Bronx (and later Harlem), in New York City, who were doing something new. This new thing would be called "hip-hop."

HIP-HOP EVOLVES

Given the ubiquitous nature of personal music today, via smart phones, iPods, iPads, and other MP3 players, it may seem difficult to imagine the days of loud "public" music through boom boxes, where urban youth strolled the streets with a heavy machine perched on their shoulders blasting their favorite songs. In late 1970s and early 1980s, those with the largest boxes earned the most respect, or "street cred." To enhance their reputations, groups of youth like the Ghetto Boys began connecting up larger and larger amplifiers to instruments and speakers to host block parties, mixing samples of existing records and shouting over portions of the songs. The DJs (or record sampler-spinners) would pay close attention to the crowds and continually repeat those portions of songs that seemed to excite and rev them up. While the recorded music was initially the focus of the parties, slowly but surely the voice-overs or MCs began to take on more prominence. Their talk over the songs became known as "rap," and many would begin to call the entire genre "rap" (or "rap music") (Chang, 2005). For years, these block parties were neighborhood events where word of mouth and handmade flyers let partygoers know where the action was.

Those who know little of the hip-hop cultural phenomenon believe that it is synonymous with rap; but while rap is hip-hop, hip-hop is a cultural movement that incorporates a variety of elements. Like Art Deco or mid-century modern design styles, there are parts of hip-hop that extend beyond the more recognizable element of rap music. The four main elements are tagging (graffiti art), b-boying (break dancing,), DJ-ing (spinning and scratching records), and emcee-ing (MC-ing) or rapping. Other elements include written and spoken word and style (e.g., clothing and other objects of fashion).

The roots of hip-hop come from a variety of African-influenced musical styles—gospel, blues, jazz, and R&B, calypso, salsa, ska, and reggae—and although most popular music historians start with sounds that came out of the South Bronx, in New York City, the story of hip-hop is not a linear one (Chang, 2005). As stated earlier, music as a form of Black resistance permeates institutions everywhere—the church, the clubs, the mainstream music industry—and makes its way throughout the world.[2]

Some scholars argue that the first documented example of hip-hop harkens back to 1925 when a dancer named Earl Tucker (a.k.a. "Snake Hips") performed at the Cotton Club in Harlem and invented dance moves that looked strikingly similar to later day break-dancing (Wintz & Finkelman, 2004; Hazzard-Gordon, 1990,). Another early indication of the longevity of the music forms shows up in 1940, when a Chinese Jamaican hardware merchant named Tom Wong (a.k.a. Tom the Great) played music from US artists on a booming sound system to steal dance hall patrons from local bands. In 1950, Clement "Sir Coxsone" Dodd engaged in a sound clash battle with Duke Reid to initiate DJ battling (Katz, 2004). In 1962, James Brown recorded live during his Apollo Theater concert where his drummer, Clayton Fillyau, influenced a sound known as the "break beat" that would later form the basic rhythm for break dancing (Payne, 2006).

In 1967 a young Jamaican immigrant, Clive Campbell, introduced the portable music scene to the West Bronx, and with a powerful sound system he dubbed himself "DJ Kool Herc" and laid the foundation for what we now know as hip-hop. Kool Herc was known for parties at the recreation room of his family's apartment on Sedgwick Avenue. Unlike other DJs who merely played a steady stream of songs, Kool Herc paid close attention to the dancers and used two turntables to switch back and forth and repeat sections of a song that the crowd seemed to like and began toasting or shouting out over the songs to increase the crowd's enthusiasm.

As the popularity of DJ Kool Herc's parties grew, they migrated to the streets, where he employed other MCs like Coke La Rock and Clark Kent to serve as emcees. It is at this point that the toasting expands to poetry and rapping. Kool Herc became something of a hero to two young men who became known as Afrika Bambaataa (Kevin Donovan) and Grandmaster Flash (Joseph Saddler), who are considered the godfathers of hip-hop. Bambaataa was a member of a street gang, the Spades, but he used his newfound interest in music to bring peace to the streets. According to Steven Hager (1982),

> For over five years the Bronx had lived in constant terror of street gangs. Suddenly, in 1975, they disappeared almost as quickly as they had arrived. This happened because something better came along to replace the gangs. That something was eventually called hip-hop. (p. 69)

Grandmaster Flash and his MCs, the Furious Five, were able to play to packed houses at the Audubon Ballroom in Manhattan, but nervous venue owners forced the DJs back to the clubs, community centers, and high school gyms of the Bronx. Grandmaster Flash used his father's collection of music and his knowledge of electronics to create new forms of DJ-ing called punch phrasing, scratching, and beat box. This form of hip-hop moved through houses and street parties until the 1980s, when hip-hop found its way to the first radio show, "Mr. Magic's Rap Attack," which premiered on WBLS in New York City.

Over the next 20 years, hip-hop would shift and morph into different styles and across racial, gender, and cultural lines. Sugar Hill Records, which was the premier label of hip-hop, died but was replaced by Def Jam Records. Female rappers like Salt-N-Pepa, Queen Latifah, and MC Lyte broke hip-hop's glass ceiling and made it easier for artists like Mary J. Blige and Lauryn Hill. Public Enemy brought a decidedly Black Nationalist flavor to hip-hop and the genre began expanding from the northeast United States to its West Coast. By 1988, hip-hop became a part of the music video scene with the show "Yo! MTV Raps."

Before long, hip-hop artists like Ice T, Snoop Doggy Dog (now just Snoop Dog or Snoop Lion) introduced gangsta rap, which glorified gang violence, drugs, and misogyny. However, alongside gangsta rap there emerged artists more interested in sociopolitical statements and Black pride. Some of the popular artists who embraced what was termed "conscious rap" were Wu Tang Clan, Tupac Shakur (2Pac), N.W.A., KRS-One, and Mos Def. Although Michael Eric Dyson argues that conscious rap gets little air play, many in the mainstream audience cannot deny having heard Public Enemy's pulsating rhythm of "Fight the Power" in Spike Lee's classic film *Do the Right Thing*, or Coolio's "Gangsta's Paradise" in the film *Dangerous Minds*.

Public Broadcast System's "Independent Lens" produced a critical film titled *Beyond Beats and Rhymes* (Hurt, 2006), which it accompanied with a website (http://www.pbs.org/independentlens/hiphop/film.htm) that includes a link that creates a periodization (by decades), which I referenced earlier when describing the work of the historian. Independent Lens divides the modern hip-hop movement into the following: the 1970s: The Early Years; the 1980s: The Rise to Radio; the 1990s: From Conscious Rap to Gangsta Rap; and the 2000s: Bestsellers and Bling. Some of the key events in the 1970s include the release of debut recording by "The Last Poets" spoken word collective that mixed music and politically conscious poetry, as well as the rise of the block party and the DJ. The decade ended with the release of The Sugar Hill Gang's "Rapper's

Delight." In the 1980s Kurtis Blow became the first "rapper" to earn a national audience by appearing on the popular televised dance program, "Soul Train." At the end of the 1980s, "rap" received its own Grammy category, but awards to artists in this category were not broadcast along with the mainstream Grammy awards. Although the 1990s hip-hop era opened with the arrest of the members of 2 Live Crew for explicit and lewd lyrics, the 1991 video recording of Los Angeles police officers savagely beating motorist Rodney King, a Black man, sparked both unrest in Los Angeles and hip-hop artists who were willing to speak against the police. When the not-guilty verdict against the police who beat Rodney King was handed down, hip-hop artists like Ice T and Public Enemy's Chuck D were asked to comment to the media, making them de facto spokespeople for the African American community—rather than more established (and perhaps more respectable) civil rights leaders from organizations like the NAACP, the Urban League, Operation PUSH, and the Southern Christian Leadership Conference (SCLC). In the meantime, Dr. Dre and Suge Knight formed Death Row Records and introduced Snoop Doggy Dogg.

In 1994, Atlanta's Outkast released its first album and moved the hip-hop focus away from the East Coast–West Coast rivalry. In 1996 the Fugees released "The Score," which combined hip-hop, R&B, and reggae. That same year, Tupac Shakur was shot and killed, and his death heighted the tension between East Coast and West Coast hip-hop artists. The following year (1997), East Coast rapper Notorious B. I. G. was killed after leaving a party for the Soul Train Music Awards in Los Angeles. In 1998, Jay-Z (Sean Carter) released a third album ("Vol 2: Hard Knock Life") that caused a meteoric rise in his popularity, and Puerto Rican rapper Big Punisher (Big Pun) (from the South Bronx) released "Capital Punishment," which made him the first Latino to produce a platinum album. That same year, the White rapper Eminem released "The Slim Shady," which became a billboard sensation. Also in 1998, *Forbes* magazine listed Russell Simmons, Master P, and Puff Daddy among its top moneymakers in entertainment. In 1999, Lauryn Hill, who had left the Fugees, released her first solo album, "The Miseducation of Lauryn Hill," winning five Grammy awards.

By the new century, hip-hop took a sharp turn toward glamorizing alcohol, drugs, women as sex objects, and conspicuous consumption. The music of the era focused on creating a "gangsta" (gangster) persona—living fast and "large" (i.e., big homes, expensive cars and clothes, and extravagant jewelry). Perhaps the song (and video) that best epitomizes this era is the album by Jay-Z and Kanye West, "Watch the Throne" with its very popular "N**gas in Paris." In the song the rappers brag about owning Rolex watches, spending exorbitant amounts of money, and disposing of women as if they were paper cups. Of course, because hip-hop has always been a dialectic art form, with artists speaking back and forth to each other and engaging in cyphers where artistic battling is an accepted form of settling disputes, the Jay-Z/Kanye West song was met with a political response from Yasiin Bey (formerly, Mos Def) titled, "N**gas in Poorest." Yasiin Bey's song describes the ongoing struggle of everyday people to make ends meet and centers around a hook that says, "Don't get caught up in no throne!"

HIP-HOP AS A GLOBAL PHENOMENON

This brief history of hip-hop music serves as a precursor for discussing the ways that new forms of music can be incorporated into social justice education. Michael Eric Dyson (2007) has dubbed hip-hop the most original and creative form of culture to which we have access. Neate (2004) begins his book by describing his encounter with hip-hop music in a village 10 miles from Chippenham, Gloucestershire, in the United Kingdom. In an extended quote from Tony Mitchell's edited volume, *Global Noise: Rap and Hip-Hop Outside the USA* (2001), the editor states:

> In his track, "Another Root," the African French rapper, Ménélik marks out a new era of confident, emergent global hip hop that has evolved from Tunis to Honolulu. He illustrates it by rapping in French on a 1994 album by the Japanese jazz musician Nobukazu Takemura, which was recorded in London, Paris, Osaka, and Tokyo. [In this volume] we will encounter Japanese b-boys struggling with the hyper-consumerism of Tokyo youth culture, Italian posses promoting hard-core Marxist politics and alternative youth culture circuits, and Basque rappers using a punk rock-hip hop syncretic to espouse their nationalist cause and promote the rights of ethnic minorities globally. Rappers in war-torn Bosnia declare their allegiance with the violent lives of gangsta rappers in South Central Los Angeles, and a rap group in Greenland protests that country's domination by the Danish language.

To this reality Mitchell concludes that

> [h]ip-hop and rap cannot be viewed simply as an expression of African American culture; it has become a vehicle for global youth affiliations and a tool for reworking local identity all over the world....Rap and hip-hop outside the USA reveal the working of popular music as a culture industry driven as much by local artists and their fans as by the demands of global capitalism and U.S. cultural domination. But the flow of consumption of rap music within the popular music industry continues to proceed hegemonically, from the USA to rest of the world, with little or no flow in the opposite direction. (pp. 1–2)

Perhaps one of the more surprising manifestations of hip-hop was its influence in what has been termed the "Arab Spring." Syrian American rapper Omar Offendum, along with Amir Suliman, Narcissist, Freeway, and Ayah, created a song entitled "Hashtag January 25," symbolizing the powerful impact of social media like "Twitter" to mobilize social activists and masses of people against oppressive and dictatorial regimes. Both the underground hip-hop music scene and its global manifestations are linked to social justice fights against repressive governments, global poverty, income inequality, racism, sexism, and heteronormativity. These emphases provide an opening for teachers to introduce hip-hop in the classroom.

MOVING HIP-HOP TO THE K–12 CLASSROOM

One of the challenges for K–12 educators is determining the place of hip-hop in the classroom. From the music educator's perspective, hip-hop can be included in the classroom from the standpoint of expanding music genres. Such inclusion does not necessarily require critical analysis. Just as a teacher may present music of the Baroque period by providing surface-level information about the period, she can do the same when introducing hip-hop. However, the decision to introduce hip-hop as a form of protest and social justice art requires a series of pedagogical decisions. Work on culturally relevant pedagogy (Ladson-Billings, 1995, 2009) suggests that teachers who focus on student learning, cultural competence, and critical consciousness are more likely to be successful with students of color who have struggled to experience school-based excellence.

Student learning represents more than the narrow notions of academic achievement linked to standardized test performance. Culturally relevant pedagogy (CRP) suggests that students learn much more than can be tested—a broader range of curriculum and experiences—and that students' growth, not merely their static scores, can be a more robust indicator of their learning. Cultural competence refers to students' deep understanding of their culture of origin, coupled with a fluency in at least one additional culture. For students of color, this may mean a deep understanding of their home culture and an ability to pull upon the "funds of knowledge" (Moll, Amanti, Neff, & Gonzales, 1992) of those cultures, along with acquiring the ability to be facile in the dominant culture. In the case of White students, this means that they, too, should become fluent in at least one other culture. They also need to be cognizant that their culture is just that—a culture, not the universal way, or the "right" way of doing things. Third, cultural relevance requires teachers to help students engage in critical consciousness—an ability to decipher the meaning of what is obvious and what is missing. Critically conscious students will be able to ask questions about the nature of what they are studying, including why they are not studying certain things. For example, a critically conscious student will want to know why he is only studying Black history in February and Women's history in March. That same student might ask why hip-hop is excluded from the music curriculum.

Culturally relevant pedagogy is at least 20 years old and is evolving through its incorporation of youth culture—specifically hip-hop (Ladson-Billings, 2014). Thus conversations about culture are taking on new and dynamic meanings. Gutierrez and Rogoff (2003) remind us that rather than a static, fixed notion of culture, we must attend to the cultural practices that people engage in. Thus, in the case of hip-hop we are not merely talking about some constructed notion of "Black culture," but rather a set of practices that youth around the world engage in to express their opposition to and independence from what they see as oppressive regimes on local, national, and global levels.

Hip-hop in the K–12 classroom necessarily requires a focus on specific artists in the same way that teaching English requires selecting specific texts. The work has to be vetted and linked to bigger ideas, rather than a voyeuristic consumption of the other. Fortunately, despite the rampant corporate promotion of violent, obscene, racist, misogynistic, and homophobic rap music, there is a growing group of socially and politically conscious artists in both underground and mainstream hip-hop. Underground artists like Immortal Technique, Jasiri X, and Wise Intelligent join mainstream artists like Kendrick Lamar, Yasiin Bey, and Lupe Fiasco to challenge student thinking and to use hip-hop to change the world.

One of the concerns that many teachers have about introducing hip-hop in the classroom is their own limited understanding and conception of the genre. Thus, they believe they are ill-equipped to use hip-hop as a pedagogical tool. Perhaps the simplest way to think about linking hip-hop to classroom practice is to follow the admonition of hip-hop educator Sam Seidel (2011) to borrow the "forms" of hip-hop rather than the "substance." Rather than teaching hip-hop, hip-hop educators seek colleagues who are willing to "be" hip-hop. This means being willing to do the kind of blending and bending of genres that are so prevalent in hip-hop. For example, mixing poetry and mathematics represents "being" hip-hop. Another hallmark of hip-hop is the need to "stay fresh." In the K–12 classroom, this requires teachers to come up with new approaches to concepts and skills they may have taught for many years. For example, the English teacher who teaches *Romeo and Juliet* could update it by making it a "musical" where students use contemporary music or write their own verses. Another example of being hip-hop is what hip-hop heads term "flipping something out of nothing." In hip-hop culture, this was scratching old vinyl records to create new sounds or using discarded pieces of linoleum as a dance floor. In a science class, a teacher might do project-based learning in which students take recycled and found materials to create new uses for them. A final example of being hip-hop is sampling from older elements to create new elements. Cognitive psychologists call this skill "synthesizing." In a history class, students could take a series of historical photos linked by a specific theme and sample music to create a video montage or slide show. In each of these examples, the teacher does not have to be deeply involved in hip-hop; rather, she has to allow hip-hop as a genre students can employ in representing what they know.

In addition to incorporating hip-hop into the K–12 classroom, we recognize the ways in which hip-hop has become a presence in the academy. In recent years, Ohio State University and Stanford University have hosted hip-hop conferences. Cornell University, California University of Pennsylvania, St. Cloud State University, and City College of New York also have hosted hip-hop conferences, and Harvard University houses the Hiphop Archive, which is the repository of all things hip-hop.

The University of Wisconsin has a unique spoken word program. Through its Office of Multicultural Arts Initiatives (OMAI), the university searches out talented spoken word and other hip-hop arts students to receive full tuition scholarships. Once at the university, the students pursue one of the extant majors while they hone their artistic craft and perform in a variety of venues. The program, First Wave, will welcome its eighth cohort of students in the fall of 2014. First Wave students have performed at the 2012 London Cultural Olympics, on Broadway, for the American Sociological Association (ASA), and others. Their presence is pushing universities to create courses and academic opportunities that incorporate hip-hop culture and arts. Most universities include some type of hip-hop culture, learning through courses in cultural studies, African American studies, music, and the arts. Increasingly, a cadre of young bright scholars like Marc Lamont Hill (Teachers College), Jeff Duncan Andrade (San Francisco State University), H. Samy Alim (Stanford University), and Django Paris (Michigan State University), among many others, are incorporating hip-hop studies and culture into their work in education, literacy, linguistics, and social work. Their intellect, coupled with their knowledge and understanding of youth culture (specifically, hip-hop), will provide a powerful tool for leveraging students on campuses (and in K–12 classrooms) who represent more diverse and globally conscious student bodies.

DEMOCRACY—WHAT A CONCEPT

Anyone who has paid close attention to hip-hop realizes that one strand of it is ultimately about democracy. Consider that our schools, with their official curricula, standards, and high stakes assessments, are becoming less democratic, and our students are the ones creating the only sites of democracy they know how to—through their art. Topics like global warming, war and peace, unemployment, and poverty do not show up in the school schedule or on the state tests. They show up in students' artistic expression. The larger question is how to re-situate democracy in the school, so that students begin to understand how issues of rights, fairness, equality, and equity can and should exist within the school and its practices, rather than as abstract concepts to be applied at some later date.

Most people think the hardest thing we have to do in our schools is figure out how to teach students how to read, write, and compute. In far too many urban schools, we also think the big task is how to get students to behave in school—how to sit quietly, listen to and obey adults, and comply with rules. The importance we have attached to these things—basic skills and compliance—is borne out in the emphasis we give them. We have zero tolerance policies and test prep sessions. However, the hardest thing we have to do actually is making democrats in undemocratic spaces. This is close to impossible. Instead, our schools have become prison preparatory plantations.

In his "Talk to Teachers," James Baldwin (1985) reminds us that no nation truly wants educated citizens because such citizens are dangerous. These are the citizens that ask questions about social inequities and social contradictions. More specifically, Baldwin states, "What societies really, ideally, want is a citizenry which will simply obey the rules of society. If a society succeeds in this, that society is about to perish. The obligation of anyone who thinks of himself as responsible is to examine society and try to change it and to fight it—at no matter what risk."

If we consider that—a compliant society is a society that is about to perish—then perhaps we will develop a sense of urgency about what we teach in our schools. Today's schools are more coercive and regimented—particularly those schools serving urban youth in poverty. We have draconian rules about managing schools and disciplining teachers and students. We claim to want parents to engage and yet we set up schools as places that are totally unfriendly to parents. We are developing the most highly techno-logical and sophisticated society the world has ever seen, but we expect our students to do the same mundane curriculum we did 50 years ago. We mistakenly think we can fit a hip-hop generation into a 1950s crooner-sweater-vest life.

For 40 years "adults" have proclaimed that hip-hop would not last. However, we are now teaching students whose parents were part of a hip-hop generation. The art of hip-hop is unlikely to leave us anytime soon. Just as popular genres like punk rock and heavy metal have been taken up by more "mainstream" genres, hip-hop will continue to be simultaneously incorporated into the mainstream and push back against the main-stream. In its attempt to serve as the protest voice for youth, hip-hop will always stand outside standard forms. However, if we are wise, we will learn to use it to engage youth in important social justice work that may transform our society and the world.

NOTES

1. In the tracing of this music history I am excluding much of the branch that continues on through sacred music that results in hymns, anthems, and gospel to tell a story of secular Black music.
2. In Jamaica and other Caribbean countries, disc jockeys began performing in dance clubs by "toasting," which is a kind of scripted or improvised talking while playing a record. This later becomes what is known as either "talk over" or "dub."

REFERENCES

Adams, N. (2013, August 28). The inspiring force of "We Shall Overcome," audio recording, *All Things Considered*, National Public Radio. Retrieved May 17, 2014, from http://www.npr.org/2013/08/28/216482943/the-inspiring-force-of-we-shall-overcome.

Baldwin, J. (1985). A talk to teachers. In J. Baldwin (Ed.). *The price of the ticket: Collected non-fiction 1948–1985*. New York: Saint Martins Press.

Chang, J. (2005). *Can't stop, won't stop: A history of the hip hop generation*. New York: St. Martin's Press.

Dyson, M. E. (2007). *Know what I mean? Reflections on hip-hop*. New York: Basic Books.

Digital History website. Retrieved June 4, 2014, from http://www.digitalhistory.uh.edu/index.cfm.

Fisk Jubilee Singers. Retrieved December 19, 2013, from www.fiskjubileesingers.org.

Gutierrez, K. & Rogoff, B. (2003). Cultural ways of learning: Individual traits or repertoires of practice. *Educational Researcher*, 32(5), 19–25.

Hager, S. (1982, September 12). Afrika Bambaataa's hip-hop. *Village Voice*, pp. 69, 72–73.

Hazzard-Gordon, K. (1990). *Jookin': The rise of social dance formations in African American culture*. Philadelphia: Temple University Press.

Hurt, B. (Director). (2006). *Hip hop: Beyond beats and rhymes*. Film recording. San Francisco: ITVS.

Katz. D. (2004, May 5). Clement "Sir Coxsone" Dodd: Pioneering producing of Jamaican reggae music scene and founder of studio one. Retrieved May 18, 2014, from http://www.theguardian.com/news/2004/may/06/guardianobituaries.artsobituaries.

Kuhn, T. (1996). *The structure of scientific revolutions* (3rd ed.). Chicago: University of Chicago Press.

Ladson-Billings, G. (1995). Toward a theory of culturally relevant pedagogy. *American Educational Research Journal, 32*(3), 465–491.

Ladson-Billings, G. (2009). *The dreamkeepers: Successful teachers of African American children*. San Francisco: Jossey Bass.

Ladson-Billings G. (2014). Culturally relevant pedagogy 2.0, a.k.a. the remix. *Harvard Educational Review, 84*, 74–84.

Lawrence-McIntyre, C. C. (1987). The double meanings of spirituals. *Journal of Black Studies, 17*(4), 379–401.

Mitchell, T. (Ed.) (2001). *Global Noise: Rap and hip-hop outside the USA*. Middletown, CT: Wesleyan University Press.

Moll, L., Amanti, C., Neff, C., & Gonzalez, N. (1992). Funds of knowledge for teaching: Using a qualitative approach to connect homes and classrooms. *Theory into Practice, 31*(2), 132–141.

Neate, P. (2004). *Where you're at: Notes from the frontlines of a hip-hop planet*. New York: Riverhead Books.

Oakley, G. (1997). *The devil's music: A history of the blues*. New York: Da Capa Press.

Payne, J. (2006). *The great drummers of R & B: Funk and soul* (2nd ed.). New York: Face the Music Productions.

Seidel, S. (2011). *Hip hop genius: Remixing high school education*. Lanham, MD: Rowan & Littlefield.

Thomas, V. M. (2001). *No man can hinder me: The journey from slavery to Emancipation through song*. New York: Crown Publishers.

Ventura, M. (1985). Hear that long snake moan. In M. Ventura (Ed.), *Shadow dancing in the USA*. New York: St Martin's Press.

Wintz, C., & Finkelman, P. (Eds.) (2004). *Encyclopedia of the Harlem Renaissance*, Vol 2 (2nd ed.). New York: Taylor & Francis.

Wynter, S. (1984). The ceremony must be found: After humanism. *Boundary 2 12*(3)/13(1), 19–69.

TOWARD SOCIAL JUSTICE PEDAGOGY

Problems and Opportunities

INTRODUCTION

Rethinking the Ways We Engage with Others

GARY SPRUCE, SECTION EDITOR

TAPPER (2005) suggests that "[o]ne way to deepen our understanding of social justice in education is to look at the ways it manifests in terms of ideology and practice" (p. 412). The chapters in this section seek to deepen our understanding of social justice in music education through exploring the ways that social justice is manifested or inhibited both within and through particular music and music education contexts, practices, and sites of learning. These contexts, practices, and sites include schools, community spaces, music technologies, choral music making, and the ways in which musical value and achievement are assessed and evaluated.

Many chapters draw on vignettes and case studies based on the direct experiences of the authors or the firsthand experiences of those musicians and teachers being reported on. These vignettes and case studies range widely: from the reflections of a music teacher in a secondary (aged 11–16) school in South London (Philpott with Kubilius, Chapter 26) to the experiences of a Chinese musician working in a community in the Henan province in central China (Higgins, Chapter 27), and from music programs with American prisoners in high security "correctional institutions" (de Quadros, Chapter 31) to teachers using music technology with students with emotional and behavioral difficulties in an urban area in northwest England (Savage, Chapter 30).

A number of chapters draw attention to how those musical and educational ideologies that can perpetuate social injustice are promoted either explicitly through official discourses such as educational policies, legislation, and examination specifications (Philpott with Kubilius, Chapter 26; Savage, Chapter 30) or implicitly through the valorization of particular, dominant music practices—most often those associated with Western art music (Higgins, Chapter 27; Louth, Chapter 29; Fautley, Chapter 32). Gaztambide-Fernández and Stewart Rose point out in Chapter 28 how such valorizations are sometimes sustained through narratives that posit hegemonic practices in terms of a social justice agenda—for example, through providing access to dominant musical practices for "disadvantaged" groups. However, these narratives carry with them the implication that those who engage in other, less dominant, practices "lead lives bereft of musical experiences."

Other themes explored include how dominant ideologies can be sustained and reinforced by unquestioned "understandings" about what is meant by particular terms or concepts such as "urban music" (Gaztambide-Fernández and Stewart Rose, Chapter 28), or assumptions that particular pedagogies inevitably result in more equitable and democratic pedagogies. For example, both Louth (in Chapter 29) and Savage (in Chapter 30) warn that, although music technologies have the potential to disrupt "the reproduction of existing social relations by enabling constructivist, collaborative approaches to music teaching" (Louth), they can equally be used to perpetuate and reinforce inequalities and arbitrary distinctions based around, for example, gender.

For a number of authors there is also the concern that music education is increasingly subject to a quasi neoliberal agenda, where young people are seen primarily as consumers of a commoditized pedagogy (Philpott with Kubilius), resulting in the construction of a "consumerist mentality" (Louth). These consumerist mentalities encourage a kind of political passivity that acts as a barrier to what Freire (1974) describes as the process of "conscientization," in which young people and their teachers come to a greater awareness of their world and the power relationships, inequalities, and anti- or undemocratic practices that exist within it. Picking up on this theme, Cooke in Chapter 33 posits the central role of critical reflection in promoting social justice, arguing for the importance of teachers and students engaging "with the historical, social and political ideas that surround music and musical learning" as a means by which they might come to imagine alternative musical futures to those that are projected or imposed through dominant educational and musical discourses and ideologies.

Although almost all chapters identify ways in which social injustices are constructed and perpetuated within music education, they equally offer ways forward toward more socially just paradigms, often through describing particular examples of socially just practices "in action." Sometimes these socially just practices take place against political or ideological backdrops that promote or sustain social injustices or inequalities. Jason Kubilius, a practicing music teacher (Philpott with Kubilius, Chapter 26), describes how, within the context of an increasing "academicization" of English music education, he tries to maintain the classroom as a space open to all the musical practices that young people bring with them into the classroom from outside school. De Quadros in Chapter 31 demonstrates how choral music making in prisons and in Arab towns in Galilee provide opportunities for personal agency, community bonding, and acts of conciliation against backgrounds of intimidation, coercion, or repression. Many of the music education practices described provide examples of social justice practices which seek to enable "'otherwise silenced' voices to be heard." (Louth).

Enabling "silenced voices" to be heard is a concern for many authors. Higgins addresses this issue directly in Chapter 27, arguing for a "hospitable" approach to music education that responds to the call from the "Other" for forms of collaborative music making that can provide occasions where silenced voices might be heard. Gaztambide-Fernández and Stewart Rose similarly argue in Chapter 28 for music education practices that allow students' voices to be heard through acting as "agents of knowledge and cultural production" and as "creators of musical knowledge," rather than simply consumers of a predetermined curriculum or "method." Following this line of thinking, Fautley in Chapter 32, regarding the matter of assessment, suggests that "musical quality" cannot and should not be determined exclusively by "external arbiters" but that students will, if supported appropriately, develop and progress most effectively if their voice is heard in judging their own music making by "their own standards."

In the final chapter of this section, John Sloboda brings the multiple perspectives of musician, empirical psychology researcher, and political activist to bear on social justice in music education. He suggests that in order to make the case for music and musical education as a tool for the promotion of social justice, "rigorous and large-scale evaluations of the effects of this work on its recipients—the young people" are required.

All the writers in this section recognize the critical importance of social justice being theorized, problematized, and embedded in a coherent philosophical framework. However, the manifestations of social justice in practice must be, as they demonstrate, located in these specific historical, social, and political circumstances in which individuals and communities find themselves and within which their music making takes place and has significance.

References

Freire, P. (1974) *Education for critical consciousness.* London: Continuum.

Tapper. A. J. H. (2005) A pedagogy of social justice education: Social identity theory, intersectionality, and empowerment. *Conflict Resolution Quarterly, 30*(4),411–445.

CHAPTER 26

....

SOCIAL JUSTICE IN THE ENGLISH SECONDARY MUSIC CLASSROOM

....

CHRIS PHILPOTT WITH JASON KUBILIUS

INTRODUCTION

THERE has been an ongoing sense in English music education that social justice is a problem to be solved, in that access to achievement and "music for all" has been an elusive goal, and especially so in the secondary music classroom. The seminal, and to a certain extent mythical, root of the issue arose from the paradox identified in the Schools Council report of 1971. Here the adolescents surveyed suggested that while music was their least favorite school subject, it was the most important discipline to them outside school. The assumption has been that this paradox has had a negative impact on the access of students to success in the secondary music classroom, and other studies have verified the persistence of the problem (see Harland et al., 2000; Lamont & Maton, 2008, 2010).

Of course such issues with classroom music did not start in 1971. However, it *can* be said that the most recent and significant moments in the history of music education in England have, on the face of things, aimed to provide a solution to the problem. As such, one of the main aims of recent initiatives, writings, and policy in music education has been for greater inclusion and social justice in the music classroom. These developments in music education have always had the aim of facilitating a wider distribution of access to achievement and success in the secondary music classroom ("music for all"), even if such aims have been implicit rather than explicitly expressed.

The following questions have been used to structure the argument of this chapter:

- What is meant by social justice in the music classroom?
- What are the indicators for a socially just music classroom?
- In what ways have significant moments in the history of classroom music aimed to promote social justice?

- In what ways have the aims of significant moments in the history of classroom music been confounded in relation to social justice?
- What does this analysis mean for a school in the early twenty-first century?

In critically exploring these questions, the chapter will focus very specifically on the English secondary classroom where *all* students have been expected to study music as part of the curriculum over the past 50 years between the ages of 11 and 14. By way of exemplification of the issues raised in this chapter, the thoughts of a head of a music department, with a strong reputation for leading inclusive music education in multicultural, comprehensive, and urban secondary schools, are inserted at significant points. These vignettes serve to illustrate how issues of social justice impinge upon the day-to-day work of a music teacher in an English classroom.

WHAT IS MEANT BY SOCIAL JUSTICE IN THE MUSIC CLASSROOM?

There are at least two levels to the discourse about social justice in the music classroom. On the one hand, there is the "democratic" discourse that can be found in many writings, curriculum documents, and initiatives at national, local, and school levels. Spruce characterizes the democratic discourse as "participation, diversity and inclusion" and these concepts are "understood as a triumvirate which are fundamental to social justice" (2013, p. 23). At this level, social justice in the music classroom involves making sure that *all* students are able to take part and ensuring that a wide variety of musical knowledge and perspectives are fully embraced.

However, Spruce also draws out implications for an "emancipatory" discourse in which the development of emancipatory knowledge "enables individuals and communities to recognise and understand the power-relationships that exist in their world and to draw on this understanding as a means of interacting with, and fully participating in, that world" (2013, p. 23). Such knowledge, he suggests, helps us to see the world "as a dynamic phenomenon upon which, and within which, a person consciously acts in the construction of knowledge and understanding" (Spruce 2012a, p. 191).

This transformative theme is picked up by Woodford (2012), who maintains that social justice goes beyond an inclusivity of curriculum content and being responsive to students' cultural needs. He targets his critique of the democratic discourse in relation to the many developments that have taken place in the United States and Britain, at the end of the last century, under the slogan of "music for its own sake."

> By declaring that music should be taught for its own sake, divorced from the world and its problems, music teachers were aligning themselves with democratic realists who believed in rule by social elites and experts and who were deeply suspicious of notions of social justice that attempted to go beyond negative rights such as equality of opportunity. (2012, p. 86)

Furthermore, Woodford notes that "proponents of social justice in music education often emphasize musical diversity and inclusivity while neglecting to explicitly teach students how music and music education related to politics and other forms of experience" (2012, p. 85).

Philpott and Wright (after Bernstein, 1996) echo the implications of both Spruce and Woodford by viewing democratic concepts through an emancipatory lens where *inclusion* means "the right . . . not to be absorbed"; *enhancement*, "the right to . . . critical reflection [on] possible new futures"; and *participation*, "the right to participate in situations where order is formed and changed" (2012, p. 454).

These democratic and emancipatory discourses elicit distinctive indicators for social justice in the classroom, which can be used as headline criteria to analyze initiatives, policy, and curriculum developments.

WHAT ARE THE INDICATORS FOR A SOCIALLY JUST MUSIC CLASSROOM?

We would like to propose a set of indicators for social justice in the music classroom that can be drawn out from the theory and practice of the democratic and emancipatory discourses. The democratic discourse leads us to propose the following indicators:

1. Curriculum, pedagogy, and assessment
    a. A wide conception of what counts as musical knowledge;
    b. A wide conception of what counts as musical learning and development;
    c. A wide conception of what counts as musical achievement;
    d. A wide distribution of musical achievement among various social and cultural groups;
    e. Assessment practices that are able to recognize the same;
    f. Assessment strategies that validate a wide range of musical achievement;
    g. A wide range of resources (human and technological) that promote inclusion.

Vignette 1

An essential way of considering an inclusive music department's success is to look at the strength of the formal curriculum. It is in the day-to-day teaching that you meet all students and that all students have a chance to make music. The rest is extra—important, but an addition to what should be an already inclusive department. It is important to recognize that in terms of inclusion, many students making music at many different levels is more important than a few students playing at a very high level.

In trying to widen what counts as musical knowledge, it is important to recognize the act of music making as the central way we come to express our knowledge, understanding, and skills in music. This means a more co-constructed approach to teaching and learning where music is often created in dialogue with the students and where aesthetic/compositional choices are negotiated and discussed along with possible success criteria.

From the curriculum can come much of the showcasing of students' work. We can try to recognize the real-life musicianship that many students bring, rather than look to how they fulfill the criteria of the statutory levels or examination syllabus grades. We can also use as many opportunities as possible to celebrate the various musical traditions in the school.

However, an open policy to what counts as musical knowledge is increasingly difficult to maintain. Still, it is important that all students are treated as musicians through emphasizing the support and development of their musicianship in the classroom.

2. Inclusion, participation, and diversity
   a. Students having ownership of and responsibility for their knowledge and learning;
   b. Students having some choice over the musical practices they engage with;
   c. Teachers and students making music together as "real" musicians do;
   d. An inclusive conception of who is regarded as a musician among staff and students;
   e. Respect for a wide range of cultural traditions;
   f. Students' own cultural image reflected in school curriculum;
   g. The open accessibility of resources (physical and human);
   h. High levels of motivated participation at all levels of schooling and in wider society;
   i. A lifelong approach to musical learning.

Vignette 2

Social justice starts with the curriculum, a curriculum designed so that it enables all students to make music and that connects in some way with their own sense of musicality. There needs to a space in the curriculum that allows students to see themselves and who they are reflected in the music that they make. Some believe that we should be presenting the best that culture as to offer, and this means the agreed and accepted greats of Western music, but of importance are the relationships between the people who make music and the actual music making itself, not the quality perceived or otherwise of the music.

However, and more controversially, the emancipatory indicators imply a significant realignment of the relationships between teachers, students, and musical knowledge and include

3. Criticality and reflection.
   a. A dialectical construction of knowledge and pedagogy between students and teachers;

b. An awareness of the political dimensions to culture and musical practices;
c. Critical reflection on cultural "givens" and possible futures (teachers and students);
d. Critical reflection on curriculum, pedagogy, and assessment (teachers and students);
e. The student as cultural and educational critic;
f. An openness to change in musical practices that can be instigated by students and teachers.

These emancipatory indicators have significant implications for student and teacher agency and a critical pedagogy. In light of his critique, Woodford proposes that social justice in music education can *only* be achieved through a critical pedagogy that is nothing less than social and political activism through "empowering teachers and students to reclaim ownership over the design and direction of their musical lives by helping them to see and hear the world with critical eyes and ears" (2012, p. 98). A similar critical pedagogy is implied by Spruce in which the emancipatory discourse is "manifest through the involvement of individuals and communities in deciding what is worthwhile musical 'knowledge' and how that 'knowledge' is best learnt" (Spruce, 2013, p. 23).

Critical pedagogy in an emancipatory discourse promotes the importance of human agency in social justice—the implication being that the democratic discourse will not by itself lead to the changes that have characterized previous injustices in the English music classroom. The implications of the emancipatory discourse for social justice in the music classroom are controversial and challenging, and we shall return to these later.

SIGNIFICANT MOMENTS IN THE HISTORY OF SOCIAL JUSTICE IN THE ENGLISH MUSIC CLASSROOM

Recent initiatives and policy in England have focused on social justice in the music classroom through explorations in epistemology, pedagogy, and technology, and these, as we shall see, can be been predominantly characterized as being part of the democratic discourse.

Epistemological developments in the history of English music education have related to either (a) content knowledge, or (b) the nature of musical knowledge. While this is not the place for a full historical analysis, an example of (a) can be seen in the early 1960s, where there were calls for "pop" music to be included as a valid curriculum content (see Vulliamy, 1977), as well as knowledge of the dominant Western classical tradition. An example of (b) can be seen in the work of Swanwick (1988), who had an important influence on the formation of the first English national curriculum for music in 1992.

Swanwick argued for a wider conception of knowledge based on the nature of music itself and emphasized the primacy of our lived relationship with music in education. Each of these examples serves to illustrate a tendency toward a wider conception of what counts as musical knowledge and thus what counts as achievement in a (potentially) more democratic and socially just classroom.

The pedagogical developments in various initiatives and policy have related to (a) the ways in which we learn music, and (b) the relationships between teacher and learner. An example of (a), from the 1970s, can be seen in the work of Paynter and Aston (1970), who maintained that the way to learn how to compose is to actually do it, and who developed a sophisticated pedagogy to underpin an approach that placed children as creative agents at the center of the music curriculum. This, of course, also exemplifies (b), where the relationship between the teacher and learner is fundamentally changed and the flow of knowledge is no longer one way, as was the case in the "traditional" music classroom. The radical implications of this idea can now be seen in the self-directed learning associated with projects such as *Musical Futures*, which is an ongoing curriculum development project focusing on students' ownership of musical learning. Again, the principal aim of such pedagogical developments was to facilitate social justice in the music classroom through, it is argued, a more democratic set of pedagogical relationships.

Technology is at the heart of how we engage with and mediate music at a very fundamental level. Technology enables us to "do" music and can also provide access to it. Whether intentionally or not, it can be argued that all technological developments have facilitated a more inclusive, accessible, and thus socially just music classroom from the use of Orff instruments to the tape recorder, to electronic keyboards, and to the use of mobile technology. The development of diverse technologies has underpinned both epistemic and pedagogic aims for democracy and social justice in the music classroom through aiming to make musical learning more accessible

Table 26.1 draws together a summary of some key moments in the development of classroom music in England, cross referenced with the most significant of the indicators proposed at the beginning of this chapter. Again, it is worth noting that this analysis focuses on the English secondary classroom for students aged 11–14.

Necessarily all these snapshots are problematic distillations that miss many nuances of actual practice (if they ever permeated many classrooms at all). For example, some involved in the "creative movement" have been accused of having a "closed" approach to creativity through focusing on models inspired by Western avant-garde art music (see Green, 2008). Similarly, self-directed music in the classroom has often been criticized for having a "closed" view of content based on "pop" music.

However, what is true about each is that democratic indicators dominate successive attempts toward a more socially just music classroom. Each instance exemplified in Table 26.1 has aimed in good faith to validate and recognize a progressively wider conception of what counts as musical knowledge, pedagogy, and achievement in the classroom. All have contributed to progress in relation to what we have called the democratic discourse surrounding social justice through epistemological, pedagogical, and technological developments in English classroom music.

Table 26.1 Policy and Initiatives for the English Music Classroom and Indicators of Social Justice

	Epistemology: The content of the curriculum, the nature of music, and our relationship to it	Pedagogy: The ways in which we learn and relationships between teacher and learner	Technology: How we engage with and mediate music
Traditional "baseline"	Closed curriculum content based on singing (traditional songs), appreciation (of classical music), and theory (notation)	A closed pedagogy involving didactic learning and based on choices made by teachers	Closed choices of technology limited to the voice and gramophone
Late 1960s, early 1970s: Developments inspired by the sociology of knowledge (see Vulliamy, 1977) to validate "pop" music [1a, 1c]	A wider conception of content knowledge if still located in a "closed" curriculum	Conceptions of learning closed, with teachers still making pedagogical choices	Wider technology (if still limited) including recording and playback technology
Late 1960s, early 1970s: Developments inspired by the "creativity" movement (Paynter and Aston, 1970; Schafer, 1965) to validate composition in the classroom [1a, 1b, 1c, 2a, 2b, 3a]	A more open conception of content where children are seen as creators of musical knowledge	More open and less hierarchical relationships between learners and teachers	The addition of "accessible" Orff instruments for creative music making
Late 1980s, early 1990s: The first national curriculum for music (DES, 1992), an eclectic curriculum integrating listening, composing and performing [1a, 1b, 1c, 1d, 1f, 1g, 2a, 2b, 2e]	A wide breadth of content now drawing in world musics (see Kwami, 1996) and focusing on making music	A mixed pedagogy based on "instruction and encounter" (see Swanwick, 1988)	The addition of popular "democratic" electronic keyboards, sequencing, and sampling technology
Early 2000s: Self-directed learning (see Green, 2008, and *Musical Futures*) [1a, 1b, 1c, 1d, 1g, 2a, 2b, 2e, 2c, 2d, 2e, 2g, 2i, 3a]	Open content based on children making choices about the music that they play	An open pedagogy with teachers as facilitators and children making pedagogical choices	The addition of authentic instruments and mobile technology

Having said these things, there is evidence to doubt the critical success of these predominantly democratic developments in producing a more socially just music classroom. It would appear that wider cultural and sociological processes have confounded aims for a more socially just music classroom. If this is the case, how have these mechanisms worked to do this?

Reform in the Music Classroom and Social Justice

Over the period of time outlined in Table 26.1, there is no doubt that the political and economic agenda has delivered significant gains for the funding and provision of classroom music in England. This has been a period of unprecedented attention for all aspects of music education with the avowed aim of a more democratic and socially just music education in which all students have greater access to participation and achievement in music. However, various commentators and critics have also suggested that the impact of these democratic reforms has been confounded by a range of social and cultural mechanisms.

How do we know that the issue of social justice in the music classroom remains a problem to be solved? Given the relatively low status of music as a *curriculum subject* in schools, as opposed to a set of *extracurricular activities*, there are few studies that get to the heart of social justice in the music classroom. Classroom music in schools in England competes not only with music outside the curriculum for importance, but also with all other subjects in school. However, one measure of participation is the number of those opting to study music beyond the compulsory age of 14. This continues to drop for music in most recent times from over 48,000 in 2011 to just over 41,000 in 2013, compared with over 70,000 who studied drama in 2013; and, unlike music, drama has not been compulsory for 11–14-year-olds as part of a national curriculum. While it is acknowledged that music is different from some other subjects, in the sense that participation can take place outside the classroom, it is argued that greater inclusion for 11–14-year-olds would mean greater numbers studying beyond the compulsory age.

While there are various other explanations of this issue, for example, the pressures on schools to achieve highly in the English Baccalaureate, which contains no compulsory arts subjects (and thus no drama also!), it remains the case that, as Evans has pointed out, "It has proved difficult to reverse the position where approximately nine out of ten students turn their backs on 'school music' at the earliest opportunity" (Evans, 2012, p. 197).

This situation transcends recent initiatives and policy, where historically low levels of participation beyond the compulsory curriculum (and thus the wide distribution of achievement) would appear to have consistently confounded social justice in the music classroom. While on the face of things social justice has been actively promoted (through a more "democratic" approach to social justice), it is argued here that these developments (even those seemingly radical ones) have been appropriated by powerful cultural and sociological forces, thereby neutering attempts at a socially just music classroom. There is a range of strong and implicit reasons for continued injustices and it is to these that we now turn.

CONFOUNDING SOCIAL JUSTICE IN THE MUSIC CLASSROOM

The literature indicates that there are several mechanisms at play that confound social justice in the music classroom, in spite of democratic developments, and these include

- subtle mechanisms that perpetuate the pervasive and exclusive elitism of the Western classical tradition;
- the related socialization of music teachers both in their own training and when working as teachers in schools;
- the construction of and justification for music in the classroom that promotes a hierarchical dichotomy with other school subjects and an impoverished discourse on the nature of music as a discipline.

We will explore each of these in more detail.

Perpetuating the Exclusive Elitism of the Western Classical Tradition

There is a well-established critique of classroom music that relates to the pervasiveness of the Western classical tradition, and this pervasiveness is both explicit and implicit. In confounding social justice in the music classroom, the Western classical tradition, it is argued, has the power to define what counts as "good" music by appearing to have values that are autonomous and universal, through the objectification of these values when music is regarded as an object, and through these values being measured and characterized by "complexity."

"Good" Music as Having Values That Are Autonomous and Universal.

Of explicit significance here is the transcendental status of Western classical music being autonomously, universally, and self-evidently perceived as a measure of ultimate value in music. Here "great music is made to appear, and required to appear, eternal, natural and universal . . . poor music is rooted in society . . ." (Green, 1988, p. 101). An example of the socially unjust consequences of this is where:

> . . . western classical music is then rationalised by evaluating non-art music (*pop*) on art music's (*classical*) terms: as an autonomous object, detached from its social and cultural context, valued only in terms of relationships between its musical materials. An exercise in which non art music can only come off worse. Thus the bourgeois aesthetic is confirmed as intrinsically superior and, by association, so are its consumers and creators. (Spruce, 1999, p. 79)

Furthermore, the self-evident universal value of Western classical music has meant that classroom music in England has struggled to shake off the perception of youngsters that it is underpinned by a "bourgeois aesthetic." For example, Lamont and Maton (2008, 2010) have suggested that students perceive post-14 music courses to have an "elite" content based on possessing specialist knowledge against which they are reluctant to be judged. These factors may account for some of the lack of participation in English class-

Vignette 3

Recently exam specifications have started to redirect and reshape our teaching and particularly expectations surrounding "musical literacy." Naturally I am sometimes worried about the impact of a lack of "musical literacy" for students. Of course the issues are around how overwhelmingly classically centred the "language" around musical literacy is for GCSE examinations, which nearly always points to students using staff notation whether or not it is relevant or helpful. Here there is a real pressure to try to ensure that the students succeed, but it does encourage a hoop-jumping exercise and a narrower vision of what is acceptable musical knowledge. This is a tension that can restrict what we celebrate as valid musical knowledge.

One gifted pianist I taught whose harmonization of melodies was incredibly sophisticated had difficulty finding a C on a piano. How's that for progress? Then of course I have known a number of students who primarily see themselves as MCs/rappers, and this is very difficult to recognize through officially sanctioned assessment criteria.

room music beyond the age of 14 and thus a lack of social justice.

Music as Object

Closely related to values that appear to be autonomous and universal is the objectification of music. The notion of music as object means that

> [t]he ideology of music being 'out there' is promoted particularly in the western classical tradition through the idea that the objectified forms of music—the scores and recordings—are synonymous with 'the music'. Music—or one of its objectified forms—then becomes an object to be taught. (Spruce, 2012a, p. 188)

One of the consequences of music as object is that it becomes susceptible to reification and commodification, resulting in an alienated relationship between learner and musical knowledge that can explain, at least in part, the paradox that students identify more with music outside school than they do in the classroom.

> Alienation arises as a result of disjuncture between the material nature of musical learning ... and how it is experienced as part of a socially mediated school music curriculum. ... In music education this can be illustrated by a disjuncture between most pupils' experience of music outside of school ... and music in the classroom. (Philpott, 2010, p. 83)

The power of music as object to permeate curriculum developments can be seen in the way in which a seemingly more socially just national curriculum (in all of its incarnations), which included a wide range of "musics," was commodified through taking a "museum" approach to the study of musics. Here programs of study promoted the notion that "musics" can be objectified as musical processes to be studied as objects quite separate from the cultural context in which they had been used and produced. "The consequence was a music curriculum in which music took on the charter of a *commodity* to be 'done' in the roundabout of curriculum coverage" (Philpott, 2010, p. 83).

In summary, it has been argued that, when working together, the concepts of "good" music exhibiting values that are autonomous and universal *and* music as an alienated object can subtly confound social justice in the music classroom.

Good Music Being Characterized by Its Complexity

Once again closely related to values that are autonomous, universal, and objectified in the Western classical aesthetic is the idea that good music can be "measured." These criteria have underpinned approaches to formative and summative assessment in the music classroom (see Philpott, 2012b) and include the notion that "good" music can be characterized through its

- complexity;
- originality;
- difficulty;
- breadth of influence(s); and
- linearity of associated musical learning and development.

These socially and culturally derived assumptions, characteristically promoting "more is good," impinge upon the curricula and assessment regimes of classroom music at all levels in England, taking on the appearance of being universal; and yet, as Swanwick argues:

> Complexity by itself is no virtue. Performing a wide range of complex music without understanding would definitely not count as a high level of achievement. And it is

certainly possible to perform, compose and enjoy a high quality musical experience without any great complexity. (1999, p. 78)

The result is an exclusivity that impinges upon social justice in the music classroom through an implicit definition of what counts as "good" music and thus the recognition of what counts as achievement.

There is evidence that this implicit pervasiveness has the power to appropriate even the most radical (and potentially emancipatory) of developments such as the self-directed learning associated with *Musical Futures*. As an example, the project published assessment criteria compatible with what, at the time, was the current statutory national curriculum (see Philpott, 2012b), within which "more is good" is implicit. Sanctioning such criteria has the potential to be prejudicial to "good" music exhibiting other characteristics such as simplicity of structure, of melody, of harmony (i.e., music that champions that simplicity *can* be great music). Given that much of the self-directed musical learning identified in the *Musical Futures* research (Green, 2008) showed that it could be characterized by the quality of music making above any quantitative measure of difficulty or breadth, it is questionable whether such criteria, derived from the dominant ideology of Western "art" music, are appropriate for self-directed learning. In short, summative and formative assessment criteria based on the assumptions and values of Western art music can impinge upon social justice for students in terms of what can be recognized as worthy achievement.

Vignette 4

To what extent are we trying to broaden horizons? This has been an ongoing debate for me. I don't really remember focusing on more than one instrument and one particular style in my teens (classical music) and really, when it came down to it, studying just a handful of composers never seemed to penalize me. However, being an MCer is nearly always (and unfortunately) seen negatively as a lack of real musical knowledge, a serious restriction and focus that is unhealthy—almost non-musical.

The Socialization of the Music Teacher and Student

The socialization of music teachers and students in their musical training and the culture of schooling in England can serve to perpetuate injustice in the music classroom and reinforce the pervasiveness of the Western classical aesthetic.

There is some evidence to suggest that the professional backgrounds of music teachers are liable to reinforce and perpetuate the values wrapped up in "good" music being constructed as object, as having autonomous and universal values and being characterized by complexity. Green has suggested that the "majority of school music teachers in the UK ... have classical backgrounds" (2008, p. 27), and Finney (2007) also notes that music teachers' backgrounds and training enable them to empathize with the elite "codes" wrapped up in officially sanctioned curricula and assessment criteria.

Quite apart from the role of music teachers' training in perpetuating these values, this issue is also played out through the socialization of class music teachers into a culture of accountability through assessment. Here the power of league tables and the measurement of student progress serves to perpetuate a culture of good equals complexity (more is good). This has led to what often amounts to the over-assessment of students in the music classroom when using quantitative criteria derived from statutory documents.

Even the Office for Standards in Education (Ofsted, 2012), whose job it is to inspect for accountability in England, has noted the pernicious impact of such socialization on the quality of music teaching "linked to schools' requirement for teachers to provide half-termly numerical levels and sub-levels of attainment for every student" (2012, p. 37). In addition,

> [w]hile it is important to demonstrate, measure, track and challenge students' progress through comparison of their work and achievement over time, this led to frequent instances of teachers artificially and inaccurately dividing the levels into sub-grades or assessing isolated areas of musical activity, rather than considering students' musical responses holistically . . . considerable amounts of teaching time were spent on the mechanics of assessment procedures. This often had a negative impact on students' engagement, enjoyment and achievement. . . . (Ofsted, 2012, p. 37)

Vignette 5

I have tried to avoid indiscriminately "leveling" students' work using the national curriculum criteria, and this has not seemed to matter to Ofsted or senior leadership teams. Avoiding class discussions around abstract levels has allowed more focused discussion on the music making in front of us, not on "how does this music fit the criteria" but more on its own terms and what makes this good.

However, the tension of accountability and autonomy in teaching and learning has begun to influence more day-to-day teaching. The issue of showing progress in lessons and over time can make some lessons more "conservative" with a sense that teachers needed to intervene to ensure maximum progress for all students and to show "impact." This is probably not unique to music. There is a tension between seeing music education as about developing your music making as part of your cultural practice and linear progression of the mastery of certain skills and knowledge. The latter used for accountability, as evidenced in "progression," can restrict and reshape your views on what is important in the music classroom.

In short, it is argued that the hegemonic assumptions wrapped up in music curricula and approaches to assessment in England are embedded in a culture of schooling dominated by accountability. The values of complexity, difficulty, breadth, and linearity of learning are eminently measurable (if not musical or inclusive), and the "ease" of quantitative measurement is facilitated through criteria incrementally written to assess various curricula and syllabi. These are implicit influences on the socialization of music teachers that militate against social justice for all students.

Of course, these influences play out equally on the socialization of students. The playing of certain types of instruments (from the Western classical tradition and usually learned outside the classroom) and certain types of musical backgrounds are more likely to predispose a pupil to success. Those who have benefited from an aesthetic that is consonant with the Western classical tradition are most likely to succeed, to the exclusion of others who may have ambitions in relation to other musical traditions (see Philpott, 2001). There is also some evidence to suggest that those who play a "classical" instrument are more likely to opt for music at after age 14 (see Bray, 2000).

The Construction of and Justification for Music in the Curriculum

Finally, there would appear to be a set of issues surrounding the social and cultural construction of music and its justification in the curriculum that additionally serve to challenge the impact of developments in the music classroom on social justice.

Justifications for music in the curriculum most commonly come in the following extra-musical constructions (see also Philpott, 2012a):

- instrumental justifications, in which the study of music is said to be able to develop, for example, mathematical skills, spatial skills;
- therapeutic justifications, where music can have cathartic and healing powers;
- civilizing justifications, where music makes us a better and more rounded human being; and
- emotional justifications, where music facilitates the development of our emotional intelligence.

Music is also commonly justified in the curriculum for the contribution of music education to a personal, social, and economic good. This is most easily exemplified through most recent policy statements such as, "The value of music as an academic subject lies in its contribution to enjoyment and enrichment, for its social benefits. . . ." (DfE, 2011, p. 6).

Instrumental justifications for music in the curriculum most commonly suggest that music is "good" for us (see also Philpott, 2012a), and these overarchingly instrumental justifications are problematic for social justice in the music classroom. It is also the case that one of the tacit assumptions of such justification is that the music that is good for us is "good" music (i.e., the music of the Western classical tradition).

There are two seemingly contradictory nuances to this construction. First, there is the construction of music as an amelioration and counterpart to a more rational and (more important) scientific world, which promotes a stratified, hierarchical epistemology that militates against the arts. Such a construction adopts a dualism that has subjugated music (and the arts) beneath other "harder" subjects, thus establishing a hierarchical dichotomy. However, while on the one hand music is constructed as a "soft" subject whose strengths lie in our inability to "measure," paradoxically it is justified for its transferable and measurable impact on other aspects of our life. In a culture of accountability, politicians who "sponsor" initiatives and statutory curricula are attracted by evidence that can show the potential impact of music on wider educational success and thus economic good. This is another manifestation of a hierarchical epistemology.

The inherent hierarchical dichotomy here has undermined the case for music and the arts through emphasizing its independent autonomous (and "soft") values that separate it from an emancipatory discourse through a partial and impoverished exposition of the nature of musical expression, meaning, and understanding.

> The contention is then that the 'soft' justifications have made it easier to take music (and the arts) less seriously and that they are derived from a partial analysis of musical meaning. Given that any symbolic mode is subject to wide and powerful political, social and cultural forces, this construction of educational music has not helped the cause. (Philpott, 2012a, p. 50)

The argument here is that what appear to be strong constructions and justifications for music in the curriculum result in a subversion of its importance in relation to what are "harder" disciplines. The result has been an underplaying of music as a curriculum subject (e.g., in terms of the curriculum time devoted to it) that amounts to a lack of access and thus social justice for students. Furthermore, such constructions serve to perpetuate values of autonomy, universality, and objectification.

By way of summary to this section, we have seen that there are important critiques of what we have called democratic developments in the music classroom, and that explicit and implicit aspects of school music, which are strongly informed by an elitist Western classical tradition, have served to perpetuate long-standing injustices in the music classroom. These are subtle and nuanced forces that confound the avowed aims of the democratic discourse and which add up to injustice for many students who participate in the English music classroom.

Concluding Discussion

Previously we have seen that much progress has taken place in the English music classroom in relation to the democratic discourse surrounding policy and initiative. However, we have also seen arguments that developments in the democratic discourse have been appropriated by sociological and cultural mechanisms that have negated significant gains in social justice.

The difficult question remains as to what we can conclude from this analysis. It would appear that of and by itself the democratic discourse is not enough. What are the possibilities for an emancipatory discourse, and how might this manifest itself in the classroom? There are three main implications arising from the analysis for an emancipatory discourse that can be drawn out:

- a critical pedagogy;
- teacher and pupil agency; and
- the possibility of moving music out of the curriculum and compulsory classroom.

What is a critical pedagogy? A critical pedagogy suggests going beyond democratic discourse to an emancipatory discourse that engages with the complex meanings of music as valid curriculum content, and where tacit political and cultural meanings are part of the pedagogical transaction of students and teachers. By way of example, Woodford (2012) has suggested that the reasons that ambitions for social justice in music education have been confounded relate to our passive acceptance of mechanisms that are functions of a neoliberal and corporate political agenda. Green (1995, 1996) has suggested that wider social processes can be seen in the prejudicial gendered meanings inherent in music and that the stereotypes arising need to be challenged. A critical pedagogy would aim to open up the implicit politics of music in the classroom and, by so doing, enable teachers and students to understand the ways in which music is subject to powerful social and cultural forces as part of their learning and teaching. Such a process, it is argued, has the potential to be emancipatory and promotes teacher and pupil agency. Where is the "space" for teacher and pupil agency to influence the course of social justice as part of a critical pedagogy and emancipatory discourse? Philpott and Wright (after Bernstein, 1996)) suggest that

> [t]he power to influence change . . . is apparent in the gaps between the various sites for the recontextualization of curriculum and pedagogy i.e. at the levels of *state, school,* and *individual teachers and pupils.* It is here that agency can operate. . . .
> (2012, p. 456)

What does it mean for teachers and students to have agency when working in "discursive gaps"? The argument here suggests that teachers have power to change the status quo when they work in the gaps between policy and practice. The power to influence real change in social justice (for teachers and students) is apparent in the gaps between the various sites for the re-contextualization of curriculum and pedagogy, that is, at the levels of *state, school,* and *individual teachers and students.* It is here that agency and an emancipatory discourse can operate as students and teachers reinterpret policy and initiatives.

However, these important implications for an emancipatory discourse are problematic on many different levels for the "jobbing" music teacher in the secondary classroom. It would be invidious to not recognize the power of what Bernstein calls the "regulative discourse," related as it is to wider social and cultural structures, for as we have seen there is a long history of the status quo embracing change with potentially little or no redistribution of access to achievement and success in the music classroom.

Vignette 6

There are tensions between developing and challenging the students' musical horizons and allowing students to explore their own. This is part of a long-standing debate. Musical Futures has been for me the most important recent curriculum intervention and is a good example of a "ground-up" approach, with much of the work coming from teachers or based on research working with teachers. The influence of student voice became stronger because of Musical Futures.

Teachers and students are inevitably subject to powerful structural processes of socialization, which are all the more pervasive where there is a strong culture of external accountability. For example, it takes some courage to eschew assessment practices that are based on regular "leveling" using criteria dominated by values of complexity. Such expectations are often most strongly articulated at the level of individual schools, and in such circumstances emancipation is rarely high on the agenda for most music teachers.

There is an inevitable tension between a democratic discourse and an emancipatory discourse when the implicit politics of music are laid bare. For example, in self-directed learning, who chooses the "what" and "when" of the critical revelation? And, if the teacher, then does this risk further alienation of students should they not wish to have the politics of their self-directed learning revealed? This is a tension that a pedagogy for social justice will need to resolve if it is to be both democratic and emancipatory. The problem with much critical thinking about music is that it is a discourse *about* music rather *in* music. Furthermore, this can be someone else's critical thinking (the teachers?) and, as we have seen, social justice has often been confounded through pupil alienation from the "reified" musical knowledge of others. The challenge here is for pupil "ownership" of the discourse *about* music as well as the discourse *in* music.

Vignette 7

Possibly the area that I have engaged in less is the more critical approach to music, that is, the more historical and social aspects of music making. What would it mean to put the rather silly masculinized posturing of some of the MC/rapping lyrics in context, if at the same time we did not look at sexist practices in other musics? Sexism in classical music is well documented, but how many music teachers would be happy to situate classical music making as the sexist white middle class hegemonic practice it has become? I know most teachers would be much more comfortable pointing out heavy metal's sexist lyrics or reggae's homophobia—without really addressing the complexity of the issue—that is, the recognition that rappers challenge sexism, that a lot of rap addresses issues of class/race and gender, and that everyone (white) likes to focus on the more extreme of rap at the expense of much other rap music.

Given the rather conservative nature of most music teachers, I imagine much critical discourse about music to be reinforcing and essentializing notions of the "Other," problematizing popular music and critiquing text at the expense of the acknowledgment of context. I imagine the power of the music teacher to label approval at certain musical practices and disapproval at others is too strong to make the discussion useful. I doubt people sufficiently recognize that who they are socially and culturally gives them a partial view of other people and that their own partial view needs critiquing and challenging. I imagine most people are of the view that young people need to be taught and that our experience and knowledge gives us an authority to speak with wisdom and insight.

The complexities of discussing critically different music might just reinscribe the difference and the power inequalities we wish to challenge.

There is much work to be done here on what is a sophisticated and complex pedagogy. Making progress in social justice in the music classroom will require courageous music teachers and senior leaders in schools who promote music being treated as the dominant language of the classroom, where music making itself *is* the critical discourse, and not words about music (although these have their place). The vision here is for a classroom music that is both democratic and emancipatory in its approach to social justice and where music is the discourse that underpins both a critical pedagogy and the exploitation of "discursive gaps."

The aim is for the music classroom to be democratic, in the sense of the inclusivity of the musical discourse, and where there is a conspicuously wider distribution of musical achievement. The aim is also emancipatory, in the sense of the criticality implicit of the discourse *in* music and, where there is discourse *about* music, that this arises from the students' ownership of making and thinking in music. The implication is for a complex, subtle, and nuanced pedagogy for social justice, and there is still much research and thinking to be carried out here.

Postscript

By way of a final thought (and the third implication for an emancipatory discourse noted earlier), we also ought to consider the proposition that curriculum classroom music is destined to be a place for injustice in music. Given the cultural and social forces at play, which have been reported here, it could be that music in the classroom is always held in the bind of such forces. In this context, the "space" for a critical pedagogy and genuine pupil and teacher agency as part of an emancipatory discourse seems an increasingly distant prospect. This is especially so when, at the time of writing, the epistemological and pedagogical implications of the most recent (and as yet not fully operational) developments in England are set to backtrack on even the democratic discourse (see Spruce

2012b, 2013) and where examinations in music and the arts are to become, in the discourse of government policy, "tougher and more rigorous," focusing on the "best" of our culture. Such issues should cause all to ask fundamental questions about the purpose of compulsory classroom music in the English secondary school: whether it needs to be a weekly timetabled subject with a formal curriculum, what physical resources are most appropriate, and who should be the teachers.

Perhaps we should countenance taking music *out* of the compulsory curriculum both for its own sake and for the sake of social justice; this will also take courageous leadership. Perhaps the radical implications of a critical pedagogy, student and teacher agency, and an emancipatory discourse are best served by other ways of organizing music in schools. The self-directed learning model of *Musical Futures* promised much in this regard, and one of the more radical implications of such work is for music to be arranged in non-compulsory open curricula, in open classrooms and with open resources, where criticality *in* music has a higher chance of flourishing in an ever open "discursive gap." If criticality, agency, and emancipation are so important to social justice in music education, as outlined here, then we should at least consider these options. To do otherwise risks ignoring the lessons of the past and perpetuating the ongoing problem of social injustice in the English secondary music classroom.

References

Bernstein, B. (1996). *Pedagogy, symbolic control and identity: Theory, research, critique.* London: Taylor and Francis.

Bray, D. (2000). An examination of GCSE music uptake rates. *British Journal of Music Education, 17*(1), 79–89.

Department for Education and Science (DES). (1992). *Music in the National Curriculum.* London: HMSO.

Department for Education (DfE). (2011). *The importance of music—A national plan for music education,* London: DfE.

Evans, K. (2012). Music 14–19: Choices, challenges, and opportunities. In C. Philpott & G. Spruce (Eds.), Debates in music teaching (pp. 197–208). London: Routledge.

Finney, J. (2007). Music education as identity project in a world of electronic desires. In J. Finney, J. & P. Burnard (Eds.), *Music education with digital technology* (pp. 9–20). London & New York: Continuum.

Green, L. (1988). *Music on deaf ears,* Manchester: Manchester University Press.

Green, L. (1995). Gender, musical meaning and education. In G. Spruce (Ed.), *Teaching music* (pp. 117–124). London: Routledge.

Green, L. (1996). The emergence of gender as an issue in music education. In C. Plummeridge (Ed.), *Music education: Trends and issues* (pp. 41–58). London: Institute of Education, University of London.

Green, L. (2008). *Music, informal learning and the school: A new classroom pedagogy.* Aldershot, UK: Ashgate.

Harland, J., Kinder, K., Lord, P., Stott, A., Schagen, I., & Haynes. J. (2000). *Arts education in secondary schools: Effects and effectiveness.* Slough, UK: NFER.

Kwami, R. M. (1996). Music education in and for a multicultural society. In C. Plummeridge (Ed.), *Music education: Trends and issues* (pp. 59–78). London: Institute of Education.

Lamont, A., & Maton, K. (2008), Choosing music: Exploratory studies into the low uptake of music GCSE. *British Journal of Music Education*, 25(3), 267–282.

Lamont, A., & Maton, K. (2010). Unpopular music: Beliefs and behaviours towards music in education. In R. Wright (Ed.), *Sociology and music education* (pp. 63–80). Farnham, UK: Ashgate.

Office for Standards in Education (Ofsted). (2012). *Music in schools: Wider still and wider*. London: Ofsted.

Paynter, J., & Aston, P. (1970). *Sound and silence: Classroom projects in creative music*. Cambridge: Cambridge University Press.

Philpott, C. (2001). Equality of opportunity and instrumental tuition. In C. Philpott & C. Plummeridge (Eds.), *Issues in music teaching* (pp. 21–31) London: Routledge.

Philpott, C. (2010). The sociological critique of curriculum music in England: Is radical change really possible? In R. Wright (Ed.), *Sociology and music education* (pp. 81–92). Farnham, UK: Ashgate.

Philpott, C. (2012a). The justification for music in the curriculum: Music can be bad for you. In C. Philpott & G. Spruce (Eds.), *Debates in music teaching* (pp. 48–63). London: Routledge.

Philpott, C. (2012b). Assessment for self-directed learning in music education. In C. Philpott & G. Spruce (Eds.), *Debates in music teaching* (pp. 153–168). London: Routledge.

Philpott, C., & Wright, R. (2012). Teaching, learning and curriculum content. In G. E. McPherson, & G. F. Welch (Eds.), *The Oxford handbook of music education* (Vol. 1, pp. 221–459). New York: Oxford University Press.

Schafer, M. (1965). *The composer in the classroom*. Ontario: Canada BMI.

Schools Council. (1971). *Music and the young school leaver: Problems and opportunities*. Working Paper 35. London: Methuen Educational.

Spruce, G. (1999). Music, music education and the bourgeois aesthetic: Developing a music curriculum for the new millennium. In R. McCormick & C. Paechter (Eds.), *Learning and knowledge* (pp. 71–87). London: Oxford University Press.

Spruce, G. (2012a). Musical knowledge, critical consciousness, and critical thinking. In C. Philpott & G. Spruce (Eds.), *Debates in music teaching* (pp. 185–196). London: Routledge.

Spruce, G. (2012b). Unanswered questions. *National Association for Music Educators Magazine*, 35, 4–5.

Spruce, G. (2013). Participation, inclusion, diversity and the policy of English music education. In C. Harrison & P. Mullen (Eds.), *Reaching out: Music education with "hard to reach" children and young people* (pp. 23–31). Salisbury, UK: Music Mark.

Swanwick, K. (1988). *Music, mind and education,* London: Routledge.

Swanwick, K. (1999). *Teaching music musically*. London: Routledge.

Vulliamy, G. (1977). Music as a case study in the "New Sociology of Education." In J. Shepherd, P. Virden, G. Vulliamy, & T. Wishart (Eds.), *Whose music? A sociology of musical languages* (pp. 201–232). London: Latimer.

Woodford, P. (2012). Music education and social justice. In C. Philpott & G. Spruce (Eds.), *Debates in music teaching* (pp. 85–101). London: Routledge.

CHAPTER 27

HOSPITABLE MUSIC MAKING

Community Music as a Site for Social Justice

LEE HIGGINS

INTRODUCTION

ALTHOUGH the term "community music" can be understood in a variety of ways, reflecting a myriad of possible contexts and musical situations (Veblen, Messenger, Silverman, & Elliott, 2013), this chapter has its focus on community music as an active intervention between a music leader and the participants with whom he or she is working (Higgins, 2012). As a form of thoughtful disruption, intervention denotes an encounter with "newness," a perspective that seeks to create situations in which new events innovate and interrupt the present toward moments of futural transformation (Bhabha, 1994). Although there might be a danger that those who intervene are seen as an all-knowing Other, my particular location of intervention follows postmodern thinking inasmuch as there is an insistence of the emergence of the in-between, of boundary crossing through negotiation. Actions of interventions, which could include leading workshops, facilitating discussions, or supporting groups in their musical endeavors, demand deliberate strategies that seek to enable people in finding self-expression through musical means. Using teaching concepts rooted in non-formal education (A. Rogers, 2004), such as facilitation (Hogan, 2002), the pedagogic approaches employed by community musicians place an emphasis on negotiation through collaboration, and thus learning takes place through a "bottom-up" rather than "top-down" approach. With a heart toward coauthorship, collaborative group work, and a belief in the creative potential of all sections of the community, those who work in, and advocate for, community music have attempted to transform attitudes, behaviors, and values toward music making through their practice. This in turn has led to critical questioning surrounding the appropriateness of current music education provision in areas such as inclusion, community responsibility, creative opportunities, diversity, and preparation for a life in music making. This chapter has its focus on the creation of musical spaces that are open to each individual participant. Through two illustrative cases and a conceptual framework informed by Jacques Derrida's writings on justice, I reveal why these music projects can be understood as sites for social justice and thus examples of hospitable music making.

HOSPITABLE JUSTICE

In order to address the central concern of this chapter, an argument for the importance of hospitable music making through Jacques Derrida's account of justice is pertinent. Derrida's detailed and insightful probing is useful, not because it formulates a workable theory of social justice or provides a tight structure to follow, but because it invites us to return to the question of justice.[1] Key to Derrida's analysis of justice is the distinction between justice and law. Law is constructed and constructible and is violent at its origin, in the sense of needing an aggressive and willful power in order to create and embed it. In other words, the foundations of law are structurally always prior to questions of legitimacy. As Simon Wortham (2010, p. 80) notes, "Law cannot found itself lawfully, since the very question of legality obviously cannot be put until law has established itself." Laws are therefore prescriptive and demand that those who fall under their jurisdiction are in compliance within a given authority. Although laws vary dramatically in degree from place to place and from culture to culture, certain forms of law are deemed important for the lives we live. Some obvious examples from the industrial nations might include designated speed limits on motorways, regulations on alcohol and drug consumption, and censorship classifications of films and video games. Implementations of laws do, however, inevitably reduce individual and group decision-making and as a consequence may be said to limit responsibility. For example, when parents adhere to the Board of Film Classifications without inspecting the material themselves, they are entrusting their children's viewing to people they do not know and to the judgment of the panel regarding what is, and what is not, suitable for their child.

In contrast, simply following or applying set laws cannot be said to provide justice, as the truly "just" decision (if there can be such a thing) "must stem from a fundamental responsibility that cannot prop itself up through mere reference to statutory or case law" (Wortham, 2010, p. 80). Justice can therefore be said to come about through the force of law, although there is reciprocity between both; for example, we might say justice needs laws to be justice. Following mathematician and Christian philosopher Blaise Pascal (1958, p. 144), who writes, "Justice without might is helpless," Derrida (2002) concludes, "Justice is not justice, it is not achieved if it does not have the force to be 'enforced'; a powerless justice is not justice, in the sense of law" (p. 238). One might say that justice cannot be constructed and is beyond any legal system and is therefore unable to be calculated in terms of an exchange value within an economy of the law. Laws then have their purpose toward this type of unconditional justice: "Justice is what gives us the impulse, the drive, or the movement to improve the law" (Derrida, 1997, p. 16). As an affirmative gesture, justice is more than simply a response; it is an invitation toward that which is unforeseeable.

Justice considered this way should not be confused with the Platonic form (as this would indicate that we could describe the future situation of justice today) or a Kantian regulative idea (which would imply a description of what justice is, although with the implication that the ideal is not expected to be ever present in some future) (Biesta, 2001, p. 48). Why? Because experienced as an invitation, justice is structured toward an unforeseeable future, calling us to always rethink and reinvent the conditional forms suggested by the law. Justice solicits us from afar, rather than presenting something we could accurately describe and know. Justice is not therefore a foreseeable idealization, something that can be concretely understood. Following John Caputo (1997), justice is always to come and will never fully arrive. Justice is then a call toward something never fully knowable but always worth striving for. Considered in this way, justice is inhabited by a *memory* of those who have died in its name, those who are, and who continue to be, oppressed, as well as those who have been liberated under its call. Justice is also inscribed by *hope*, an appeal to others that can never be fully delivered. As a hopeful enterprise, humans who have a heart toward justice make promises to each other. It is this power of the promise—an affirmation or giving that structurally opens the possibility of the Other as Other, a conscious focus towards individuals beings as individuals—that seeks to commit beyond abstract ideals to the production of happenings such as music making. How can such a promise to justice help us think about community music practice? The next section frames this as hospitable music making.

Hospitable Music Making

At the heart of hospitable music making lies the *decision*, a thought and action that operates as an interface between what is known and what is unknown. For many musicians who work in environments that they see as representing aspects of social injustice, such as areas of conflict or former conflict, prisons, schools, care homes, and so on, their decision means that they step out into the unknown—at least partially. As Derrida (2002, p. 251) suggests, "Each case is other, each decision is different and requires an absolutely unique interpretation." Therefore to decide on that which is already decidable is, in some ways, no decision at all and as a consequence does not serve claims to justice very well. Community musicians often work under the banner of equal opportunities and are therefore making decisions based on a law that sets out to be equal for all, while also attempting to respect and respond in the ways that treat each case differently.

Of course there are certain calculations, certain laws and rules to think about and even to adhere to, but in order to respond to a situation that musicians who work this way perceive as unjust, their actions move toward that which they cannot fully know. The radical decision, a gesture that cannot be based solely on reason or knowledge, enables the musicians and the participants to find positions that prepare themselves for the potential experience of hospitable music making—that is, music making primed for the possibility of responding to issues of social justice. Making these types of decisions can provide the opportunity to energize citizenship and make political action responsible (Sokoloff, 2005). In the context of this chapter and illustrated in the following sections, three musicians make decisions in the name of people, musical participation, context, inclusivity, and diversity. Decisions that are contextualized in this way are always being made in the light of not having all the evidence at hand. A decision to intervene and thus respond to a call for musical participation is always made in a context that is not fully calculable.

"Left-Behind" Children in Taikang

Wang LinLin is a musician studying in the China Conservatory in Beijing. Since moving to the city, Wang LinLin has spent time reflecting on her good fortune in having parents who have been able to support her throughout her education and training as both a professional musician and music therapist. Studying music full-time at most of the world's universities or conservatoires requires particular privileges that are linked to one's past: for example, economic, financial investments that stretch back to the first private lesson; opportunity, having access to a quality music education and/or a music education that meets our expectations; and support from family and friends, those who nurture and protect us physically, emotionally, and spiritually. Wang LinLin's reason to be appreciative of her current situation is set against the context of the town where she spent her formative years. Located in the Henan province in central China, the county town of Taikang is one of many examples of how the economic disparities between China's rural communities and the rapid growth of urban wealth have severely affected community life. Brought about through a widening gulf between those who have and those who have not, parents are forced to leave their children while they go off to the large cities in search of a stable income. This has resulted in many children being left in places where they are looked after and schooled until they are around 9 or 10 years of age. Many rural children are sent to Taikang because a number of the schools can provide room and board from birth. The staff also take responsibility for the children's safety, but this results in not allowing the children out during the days they are in attendance. During the time at the school the children see their parents once, maybe twice, a year. For many children, achieving their professional ambitions seems an impossible task. Wang LinLin evaluates her own narrative against this background and feels that she has been blessed with good fortune and wishes to give back to the community she loves so dearly.

Working with music in the town of Taikang, Wang LinLin creates environments in which the children can express their feelings through rhythm and song. Simple rhythmic games give the children opportunity to add their own words and lyrics and traditional Chinese songs provide a sense of unison. Through the music making, Wang LinLin cultivates a trust between herself and the children. There is an openness to the possibility of change, a sense of humanity and a sense of the "just," what Lithuanian philosopher Emmanuel Levinas (2006) might describe as a humanism of, and for, the Other. Speaking through an interpreter, she admits that there is a "numbness" among the children: "They don't know their parents' love," Wang LinLin laments, "but the songs we sing provide opportunities of emotional release."

Through her interventions with the children as individual and precious human beings, Wang LinLin evokes a friendship and gives them a certain type of permission to express their inner thoughts. Her actions reflect Derrida's notion that justice is a vocation, an affirmative step toward another human being. The children will initially say, "I'm not angry that my parents are gone because I know they are making a better life for me." After a time of music making, some of the children reveal that they miss their parents and ask, "Why did they leave me here?" Wang LinLin's work is driven by a sense of the unjust: Why are these children left alone? This doesn't seem fair, not for the parents, not for the children, and not for China's society. In the future, Wang LinLin wants to try to make music students studying in Beijing aware of this situation. Wang LinLin is convinced that if she can, somehow, showcase her work to those who are privileged and studying in the city, then they too will be empathetically touched and will be inspired to head to the rural villages as community musicians.

Music in a Massachusetts Correctional Institution

Jamie Hillman and André de Quadros are two choral conductors who have run a participatory music-making course in a Massachusetts correctional institution for men. The course was part of a university prison education program run by Boston University in the United States. Drawing upon facilitatory techniques honed by the Brazilian dramatist August Boal (2002), Hillman and de Quadros created a "safe" environment where musical risks could be taken. These included singing solo and reciting self-penned poetry and song lyrics. Over the duration of their time together, inmates learned to trust the group leaders and, perhaps more crucially, learned to trust and respect each other.

Chosen for the powerful words, a Handel aria, *Lascia ch'io Pianga*, was the first song the group learned and performed together:

> Let me weep for my cruel fate
> And sigh after freedom!
> And let me sigh
> Sigh after freedom!

Although cognizant of the positive impact that music might have within the context of a prison or secure environment, it took the inmates to reveal that they were singing *Lascia ch'io Pianga* in the shower for Hillman and de Quadros to realize just how much their work was affecting the daily lives of the men involved (Seligson, 2012). I was lucky enough to contribute to this course, and my own experience brought me face to face with a group of men willing to share, collaborate, and step out of their comfort zone. Among the group there was willingness to try new and inventive things. Using teaching strategies that encouraged individual and group input, we were able to work toward percussive grooves that reflected individual "voices" while attempting to consolidate group cohesiveness. Group musical activities, such as learning cultural-specific rhythms using the voice and body percussion, were woven into a free musical "jam." Because of its informality, this session lent itself toward the men feeling relaxed enough to discuss aspects of their lives both inside and outside the prison. This enabled conversations about musical interests and past musical involvement.

During my time with the men, it was clear that Hillman and de Quadros had skillfully crafted a safe and creative working environment for the participants and the music leaders. By building a working space that put trust and respect at the forefront, the group could rely on each other's actions and decisions. By taking responsibility for the bond between music facilitator and participants, Hillman and de Quadros had provided an outlet for self-expression and discovery while empowering and validating the participants. Grounded in what US psychologist Carl Rogers (1994) describes as "empathic understanding," the music leaders had, over the weeks of the course, created relationships without presenting an "expert" front or a façade. This non-directional approach encouraged the participants to do likewise and thus opened the possibility for both sides to journey together, a chance to venture "safely" into the unknown. Indeed, both parties' experience, expertise, and knowledge were different, and their goals may also have been different, but through a facilitative process that placed faith in the realness of the relationship, trust, respect, and responsibility flowed.

Encouraged to keep reflective accounts through blogs and journals, the writings of one attendee described the communicative transformation in and around parts of the prison site and evocatively captures the impact that music making had on the group:

> The shared experience of making music, in its most primitive form, gave us a tribal sense of community. This bonding became evident outside of the classroom when by chance we would encounter one another, and exchange a secret smile, a salutation, or break into some song or exercise, which we had learned.[2]

Continuing, the writer notes that

> [t]his sense of good will is noticeably contagious. When we see one another and interact in passing, it invariably requires some explanation with fellows who observed the odd exchange. In so doing we spread the good will, this sense of communion with others. It even sparks curiosity in some, or a longing for the sense of community, which they have witnessed.[3]

It is clear from these comments that those running the music sessions "worked with" rather than "worked on" the participants. Those involved were collaborators embarking on a musical journey together. Resisting a perspective that would render the inmates a "crowd," Hillman and de Quadros employed a sense of compassion and thus cultivated relationships that ignited a passion for life and each other. Their pursuit of justice, in the Derridian sense of an invitation toward that which is unforeseeable, enabled a type of interaction, musical or otherwise, that many of the men may not have experienced before. If community music projects like this can, as one inmate suggests, "answer the question of who men really are," then there is much to learn from the practices and processes of community musicians. Opening avenues to assist people in empathizing with others and to sharing in what it means to be human takes substantive steps toward a more just world.

Both of these examples have been driven by musicians who feel that certain injustices are at work within sections of the community. Wang LinLin feels that the current economic situation in her town Taikang in the Henan province has created an unjust situation. Hillman and de Quadros feel that finding meaningful ways to enable human interaction among incarcerated men is the right thing to do. These projects illustrate what I am describing as *hospitable* music making—musicking that is a response from the call of the Other and is sparked into life through an encounter of a promise toward justice. Wang LinLin made a decision to return to her village to work with those who she felt were not getting the love and support needed to reach full human potential. Hillman and de Quadros made the decision to work in a Massachusetts correctional institute and engage the men in creative music making, rather than teach a course on music appreciation. All three musicians were active in the process of decision-making that led to a promise toward creating environments for hospitable music making—music making with justice as a significant feature, both in terms of the conception and the action itself. However, none of the musicians really knew what to expect, and it was their willingness to embrace the unknowable that led the musical interactions that eventually took place.

Conclusion

Human encounters, connected through a call, a response, and a welcome, are what binds these examples. In some cases the call is direct, people vocalizing a desire to be included in music making, while others require the music leaders to make themselves and their resources available on the off chance that something might happen. Whatever the context, there is, at some point, a moment of decision, a moment to affirm, a moment to utter "yes." The two examples I have highlighted are single cases, non-repeatable events ignited through a decision and a desire for justice.[4] It would, however, be wrong to assume that this type of justice, a justice that is to come, a justice residing in an unforeseeable future, is politically impotent—quite the opposite: it is an urgent and non-programmable justice. Marked by justice beyond the law, this is not a question of utopia, but a promise, an urgent and passionate justice that is always in a heterogenic relation to the Other.

With cultural democracy acting as a political compass, community music practice attempts to move toward the Others' call, not in the name of horizons of perfectibility and foreseeable ideals but, rather, in a response to the urgency of hospitable music making. By engaging with the conceptual apparatus of hospitable justice and the teaching practices commonly found in non-formal education, much of the work of community musicians, such as Wang LinLin, Hillman, and de Quadros, encourages critical questioning surrounding the appropriateness of current music education provision. Questions might include:

- What does it mean to respond responsibly in a music-making context?
- How might the decisions I make affect issues important for those individuals and groups with whom I work?

Inclusion, community responsibility, creative opportunities, diversity, and lifelong learning are areas of concern within music education. Although not unproblematic, these areas might be framed in the following ways:

- Do current teaching strategies encourage inclusive music participation?
- How important is it that music students nurture a sense of collective responsibility— in terms both of working in ensembles and community engagement?
- Are students being encouraged to take risks and make their own music?
- How are school music programs reflecting the musical diversity of their local community?
- What structures and pathways are in place to support lifelong musical learning?
- How are the conservatories, universities, and schools of music responding to the inclusivity agenda?[5]

Questions such as these can be understood as a desire to reveal the injustices that currently infiltrate many institutionalized music education programs. These include discriminatory distinctions between classical and vernacular music, and the promotion of music elitism, pursued through pedagogic structures that are validated through sets of standards created by self-nominated gatekeepers of musical culture. Community music practice as a site of social justice relies on those working in it to constantly make radical decisions. These types of decisions, decisions that have an unknown fate, fuel an aspiration for justice by engaging participants as individuals. In this formulation, the Other is treated as the Other and, as such, musical learning begins as a site for justice. The projects from Taikang and the Massachusetts correctional institution began from a radical decision: a promise made by musicians who quite frankly did not know what they were getting themselves into! The decisions made by Wan LinLin, Hillman, and de Quadros were made not knowing what the precise outcomes would be. However, each person carried with him or her a deep sense that something needed to be done. It was this combination—a sense of a current injustice and a desire to intervene—that ignited their actions toward what I would call hospitable music making. Let's be clear: hospitable music making can never truly *be*, but can come to us through decisive moments of justice, an open embrace toward those who wish to participate in active music making and those who just might. In a broader sense, educating within a context that celebrates peoples differences, or at least thinking about it, might encourage a greater sensitivity toward issues of social justice.

As a field of practice, community music attracts musicians who have a heart for social justice. The work of musicians such as Brydie Leigh-Bartleet, Mary Cohen, Don Devito, Gillian Howell, Magali Kleber, Phil Mullen, and Catherine Pestano supports this notion.[6] Whether working with those at risk, in youth detention centers, or marginalized through disability, poverty, gender, or ethnicity, a common feature of those working in community music has been an outstretched hand toward those who have been excluded. Through a Derridian lens, justice is a vocation, a positive response to the Other in the shape of a call, rather than a matter of knowledge. Justice is therefore ignited through the encounter and as such lies at the heart of any educative experience. Structured as an unforeseeable future, justice thought of in this way invites community musicians (as well as music educators more generally) to question what it means to respond to those who we know wish to be involved in active music making. Importantly, and perhaps crucially, justice conceived in this way turns our head toward those we do not yet know—those whose voices have been suppressed or those whom we have yet to meet. For an education experience—music or otherwise—to resist being unjust, I suggest that some form of recognition of the Other as Other, is essential. Derrida's conception of justice, formulated as hospitable music making, helps us understand what this might mean not only in a theoretical way, but also in a very practical sense.

Notes

1. Derrida's ideas are woven throughout a large body of work, so it is often difficult to give an exhaustive list of texts that deal with any one idea. In this instance the go-to text would be "Force of law: The 'mystical foundation of authority'" (2002), the first part of which was published by the *Cardozo Law Review* in 1989 and subsequently republished and critical analyzed by the colloquium convener Drucilla Cornell in the book *Deconstruction and the Possibility of Justice* (1992).
2. Prose written by one of the men and shared with consent.
3. Prose written by one of the men and shared with consent.
4. The music projects and those that run them are not to be understood as "just" because justice never fully arrives, and this is its power. Although responding within a different theoretical framework, Elizabeth Gould's (2007) notion of "stretching the boundaries of power" resonates with this idea (p. 235).
5. In personal conversation, Phil Mullen helped me think about categorizing these questions into three groups: inclusion, diversity, and creativity. Community music may be described as trying to create the circumstances through which these three things can take place.

6. For illustrations of this work, see past issues of the *International Journal of Community Music*. See also Higgins (2012); Veblen et al. (2013).

REFERENCES

Bhabha, H. K. (1994). *The location of culture*. London: Routledge.

Biesta, G. J. J. (2001). "Preparing for the incalculable": Deconstruction, justice, and the question of education. In G. J. J. Biesta & D. Egea-Kuehne (Eds.), *Derrida and education* (pp. 32–54). New York: Routledge.

Boal, A. (2002). *Games for actors and non-actors* (A. Jackson, Trans., 2nd ed.). London: Routledge.

Caputo, J. D. (1997). Justice, if such a thing exists. In J. D. Caputo (Ed.), *Deconstruction in a nutshell: A conversation with Jacques Derrida* (pp. 125–155). New York: Fordham University Press.

Derrida, J. (1997). The Villanova roundtable. In J. D. Caputo (Ed.), *Deconstruction in a nutshell: A conversation with Jacques Derrida* (pp. 1–28). New York: Fordham University Press.

Derrida, J. (2002). Force of law: The "mystical foundation of authority." In G. Anidjar (Ed.), *Acts of religion* (pp. 230–298). London: Routledge.

Higgins, L. (2012). *Community music: In theory and in practice*. New York: Oxford University Press.

Hogan, C. (2002). *Understanding facilitation: Theory and principles*. London: Kogan Page.

Levinas, E. (2006). *Humanism of the Other* (N. Poller, Trans.). Urbana: University of Illinois Press.

Pascal, B. (1958). *Pensées*. New York: Dutton Paperback.

Rogers, A. (2004). *Non-formal education: Flexible schooling or participatory education?* Hong Kong: Comparative Education Research Centre, University of Hong Kong.

Rogers, C. R. (1994). *Freedom to learn* (3rd ed.). New York: Macmillan College.

Seligson, S. (2012). What "makes us fundamentally human." *BU Today*. Retrieved from http://www.bu.edu/today/2012/what-makes-us-fundamentally-human.

Sokoloff, W. W. (2005). Between justice and legality: Derrida on decision. *Political Research Quarterly*, *58*(2), 341–352.

Veblen, K., Messenger, S. J., Silverman, M., & Elliott, D. J. (Eds.). (2013). *Community music today*. Landham, MD: Rowman and Littlefield.

Wortham, S. M. (2010). *The Derrida dictionary*. New York: Continuum.

CHAPTER 28

SOCIAL JUSTICE AND URBAN MUSIC EDUCATION

RUBÉN GAZTAMBIDE-FERNÁNDEZ
AND LESLIE STEWART ROSE

INTRODUCTION

THE urban classroom has presented a unique set of challenges for music educators that have been broadly addressed by a number of scholars and practitioners. While many of these challenges are not unique, such as issues related to poverty and the general lack of resources that pervade schools in large and underfunded urban districts, these manifest in particular ways in music classrooms. As priority is given to literacy and numeracy, even fewer resources are allocated for music programs, resulting in significant lack or absence of time, space, and other necessary resources, such as instruments and new technology. Moreover, the cultural diversity that characterizes urban classrooms raises profound questions about the relevance of mainstream music programs and complicates the question of multiculturalism. Even more significant is the issue of not just how to develop and implement music programs in the context of poverty, but also how such programs might respond to and take responsibility for addressing the gross economic disparities that shape and characterize urban schooling. Implied here, of course, is the assumption that music education programs in urban schools *should* address such challenges and not simply assume the value of a music education removed from the social and cultural context within which it takes place.

The argument that music education in urban schools should be premised on a commitment to social justice has been strongly developed elsewhere (e.g., Allsup, 2007a; Bowman, 2007; Gaztambide-Fernández, 2010; Gould, Countryman, Morton, & Stewart Rose, 2009; Jorgensen, 2007; Schmidt, 2011). In this chapter, we want to point to some of the quandaries that emerge when engaging music education in urban classrooms through social justice commitments, particularly given the thorough and sometimes devastating critiques that have been leveled against music education and its role in social, cultural, and economic reproduction. These critiques have taken many important directions. For instance, scholars like Beynon (2009), Gould (2005), Koza (1993, 1994, 2003), and Lamb (1994, 1996) have demonstrated the role of music education in reproducing gender hierarchies and heteronormativity. Similarly, scholars have pointed out how music plays a role in asserting White supremacy (Bradley, 2006, 2007, 2009; Bradley, Golner, & Hanson, 2007; Koza, 2008), imposing classed conceptions of taste (Bryson, 1997; Peterson & Simkus, 1992), and normalizing able-bodied imaginaries (Lubet, 2009, 2010). Others have taken up a critique of the role of music education in imperial conquest and nation-building through colonial settlement (Vaugeois, 2013). These critiques can have a paralyzing effect, leaving music educators who are committed to social justice without clear direction and reluctant to engage in social justice projects. Remaining paralyzed by these critiques, however, would be to remain complicit and to some extent akin to remaining naïve (see Vaugeois, 2013).

These critiques demonstrate that the problem of how to approach social justice is not external to music education, but rather it is deeply embedded in how music education has evolved as a field and how it is conceptualized as a practice. It is crucial, then, to develop an approach to social justice that does not remain loyal to prior conceptualizations of music education, but rather reframes music education through a different paradigm, one premised on a dynamic conception of culture and social change. More specifically to urban classrooms, such a reconceptualization requires a shift in how music educators understand the very idea of "the urban," both in relationship to urban schools and to what counts as urban music. As such, in this chapter we offer a discussion of some of the approaches to social justice that music educators in urban schools have embraced, highlighting key commitments and practical strategies. First, we describe the contours of what it means to conceptualize urban music education as cultural practice, unpacking the relationship between notions of the urban and musical practice. Second, we provide a brief introduction to various understandings of social justice and lay out key concepts for understanding the approaches that we discuss. We then present four different ways of approaching social justice that highlight key concerns with issues of access, representation, pedagogy, and ideology. We argue that a comprehensive approach to social justice in urban music education must tackle each of these concerns through an understanding of music education as cultural practice that places a dynamic conception of the urban and social justice at its core.

CONCEPTUALIZING URBAN MUSIC EDUCATION AS CULTURAL PRACTICE

Some aspects of the argument we outline in this chapter are not only relevant for urban music education in particular, or even urban schools in general. Indeed, much of what we discuss here can be directly or indirectly relevant to music educators working in schools and communities in other settings, whether rural, suburban, or many other international settings. We focus on the urban, in part, because it has been the primary focus of our own work and because of our commitment to addressing the stark social inequalities that are made manifest through and that shape urban classrooms, as well as the specific challenges and needs of the urban context. We also focus on the urban because it has particular conceptual significance; our approach to understanding the intersection between social justice and music education as cultural practice is best expressed and illustrated through the particularities of the urban context. A focus on the urban context brings inequality into relief because it is defined by proximity and enlivened by constant movement and encounters with difference (Gaztambide-Fernández, 2011). Urban spaces are defined by the explicitness of the structures and rules that regulate but, as DeCerteau (1984) has argued, do not entirely constrain cultural practices such as music making.

Elsewhere, Gaztambide-Fernández (2011) presents a three-pronged conception of the "urban" as a space constituted at the intersection of specific material realities, symbolic imaginaries, and embodied cultural practices. First, the urban is defined by the "material reality" of population density and close proximity in relationship to extreme economic inequalities. This conception of the urban highlights disparities in material conditions through the juxtaposition of extreme wealth and poverty, as well as how the two define each other. Second, these material disparities also produce different "imaginaries" of the urban, which are not typically understood in relationship to each other. Gaztambide-Fernández (2011) highlights how "the urban is imagined both positively and negatively; it is imagined positively through the notion of the *urbane—the* center of civilization, cultural refinement, and progress—and it is imagined negatively—as a place of decay, poverty, and danger" (p. 19). Finally, a "practice" conception of the urban focuses on the ways in which the urban landscape is constantly being made through the ways in which individuals come into contact with each other and with the structures and institutions constituting the city (DeCerteau, 1984). A practice conception of the urban requires a complex accounting of both the material realities as well as the imaginaries through which the urban is continually produced and comes into being.

Previous work in music education that focused on urban contexts has tended to embrace a narrow conception of the urban that collapses often essentialized views of youth of color with the material conditions of poverty. This leads music educators to misrecognize the broad and complex dynamics of inequality that constitute the urban. Thinking of the urban as constituted at the intersection of particular material realities, symbolic imaginaries, and daily practices provides an alternative lens for thinking about urban music education and how social justice might figure in it as a field. For instance, when we think about urban music as more than what the label references in the context of popular music, we come to appreciate the wide range of musical practices that exist within and that constitute the urban. This includes not only the musical practices associated with youth of color, such as rap or reggaeton, but also the classical repertoire that is the core of musical organizations in major cities, musicals, and even the so-called muzak that adorns the hallways of malls everywhere. Such an expansive categorization stands in tension with both common sense as well as musicological notions of "urban music" (see Gaztambide-Fernández, 2011). This dissonance is crucial because it highlights inequality, whereas a narrow conception of urban music tends to obscure the role that the full range of musical practices that constitutes the urban play in the production of social inequality.

This way of understanding urban music pushes the boundaries of what counts as music education, expanding the repertoires and the practices that can be integrated as part of the curriculum and pedagogy. Ostensibly, this is about taking the standard repertoires and practices of music education and placing them alongside a wider range of practices, such as DJ-ing, slam poetry, street dancing, and jams. Yet, this is not simply about a more inclusive music education. Rather, embracing an expansive view of urban music in music education opens the door for taking cultural practices seriously as central to an urban education project focused on social justice.

SOCIAL JUSTICE COMMITMENTS, DEFINITIONS, AND DILEMMAS

Education scholars have noted that social justice is mobilized for a wide range of rhetorical purposes, often without a clear definition (Ayers, Quinn, & Stovall, 2008; Clark, 2006; Hytten & Bettez, 2011; North, 2006, 2008). What precisely constitutes justice? What are the perceived challenges for the achievement of justice? What and how should educators contribute toward accomplishing justice? Before we elaborate on the various issues related to a social justice commitment in urban music education, in this section we discuss key points for thinking through the question of social justice in relationship to urban music education.

In the broadest sense, social justice commitments typically imply that there are aspects of contemporary society that are either inherently unjust or that undermine the desire for justice, usually because of some form of inequality or disadvantage (Harvey, 1973, 2008; North, 2008; Sen, 1992). Such inequalities and/or disadvantages are sometimes framed in relationship to differences in social, political, or economic conditions that affect the well-being of groups and/or individuals and their capacity to participate fully in society. From this view, social justice efforts are focused on the equal "redistribution" of resources in order to make conditions more equitable for participation (Fraser, 1997; Harvey, 1973). Other times, inequalities and disadvantages are understood as being related to differences in the perceived or presumed characteristics of individuals and groups, whether these differences are construed as biological, cultural, or social. From this view, social justice efforts are focused on the equal "representation" of different ways of being and expressing oneself and one's desires, as well as different modes of participating in society based on the unique particularities that characterize groups and individuals (Kymlicka, 1996; Young, 1990, 2001).

Drawing on Fraser's (1997) attempt to "synergize a politics of recognition with a politics of redistribution," North (2006) identifies two additional "frictions" that "indicate the importance of contextualizing discussions about and political challenges to social injustice in the field of education" (p. 508). As she notes, central to the problem of redistribution versus recognition is the problem of how to understand equality, whether in terms of ensuring sameness or protecting difference. That is, while a focus on redistribution is concerned with ensuring sameness in terms of access to valued resources and opportunities for participation, a focus on recognition is concerned with ensuring differential access on the basis of the characteristics of particular groups and the varying needs of individuals based on their particular identifications. Moreover, whether the focus of justice efforts is on macro-level processes, such as policymaking, or micro-level processes, such as individual interactions, also shapes how these efforts are articulated. Thus, while policies are typically intended to apply to all participants equally as a strategy to ensure equal access and accountability, attention to the needs of students typically requires addressing the particular needs of individuals in context.

Framing social justice education around different understandings of oppression, Kumashiro (2000) describes how different approaches construe the pedagogical strategies necessary for addressing inequality. The first approach, "education for the Other," focuses on equalizing the conditions for, as well as the expectations from, the educational opportunities available for those who experience marginalization or oppression, whom Kumashiro defines as the "Other." Reflecting the tension between sameness and difference described by North (2006, 2008), this approach focuses on ensuring equal access to educational opportunities, as well as providing "spaces where students who face different forms of oppression can go for help, support, advocacy, resources, and so forth" (Kumashiro, 2000, p. 28). The second approach, "education about the Other", focuses more directly on issues of representation, not only by incorporating more, and more accurate, knowledge about the experiences of the Other, but also by challenging hierarchies that reinforce dominant views about what is valuable knowledge.

Attention to questioning knowledge hierarchies is central to what Kumashiro labels as "education that is critical of privileging and Othering," which focuses on developing a critique of power and the hierarchies that impose dominant conceptions of knowledge and produce marginalization. Unlike the first two, this third approach "calls on educators not only to teach about oppression but to try to change society as well" (p. 38). Through processes of "conscientization," all students, whether or not they experience marginalization, are expected to take action by engaging in political participation (p. 38). The fourth approach, "education that changes students and society," turns the focus away from structures of inequality toward the discourses that "frame how people think, feel, act, and interact" (p. 40). By turning attention not only to the meanings and ideas that shape interactions, this approach highlights the role of desires, feelings, and the various citation practices that reinforce oppression through language and symbolic exchange.

Kumashiro (2000) notes the opportunities as well as the limits of each of these approaches to anti-oppression education, highlighting the importance of bringing these approaches together into an "amalgam" that reflects the particular needs of students. In what follows, we describe how some of the various notions of social justice manifest through different approaches to social justice in urban music education.

ILLUSTRATIONS AND APPROACHES

Committed to disrupting marginalization and inequitable distributions and representations, music educators have theorized and critiqued the multiple ways that power and value are practiced in North American urban music classrooms. In parallel, music teachers have explored what a commitment to addressing social justice might look and feel like, particularly when music education has historically been entrenched within dominant practices that are particularly resistant to change. The aim of this section is to describe ways that issues of social justice have been addressed in practical ways and how different conceptualizations of injustice dictate, limit, or impede fulsome enactments of social justice. While we discuss these approaches separately, we note that these are not discrete or necessarily exclusive practices. Rather, teachers committed to social justice often find ways to combine these practices in order to address the challenges faced by students in their particular classrooms. We discuss various approaches to social justice in urban music education by considering how these approaches deal with four key problems:

- providing access (who is participating?);
- ensuring representation (what and whose music is being taught?);
- rethinking pedagogy (how is music being taught?); and
- questioning ideology (how is music political? what are the politics of music?).

Providing Access: Who Is Participating?

The goal of equalizing access to and redistributing resources for music education begins from the acknowledgment that opportunities for participating in music education programs are particularly absent in schools that are affected by poverty, which in the United States and Canada are often schools in urban areas serving students of color. Typically, the redistribution of opportunities to study music focuses on three broad questions: Who has access to the music education programming available? Who is included or excluded from particular kinds of music education opportunities? And whose well-being, needs, and/or desires are being served by the music education opportunities available? (see Bartel, 1995, 2001).

Social justice music education committed to redistributing access is often focused on securing more funding, more specialist teachers, continued advocacy, and better supports and training for generalist teachers (Coalition for Music Education in Canada, 2010). The programs being promoted might include primary schoolchildren's choirs, recorder ensembles, band or string class, classical (i.e., European) music notation, and sometimes music appreciation classes that might include visits to the local symphony. The assumption behind these mainstream music programs is that being exposed to the European musical canon and participating in its corresponding musical ensemble models will enrich and even enhance the lives of *all* students. Within urban schools, the concern is that most students do not have access to such opportunities, and the goal of social justice is to address this lack and ensure that poor students and students of color have equal access to the *great* works of European music. How these works are supposed to be engaged and even how they are meant to be experienced is prescribed, and thus the aim is to ensure that all students have the *right* kind of experience, with the *right* kind of music.

This commitment to redressing the lack of access is premised on what Gaztambide-Fernández (2011) calls a "civilizing approach" to urban music education, in which the goal is to further assimilate marginalized or otherwise *uncivilized* students through opportunities to participate in dominant modes of music making. This approach reflects what Kumashiro (2000) calls an "education for the Other," as it seeks to change the presumed harm done by providing equal access to what is assumed to be good for everyone. Often these approaches assume that participation in music has the effect of rescuing students from their social and economic conditions. Music teachers are construed as saviors who can ensure access to dominant musical practices and values.

Beyond schools, outreach and community programming also seek to provide access to those who lack what is assumed to be the right kind of music education for the purpose of transforming their lives. The world-renowned music outreach program *El Sistema*, for example, describes itself as a "new model for social change" and a "visionary global movement that transforms the lives of children through music" by "preparing for participation in orchestra ensembles" (National Alliance of El Sistema Inspired Programs, n.d.). Rather than changing society, the aim is to change the individuals who have the opportunity to participate in a mainstream musical organization. Moreover, the salvation narrative assumes that those who do not have such access lead lives bereft of musical experience, as any non-dominant musical practices are not perceived as worthy of the label. Of course, not every program that seeks to provide music education to all students who are presumed to lack such opportunities assumes the singular value of dominant musical practices.

Ensuring Representation: What and Whose Music Is Being Taught?

A second approach toward social justice in urban music education aims to address questions of representation, often taken up by considering "whose music" will be the content of the curriculum (Campbell 2004, 2005; Reimer, 2002; Schippers, 2010). This approach aims to meet the goals of social justice by including musical practices assumed to belong to groups of students who experience marginalization. Kumashiro (2000) describes this approach as "education about the Other," which attempts "to work against oppression by focusing on what all students—privileged and marginalized—know and should know about the Other" (p. 31). Since what is valued is worth learning, the inclusion of many musical practices and styles attempts to disrupt the dominance of the Eurocentric classical canon as the definitive music. This goal becomes particularly important in urban spaces that are defined by diversity and closeness, where the students themselves bring musical traditions, both contemporary and traditional, from a multiplicity of geographic regions.

Social justice approaches that focus on representation are often premised on what Gaztambide-Fernández (2011) calls a "culturalist" approach, as these aim to increase the visibility of non-dominant cultural practices. Much like the civilizing logic that is the premise of social justice projects focused on access, the culturalist approach tends to assume a fixed understanding of culture and cultural practices, in which particular groups are assumed to have particular musical practices that uniquely belong to them and that are somehow fixed in time. This is often manifested by a focus on authenticity necessary for making distinctions and assigning labels to a wide range of practices, in order to distinguish them from dominant forms and from each other. Notions of authenticity, however, are often based on stereotypes and essentialized views of non-dominant musical practices that are then viewed as exotic and are commodified as "world music" (Brennan, 2001; Connell & Gibson, 2004; Taylor, 2007).

A focus on representation is particularly important in urban schools, where there is more cultural diversity and where students may be more familiar with a plethora of non-dominant musical forms. However, this commitment often takes an additive approach to multicultural curriculum, in which a few discrete examples are presented in politically neutral ways and in relationship to a predominantly Western viewpoint (Banks, 2007). This can lead to gross reductionism, for example, when the music of a particular country is used to represent the music of an entire continent. Moreover, the assumption that the "culture" of individual students who experience oppression must be somehow included often relies on essentialisms based on historical representations. This is particularly challenging when the aim is to include representations of Indigenous cultural practices, which are often assumed to be extinct or frozen in the past, as if Indigenous people were no longer engaged in complex processes of cultural creation.

A focus on representation also raises questions about who is responsible and/or qualified to teach non-dominant musical practices. An essentialist focus on authenticity would suggest that, for instance, only Latin American teachers can teach Latin music, or only teachers from the English-speaking Caribbean can lead a steel drum ensemble. This is also associated with questions about what competences are necessary to properly teach non-dominant musical practices; for instance, what kind of training is necessary to introduce students to rock bands or DJ-ing. Moreover, given that most music teachers are trained within a dominant understanding of music and musical practices, there is also a tendency to impose European classical music frameworks, such as "the elements of music" (Stewart Rose & Countryman, 2013), and Western theory systems on non-Western/classical traditions (see McClary & Walser, 1990). Ultimately, these challenges point to a third approach to social justice in music education, focusing not only on redistribution and representation, but more importantly on the pedagogical approaches to music education.

Rethinking Pedagogy: How Is Music Being Taught?

A third common approach to social justice in music education reconsiders questions about how to approach learning and teaching. This approach challenges the "highly prescriptive pedagogies and methodologies" that are typical of mainstream music education and that often "stifle the individual creativity and thinking of students and teachers alike" (Woodford, 2005, p. 30). Those who approach social justice commitments through a critique of pedagogy are not always directly focused on particular groups who are excluded or on expanding musical content beyond European traditions, although both of these are often at stake. Rather, they are concerned with the oppressive character of traditional approaches to music based on the complete control and authority of the teacher and/or conductor and how these undermine commitments to democracy and participation (e.g., Allsup, 2003, 2007b; Woodford, 2005).

At stake in this approach is an examination of the power relations between students and teachers and a focus on new modes of participation, which sometimes are based on musical practices that contrast with classical training. This may involve attempts at decentering—or eliminating—the traditional role of the conductor/teacher (see Friesen, 2009; Snell, 2009). Instead, the focus might be on student-led small groups, sometimes inspired by the musical practices associated with the music that students engage throughout their lives outside schools, or what is often referred to as popular music. In order to shift power relations, some music educators turn the focus away from performance and technique, toward composing, improvising, recording, and performing with rhythm sections, computers, and new media (see Bolden, 2009, 2013; Green, 2002; Lashbrook & Mantie, 2009; Younker & Hickey, 2007). These teachers often aim to share decision-making, to engage students through inquiry and self-governance, and to invoke circle pedagogies in an effort to promote participation and practices of democracy.

Teachers concerned with questions of pedagogy struggle with the dilemma of how to define democracy, first recognizing that the teacher, no matter the intent, holds more power than the students. For instance, questions around consensus versus majority rule point to implicit dynamics of coercion and bullying that can often undermine lofty commitments (Gould, 2007). Whether students' particular interests can come to occupy the proverbial center stage of the curriculum is also often a challenge in this approach, as it raises questions about what is appropriate within the context of schools. Recently, issues of copyright have also become of concern, as the interests of corporations clash against practices such as sampling, remixing, and other creative practices that challenge how legal frameworks understand authorship. These questions seem to be exacerbated when the wide range of cultural practices that coexist within the urban context come into contact with each other within a music classroom.

Finally, a focus on the process alone can sometimes yield to a naïve conception of music making, as if it were removed from the larger social and political context that surrounds it, ignoring the fact that while power relations might be undermined within the classroom, they continue to persist outside. This becomes an issue, for example, when issues of gender and sexuality—topics that are common in the genres that students usually engage outside school—are raised. The extent to which teachers should challenge, question, examine, or simply accept the ways in which students engage these topics becomes a thorny question, particularly when teachers are either unable or unwilling to engage students in discussions about how politics, ideology, and other social dynamics shape how music making takes place.

Questioning Ideology: How Is Music Political? What Are the Politics of Music?

A fourth approach to social justice in urban music education directs attention to the social and political context of urban music, how ideology shapes music, and how music can serve the interests of the dominant social order. This approach pays less attention to the actual practice of music, and more to the historical, social, cultural, and political context of music making, creating opportunities to identify, name, and discuss power and the role of music in processes of marginalization and the privileging of some groups over others. Drawing on critical pedagogy, the focus of this approach is to engage students—particularly those who experience marginalization—in an examination of how structures of power work at individual, institutional, and systemic levels, what Kumashiro (2000) describes as "education that is critical of privileging and Othering" (pp. 25, 35). This "critical" approach seeks to "interrupt normative and essentializing ways of thinking about culture, mainly by illuminating how power dynamics shape whether and how particular kinds of music come to be accepted as legitimate and/ or authentic" (Gaztambide-Fernández, 2011, p. 31). Here, a broad conception of urban music, as articulated earlier in this chapter, becomes essential as a locus of analysis for examining the role of musical practices in social inequality.

The conceptual premise of this approach is that culture is always a socially constructed practice, bound by socially constructed webs of power, in which all musical practices are connected to each other. The object of learning becomes the analysis of the politics that shape and are shaped by musical worlds, past and present. This might include an examination of the economic aspects of music and how the music industry shapes music making, usually by considering already existing musical works and how these are circulated and engaged. That is, rather than music making, teachers look for

opportunities to use existing musical products to examine how musicians both participate and resist the political and economic context that surrounds them and engage in
a social-cultural critique of power relations in music (e.g., McClary, 1991; Taylor, 2007;
Walser, 1993).

While a focus on ideology is critical of dominant understandings of what counts as
music and what are accepted musical practices, this "critical approach" is also premised
on a deficit model that positions students as lacking, if not the access to the *right* kind
of music, then the *right* kind of musical understanding. The teacher's job is to ensure
that students can lift the mantle of dominant ideology and embrace the radical political stance toward social justice that the teacher has presumably already achieved. This
involves an intellectual process that eschews feelings, unconscious desires, and needs, in
favor of reason as the proper way to experience music. This

> rationalist approach to consciousness-raising assumes that reason and reason alone
> is what leads to understanding. However, rational detachment is impossible: one's
> identities, experiences, privileges, investments, and so forth always influence how
> one thinks and perceives, what one knows and wills not to know. (Kumashiro,
> 2000, p. 39)

Moreover, by focusing on music and music practices as objects, this "critical approach"
often lacks any substantial engagement with music making. This focus on the *study* of
music, rather than the *making*, can sometimes stem from an ironic paralysis that results
from such analysis. For instance, an examination of how dominant institutions appropriate and exoticize non-dominant cultural practices might result in a refusal to find
ways of engaging such practices within schools (e.g., Bradley, 2009; Countryman, 2009).
Of course, many music teachers do find ways to create conditions for engaging a range
of musical practices, while at the same time remaining aware of the power dynamics that
surround music making (see Younker & Hickey, 2007). Often this involves shifting the
focus to the process of creating new music, rather than performing music composed by
others, and creating the conditions for students to bring the musical practices that are
more important and relevant to them into the process (Hickey, 2003).

RETHINKING SOCIAL JUSTICE IN URBAN MUSIC EDUCATION: TOWARD A COMPREHENSIVE APPROACH THROUGH CULTURAL PRODUCTION

The approaches to social justice in urban music education discussed in the preceding
sections can, to some extent or another, be seen as either complementary or contradictory. Attention to the distribution of opportunities, when based on the assumption that

only certain ways of experiencing music are valid, would undermine a commitment to representation; a commitment to representation, even if based on the assumption that non-dominant ways of experiencing music are more important for some students, would also require the demand for more resources and opportunities to support such engagement. While a commitment to more democratic and participatory ways of engaging students might contradict the traditional role of the conductor (or the teacher, for that matter), it might still engage dominant styles of music, and surely would require attention to how resources are distributed.

An integrated approach to social justice in urban music education would, as we will argue in this final section, require close attention to all four of the concerns raised by the approaches described earlier, even as contradictions are raised in the process. A cultural production approach to social justice provides a strong foundation and the underlying logic for an approach to music education that addresses all four concerns. Such an approach begins from the assumption that social inequality and marginalization are structural problems that reflect flaws in the institutionalization of dominant ideology. That is, rather than locating the problem of justice within the students (e.g., it is the students who lack exposure to the right music, or it is the students who have to learn how to engage in democracy, etc.), it assumes that the problem of justice requires the transformation of society itself, along with the students (and the teacher).

A cultural production approach pays heed to the four concerns discussed earlier, acknowledging issues of access, representation, ways of participating, and recognizing, examining, and understanding the powers and structures that oppress. This includes the assumption that schools themselves are key to the reproduction of inequality, while also a location for the examination of subjectivity and engagement in transformative action. In fact, a cultural production approach takes as a starting point the somewhat untenable or contradictory position of the teacher, who is at once implicated in the production of inequality while also located in a unique position to challenge it (Gaztambide-Fernández, 2013a). It views the problem of justice as central to the ethical responsibilities of teachers.

To address the challenges outlined earlier, a cultural production approach to music education begins from the assumption that music and musical practices are part of everyone's everyday life (Small, 1998). Embracing the notion of "musicking" as developed by Small, a cultural production approach begins by asking: What are the musical practices that animate the lives of the particular students in this particular classroom or learning context? Such practices may range from playing classical instruments to creating playlists in a mobile device; from singing songs within a religious organization to singing songs in the shower; from humming along to the soundtrack of a videogame to using software to create the music for a new stop-motion movie, and so on. Being able to understand the importance of these practices requires paying attention to local needs, desires, and the particular social arrangements that allow for practices to unfold.

Viewing culture as a practice (or set of practices) that must be enacted over and over again, a cultural production approach assumes that cultural processes are always fluid and open to transformation. Because culture is never complete, it is always open to reinterpretation and rearrangement, albeit within institutional and material constraints. In fact, it is precisely because cultural practices and identifications are always fluid that social change is possible through the transformation of the dominant symbolic arrangements that support inequality. Yet, as noted earlier, because the role of the teacher (and the institution of schooling) relies on these very dominant symbolic (and material) arrangements, teachers can be caught in the contradiction of challenging the very structures that enable them to do their work as teachers. For this reason, and as a final premise, a cultural production approach requires a deep reflexive engagement and the ability to strategically negotiate the institutional context of the school (Gaztambide-Fernández, 2013a, 2013b).

Rethinking musical practices in urban music education classrooms through a cultural production approach requires that teachers deeply engage pedagogical approaches that are indeed challenging, like student-centered teaching that views students as agents of knowledge and cultural production. It requires seeing students as creators of musical knowledge by centering the experiences, points of views, and identifications that are often "checked at the door" or left outside the school context (Giroux, 1992). In urban classrooms, this means engaging the conditions that constitute the urban as sources of strength and inspiration by thinking through the ways in which differences rub against each other within the density and the closeness of the city. It means not only recognizing, but also challenging, material inequalities by calling attention to the disparities that shape urban schooling and that produce violence. That is, a cultural production approach requires the recognition that things like violence and low academic achievement are the outcome of persistent economic inequality, not of individual deficits associated with cultural differences. Indeed, cultural differences are themselves constructed and enacted within the specificity of the city, and as such can be both a source of distraction as well as a source of clever playfulness and wit. As such, cultural production spurs creativity as a culturally affirming pedagogy.

Premised on an understanding of urban music education as cultural practice, a cultural production approach to social justice seeks to create opportunities for new relationships with and through musical practice. It highlights not only the practices, but also the meanings that students bring to musicking, by focusing on the production of a space for creative play where subjective experiences can be expressed and reimagined; where self-understandings can be transformed by embracing the rich musical knowledges and skills that students bring into the classroom. We believe, in fact, that to the extent that musicking involves communication through sounds, it provides conditions for what we might call *radical symbolic play*, as it is not constrained by language rules, yet it may draw from linguistic material. This opens a space for the possibility of different types of identity work that might, in some instances, challenge received categories of race, gender, sexuality, ability, and so on. The fact that the relationships that students have to these categories are fluid is evident in research that demonstrates the complex ways in which youth consume and produce media (see Buckingham, 2003).

Kumashiro's (2000) call for an "education that changes students and society" (pp. 25, 40) invites the active construction of new patterns of behavior, including new modes of cultural—and in this case musical—practices. This requires a centering of difference and of the dynamic interaction that produces difference and that brings a range of musical practices together into new forms of expression. Recognizing and valuing difference as a source of learning also means being "alert to tendencies to suppress or assimilate differences" (Reynolds & Trehan, 2001, p. 357). It draws attention to our obligation to act and transform unjust and unequal situations, understandings, and how they shape musical practices. This way, cultural production as a framework for social justice in urban music education also allows for living in the present, working with what is, and with who students are the moment they enter the classroom. It is not an education to learn about the past, or one to prepare for the future. It allows students to be who they are, to bring themselves and the full complexity of their musical lives into the classroom. As such, cultural production is also a framework of possibilities as it deliberately aims to decenter the norm by focusing on the plural, the contingent, and the unexpected.

REFERENCES

Allsup, R. E. (2003). Mutual learning and democratic action in instrumental music education. *Journal of Research in Music Education, 51*(1), 24–37.

Allsup, R. E. (Ed). (2007a). *Music Education Research: Special edition: Music education, equity, and social justice, 9*(2).

Allsup, R. E. (2007b). Democracy and one hundred years of music education. *Music Educators Journal, 93*(5), 52–57.

Ayers, W., Quinn, T., & Stovall, D. (Eds.). (2008). *Handbook of social justice in education.* New York: Routledge.

Bartel, L. R. (1995). Cultural equity in music education. *The Recorder, 37*(2), 51–54.

Bartel, L. R. (2001). Music education's rehearsal model. *Canadian Music Educator, 43*(1), 16.

Banks, J. (2007). *An introduction to multicultural education* (4th ed.). New York: Pearson.

Beynon, C. (2009). (Re)constructing and (re)mediating societal norms in masculinity: Reconciling songs of war. In E. Gould, J. Countryman, C. Morton, & L. Stewart Rose (Eds.), *Exploring social justice: How music education might matter* (pp. 38–51). Waterloo, ON: Canadian Music Educators' Association/L'Association canadienne des musiciens éducateurs.

Bolden, B. (2009). Teaching composing in secondary school: A case study analysis. *British Journal of Music Education, 26*(2), 137–152.

Bolden, B. (2013). Learner-created podcasts: Students' stories with music. *Music Educators Journal, 100*(1), 75–80.

Bowman, W. (2007). Introduction: Theorizing social justice in music education. *Action, Criticism, and Theory for Music Education, 6*(4). Retrieved, from http://act.maydaygroup.org/articles/BowmanEditorial6_4.pdf.

Bradley, D. (2006). Music education, multiculturalism, and anti-racism—Can we talk? *Action, Criticism, and Theory for Music Education, 5*(2). Retrieved, from http://act.maydaygroup.org/articles/Bradley5_2.pdf.

Bradley, D. (2007). The sounds of silence: Talking race in music education. *Action, Criticism, and Theory for Music Education, 6*(4), 132–162. Retrieved, from http://act.maydaygroup.org/articles/Bradley6_4.pdf.

Bradley, D. (2009). Global song, global citizens? The world constructed in world music choral publications. In E. Gould, J. Countryman, C. Morton, & L. Stewart Rose (Eds.), *Exploring social justice: How music education might matter* (pp. 105–119). Waterloo, ON: Canadian Music Educators' Association/L'Association canadienne des musiciens éducateurs.

Bradley, D., Golner, R., & Hanson, S. (2007). Unlearning whiteness, rethinking race issues in graduate music education. *Music Education Research, 9*(2) 293–304.

Brennan, T. (2001). World music does not exist. *Discourse, 23*(1), 44–62.

Bryson, B. (1997). What about the univores? Musical dislikes and group-based identity construction among Americans with low levels of education. *Poetics, 25*(2), 141–156.

Buckingham, D. (2003). *Media education: Literacy, learning and contemporary culture.* London: Polity.

Campbell, P. S. (2004). *Teaching music globally: Experiencing music, expressing culture.* Global music series. New York: Oxford University Press.

Campbell, P. S. (2005). *Cultural diversity in music education: Directions and challenges for the 21st century.* Queensland: Australian Academic Press.

Clark, J. A. (2006). Social justice, education and schooling: Some philosophical issues. *British Journal of Educational Studies, 54*(3), 272–287.

Coalition for Music Education in Canada. (2010) *A delicate balance: Music education in Canadian schools.* Prepared by Hill Strategies Research. Retrieved, from http://musicmakesus.ca/wp-content/uploads/2010/10/Music_Education_fullreportE2010.pdf.

Countryman, J. (2009). Stumbling towards clarity: Practical issues in teacher global musics. In E. Gould, J. Countryman, C. Morton, & L. Stewart Rose (Eds.), *Exploring social justice: How music education might matter* (pp. 23–37). Waterloo, ON: Canadian Music Educators' Association/L'Association canadienne des musiciens éducateurs.

Connell, J., & Gibson, C. (2004). World music: Deterritorializing place and identity. *Progress in Human Geography, 28*(3), 342–361.

DeCerteau, M. (1984). *The practice of everyday life* (Steven Rendall, Trans.). Berkeley: University of California Press.

Fraser, N. (1997). *Justice interruptus: Critical reflections on the "postsocialist" condition.* New York: Routledge.

Friesen, D. (2009). That teacher pedestal: How alternative methods challenged my concept of the teacher role. In E. Gould, J. Countryman, C. Morton, & L. Stewart Rose (Eds.), *Exploring social justice: How music education might matter* (pp. 253–260). Waterloo, ON: Canadian Music Educators' Association/L'Association canadienne des musiciens éducateurs.

Gaztambide-Fernández, R. (2010). Wherefore the musicians? *Philosophy of Music Education Review, 18*(1), 65–84.

Gaztambide-Fernández, R. A. (2011). Musicking in the city: Reconceptualizing urban music education as cultural practice. *Action, Criticism, and Theory for Music Education, 10*(1), 15–46. Retrieved, from http://act.maydaygroup.org/articles/Gaztambide-Fernandez10_1.pdf.

Gaztambide-Fernández, R. (2013a). Why the arts don't *do* anything: Toward a new vision for cultural production in education. *Harvard Educational Review, 83*(1), 211–237.

Gaztambide-Fernández, R. (2013b). Thinking otherwise about the arts in education: A rejoinder. *Harvard Educational Review, 83*(4), 636–643.

Giroux, H. A. (1992). *Border crossings: Cultural workers and the politics of education.* New York & London: Routledge.

Gould, E. (2005). Desperately seeking Marsha: Music and lesbian imagination. *Action, Criticism, and Theory for Music Education*, 4(3). Retrieved, from http://act.maydaygroup.org/articles/Gould4_3.pdf.

Gould, E. (2007). Social justice in music education: A problematic of democracy. *Music Education Research*, 9(2), 229–240.

Gould, E., Countryman, J., Morton, C., & Stewart Rose, L. (Eds.) (2009). *Exploring social justice: How music education might matter.* Waterloo, ON: Canadian Music Educators' Association/L'Association canadienne des musiciens éducateurs.

Green, L. (2002). *How popular musicians learn: A way ahead for music education.* London & New York: Ashgate Press.

Harvey, D. (1973). *Social justice and the city.* Baltimore, MD: John Hopkins Press.

Harvey, D. (2008). The right to the city. *New Left Review*, 53, 23–40.

Hickey, M. (2003). *Why and how to teach music composition: A new horizon for music education.* Lanham, MD: Rowman & Littlefield.

Hytten, K., & Bettez, S. C. (2011). Understanding education for social justice. *Educational Foundations*, 25(1–2), 7–24.

Jorgensen, E. R. (2007). Concerning justice and music education. *Music Education Research*, 9(2), 169–189.

Koza, J. (1993). Big boys don't cry (or sing): Gender, misogyny, and homophobia in college choral methods texts. *The Quarterly: Journal of Music Teaching and Learning*, 4–5(5–1), 48–64.

Koza, J. (1994). Aesthetic music education revisited: Discourses of exclusion and oppression. *Philosophy of Music Education Review*, 2(2), 75–91.

Koza, J. (2003). *Stepping across: Four interdisciplinary studies on education and cultural politics.* New York: Peter Lang.

Koza, J. E. (2008). Listening for whiteness: Hearing racial politics in undergraduate school music. *Philosophy of Music Education Review*, 16(2), 145–155.

Kumashiro, K. (2000). Toward a theory of anti-oppressive education. *Review of Educational Research*, 70(1), 25–53.

Kymlicka, W. (1996) *Multicultural citizenship: A liberal theory of minority rights.* Oxford: Clarendon Press.

Lamb, R. (1994). Feminism as critique in philosophy of music education. *Philosophy of Music Education Review*, 2(2), 59–74.

Lamb, R. (1996). Discords: Feminist pedagogy in music education. *Theory into Practice*, 35(2), 124–131.

Lashbrook, S., & Mantie, R. (2009). Valuing subjugated experience: The One World Youth Arts Project. In E. Gould, J. Countryman, C. Morton, & L. Stewart Rose (Eds.), *Exploring social justice: How music education might matter* (pp. 292–303). Waterloo, ON: Canadian Music Educators' Association/L'Association canadienne des musiciens éducateurs.

Lubet, A. (2009). The inclusion of music/the music of inclusion. *The International Journal of Inclusive Education*, 13(7), 727–739.

Lubet, A. (2010). *Music, disability, and society.* Philadelphia: Temple University Press.

McClary, S. (1991). *Feminine endings: Music, gender, and sexuality.* Minnesota: University of Minnesota Press.

McClary, S., & Walser R. (1990). Start making sense!: Musicology wrestles with rock. In S. Frith & A. Goodwin (Eds.), *On record: Rock, pop, and the written word* (pp. 237–249). New York: Pantheon Books.

National Alliance of El Sistema Inspired Programs. (n.d.). *El sistema*. Retrieved, from http://elsistemausa.org/el-sistema/venezuela/.

North, C. (2006). More than words? Delving into the substantive meaning(s) of "social justice" in education. *Review of Educational Research, 76*(4), 507–535.

North, C. (2008). What is all this talk about "social justice"? Mapping the terrain of education's latest catchphrase. *The Teachers College Record, 110*(6), 1182–1206.

Peterson, R., & Simkus, A. (1992). How music taste marks occupation status groups. In M. Lamont & M. Fournier (Eds.), *Cultivating differences: Symbolic boundaries and the making of inequality* (pp. 152–186). Chicago: University of Chicago Press.

Reimer, B. (Ed.). (2002). *World musics and music education: Facing the issues.* Reston, VA: MENC, National Association for Music Education.

Reynolds, M., & Trehan, K. (2001). Classroom as real world: Propositions for a pedagogy of difference. *Gender and Education, 13*(4), 357–372.

Schippers, H. (2010). *Facing the music: Shaping music education from a global perspective.* Oxford: Oxford University Press.

Schmidt, P. (2011). Music education in urban contexts: A redress. *Action, Criticism, and Theory for Music Education, 10*(1), 1–14. Retrieved, from http://act.maydaygroup.org/articles/Schmidt10_1.pdf.

Sen, A. 1992. *Inequality reexamined.* New York & Cambridge, MA: Russell Sage & Harvard University Press.

Small, C. (1998). *Musicking: The meanings of performing and listening.* Middletown, CT: Wesleyan University Press.

Stewart Rose, L., & Countryman, J. (2013). Repositioning the *elements of music*: How students talk about music. *Action, Criticism and Theory for Music Education, 12*(3), 45–64.

Snell, K. (2009). Democracy and popular music in music education. In E. Gould, J. Countryman, C. Morton, & L. Stewart Rose (Eds.), *Exploring social justice: How music education might matter* (pp. 166–182). Waterloo, ON: Canadian Music Educators' Association/ L'Association canadienne des musiciens éducateurs.

Taylor, T. (2007). *Beyond exoticisim.* Durham, NC: Duke University Press.

Vaugeois, L. (2013). *Colonization and the institutionalization of hierarchies of the human through music education: Studies in the education of feeling.* Unpublished doctoral dissertation, University of Toronto.

Walser, R. (1993). *Running with the devil: Power, gender, and madness in heavy metal music.* Hanover, NH: Wesleyan UP.

Woodford, P. (2005). *Democracy and music education: Liberalism, ethics, and the politics of practice.* Bloomington: Indiana University Press.

Young, M. (1990). *Justice and the politics of difference.* Princeton, NJ: Princeton University Press.

Young, M. (2001). *Inclusion and democracy.* Oxford: Oxford University Press.

Younker, B., & Hickey, M. (2007). Examining the profession through the lens of social justice: Two music educators' stories and their stark realizations. *Music Education Research, 9*(2), 215–227.

CHAPTER 29

SOCIAL JUSTICE AND MUSIC TECHNOLOGY IN EDUCATION

PAUL LOUTH

INTRODUCTION

THIS chapter will discuss various connections among technology, music education practices, and social justice, with the dual objectives of exploring uses of technology that further the cause of social justice, and problematizing technology as a potential hindrance to social and economic equity. The latter would occur, it will be argued, when music technologies are perceived as wholly transformative in their own right, or merely as means to better or more current music instruction. The more desirable alternative is that technology be perceived and presented to students as a medium that alters teaching and learning processes in ways that either challenge or reinforce dominant ideologies.

Discussions about technology and social justice date back to the writings of mid-twentieth century thinkers such as Lewis Mumford (1934, 1954) and Jacques Ellul (1964), who were concerned about the nihilistic consequences of considering technology as an end in itself. Although ostensibly pessimistic about technology's influence on the human condition, these early authors were attempting to make their readership aware of technology's mediating qualities in the hopes of helping them to regain some control over their technological environments and thus work toward more humanistic outcomes. Whereas true technological determinism is the belief that technological development cannot be influenced by moral choices apart from its own technically driven imperatives, this chapter takes the position that this is a potentially dangerous and irresponsible assumption. The determinist stance is related to the notion that whatever can be done in the realm of technology should be done, a position that Heather-Jane Robertson dubs "the technological imperative," and one that arguably represents a numbing of critical thought and an abandonment of ethics in teaching (Robertson, 1998). Drawing on a disparate sample of research on the subjects of music education technology and critical pedagogy, and aiming for a dialectical exposition of the arguments presented in said literature, I take as my point of departure the assumption that music educators should examine closely the various ways in which technology mediates instruction with the potential to either transform it in emancipatory ways or to reinforce social and economic inequities.

Drawing on the work of Marshall McLuhan, Postman reminds us

> that embedded in every tool is an ideological bias, a predisposition to construct the world as one thing rather than another, to value one thing over another, to amplify one sense or skill or attitude more loudly than another. (1993, p. 13)

This is of course what McLuhan meant by his famous aphorism, "the medium is the message." To say that technology shapes and influences our environment, however, is not to say that it determines precisely what that environment will be. Although McLuhan argues that any technology, as a type of media, "has the power of imposing its own assumptions on the unwary," he nevertheless maintains that "prediction and control [are possible by] avoiding this subliminal state of Narcissus trance" (McLuhan, 1966, p. 30).

Opposing the view that technology determines musical outcomes is the view that the creative individual transforms technology and uses it to his or her advantage. Writing about a British composer, the focus of a case study who became extremely successful learning to use digital technology, despite (or perhaps because of) his lack of formal training, Savage states:

> Alex is not dictated to by the pieces of technology in his studio. Rather, he uses and abuses hardware and software for his creative ends. The context of ideas that he develops about a particular project and his broad aesthetic awareness are all driving forces in his musical expressions through the studio. (Savage, 2005a, p. 5)

Savage's study participant, Alex, appears to embody the emancipatory potential of music technology, in this case the constructivist, learner-centered approach to musical creation, whereby technology has enabled him to compose music without necessarily subjecting himself or his music to the values associated with the traditional Western art music canon. Speaking of these traditional norms, Savage states that "new technologies have allowed Alex to bypass some of these concerns and focus on more direct expressive issues of musical composition" (p. 5). Inasmuch as I agree with Savage's assertion that Alex's journey to learn to compose music in this way represents a potentially liberating pedagogy, we must be careful not to go so far as to claim that technology gives Alex *direct* access to expression. This would overlook the mediating effects of any technology—its ideological biases, if you will, or what Janet Mansfield refers to as technology's "enframing and manipulative qualities" (Mansfield, 2005, p. 141). It is this aspect of technology that should interest music educators most, since ignoring its mediating effects carries the risk of subjecting students to whatever ideological biases exist in current technologies and, by extension, to any authority whose interest is served by such biases. In order to counter such possible effects, I argue that music educators concerned about social justice are ethically obligated to foster, as Mansfield succinctly puts it, "a critical aware-ness of a technologically mediated music education environment" (p. 141). What fol-lows is a discussion of two different aspects of technology-based music instruction that have the potential, through their mediation, to either positively or negatively influence the cause of social justice. I speculate that the conditions under which this positive or negative influence might occur include socioeconomic forces, the design and choice of technologies themselves, the educational contexts, and (probably most important) the teaching approaches that frame technological instruction.

EMPOWERMENT VERSUS CONSUMERISM?

I would first like to highlight the tension that exists between the potential of information and communication technologies to empower students by transforming pedagogy along constructivist lines, and their potential to perpetuate free market ideologies by reinforc-ing a consumerist mentality among students and indirectly disenfranchising those who are economically disadvantaged. On one hand, the advent of computer-assisted music instruction has sparked considerable interest in how electronic technologies can pro-mote constructivist pedagogies that can challenge and transform traditional pedagogies (Webster, 2011). This can happen in at least two important ways.

First, to take computer-assisted composition as an example, since high-speed Internet and home computer use have become relatively widespread, many people "who up until now did not perceive themselves to be musicians" can manipulate sounds and create music with the aid of inexpensive software and in the absence of formal training (Crow, 2006, p. 123). For some, the economic barriers to creating music are now much lower when comparing the cost of many software programs to that of traditional instruments and considering the fact that the computers on which such software runs are already in most homes. Additionally, the barrier of formal training is also removed for those who choose to use computer programs with intuitive user interfaces that in many cases require minimal knowledge of theoretical concepts or traditional performance skills. This would certainly seem to be an example of mediation that facilitates access to the world of musical creation.

Second, there are several aspects of new technology that are particularly well suited to constructivist pedagogy. Chief among these is the advent of communications tech-nology, such as interactive software and numerous tools associated with "Web 2.0" that allow for user-generated content and collaborative work between student and teacher or student and student. Additionally, Internet and computer technology are generally considered to be "native" concepts for most students—natural features of the landscapes in their world—and therefore using computers to learn about or create music is a way of connecting with their preexisting inclinations to communicate and learn in this way (Bolton, 2008). In his 2011 review of key research in music technology as it applies to music learning and teaching, Peter Webster notes that there is sustained interest in linking music technology with constructivist forms of pedagogy that begin with the foundational belief that what students bring to the learning situation from their lived experiences is well worth building on.

On the other hand, and despite a number of projects examining possible uses of open source software in music education settings in various countries, the tools with which this is all being accomplished are being forged primarily by private industry. There are three major concerns that have surfaced in response to this situation. First, that the promotion of commercial software in schools, and even the manner in which technology alters teaching and learning, encourages consumerism and fosters neoliberal notions of education; second, that the cycle of software development (or planned obsolescence, depending on one's view) is so short that students may be forced into similar cycles of repurchasing and constantly upgrading their technical skills; and third, that much technology is still simply not economically available to a significant portion of students.

To expand on the first complaint, Myllykoski (2012) notes that free and open source music education software is minimally present in educational settings worldwide, a situation that he largely attributes to "strong resistance from the side of commercial, for-profit software companies" (p. 160). While accessing the main page of Apple's website while preparing this chapter, I noticed that two of the top six technology "news" articles visible were advertisements for the educational success of the company's software, including the headline that queried, "Can the iPad Rescue a Struggling American Education System?" The obvious risk of music curricula becoming increasingly centered around commercial technology is that students may become conditioned to be consumers, not to mention that these various products have the potential to steer curriculum in the direction of private interests. A further consideration is that when families can afford to purchase technologies that are being taught in school for home use, compatibility requirements dictate that educators are effectively working for corporations when they make decisions about educational technology since they are simultaneously creating a demand for specific brands of compatible home software (Robertson, 1998). Taylor (2011) goes so far as to argue that a technology-driven curriculum by its very nature perpetuates neoliberal capitalist ideology by focusing teaching on the production of artifacts for student consumption (for example, lectures as podcasts, PowerPoint slides, etc.), which is encouraged and greatly expanded by the array of educational choices now offered via technology.

The second point, which deals with the perpetual cycle of obsolescence, also carries some interesting implications for the potential obsolescence of skills and knowledge. This can perhaps be illustrated with reference to the concept of "de-skilling." Defined as a separation of conception from execution such that a worker no longer controls the entire process of his or her work, de-skilling is seen by Michael Apple as a mode through which corporations indirectly use formal educational settings to reinforce social inequities by annulling critical thought through the development and sale of prepackaged curricula that specify "appropriate" classroom activities, teacher directives, student responses, and evaluation methods (Apple, 1996). Wayne Bowman (2005) warns that "sustained engagements with challenging problems is anathema" to prepackaged curricula in music education (p. 31). Since computer-assisted instruction (CAI) can often consist of such prepackaged curricula, educators who fail to seek out CAI resources that are malleable and can be adapted to their specific curricular needs may risk this potentially negative outcome.

But to speak to the original point, perhaps of greater concern than teacher de-skilling is student de-skilling, which might manifest itself if more time is spent on learning to manipulate a user interface than on using the software to acquire conceptual knowledge of music. For example, when creating music with computer technology, knowledge of the keystrokes or mouse clicks required to execute particular musical functions—such as transposing a phrase or rendering a musical idea performed on a MIDI keyboard into notation or some other visual format—are, as already noted, not necessarily dependent on an understanding of the musical concepts in question. I reiterate that this is in one sense emancipating for students, who gain access to composition through nontraditional means. As Roberta Lamb (2010) correctly points out, in cases where students are engaging in self-directed learning and venture into music through their interest in such technology as *Guitar Hero* or *Garage Band*, music educators should support their interests and help them to develop their musicianship instead of treating them as second-class musicians. But at the same time, if understanding how to use the software that mediates that process is overly dependent on a unique set of skills and knowledge that are controlled by commercial interests, then de-skilling, in this case separation of musical conception from (digitally mediated) execution, may become an issue.

I submit, then, that de-skilling may present itself in two situations. First, it would be of concern in situations where music technologies were intentionally being used to teach traditional skills and concepts. For example, the ease with which scores can be created using various kinds of notation software may hamper the development of aural skills for some students. Although such software does not prevent students from creating scores without the touch of a single key, its particular ideological bias encourages the quicker option (Argersinger, 1993). Second, it is a risk for those students mentioned earlier who learn about music in nontraditional ways, owing to the vagaries of the marketplace. As Thorgersen (2012) points out, users must invest significant time in learning to manipulate the interface of any software program in order to maximize its potential. So, as software inevitably changes and rapidly comes in and out of use in response to market forces, students who are dependent on an understanding of its user interface in order to learn about and do various things with music risk seeing their skill set—and, perhaps ironically, their access point to music—vanish.

Regelski (2012) argues for music educators to adopt an ethical stance based on the premise that they constitute first and foremost a category of "helping" professionals, which, by definition, implies that they should contribute to the well-being of their students, thus partaking in ethical practice. Among those ethical duties he cites as paramount is "the duty to allow and promote free expression [which] flows from a basic conception of human rights" (p. 291). This freedom of expression is promoted for students by making available "options from which to choose," as well as "criteria for their choices" (p. 291). Thinking constantly about choice is another way to view the issue of "using versus abusing" technology in music instruction. Applying Regelski's idea, we can say that freedom of expression expands so long as technological mediation enables the expansion of musical options, and conversely it becomes limited as creative musical options are limited. For example, as long as a program like *Garage Band* is used in such a way as to allow students access to more genres and execution of a wider array of sounds than they would be able to using traditional means, freedom of expression would appear to be promoted. But Regelski's notion of having to supply criteria for choices is an important caveat. Performing and composing of music always occurs within some cultural context, not in a vacuum, and, as Kratus (2012) argues, the stylistic parameters of various genres and practices constitute criteria in the form of some musical syntax, whether its understanding is formalized or not (more on this presently). Beyond an understanding of musical syntax, Kratus stipulates two more "capabilities" that must be present in the creator of any composition (in the sense of a musical product). These are audience awareness and, above all else, the ability "to audiate (to hear inwardly with meaning) so that the physical actions required to make the musical sounds match the mental images of those sounds" (p. 371). Because of the very real possibility of de-skilling, nurturing these capabilities, the acquisition of *a* musical (not necessarily Western art music) syntax and the ability to hear inwardly—at least as much of the time as teaching students to manipulate the user interface—should be the priority for music educators when teaching students to use electronic technologies as a means of musical expression.

To speak briefly to the third complaint mentioned at the beginning of this section, we cannot overlook the fact that the benefits of technology are simply not distributed equally among populations. I teach in a city that, as of 2011, had the highest rate of concentrated poverty among the 100 largest metropolitan areas in the United States (Kneebone, Nadeau, & Berube, 2011). Needless to say, there are students who live not far from where I work who cannot afford a few dollars a year for a repair fee that is charged to borrow a traditional instrument, and many cannot dream of owning a computer. Webster (2011) states that we need more research devoted to the issue of equity in accessibility to technological resources, and this would certainly appear to be true.

But what of the alternatives to commercially produced technology? Despite the fact that they have not made much headway in terms of implementation, free or open-source software development projects undertaken by individuals in collaboration with researchers, educators, and companies or governments are an attractive option with the potential to overcome many of the problems cited above and to tip the scales in favor of empowerment over consumerism. As Myllykoski (2012) explains, schools have a prominent role to play in such projects, where the development of software is conceived as a knowledge-building process or a type of action research. Open source licensing, in which the software code is free to use, distribute, and alter, can be a potential remedy for many accessibility problems. However, besides strong opposition to its development and wide distribution by commercial interests, there are several inherent challenges with this path. As Steve Dillon (2012) points out,

[a]ll these software dependencies develop along their own path and reasons for changes in the open-source world can be arbitrary. There is no coordinating organization to ensure compatibility or consistency with any other component the software relies on. The tendency for things to break over time is high. (p. 176)

Another alternative to moderately or high-priced stand-alone software is the plethora of web-based software (such as Noteflight, a popular web-based notation program) that offers users access to music technology via a reasonably fast Internet connection and a website interface. The exciting aspect of these services is that many of them have interactive, Web 2.0 characteristics that allow for cooperative and/or student-centered learning via communication with instructors, collaborative online music making, and such. There is generally a required revenue stream of some sort, however, and that means either advertising or membership or subscription fees to the user. Further, one can easily argue that encouraging students to adapt their skills to commercial web-based software could lead to the same consumerist results as enculturating them to stand-alone commercial software.

DE-POLITICIZING VERSUS CONTEXTUALIZING MUSICAL MEANINGS

The second example of mediation focuses on the compositional uses of electronic technology. One of the potential mediating effects that technologies possess is the ability to either de-politicize musical meanings or better contextualize them, depending on use and design. Music software has the ability to allow preexisting sounds to be moved about, fragmented, and reordered, a legitimate mode of musical composition and one that, as already mentioned, has the potential to emancipate students from the ideological effects of the theoretical rules of Western art music by avoiding the issue of notation altogether and allowing preassembled fragments of sound to become the building blocks of new music. Along these lines, Bolton (2008) describes a collaborative learning project in which New Zealand primary school students were involved in learning to compose using the software program *Garage Band*. The project "deliberately [made] use of intuitive music software that allows musical concepts to be easily accessible, visually and aurally, without the need for much prior musical knowledge, traditional performance skills, or understanding of music notation" (p. 44). The results of a narrative study on one of the students involved in the project show that for that individual student it was clearly empowering and motivating (p. 51). Savage (2005b) explains the shift in electronically mediated composition as one away from symbol and toward sound. In describing the results of three early case studies on computer-assisted composition projects carried out in British schools between 1999 and 2000, he states:

> Pupils enjoyed exploring the sounds within a pedagogical framework of exploration and discovery rather than in the context of right or wrong compositional choices. But more than this, the technologies themselves brought about a shift of emphasis in compositional enquiry, away from thinking about melody, rhythm or harmony towards an increasing focus on dealing with the sound itself, and its intrinsic value and place in a wider musical structure. (p. 171)

Savage explains how working outside symbol systems provides a unique opportunity for students to have more direct access to sounds and that this enables them to challenge and transform traditional musical practices (p. 168). What is left unaddressed in this and many other accounts of students' compositional efforts with electronic technology, however, is the issue of musical meanings associated with sounds apart from purely aesthetic or formalistic connotations.

Elsewhere, Savage writes:

> It is not that traditional musical concepts, forms and devices have had their day. Rather, it is a reprioritising and reordering of what is important at any one given moment in that particular educational context that matters. (2005a, p. 6)

I would add that the educational context should be governed by the musical context: the style or genre (or combination of such) under consideration should determine which concepts, forms, and devices are appropriate for students to learn. For there *are* concepts, forms, devices (and nomenclature) appropriate to a given genre, and unless these are willing to be explored from the perspective of the musical culture(s) under consideration, one of two outcomes will occur. Either students will believe that they are under the influence of no rules or restrictions while composing in this manner, or they will eventually learn such "universal" compositional strategies as the imposition of large-scale form, without necessarily exploring any of the stylistic parameters that apply to the particular culture(s) associated with either their inspired ideas or their preexisting sound samples. The latter situation would be unfortunate because it would erase traces of cultural meaning associated with particular sounds, and the former situation would be unfortunate because student composers who think they are free from rules are simply functioning under the influence of the unspoken values of whatever musical culture they are most heavily exposed to in their lives. Lucy Green provides an excellent example of this problem with the case of the "creative music" movement in the United Kingdom. Students were encouraged to compose music in a manner that was seemingly free of rules or restrictions of any kind, which, she argues pointedly, simply results in a false sense of subjectivity (1988).

What I am suggesting is that a *purely* aestheticized approach to electronically mediated composition and, in particular, compositional remixing may contribute to the reproduction of existing social relations through de-contextualized, and therefore a de-politicized, view of musical culture. This would result if the elements of composition (either traditional ways of organizing sound, or composite audio samples) are perceived as merely free-floating signifiers that become completely detached from particular, contextual meanings. This can perhaps be best illustrated with references to the work of two quite different scholars: the critical pedagogue Henry Giroux, and the music education scholar Lucy Green.

Giroux speaks about the importance of refusing to consider cultural products as merely free-floating objects under no one's control. As he explains, one of the strategies that corporate culture uses to deflect criticism from itself is to dissolve the political into the purely representational (1994). Music is arguably one of the most prominent "public pedagogies" to permeate young people's lives. The phrase denotes a site of learning created largely by electronic media and technology that shape children's lives and whose (often adverse) effects educators should feel ethically obliged to scrutinize (Giroux, 2000). Granted, the meanings ascribed to music are clearly more contestable than those ascribed to images or text (and perhaps this is why Giroux avoids musical analyses in his work). But this does not mean that educators should avoid discussions of these meanings. The speed with which technology can facilitate the transportation, manipulation, fragmentation, and reconfiguration of preexisting musics has the potential to accelerate "artificially" the process by which music is dislocated from its culturally delineated meanings, and this is potentially very disconcerting.

Along similar lines, Lucy Green theorizes that we are essentially forced to collapse unconsciously the categories of inherent and delineated meanings when we listen to music. As she puts it, the delineated meanings "appear to come to us as if they were a part of the inherent meanings, the 'music itself' " (2005, p. 90). This need to collapse delineated into inherent meaning has, over significant time, caused us to associate certain socially constructed attributes, such as timelessness, autonomy, and the ability to speak to the human condition, with Western art music and has shaped a governing aesthetic position "that was fundamentally derived from classical paradigms, and was not necessarily applicable to most of these 'other' musics in the world outside the school" (p. 88). Once popular and world musics were mandated into the curriculum (at least in Great Britain), the problem of music serving to reproduce existing social relations did not go away because the dominant aesthetic paradigm that celebrated autonomy and universality was used to analyze, gauge, and teach these other musics. As Green points out, most music educators (in the West) are still trained primarily if not exclusively in classical music, and this perpetuates the problem of music being valued only for its so-called autonomous qualities (p. 88).

Green concludes that most music teachers continue to focus on a concept of delineated musical meanings that essentially equates them with non-musical meanings as a result of said teachers' conditioning in the Western art music aesthetic. What this means is that music educators who work with technology that enables students to work creatively with sound may be more likely to ignore issues of delineated meaning (as "non-musical") and treat appropriated (pre-recorded) musical sounds as free-floating, autonomous objects to be aesthetically assembled. Yet to treat music in this way would be to ignore its political and sociocultural meanings, and run the risk that students may conceptualize the act of musical creation as a purely aesthetic undertaking, regardless of the cultural meanings associated with the sounds that they appropriate.

As Green indicates, the very emphasis on individualism and autonomy with regard to musical materials may reproduce the Western classical aesthetic in the classroom (or MIDI lab, as the case may be). Paul Woodford (2012) offers a historical perspective on this problem, pointing out that music educators have generally been complicit in failing to address issues of social justice in the classroom by choosing instead to bow to political and economic pressures in adopting an aesthetic stance that projects music study as a collection of "abstract skills and knowledge divorced from real world problems" (p. 90). Thus the pedagogy of technologically mediated composition may be in a position to contribute to the perpetuation of such a neutral, aestheticized view of music.

Perhaps the greatest risk of over-aestheticization, for lack of a better term, inheres in the process of compositional remixing. Various scholars have weighed in on the issue of whether the trend (or opportunity, depending on one's position) of manipulating fragments of sound (loops) from commercially produced recordings as a form of musical creation is a good or bad thing. Mark Campbell (2009) feels encouraged about this activity, sometimes called "remix culture," arguing that it has the potential to disrupt the culture industry's hold on the chain of production/consumption of (popular) music as a commodity. As evidence, he cites DJ Danger Mouse's juxtaposition/integration of the Beatles' music with that of African American rap artist Jay-Z, which occurred in the form of *The Grey Album* (2001). This remix "provided a powerful critique of black/white cultural relations in the United States, contradicting . . . the separateness of the social constructs of both whiteness and blackness" (p. 360). He argues that it is precisely this sort of re-appropriation and manipulation of commercially produced music that will enable students to resist ideology by creating new musical products that question, through juxtaposition, the one-dimensional notions surrounding cultural identities that are often circumscribed by mass-produced music.

Janet Mansfield, on the other hand, reacting to a prescribed music education technology curriculum in New Zealand, believes that the use of "packaged resources" when creating music through sound manipulation via technology is likely to remove students from the realm of meaningful music making that is unencumbered by capitalist interests. At issue for Mansfield is the extent to which students and educators are dominated by the forces of global capitalism that act to decenter cultural knowledge. Mansfield (2005) states:

> Under globalizing musical culture, modernism's unifying universalist principles and ethos which had assumed that music practice was merely the product of free, autonomous individual expression, have been unsettled and replaced by relativistic perspectives and questions of 'difference.' However, simultaneous yet contradictory processes occur relating to globalization as the twenty-first century begins. . . .

As a result, national, ethnic or religious groups, professions, businesses and cultures become further and further enmeshed. (pp. 134–135)

She maintains that the conditions of globalization and, in particular, corporate transnational interests that produce music are commodifying "cultural resources [that are] appropriated from different parts of the world by roaming musical marketeers" at an alarming rate (p. 135). This means that the original (cultural) meanings ascribed to certain sounds may already be lost (i.e., commodified) by the time a musical product is packaged for the marketplace. Because prepackaged musical sounds can act as raw materials for remixing and other forms of sound manipulation, Mansfield is concerned that "these trends must shape possibilities for artistic and musical cultural expression and production and be affected by the increasing gaps between wealthier and poorer nations" (p. 135). These concerns are echoed by Randall Allsup, who speaks of global capitalism's potential to misappropriate the very quality of "*différance*" in producing musical commodities that, by the nature of their artificially induced hybridity, may be culturally exploitive (2006).

Both viewpoints have merit. Whether compositional remixing in music education is beneficial or detrimental to the cause of social justice depends on whether the "original" contextual meanings of the musical sounds used (as contested and multifaceted as these may be) are able to be considered. As Webster states, "It is no longer possible to discuss music technology in instruction and learning without careful consideration of social context" (2011, p. 116). Critically minded educators should consider, then, ways in which contextual information about musical sounds might be accessed by students when composing in this manner. How might such a pedagogy look? Might students be required to research or, through guided discovery, to reveal and explain the cultural significance of the sounds that they appropriate or the sounds that influence their choices when composing "purely" imaginatively? Might composition/sound editing software be designed to help students access cultural information about musical ideas and "prepackaged" sounds?

If we encourage our students to consider the ways in which technology can either reinforce ideology (by commodifying cultural products in the manner that Mansfield describes) or resist it (by pitting commercially produced music against itself in the manner that Campbell suggests), then we may be able to reach some truly socially significant outcomes. Campbell suggests some very imaginative and potentially emancipatory strategies for using media technology and music software to raise questions about social justice through teaching high school students about the various roles that media and technologies play in forming general attitudes and beliefs. The lessons all focus on using remix technology to disrupt the messages, and thereby question the assumptions embedded, in various movies and songs, including the Canadian national anthem (2009). Although Campbell's lesson plans are geared toward such classes as media studies, civics, and sociology, there is no reason they could not be adapted for a computer-assisted composition class.

Conclusion

As Lamb points out, "music for most young people is electronic, mediated, and virtual, rather than acoustic and performance-based" (2010, p. 34). Technology can and should be used in the music classroom to validate the identities and musical efforts of many individuals who do not identify with the traditional concept of what a "music student" is. It can be used to tap into knowledge about other musical cultures and practices and to shatter stereotypical ideas. Software and hardware that facilitate feedback and cooperative learning among students represent potential modes of disrupting the reproduction of existing social relations by enabling constructivist, collaborative approaches to music teaching that may enable otherwise "silenced" voices to be heard. Further, when technology is itself presented as an object of inquiry, critically minded educators can demonstrate the ways in which it shapes our understanding of reality. But there is also a darker side to technology use.

It has been the aim of this chapter to argue that music educators have an ethical responsibility to consider new technologies as media that potentially shift learning toward emancipatory or ideological ends. Whether technology use in music education leads to constructivist pedagogies that empower students by calling into question the assumptions underlying both instructional methods and musical creation, or whether it leads to de-skilling, de-contextualizing, or reinforcement of a consumerist mentality would seem to depend on the extent to which educators can raise awareness of technology's mediating qualities and negotiate its primarily free market model.

References

Allsup, R. E. (2006). Species counterpoint: Darwin and the evolution of forms. *Philosophy of Music Education Review*, 14(2), 159–174.

Apple, M. (1996). *Cultural politics and education*. New York: Teachers College Press.

Argersinger, C. (1993). Side-effects of technology on music and musicians. *Jazz Educators Journal*, 26(1), 33.

Bolton, J. (2008). Technologically mediated composition learning: Josh's story. *British Journal of Music Education*, 25(1), 41–55.

Bowman, W. (2005). Music education in nihilistic times. *Educational Philosophy and Theory*, 37(1), 29–46.

Campbell, M. (2009). Remixing the social: Pursuing social inclusion through music education. In E. Gould, J. Countryman, C. Morton, & L. Stewart Rose (Eds.), *Exploring social justice: How music education might matter* (pp. 359–370). Toronto: Canadian Music Educators' Association.

Can the iPad Rescue a Struggling American Education System? Retrieved, from http://www.apple.com/startpage

Crow, B. (2006). Musical creativity and the new technology. *Music Education Research, 8*(1), 121–130.

Dillon, S. (2012). An open-source approach to music education through jam2jam XO. *Journal of Music, Technology and Education, 5*(2), 171–180.

Ellul, J. (1964) *The technological society.* New York: Vintage Books. Originally published (1954) as *La Technique ou l'enjeu du siècle.* Paris: Librarie Armand Colin.

Giroux, H. (1994). *Disturbing pleasures: Learning popular culture* (New York: Routledge).

Giroux, H. (2000). *Stealing innocence: Youth, corporate power, and the politics of culture.* New York: St. Martin's Press.

Green, L. (1988). *Music on deaf ears: Musical meaning, ideology, education.* Manchester, UK: Manchester University Press.

Green, L. (2005). Musical meaning and social reproduction: A case for autonomy. *Educational Philosophy and Theory, 37*(1), 77–92.

Kneebone, E., Nadeau, C., & Berube, A. (2011). *The re-emergence of concentrated poverty: Metropolitan trends in the 2000s.* Metropolitan Policy Program at the Brookings Institute. Retrieved, from http://www.brookings.edu/~/media/research/files/papers/2011/11/03%20 poverty%20kneebone%20nadeau%20berube/1103_poverty_kneebone_nadeau_berube. pdf.

Kratus, J. (2012). Nurturing the songcatchers: Philosophical issues in the teaching of music composition. In W. Bowman & A. Frega (Eds.) *The Oxford handbook of philosophy in music education* (pp. 367–385). New York: Oxford University Press.

Lamb, R. (2010). Music as sociocultural phenomenon: Interactions with music education. In H. F. Abeles, & L. A. Custodero (Eds.), *Critical issues in music education: Contemporary theory and practice* (pp. 23–38). New York: Oxford University Press.

Mansfield, J. (2005). The global musical subject, curriculum, and Heidegger's question concerning technology. *Educational Philosophy and Theory, 37*(1), 133–148.

McLuhan, M. (1966). *Understanding media: The extensions of man* (2nd ed.). New York: McGraw Hill. First published in 1964.

Mumford, L. (1934). *Technics and civilization.* New York: Harcourt, Brace.

Mumford, L. (1954). *In the name of sanity.* New York: Harcourt, Brace.

Myllykoski, M. (2012). Open-source software projects in music education: Stakeholders, structure, and the development cycle. *Journal of Music, Technology and Education, 5*(2), 159–170.

Postman, N. (1993). *Technopoly: The surrender of culture to technology.* New York: Vintage Books.

Regelski, T. (2012). Ethical dimensions in school-based music education. In W. Bowman & A. Frega (Eds.) *The Oxford handbook of philosophy in music education* (pp. 284–304). New York: Oxford University Press, 2012.

Robertson, H. (1998). *No more teachers, no more books: The commercialization of Canada's Schools.* Toronto: McLelland & Stewart.

Savage, J. (2005a). Information communication technologies as a tool for re-imagining music education in the 21st Century. *International Journal of Education and the Arts 6*(2). Retrieved, from http://www.ijea.org/v6n2/.

Savage, J. (2005b). Working toward a theory for music technologies in the classroom: How pupils engage with and organise sounds in the classroom. *British Journal of Music Education, 22*(2), 167–180.

Taylor, T. D. (2011). The seductions of technology. *Journal of Music, Technology and Education, 4*(2–3), 227–232.

Thorgersen, K. (2012). Freedom to create in the cloud or in the open? A discussion of two options for music creation with digital tools at no cost. *Journal of Music, Technology and Education, 5*(2), 133–144.

Webster, P. (2011). Key research in music technology and music teaching and learning. *Journal of Music, Technology and Education, 4*(2–3), 115–130.

Woodford, P. (2012). Music education and social justice. In C. Philpott & G. Spruce (Eds.), *Debates in music teaching.* New York: Routledge.

....

CHAPTER 30

MUSIC FIRST AND LAST

*Developing a Socially Just Pedagogical Approach
to Music Education with Technology*

....

JONATHAN SAVAGE

INTRODUCTION

....

WHAT does social justice mean for music education with technology? At the most general level, social justice implies fairness for all, a responsibility toward one another, and a commitment to ensure that everyone has an equal chance to succeed. However, the balance between social equality and individual freedom is a complex one. It is helpful to see these as being in tension and to consider how they can be balanced against one another within the context of music education and the specific context of music education with technology. Here, perhaps, issues associated with social justice are particularly acute. At the most obvious level, music technologies, like many musical instruments, are often expensive and difficult to access. Like the provision of music education opportunities generally, access to music technology as a resource is dependent on decisions made by teachers, head teachers, or other administrators who may or may not prioritize music technology in their budgets. But at a deeper level, the systems through which music education take place, and the policies that underpin these systems, can also be seen to be influencing the extent to which music technology within music education could be portrayed as socially just or unjust.

Technology is not a neutral force, nor is it an unwielding master. It exists within particular educational contexts and shapes the various actions that occur within them. One of the most important keys for any music educator is to find the tools by which to analyze these interactions and consider how to shape them for the educational benefit of all involved. This is far from simple. As Mansfield (2005, p. 150) puts it, all music educators are ethically obligated to foster "a critical awareness of a technologically mediated music education environment." The word "critical" is vitally important in this sentence.

This chapter will explore the issues of social justice in music education with technology in a variety of contexts. The first of these relates to the provision of examinations in music and music technology within the United Kingdom. The second recounts a project conducted in Manchester, northwest England, that drew together two groups of students from very different musical social backgrounds within a technologically rich, music education environment. I will use these two contrasting contexts to highlight a number of issues relating to our chapter's key themes of social justice, technology, and music education. Along the way, I will draw on a number of other observations from educational policy within the context of the United Kingdom and from observations of schools and music education hubs. Following this, I will draw together a range of discussion points relating to how we can build a more socially just model of music education with technology.

"THOSE WHO CAN DO MUSIC; THOSE WHO CAN'T DO MUSIC TECHNOLOGY"

Robert Benchley, the famous American columnist, once quipped that "there are two kinds of people in the world: those who divide the world into two kinds of people, and those who don't." I was reminded of the quote when interviewing a number of teachers for a piece of research for Roland UK, a leading manufacturer of music technology (Savage, 2010). During one interview, I was taken aback by the bluntness of the teacher's view in relation to the examination courses being offered at Key Stage 4 (for students aged 14–16). When asked whether a student would be encouraged to take the General Certificate of Secondary Education (GCSE) in music or an alternative (vocational) qualification (a BTec) in music technology, the teacher replied, "Those who can do music; those who can't do music technology."

This teacher's sharp division in terms of their students' suitableness for studying music, or music technology, troubled me. It made me wonder whether such views were commonplace or whether they had been fostered within a particular educational climate within the United Kingdom. Over the past few months it led me to do a little historical analysis of our examination frameworks within the United Kingdom.

For the last 16 years, students have been able to study for a separate Advanced Level (A Level) qualification in music with technology, an examination usually taken at the age of 18; more recently, during the first decade of the 2000s, vocational qualifications in music with a significant, if not entire, course content devoted to music technology (e.g., recording, production, and other technologically mediated musical activities) have been available to students from the age of 14 onwards. Alongside these specialist courses, references to music technology and its use have continued to appear in National Curriculum Programmes of Study in various forms.

What is quickly apparent from a cursory overview of the curriculum and qualification frameworks within the United Kingdom is that students' experience of music technology begins as part of broader music curriculum experience within the school but quickly becomes specialized around the age of 14 into discrete qualifications that focus, to a greater or lesser extent, on the specialist skills associated with music technology.

An analysis of the number of students taking these examinations is informative. Research (Cambridge Associates, 2013a, 2012a, 2011a) demonstrates that the number of students studying for both an A level in music and an A level in music technology have fallen by around 35 percent over the last three years. While the gender balance in relation to A Level music slightly favors boys (16 percent more boys than girls studied for this examination in 2012), the differences in terms of gender within the A Level music technology intake are significant. Between 2010 and 2012, for example, 85 percent of entrants for this examination were male.

In terms of the "vocational" curriculum offered through qualifications such as the BTec First and BTec national examinations, a similarly marked difference in gender is noted (Edexcel 2012, 2013). Across the entire portfolio of examinations (i.e., in every subject) offered by Edexcel (the awarding body), male students favor female students by 52 percent to 48 percent. However, within the music courses that, as stated, have a core element of music technology within them, the gender imbalance is significant. Over the last three years, within the Level 2 BTec First, male students account for around 63 percent of the total student entries; at Level 3 (BTec National), they account for 80 percent of the total student entries.

Against this backdrop, the GCSE music examination has been taken by around 11 percent fewer students in 2012 compared to 2010 (Cambridge Associates, 2011b, 2012b, 2013b). The gender imbalance has narrowed from around a 10 percent gap (with boys outnumbering girls) in 2010 to a 3 percent difference in favor of the boys in 2013.

> I have dwelt on these figures for a number of reasons. First, and obviously, the separation of the study of music technology from the study of music in the United Kingdom's curriculum and examination framework has created a significant gender imbalance. This is something that numerous writers have observed for many years concerning technology generally, and computing specifically. Clegg, writing in 2001, commented that[t]he dominant discourse in computing is shaped by social practices which have institutionalized the power of experts, mostly male, to define what counts as computing in education . . . these ideologies in turn shape the climate which women have to negotiate. (Clegg 2001, p. 308)

There a few things in education more "institutionalized" than the examination system! The concepts and hierarchies imposed within this system shape, in very powerful ways, notions of gendered subjects—both male and female. As Francis points out, this benefits neither boys nor girls:

> Gender difference is socially produced and often limiting to both sexes. Moreover, this social construction of gender difference holds important consequences in terms of power, because in the dichotomous construction of gender, power is located in the male, and the female is subjugated. . . . The main point about discourses is that

they carry power in their ability to position things and people as negative or positive, powerless or powerful. (Francis 2001, p.19)

While the number of boys studying for a formal qualification in music or music technology always outnumbers the number of girls studying for the same qualification, the more music technology content that is included within the examination itself, the greater the gap between male and female students (at its largest, a massive 80 percent difference with the Level 3 BTec qualifications).

Gender issues associated with music technology within the school have been explored in Armstrong's recent book (Armstrong, 2011). Through a number of chapters she explores the processes and practices that contribute to the gendered culture of a classroom when music technology is used within compositional tasks. She analyzes specific elements, such as how institutional factors shape (and are shaped by) gender-technology relations, the nature of technological talk and how this impacts on the ways in which boys and girls learn differently about technology, and the default masculine role in controlling technology and technological information. One of her key points relates to how a teacher's pedagogy is gendered and the negative effects this can have on students' sense of ownership of their work. Throughout her book, Armstrong argues that historical and cultural forces have confined women to a particular compositional space; this, she argues, needs to be reclaimed,thereby facilitating a greater degree of agency for young female composers. What is true in relation to Armstrong's arguments in terms of musical composition within the classroom is also the case for the wider application of music technology throughout our educational system, as evidenced by the statistics presented earlier.

In addition to gender segregation, while the decline in students taking GCSE and A Level examinations in music has been marked, during the same period of time the total number of students taking vocational qualifications such as the BTec courses has increased by around 22 percent from 2012 to 2013. What are perceived as academic qualifications, on the one hand, have diminished, while those relating more closely to technological skills, popular musical styles, and perceived employability, on the other, have prospered. I make no value judgments here, but the change in fortunes is stark.

Within the United Kingdom, the move in the 1990s to distinguish music without technology (in a general sense) from music with technology has resulted in such a highly unhelpful, gendered, and rigid delineation of musical content, activity, perceived relevance in terms of "employability" and technologically mediated practice to such an extent that it is difficult to see any way in which this could be reversed. The impact of these changes within the examination framework encompassing schools have been felt higher up the educational system within the United Kingdom, too, with the number of male applicants to universities increasing rapidly in recent years (Armstrong, 2011, p. 3). As music education has focused increasingly on technology, "what we are witnessing is a shift from a traditionally 'feminine' subject to a subject that has increasingly masculine connotations" (ibid).

DUBDUBDUB, THE SOUNDS OF THE WORLD WIDE WEB

Within this context of sharp categorizations of what counts as "proper" music, with or without technology, certain projects have tried to explore a more unified approach to music education. DubDubDub was one such project, conducted by staff and students from Egerton High School and Manchester Metropolitan University. The project was supported by a not-for-profit software development company, UCan.tv. The name DubDubDub references the three "w"s of Internet URLs. It introduced a new type of digital musical instrument to the classroom, the DubDubDub player, which developed students' musical performance skills by drawing on the sonic environment of the Internet. Within this context, users of DubDubDub remixed the sonic content of the Internet, arranged sounds, and prioritized them in real time to form new musical works. The initial aim of the project was to develop an intuitive software instrument that would facilitate effective control of live Internet audio and then to use this tool in a performance setting. The first DubDubDub performance took place with a string quartet from the Royal Northern College of Music and a group of MCs and DJs drawn from an extended schools project held at Egerton High School at the Discourse, Power and Resistance conference (hosted by the University of Plymouth and Manchester Metropolitan University) on April 21, 2006 (MMU, 2006).

The performance moved through three sections. A string quartet opened with a traditional performance of Pachelbel's *Canon*. During the second stage of the performance, this was deconstructed as students moved away from their string instruments, one at a time, to add sounds and music using the DubDubDub interface on four, Internet-enabled laptop computers. The resulting mix of sounds from the Internet formed the middle section of the performance. One student searched for Google videos of violinists performing the same opening piece, and this provided a simple conceptual link to the first section of the performance. The nature of the DubDubDub player meant that each performance was uniquely different because the content relies on *live* Internet, in this case complete with its quirky connection status. The final movement of the performance involved the MCs and DJs from Egerton High School and the extended school's project. They introduced and blended in some contemporary grime beats using an MP3 player, a CD deck, and a cross-fade mixer. Quite naturally, they started spitting lyrics over the resulting sounds. Through these lyrics they introduced themselves, who they were reppin (representing), and established their style. Much of this was freestyling (a kind of vocal improvisation) combined with the inclusion of existing bars (sections of lyrics) that they had written to suit the occasion. During this final stage of the performance the string quartet/DubDubDub players gradually moved back to their string instruments from the laptops and improvised with the MCs and DJs. At the end of the performance, all performers were contributing to the piece. The string players were improvising with the MCs and DJs, using the wider harmonics of their instruments to compliment the grime beats through emulating scratch sounds, sub-bass riffs, bass drum grooves, and claps. The original Baroque piece had been transformed through a DubDubDub-inspired breakdown into a unique presentation of improvised music and expression.

So, how did DudDubDub explore an alternative approach to social justice in music education?

1. By Starting with the Students

"Adults fink they no bout lyf."

(Lyric from UK TRAP delivered during the DubDubDub project by "Impulse," a Year 10 student "reppin" [representing] the L.T.C. (Lyrically Talented Crew).

Egerton High School is a special school for students with social, emotional, and behavioral difficulties in the metropolitan borough of Trafford in southwest Manchester. All students have been excluded from mainstream schools in the local authority. Many of the inspirational features of this work came from the students at the school themselves. For them, music, rapping, beats, DJ-ing, and MC-ing are common features of a rich artistic sense of self-expression and a normal part of their day-to-day lives. Through working alongside these students as an artist, teacher, and co-learner, the project leader developed an interest in how chance informed both his own and their work. In particular, the synergy between music, visual media, and technology was a source of inspiration. The freedom of expression that this synergy brings allowed students to make sense of the ubiquitous violence and problems that permeate their lives, sharing and communicating solutions through forming and performing in music-focused "crews." These groups include DJs, MCs, beat programmers, and producers. Lyric writing (the construction of "bars") is prolific, their use of music hardware highly skillful, and students are adept at using a range of freeware, open source, and professional software tools for musical composition.

The effective engagement of these disaffected students at Egerton High School through allowing them to direct their own learning, develop a high level of multimedia ICT skills, and develop their passion for music and verbal expression led to early Expressive Arts GCSE examination entry and successful results for students aged 14 and above. It was this richly talented and artistic, yet challenging, group of young people that provided the opportunity to develop the DubDubDub project from a concept to reality.

Some of the key themes of social justice are fairness, equal access, and equal ability to succeed. Working with such a potentially challenging group of young people has forced the staff at Egerton High School to think in a completely different way about the educational provision provided by the school. As these teachers know, this must start with the students themselves. A socially just approach to music education embraces students' natural musical expression and uses this as a starting point for collaboration and inquiry. It adopts technologies that are familiar to students and explores these in creative ways, rather than seeking to impose new or unfamiliar instruments within the classroom. It conceptualizes music education within a relevant curriculum context that is relevant to their experience but that does not patronize them. Rather, it seeks to inspire and motivate them to succeed.

2. By Promoting a Responsive Curriculum

DubDubDub was part of a "Super Learning Week" on Recycling. The timetable at the school was collapsed for a week and students worked in vertical groupings (i.e., with a mixture of students from each year) looking at aspects of recycling across the curriculum. There was an interdisciplinary emphasis to activities. The Expressive Arts program of study related the work that these artistically literate pupils had been doing to the concept of recycling by re-using audio from the Internet in a random and nonlinear way to form compositions. Entitled "Recycled Audio Portraits," the students were free to use the Internet as they wanted for an hour, providing that they recorded all the incidental sounds that they discovered through the computers' sound card. Students were informed that the resulting sounds would be used to create an individual aural portrait of their Internet usage. For this reason, it was suggested that they place an emphasis on visiting bookmarked sites so as to present as broad a reflection of themselves as possible. A complimentary task involving recycling prose by cutting words out of poems and picking them out of a bag at random to form new syllabic expressions. Pasting words in new orders reinforced the recycling concept, and pupils were encouraged to record their new verbal pieces on the computer and mix it into their Internet-inspired audio portraits. Many initial recordings drawn from the Internet were edited to fit the length of the recorded vocal track. This provided a simple way of delineate the length of the piece. All the finished tracks were mixed together by a student as an extension task, and the result was played as part of a series of performances on the Friday afternoon that celebrated the work done during "Super Learning Week." Critical studies during the week included an investigation of the Dada and Surrealist art movements, including art, games, and films, and the cut-up technique used and developed by William S. Burroughs and others, as popularized by David Bowie.

The recycling of digital audio sourced from the Internet, along with the other simple sound generation ideas explored earlier, demonstrates very clearly how all students were given an equal chance to access musical composition within the project. This is not to say that all students succeeded equally within the activities. Judgments can be made about the appropriate selection of sounds, how they were edited, effected, and mixed together, the expressive impact of resulting pieces and their effectiveness in terms of the wider interdisciplinary project that the students worked within. It is important to note that this kind of musical composition is not a soft option. It is educationally and musically rigorous and demands a range of skills that students need to learn and a sophisticated musical understanding that can develop over time. The key point here is that the point of entry is accessible to the majority when compared to other types of musical composition that rely on conventional instruments or technologies. Part of the success of DubDubDub was the careful curation of digital technologies to ensure that all students were given an equal and fair chance to participate and succeed.

3. By Carefully Curating Technology

Audio exists on the Internet for a variety of reasons and serves a number of functions. It may arise incidentally by way of an embellishment to a corporate website, or it may have a specific function, such as a radio station. The DubDubDub player was a free, simple, and intuitive performance instrument through which students could control live audio sourced from the Internet. It comprised a specially prepared Internet browser with multiple tiled windows, basic volume and mixing controls, and video content sourced from Google Video (now YouTube).

The DubDubDub player worked on the principle that the various sounds contained within web pages will resonate together and that it is the user's skill, practice, and sensibilities toward these sounds and processes that produce effective improvisations. This type of musical skill or understanding is not dissimilar to the sensibilities needed in a range of other musical activities with which pupils were familiar, for example, through learning to play vinyl decks, CD turntables, or PCs as instruments, students were able to develop a range of transferable skills.

The creation of the DubDubDub instrument as an Internet browser-based instrument was an important element in its success. Original plans had been to develop a new piece of software, and this did go through several design stages. However, the adoption of the "Avant Browser" that, at the time, was innovative in its ability to offer the user multiple windows that could be tiled across the computer screen, together with independent volume controls for each window, proved to be a wise choice. It offered students a basic extension of the traditional browser environment that they were familiar with using to access the Internet. There were obvious limitations to this approach, not least that the triggering of live sound from numerous websites was not always a precise science, but this did not seem to concern students at all. As will be discussed further, this instrument can be categorized as an "infra-instrument" (Bowers & Archer, 2005, p. 6). It allowed students to do one or two things very easily, at very low cost, and with minimal traditional instrumental ability. But while instant musical engagement of this type might be considered important in a socially just music education program, this does not mean that it is unskillful; nor does it lack the opportunity for students to be musically expressive and creative. In fact, it allowed students a point of entry to a musical discourse that was richer and more diverse than they could have ever anticipated.

4. By Sharing Improvised Music with the "Other"

Prior to the first DubDubDub performance, a number of extended teaching sessions were held at Egerton High School with student teachers joining the group of school students. They worked with the school students to develop their skills with the DubDubDub player. During these sessions, the MCs and DJs shared their enthusiasm for music, demonstrated their skills, and discussed ideas for the performance with the university students. There were many interesting conversations between the university students and schools around the construction of an indeterminate, process-oriented piece of musical performance, albeit with a range of pre-established reference points that informed their decision-making process (e.g., bookmarks of Internet sites, pre-written lyrical content and musical beats, etc.).

We were pleased to note that both groups of young people were not afraid to explore the improvisational process as an integral element of the musical performance. More widely, many of them were able to incorporate ideas about improvisatory practices drawn from a range of other work that they had recently completed. For the students from the Manchester Metropolitan University, this included elements of improvisation pedagogy drawn from their Dalcroze studies, particularly principles from eurhythmics classes. For the Egerton High School pupils, the projects discussed earlier placed the DubDubDub project in a wider context of multimedia work centered around preparations for a GCSE in Expressive Arts (which pupils undertake in Year 9).

In some ways, it was hard to imagine two groups of students who could be more different in terms of their musical interests, instrumental experience, and educational experiences. The Egerton High School students were male, brought up in south Manchester, and all had been excluded from mainstream schools in Trafford; the MMU students were female, string players, had music degrees, and were studying for a postgraduate teaching qualification.

Yet these students found that they had much in common. The MMU students were intrigued by the technologies that the Egerton students were using. They enjoyed learning to use the various pieces of software and were even given lessons in using a DJ deck. Similarly, the string instruments played by the young women fascinated the Egerton High School students. This resulted in several impromptu violin lessons during the project! Musical conversations and engagement flowed quite naturally between the students despite their apparent differences.

Music is not a universal language. The musical languages that these two groups of students were familiar with were, at one level, very different. But within the specific musical utterances and gestures within their favored genres or styles, there was enough in common for these students to collaborate, meaningfully, with each other. The use of the digital technologies within DubDubDub provided a platform from which this could be facilitated. The technologies (traditional string instruments or Internet browser-based) were authenticated in the context within which they were used. It did not matter that they were simple or restrictive. For the teachers within DubDubDub, the key was to find a way to integrate music technology into inclusive musical activities, games, curricula, and conversations with their students in a way that facilitates their creativity and engagement with music itself. This was the basis from which musical conversations with the "Other" could be initiated. DubDubDub proved that a socially just approach to music education that does not depend on students having had the opportunity to learn to play a musical instrument, or even having the ability to afford to buy a musical instrument in the first place. A shared and common musical passion and commitment brought together two contrasting sets of students and sustained a shared process of musical composition and improvisation, which both found intrinsically rewarding.

Developing Positive Approaches to Social Justice in Music Education with Technology

Up to this point, this chapter has presented two contrasting visions of music education with technology. The first is disappointing, characterized by segregation, stereotype, and difference; the second is celebratory, characterized by simple technologies, collaborative working, and a shared commitment to music expression. It is clear where the more socially just model is evidenced.

In broader musical life outside formal education, contemporary musicians and artists are exploring the potential of new technologies as musical performance tools. In what is a very gradual, but well-documented, process, these new technologies are beginning to be applied and explored within educational contexts in the United Kingdom (Savage 2005, 2007). The whole skill set that underpins the use of these technologies is very different from a classical or conservatory model of musical learning. Yet often, it seems, the world of music education has been slow to embrace change and has imposed sharp, negative, socially unjust, and divisive categorizations of the type we explored at the beginning of this chapter.

DubDubDub has provided an alternative approach. It utilized a new type of musical instrument that was deliberately situated much closer to technologies that students were already using in their everyday lives, that is, the Internet browser. Blaine encourages us to re-conceptualize the notion of a musical instrument for the twenty-first century (Blaine 2005, p. 32) in line with lessons learned from game theory. Specifically:

> Musical instruments must strike the right balance between challenge, frustration and boredom: devices that are too simple tend not to provide rich experiences, and devices that are too complex alienate the user before their richness can be extracted from them. In game design, these same principles or 'learnability' are the fundamental principles of level design used to build an interest curve to engage players. (Blaine 2005, p. 28)

DubDubDub signals that the creation of such new instruments can lead to a more socially just and inclusive model of music education, in which students with diverse sets of musical skills and experiences can collaborate meaningfully together. It is important to note that this did not require any particular changes to the classical instruments that were brought into the project. Quite the reverse, in fact. These were a source of fascination, and the compositional and performance opportunities they facilitated were highly valued by both sets of students.

Associated with this change in mindset is the opportunity to re-analyze the process of musical performance and improvisation. There is an opportunity to get beyond the stereotypical notions of technique, interpretation, and recreation as being central to instrumental performance and to use new, technological innovations in such a way as to support the development of generic, accessible, and intuitive musical performance skills.

Within the United Kingdom, it is unlikely that many of the broader social and economic issues associated with access and privilege in music education are going to change. Despite public programs that give primary school students instrumental tuition for a short period, the reality is that students are not able to choose what instrument they want to learn, the continuation rates from this experience are poor, and the wider entitlement to a sustained instrumental music education are highly variable, depending on which part of the country one lives in.

The opportunities for production of a socially just model of music education lie within the hands of the open-minded music teacher. Infra-instruments, based on the principles explored with DubDubDub, may be one way forward. Despite the apparent reversals of instrument design (i.e., they are deliberately simple and easy to engage with), Bowers and Archer argue that they are nonetheless "aesthetically engaging and technically intriguing" (Bowers & Archer, 2005, p. 6) and worthy of further study. Their findings have some relevance to our discussion here, particularly that infra-instruments are evaluated best within the context of a "performance setting":

> Handling an assembly of 'stuff' is often facilitated by an infra-instrument designing philosophy, where each device plays its part in a manageable hybrid environment. . . . The whole performance setting becomes the unit of analysis, design and evaluation, not just a single 'new interface for musical expression' (Bowers & Archer, 2005, p. 6).

This reflects another theme in Bower's work, that of "performance ecology." This has a rich resonance for those involved in formal, classroom-based music education. By "performance ecology," Bowers means a closer analysis of the places for practical action and its display to others (co-performers or audience). Examples include desktop performance ecologies (or even classroom performance ecologies) that may

- be differentiated (a place for the computational, for the acoustical, and for other tools);
- be integrated in a variety of ways;
- allow opportunities for juxtapositions and for legible, embodied conduct (how performers look for, reach for, touch, communicate in nonverbal ways, etc.).

These notions of "infra-instruments" and a "performance ecology" remind us of the broader social context within which all music education takes place. Regardless of whether students are utilizing violins, laptops, the Internet, or a traditional score, the sounds, conversations, and interactions that they facilitate need to be understood in the context of a wider performance ecology. An important part of this ecology is the requirement for it to be socially just. It needs to be fair to all, to facilitate an equality in musical conversation and not bar anyone from being able to access it in a simple way. The DubDubDub project is an example of how extreme difference in terms of musical experience, types of musical skill, and education opportunity does not need to be a barrier to meaningful musical engagement and production. The contingent practical context of music education is fundamental and integral to this process of creating music with technology. It is only through a strong commitment to allowing intricate relationships to develop that a true (or at least a defensible) understanding of what a socially just music education really is can be created.

Understanding these elements is important if we are to truly understand and know how a student's musical learning has developed within a social context. It is also crucial if we are to take meaningful actions against socially unjust models of music education of the type explored at the beginning of this chapter. Only by developing a rich understanding of the broad context within which students' work has been produced can you begin to understand why they have made their particular musical choices. This understanding is not helped by simplistic and reductionist categorizations of the type presented within our current examination system within the United Kingdom. The social forms of control that examination frameworks facilitate only serve to atomize our understanding of what constitutes meaningful musical expression and prevent us considering the real essence of what it means to be a musician (and a music educator).

Conclusion

Technologies are integral to all music making, digital or otherwise. I would argue, philosophically, that there is not much difference between the development of the sustain pedal on the pianoforte in the nineteenth century and the latest Boss guitar effect pedal in 2015. Technologies of any type can help enforce the social order, or they can negate it and encourage alternative forms of expression; they can facilitate a meshing of ideas and responses, or they helpfully or unhelpfully disrupt them.

The rich technological context of music education extends beyond our choice of instruments and their use in educational settings. The broad array of technology that mediates our students' lives implicates, fundamentally, their engagement with us, as teachers, and with music more broadly. One cannot escape this, and it is ridiculous to imagine that one can.

Within the United Kingdom, for the foreseeable future, teachers and their students will work within examination and curriculum frameworks that are seeking to divorce musical skills and processes from those categorized as being tainted with or by "music technology." This is a system that prioritizes certain forms of knowledge in a simplistic and unhelpful way; for example, the rewards of studying for an A Level in music, as opposed to music technology, are more favorable (e.g., in accessing an undergraduate course of higher education). As we have seen, it also creates artificial and unhelpful barriers in terms of the gendered discourse surrounding music itself. They are socially unjust and serve to protect a musical elite and to disempower large swaths of our young people in a most unhelpful way.

The study of music and the provision of music education within the context of an individual teacher's work is a location where it may be possible to begin to chip away at some of these socially exclusive barriers. Teachers have a responsibility *not* to buy into the narrative that music technology is only for some students, that is, for those who cannot access music in the "proper" way, or who are male! They need to realize that the skill sets that they need to implement a broad and appropriate range of music technology within their work is their own responsibility, and not something that should be hived off to a technician or support staff. Most important, their conceptual models for music education and how it is organized must be built upon an understanding of an authentic musicianship that embraces technology, of any shape and form, and sees it as integral to musical expression. Music technology is too important to be categorized as being solely within the domain of the "digital musician" (Hugill 2008) and left at the doorstep in the experiences of so many others. Artificial categorizations only divide; what music education needs to develop first and foremost are students with a rich and authentic music expression, regardless of the tools they choose to use.

References

Armstrong, V. (2011). *Technology and the gendering of music education*. Aldershot, UK: Ashgate.

Blaine, T. (2005). The convergence of alternate controllers and musical interfaces in interactive entertainment. *Proceedings of the 2005 International Conference on New Interfaces for Music Expression* (pp.27–33). Canada, Vancouver, BC.

Bowers, J., & Archer, P. (2005). Not hyper, not meta, not cyber but infra-instruments. *Proceedings of the 2005 International Conference on New Interfaces for Music Expression* (pp.5–10). Canada, Vancouver, BC.

Cambridge Associates. (2011a). Uptake of A level subjects 2010: Statistics report series No. 28—revised. Retrieved, from http://www.cambridgeassessment.org.uk/Images/109918-uptake-of-gce-a-level-subjects-2010.pdf.

Cambridge Associates. (2011b). Uptake of GCSE subjects 2010: Statistics report series No. 35—revised. Retrieved, from http://www.cambridgeassessment.org.uk/Images/109925-uptake-of-gcse-subjects-2010.pdf.

Cambridge Associates. (2012a). Uptake of A level subjects 2011: Statistics report series No. 42. Retrieved, from http://www.cambridgeassessment.org.uk/Images/109931-uptake-of-gce-a-level-subjects-2011.pdf.

Cambridge Associates. (2012b). Uptake of GCSE subjects 2011: Statistics report series No. 44. Retrieved from http://www.cambridgeassessment.org.uk/Images/109933-uptake-of-gcse-subjects-2011.pdf.

Cambridge Associates. (2013a). Uptake of A level subjects 2012: Statistics report series No. 55. Retrieved from http://www.cambridgeassessment.org.uk/our-research/all-published-resources/statistical-reports/.

Cambridge Associates. (2013b). Uptake of GCSE subjects 2012: Statistics report series No. 57. Retrieved January 27, 2014, from http://www.cambridgeassessment.org.uk/our-research/all-published-resources/statistical-reports/.

Clegg, S. (2001). Theorising the machine: Gender, education and computing. *Gender and Education*, 13(3), 307–324.

Edexcel (2012). BTEC results day 2012. Retrieved from http://www.edexcel.com/btec/Documents/BTEC-Results-Day-2012-External.ppt.

Edexcel (2013). BTEC results day 2013. Retrieved from http://www.edexcel.com/btec/news-and-policy/.../BTEC_results_day_2013.ppt.

Francis, B. (2001). Beyond postmodernism: Feminist agency in educational research. In B. Francis & C. Skelton (Eds.), *Investigating gender: Contemporary perspectives in education*. Philadelphia: Open University Press.

Hugill, A. (2008). *The digital musician*. London: Routledge.

Mansfield, J. (2005). The global musical subject, curriculum, and heidegger's question concerning technology. *Educational Philosophy and Theory*, 37(1), 133–148.

MMU. (2006). DubDubDub performance from the Discourse, Power & Resistance conference. Retrieved from https://www.youtube.com/watch?v=PBsPXorwXpI.

Savage, J. (2005). Working towards a theory for music technologies in the classroom: How pupils engage with and organise sounds with new technologies. *British Journal of Music Education*, 22(2), 167–180.

Savage, J. (2007). Reconstructing music education through ICT. *Research in Education*, 78, 65–77.

Savage, J. (2010). A survey of ICT usage across English secondary schools. *Music Education Research*, 12(1), 47–62.

CHAPTER 31

RESCUING CHORAL MUSIC FROM THE REALM OF THE ELITE

Models for Twenty-First-Century Music Making—Two Case Illustrations

ANDRÉ DE QUADROS

INTRODUCTION: SETTING THE CONTEXT

THE practice of music has long been a vehicle for both inclusion and exclusion. Recent progressive and inclusive practices have questioned this practice, resulting in the democratization of the music classroom (Woodford, 2005). The practice of education possesses the societal constructs of exclusion and elitism (Freire, 1985), and there is no reason to suppose that music education is any different. Indeed, as Koza (2008) points out in "Listening for Whiteness," ". . . the construction of musical difference, which is an effect of power and is accompanied by the materialization of styles of music, plays a role in the systemic inclusion or exclusion of people whose bodies have already been raced through a similar process of sorting and ordering" (p. 146). Music educators have variously dealt with inclusion by way of choice of repertoire, access and equity, teacher-student relationship and student-student relationship, and the usual considerations of power and knowledge in Foucauldian and Freirean senses (see, for example, Tenorio, 2008; Kumashiro, 2004).

The music education enterprise is frequently focused on the acquisition of skills and knowledge, as evidenced by the emphasis on key competencies and technical facility, frequently subverting the larger goals of personal meaning in favor of the acquisition of technique (Schippers, 2009). In choral music, the proliferation of competitions emphasizes the need for technical prowess as a goal. As music educators, we are, after all, a product of our own musical experiences and education, in which most of us have sought technical mastery of our chosen instruments as part of the educational systems prevailing in conservatories and other institutions of music in higher education.

Choral music is frequently regarded as the most widespread form of participatory music making and has long been utilized as a locus for personal agency, community bonding, and social change (Ahlquist, 2006; de Quadros, 2012). Some little known examples of this kind of choral music include Saregam, a transgendered choir in Nepal, and the Muslim Brotherhood choir in Cairo. More widely known are the choirs in the Gay and Lesbian Association (GALA) movement, mainly in North America, where thousands of singers have been seeking choirs based on similar sexual orientation. In New York City, the Young People's Chorus, led by Francisco Núñez, continues to explore issues of diversity and inclusion. However, the dominant aesthetic paradigm, choice of repertoire, leadership dynamic, and relationship of performance to stage and location speak for an exclusionary practice, one in which individual voices are repressed and the oligarchy of the profession holds sway, thus preventing a truly consensual and inclusive enterprise. Power in a choir, as in an orchestra, band, and other conducted ensembles, is constituted by a quality of authority that is almost unrivaled in any other aspect of civic life, resembling the absolute authority in the armed forces and other areas of uniformed life. While there is a certain logic attaching to the governance of a large musical ensemble on matters of tempo, dynamics, and so forth, the suppression of individuality in most matters to do with the artistic enterprise is relatively unchallenged and largely uncontested by the music education profession. O'Toole's article titled "I Sing in a Choir but I Have 'No Voice'!" speaks to the heart of this problem (O'Toole, 2005).

This chapter presents alternatives to the choral practice as described above and refers to social exclusion (Agulnik, 2002) as a potent force that many are seeking to displace, even while others argue, as Dorling (2010) points out, that exclusion is necessary or inevitable. The two case illustrations in community choral music grounded in inclusion, communal participation, bonding, and resistance emerge from my personal encounters in the US incarceration system and in an Arab town in Galilee. Through these examples—which are completely different—I seek to describe processes that resist exclusion, recognizing it as an institutionalized form of injustice. I have adopted a narrative approach to presenting this material because it affords a means of exploring these two illustrations through story, incident, and chronology. I also use elements of portraiture as a research approach, acknowledging a common purpose, where portraiture seeks "... not to test previously established theories or hypotheses. Rather, like most qualitative methodologies, the purpose is to explore participants' experiences and the complexities of how meanings are produced within a particular context" (Gaztambide-Fernandez et al., 2011, p. 4). In *Telling Stories: The Use of Personal Narratives in the Social Sciences and History*, Maynes, Pierce, and Laslett (2008) emphasize that the positionality of the narrator is intrinsically connected to the narrative and indeed shapes it. In this chapter, I function in the triple role of collaborator, narrator, and analyst. When these roles are combined, they lead to a unique intersubjectivity and insight, which I attempt to share in the following narrative.

Social exclusion, sometimes referred to as "marginalization," is commonly defined as a concept involving deprivation, relativity, agency, and dynamics:

> ... multiple deprivation implies that social exclusion is about more than simply income poverty or lack of employment. Other factors are also important, such as absence of community or social interactions. Relativity refers to the fact that people are excluded from a particular society in a particular place at a particular time: there is no 'absolute' social exclusion, whereby someone can be judged excluded solely by reference to his or her circumstances in isolation. The issue of agency arises because exclusion is an act, implying that there are agents who undertake that act.... The dynamics element arises because exclusion implies... with little prospects for the future. (Richardson & Le Grand, 2002, pp. 3–4)

The persistent disadvantage that besets most industrialized societies can result in severe exclusion, where citizens are prevented from routine social engagement such as finding employment, gaining access to social services, and engaging in cultural life. The rising income inequality in the United States, Australia, the European Union, and in several other countries in the Majority World, such as India and China, is an indication of institutionalized injustice (Reich, 2010; Wilkinson & Pickett, 2010), where no one is served by inequality, neither the rich nor the extremely poor.

Case Illustration 1: A Prison Music Program Based on the Aesthetics of the Oppressed

Even America's own citizens are largely unaware of the full extent of its incarceration system in numbers, ethnicity, and economic and class parameters. With 5 percent of the world's population, the United States has more than 25 percent of its prisoners, with the total number being close to 2.5 million.[1] The Bureau of Justice Statistics reported that the number of adults under correctional supervision in the United States in 2010 was over 7.2 million if one includes parole, probation, and multiple forms of detention.[2] Incarceration has reached a level of a social disease on a massive scale (Drucker, 2011), with Americans becoming a punitive society, locking up an increasing proportion of the population, while showing no evidence that the country is any the safer or healthier as a result (Loury, 2008). In a book devoted to social justice, the obvious injustices in the criminal justice system need to be emphasized, for it is not only the large numbers of incarcerated people, but the obvious disparities in class and race that are at stake (Alexander, 2010; Reiman & Leighton, 2010). To cite a few data, the NAACP states:

> One in six black men had been incarcerated as of 2001. If current trends continue, one in three black males born today can expect to spend time in prison during his

lifetime...1 in 100 African American women are in prison.... Nationwide, African Americans represent 26% of juvenile arrests, 44% of youth who are detained, 46% of the youth who are judicially waived to criminal court, and 58% of the youth admitted to state prisons (Center on Juvenile and Criminal Justice).... About 14 million Whites and 2.6 million African Americans report using an illicit drug...5 times as many Whites are using drugs as African Americans, yet African Americans are sent to prison for drug offenses at 10 times the rate of Whites.[3]

Putting these figures in perspective, and extrapolating National Center for Education Statistics reported by Elpus and Abril (2011), there were approximately 2.5 million music students in US high schools in 2004.[4] Thus, given the comparison between high school music enrollment and those currently behind bars in US prisons, it is both clear and surprising that music education has largely failed to reach a large population, and one may appropriately ask why this population has been neglected by all sectors of the education profession. Part of the reason may lie in the training of music teachers, which focuses on music in schools rather than music in other settings, but we must consider whether this neglect is also part of a societal trend of a lack of attention to social justice; music educators are, after all, creatures of their context.

Since 2012, my two colleagues, Jamie Hillman and Emily Howe, and I have worked in two prisons, the Massachusetts Correctional Institution—Norfolk, and the Massachusetts Correctional Institution—Framingham. The Norfolk facility is a medium-security prison housing approximately 1,500 men, many of whom are serving life sentences, and the Framingham prison for women has approximately half that number.

At least two of the men with whom we work have been held since their teenage years, sentenced as minors to die in prison, serving for life without parole—this in spite of the 2012 ruling of the US Supreme Court in its consideration of the *Miller v. Alabama* case (Del Carmen et al., 2008).[5] In this case, the Court ruled that it is unconstitutional to sentence a minor to die in prison, a life sentence without parole. The United States is permitted to deliver sentences of this kind because it has not ratified the International Convention on the Rights of the Child.[6] One of these two men is among our most committed students, and we have observed a steady transformation over the years of his participation in music. He sings with greater confidence, he finds ways in which songs inspire him to reflect on his life and his circumstances. The women's group consists of people convicted of a range of offenses, from nonviolent to violent.

The prison music programs that do exist serve to provide opportunities for musical participation through singing, choral work, acquisition of musical literacy, composition and song writing, and other similar activities (Cohen, 2007; Cohen & Silverman, 2013). My colleagues and I have developed a distinct interdisciplinary arts approach that is titled the "EMPOWERING SONG" approach, rooted in improvised song, poetry, bodywork, movement, and imagery for personal and communal transformation. This philosophy of teaching, nurturing, and leading is located in a number of participatory paradigms (Higgins, 2012; Silverman, 2012; Stige, 2010), but most particularly in Boal's revolutionary work with oppressed peoples (1985; Boal & Jackson, 2006). The hallmark of this approach lies in its democracy, with an open-ended quality, where starting points for sessions are frequently set by us, but the conduct of the session is guided by the responses and ideas from the prison participants. In its interdisciplinarity, its focus on the body, and its experimental processes linked to personal meaning and community, EMPOWERING SONG may well be breaking new ground. While Boal's work with the oppressed is central to community theater, there are few comparable approaches in music education. We see this approach as aligning with these more subversive and discursive approaches.

Several of the activities in the prisons aim to displace the highly regulated authoritarian prison system while the sessions are underway. Two examples will serve to illustrate. We start every session singing in a circle, usually holding hands. For male prisoners to hold hands is unheard of in an open, legitimate way. The second illustration emerged from a Society for Ethnomusicology conference, in which I attended a session given by an ethnomusicologist who had been incarcerated. He noted that eye contact between prisoners is usually avoided; frequently such contact can lead to violent trouble. In one session, I asked participants to gaze into each other's eyes and sing. These activities serve to empower the participants and to allow them to experience a democratic classroom within a brutal penal system—a zone of safety, security, and integrity.

We have found that adopting a theme for our work encourages all of us to anchor our songwriting, poetry, visual art, and other improvisational work. We took a line from the Anglo-Celtic song *O Waly, Waly*: "And neither have I wings to fly." The prison participants used these words in various ways, to comment on the justice system, to reflect on their own reality, and to express hope and pessimism, optimism and desperation. One elderly African American man wrote the following, which I have reproduced with the exact spelling and punctuation of the original:

> ... Men disregard the potential of my African mind; trialed, sentenced, and convicted as my hawk's wings are clipped as human justice is derailed, my new slavery, condition is jail. . . . and Neither have I wings to fly, to justify my being, what I believe in, the crimes against me, my black face, some can call treason, an injustice that has touched us, deeply in the history of time. Justice has never been designed to be mine, . . .

Another man in his fifties, a victim of childhood sexual abuse, produced a painting as inspiration from the song. The readers need to know that there are no resources in the prison for painting. Frequently, the men use paintbrushes fashioned from their own hair and dissolve M&Ms to create paint. In the women's prison, we had a mural painting session during the term, in which the theme was taken from *Amazing Grace*. The theme "I once was lost but now am found" gave rise to the mural in Figure 31.1.

In both these examples, visual and textual, the song gave rise to reflections on "prisonization," the term that Clemmer (1940) used to connote the extent to which prisoners accept and contest the culture of incarceration in the United States that is located in poverty and race.

FIGURE 31.1 Mural created in the Framingham women's prison.

CASE ILLUSTRATION 2: A MUSIC PROGRAM IN ARAB ISRAELI GALILEE

It may not be commonly understood in the Western world that there is a substantial population of Arabs living within the state of Israel as full-fledged Israeli citizens. They are neither residents of the West Bank nor of Gaza. Indeed, as Israeli citizens they are forbidden from visiting either the West Bank or Gaza. Most of these Arabs, absorbed into the state of Israel in 1948, live in cohesive Arab communities dotted throughout the country, which typically do not include Jews. Correspondingly, most villages in Israel are exclusively Jewish Israeli, with only rare examples of Arabs living side by side with Jewish Israelis. The segregation of Israeli citizens is on such a scale, not only between Jewish Israelis and others, but also within the Jewish and Arab communities (Al Haj, 2004; Goldberg, 2006; Khattab & Miaari, 2013; White, 2012), that towns and regions are frequently organized around ethnic, linguistic, and religious affinities.

The *New York Times* refers to the Arabs from the 1948 absorption as "Palestinian Israelis" or as "Israeli Arabs," but I will refer to them in this chapter also as Palestinians, a term that they use for themselves, knowing full well that the term has other connotations.

In the Galilee area, some two and a half hours driving distance north of Jerusalem, a few minutes away from Nazareth, and not far away from Jericho, lies Shefar'amr, a small Arab town, captured in 1948 by the Israeli army (Morris, 1999) and kept under military rule until 1966. This town, with its majority Sunni Muslim population and substantial Christian and Druze minorities, has, for over the best part of the last three decades, been the site of a unique experiment in inclusion and participation. Rahib Haddad, a pianist and music teacher, has created a choral program consisting of three choirs: Al Baath

Arab Voices of Galilee, the Sawa Choir, and the Sawa Children's Choir, for adults, youth, and elementary school children, respectively.

Rahib Haddad started in 1986 in a modest way with the initiation of a community Arab choir for adults, pictured in Figure 31.2. Mindful of the dispossession of identity that these Israeli Arabs feel, he was eager to give voice to Arab culture and Palestinian identity through founding the choir. Israeli Arabs frequently feel excluded by several constituencies (Kook, 2002; Rabinowitz, 1997). Unlike the Palestinians from the West Bank and Gaza, the Israeli Arabs are given scant attention by the public narratives about Palestinians, perhaps understandably so. Possessing Israeli passports and considerable measures of citizen equality, they are not engaged in the daily fight for land rights, as are their West Bank and Gaza compatriots (Ophir, Givoni, & Ḥanafi, 2009). Thus, although they have a kinship with their Palestinian compatriots in East Jerusalem, Jordan, the Occupied Territories, Lebanon, and Syria, they are almost completely isolated from them, and with their Israeli passports, are barred from traveling to several of these areas. The profound sense of exclusion that these Arabs suffer in towns like Shefar'amr (Raven, Albregtse, & Zevulun, 2008) inspired Haddad to develop a musical community that would exercise its Palestinian identity. For over 25 years, this community chorus, Al Ba'ath Arab Voices of Galilee, has continued without interruption, and with several of its original members.

In 2004, Rahib Haddad entered into a new phase of his work by including young people. Maya Shavit, a Jewish Israeli, and conductor of the Efroni choir from the Jewish town of Emek Hefer, together with another Jewish colleague, Eva de Mayo, approached Haddad to form an Arab youth choir to participate with the Efroni Choir in the Peace Camp at Forum Barcelona.[7] This led to the birth of the Sawa Choir, a choir predominantly of teenagers, which has since become a permanent choir after this initial impetus. A strong partnership sprang up between the Sawa Choir and the Efroni Choir, which lasted well beyond the Barcelona project. The collaboration between these two choirs necessitated the Jewish youth coming to Shefar'amr and the Sawa singers traveling to Emek Hefer for workshops, rehearsals, and joint performance projects. For almost 10 years, Eva de Mayo, the Jewish conductor, jointly directed the Sawa Choir and was received without any reservation by the Shefar'amr community. I was surprised to observe that Eva de Mayo conducted the rehearsals in Hebrew, with no opposition from any of the Arabs.

Based on my interviews, de Mayo, Haddad, and Shavit generally concur that the objective of collaboration between the two choirs was less about being a model for peace- making than it was concerned with building understanding between two groups of young people whose worlds simply do not normally intersect—an exercise in inclusion. In interviews with the young singers from both choirs, this feeling was shared by many singers, asserting that they felt strong kinship with each other.

These collaborative activities do not meet with universal acceptance. In 2009, the two choirs planned a joint activity with a third choir, the Yasmeen Choir from East Jerusalem, a Palestinian youth choir directed by Hania Soudah Sabbara in the Franciscan monastery of the old city of Jerusalem. The difficulties of collaborating arose principally

FIGURE 31.2 Al Baath Arab Voices of Galilee

from the international BDS (boycott, divestment, sanctions) campaign initiated by Palestinian civil society (Barghouti, 2011). The campaign opposes Israeli-Palestinian interaction and any activities that resemble the normalization of relations. The collaboration between these three choirs has been documented in the progressive Israeli newspaper, *Haaretz*,[8] but I provide some details here. As a result of the unrest, the bishop of the church that originally agreed to host this event, the Augustus Victoria Church, decided to make the church unavailable. The entire project was doomed until the Franciscan monastery offered its facilities to host this event. It lies beyond the scope of this chapter to evaluate the validity of BDS opposition against such activities; I simply observe and remark on the genuine difficulties that such collaborations encounter (see, for example, Brinner, 2009).

Another exercise in social inclusion arose from a period of civil strife in Shefar'amr between the Christian and Druze communities. In 2004, the murder of a young woman by her father-in-law resulted in bitter strife between the Christian and Druze communities, with property damaged and several people wounded. This period of strife continued for five years, ending in 2009 with the signing of a reconciliation agreement between all parties. Rahib Haddad, determined to find ways to contribute to the reconciliation process, started a children's choir for Christians, Druze, and Muslims. Twice a week, a bus from the Sawa Centre travels through the neighborhoods of Shefar'amr to collect these young children to bring them together for an evening of song. In my observations of the group, it was clear that the communal barriers between these communities had been lifted, and the children were interacting as a group of elementary school children would, with all the differences of energy, ability, and attention, and normal types of peer interaction.

Rahib Haddad's various initiatives and collaborations with Eva de Mayo and Maya Shavit have recently coalesced under the umbrella of a project with the title *Community Heartsong*, indicating the centrality of singing, community, and love. The *Community Heartsong* has also offered an annual conducting course for Arab and Israeli conductors for one week in Jerusalem, which I have taught every year from its inception in 2010 until 2013. In 2014 and 2015, I have offered workshops in the West Bank for community music leaders. This project seeks to continue to work in the more difficult territory of the West Bank, where there is a genuine interest in community music activities with school children and those who live in the refugee camps.

COMMENTARY

Both case illustrations point to choral music as a locus of potential, offering possibilities for inclusion and justice. While choral music can be an exercise of the elite, it can also be an inclusive practice. Indeed, several choirs and conductors around the world are utilizing the possibilities of choral music for the exercise of justice in settings rife with alienation, racism, poverty, and discrimination on the basis of sexual orientation, religion, and several other factors.

In the case of the two prisons, the specific nature of the Empowering Song Approach allows participants to engage in deeply reflective exercises on their prisonization. My observations suggest that even some of the long-term prisoners have come to new understandings, sometimes uncomfortably so, as a result of the musical process. While this approach has emerged from prison teaching and has been particular to the incarcerated context, its transferability to the general music classroom is being explored.

The second illustration, in one of the most hotly debated political and social issues of our time, is written from the desires and feelings of injustice that Palestinians experience. In so doing, I understand that Palestinians do not have a monopoly on injustice and suffering. Nevertheless, this is an example of action and resistance through music, in the pursuit both of justice and understanding. With this case, the music education activity is not distinctive. But the setting and context, ridden with conflict and division, create singularities where ordinary music education can provide extraordinary outcomes.

In this chapter, social exclusion as an expression of injustice serves to offer an understanding of how power is constituted, formed, and played out in these two settings. Musical activities that counter social exclusion allow us to understand the ways in which people see themselves isolated from the dreams and narratives of the mainstream, and the ways, through music, that such yearnings may be altered and shared.

Notes

1. International Centre for Prison Studies, http://www.prisonstudies.org/country/united-states-america.
2. http://bjs.ojp.usdoj.gov/content/pub/press/corrections09pr.cfm, accessed May 16, 2012.
3. http://www.naacp.org/pages/criminal-justice-fact-sheet.
4. Ken Elpus and Carlos Abril, "High School Music Ensemble Students in the United States: A Demographic Profile," *Journal of Research in Music Education,* 59(2) (2011). Elpus and Abril reported 621,895 high school seniors in band, orchestra, or choir in 2004.
5. http://www.leagle.com/decision/In%20SCO%2020120625000T.
6. http://www.unicef.org/crc/.
7. http://www.fundacioforum.org/b04/b04/media.barcelona2004.org/en/convocatoria335a.html?id=2741.
8. http://www.haaretz.com/culture/arts-leisure/soundbox-working-in-concert-1.263923.

References

Ahlquist, K. (Ed.). (2006). *Chorus and community.* Urbana: University of Illinois Press.

Agulnik, P. (2002). *Understanding social exclusion.* New York: Oxford University Press.

Alexander, M. (2010). *The new Jim Crow: Mass incarceration in the age of colorblindness.* New York: New Press.

Al Haj, M. (2004). *Immigration and ethnic formation in a deeply divided society: The case of the 1990s immigrants from the former Soviet Union in Israel.* Leiden: Brill. Retrieved June 26, 2014, from http://site.ebrary.com/id/10089756.

Brinner, B. E. (2009). *Playing across a divide: Israeli-Palestinian musical encounters.* Oxford: Oxford University Press.

Barghouti, O. (2011). *BDS: boycott, divestment, sanctions: The global struggle for Palestinian rights.* Chicago: Haymarket Books.

Boal, A. (1985). *Theatre of the oppressed.* New York: Theatre Communications Group.

Boal, A., & Jackson, A. (2006). *The aesthetics of the oppressed.* London: Routledge.

Clemmer, D. (1940). *The prison community.* Boston: Christopher.

Cohen, M. L. (2007). *Christopher Small's concept of musicking: Toward a theory of choral singing pedagogy in prison contexts.* PhD diss., University of Kansas.

Cohen, M. L., & Silverman, M. (2013). Personal growth through music: Oakdale Prison's community choir and community music for homeless populations in New York City. In K. K. Veblen, D. J. Elliott, S. J. Messenger, & M. Silverman (Eds.), *Community music today* (pp. 199–216). Lanham, MD: Rowman & Littlefield.

De Quadros, A. (Ed.). (2012). *The Cambridge Companion to Choral Music.* Cambridge: Cambridge University Press.

Del Carmen, R. V., B. A. Witt, & Ritter, S. E. (2008). *Briefs of leading cases in corrections.* Newark, NJ: LexisNexis Anderson Pub.

Dorling, D. (2010). *Injustice: Why social inequality persists.* Bristol, UK: Policy Press.

Drucker, E. M. (2011). *A plague of prisons: The epidemiology of mass incarceration in America.* New York: New Press.

Elpus, K., & Abril, C. (2011). High school music ensemble students in the United States: A demographic profile. *Journal of Research in Music Education,* 59(2), 128–145.

Freire, P. (1985). *The politics of education: Culture, power, and liberation*. South Hadley, MA: Bergin & Garvey.

Gaztambide-Fernandez, R., Cairns, K., Kawashima, Y., Menna, L., & VanderDussen. E. (2011). Portraiture as pedagogy: Learning research through the exploration of context and methodology. *International Journal of Education & the Arts, 12*(4), 1–29.

Goldberg, D. J. (2006). *The divided self: Israel and the Jewish psyche today*. London: I. B. Tauris.

Higgins, L. (2012). *Community music: In theory and in practice*. New York: Oxford University Press.

Khattab, N., & Miaari, S. (2013). *Palestinians in the Israeli labor market: A multi- disciplinary approach*. New York: Palgrave Macmillan.

Kook, R. B. (2002). *The logic of democratic exclusion: African Americans in the United States and Palestinian citizens in Israel*. Lanham, MD: Lexington Books.

Koza, J. E. (2008). Listening for whiteness: Hearing racial politics in undergraduate school music. *Philosophy of Music Education Review, 16*(2), 145–155.

Kumashiro, K. K. (2004). *Against common sense: Teaching and learning toward social justice*. New York: RoutledgeFalmer.

Loury, G. C. (2008). *Race, incarceration, and American values*. Cambridge, MA: MIT Press.

Maynes, M. J, Pierce, J. L., & Laslett, B. (2008). *Telling stories: The use of personal narratives in the social sciences and history*. Ithaca, NY: Cornell University Press.

Morris, B. (1999). *Righteous victims: A history of the Zionist-Arab conflict, 1881–1999*. New York: Knopf.

Ophir, A, Givoni, M., & Ḥanafī, S. (2009). *The power of inclusive exclusion: Anatomy of Israeli rule in the occupied Palestinian territories*. New York: Zone Books.

O'Toole, P. (2005). I sing in a choir but I have "no voice"! *Visions of Research in Music Education, 6*. Retrieved from http://www-usr.rider.edu/~vrme/v6n1/visions/O%27Toole%20I%20Sing%20In%20A%20Choir.pdf.

Rabinowitz, D. (1997). *Overlooking Nazareth: The ethnography of exclusion in Galilee*. Cambridge: Cambridge University Press.

Raven, D., Albregtse, M., & Zevulun, D. (2008). *Home is where the hatred is? Sense of belonging and exclusion of Galilee Bedouins with regard to the Jewish state, Israeli-Jewish and Israeli-Arab citizens*. Retrieved from http://hdl.handle.net/1874/30287.

Reich, R. B. (2010). *Aftershock: The next economy and America's future*. New York: Alfred A. Knopf.

Reiman, J. H., & Leighton, P. (2010). *The rich get richer and the poor get prison: A reader*. Boston, MA: Allyn & Bacon.

Richardson, L., & Le Grand, J. (2002). *Outsider and insider expertise: The response of residents of deprived neighbourhoods to an academic definition of social exclusion*. London: CASE, London School of Economics. Retrieved from http://eprints.lse.ac.uk/4647/1/Outsider_and_Insider_Expertise_The_response_of_residents_of_deprived_neighbourhoods_to_an_academic_definition_of_social_exclusion.pdf.

Schippers, H. (2009). *Facing the music: Shaping music education from a global perspective*. New York: Oxford University Press/Oxford Scholarship Online.

Silverman, M. (2012). Community music and social justice: Reclaiming love. In G. McPherson & G. Welch (Eds.), *The Oxford handbook of music education* (pp. 155–167). New York: Oxford University Press.

Stige, B. (2010). *Where music helps: Community music therapy in action and reflection*. Farnham, UK: Ashgate.

Tenorio, R. (2008). Music for social justice. In A. Pelo (Ed.), *Rethinking early childhood education* (pp. 215–218). Milwaukee, WI: Rethinking Schools.

White, B. (2012). *Palestinians in Israel: Segregation, discrimination and democracy.* London: Pluto Press.

Wilkinson, R. G., & Pickett, K. (2010). *The spirit level: Why greater equality makes societies stronger.* New York: Bloomsbury Press.

Woodford, P. (2005). *Democracy and music education: Liberalism, ethics, and the politics of practice.* Bloomington: Indiana University Press.

CHAPTER 32

MUSIC EDUCATION ASSESSMENT AND SOCIAL JUSTICE

Resisting Hegemony Through Formative Assessment

MARTIN FAUTLEY

INTRODUCTION

ASSESSMENT in music education is a problematic and contested area. There are multiple uses and purposes of assessment, and a range of views and interests   vested and otherwise—concerning it. This chapter will consider the role that assessment, particularly formative assessment, has to play with regard to social justice purposes in music education, focusing particularly on the way that formative assessment can be utilized to resist the prevailing hegemony. It suggests ways in which assessment can be used to open the sphere of music education to democratization, and challenges some of the customs and practices in music education that have developed over the years.

To begin with, we need to be clear on the topics this chapter will be addressing. There are a number of different terminologies used with regard to assessment, and it is important to understand these at the outset. Principal among these are the two common notions of *formative* and *summative* assessment. Although these terms are frequently encountered, and to some extent understood, there are considerable differences in the ways in which understandings are applied; this is especially true for formative assessment. Summative assessment is, in essence, an assessment that *sums up* the attainment of a learner, and does so by ascribing a grade, mark, or level. Summative assessment is normally undertaken at a significant point, such as the end of a course of study, a unit of work, a term, or a year. This assessment is designed to yield data that will be used for specific purposes, as Harlen observes:

> ... in the case of summative assessment there are various ways in which the information about student achievement at a certain time is used. These uses include: internal school tracking of students' progress; informing parents, students and the students' next teacher of what has been achieved; certification or accreditation of learning by an external body; and selection for employment or higher education. (Harlen, 2005, p. 208)

It is summative assessment that often assumes primacy both in educator discourse and public perception. It could be said of summative assessment that it is well understood, and embedded into educational thought and practice. The same cannot be said of the other significant assessment terminology, *formative assessment*. This can also be known as assessment for learning (AfL) which is actually a helpful way of describing this form of assessment and what it does. The equivalent terminology for summative assessment is assessment *of* learning; and it is the differences, between *of* and *for*, that most adequately encapsulate what is going on in each mode of assessment. Assessment of learning summarizes for the audience (whoever that might be) a level of attainment of the individual. Assessment for learning, on the other hand, has as its primary focus improving learning and activity for the learner. What this means is that formative assessment does not necessarily need to involve grading, marking, or leveling. Instead, it is concerned with teacher and student discussing what specifically the student needs to do next, and how the student can take their learning and attainment to the next stage.

Assessment and Testing

One of the problems that has arisen is that the use of the word "assessment" as employed in the terminology 'formative assessment' troubles conceptions that equate assessment with testing. As Dylan Wiliam, a key researcher in educational assessment, observed in an interview published in *The Times Educational Supplement*:

> The big mistake that Paul Black and I made was calling this stuff 'assessment'... Because when you use the word assessment, people think about tests and exams. For me, AfL is all about better teaching. (Stewart, 2012)

This has given rise to a situation in which formative assessment has become in practice two different things entirely: formative assessment per se, and what might better be termed as *the formative use of summative assessment*. True formative assessment, that which involves teacher and student in a dialogue about the music produced, and has as its primary aim to develop the music that the student has produced, is very different from the formative use of summative assessment, where the student is told what grade they have scored in a test, and this is then used to provide a target for the student to aim at next time a test is given. As Wiliam noted:

> In the United States, the term 'formative assessment' is often used to describe assessments that are used to provide information on the likely performance of students on state-mandated tests—a usage that might better be described as 'early warning summative'. In other contexts it is used to describe any feedback given to students, no matter what use is made of it, such as telling students which items they got correct and incorrect. (Wiliam, 2004)

These differences can be clearly seen in music learning contexts throughout the Western world.

ASSESSMENT AND VALUING

Allied to this issue, we have in music education an ongoing and deep-rooted history of valorization of Western art music as the highest form of achievement. This hegemonic view places Western art music at the apex, with all other forms falling short in some way:

> ... the music that is typically and unquestioningly assumed by many to have the highest status, music of the Western classical tradition, has attained this hegemonic status through its association with a dominant cultural order and has come to be one means by which such a hegemonic order is maintained.... (Spruce, 2007, p. 19)

Sometimes this can be stated overtly, as in this instance:

> It is surely not difficult to establish the superiority of Cole Porter over R.E.M.; one has only to look at the incompetent voice-leading in *Losing My Religion*, the misunderstanding of chord relations, and the inability to develop a melodic line in which the phrases lead into one another with a genuine musical need.
>
> But once you look at modern popular music in this way, you will come to see how gross, tasteless and sentimental it mostly is, and how far it is from our tradition of meditative polyphony.... (Scruton, 1996)

This viewpoint is at least clear in its valorization. There are occasions in music education where we see examples of thinking that has not even gotten as far as this, containing tacit assumptions that "West is best," and excluding many (or, in some cases, all) other forms of music. This has important ramifications for assessment in music education, not least because, as Spruce observes:

> [Classical music] still exerts its influence through the assumptions we hold about music: assumptions about the way in which musical quality is best evaluated.... (Spruce, 2007, p. 19)

This point is one that has been part of the discourse in mainstream music education for many years. As long ago as 1977, Shepherd et al. (1977) were asking the question "whose music" should be studied in music education, and in 1991 Janet Mills observed that

> [First] . . . in a multi-cultural society our culture is not just European. Second, a notion that high art is great and other forms of European music are not great is open to question. Third, the transmission of our cultural heritage, whatever we mean by this, is only one part of music education. (Mills, 1991, p. 108)

More recently, writing about music education in the United States, Kratus observed that

> . . . the music made in schools, largely based on classical, folk, and sometimes jazz traditions, represents a small and shrinking slice of the musical pie. Students perform music in school that they rarely, if ever, hear outside of school. (Kratus, 2007, p. 45)

The points raised by Spruce, Mills, and Kratus lie at the heart of what a consideration of assessment in music education for the twenty-first century should involve. Music is a dynamic, vibrant, lived culture, which has importance in terms of identity formation, socialization, and relevance to a huge number of young people, and this has been the case for many years. And yet if Kratus's observation is correct, then the music that young people encounter in school can be a long way removed from their personal interests and involvement. Why does this matter? It matters because if a separate category of music exists that can be defined as "school music," then it begs the question as to why this has any relevance beyond the immediate and circular self-referential format of its own devising. It matters, too, if we want our young people to develop in music making beginning with and on their own terms, and have their horizons not just broadened, but also deepened. Let us examine this in a little more detail.

We know that young people bring with them a raft of personal knowledge, experience, and attitudes that are highly relevant to them on a personal basis. Making music falls into this category. Many young people want to make music that is relevant to their lives, and that emerges from their own experiences. This is not to say that they should be constrained within the limitations of their own knowledge and experience, but that the enthusiasm and energy they have for wanting to make music, and improve at making music, should be part of classroom ontology. This point was recognized many years ago by Mrs. Curwen in her piano method of 1886, when she recommended that music teachers "[p]roceed from the known to the related unknown" (Curwen, 1886, p. 104). As the pupils are fully acquainted with what they know, they also tend to like what they know. The job of the teacher therefore becomes that of leading them to the "related unknown."

This finds its most obvious outworking in music education in the choice of materials for pupils to engage with. Social justice is not served if the predominant modality of musical encounter that is planned for and enacted is one that privileges Western art music culture, which (as Kratus said above) "they rarely if ever hear outside of school," over the lived experiences and enthusiasm of the young person. As we have seen, what all too frequently tends to occur is that there is a school-based hegemony resulting from a privileging of certain types of musical styles and genres over others. Thus Western art music tends to trump all other types; dubstep, rap, scratching, toasting, DJ-ing, MC-ing, heavy metal, and many others, become marginalized and their existence disavowed. In the urban twenty-first-century high school, many of our pupils come from non-Western cultures, and so the same happens to bhangra, dhol, township, gamelan, and many other types of world music.

But it is not only in the choice of materials that social justice issues come to the fore. Assessment practices that are based on music that is thought to be "other" in comparison can also cause problems. Assessing a dhol drummer using criteria or rubrics that were designed for an orchestral player will be difficult. What tends to happen as a result of this is that there is a concomitant stratification of assessment practices that render otherwise valid forms of musical expression as becoming inadmissible for assessment purposes; so the dhol drummer realizes that his/her performance is not valued in and by the dominant assessment culture, and retreats away from "school music."

This is not the sole prerogative of non-Western music, though. In many music education systems, the archetypal apotheosis is the performer. It is the expert performer (in the Western classical tradition) who is highly valued, lauded, and held as paragon exemplar. Even within the Western classical art tradition, this means that the process of composing, of creating music, can often feel undervalued in comparison—only taught, if taught at all, and learned in limiting (and limited) ways, and only problematically admitted to the periphery of the canon of admissible musical experiences (as one inner-city pupil observed in a research site I was investigating, "Does you have to be dead to be a composer?").

ASSESSMENT AND HEGEMONY

So how can music education assessment address these issues, and remake itself in such a way that it is not solely the purveyor of a single hegemonic structure? One way of doing this is to begin by considering that which Spruce refers to as

> ... the manner in which musical achievement is defined and assessed [that] inevitably articulates a set of philosophical and political principles about the nature and purpose of learning, the subject being assessed, and the relationship between school and society.... (Spruce, 2001, p. 118)

This is the point that *Musical Futures* (see, *inter alia*, Hallam et al., 2008; Price, 2006) endeavors to address by starting from the very aspects of music that young people bring with them to the classroom. Important and useful though this is, it is not the only way in which social justice can be served. One important aspect of musical learning that can be developed is that of emerging proficiency in the music that the young person wants to make, and doing so on their own terms. What this means is that assessment criteria that are negotiated between learner and teacher, and are aimed at developing whatever aspects of the music are appropriate, and amenable to development, need to be negotiated. To do this, some music educators feel that they lack the necessary background and knowledge of musical styles and types other than that of their specialism. Yet music educators are teachers, and should be able to discuss with students what it is that is important in the music which is amenable to intervention. For example, with regard to the issue of quality, key questions for music educators to ask of their pupils are these:

- What are the key characteristics of this type/style/genre of music?
- Is this a good example of a piece of music of this type?
- Is your composition/performance within the context requirements of the type/ style/genre?

And a further question, to tease out understandings, would be

- Why? (Fautley, 2010, pp. 80–81)

To do this requires a shift in the balance of power, however. This does *not* require the teacher to be the sole expert arbiter of quality, but instead democratizes the process of valuing. It involves the pupil in co-construction of criteria for what will be done, what will be worked on, and what will be the focus. This point was recognized by Hickman with regard to art education, when he observed that

> [i]f criteria are considered to be necessary ... the community decides on criteria for assessment, but we need to determine the size of the community; I would advocate that the learner's own criteria be used, which means that the community is a minimum of two people. . . . (Hickman, 2007, p. 84)

In other words, the domain of quality is not to be determined solely by external arbiters. Csikszentmihalyi (1996) argued that for creativity to occur, there had to be an interplay between the individual, the domain, and the field. The domain he saw as a ". . . set of symbolic rules and procedures" (Csikszentmihalyi, 1996, p. 26). The field he defined as ". . . all the individuals who act as gatekeepers to the domain. It is their job to decide whether a new idea or product should be included in the domain" (Csikszentmihalyi, 1996, p. 28).

Negotiating criteria between student and teacher means that Csikszentmihalyi's notions of field and domain are allied with what Lave and Wenger (1991) refer to as a *community of practice*. In this case, the community of practice will more properly be *communities*, as a number of different communities will overlap and elide.

What all this means in practical terms is that the application of assessment needs to shift from one in which the primary purpose is certification through summative assessment, and toward one in which what really matters is developing learning and achievement through formative assessment. In many ways, this is not a major shift in *direction* for most music educators, but it does involve a repositioning of mindset. This is because for many years summative assessment, or at best the formative use of summative assessment, has been the dominant modality of assessment discourse. In order to truly develop music education for all pupils, then formative assessment, assessment *for* learning, needs to be significantly privileged in this regard. So, how can this be achieved?

DEMOCRATIZING MUSIC EDUCATION

To begin with, we need to question the very role of what music education is, and what it entails. For many years in the United Kingdom, and many other jurisdictions as well, music education has been both conceptualized, and legislated for, as consisting of three more or less equal components: listening, performing, and composing. This triumvirate is somewhat different from those parts of the world where music education occupies a position solely centered on performance. Although we know that performing is a creative act, there are differing levels of creativity employed. By thinking about what music is (or could be) we start to wrestle power away from a hegemonic perspective that situates performance at the educational apex. This attitude has persisted for a surprisingly long time in some quarters, and composing can still be looked on with some doubt and suspicion; but in these technologically plugged-in, switched-on times, it is clearly untenable. The proliferation of free or low-cost music software means that anyone with a phone, iPad, tablet PC, or laptop has access to sophisticated music production apps that would have been unimaginable only a few years ago. This means that students can create, edit, and store their own music with ease; not only that, but they can do so in styles that may not even have a name-label yet. Creation of new songs does not necessarily require technique on an instrument; there are many computer programs and apps that involve variations on the drag-and-drop principle so that students can create and be original.

This democratization of the production of music places a greater responsibility on the shoulders of music educators. It is not sufficient in the twenty-first century simply to shrug, walk away, and retreat into conducting the school wind band playing great movie themes. As Woodford observes:

> [music teachers] are charged with helping children to develop, warrant, and defend their own beliefs and ideas—their own values and choices—while simultaneously opening themselves up to the world and possible criticism. (Woodford, 2005, p. 31)

The music produced by young people for themselves should be worthy of as much attention in the music room as, say, the paintings and sculptures produced in the school art room warrant. We do not, in most high schools, see school artwork consisting solely of novice reproductions of Rembrandt and Rubens; instead we see exciting, relevant, sometimes "edgy" pictures that have meaning for the young people who produced them. Assessment that follows the democratization of music for social justice purposes therefore needs to be grounded in the requirements of music production and creation, as well as in performing.

Formative Assessment
for Social Justice

So let us take a closer look, then, at what implementing formative assessment for social justice purposes in music might entail. We have already seen that the democratization of music education content matter questions a performance tradition that overly privileges Western art music. What is the role of formative assessment in developing more socially just ways of working?

In order to do this, we really need to come to grips with formative assessment—and what it is not. Much has been written concerning formative assessment, and, as we saw earlier, a lot of it misses the point. Central to the notion of good formative assessment is that quality is developed by personal human interaction between teacher and student. At the heart of this is the notion of *feedback*, or, as some would put it, *feedforward*. This takes place in the moment, as music making is proceeding, and while the process is still unfolding. Doing this renders the *process* of musicking significant, as opposed to the *product*. In many cases of summatively assessed music creation, it is the final product that is marked and graded. The processes that were gone through in order to arrive at the product can be either invisible, or ignored by the assessment regime. In the case of some examinations, what this means is that it is only the finished work resulting from the process, whether this be composing or performing, that gets any credit. When such assessment is the result of external assessment, teachers would argue that there is little they can do about it, and they may be right. But this does not mean that in preparation for such final high-stakes examination an identical assessment modality needs to be followed. This is an especially worthwhile consideration, as there are direct causal and correlational linkages between an improvement in process leading to a concomitantly improved product. The role of formative assessment, therefore, in addressing the processes of the activities of learning, will have direct consequences for the non-process-based summative assessment that ensues.

Feedforward, then, involves discussion of improvement. We have already seen how the teacher does not need to be an expert in all styles of music in order to be able to make helpful interventional judgments in this regard. We have also seen how the students themselves can be involved in the creation of assessment criteria that help them understand what they need to do in order to get better. The implications of this are that one of the most powerful tools of assessment, and one that foregrounds social justice, is the notion of *ipsative* assessment. Ipsative (from the Latin *ipse*: "of the self") assessment is where students are concerned with their own development and progress against their own previous performance (either in the musical or non-musical sense). Students themselves set their own baselines against which improvements are made and judged. We see this very commonly in sports, where rather than trying to beat standardized targets, athletes aim for their own "personal best." The same is true in music; examples include the teenage guitarist practicing speeding up licks in the privacy of her own bedroom, the drummer trying to do faster rolls, the cornet player trying to play very fast passages, the pianist practicing their scales at increasing speeds, the vocalist holding notes longer, and so on. Ipsative assessment can also be used for composing and music creation. This can include understanding how to extend a verse and chorus with the introduction of a middle eight, the use of effective key-shifts, ways in which the *affekt* of music can be developed, and many more. For composers using technology, it can include not only increasing complexity, but also more nuanced control of sound sources.

All of these examples show how involving students in the development of their own musical learning, and the importance of attention to process, can result in improved personal performance. It should also be clear from these discussions that doing this does not, and should not, represent a diminution of standards in any way; this is not "dumbing down" for the sake of it. What it is instead is using formative assessment to develop students' personal interests in their own music making, and by doing so, taking them to the next level incrementally, so that their own music making, judged by their own standards, improves, develops, and progresses.

RECASTING MUSIC EDUCATION ASSESSMENT IN LINE WITH PRINCIPLES OF SOCIAL JUSTICE

The reconceptualization of assessment discussed in this chapter requires a shift in perspective as to what assessment in music education is, and how it is undertaken. As Freire observed, "education is a political act" (Freire, 1985, p. 188) and within education as a whole, assessment too has a political dimension, as Broadfoot points out:

> Assessment procedures are the vehicle whereby the dominant rationality of the corporate capitalist societies typical of the contemporary Western world is translated into the structures and processes of schooling. (Broadfoot, 1999, p. 64)

While this may seem an extreme stance, nonetheless the disenfranchising of vast swaths of world music, pop, rock, and jazz happens on a daily basis in music classrooms, studios, and rehearsal halls all over the Western world. Add to this the potent mix of curricular neglect and public examination valorization procedures, and it is becomes clear that the dominant hegemony is busily reproducing itself in many music education contexts today. But just because something is so, does not mean that the *status quo* is right. There are ways in which music education can be reconceived from the perspectives of social justice.

One way in which teachers can take the first tentative steps in this regard is by a consideration of the question of who it is that any assessment is intended for. As we have seen, summative assessment's role is to mark, grade, or level any piece of work. We have also seen that this can play a role in developing student work if it is used in a formative fashion; however, all too often this is not the case. Summative assessment is also used for accountability purposes, of both teacher and students, as well as of the institution in which it takes place. What this means is that there are potentially multiple audiences for the same item of assessment data. For the music teacher, addressing the question of whom the assessment data is for can be reduced to three essential items:

- the student;
- the teacher;
- the system.

The students are, or should be, the most important of these, as it is their learning, their music making, and, ultimately, their grades, that should be the focus of attention. The teacher will want access to assessment data, formative and summative, in order to monitor student performance and progression, and to determine how to tailor the work plan for the students to help them progress to their maximum potential. This is an important aspect of formative assessment. It should not be the case that teaching and learning proceed solely along linear and pre-established non-deviational pathways, although the teacher will have some idea of the route, inevitably. Instead, a good teacher will use the results of formative assessments to plan for subsequent pedagogic activity, personalizing materials so as to take account of what they know that the student needs to do next, and differentiating tasks for whole classes so that appropriate challenge is available to all students in a group.

It can sometimes be the case that the systemic requirements of assessment can seem to outweigh the other audience groups, especially when dealing with school, regional, and national requirements for assessment data for accountability purposes. At the systemic level, the performance of an individual student matters not a jot; it will be subsumed within a range of statistics. For the teacher, though, the student will not just be a number, they will have a name. The teacher will know about their likes, dislikes, preferences, and foibles. This relationship matters to the success of the teaching and learning encounter, and this can be especially true in music education, where the importance of the personal should not be downplayed.

CONCLUSION

We have seen in this chapter that formative assessment in music education can play a powerful role in resisting hegemony. Formative assessment undertaken in the ways suggested becomes assessment for social justice, as it involves learners in becoming agentive in the processes of their own learning, and although interventionist to some extent, it is personalized purposefully so that the learning journey is negotiated, not imposed. It is underused in some music education contexts, and yet implementing it does not, in many cases, require a huge shift on the part of the teacher. We have also invited music educators to reflect on their own professional practice, in terms of what is taught and learned and, by so doing, to think about ways in which the contents of music education curricula publicly display the values that lay behind their inclusion. We have also reflected on the democratization of the assessment processes, and of ways in which this can be addressed.

Hopefully a consideration of the issues raised here, and throughout this Handbook, will cause music educators to ask difficult questions of their own customs and practices, and will enable subsequent generations of teachers and learners to benefit.

REFERENCES

Broadfoot, P. (1999). Assessment and the emergence of modern society. In B. Moon & P. Murphy (Eds.), *Curriculum in context* (pp. 63–91). London: Paul Chapman/Open University.

Csikszentmihalyi, M. (1996). *Creativity: Flow and the psychology of discovery and invention.* New York: HarperCollins.

Curwen, A. J. (1886). *The teacher's guide to Mrs. Curwen's pianoforte method (the child pianist). Being a practical course in the elements of music.* London: Curwen's Edition.

Fautley, M. (2010). *Assessment in music education.* Oxford: Oxford University Press.

Freire, P. (1985). *The politics of education: Culture, power, and liberation.* Hadley, MA: Bergin & Garvey.

Hallam, S., Creech, A., Sandford, C., Rinta, T., & Shave, K. (2008). *Survey of Musical Futures for the Paul Hamlyn Foundation.* London: Institute of Education.

Harlen, W. (2005). Teachers' summative practices and assessment for learning: Tensions and synergies. *The Curriculum Journal, 16*(2), 207–223.

Hickman, R. (2007). (In defence of) whippet-fancying and other vices: Re-evaluating assessment in art and design. In T. Rayment (Ed.), *The problem of assessment in art and design* (pp. 77–87). Bristol, UK: Intellect Books.

Kratus, J. (2007). Music education at the tipping point. *Music Educators Journal, 94*(2), 42–48.

Lave, J., & Wenger, E. (1991). *Situated learning: Legitimate peripheral participation.* Cambridge: Cambridge University Press.

Mills, J. (1991). *Music in the primary school.* Cambridge: Cambridge University Press.

Price, D. (2006). *Redefining music training: Shaping music education, an emerging vision.* Pamphlet 5, Musical Futures Project. London: The Paul Hamlyn Foundation.

Scruton, R. (1996, October 24). Review of Simon Frith: Performing rites: On the value of popular music. *The Times* (London).

Shepherd, J., Virden, P., Vulliamy, G., & Wishart, T. (1977). *Whose music? A sociology of musical languages.* London: Transaction Books.

Spruce, G. (2001). Music assessment and the hegemony of musical heritage. In C. Philpott & C. Plummeridge (Eds.), *Issues in music teaching* (pp. 118–130). London: RoutledgeFalmer.

Spruce, G. (2007). Culture, society and musical learning. In C. Philpott & G. Spruce (Eds.), *Learning to teach music in the secondary school: A companion to school experience* (2nd ed., pp. 16–27). London: RoutledgeFalmer.

Stewart, W. (2012). Think you've implemented Assessment for Learning? *Times Educational Supplement.* Retrieved from http://www.tes.co.uk/article.aspx?storycode= 6261847.

Wiliam, D. (2004). *Keeping learning on track: Integrating assessment with instruction.* Paper presented as the invited address to the 30th annual conference of the International Association for Educational Assessment (IAEA), Philadelphia.

Woodford, P. (2005). *Democracy and music education: Liberalism, ethics, and the politics of practice.* Bloomington: Indiana University Press.

CHAPTER 33

CRITICAL REFLECTION FOR SOCIAL JUSTICE AND INCLUSION IN MUSIC EDUCATION

CAROLYN COOKE

INTRODUCTION

CRITICAL reflection is often cited as central to addressing issues of social justice (Benedict & Schmidt, 2007; Freire, 1970; Ingram & Walters, 2007; Kemmis et al., 1983; Wright, 2013). However, very little is written about the relationship between critical reflection in music education, social justice, and inclusion, in terms of how teachers can facilitate critical reflection for the purposes of social justice and inclusion, as well as how teachers and students might view critical reflection as central and inseparable to their identities as musicians. To understand how critical reflection can be used as a pedagogical tool for social justice and inclusion requires us to explore in more detail how critical reflection might sound or look like within a music education context.

This chapter will explore

- the role of critical reflection in promoting social justice and inclusion;
- the nature of critical reflection within music education;
- the conditions necessary for facilitating critical reflection within the music classroom; and
- music pedagogies that support critical reflection for social justice and inclusion.

Much has been written to define critical reflection and its potential in relation to education (Finlay, 2008; McGregor & Cartwright, 2011). For the purposes of this chapter, critical reflection will be defined as a process by which students and teachers engage in "the active, persistent and careful consideration of any belief or supposed form of knowledge in the light of the grounds that support it" (Dewey, 1933, p. 118).

THE ROLE OF CRITICAL REFLECTION IN PROMOTING SOCIAL JUSTICE AND INCLUSION

A brief analysis of how different authors perceive the role of critical reflection in relation to social justice highlights some key themes that have implications for teachers and students.

First, many see a strong correlation between critical reflection and discussions of questioning, challenging and understanding the assumptions, beliefs, and values that underpin education (Cerecer et al., 2010; Ingram & Walters, 2007; Wright, 2013). As discussed by Ingram and Walters, teachers and students are products of cultural conditioning, and schools cannot in themselves be viewed as neutral (Ingram & Walters, 2007). It is this lack of neutrality that Ingram and Walters argue can be brought to the surface and addressed through critical reflection, as it can be used to break down seemingly certain views and beliefs, thereby opening up students and teachers to more socially just alternatives. At a practical level, they suggest that this "requires habits of mind of openness, skepticism, and suspended judgment . . . and . . . begins with examining one's own values, beliefs, and dispositions" (Ingram & Walters, 2007, p. 8).

Second, some authors highlight how critical reflection can be used to promote a vision of a better or different future and an individual's ability to act on this. Wright, in quoting Friere's concept of a liberatory education, argues that this happens through students critically reflecting on the circumstances in which they live, critiquing the "givens" in their world and allowing them to see lives in a sequential fashion as having a past, present, and possibly different future (Wright, 2013). Woodford argues that criticality plays a similar role in "empowering teachers and students to reclaim ownership over the design and direction of their musical lives" (Woodford, 2012, p. 98). In the eyes of both of these authors, critical reflection is seen as a tool to help students see or imagine an alternative way of being.

Third, social justice can be perceived in the context of giving voice to, and minimizing injustice to minority groups (e.g., based on race or class). However, conceptualizing social justice only in relation to what may incorrectly be perceived to be homogenous groups has the potential risk of excluding individual voices and thus creating different inequalities and injustices (Jorgensen, 2007). Jorgensen argues that it is through critical reflection, at an individual as well as a group level, that all students (and teachers) are given a voice.

Finally, a number of authors discuss the significance of critical reflection as an essential tool for teachers to increase their awareness and to address issues of inequality and injustice in their own practice and classrooms. Howard argues that it is through critical reflection that teachers can "acknowledge how one's own worldview can shape students' conceptions of self." He goes on to quote Palmer, who states, "We teach who we are" (Howard, 2003, p. 198).

Whereas these four themes—questioning underpinning beliefs and assumptions; promoting alternative futures; giving all individuals a voice; increasing teachers' awareness of their role in creating and sustaining inequalities and injustices—establish a role for critical reflection in addressing issues of social justice, they arguably do little to enlighten us as to exactly what these themes might mean within a music education context. Fundamentally, they tell us little about how critical reflection might be experienced within the music classroom.

Reflection and Musical Learning

In order to explore the potential of critical reflection for social justice in a music education context, it is worth considering for a moment whether it is appropriate to be discussing the notion of critical reflection in isolation at all. Many authors have argued that experiences or events and critical reflection are inseparable (Adams, 2010; Cerecer et al., 2010; Ingram & Walters, 2007; Kemmis et al., 1983). Cerecer et al. argue that to bring about change "social justice must connect critical thinking with action" (Cerecer et al., 2010, p. 150). This triangulation of social justice, action, and critical thinking suggests a role for critical reflection both "in action" and "on action," but not in isolation. This inseparable link between critical reflection and action can be observed in reflective learning models such as those of Atkins and Murphy (1993), Gibbs (1988), and Kolb (1984). These models demonstrate how reflection serves as a catalyst for changes to understanding, knowledge, or practice. It is this change that then informs subsequent cycles of learning. All of the above-mentioned models include experience as a core feature of the reflective cycle, thereby cementing the relationship between reflection and experience. Joplin argues that "experience alone is insufficient . . . it is the reflection process which turns experience into experiential education" (Joplin cited in Adams, 2010, p. 15).

Therefore to discuss the use of critical reflection in music education requires us to discuss the practices and experiences of students. This link between experience and reflection has significant implications for a subject like music, where high value is placed on students learning from engaging in experiences as musicians (i.e., as performers, composers, and listeners). In this context, it is arguable that it will be the choice and structuring of musical experiences that will enable critical reflection to address social justice and inclusion issues. It suggests the importance of experiences that allow (or even require) "reflection-in-action" as well as "reflection-on-action" (Dewey, 1933), as it is in this way that critical reflection can be seen as integral to the learning process. At a practical level, it is easy to conjure up examples of "reflection-in-action" within musical experiences: for example, a student may realize the part she is playing is unbalanced with the rest of the group and then adjusts her dynamics accordingly, or she may remember how another member of the group articulated a particular musical motif and she then reflects this in her playing.

The idea of critical reflection as integral to experiential learning also supports the idea that reflection is not limited to dialogue, discussion, or writing, but can be applied to the act of making music itself. This viewpoint expresses a belief that all students will be creating a personal, internal dialogue about the musical learning they are engaged in at the very point at which it is happening. This challenges common practices around reflection as an activity that is often teacher-led and teacher-structured, used as a conclusion to a project or unit of work or used as part of summative assessment. If reflection on musical learning is integral to the process of learning (i.e., happens in tandem with experience, rather than as a separate activity) and is potentially musical, personal, and internal rather than teacher-led, then the possibility for addressing social justice and inclusion through critical reflection becomes a possibility.

This link between critical reflection and musical experiences in the classroom suggest the nature of critical reflection will be

- heavily influenced by the context and nature of the learning experience—that is, critical reflection for social justice and inclusion in music will be different from other subjects;
- an integral part of the musical learning experience;
- something that can be formal (organized and led by teachers or students) or it can be personal or informal (internal dialogue and understanding at any time and in any place where they have a musical experience).

This suggests that for musical learning to become a vehicle for addressing issues of social justice and inclusion, we need to consider carefully the students' experiences and how reflective activities are discussed and facilitated within the classroom.

CRITICAL REFLECTION FOR SOCIAL JUSTICE IN A MUSIC CONTEXT

To begin to develop a practical understanding of what critical reflection for social justice in music education may look or sound like, we can usefully utilize Ingram and Walter's *Social Justice Critical Reflection* model (Ingram & Walters, 2007). Originally developed in relation to the use of literature as a way of infusing social justice issues into education, it argues that the study of literature

- allows the reader to "obtain . . . information" and enables "an aesthetic stance which attains to dialogic thinking";

- "engages the imagination and introduces the reader to people who are both like and different from themselves in time, location, and socio-political contexts";
- offers "lenses for viewing the . . . effects of poverty and culturally constructed discrimination";
- "allows readers to experience the anguish, feelings, hopes, and emotions of other people";
- "can stretch the mind to derive awareness that dominant forces have shaped us." (pp. 5–6)

There are clearly strong resonances here with music as for the most part substituting the word "music" for "literature" and "musician" for "reader" provides an equally compelling argument for drawing on this model within a music education context and the potential impact that music education might have on promoting social justice. These summary bullet points alone point the way towards a socially just and inclusive music pedagogy, but the model itself highlights the particular role of critical reflection in achieving this. The model is based on five interrelated schemata, as shown in Figure 33.1.

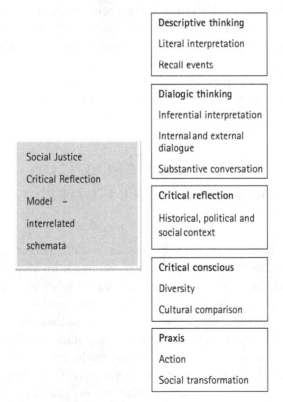

FIGURE 33.1 The interrelated schemata of the Social Justice Critical Reflection Model (Ingram and Walter).

Table 33.1 Ingram and Walter's Critical Reflection Schemata (2007)	
Theme	Issues
Historical context	Enduring problems
Political context	Common patterns
	Power
	Privilege
	Policy
Social context	Norms
	Culture
	Ethos

It is through these five interrelated schemata that Ingram and Walters argue for a broader pedagogy that addresses social justice issues through descriptive thinking, dialogic thinking, critical reflection, critical consciousness, and praxis. They argue that it is through this broader pedagogy that learners can deconstruct and reformulate schema, leading to transformative learning.

Ingram and Walters see critical reflection for social justice as relating to three specific themes: the historical context, political context, and social context (Ingram & Walters, 2007). For each of these three themes, they outline particular issues to consider, as shown in Table 33.1.

Although these three themes were originally conceptualized in relation to literature, again we see strong parallels with music that can begin to shape our thoughts as to what critical reflection in music would sound or look like.

CRITICAL REFLECTION
ON HISTORICAL CONTEXTS

Music is replete with examples of how the historical context of pieces has shaped them and their reception, from *Quatour pour la fin du temps* by Messiaen to Paul Simon and Ladysmith Black Mambazo. In these examples it is relatively easy to consider how descriptive thinking, led by the teacher, could shed light on the implications of the historical context on issues of social justice. However, this descriptive engagement alone is not maximizing the opportunities for transforming student and teacher understanding. Ingram and Walters argue that reflecting on the historical context should involve surfacing "enduring problems" and "common patterns" (Ingram & Walters, 2007). It could be argued that within a music education context this might involve developing students' awareness of

Table 33.2 Opportunities for Critical Reflection on Historical Contexts

Historical context	Developed through:
Awareness of development and impact of musical canon	Experience of a wide range of musical repertoire from different genres, traditions and styles including music which is considered 'inside' and 'outside' the canon (e.g. underground music, protest music, prohibited music, crossover music)
Perception of 'high' and 'low' art	Challenging student, teacher or others views about the value of different types of music. Experiencing music that challenges their own perceptions of what is musically valued.
The impact of 'music as product' on different musics	Exploring music that challenges 'product' norms (e.g. aural tradition, music that is difficult to notate or capture, music that is social context dependent and cannot be separated out to 'sell' as a CD)
Impact of technological developments	Developing students understanding of the technologies available at the time and their impact on the music (e.g. limitations of recordings at the start of the 19th Century, increasing issues of authenticity, performing rights and authorisation to market musics, the democratic but problematic effect of the internet on live and recorded music).

- the musical canon and how through historical, political, and social means it has been created;
- the dominant perception of low and high art and its impact on people's beliefs and assumptions about the creation and performance of different musics;
- the distribution and consumption of music as a "product," and the impact this has on the ability of particular composers, performers, or musical traditions to be "heard";
- the effect of technological developments, particularly the Internet, for gaining access to music and experiences from around the world.

Supporting the development of this level of awareness in students will quite obviously span many different musical experiences, but the important aspect to note is that in all of these instances, students are able to employ critical reflection-in-action to develop their awareness. Put another way, awareness of social justice issues through critical reflection on historical contexts can and should be achieved through engaging in musical experiences. In this way, the critical reflection allows them to explore and address these issues in their practice as musicians, as demonstrated in Table 33.2.

CRITICAL REFLECTION ON POLITICAL CONTEXTS

Much of the discussion around critical reflection on historical contexts can be equally applied to the political context of music. However, Ingram and Walters indicate three specific issues within this theme: policy, power, and privilege (Ingram & Walters, 2007). Of course, politics can be considered at many different levels: national, regional, school, classroom, or even small group. Developing an awareness of social justice issues through reflection on the political context can relate to all these layers of influence. However, within the context of the classroom there are some specific implications of moving away from the potentially oppressive politics of power, privilege, and policy and toward developing a socially just and inclusive classroom. Fundamental to this is breaking down the model of "teacher as expert" to develop a more democratic view of musical learning that draws on peers and others. This might include

- embedding students' critical, reflective voices in shaping and developing the curriculum and their experience of it;
- supporting students in reflecting critically on their contributions to making musical decisions and solving musical problems;
- through critical reflection, providing opportunities to challenge views that promote hierarchies within the classroom (e.g., redressing the balance of representation between students who have instrumental lessons beyond the class and those who don't);
- challenging negative or exclusive notions of musicianship (e.g., being a musician involves reading and using Western art notation, or musical participation relies on particular kinds of instrumental or vocal technique).

Again, it is possible to consider how this should be achieved through musical experience, as outlined in Table 33.3.

CRITICAL REFLECTION ON SOCIAL CONTEXTS

Third, Ingram and Walters define critical reflection on social context in relation to three issues: norms, culture, and ethos (Ingram & Walters, 2007). It can be argued that this theme, more than historical and political contexts, provides a wealth of opportunity for music educators to address issues of social justice and inclusion due to the fundamentally social nature of musical learning. Social interaction and the influence of society

Table 33.3 Opportunities For Critical Reflection on Political Contexts

Political contexts	Developed through:
Students critical reflections on the curriculum and their own learning experiences	...providing musical experiences which can be developed in a number of different directions depending on the student's interests and critical reflection on the musical task (e.g. allowing them to challenge how the task has been presented or directions for completion).
	...developing opportunity for students to critically reflect on whether their musical experiences have led to meaningful musical learning, and allowing them to suggest alternatives (e.g setting out own process or targets, or choosing alternative genres or styles that can be used to meet outcomes).
	... providing multiple occasions for all individuals to express their own opinions about school music, the curriculum and what they feel they want to develop (e.g. what do they feel they would gain most from experiencing? How do they feel about the relevance of school music to what they experience as a musician beyond the classroom?)
Students critically reflecting on their contributions to and the process of making musical decisions and problems solving	... creating opportunities to consider what it means to be democratic in the decision making process in a musical context (e.g. promoting student led, rather than teacher led decision making and encouraging those who may be less able to voice their opinions gain the confidence to do so)
	... creating experiences that support students in understanding alternative viewpoints or distinct musical problems
Challenging negative or exclusive notions of musicianship	... facilitating musical experiences that allow *all* students to engage musically and achieve and receive recognition for this.
	... supporting students to acknowledge that we all hold perceptions of what it means to be musical, and that there are alternative views.
Challenging classroom hierarchies and creating a democratic view of musical learning	... acknowledging the limits of the teacher expertise and encourage them to find alternative sources of support
	... demonstrating that you as the teacher are a learner of music, modelling learning processes and participating as co-learners alongside the students.
	... encouraging students to use each other as teachers and facilitators.

plays out in every musical learning context and in every musical interaction that is made. As recognized by Joplin, this social element is central to the idea of experiential education, with a pedagogy for social justice "encouraging students to visit each others'... turfs" (Adams, 2010, p.61). This social awareness and ability to reflect critically on its implications can in many ways be seen to underpin a student's (and teacher's) ability to engage in the type of transformative critical reflection and subsequent learning that this chapter is promoting.

However, there is a fundamental difference with the notion of "visiting others' .turfs" within a music education context. First, as recognized by ethnomusicologists and anthropologists, being able to actually "live" another person's music is practically impossible. Second, there are inherent dangers of visitors acting as colonizers, transferring their own musical practices, values, and ideals onto those of others (quite possibly unconsciously). Finally, it is arguable that classroom music can never achieve authentic replications or "visits" of social musical practices where the system is tied to set lessons, curricula, numbers of students in a class, limited funds or opportunities for bringing in expertise, and standardized assessment models. This is not to completely dismiss Joplin's idea within a music context, but it is important that we focus on the idea of "visiting," possibly with the addition of the term "experiencing," while recognizing its limitations. If students, over the course of the curriculum, are able to visit and experience different musical practices that highlight cultural norms and ethos, and are able to reflect critically on the implications of these in relation to their own musical understanding and development, then this is the juncture at which critical reflection can be transformative in relation to social justice.

In practice this will be achieved through

- encouraging students to critically reflect on the culture, social norms, and ethos surrounding musical practices both within their own experiences and beyond them (i.e., analyzing and understanding why there are differences and similarities between their experiences of musical practices—for example, the use of notation, type of rehearsal practices, or how the music is performed);
- developing students' (and teachers') critical awareness of how school culture, norms, and ethos impact the way in which the music curriculum is experienced;
- surfacing individuals' beliefs and assumptions about music in society and providing the opportunity to challenge these.

The realization of this practice is more difficult to exemplify, as it will be dependent on individual interactions (student/student and teacher/student), class dynamics and relationships, the nature of the school and curriculum, and the society within which the school and the students are positioned. However, as recognized by Kemmis in his work on the socially critical school, "education must engage social issues and give students the experience in working on them" (Kemmis et al., 1983, p. 18). This active participation with society (not just within the classroom, but also the local community) is central to Kemmis's argument for a curriculum that is not separated from society, or merely a reflection of it, but a critical and active part of it. This has implications for using critical reflection as part of a broader socially just and inclusive music pedagogy, as will be discussed later.

Student and Teacher as Historically, Politically, and Socially Aware Beings

We have, in the previous three sections, discussed students as if these issues will be new to them, as if they will be facing these challenges for the first time. Of course we know that this is far from the reality. Many students in a music classroom, even at a relatively early age, will have become acculturated into particularly ways of thinking about, engaging with, and perceiving music historically, politically, and socially. Equally, the discussion thus far has assumed a position that suggests all teachers are explicitly aware of these social justice issues—open, willing, and active participants in challenging and transforming their own personal views (as well as the views of others) through critical reflection. Again, it is clear that this is not always the case. Therefore there is a need to develop a pedagogical approach that challenges and motivates all participants (students and teachers) to engage in critical reflection for the purpose of social justice and inclusion.

Pedagogy for a Critically Reflective Music Classroom

Scheffler defines human potential as relating to three notions (Jorgensen, 2007):

1. capacity or physical possibility of . . .
2. predictive notion of potential to do. . . .
3. individual decision to do. . . .

These notions can be usefully summarized as *imagining, predicting,* and *doing* beyond one's own existing experience or perceived opportunities. These three notions may serve useful in developing a critically reflective music pedagogy that addresses inclusion and social justice. It is through experiencing music that teachers and students are challenged to reconceptualize what is possible—developing a critical consciousness of the impact of social, historical, and political influences, being able to imagine alternative ways of engaging or experiencing music and learning, and enabling each other (both as teachers and peers) to follow an individual musical journey—that social justice issues and inclusion can become meaningfully interwoven within music pedagogy.

This requires of teachers and students a potential change in outlook about the nature of music education.

THE TEACHER'S ROLE

Facilitating critical reflection in the music classroom can be seen to involve teachers becoming increasingly aware of their own positions within the classroom, school, and society, and how their beliefs and values impact the students' understanding of social justice within a music context. There are some particular opportunities that teachers can make and take to establish a climate of critical reflection. These might include

- modeling their own learning and acknowledging the limits of their own knowledge and understanding;
- explicitly acknowledging their own assumptions and beliefs and the impact they have on their view of music and musical learning;
- demonstrating the ability to understand something in a new light or experience something in a new way through musical interactions with students;
- questioning the existence of and arguing the case for a more democratic and less hierarchical view of music and musical learning;
- instilling the ideals of equality of rights and access within the music classroom in relation to musical excellence, musical ideas, and the decision-making processes;
- developing a curriculum that allows students to experience musical practices that will challenge and extend their views of music and musical learning;
- explicitly discussing and practically demonstrating the impact of historical, political, and social influences on music.

THE STUDENT'S PERSPECTIVE

Creating an environment where students have the confidence and resources to engage in critical reflection and the ultimate transformation of their ideas might include

- having the confidence to ask questions, suggest alternative viewpoints, and consider *why* music and music practices are approached in certain ways;
- acknowledging that everyone in the class has a valid musical contribution to make and reflecting this through their approach to participating in musical decision making;
- seeking to understand others' beliefs and values about music or musical practices in order to learn from them;

- recognizing the potential of a different approach, and knowing how to pursue it;
- approaching all musical experiences and discussions as opportunities to challenge and change their understanding.

It is through developing and facilitating these behaviors that we can develop students' notions of their potential as musicians.

CONCLUSION

This chapter has argued for developing music pedagogy that forefronts critical reflection as a way of furthering students' (and teachers') awareness of inclusion and social justice within a music context. It has highlighted that to develop a critically reflective environment within the music classroom requires teachers and students to engage with historical, social, and political ideas that surround music and music learning. It has also argued that, in practice, critical reflection on issues of inclusion and social justice requires an integrated approach, in which critical reflection is interwoven into a pedagogy that promotes students thinking and behaving as musicians. It is through these experiences, the development of students' ability to critically reflect on them, and the development of an environment in which critical reflection is valued and celebrated that issues of social justice can be addressed.

REFERENCES

Adams, M. (2010). Roots of social justice pedagogies in social movements. In T. Chapman & N. Hobbel (Eds.), *Social justice pedagogy across the curriculum: The practice of freedom* (pp. 59–85). New York: Routledge.

Atkins, S., and Murphy, K. (1993). Reflection: A review of the literature. *Journal of Advanced Nursing, 18*, 1188–1192.

Benedict, C., & Schmidt, P.K. (2007). From whence justice? Interrogating the improbable in music education. *Action, Criticism and Theory for Music Education, 6*(4), 21–42.

Cerecer, P. D. Q., Gutierrez, L., & Rios, F. (2010).Critical multiculturalism: Transformative educational principles and practices. In T. Chapman & N. Hobbel (Eds.), *Social justice pedagogy across the curriculum: The practice of freedom* (pp. 144–163). New York: Routledge.

Dewey, J. (1933). *How we think*. Madison: University of Wisconsin Press.

Finlay, L. (2008). *Reflecting on "Reflective practice."* UK: Open University. Retrieved from http://www.open.ac.uk/opencetl/resources/pbpl-resources/finlay-l-2008-reflecting-reflecti ve-practice-pbpl-paper-52.

Friere, P. (1970). *Pedagogy of the oppressed*. New York: The Seabury Press.

Gibbs, G. (1988). *Learning by doing: A guide to teaching and learning methods*. Oxford: Oxford Polytechnic Further Education Unit.

Howard, T. C. (2003). Culturally relevant pedagogy: Ingredients for critical teacher reflection. *Theory into practice, 42*(3), 195–202.

Ingram, I. L., & Walters, T. S. (2007). A critical reflection model to teach diversity and social justice. *Journal of Praxis in Multicultural Education*, 2(1). Retrieved from http://digitalscholarship.unlv.edu/cgi/viewcontent.cgi?article=1021&context=jpme.

Jorgensen, E. (2007). Concerning justice and music education. *Music Education Research*, 9(2), 169–189.

Kemmis, S., Cole, P., & Suggett, D. (1983). *Orientations to curriculum and transition: Towards the socially-critical school*. Melbourne: Victorian Institute of Secondary Education.

Kolb, D. A. (1984). *Experiential learning: Experience as the source of learning and development*. Englewood Cliffs, NJ: Prentice Hall.

McGregor, D., & Cartwright, L. (2011). *Developing reflective practice: A guide for beginning teachers*. Berkshire, UK: Open University Press.

Woodford, P. (2012). Music education and social justice: Towards a radical political history and vision. In C. Philpott & G. Spruce (Eds.), *Debates in music teaching* (pp. 85–101). Abingdon, UK: Routledge.

Wright, R. (2013). Thinking globally, acting locally: Informal learning and social justice in Music Education. *Canadian Music Educator*, 54(3), 33–36.

CHAPTER 34

CAN MUSIC TEACHING BE A POWERFUL TOOL FOR SOCIAL JUSTICE?

JOHN SLOBODA

INTRODUCTION

I was honored to be invited to contribute some reflections to this volume. Unlike the vast majority of contributors to this volume I am not a professional music educator. This means that my observations are very much those of an outsider, and I offer them with apologies for inevitable oversimplifications based on ignorance both of practice and of the enormous literature that informs this volume. My agreement to offer a chapter stems from two somewhat independent areas of activity that I have engaged in. For 40 years I have worked as an empirical psychology researcher, both alone and in productive collaborations, attempting to uncover and explain key facts about music, its effects, and its development as a skill over the lifespan. For the last 15 years, I have also increasingly devoted my attention to a different issue, contributing with others to understanding the extent of, and advocating for better and deeper knowledge of the civilian casualties of conflict.

MUSIC FIRST OR SOCIAL JUSTICE FIRST?

Social justice has not been an explicit focus of my work in music. Indeed, a word search on my previous publications would likely yield no instance of the term "social justice." However, I have been very interested in the conditions under which musical expertise develops, and—as a corollary—the conditions under which such development appears to be thwarted. The empirical investigations I have contributed to have supported the assertion that many more people in post-industrial Western society have the capacity to develop as musicians than are actually enabled to do so by the structures and institutions of that society (Sloboda, 2001, 2005a; Sloboda, Davidson, & Howe, 1994). These institutions (and associated cultures and discourses) generate strong beliefs (including self-beliefs) that label individuals as "non-musical" (Wise & Sloboda, 2008). I have also had a strong interest in how people use and value music in their everyday lives—in ways that can be quite dissimilar to those promoted by musical elites, yet richly and adaptively suited to their life situation and needs (Sloboda, 2005b; Sloboda, O'Neill & Ivaldi, 2001). Some of these findings may indeed be supportive of, and usable by, those working for social justice within music education. But it would be a mistake to characterize my music psychology research career as motivated by social justice concerns, or even by giving such concerns a central place within the research. Rather, such concerns grew gradually as I discovered more about the nature and causes of high levels of musical skill within individuals.

Social justice has, by contrast, been explicitly at the center of my work on conflict, which was motivated in great part by the huge disparity between how much we in the West know (and care) about British and American soldiers killed in modern conflicts such as Afghanistan and Iraq, and the little we know (and care) about the civilian deaths caused in these conflicts. Each British soldier killed is given a hero's commemoration, and his or her name is inscribed for posterity on the Armed Forces Memorial at the National Arboretum. In contrast, for example, among the 142,000 civilian victims of the Iraq War who were documented on the www.iraqbodycount.org website by the beginning of August 2014, only 7.5% (10,700) were yet identified by name. The organizations that I work for and with (see www.everycasualty.org) are committed to eliminating this gross disparity worldwide, by campaigning for and assisting others to work toward the prompt, accurate, and public acknowledgment of every victim of armed violence worldwide, regardless of location, age, gender, nationality, religion, or status.

I could perhaps summarize the contrast between my two areas of work bluntly. I work on music because music fascinates me and it is a pleasure to go more deeply into it. It is an added bonus if the work sometimes has social justice implications, but that is not why I study music. In contrast, I abhor war and would never choose to spend time and effort studying it unless I believed that by doing so I could be contributing directly to social justice.

I make these opening remarks precisely because I believe that the way musicians and music educators can approach issues of social justice in music education will depend on whether they come to the work primarily from a music perspective, or primarily from a justice perspective. In the former case, social justice considerations may be one of several ways in which a musician/music educator might enhance and enrich his or her music practice. In the latter case, music may be one of several means that a social justice activist will participate in as a tool for his or her justice goals. There are, of course, "shades of gray" here, and some educators may move from being more dominated by one perspective than another over time.

In the absence of knowledge of any data on this topic, I'd suggest that a plausible null hypothesis is that love of (and skill in) music, rather than love of social justice, is the reason that most people become music teachers. Prioritizing social justice is more likely to be a special interest for the few, and an emerging interest for others. Of course, there are some specific issues of social justice that pertain to music and music education alone (e.g., concerning repertoire) and cannot be addressed other than through the decisions a music educator makes about how to practice his or her profession. So I'm not suggesting that prioritizing a music education perspective means that social justice issues are ignorable. But there are many important social justice issues that extend far beyond what most music education needs to grapple with.

People whose primary motivation is social justice might not consider music or music education as the obvious means to that end, but might instead opt for intensive engagement in politics, international development, humanitarian aid, religion, and so on. Those who see education as the focus for their social justice work might not choose music as their educational specialism, but rather sociology, history, literature, and so on; or they may seek to engage with education at a national policy level. If such individuals do take up music as the tool for their social justice ends, it will be on a rather different basis from those who come from within music education. Presumably it will be based on an assessment that music is the best tool to achieve the justice ends they have in mind. In other words, there will need to be a case made for why music is more suited to enacting social justice than literature, art, or mathematics. There are few references in this volume to how music educators have forged, or might forge, alliances with teachers of other school subjects to promote social justice on an institution-wide basis. It is important to consider such alliances, as children do not experience music education in isolation from all the other influences that they will encounter in the course of a school week. Similarly, music educators do not operate in a vacuum, but in the context of complex institutions in which they have a small, but potentially significant, role.

These considerations naturally lead me, as a scientist who has studied the lives of others, and the conditions under which they developed as they did, to be curious about the authors who have contributed to this volume (and the music educators whose work they describe). What life experiences and developmental paths brought about their prioritizing of social justice in music education as their personal and professional focus? Are these experiences and paths widely available to music educators, and what might be done to promote them?

INTERVENTIONS ASSESSED

The achievement of social justice is a macro-issue. For significant advances in social justice, large numbers of people (measured in the thousands or hundreds of thousands) need access to resources and support that are currently denied to them. Therefore if music education is to be a tool for the achievement of social justice, the initiatives that bring it about need to be macro-initiatives—initiatives that can be rolled out in multiple local contexts.

Musicians and teachers working at a local level, with individual groups of learners, may well provide rich and even transformational experiences for the 20, 50, or 100 people that they are working with, but these experiences may not lead to sustained and replicable advances in social justice unless these practices spread to other teachers, and are backed up with training, support, and finance—over the long term, and in a way that is transferable, scalable, and sustainable.

I was therefore particularly interested to see the ways in which authors in this section thought about, or reported on, issues of spreading support in practices claimed to uphold social justice.

Some of the interventions reported appear to be unique "one-offs" (e.g., the interventions of Hillman and de Quadros in a single Massachusetts correctional institution, as described in Chapter 27 by Lee Higgins; and the "DubDubDub" project bringing together students from two very different educational institutions in one city, as described by Jonathan Savage in Chapter 30). It is, of course, very important that individual music educators innovate locally, and respond creatively to the people and materials they have in front of them. However, if innovations are judged significant enough to report on in print, this suggests that they could benefit from having their methods and results mediated within the networks of practice and influence that can inspire others to learn from these innovations and be empowered to take analogous steps in their own situations. Without such rollout, well-designed and locally inspiring initiatives risk failing to have substantive influence on the wider field.

One way in which educational innovations can spread is through some form of manualization that then allows organizations with wide networks of influence and access to push forward an initiative on a larger scale. These organizations can include governments or government-funded agencies (as in the case of the UK National Curriculum described by Chris Philpott and Jason Kubilius in Chapter 26, or as in the case of El Sistema as discussed by Rubén Gazamtbide-Fernández and Leslie Stewart Rose in Chapter 28), or independent and charitable organizations (such as the Paul Hamlyn Foundation that hosts the Musical Futures informal learning initiative based on the work of Lucy Green (2008), as discussed by Chris Philpott and Jason Kubilius in Chapter 26).

The opportunities and threats of such "systematization" are well noted by more than one author. Opportunities include the spreading of resources and support over a wider body of children than any individual and local initiative could offer. Threats include the imposition of a cultural uniformity which excludes or de-prioritizes other valid approaches. For instance, El Sistema, as developed in Venezuela, prioritizes a non-indigenous Western classical tradition over the rich and vernacular informal and folk musical traditions embedded in that society. Such traditions appear universally embedded in a sustainable way that should be the envy of others, particularly those of us who inhabit societies where such traditions have all but disappeared.

INCLUSIVITY AND SUSTAINABILITY

I have argued elsewhere (Sloboda, 1998, 2001) that one of the reasons for the decline of active communal music making in contemporary Western societies is the decline and fragmentation of precisely those institutions that could provide authentic community-based wide-scale and replicable support for practical musical engagement across an entire society. In the case of Britain, until the 1960s almost every young person in education was also involved to a greater or lesser extent in organized Christianity. Christian churches offered a nationwide network of coherent musical practices (based on hymns and chants) that exposed every child to a somewhat unified corpus of musical materials, and allowed many opportunities for participation at different levels (from the all-comer involvement in congregational hymn singing, to more specialist contributions offered by a choir or music-support group). In some parts of the country, these opportunities were augmented by allied folk music traditions, where all members of the society were welcome to participate in such cultural forms as the Ceilidh (Ireland), or the Eisteddfod (Wales). These latter regional traditions still survive in a somewhat robust form, but have limited geographical span. Of course such cultural forms do not and did not embody all relevant categories of social justice, but they did at least offer a musical inclusivity that few other institutions are able to do.

These forms of musical engagement were authentic expressions of vernacular culture, which sustained people through the life span into adulthood and old age, and into which the work of music educators in schools and elsewhere could feed. They also were underpinned by the voluntarism that sustains authentic community culture, ensuring a sustainability that did not have to be excessively propped up by statutory means (or worse, by corporate sponsorship).

One deep concern expressed within music circles is the increasing loss of such specific local musical cultures in the face of globalization and market forces, which privilege mass-consumed commercial popular music. Vernacular musical traditions that have survived for generations are facing unprecedented challenges across the world, and it is unclear that new and vital forms of community music are replacing those that die out. One of the important aspects of a sustainable musical culture is that it offers points of contact and engagement for all sectors of a society, old and young, male and female. This means that what you learn in childhood is usable and relevant in old age.

Many contemporary musical cultures are more or less exclusionary of particular categories of person, based on age, gender, or other characteristics. Therefore a critical analysis of the musical cultures that young people bring with them into schools is necessary for the determination of if and how an inclusive and sustainable educational practice can be built on them. It cannot be assumed that every musical subculture is equally suitable for a social justice approach.

One issue, for instance, relates to intergenerational cohesion within a society, whether at a family or macro-level. From this perspective, a question that one might ask of a particular musical activity proposed as a promoter of social justice would be—is this a musical activity that speaks to and has meaning to people of all generations, including the elderly? And, equally—can older allies to young people in the community support that particular musical activity when they are not in the presence of a teacher or within an educational establishment?

What a child learns, and how he or she learns it, is to some extent influenced by what is provided by school and other education outside the home. But by far the most profound influence on a child's overall learning and development is the family and the home. Families where active music making is prized and a norm are those most likely to nurture musical development in their children. One aspect of music education and social justice that seems to be relatively unexplored within this volume is how music educators have worked, or might work, with parents and other family members to give them the skills and confidence to better support their children's musical activities. Some successful educational programs (such as the Suzuki string method) are premised on parents and children learning together, so that the parent becomes equipped to be the child's principal early tutor. Where such programs are elective and commercialized, then, of course, they tend to favor the already privileged—but there is no reason that such practices cannot be incorporated into programs that target the less privileged.

In that respect, I was very interested to learn of the work of Wang LinLin as reported by Lee Higgins in Chapter 27. It is highly commendable that she has targeted a particularly vulnerable group of children who are suffering long-term separation from their parents. However, one might question the extent to which meaningful social justice has been achieved for these children through opportunities to express their loss in music. From a pure social justice perspective, one might have advocated other interventions (for example, a public campaign to encourage employers to provide the necessary support for workers to have their children live with them wherever they happen to work). Empowering parents through political and psychological support might, in this case, be a more obvious and effective strategy than inspiring music students to work with such children, which is Wang LinLin's stated strategy. The question then becomes to what extent a particular music educator is willing or able to step outside his or her professional role to exercise wider social action as a citizen and political agent.

VALUES AND PROFESSIONAL CHOICES

So this returns full circle to the dilemma I posed at the beginning of these observations. Is your priority social justice, or is it music? It should not be assumed that, if social justice is the priority, then music is the most effective route to its achievement. That will depend on a careful assessment of the need, and an evaluation of the best strategies available to meet that need.

In a semi-autobiographical account of how these dilemmas have played out in my own professional life (Sloboda, 2005c), I tried also to characterize in a somewhat formal way the different approaches that a professional (in my case an academic) could apply to his or her work. I postulated four levels of social engagement, starting with "sensitivity to historic professional norms" (in the case of academia, such things as public access to findings, and full citation of sources), moving through "sensitivity to applicability" and "focus on applicability," to "focus on values." I argued that putting a focus on values (such as social justice) may require a re-evaluation of one's professional field of activity, and the possible abandoning of it for a different field more suited to one's values.

For reasons I outlined in the chapter, the international events of the early part of the first decade of the century (9/11 and what followed from it) convinced me that I needed to refocus my activity on highlighting the enormous damage done to people around the world by the actions of the US and the UK governments while led by George W. Bush and Tony Blair, and while politically supported by Congress and Parliament, and fiscally supported by every taxpayer. In this shift of focus, I judged that my musical interests and expertise could play no significant role, and were irrelevant as compared to other types of expertise and activity I had or could develop. This is a view I still hold, in light of more than 10 years of research and activism on conflict.

MUSIC AND CONFLICT

From time to time I have been encouraged to look at the possible intersection between music and conflict, to see whether there is some useful way to bridge the gap between my two disparate interests. In this I am particularly indebted to Arild Bergh, a researcher on the role of music in conflict and conflict transformation, who invited me to be second author on a review of the field (Bergh & Sloboda, 2010). In that review, we concluded that, for the potential for music to be a significant influence in conflict transformation, very specific and exacting conditions had to pertain. The existing evidence is that much music has no significant positive effect on conflict, and in many documented cases is actually a spur to conflict and ethnic hatred.

As I write (August 2014) the apparently intractable Israel-Palestine conflict has recently flared up, with appalling loss of civilian life, mostly of Palestinians within Gaza. Over the years, a number of musical initiatives have been set up to bring Israeli Jews together with Palestinians and Arabs. The most high-profile and long-lasting of these is probably the West-Eastern Divan project, led by Daniel Barenboim, which brings together student musicians working toward careers as professional orchestral players, for intensive musical and political interactions over a two-month period every summer, ending with concerts in both Israel and the West Bank. If high-quality music making under an inspirational leader were sufficient to achieve mutual tolerance and understanding between these two ethnic groups, then this project should have achieved outstanding results. However, excellent and detailed ethnographic research (Beckles Wilson, 2009) shows that attitudinal change toward the other group among the young musicians was minimal, with most participants justifying their participation in terms of their musical career prospects rather than any commitment to, or hope for, reconciliation with the other group.

It is therefore encouraging to learn of a less high-profile initiative reported in this volume by Andre de Quadros in Chapter 31 that has involved the collaboration, over a ten-year period, of the Efroni Choir (for Israeli Arabs) and the Sawa Choir (for Israeli Jews). Interviews with the young singers from both choirs revealed that they had developed a strong sense of kinship with the other. An analysis of what factors allowed these bonds to develop in this project, while failing to do so in the West-Eastern Divan, would be a very substantial contribution to future understanding of the potential role of music in such conflicted societies.

I do, however, fear that forces far more powerful than those that can be marshaled by musicians will be the ultimate determiner of what happens in this (and other similarly) conflicted parts of the world. In a situation where 96 percent of Israelis believe that the Israel Defence Force was justified in its summer 2014 use of force against the civilians of Gaza (Israel Democracy Institute, 2014), it is hard to be hopeful that any cultural intervention, whether musical or otherwise, can make any dent on the hardened, and increasingly hardening, attitudes found in this traumatized region.

END NOTE: EVALUATION

Advocating for the benefits of music and music education is important, but it is also important not to be seen to be indulging in special pleading, or going beyond what the evidence supports. As authors in this volume have noted, multiple claims have been made in the research and advocacy literature for the role that music and music education can play in social, psychological, personal, and cultural development. Some of the least nuanced claims come from those who have a direct interest in maintaining or increasing the amount of paid work for musicians and music teachers, and increasing the income of commercial organizations offering musical products and services. These are not helpful for the field as a whole. The far stronger voice comes from the beneficiaries, not the providers.

I hope, as the growing social justice in music education movement goes forward, it is able to benefit from a greater number of rigorous and large-scale evaluations of the effects of this work on its recipients—the young people. This will require the further development of clear and transparent indicators of advances in social justice, so that different programs might be assessed by comparable metrics. It is also important that longer-term effects are assessed. It is always difficult to track people over months and years, but it is important to do so.

I am confident that long-term effects are recordable. My own experience as a musician, supported by a range of research (e.g., Gabrielsson, 2011; Sloboda, 2005d) is that single short-lived musical experiences can be transformational across the life span—and remembered as such decades later. We now know enough about the antecedents of such "peak experiences" to understand what situations are more or less likely to engender them. I have an intuition and a confident hope that many musical experiences devised with social justice in mind may have a similarly life-transforming impact, and may be explicitly recalled by participants as such. But in this area, as in most, good intentions and hope are not sufficient. Rigorous and assessable results are what count.

REFERENCES

Beckles Willson, R. (2009). The parallax worlds of the West-Eastern Divan Orchestra. *Journal of the Royal Musical Association, 134*(2), 319–334.

Bergh, A., & Sloboda, J. A. (2010). Music and art in conflict transformation: A review. *Music & Arts in Action, 2*(2), 1–17.

Gabrielsson, A. (2011). *Strong experiences with music.* Oxford: Oxford University Press.

Green, L. (2008). *Music, informal learning and the school: A new classroom pedagogy.* Farnham, UK: Ashgate.

Israel Democracy Institute (2014). July 2014 Peace Index. Retrieved from http://en.idi.org.il/about-idi/news-and-updates/july-2014-peace-index/.

Sloboda, J. A. (1998). Music: Where cognition and emotion meet. *The Psychologist, 12*(4), 450–455.

Sloboda, J. A. (2001). Emotion, functionality, and the everyday experience of music: Where does music education fit? *Music Education Research, 3*(2), 243–253.

Sloboda, J. A. (2005a). Are some children more gifted for music than others? In J. A. Sloboda, *Exploring the musical mind* (pp. 297–316). Oxford: Oxford University Press. [Originally published in Italian as "Dotu musicali e innatismo?" In J. J. Nattiez (Ed.). (2002). *Enciclopedia della Musica,* Vol II: *Il sapere musicale* (pp. 509–529). Torina: Giuilio Einaudi Editore.]

Sloboda, J. A. (2005b). Everyday uses of music listening: A preliminary study. In J. A. Sloboda, *Exploring the musical mind* (pp. 319–331). Oxford: Oxford University Press. [Originally published in S.W. Yi (Ed.). (1999). *Music, mind & science* (pp. 354–369). Seoul: Seoul National University Press.]

Sloboda, J. A. (2005c). Assessing music psychology research: Values, priorities and outcomes. In J. A. Sloboda, *Exploring the musical mind* (pp. 395–429). Oxford: Oxford University Press.

Sloboda, J. A. (2005d). Music as a language. In J. A. Sloboda, *Exploring the musical mind* (pp. 171–190). Oxford: Oxford University Press. [Originally published in F. Wilson & F. Roehmann (Eds.), *Music and child development: Proceedings of the 1987 Biology of Music Making Conference.* St. Louis, Missouri: MMB Music.]

Sloboda, J. A., Davidson, J. W., & Howe, M. J. A. (1994). Is everyone musical? *The Psychologist, 7*(7), 349–354.

Sloboda, J. A., O'Neill, S. A., & Ivaldi, A. (2001). Functions of music in everyday life: An exploratory study using the Experience Sampling Methodology. *Musicae Scientiae, 5*(1), 9–32.

Wise, K. J., & Sloboda, J. A. (2008). Establishing an empirical profile of self-defined "tone deafness": Perception, singing performance, and self-assessment. *Musicae Scientiae, 12*(1), 3–26.

SOCIAL JUSTICE IN PRACTICE

Examples of Educational Projects from Beyond the Schools and Around the World

INTRODUCTION

Description, Questions,
and Challenges for Researchers

PAUL WOODFORD, SECTION EDITOR

THE chapters in the previous sections on this Handbook were more often than not about conceptualizing social justice and ideas relating to history, policy, citizenship, racism, ableism, sexual diversity, informal music learning, creativity, pedagogy, youth empowerment, elitism, technology, and inclusiveness. The authors of this concluding section of this Handbook, by contrast, were asked to take a more practice-based approach in which some of these and other ideas were applied to pedagogy and real-life teaching situations or contexts. Two chapters (Chapter 35 by Mary Cohen and Stuart Paul Duncan and Chapter 38 by Maud Hickey) address social justice in the very challenging contexts of prisons or youth detention centers, respectively. Cohen and Duncan first define two conceptions of social justice that are particularly relevant to those contexts (i.e., restorative and transformative justice), which they believe can inform and enrich music programs operating in those facilities in ways that are new and exciting, and that might also be relevant to school-based music programs. Hickey shares the same research interest as Cohen and Duncan, albeit in relation to incarcerated youth more so than to adults, while also exploring some of the questions and implications arising therein for music in schools and other venues. Motivating all three of these authors is a shared interest in empowering individuals, regardless of age, and whether in prisons, youth detention centers, schools, or other venues, to transform their lives through musical participation.

Joseph Abramo outlines in Chapter 37 a strategic pedagogical approach for challenging high school students to think more critically about the social themes embedded in the popular music they consume, so that they become more critically aware of, and thoughtful about, problems relating to power and privilege in its production and reception. Abramo's strategy involves inviting students to generate and discuss their own evidence-based interpretations of popular music videos, which begs the question of how this might work to promote social justice. Several convincing answers to this question are provided by him. Among the challenges that this strategic pedagogy presents, of course, is how teachers can ensure that students remember to also focus on the musical sounds themselves, rather than on just the video or lyrics.

This idea of promoting critical awareness of the effects of power and privilege in shaping individual and societal consciousness in and through music—and also music education—underscores many, if not all, of the chapters in this Handbook. In Chapter 36, Eric Shieh models what this critical thinking might look like as he struggles to gauge the success of the renowned Venezuelan El Sistema orchestral program in furthering the cause of social justice. There is a strong tendency among many people both within and outside El Sistema to glamorize the program, even though, as Shieh wryly observes, its structure remains something of a mystery. Others take a more cynical stance, viewing the program as yet another instance of colonialism because it is based on the model of the European orchestra and the so-called "great" music of the classical and romantic traditions. Shieh takes a welcome balanced approach in attempting to reveal the program's sometimes murky purposes, structure, and pedagogical practices while troubling them, asking difficult questions about power, politics, race, and privilege—including ones about the program's reliance on the music of the European orchestral tradition—not to denigrate or disprove, but to obtain a better understanding of why, despite whatever problems it might have, the El Sistema program continues to enrich the lives of many Venezuelan children.

Sheila Woodward (Chapter 39) and Amanda Soto (Chapter 40) propose pedagogical practices involving music as a means of combating racism and colonialism encountered in educational and public spaces. Soto complains that, although Mexican American children represent a significant and growing proportion of the school population in the United States, there continues to be a gap between the music of their own culture and that represented in the music they listen to, study, and perform in schools. A socially just music education for those children must recognize and validate their cultural identity by ensuring that their music is adequately represented in the curriculum. Woodward's chapter is radical in comparison, documenting and illustrating some of the history of resistance and rebellion against apartheid in her native South Africa in which music and song played important roles, and revealing some of the many ways that music in education can be used to further the cause of social justice, including as a tool for resisting oppressive authority. Among the questions that music teachers should ask their pupils, Woodward proposes, is "What part will they play, as musicians, in impacting change in the world?"

The remaining two chapters in this section (Chapter 41 by Australians Julie Ballantyne and Carmen Mills and Chapter 42 by Janet Barrett) allow for varying degrees of synthesis of the ideas and practices discussed and illuminated in this book. Ballantyne and Mills provide a helpful overview of the empirical research literature in music teacher education relating to social justice, presenting evidence of the research that has already been accomplished and recommending areas in which further work is required. Barrett's chapter, it must be noted, was commissioned by the editors as an epilogue and frames much of the discussion in this Handbook, while offering commentary on the success of music teacher educators in accomplishing what many believe should be their primary goal. Like Joel Westheimer and other authors throughout this Handbook, Barrett emphasizes music teacher education's potential for furthering the cause of social justice by contributing to the recognition among politicians and others of the essential dignity and worth of persons, in contradistinction to those who would reduce education to technocratic or vocational training. This, of course, will be no easy task, requiring courage, perseverance, imagination, and critical thinking, coupled with a concern for professional ethics and the welfare of the less fortunate and marginalized. Hopefully, as Barrett says, the contents of this Handbook will inform, challenge, and inspire, while prompting and guiding future action. Her chapter thus provides a fitting conclusion to this Handbook.

CHAPTER 35

BEHIND DIFFERENT WALLS

Restorative Justice, Transformative Justice,
and Their Relationship to Music Education

MARY L. COHEN AND STUART PAUL DUNCAN

WILLIAM Ayers, Therese Quinn, and David Stovall (2009) define the purpose of education as the building of "societies in which people can learn, love, and imagine more and suffer less" (p. i). How can music education support this purpose? These authors establish three principles of social justice education: equity, activism, and social literacy. Each of these principles plays a role in rethinking music education. The third principle, social literacy, described as "nourishing awareness of our own identities and our connection with others" (p. xiv), aids in building just and humane societies within music education settings.

This notion of social literacy is vital for positive and meaningful music education. Overt or hidden conflict occurs in music education contexts. Conflict can arise particularly when students, parents, and/or administrators advocate differing ideals or misinterpret some aspect of a learning activity or a musical composition. One example of an overt conflict might involve a music teacher who introduces Gregorian chant to his or her students with the intention of sharing a past musical style, but students or parents perceive the religious music as conflicting with their own belief systems. One example of a hidden conflict occurs when a music teacher establishes a full-school sing-along, in which one of the other teachers is reluctant to sing in front of the students due to a negative choral experience as a youth, when he or she was told to just mouth the words during performance. Although music teachers generally do not complete sociological studies in their preservice training, their interactions with people and musical activities naturally demand a solid understanding of how to deal with conflict and harms that occur within their jobs.

Bradley (2007) argues that music educators do not often consider deeper levels of social injustice in the classroom. She explains that in music education curricula, colonialism and re-colonization occur through the validation of past cultures related to the

Western musical canon. Through an emphasis on performing styles and instruments within the Western musical canon, other musical practices may be marginalized or omitted (p. 134). Bradley suggests that music educators should speak directly about race and racial inequality, discussing what has until now been a hidden conflict.

Restorative justice and transformative justice are two potential conceptual apparatuses that can aid music educators' ability to work through conflict. Restorative justice provides alternative ways of thinking about offending behavior, whether those actions occur on the streets, in prisons, in schools, or elsewhere. Many thinkers have employed restorative justice to examine victims' needs and offenders' responsibilities for repairing harm. Restorative justice cultivates outcomes that develop healing, reparation, and responsibility for all (Zehr, 2002). On the other hand, transformative justice focuses on the potential to address deeper, ingrained issues associated with the causes and circumstances surrounding harmful behaviors. Concepts of restorative and transformative justice have the potential to inform music education practices in new ways not yet imagined. Implementing these frameworks can lead to fresh approaches to classroom management and positive school-wide changes through relationship building, the construction of new underlying goals for creative music making (i.e., songwriting, improvisation, composition, arranging), and new pedagogical approaches that incorporate ideas from critical race theory (Ladson-Billings, 2001, 2005a, 2005b), ethics of care (Noddings, 2003), and positive youth musical engagement (O'Neill, 2006).

When applied to music teaching in a mindful and effective manner, restorative and transformative justice reframe pedagogy to be more sensitive to the relationships that occur among students and instructors, social interactions within learning activities, and the experiences of audience members who attend musical ensemble performances. Reconsideration of underlying learning goals may lead to more inclusive attitudes within schools and within the curriculum in the institutions that train the teachers. Music educators might pay greater attention to the depth of relationships not only among sounds, but also among the people in their charge. As bell hooks (1994) cautioned in *Teaching to Transgress: Education as the Practice of Freedom*, "theory is not inherently healing, liberatory, or revolutionary. It fulfills this function only when we ask that it do so and direct our theorizing towards this end" (p. 61). This chapter examines how the theories of restorative and transformational justice can be put into practice within music education.

Scholars have primarily examined restorative and transformative justice in criminal justice contexts (i.e., Rugge & Cormier, 2005; Schiff, Von Hirsch, & Roberts, 2004); however, these frameworks have also been applied in workplaces, schools, and religious institutions (Zehr, 2002, p. 4). Beyond these institutions, a recently emerging area of scholarship has begun to explore restorative and transformative justice from the perspective of music education within prisons. Through two prison case studies—a choral singing program and a music appreciation course—this chapter demonstrates the applicability of the concepts of restorative and transformative justice within the music classroom and reflects on their usefulness, more broadly, for the music education community. A short introduction to the terms "restorative" and "transformative" follows, which will build the foundation for a deeper discussion of their implementation in music education.

RESTORATIVE JUSTICE

In *Restoring Justice: An Introduction to Restorative Justice*, Karen Strong and Daniel Ness (2010) discuss the difficulty of defining the term "restorative justice." In their overview of the various uses of the term, they describe three categories within which definitions of restorative justice fall. Their first category involves a definition that emphasizes meetings among the victim, the offender, and the community (also defined in various ways). Their second category involves a definition that focuses on healing harms caused to the victim, offender, and/or community, rather than requiring meetings. As Strong and Ness point out, this category "is not limited by the inability or unwillingness of the parties to meet" (p. 42). Their third category places the concept of transformation within a broader concept that addresses a myriad of social issues such as racism, sexism, and classism and the roles these play in broken relationships. For Strong and Ness, this broader conception "is therefore a way of life because it addresses all of our relationships, and it offers a way in which broken relationships can be repaired (often through challenging existing societal injustices)" (p. 42).

Common to all three of these definitions of restorative justice is the importance that the offender plays in the healing process. Paulo Freire's (1970) classic text, *Pedagogy of the Oppressed,* highlights the problems involved in the initial stages of the processes of reconciliation when, rather than strive for liberation, the victims tend to become oppressors themselves, and bipartisanship becomes no longer possible (p. 45). In order to overcome oppression, the mechanisms of oppression must be recognized and made explicit. The key point here is that the process "must be forged *with*, not *for* the oppressed" (emphasis in original, p. 48), and that in order to reach a state of reconciliation the causes of harm must be addressed. In today's society, people, acting as "the community," tend to act as judge and juror, thus excluding the oppressor from any mediation. This notion of removing power dynamics and giving equal attention to the participants within a conflictual situation is a central aspect of restorative practices and has been employed in a variety of contexts, including schools.

Restorative justice, also termed restorative principles, practice, or measures, has been used within school systems in the United States, Canada, New Zealand, and the United Kingdom with the intentions of fostering a positive school-wide climate through processes of mediation (i.e., Hopkins, 2004; Morrison, 2005). These processes involve key individuals coming together to interact through storytelling, inquiry, and conferencing. Conferencing involves victims interacting face to face with offenders, with a mediator present, where the offenders hear how their criminal behavior impacted the victims' lives. The goals of this process are to heal harms and empower all involved to move constructively beyond the difficulties related to the conflict. The New Zealand model of conferencing used for serious juvenile offenders involves the presence of police, a neutral facilitator, and private time for the young offenders and their support networks where underlying problems can be identified and addressed by family and friends (Vanfraechem, 2005). Employed in schools, restorative justice emphasizes equal opportunity for all students to feel connected, to feel as if they can be themselves and still be friends with others whom they perceive are different from them (Morrison, 2005).

The use of restorative justice in the school system likely draws from a desire to avoid more punitive-based disciplinary methods. As Sharkey and Fenning (2012) argue, zero tolerance policies exacerbate problems in schools. Recent research suggests that expulsions, suspensions, and other punitive tactics push students out of schools, setting them on the fast track to prison, and leaving social problems unsolved (Meiners, 2007). Applications of restorative justice in schools align closely with Ayers, Quinn, and Stovalls' notion of social literacy. A key component of social literacy relates to increasing awareness of our own identities and our connections with others. Restorative justice frameworks enable people to self-reflect and to consider how actions impact one another and affect their communities. Self-reflection can nourish self-identity, while awareness of how actions affect communities can lead to more positive relationships with others.

Although restorative justice provides an alternate approach to working through conflict compared to many procedures employed within the traditional criminal justice system, some thinkers have pointed out flaws and concerns (Harris, 2006; Morris, 2000; Zehr, 2005). Zehr (2005) asks to what extent restorative justice practices address offender needs, attend to ethnic and cultural dimensions, are victim-oriented, and make allowances for the community. Morris (2000) argues that restorative justice is not mindful of "enormous structural injustices at the base of our justice systems, and the extent to which they function mainly to reinforce racism and classism" (p. 19). One shortcoming of restorative justice includes its inability to address, at a fundamental level, biases inherent in our judicial and social systems. Morris has suggested an alternate form of justice, named "transformative justice," that reframes offending behaviors as opportunities to establish and build more inclusive and more caring communities.

THE TERM "TRANSFORMATIVE" IN RELATION TO EDUCATION, AND ITS USE IN MUSIC EDUCATION

In addition to emphasizing healing harm, transformative justice can be used to examine the root causes of damaging behaviors, involving complex issues such as racism and classism. Its varied applications include schools, neighborhoods, families, and workplaces, in local, national, or international contexts. According to Harris (2006), both transformative justice and restorative justice work toward interpersonal and larger social change

(p. 556). The term "transformative" has been applied to education in a number of contexts. The purpose of this section is to introduce two uses of the term "transformative," noting their respective uses and the similarities and differences between them. The following terms are introduced: "transformative learning" and "transformative music engagement."

Transformative Learning

Mezirow (1997) describes transformative learning as the process of changing one's "frame of reference" (p. 5), which is defined as a "coherent body of experience—associations, concepts, values, feelings, conditioned responses" that influence one's attitudes and life choices. According to Mezirow, the two dimensions that constitute a frame of reference are "habits of mind," which are broad, abstract, orienting, habitual ways of thinking, feeling, and acting, and a "point of view," which involves the interpretation of the habits of mind through a collection of beliefs, value judgments, attitudes, and feelings (pp. 5–6). Points of view are more susceptible to continuous change, whereas habits of mind are more durable, with limited flexibility, as people tend to stick with previously learned patterns. Mezirow suggests that critical reflection is necessary to transform our frames of reference, and if what we are learning fits easily into our existing frames of reference, no transformative change is possible (p. 7). To encourage transformative learning, teachers need to guide students to develop greater self-awareness of their own assumptions, to be critical of these, and to understand assumptions that others carry (p. 10).

Transformative Music Engagement

Susan O'Neill (2012) argues for a theory of transformative music engagement. Referencing Carl Rogers (1961), O'Neill suggests that we need to emphasize the dynamic processes that are a natural part of musical learning, rather than consider such processes as static, non-changing entities. By emphasizing process, teaching and learning become more critically reflective, inclusive, permeable, integrative of experience, and differentiating (O'Neill, 2012, p. 164). Transformative music engagement operates on personal, sociocultural, and systemic levels. It is a strength-based, not deficit-based, theory, in which instructors emphasize their learners' aptitudes and avoid assuming that students either have or do not have talent: "all musical learners in all contexts of development have musical strengths and competencies" (p. 166).

In transformative music engagement, learners reflect on musical meaning, are empowered to build on their competences, and foster resilience to overcome negative constraints that hinder musical growth. O'Neill (2012) questions the notion of communities of practice—the idea that we gradually and naturally develop into various common interest learning communities through regular participation—by arguing that this way of thinking tends to simplify the rich, complex, individual musical experiences that happen within the members of the group. Interactions among people influence musical learning, and O'Neill recognizes how these interactions are dynamic, fluid, and changeable components of transformative music engagement. Due to the dynamic aspects of social affiliations, in order for a music teacher to create a supportive learning environment, a culture of care must be regularly nourished (Noddings, 2003).

In order for pedagogy to be rooted in care, and for the learning processes to be transformative, according to the authors cited earlier, a critical understanding of what has informed one's perceptions is required. For O'Neill (2012), transformation acts as a modifier for a theory of musical engagement, within which a pedagogical model is reframed from a state of being to one of becoming. Mezirow (1997) suggests that transformation occurs individually through reflection on habitual thinking and broadening one's perspective, rather than identifying it with a pedagogical approach or a subject. Frames of reference and habits of mind are central concepts that can orient our thinking toward changing embedded, preconceived notions. The common thread among these aspects of transformation lies in the awareness that teachers must bring into their learning environments regarding social literacy; social literacy is not static, it is rooted in student-centered experiences, and when both teachers and learners are mindful of their personal frames of reference and habitual thinking, they can more easily connect with others and transform themselves through learning experiences.

MUSIC EDUCATION IN PRISON CONTEXTS

Next, we describe two case studies of music education in prison contexts to illustrate how concepts of restorative and transformative justice can inform musical learning practices. The two case studies are the Oakdale Community Choir in a medium-security prison in Iowa and a music appreciation course in a maximum-security prison in upstate New York.

The Oakdale Community Choir, founded in February 2009, is unique in that its membership includes regular weekly participation with both incarcerated men (inside singers) and women and men from outside the prison (outside singers). The symbolism behind the choir's membership is significant in that people who have been accused of committing crimes against society are singing in unison and harmony alongside people who represent the society that has been harmed. Together, they prepare a unified performance. Through these social interactions, the choir provides a sense of normalcy for the inmates (Cohen, 2012a). Many inside singers do not receive regular visits, so the choir contributes to their sense of family. Additionally, the choir provides a space for transformation through the process of bringing people together and creating a safe space for them to explore, affirm, and celebrate their sense of ideal relationships (Small, 1998). As one of the inside singers wrote, "I've learned through our practices and meeting people from the outside world, that we are human and that is a very strong self-esteem builder"

(Gromko & Cohen, 2011, p. 111). In this sense, the choir contributes to a sense of wholeness and humanness for the incarcerated members.

Averaging about 60 people per season, members self-select to participate in the choir. In addition to rehearsing and performing together, members may choose to partake in reflective writing and songwriting, in addition to participation with the choir. At the conclusion of each of the two choir seasons per year, the choir performs one concert for people incarcerated at the prison and a second concert for around 85 outside guests. Approved family members and friends of the inside singers receive audio recordings of the concert performances. The choir regularly performs original songs in these themed concerts. Writing and performing original songs provide a means of healing for its members. The original songs provide sustenance for the inside singers' need for self-expression and express to outside singers and audience members a sense of their inner feelings. These experiences allow for a deeper and more personal relationship between people who are incarcerated and the outside singers and audience members who come into the prison for concerts, and family members or friends who receive concert compact discs.

Choral singing in a prison provides a space for constructing new identities and building community in an environment where one's sense of feeling human is squelched and where community building is not a primary focus. Such choral singing practices inform music education practices in contexts other than prisons in that the actual experience allows participants to develop social literacy (Ayers, Quinn, & Stovall, 2009) through increased awareness of their own identities and deeper connections with other people.

Auburn Correctional Facility, located in upstate New York, is the United States' oldest prison in operation. Known for its reformation of the Quaker's system, Auburn replaced prayer, contemplation, and humane conditions with hard labor. Given its rather hard-line status, it is surprising to find that the correctional facility works alongside local Cayuga Community College and Cornell University to grant inmates associate's degrees in a variety of different subject areas. Students register to take classes during their lunch breaks since the rest of the day involves hard labor; thus, participation is not mandatory, and it requires giving up their only free time during the day.

Owing to its maximum-security status, regular outside community participation is not an option. Furthermore, a sense of community among inmates is actively discouraged due to security protocol. Referred to by numbers, clothed entirely in green, and living in a controlled environment, the maximum-security system is designed to ensure adherence to standards of behavior and to maximize prison productivity. Facets of their prior lives—that made them individuals—are stripped away.

Given the idea that music can humanize and provide a sense of normalcy, this course was designed to prioritize students' musical experiences, as well as to acknowledge their state of incarceration. Although it is tempting to treat the environment in the same manner as a non-prison environment, such an approach negates important social, cultural, racial, and educational situations specific to being "inside" the walls. Prior to incarceration, one inmate was an actively performing jazz guitarist. His sentence stripped him of the right to express himself through guitar playing, which for him was closely connected to his sense of individuality. Because guitar strings can be used as weapons, the inmate was not allowed his guitar while incarcerated in this particular institution. But performing, for him, was also a communal activity, one where musical ideas could be shared among fellow musicians. The music appreciation course in his case was restorative in a twofold manner: first, it channeled and validated his prior experience and knowledge as a musician—an identity closely linked to playing a guitar; and second, it restored a sense of a musical community where ideas, musical or not, were safe.

The jazz guitarist's knowledge of chordal progressions and his compositional skills were sources of untapped potentiality; however, he had no way of realizing this potential given the restrictions on guitars within this prison. Keyboards, though, were allowed. Through a process of learning to transcribe his compositional ideas via notation and of learning rudimentary piano technique, he was able to build relationships with others, sharing his music beyond an environment deprived of social interaction, and developing a new channel for his compositional visions. This experience is not restorative in the sense of conflict resolution, but it has provided a means for prior knowledge and skills to develop in a new situation, enabling this individual a renewed identity, motivation to grow in new directions, and a sense of accomplishment.

The prison environment, so deeply entrenched in American society, continues to enact a toll on the individuals incarcerated within. The system divorces the incarcerated from society, strips them of their individuality, and prevents their harms from healing. Musical experience, through either choral singing or a traditional class setting, has the potential to be a transformative act, one in which the incarcerated are reconnected to an "outside" community, through programs such as the Oakdale Community Choir, or are reconnected to a musical identity suppressed behind walls, through traditional music classes such as those at Auburn Maximum Security prison. These experiences are transformative in several ways: first, they reignite, rather than seek to deny, students' past musical experiences; second, they do not seek to restore a student to his state prior to incarceration, but to validate those experiences by reconstituting them in the present; and third, the student is transformed in the sense of being given an identity, either as part of a new community, or through his identity as a musician, that is explicitly denied by the prison environment.

Applications to Music Education

Researchers and school administrators have explored applications of restorative practices in schools. Hopkins (2004) suggests that a whole school approach most effectively creates a positive school climate when every component of the school day follows restorative principles (p. 13). Given the possibility to influence many people within the school community, including students through rehearsals, and teachers, administrators, and parents in the school community through performances, music teachers may support and build restorative practices by regularly incorporating skills and values essential to restorative principles. These include remaining non-judgmental, respecting all perspectives, listening empathetically and actively, developing rapport, and empowering participants to construct solutions rather than imposing ideas, creative questioning, compassion, and patience (pp. 37–38). This section explores three applications of restorative and transformative practices in music education: (a) pedagogical possibilities, (b) types of learning activities, and (c) classroom management.

Pedagogical Possibilities

Restorative principles can be embraced within any school musical setting, including traditional ensembles and other musical groups and activities involving guitar, rock band, mariachi, songwriting, and computer-based digital musical learning and creating. As described earlier, restorative approaches emphasize two or more parties working alongside one another—*with* rather than to, at, or for. The emphasis is on equality in the learning process, in contrast to power dynamics. It is difficult to prepare a large ensemble to perform a composition without verbal or gestural directions from the conductor. If a school teacher-conductor has no training in large group or small ensemble improvisation (Oshinksy, 2008) or other student-directed learning pedagogies, he or she naturally gravitates toward a more authoritarian model when instructing the ensemble. Within large ensemble settings, the teacher-conductor who empowers student musicians to lead the group through aural warm-ups, rhythmic exercises, melodic and rhythmic call and response, and improvisation activities changes the power dynamics that tend to be inherent in large ensembles.

The establishment of the group Help Increase the Peace Project (HIPP) began in the 1990s in the United States in response to increasing violence in society and schools. The group is based on two assumptions: first, that conflict can lead to positive change; and second, that the root of a large amount of violent conflict is social injustice (Morrison, 2005, p. 41). Its aim is to create care and trust within a community, foregrounding student interests as the basis for learning. In the case of music ensembles, teacher-conductors might survey the members and incorporate their musical preferences into rehearsals and performances. If the students' preferences are musical pieces that are not arranged for a particular ensemble, the students can follow Lucy Green's (2014) approach and teach themselves from audio recordings and, as a result, develop autonomy with respect to learning and performing.

In the Oakdale Community Choir, two disparate groups combine into one musical ensemble. Music educators might take into consideration populations who have not been represented in K–12 school music programs, for example, a group of older adult musicians in an instrumental or choral ensemble. Research on intergenerational music making suggests that combining older adults and college students improves participants' attitudes toward one another (Bowers, 1998). Alfano (2008) reported on an intergenerational band class composed of adolescents and senior adults who met in a Canadian public school. The musicians working side by side were equals in the music-making and the learning processes. Music educators who explore populations living within their local communities can identify specialized groups that might be combined with school musicians into one musical ensemble.

Types of Learning Activities

Some musical activities more readily lean toward restorative and transformative approaches. For example, songwriting, improvisation, and composition are means to express one's thoughts, feelings, and needs within a given context. We acknowledge that music teachers are not trained as social workers or counselors; nevertheless, songwriting naturally allows one to express whatever emotions one is comfortable expressing. The opportunity to perform one's original song is an empowering experience for the songwriter. Through metaphor, melodies, rhythms, forms, and lyrics, a songwriter uses tools to express feelings in ways that might feel safer or more satisfying than through dialogue. Improvisation and aural training emphasize listening and responding, and enable ensemble-style interaction without difficulties associated with interpreting a score. Open-ended reflections through a discussion of "What did you notice?" among participants provide a means for a deeper awareness of how improvising together influenced their connections with one another, as well as other insightful considerations.

Another strategy for applying concepts of restorative and transformative justice in music ensemble settings is to seek out and practice new ways for people in the ensemble to connect with one another. One example implements a reflective writing component with participants, leaders, and even members of the audience (Cohen, 2012b). Writing provides a way for people to self reflect on aspects of rehearsing and performing and the literature practiced. These ideas can be shared in at least three forms: (a) individually through exchanges with the whole ensemble by reading the writing during a rehearsal, (b) in written form, and (c) with the audience during concert introductions or in program notes. In the Oakdale Community Choir, newsletters featuring original writing pieces are created periodically. Such newsletters give everyone in the choir an opportunity to learn about what individuals in the group are thinking. These newsletters can be shared with other people from the community interested in the choir. As one of the participants of the choir wrote: "It [reading newsletters] enables 'peeking' into the hearts and minds of our fellow choir members" (Cohen, Gilchrist, & Trachsel, 2010).

Classroom Management

As described earlier, schools have adopted restorative justice frameworks to alleviate issues of dropouts and conflict, and to foster a positive school climate. According to Chmelynski (2005), restorative justice is a collective, constructive means of resolving conflict. Restorative justice provides a process to reach resolution and manage future disputes. In music classrooms, teachers can apply principles from restorative justice for preventive disciplinary measures and for dealing with issues of conflict within the classroom. Some music teachers already follow restorative justice approaches. For example, when they collaborate with the students to create classroom guidelines and dialogue to decide on consequences for disruptive behavior, they observe components of a restorative model.

Sometimes conflict is implicit. In the music classroom, students and teachers regularly hold their own opinions on their favorite musical styles. And in turn, they have clear ideas on what musical genres they do not like. Depending on the maturity level of the learners and self-awareness (Mezirow's habits of mind) of the teachers, strong musical opinions can result in visible or invisible conflict. A restorative justice approach might address these conflicting attitudes toward musical styles by emphasizing that musical styles are created through people and cultural groups. From this approach, the teacher can invite the students to consider how they can still respect the people who create or perform a musical style they do not enjoy. Through repeated instances of perceiving another cultural group as fellow humans rather than the "Other," seeds may be planted to adopt a cooperative rather than competitive or divisive attitude toward other people. In other words, if a country fan who does not like rap music can view people who create rap music as humans who express themselves differently than he or she does, that country fan may more easily respect people who hold differing opinions.

SUMMARY AND CONCLUSIONS

The purpose of this chapter was to explore frameworks of restorative and transformative justice in two prison case studies and to consider possible applications to music education. As was explained, restorative justice prioritizes the question of how to heal harm from offending behaviors, while transformative justice examines the underlying causes of offending behaviors and regards offenses as opportunities for education and transformation. In the two prison case studies, we described how choral singing and musical learning were means for humanizing the lives of incarcerated individuals.

Music educators who are mindful of the frameworks within restorative and transformative justice can implement new and interesting learning activities that encourage authentic self-expression and meaningful community building among the learners. Classroom management strategies based on restorative justice emphasize building positive social relationships and deal with conflict in ways that draw attention to healing harms, rather than blaming wrongdoers.

Past generations emphasized the competitive values of formal education. Russia's launch of Sputnik fueled the US government to emphasize math and science curricula. Today, the science, technology, engineering, and mathematics (STEM) initiatives are intended to build a strong workforce that can compete globally. Now it is time for music educators to lead society toward a cooperative global community rather than emphasizing competitive global initiatives. The concepts behind restorative and transformative justice provide a means toward healing conflict, using a more humanized approach toward offending behaviors, and for all stakeholders to develop responsibility and respect when offenses occur. Research is warranted to examine short-term and long-term applications of these approaches to music education, as well as comparative studies investigating school and community programs that are already incorporating these ideas. Music educators may benefit through collaboration with experts in restorative and transformative justice for the creative implementation of essential ideas into teaching and structuring of music programs.

REFERENCES

Alfano, C. J. (2008). Intergenerational learning in a high school environment. *International Journal of Community Music, 1*(2), 253–266.

Ayers, W., Quinn, T., & Stovall, D. (Eds). (2009). *Handbook of social justice in education.* New York: Routledge.

Bowers, J. (1998). Effects of an intergenerational choir for community-based seniors and college students on age-related attitudes. *Journal of Music Therapy, 35,* 2–18.

Bradley, D. (2007). The sounds of silence: Talking race in music education. *Action, Criticism, and Theory for Music Education, 6*(4), 132–162.

Chmelynski, C. (2005). Restorative justice for discipline with respect. *Education Digest, 71*(1), 17–20.

Cohen, M. L. (2012a). Harmony within the walls: Perceptions of worthiness and competence in a community prison choir. *International Journal of Music Education, 30*(1), 47–57. doi: 10.1177/0255761411431394.

Cohen, M. L. (2012b). Writing between rehearsals: A tool for assessment and building camaraderie. *Music Educators Journal, 98*(3), 43–48, doi: 10.1177/0027432111432524.

Cohen, M. L., Gilchrist, M., & Trachsel, M. (2010, October). *Voice as intersection between music and language: The writing component of the Oakdale Prison Community Choir.* Paper presented at the *International Consortium for Research on Equity in Music Education,* Madison, WI.

Freire, P. (1970). *Pedagogy of the oppressed* (M. B. Ramos, Trans.). New York: Continuum.

Green, L. (2014). *Hear, listen, play! How to free your students' aural, improvisation, and performance skills.* New York: Oxford University Press.

Gromko, J. E., & Cohen, M. L. (2011). Choir in prison: The relationship of psychological needs to perceptions of meaning in music. In P. Madura (Ed.), *Advances in social psychology and music education research* (pp. 107–114). London: SEMPRE (Society for Education, Music, and Psychology Research).

Harris, M. K. (2006). Transformative justice: The transformation of restorative justice. In D. Sullivan & L. Tifft (Eds.), *Handbook of restorative justice* (pp. 555–566). New York: Routledge.

hooks, b. (1994). *Teaching to transgress: Education as the practice of freedom.* New York: Routledge.

Hopkins, B. (2004). *Just schools: A whole school approach to restorative justice.* Philadelphia, PA: Jessica Kingsley.

Ladson-Billings, G. J. (2005a). *Beyond the big house: African American educators on teacher education*. New York: Teachers College Press.

Ladson-Billings, G. J. (2005b). Is the team all right? Diversity and teacher education. *Journal of Teacher Education, 56*(3), 229–234.

Ladson-Billings, G. J. (2001). *Crossing over to Canaan: The journey of new teachers in diverse classrooms*. San Francisco, CA: Jossey Bass.

Meiners, E. (2007). *Right to be hostile: Schools, prisons, and the making of public enemies*. New York: Routledge.

Mezirow, J. (1997). Transformative learning: Theory into practice. *New Directions for Adult and Continuing Education, 74*, 5–12.

Morris, R. (2000). *Stories of transformative justice*. Toronto: Canadian Scholars Press.

Morrison, B. (2005). Restorative justice in schools. In E. Elliott & R. M. Gordon (Eds.). *New directions in restorative justice: Issues, practice, evaluation* (pp. 26–52). Portland, OR: Willan.

Noddings, N. (2003). *Happiness and education*. Cambridge: Cambridge University Press.

O'Neill, S. (2012). Becoming a music learner: Toward a theory of transformative music engagement. In G. E. McPherson & G. Welch (Eds.), *The Oxford handbook of music education* (Vol. 1, pp. 163–186). New York: Oxford University Press.

O'Neill, S. (2006). Positive youth musical engagement. In G. E. McPherson (Ed.), *The child as musician: A handbook of musical development* (pp. 461–474). New York: Oxford University Press.

Oshinksy, J. (2008). *Return to child: Music for people's guide to improvising music and authentic group leadership*. Goshen, CT: Music for People.

Rogers, C. (1961). *On becoming a person*. Boston: Houghton Mifflin.

Rugge, T., & Cormier, R. (2005). Restorative justice in cases of serious crime: An evaluation. In E. Elliott & R. Gordon (Eds.), *New directions in restorative justice: Issues, practice, evaluation* (pp. 266–277). Collumpton, UK: Willan.

Schiff, A., Von Hirsch, A., & Roberts, J. (2004). *Restorative justice and criminal justice: Competing or reconcilable paradigms*. Oxford, UK: Hart.

Sharkey, J. D., & Fenning, P. A. (2012). Rationale for designing school contexts in support of proactive discipline. *Journal of School Violence, 11*(2), 95–104. doi: 10.1080/15388220.2012.64 6641.

Small, C. (1998). *Musicking: The meanings of performing and listening*. Hanover, NH: Wesleyan University Press of New England.

Strong, K., & Ness, D. (2010). *Restoring justice: An introduction to restorative justice* (4th ed.). New Providence, NJ: Matthew Bender.

Vanfraechem, I. (2005). Evaluating conferencing for serious juvenile offenders. In E. Elliott & R. M. Gordon (Eds.), *New directions in restorative justice: Issues, practice, evaluation* (pp. 278–295). Portland, OR: Willan.

Zehr, H. (2005). Evaluation and restorative justice principles. In E. Elliott & R. M. Gordon (Eds.), *New directions in restorative justice: Issues, practice, evaluation* (pp. 296–303). Portland, OR: Willan.

Zehr, H. (2002). *The little book of restorative justice*. Intercourse, PA: Good Books.

CHAPTER 36

....

RELATIONSHIP, RESCUE, AND CULTURE

How El Sistema Might Work

....

ERIC SHIEH

GIVING a keynote at the 2012 El Sistema symposium in New York City's Carnegie Hall, the conductor and education administrator Leon Botstein effectively captured the excitement surrounding El Sistema's growth with two claims that electrified an audience of music educators, classical musicians, and classical music patrons. "There are no comparable examples of the use of music as a social activity," he declared, "which at the same time renders the music persuasive." First, then, was the claim that El Sistema had produced, on an unprecedented scale, an application for music education in social change; and second, that its efficacy was tied to musical quality, defined by Botstein as "great music and great performance and very high standards" (para. 1).

The hope that music might matter in this regard, and that all the trouble music educators undergo to ensure that students play with great technical skill might also matter, certainly touched some of the most cherished dreams of those in the audience. To that dream, Botstein (2012) added a third rousing claim: "The traditions of orchestral and choral music," he proclaimed—"that they are somehow the result of a privileged, aristocratic, white, European, male community . . . that they were a thing of the past, a historical artifact that would atrophy, turns out to be wrong" (para. 1).

El Sistema's successes have been enormously captivating. In recent years, Venezuela's program (officially named the Fundación Musical Simón Bolívar) has roared onto the international music scene, offering a rare, large-scale example of the explicit participation of music education in social policy. Funded publicly as an anti-poverty initiative and realized through the creation of almost 300 free music education centers (called *núcleos*) across the country, its brand has become associated abroad with the social and economic advancement of the country's poor. That its musical medium is primarily orchestral and choral, transplanted to the neighborhoods of the Latin American poor and manifested in high-achieving performing ensembles, has only fueled growing international interest. Since 2010, El Sistema has inspired over 100 programs across the globe,[1] addressing not simply issues of poverty but also a variety of individual developmental aims, from greater executive functioning and cognitive skills to self-efficacy and self-esteem.[2]

At the same time, the questions inherent in Botstein's claims, and the claims of many of El Sistema's adherents, are difficult to overlook. How, specifically, do the music and music education in its programs function as social intervention? What precisely constitutes "great music" and "very high standards," and what roles do they play? And, recognizing the sizable literature questioning the large-ensemble tradition as an ideal paradigm for education (e.g., Bartel, 2004; Kratus, 2007), not to mention the hubris in denying its "privileged, aristocratic, white, European, male" history—how exactly does this musical tradition live in Venezuela? This is not to deny El Sistema's achievements, but rather to suggest that "[t]here are effects—both intentional and unintentional—that require consideration of how something partially, contradictorily, and incompletely works" (Britzman, 1991, p. 227). The fact is that much of El Sistema's mechanics, even to its adherents, remains a mystery. One of its sharpest critics has gone so far as to call it "voodoo" (Toronyi-Lalic, 2012), and in a notable response, one of its strongest advocates has declared, "*Sistema* may be voodoo, but it works" (Govias, 2012, para. 5).

This chapter examines El Sistema as a social program, with implications for its growing role in social policy. In doing so, it references the relatively small (but growing) body of English-language research and also relies on personal experiences and interviews I conducted while on a Fund for Teachers fellowship in Caracas in 2012, and also as a participant in the global network of Sistema-inspired program builders. It is important to recognize, however, the diversity of El Sistema's *núcleos*: interpretations of its practices are incomplete and often contradictory. Though this chapter details several of El Sistema's characteristics, focusing almost exclusively on its Venezuelan program,[3] it does not attempt a comprehensive description of the numerous sites or the variety of structures that have emerged as part of the system. Rather, my purpose here is to explore particular characteristics that appear central to El Sistema's work as a social program, namely: its decentralization and potential capacity to serve as a responsive institution, its socioeconomic infrastructure and the discourse around creating a separate world for participants, and its complex engagements with classical music.

EL SISTEMA AS RELATIONSHIP

"This is like a home."
"It's like being in a family."
"All my friends come from here."

> Students from the Montalban *núcleo* in Caracas (personal
> communication, July 12, 2012)

When I asked students across a variety of age groups and *núcleos* to describe their experiences with El Sistema, few missed a beat before comparing it to being part of a family or close group of friends. Tricia Tunstall (2012), author of El Sistema's first book-length history, notes similar responses. "The best and closest friends in my life," she quotes a student, "are not my friends from high school or my friends from college. They are my friends from my *núcleo*" (p. 169).

This is easily one of the most salient features of El Sistema's educational spaces—a sense of care, bordering at times on the familial. My first impression when I walked into the classrooms of the program's flagship *núcleo* in the Montalban neighborhood of Caracas was of an educational space in which students were joyful and well cared for. The courtyard bustled with younger students chasing each other at play, older students chatting excitedly, and administrators and teachers exchanging hugs with students as they entered and left the building. Teachers in El Sistema regularly contrast the joyful, slightly chaotic spaces of the *núcleos* to the often poorly administered public schools that some of the students manage to attend (Perdomo, 2011). Certainly, they stand out compared to many schools in similarly impoverished areas of the United States, characterized by a rigidity and emphasis on control (Kozol, 2005).

When asked, many El Sistema teachers attribute the sense of family to the frequency of instruction, which consists of two to four hours a day, up to six days a week, in most *núcleos*. One teacher explained, "the teachers see the students so much they know all these students' stories" (personal communication, July 12, 2012). Another described her role as that of a friend and a mentor to students. This characteristic has often been cited as a hallmark of the program: "The degree of contact . . . plays a critical role in creating the essential environmental ethos of the program: that of fun and relaxed music-making," notes Govias (2011). "Relationships are forged and reinforced through long-term shared experiences" (p. 22).

As a consequence of such relationships, *núcleos* have developed a wide range of wraparound services for students and parents. For example, many of the larger *núcleos* in Caracas provide counseling, legal, and medical services. Those in dangerous areas have arranged transportation. In several *núcleos*, meals and clothing are provided alongside classes (Jekel, 2011; Kessler, 2012). Recounting some of the services his *núcleo* has provided, including paying for the hospital bills of parents, one administrator captures the spirit of the *núcleo* this way: "Sometimes you save a child by giving him a violin. Sometimes you save a child by saving his mother" (personal communication, July 12, 2012).

It may be odd to begin speaking of a program known primarily for its musical achievements in terms of medical care, but one framework for social justice begins with such acts of caring. Building on Nel Noddings's (1984) articulation of an "ethic of care" that is receptive to and responds to student needs, I have suggested elsewhere that it may be precisely this receptive response that constitutes an engagement with social justice (Allsup & Shieh, 2012). The decision to care, the act of engagement with diverse others, opens the possibility for a concern that reaches into a larger public realm while remaining grounded in contextual, relational understandings (see Noddings, 2002, pp. 21–22).

To what degree, then, might the care that saturates El Sistema's spaces approach such an engagement?

In this regard, one of El Sistema's strongest assets is its commitment to opening free music centers available to all, many of which are located in or adjacent to some of the country's most disenfranchised communities. Because these spaces are tied to government policy and funding, there is potential in the structure for local responses to have larger policy impacts. It is also important to note that, despite its reputation for serving the country's poor, El Sistema serves an estimated 10 to 30 percent of students from middle- and upper-class households (Tunstall, 2012, p. 36). Under such conditions, the possibility for engagement across differences and the civic capacity to address a variety of needs are increased.

El Sistema's decentralization is also key to its responsiveness: *núcleos* look and operate very differently, from a Barquisimeto *núcleo* housed in a conservatory to a La Negra *módulo* (a *núcleo* subsidiary) where classes are held in the streets and sometimes joined by neighborhood adults (Jekel, 2011). While El Sistema reportedly has a national curriculum (Tunstall, 2012, p. 176), most teachers I spoke with know it only as a list of recommended orchestral repertoire (personal communication, July 9, 2012); teachers and *núcleo* directors possess a large degree of autonomy in terms of curricular choices. And though many visitors to El Sistema are quick to generalize characteristics they believe are central to an "El Sistema pedagogy," a growing number find it more accurate to describe the absence of such characteristics when looking from *núcleo* to *núcleo*.[4] Tunstall (2012) frames much of the operation of El Sistema using a description from José Antonio Abreu, El Sistema's founder, that it is a *"ser, no ser todavia"*— "being, not yet being," which she describes as a unity of purpose, with implications for flexibility (pp. 173–175). The unity of purpose is, quite simply, the mission to address poverty through music education. The practice and theory may differ from place to place. In this way, El Sistema might be considered an example of place-centered education—one that is able to empower teachers and communities to innovate practices and policy, while simultaneously responding to the needs of particular communities (Schmidt, 2012).

But El Sistema's decentralized spaces are not completely devoid of common practices. There is, at some level, an implicit pedagogy that saturates El Sistema, driven by its foundational commitment to the large ensemble as its musical medium. To what degree does this narrow musical focus limit the capacity for pedagogical response? Certainly justification for the use of this medium as a response exists, and various advocates within and outside El Sistema will point to the way it challenges students to master a lifelong craft, constructs a shared sense of life as a collective, provides an opportunity to bring students together across differences, or engenders participation in a tradition that has a global reputation. But it is clear in El Sistema's history that the orchestra came first—and not in response to a particular need, though it has been adapted to varied ends (Creech et al., 2013, p. 40). Uy (2012) has noted what he calls an overemphasis on "the building of this orchestral machine" that seems at odds with the work of "creating a vibrant community" (p. 18). His particular concern is in the way orchestral playing permits increasing student-to-teacher ratios. Large-ensemble play-ing is not known, after all, for its reciprocal negotiation of musical practice between student and teacher, or student and student.

Another major consideration when examining El Sistema's capacity to function as a responsive institution is its so-called political "neutrality"—the (very much political) refusal of its leaders and participants to take stances critical of the reigning political regime (Waken, 2012). While this positioning has certainly aided its growth and funding through 10 different government administrations, it is worth asking whether this has limited its ability to advocate for the communities it serves, and has limited the horizons—the *not yet being*—of the work it aims to do. While meeting with community activists in one of Caracas's largest *barrios*,[5] I hear criticism of El Sistema's lack of a larger social vision. Its *núcleos* contrast sharply with other, albeit less well-funded, education programs that leverage artistic engagements toward developing critical and public voices for students.[6] If a core function of its work as a social program might be its responsiveness and capacity to advocate for low-income communities, as suggested here, its avenues for sociopolitical engagement require greater consideration.

El Sistema as Rescue

"The fundamental mission of El Sistema is not only to help children but often, literally, to rescue them."

(Tunstall, 2012, p. xii)

"People don't understand why I come back to Venezuela. I tell them I'm not coming back to Venezuela—I'm coming to the bubble of El Sistema."
Ximena Borges, Venezuelan concert soprano

(personal communication, July 8, 2012)

I was surprised in my visit to El Sistema by the number of teachers and administra-tors who regularly described their work as a kind of "rescue." When asked to elabo-rate, phrases like "an escape" or "a parallel world" were quick to surface, pointing to a belief that El Sistema removes children from a place of lack and brings them to a bet-ter one. It is language that Venezuelan conductor and El Sistema alumnus Gustavo Dudamel invokes in the documentary film *Tocar y Luchar* when he insists that he has "two homes: Venezuela and El Sistema" (Lanz, Lopez-Duran, & Arvelo, 2006). And perhaps most provocatively, alumnus Ximena Borges, who splits her time as a concert soprano between Caracas and New York City, calls El Sistema a "bubble." These descrip-tions have also found their way abroad. For example, Juan Antonio Cuellar, the director of Colombia's Sistema-inspired Batuta program, observes that "our vision [is] reaching and rescuing children through orchestral involvement" (quoted in Booth & Tunstall,

2011, A Key Priority section). Though in some ways El Sistema may lack a common pedagogy, it certainly possesses a common discourse.

It is not difficult to see how these ideas of rescue and parallel worlds live in practice. El Sistema functions not only as a collection of *núcleos* that dominate large periods of students' days, but also as a complex of educational, musical, and economic investments that might support participants for their entire lives. With El Sistema, students have access to a startling array of experiences that separate them from their non–El Sistema peers—experiences that may include traveling to see concerts, giving concerts across cities and countries, and interacting with peers from different socioeconomic backgrounds on an everyday basis. Students may even be presented with opportunities to attend a music conservatory, depending on their level of achievement, though this practice is uneven across the country. As one teacher at the Los Chorros *núcleo* emphasized, "El Sistema gives kids a clear mind—an open mind to see a path," referring to the opportunities that students discover (personal communication, July 18, 2012). In its young prisons programs, El Sistema has labored hard to create rehearsal facilities separate from the prison's operations and free of guards. Here, incarcerated adults may rehearse regularly for eight hours a day. "We make them forget they are in prison," said one of the teachers in Merida's CPRA prison *núcleo*. "Inmates say it is like being in another world" (personal communication, July 24, 2012).

As a result of El Sistema's rapid growth, students both in and out of prisons have the possibility of remaining in that world. The burgeoning classical music scene in the country supports increasing numbers of professional musicians, and El Sistema itself demands an exploding number of music teachers and *núcleo* administrators, not to mention luthiers and social service providers. "The system," an El Sistema conductor observes, "buys everything and supports everything" (personal communication, July 9, 2012). Tunstall (2012) notes the popular perception that "[e]very musician in Venezuela is connected somehow to the Sistema" (p. 183). Its reach as an economic vehicle is astonishing.

The language of rescue, then, refers most nearly to the breadth of El Sistema's socioeconomic bubble and its ability to function quite literally by moving children from one context to another, one family to another. In doing so, it sets a high bar for any program that has sought to provide economic opportunity for youth in regions marked by insecurity and economic instability, as is the case with many schools in high-need areas. But the discourse of rescue raises several challenging questions. To what extent do El Sistema's structures devalue the communities of Venezuela's poor in the creation of a parallel world, and in doing so inadvertently reduce student agency? And how does a program with claims to social change operate by creating that world, with seemingly no theory of action for working with existing communities or social structures? There is a very real concern that El Sistema, oriented to a large extent toward launching students into careers in music, has created a parallel world in which musical success and economic sufficiency are more or less equated, the "orchestral machine" drives on, and larger goals of societal transformation are left outside its bubble.

There is evidence for this concern in the answers that many of El Sistema's music teachers give when asked about community changes the program brings or what students take away with them. Though many teachers are eager to name successful students with careers in music, and El Sistema's administration is quick to publicize extraordinary musical achievements, there is a startling aporia that many researchers have observed regarding what happens to students who do not pursue careers in music (e.g., Borchert, 2012, pp. 55–57). When I asked, teachers responded vaguely that some students have become doctors and lawyers. Interestingly, more than a few teachers, both in Venezuela and in El Sistema–inspired programs abroad, quote Abreu as saying, "material poverty can be defeated by spiritual wealth." And when one of the teachers in the prison program was asked to articulate what exactly the music education is doing for the inmates, he replied seriously, "When you're studying, something changes—something has to change" (personal communication, July 24, 2012). All of these responses, while true in some sense, seem inadequate for a program that considers itself to be working for social change.

It is worth observing that outside Venezuela, non-musical aims generally exist more formally in Sistema-inspired programs. The large Youth Orchestra Los Angeles (YOLA) program associated with Gustavo Dudamel, for example, articulates an academic focus and provides tutoring.[7] Erik Holmgren, the former director of the Abreu Fellows program, which prepares a cohort each year to start Sistema-inspired programs in the United States, urges fellows to "identify a need in the community for a particular program, and build a program for that need." He notes that "if we were just building youth orchestras, it would be less compelling" (personal communication, September 5, 2013). It is a key distinction of El Sistema, where the orchestras—and the livelihood they promise—carry their own seeming end. It is also a cultural distinction. In Venezuela, no doubt in part because of El Sistema, social change can more easily be spoken of in terms of cultural and spiritual gains, with meaning and value that do not immediately demand instrumental justification.

A related question to that of what individuals gain from participation is whether El Sistema considers its impacts not simply on individual participants, but also on students' outside neighborhoods and communities. El Sistema's community outreach or participation is generally limited. Uy (2012) describes the presence of some self-run parent groups that typically hold fundraising events (p. 16), and Tunstall (2012) notes that more commonly *núcleos* may hold "concerts in public squares, in hospitals, in neighborhoods" (p. 204). A director of one of the system's largest *núcleos* suggests to me that it is not his *núcleo's* place to address larger social issues. The system, he says, is about "reforming individuals": "It is our grain of sand. It hasn't changed in 40 years" (personal communication, July 18, 2012). Certainly, for El Sistema, which has served an estimated 1 to 2 percent of the current youth population in Venezuela, ages 3–30, it is a large grain of sand and one that no doubt carries broad consequences. Another *núcleo* director makes the link this way when speaking of the individuals whose lives are transformed: "it is a shot into society, a vaccine that both prevents and cures social problems" (quoted in Uy, 2012, p. 17). Is this viable strategy?

This depends on the ways in which El Sistema's bubble is not fully enclosed—the ways in which its "rescue" is, in fact, incomplete. What happens at the end of the day, when students and teachers return home from their *núcleos*—do they have the capacity to "cure social problems"? What happens when money earned within the bubble is spent outside the bubble? Or when youth identities, which overstep the *núcleo's* cultural constrictions, travel both ways and participate in the construction of the *núcleo* and students' outside communities? To the degree that caring requires larger engagements, how might youth and teachers negotiate the act of border crossing, at its best a transgressive and transformative act, negotiated with agency? How might El Sistema attend to these acts in ways that avoid simply assuming some positive value to musical participation or performances in neighborhoods? The answers to these questions may be key for the success of programs that wish to adopt El Sistema's practices of focusing on individuals while maintaining aspirations for social change.

El Sistema as Culture

> "Culture for the poor must never be a poor culture. It must be the most excellent culture."
>
> (José Antonio Abreu)

Justifying El Sistema's prominent classical music practices in language similar to Botstein's "great music and great performance and very high standards," Abreu's statement raises concerns regarding the assumptions underlying the role that classical music plays in the program's cultural practice. Quoting a television interview with Abreu, Baker (2012) suggests that there can be little doubt that El Sistema grew out of a belief that European high art serves as an abstract civilizing tool for a Latin American country. In it, Abreu declares:

> El Sistema breaks the vicious circle [of poverty] because a child with a violin starts to become spiritually rich: the CD he listens to, the book he reads, he sees words in German, the music opens doors to intellectual knowledge and then everything begins.... [When] he is playing Mozart, Haydn, he watches an opera: this child no longer accepts his poverty, he aspires to leave it behind and ends up defeating it. (para. 9)

The idea that "everything begins" with exposure to Western European cultural practices, and that this leads to non-acceptance of poverty—as if it were a cultural choice—is grotesque. Blaming poverty on the child further excuses El Sistema from ever having to engage with Venezuela's larger sociopolitical contexts. Noddings (1999) cautions that

> [a]s I convert what I have received from the other into a problem, something to be solved, I move away from the other. I clean up his reality . . moving rapidly away

from the cared-for into a domain of objective and impersonal problems upon which
I impose whatever structure satisfies it. (p. 45)

If that structure is fixed (e.g., orchestral musicianship, middle-class values), then reciprocity is diminished and the space for a kind of social justice that demands agency for
students to enact larger social change is closed. hooks (1990) interprets this idea powerfully with attention to race, charging that, "racism has created an aesthetic that wounds
us, a way of thinking about beauty that hurts" (p. 113). There is a very real danger, growing out of colonial policies, of learning a beauty that may not permit room for oneself, to
inhabiting a desire that eclipses agency.

Investigating a charge of colonialism in El Sistema is no easy task. Certainly restricting engagement with non-native cultural practices is no solution any educator would
sanction; the question is the shape of the engagement. As educator and cultural theorist Gayatri Spivak (2012) suggests in relation to her work teaching the Western literary
canon in India, "You cannot be against globalization. You can only work collectively
and persistently to turn it into strategy-driven rather than crisis-driven globalization"
(pp. 104–105). The strategy and the practice of the music matter, not simply its content.
Despite El Sistema's origin in colonizing assumptions, I am interested in how it might
display evidence of a kind of strategy capable of mitigating deficit understandings of its
participants.

It will be useful here to detail a handful of musical engagements I have encountered
while visiting El Sistema. Many will be familiar to classically trained music educators,
including an orchestra of some hundred 14-year-olds rehearsing Shostakovich's *Fifth
Symphony*, the faces of the cello section intense and drawn while playing the symphony's
opening cry, a teacher telling me about his love for Baroque music, and how he subsequently followed that passion to the United Kingdom to study period playing, and a
young bassist, eight or nine years old, telling me how she switched to the bass that year
because she loved the sound of it. Some engagements may feel less familiar, such as the
musicians at a *núcleo* performance striking up a seemingly impromptu salsa and leading the audience in a dance-along as they make their way off stage, performances of
Venezuelan repertoire that include a quattro (a strummed Venezuelan folk instrument)
section in the orchestra behind the cellos, and a live performance of Bernstein's *Mambo*
through which the musicians shout and dance.

I share these stories, echoed hundred-fold in the documentaries on El Sistema, to
make two claims; first, that there is a very real love for the music by participants that
is difficult to dismiss simply as disempowering or false, and second, that something is
happening here that is not altogether an induction into a reified understanding of classical music. Upon closer inspection, a musical practice that is both quintessentially classical music and not quite classical music can be seen in El Sistema. It is a practice that
couples the subjectivities of its participants and the negotiations of El Sistema's institutions, understood at some level as social interventions, with classical forms—all under
the banner of classical music. Potentially, it invokes the category of classical music and
opens it to contestation. And while the examples above may seem superficial, I suggest

that there is nothing superficial about the subjectivities of several million musicians in Venezuela whose identifications skew differently from those of their European counterparts. These subjectivities must always overstep the music they play, and the musical tradition they claim must accommodate. "*El Sistema* is already transforming traditional musical archetypes," declares Venezuelan music anthropologist Ludim Pedroza (2011), "by bringing the fusion of folk, popular and academic elements into global consciousness, and by challenging the contemplative approach to traditional classical performance" (p. 9). Not induction, then, but at its best a kind of ownership that brings a power in reimagining, in reinterpreting a musical tradition with elite associations. The students own the music in a way that reflects some capacity to transform the boundaries of the practice, and in doing so claim some agency (Allsup, Westerlund, & Shieh, 2012).

On the other hand, Pedroza's declaration may be too optimistic. While it is undeniable that musical traditions do not exist as closed entities, the truth is that agency is often hard-won, and for many individuals or in the day-to-day work of education, agency is not always found. To apply Butler's (1993) celebrated formulation of gender to musical cultures, the fact that participants re-create culture in their participation does not acknowledge that re-creation is almost always reinscription. Traditions and culture systems are powerful and tend to replicate themselves upon the bodies of their participants (p. 107). The presence of quattros in an orchestra is no sure sign that agency is at work or will continue to be at work for all participants, and indeed may better symbolize the subjugation of folk musics under the orchestral regime (Baker, 2012). At this time, the introduction of popular elements into the curriculum remains relatively new and scattered; it does not carry the same capital as the classical tradition within the organization. Moreover, evidence that the global classical music tradition has transformed since El Sistema's celebrated emergence on the international scene is difficult to find.

At the individual level of participants, these negotiations become even more fraught. The love for classical music that the students display is mixed up in a love for the space and the opportunities it provides, in a pride over craft, in relationships with teachers and other students. Psychologists Hargreaves, Miell, and MacDonald (2002) have observed that in seeking out music, adolescents have a stake in "identification with groups of people who have a positive image" (p. 9). And Venezuelan researcher Veronica Zubillaga (2007) has documented the importance among youth in Caracas's *barrios* of locating identifications that provide for respect in the face of a socioeconomic system that denies many both social mobility and social connection. Students in El Sistema identify with classical music in part because of its associations with non-musical aspects of El Sistema, and I would argue that El Sistema simultaneously leverages the elitism and internationalism of the music—its wealth and Whiteness—to work toward social change.

This is in some way a strategy. Some educators and policymakers, Abreu included, do name the music's history as an asset as they attempt to grapple with a devastating situation of poverty and national insecurity. But this use seems more akin to crisis-driven, not strategy-driven, globalization—practices that are incidental rather than interrogated. We cannot rely on the sheer numbers of Venezuelan participants to engender an incidental agency. Where is the work, to use Spivak's words, to "collectively and persistently" (pp. 104–105) engage in the movement toward strategy, toward decolonization or cultural transformation?

I do not believe this work means radically re-envisioning musical practices. El Sistema is already wrestling with these questions in emerging work with folk and popular musics, in creative engagements with non-Western instruments, and a healthy debate among musicians who call for—among other things—composing in the curriculum (Mendoza, 2010). This work must also include greater engagement with the musics' histories and contexts, empowering students to recognize, respond to, and interact with a variety of musical traditions. Most of all, it involves responding to individual students and their identities with both care and critique—with a determination that they not be rescued so much as empowered. To the degree that Simon Rattle's resounding declaration in the documentary film *Tocar y Luchar* that El Sistema is "the future of classical music" is true (Lanz, Lopez-Duran, & Arvelo, 2006), and that ownership is felt by its participants, there is indeed hope for its musical practices to prove enabling.

Conclusion

What might El Sistema offer to social programs outside Venezuela, and to larger considerations of social policy? In the absence of salvation narratives around spiritual wealth and the difficulty of creating a vocational pipeline without massive public funding, its immediate applicability seems minimal. Yet, at its best, El Sistema can lay claim to spaces of care, and opportunities for that care to be magnified with access to wide-ranging resources. It can lead to greater horizons and new worlds for participants, and the capacity to negotiate multiple social spaces through acts of border-crossing. It can promise participation in a global music tradition and the power to transform it, and in doing so engender a sense of human agency in the midst of a complex cultural milieu. These claims are conditional and contextual, and require greater reflection and critique than El Sistema has yet engaged with. They are also open-ended, human investments—depending on committed, innovative educators and leaders in a policy realm often driven by concrete, dispassionate inputs and outputs. Yet these promises are as extraordinary as they are challenging, and few investments seem more worthy of our resources.

El Sistema also presents a challenge to music educators globally. Amidst a profession exhausted by instrumental justifications that it neither cares about nor pays attention to (Benedict & Schmidt, 2011), El Sistema *has* attempted to shape itself as a program for social change. Its structures, practices, and discourses are designed for broad consequences, and it challenges its communities to attend to those practices and consequences. It challenges them not simply to make music, but "to play and to fight," a reference to El Sistema's motto, *tocar y luchar*. Anne Fitzgibbon, founder of the Sistema-inspired Harmony Program in New York City, rightly asks, "What is the goal?

Is it attendance? Is it college? Is it reading scores? Not really" (personal communication, September 5, 2013). While instrumental goals such as these do serve a purpose, the space for music education in social change may very well be broader and bolder. El Sistema offers an opening for inquiry for music educators. The social question is not foreclosed or reduced. It forces a turn from the music in music education to the education, understood as ethical engagement (Bowman, 2002). The profession needs more music programs that will attend to the socioeconomic lives of their students, of all students. It is a start.

It goes without saying, however, that if El Sistema and the programs it has inspired are to grow and have lasting impacts, the turn toward attending to social needs can have no end. I remain wary of so many music programs, and the rush of newly minted Sistema-inspired programs, that appear under-interrogated in a global landscape where movements for social justice and social change may be easily co-opted. El Sistema's massive growth in Venezuela and its use for political propaganda make me worry about its ability to function critically and politically in ways that will benefit its communities. Yet the work of social justice is a process of negotiation, of responding in bolder and better ways to particular people and contexts as we better understand them. El Sistema itself continues to evolve, and to the degree that all of these programs continue to respond as living practices—in their strategies, in their music, in their relationships—they may indeed grow as a force for valuable social and, simultaneously, musical transformation.

ACKNOWLEDGMENTS

The research on Venezuela's El Sistema was funded by a fellowship from the Fund for Teachers program. I am also indebted to scores of teachers, admininstrators, parents, and students who generously gave me their time by sharing experiences and coordinating my visits, in particular: Rodrigo Guerrero, Lenin Mora, and Zobeya Márquez at El Sistema, and Erik Holmgren at the Abreu Fellows Program. I am grateful to two fellow travelers, Maria-José Bermeo at Teachers College, Columbia University, in New York, and Irene Caselli with the BBC News in Caracas, whose own observations, conversations, and translations deepened this work. Finally, thanks to Paul Woodford, Erik Holmgren, and an anonymous reviewer for comments on an early draft.

NOTES

1. For partial listings of Sistema-inspired programs, see Creech et al. (2013), pp. 133–203, http://elsistemausa.org, http://jonathangovias.com/2012/02/16/el-sistema-in-canada-2012-update/, and Hallam (2012), p. 105.
2. See http://tuneupphilly.wordpress.com/ and http://www.bsomusic.org/main.taf?p=9,5,1.

3. Throughout this chapter I refer to "El Sistema" only in reference to the Venezuelan program, using "Sistema-inspired" for programs outside Venezuela.

4. In a recent literature review of the research on El Sistema, Creech et al. (2013) find only broad commonalities such as interpersonal relationships, a nurturing approach, and a safe learning environment across descriptions of pedagogy (pp. 76–79). Similarly, a synthesis of "principles" of El Sistema from a dozen researchers resulted in several dozen such tenets (pp. 41–44), suggesting that their conclusions are heavily shaped by their own interests. Thus, while continuities in practice or principle may be found, I argue that their assumption hinders observation of some of El Sistema's more salient features.

5. The use of the word *barrio* differs from place to place. In Venezuela it is used to describe a site of "unplanned growth in a situation of relative lacking" (Zubillaga, 2007), and can be loosely translated as a slum.

6. One dramatic contrast is the community organization and after-school education space Tiuna El Fuerte in Caracas, where, in the words of one of its directors, "youth energy and resistance can be politicized and made constructive... where discourse can be created" (personal communication, July 25, 2012). Interestingly, it is also the site of a failed orchestra program.

7. http://www.laphil.com/education/yola.

References

Allsup, R., & Shieh, E. (2012). Social justice and music education: The call for a public pedagogy. *Music Educators Journal, 98*(4), 47–51.

Allsup, R., Westerlund, H., & Shieh, E. (2012). Youth culture and secondary education. In G. McPherson & G. Welch (Eds.), *The Oxford handbook of music education*. (pp. 460–475). London: Oxford University Press.

Baker, G. (2012). Scam, voodoo, or the future of music? The El Sistema debate [Blog post]. http://geoffbakermusic.wordpress.com/el-sistema-the-system/el-sistema-blog/scam-voodoo-or-the-future-of-music-the-el-sistema-debate/.

Bartel, L. (Ed.) (2004). *Questioning the music education paradigm*. Waterloo, ON: Canadian Music Educators Association.

Benedict, C., & Schmidt, P. (2011). The politics of not knowing: The disappearing act of an education in music. *Journal of Curriculum Theorizing, 27*(3), 134–148.

Bernstein, J., & Tunstall, T. (2013). Can El Sistema thrive in the U.S. and beyond? *Musical America*. http://www.musicalamerica.com/features/?fid=189&fyear=2013.

Booth, E., & Tunstall, T. (2011). An inside look at Colombia's "Sistema." *Createquity*. http://createquity.com/2011/09/an-inside-look-at-colombias-sistema/.

Borchert, G. (2012). *Sistema Scotland: A critical inquiry into the implementation of the el Sistema model in Raploch*. Unpublished master's thesis, University of Glasgow. Retrieved from http://theses.gla.ac.uk/4004/.

Botstein, L. (2012, December). *Keynote lecture*. Paper presented to El Sistema Discovery Day at Carnegie Hall, New York. Retrieved from http://www.take-a-stand.org/assets/Uploads/2-Botstein-Discovery-Day-Transcript-of-Speech-Dec-8-20125.pdf.

Bowman, W. (2002). Educating musically. In R. Colwell & C. Richardson (Eds.), *The new handbook of research on music teaching and learning: A project of the Music Educators National Conference* (pp. 63–84). New York: Oxford University Press.

Britzman, D. (1991). *Practice makes practice: A critical study of learning to teach.* Albany: State University of New York Press.

Butler, J. (1993). *Bodies that matter: On the discursive limits of "sex."* New York: Routledge.

Creech, A., González-Moreno, P., Lorenzino, L., & Waitman, G. (2013). *El Sistema and sistema-inspired programmes: A literature review of research, evaluation, and critical debates.* San Diego, CA: Sistema Global.

Govias, J. (2011). The five fundamentals of El Sistema. *Canadian Music Educator, 53*(1), 21–23.

Govias, J. (2012). In (partial) defense of a Sistema hater [Blog post]. Retrieved from http://jonathangovias.com/2012/07/19/in-partial-defense-of-a-sistema-hater/.

Hallam, R. (2012). Sistema: Where academic, educational, musical, personal and social development all meet. In C. Harrison & S. Hennessy (Eds.), *International perspectives on music education.* (pp. 104–115). Matlock, Derbyshire, UK: National Association of Music Educators.

Hargreaves, D., Miell, D., & MacDonald, R. (2002). What are musical identities, and why are they important? In R. MacDonald, D. Hargreaves, & D. Miell (Eds.), *Musical identities* (pp. 1–20). Oxford: Oxford University Press.

hooks, b. (1990). *Yearning: Race, gender, and cultural politics.* Boston: South End Press.

Jekel, L. (2011). Venezuela: Estado Guárico [Blog post]. Retrieved from http://laurajekel.blogspot.com/2011/05/venezuela-estado-guaric.html.

Kessler, J. (2012). An El Sistema lesson: Music can grow anywhere [Blog post]. Retrieved from http://telegraphcable.blogspot.com/2012/03/el-sistema-lesson-music-can-grow.html.

Kozol, J. (2005). *Shame of the nation: The restoration of apartheid schooling in America.* New York: Random House.

Kratus, J. (2007). Music education at the tipping point. *Music Educators Journal, 94*(2), 42–48.

Lanz, I., & Lopez-Duran, N. (Producers), & Arvelo, A. (Director). (2006). *Tocar y luchar* [Film]. Los Angeles, CA: Cinevolve Studios.

Mendoza, E. (2010). *La composición en Venezuela: ¿Profesión en peligro de extinción? Un análisis de contradicciones.* [*Composition in Venezuela: A profession in danger of extinction? An analysis of contradictions.*]. Paper presented to III Congreso de Compositores in Caracas, Venezuela. Retrieved from http://prof.usb.ve/emendoza/emilioweb/escritos_tema/escritos_frame.html.

Noddings, N. (1984). An ethic of caring and its implications for instructional arrangements. In L. Stone (Ed.), *The education feminism reader* (pp. 171–183). New York: Routledge.

Noddings, N. ([1981]1999). Caring. In W. Pinar (Ed.), *Contemporary curriculum discourses: Twenty years of JCT* (pp. 42–61). New York: Peter Lang.

Noddings, N. (2002). *Starting at home: Caring and social policy.* Berkeley: University of California Press.

Pedroza, L. (2011). *Save the children or save the music: Venezuela's El Sistema as syncretic aesthetic and pedagogical export.* Paper presented to the Latin American Music Center's Fiftieth Anniversary Conference "Cultural Counterpoints: Examining the Musical Interactions between the U.S. and Latin America," at Indiana University, Bloomington, IN. Retrieved from https://scholarworks.iu.edu/dspace/handle/2022/15544.

Perdomo, G. (2011). *Violencia en las escuelas.* [*Violence in schools.*] Caracas: Centro Gumilla, Universidad Católica Andrés Bello.

Schmidt, P. (2012). Music, policy and place centered education: Finding a space for adaptability. *National Society for the Study of Education, 111*(1), 51–73.

Spivak, G. (2012). *An aesthetic education in the era of globalization.* Cambridge, MA: Harvard University Press.

Toronyi-Lalic, I. (2012). Simón Bolívar Symphony Orchestra, Dudamel, Royal Festival Hall: Politics aside, the Venezuelans deliver an electrifying night of music (27 June 2012). *The Arts Desk.* Retrieved from http://www.theartsdesk.com/classical-music/simón-bol%C3%ADvar -symphony-orchestra-dudamel-royal-festival-hall.

Tunstall, T. (2012). *Changing lives: Gustavo Dudamel, El Sistema, and the transformative power of music.* New York: W. W. Norton.

Uy, M. (2012). Venezuela's national music education program *El Sistema*: Its interactions with society and its participants' engagement in practice. *Music and Arts in Action, 4*(1), 5–21.

Waken, D. (2012, February 18). Music meets Chávez politics, and critics frown. *New York Times* (p. A1). Retrieved from http://www.nytimes.com/2012/02/18/arts/music/ venezuelans-criticize-hugo-chavezs-support-of-el-sistema.html.

Zubillaga, V. (2007). Los varones y sus clamores: Los sentidos de la demanda de respeto y las lógicas de la violencia entre jóvenes de vida violenta de barrios en Caracas [Young men and their clamor: Sense of the demand for respect and logic of violence among youth living violent lives in the barrios of Caracas]. *Espacio Abierto Cuaderno Venezolano de Sociologica, 16*(3), 577–608.

CHAPTER 37

....

NEGOTIATING GENDER, POPULAR CULTURE, AND SOCIAL JUSTICE IN MUSIC EDUCATION

....

JOSEPH ABRAMO

As a music educator dedicated to social justice, I approach popular music with ambivalence. On one hand, I often find that it motivates students to become actively involved in music programs. When, as a high school instrumental teacher, I allowed students in a guitar class to choose their own repertoire and use informal music processes, such as learning by ear and peer-teaching, they invariably chose popular music. This led to an increase in student motivation and enrollment, particularly from demographics that historically did not participate in music instruction. This was, for me, a small act of democratic practice and social justice in music education; I provided a space where students "had voice," and shared their musical interests with the support of an educator who did not judge those choices (for a more in-depth discussion of this context, see Abramo [2010]).

While providing an opportunity for "student voice" was an attempt at social justice in music education, the music that students brought to class sometimes troubled me. Issues of sexism, heteronormativity, and racism were often unnoticed and sometimes celebrated by students. Some boys, for example, would ask me to help them learn songs with misogynistic, homophobic, and sexually violent lyrics. In these cases, my desire to create a socially just space, where students and I challenged sexism, heteronormativity, race, able-bodiness, classism, corporatization, and commodification conflicted with my democratic impulse to provide students with "voice" through popular music.

My ambivalence points to a tension within popular music in education. On one hand, music educators recently have *celebrated* popular music (Green, 2008; Kratus, 2007; Tobias, 2012, to name a few within a large body of research). In this celebratory strain, educators acknowledge and encourage music making previously ignored or explicitly discouraged in formal schooling. From this view, popular music gives students agency by inviting them to incorporate their interests into the classroom and allowing them to be creative in vernacular musical styles. This position has reinvigorated music education to allow for new pedagogical frameworks, the development of new skills, the implementation of technology, and a wider body of repertoire.

On the other hand, some educators, mostly outside of the discipline of music, approach popular music and culture *critically*. For critical pedagogues, popular music and culture are potentially negative influences because they often privilege heteronormativity, gender conformity, able-bodiness, and middle- and upper-class values (Apple, 2000; Daspit & Weaver, 2000; Giroux, 1994). These critical pedagogues use popular culture—toys, movies, music videos, television, and other media—to raise the consciousness of students about socially unjust practices and to confront these practices. These educational acts are socially just in the sense that they challenge privilege and power and their representation in, and reinscription through, popular culture.

This tension between the celebratory and critical strains in education arises because music education research emphasizes the performance of popular music, while critical pedagogy focuses on the reception of popular culture. But there are limitations to both of these positions. The celebratory position prevalent in music education often does not account for power within the construction of popular music. Such a position potentially assigns an untheorized, uncritical, individualist agency to the student, in which personal expression through the music is not contextualized in the historical conditions and power relations within society. Conversely, a critical pedagogy may fail if teachers adopt an overly deterministic sense of student agency. The teacher may see students as duped by media into socially unjust hierarchies and systems of oppressions. The danger of this view is in assigning little agency to students, dismissing them as oppressed victims of hegemony, unable to see how they possess the power to positively interpret popular culture for social justice or other ends.

Stuart Hall (2005) writes of this tension between popular music as a mode for self-expression and its potentially harmful commodification. Discussing popular culture in general, he sees "the popular" as "one of the sites where [a] struggle for and against a culture of the powerful is engaged. . . . It is the area of resistance and struggle" (p. 71). Popular culture either is, or was at one point, a subversive art form that criticized the status quo. To elaborate on this definition, Hall comes to this explanation of popular culture through a critique of common classifications. The first of these classifications, which he describes as "the things that are said to be 'popular' because the masses of people listen to them, buy them, read them, consume them, and enjoy them to the full" (p. 66), is what he calls the "market" or "commercial" definition of the popular. The "market" or "commercial" meaning of music, Hall explains, is "rightly associated with the manipulation and debasement of the culture of the people" (p. 66). He finds this inadequate and incomplete because it construes consumers to be "cultural dopes" (p. 66) and does not take into account how individuals think about and interact with popular culture. While there is manipulation in popular culture, a person also consumes it in individual and unique ways for his or her benefit. This tension is what Hall calls "the dialectic of cultural struggle" (p. 67), "with the alternative poles of that dialectic [being] containment/resistance" (p. 65). Audiences' interaction with popular culture is neither solely manipulative nor liberatory, but both or neither.

This delicate balance poses a challenge for educators engaged in the work of allowing personal expression through music while challenging social injustice within and through music. This chapter describes a strategy I have employed in high school and pre-service music education courses to negotiate the tension between these two approaches. Using Hall's (1980) encoding/decoding model—which provides a theory for different interpretations of cultural texts—I ask students to share their interpretations of popular culture texts, to imagine alternative interpretations, and to situate these interpretations within social contexts involving power relations and privilege. This is illustrated in the following pages through an examination of contested notions of "female empowerment" as seen and heard in Beyoncé Knowles's music video *Run the World (Girls)*. The chapter concludes with an acknowledgment of some of the limitations of this framework and approach to teaching and learning popular music, along with some practical advice for selecting age-appropriate materials and other considerations for teachers.

Polysemy and Diversity Through Dominant, Negotiated, and Oppositional Readings

Within the last several decades, there has been a shift from universal meanings of *texts* (e.g., writings, music, movies, or any other cultural artifacts) to situated interpretations within music education and the humanities in general.[1] A universalist or formalist view posits that texts derive their meanings from the construction of the works themselves. These latter meanings are not subject to localized readings or interpretations, but are instead deemed universal and revealed by an educated or cultured interpreter. As postmodernism influenced the humanities, formalism gave way to a kind of contextualism, in which texts' meanings are construed as open. A person's identity, which is influenced by the intersection of factors such as race, gender, class, and previous experience, plays an important role in shaping one's interpretations. From this perspective, texts, including music, are *polysemic*; they are open to many valid interpretations and meanings, rather than one true meaning based on the creator's intent or other definitive interpretation.

This shift toward polysemy facilitates democratic practice in education because a diversity of interpretations of a text opens up possibilities. These interpretations need not work harmoniously in a "melting pot" of ideas, but may create debate and conflict between members of an educational community. As Dewey ([1922]1957) notes, "[c]onflict is the gadfly of thought. It instigates invention. It shocks us out of sheep-like passivity, and sets us at noting and contriving" (p. 275). Competing interpretations shared in a democratic space spark reflection and lead to educational growth. As a result, from an education perspective,

> any reading of popular culture texts should reflect multiple readings that often contradict each other or act independently from each other. It means we purposively seek out those voices that do not fit our world view or our readings of popular culture texts. (Daspit & Weaver, 2000, p. xix)

While polysemy invites diversity, alone it is insufficient because, as Hall (1980) notes, "[p]olysemy must not...be confused with pluralism" (p. 134). Some interpretations become privileged in society because they receive the most attention and currency and support hegemony and so-called common sense. For example, Woody Gutherie's "This Land Is Your Land" is often understood as a form of uncritical patriotism. This interpretation is more widely propagated and more broadly assumed than Gutherie's intent for the song to serve as a populist and socialist critique of individual land rights. The patriotic version receives this privileged position because it supports good feelings of patriotism and American ideals of individualism and private property rights. Gutherie's socialist intent, conversely, is suppressed because it challenges these deeply held values and the belief that "America is the land of the free."

The differing meanings of Gutherie's song suggest that interpretations hold varying values and currencies. Because of this, Hall proposed three ways of reading a "text" to produce these differing interpretations—*dominant, oppositional,* and *negotiated*. He calls widely accepted interpretations *dominant* or *preferred meanings*. In this reading, the audience member fully embraces the text's codes and accepts the preferred reading or commonly held meaning of a text. Dominant readings "have the whole social order embedded in them as a set of meanings, practices and beliefs." They seek to "*enforce* or *prefer* one semantic domain over another" (p. 134, italics in original). Because of their ubiquity and support of the status quo, dominant readings are perceived as the intent of a text, or its "true" meaning.

While the dominant code may be the socially sanctioned interpretation of a text, audience members may have access to other frames to interpret works in ways that may be disruptive. These *oppositional readings* are employed when "a viewer perfectly understand[s] both the literal and the connotative inflection given by a discourse but chooses to decode the message in a *globally* contrary way. He or she detotalizes the message in the preferred code in order to retotalize the message within some alternative framework or reference" (pp. 137–138, italics in original). In other words, the audience member refuses the intended dominant reading by "detotalizing" or deconstructing it and then "retotalizes," or creates a new, oppositional reading. The audience member understands the dominant reading, but refuses that reading, instead opting to interpret it using alternative, subversive ways.

Finally, Hall suggests that there is a *negotiated reading*, in which the audience member's interpretation "negotiates" the dominant and oppositional readings. In a negotiated reading, the audience member might accept a dominant reading, but sometimes resists and modifies it in ways that reflects his or her experiences and position in society. Because Hall suggests that a negotiated reading still "accords the privileged position to the dominant definitions of events while reserving the right to make a more negotiated application to 'local conditions,' . . . [it is] shot through with contradictions" (p. 137). A negotiated reader may "contradict" herself because she strives toward an oppositional reading, but is still partly under the influence of a dominant reading. For Hall, then, a negotiated reader is only half-conscious. She partially questions the dominant reading, but has not come to the full understanding of an oppositional reading. From this perspective, a negotiated reading is better than a dominant reading, but not as robust and aware as an oppositional reading.

Two interpretations of Beethoven's *Symphony No. 9* serve as an example of dominant and oppositional readings. As Grout (1960) notes, the symphony, particularly the last movement, is an "Ode to Joy," celebrating "the universal brotherhood of man through joy, and its basis in the love of an eternal heavenly Father" (p. 491). Its performance at a celebration of the removal of the Berlin Wall in 1989 is an example of the dominance of the celebratory, fraternal interpretation. This interpretation, which is probably familiar to those who have taken music history courses, serves as the dominant reading of the composition. It supports the belief that classical music is universal and that musical compositions are autonomous art objects that speak similarly to all individuals.

Instead of this universality, feminist musicologist Susan McClary (1987) oppositionally interpreted Beethoven's composition as a violent type of masculinity when she infamously and shockingly described the symphony as a failed musical rape:

> The point of recapitulation in the first movement of the Ninth is one of the most horrifying moments in music, as the carefully prepared cadence is frustrated, damming up energy which finally explodes in the throttling murderous rage of a rapist incapable of attaining release. (p. 7)[2]

McClary reads the recapitulation as a repressed anger released in a violent and destructive way. McClary (1991) concludes that "[t]he Ninth Symphony is probably our most compelling articulation in music of the contradictory impulses that have organized patriarchal culture since the Enlightenment" (p. 129).

This reading has, as it might be imagined, caused controversy (see, for example, Rosen, 2000; Van den Toorn, 1995), and decades after its composition, it still causes discomfort and disagreement. But it triggers this discomfort precisely because it is oppositional. McClary's interpretation is oppositional not merely because it is an alternative reading, but because it is truly oppositional to the dominant reading of the symphony as an "Ode to Joy." Instead of the symphony being transcendent, autonomous, universal, and virtuous, it is corporeal, gendered male, and violent. This oppositional reading is informed by an oppositional discourse of feminism, which challenges the universalism, which is, in turn, couched in Grout's patriarchal language of "brotherhood" and the "heavenly Father." Oppositional reading need not be as controversial as McClary's interpretation of Beethoven, but reading through a lens of a less accepted, alternative position—in this case, feminism and a non-formalist reading of sonata form as narrative—challenges dominant structures in society.

These interpretations sit within a nexus of power, where dominant readings are the readings preferred by those in power. Dominant interpretations are products of, and maintain, dominant classes and interpretations of social relations. Because dominant readings support the status quo and do not challenge any preconceived ideas largely held in society, they appear commonsensical, accurately explaining the "real" meaning of the work. Readers can, however, challenge these texts and privilege by performing oppositional readings that (re)interpret works to expose the socially constructed and hegemonic nature of these structures of power.

Encoding/Decoding Beyoncé's *Run the World (Girls)*

How can dominant, oppositional, and negotiated readings allow educators and students to approach musical texts (e.g., songs, videos, concert performances, etc.) as polysemic and warranting multiple interpretations? How may the combination of multiple interpretations serve social justice in music education? Dominant and oppositional readings of gender in Beyoncé's music video *Run the World (Girls)* provide an example of how educators may explore multiple meanings of a text in the classroom. The following interpretations were derived from discussions of the video I conducted with high school (ages 14–17) and preservice music education students.

A Dominant Reading: Women's Empowerment

To many fans, the singer Beyoncé represents a strong woman who empowers herself through self-expression in music, fashion, and business. In songs such as *Single Ladies (Put a Ring on It)*, she sings about female empowerment. In her personal life, through her marriage to rapper Jay-Z and the highly publicized birth of their child Blue Ivy, she epitomizes the modern woman who "has it all."

This narrative of the woman who has it all pervades the lyrics, images, and music of the video *Run the World (Girls)*. The video commences with images of encaged and crucified women in a post-apocalyptic landscape littered with burning automobiles. However, the women who are subjected to these oppressive conditions quickly liberate themselves. This liberation takes on a gendered theme when an all-male battalion, outfitted in riot gear, including shields, helmets, and police batons, confronts Beyoncé and her accompanying army of women. But Beyoncé and her army of women render the men powerless by performing a dance meant to be read as a metaphor of rebellion. The women dramatically perform choreography that includes flipping their hair, kicking, and throwing their fists in the air. Nonplussed, intimidated, and disempowered by this symbolic retaliation by the women, the men halt their attack and stare in disbelief.

In addition to dancing, the video also uses animals as symbols of women's power. In one scene, a docile lion lies at Beyoncé's feet, and in another, she controls chained hyenas, representing her regality and dominance. Her supremacy over the natural world is extended to men as well. In one scene (c. 1:45), Beyoncé sexually coaxes one man to take his wallet and tackles another. The lyrics, which are explicitly about women's strength, complement these images. In the second verse, for example, Beyoncé sings, "Have me raise a glass for the college grads," referencing the increase in women's access to higher education acquired over the last several decades, and "How we're smart enough to make these millions / Strong enough to bear the children," suggesting women's increasing share of the workforce while retaining their unique ability to give birth.

Beyoncé and her cowriters and coproducers even exploit the musical elements to represent women's empowerment. This sense of empowerment is created, in part, by composing tensions in the contrasts in harmonies and rhythms between the song's verses and choruses that are finally resolved in the concluding section of the song. Table 37.1 illustrates the differences in the harmonies and rhythms between the verses and choruses and their combination in this final section.

Rhythmic tensions are achieved by contrasting the verses' marching cadences with the choruses' sustained pitches. The rhythmic marching cadences on the snare drums in the verses symbolize the power, strength, and military force, which contrast with the lyrical, sustained pitches in the background voices in the choruses. The contrast between the unchanging harmony of the verses and the chordal movement of the choruses creates harmonic tension. The verses' harmonies remain motionless by remaining on a C drone, whereas the chorus is lyrical: its chord progression begins on an A♭-major triad and eventually cadences on the tonic C-major triad. When juxtaposed, the choruses sound smooth and lyrical compared to the rhythmic and harmonically still verses. This smoothing out of the texture provides a relief to the tense rhythmic and percussive punctuation of the snares of the verse. This change in texture can be interpreted as a "release" from the tension of the verse, and this emphasizes the empowering lyrics of the choruses: "my persuasion can build a nation."

Table 37.1 Form, harmony and rhythm of *Run the World (Girls)*

Form:	Verses	Choruses	Final Section (starts at 4:14)
Rhythm:	Snare drum cadences	Sustained pitches	Snare drums and sustained pitches
Harmony: (Key of C minor)	C Drone, but the vocal melody uses A♭s and E♭s	Chord Progression: A♭→⟨m⟩→A♭→Cmaj	Chord Progression: [: A♭→C :]

Another tension between the harmonies used in the verses and choruses is found in the ambiguity between C-major and minor tonalities. The C drone of the verses mixes both major and minor modes by using A♭s and E♮s. In the choruses, modal mixture is achieved through the chord progression, which first cadences on C minor and then on C major. For both the verses and choruses, the mixture of major and minor creates ambiguity because the bright major harmonies are continually pulled back to the dark minor harmonies. This ambiguity and tension between major and minor modes resolve in the final section. The darkness of minor gives way to the brightness of major when the A♭ major chord cadences to a C major chord, similar to a Picardy Third in Baroque music, giving the song a liberating and triumphant conclusion. The tensions between the verses' rhythm and unchanging harmony and the choruses' lyricism and harmonic movement also resolve in the final section as the elements merge. The strength of the verses' military snares combine with the choruses' lyrical chord progression to accentuate *both* strength and the lyricism. This creates a sense of liberation as Beyoncé sings, "Who are we? What we run? The world."

Accompanying this triumphant final section, the video also ends with a final display of strength. In a compelling gesture, Beyoncé confidently approaches the leader of the male army and rips a military medal from his chest as he stands in disbelief. Through this act, Beyoncé symbolically strips him of the power of patriarchy he has maintained through intimidation, violence, and military coercion. After pulling the medal from his chest, Beyoncé and her dancers serve the men with a military salute. This is a final defiant, but magnanimous, act; the women symbolically demonstrate that they are unwilling to reinscribe the patriarchal violence they endured from the men. Instead of revenge, they salute in a sign of respect, symbolically instating a new order of equity and social justice. Taken as a whole—the video's lyrics, elements, and visual imagery—a dominant reading suggests that *Run the World (Girls)* is a narrative of strength and a claiming of voice for women.

An Oppositional Reading: Sexual Objectification

An oppositional reading through a feminist lens might question the video's representation of "women's empowerment." While Beyoncé sings of empowerment, the song and the video support traditional gender roles and reinforce patriarchy. Beyoncé and the other women gain power through sexual objectification. They display their bodies through sexually suggestive costumes and choreography. In many scenes, Beyoncé and her troupe lie on the ground, spread their legs, and "shake their booty." Beyoncé and her army bare their midriffs and legs and wear lingerie and other revealing clothes. Meanwhile, because the men are dressed in army fatigues, one might wonder why the women, who are also engaged in war, would not similarly dress in army apparel. Beyoncé also objectifies herself when she uses sexuality to gain power. At the point described earlier, where she coaxes the wallet from one male solider, she uses flirtation. This does not challenge the patriarchy of the objectification of female bodies, but merely reinscribes it. It suggests that women's only power is the ability to trick men with their sexuality. Similarly, while the title and the refrain of the song claim that females "run the world," the specific choice of words supports patriarchy. Why does she sing "girls" instead of "women"? "Woman" would conjure up strength, while "girls" merely infantilizes women. In other words, referring to them using the diminutive form of female, rather than the adult form, robs them of their ability to make decisions for themselves.

This reading challenges the dominant interpretation of the song and video as Beyoncé's anthem that "girls run the world." Singing an anthem that girls rule the world gives the impression that these inequalities do not exist and lulls women and men into a false sense that sexism is dead. The "woman's empowerment" narrative supports unexamined beliefs in a so-called post-feminist society, where issues of sexism are moot and feminist critiques are no longer necessary. It makes it appear that, while gender inequality occurred in the past, women now "rule." This confidence and view of contemporary equality allows an abdication of the responsibility of continually examining issues of power in gender relations and other aspects of identity. The result is that the culture industry has co-opted feminist discourses, only to enact the opposite; it infantilizes women and objectifies female bodies for the heterosexual male gaze.

This oppositional reading can be applied to interpretations of the tonality. The ambiguity between C major and minor is either unresolved or falsely resolved in the final section. It can be interpreted that the last section of the piece is not a cadence from A♭ to C major, as suggested in the dominant reading, but is an oscillation between the two chords. In this sense, there is no resolution between the ambiguity of the major and minor tonalities. The tension between the two is silenced and prematurely ended with the abrupt conclusion of the song. Or, the listener can still hear the end as a triumphant cadence on C major, but that cadence is a representation of false consciousness. Although there is a feeling of victory and agency, Beyoncé's character has done nothing to subvert gendered norms. The sanguine cadence is an illusion, and those who believe a triumph has been achieved are duped.

The Pedagogy of Readings

Performing dominant and oppositional readings, like the ones applied to Beyoncé's video, can help students create new and deeper interpretations of the music to which they listen. By conversing about cultural texts, students begin to imagine different interpretations and to understand the perspectives of historically marginalized populations and identities. Importantly, though, the encoding/decoding framework provides some distance from the text and content. When educators do not dictate the meaning of a work, and instead invite students to imagine different interpretations, educators are able to foster critique of popular music that students uncritically consume without creating an environment in which they feel personally judged by the teacher for their listening choices.

Students come to new meanings through dialogue with the teacher and other students. At times, the teacher might use the Socratic method, leading students through questioning to specific interpretations. At the same time, however, the teacher must remain open to students' interpretations and to unanticipated readings. Because of this, when exploring dominant and oppositional readings, it is important for educators to keep in mind that they do not necessarily need to agree with all aspects of those readings. The goal is to render as many different, and sometimes contradictory, meanings as possible and to imagine how different audiences might interpret a text. Most important, the teacher must continually and consistently ask students to cite evidence from the video, and sometimes from other sources, to substantiate their claims and interpretations. Also, because music educators' ostensible goal is careful study of musical *sounds*, music educators must be careful to draw their attention to the music itself. While images and lyrics are integral evidence within a reading and educators must include their study in class, continual attention to how the elements of music contribute to the meaning of the text is vital. By exploring the different meanings derived from the music, video, and lyrics, students and teacher begin to see the text in a different light, as well as start to understand how others may view that artifact, without it appearing that the teacher is voicing a personal judgment of the work or of popular music in general.

LIMITATIONS AND CRITIQUES OF THE ENCODING/DECODING FRAMEWORK

Although the encoding/decoding framework provides students an educational process for discovering and discussing alternative interpretations of a work and how privilege and power influence interpretations, there are some caveats. This section describes some of the limits of this process and suggests ways for educators to modify the framework to describe power and interpretation in music with more nuances.

Hall's (1980) encoding/decoding framework creates a binary between those who are privileged and marginalized. Poststructuralist ideas, particularly those of Foucault (1977) and the feminist postructuralists who have furthered his work (Butler, 1993, 1999; Weedon, 1997) have complicated this binary. For Foucault, power does not reside with an elite class that holds power at all times, exerting its dominance over the powerless. Rather, power is distributed in the hands of different parties at different times; it is "a productive network which runs through the whole social body" (Foucault, 1980, p. 119). This flow of power throughout society is, in part, a product of our intersecting identities. Each individual is a mix of differing identities: class, race, gender, sexuality, age, and so on. Some of these identities may be privileged, while others are not. The result is that the nuance of power is more complicated than discrete classes of oppressed and oppressors (Crenshaw, 2003).

These poststructuralist ideas of power and intersectionality of identity complicate the interpretation of texts. What exactly constitutes the "dominant" reading? In Beyoncé's video, are interpreters to assume that a "female empowerment" message is the preferred meaning? Certainly there are individuals who, at least at times, can be considered "powerful," but would reject this meaning of the text. Similarly, it could be oppositional to see any "female empowerment" as subversive. To complicate it even further, this does not take into account that the performers may be engaging in parody. Are they consciously appropriating an opposing view of their intentions in order to mock and critique? These questions require audience members to acknowledge that when interpreters label any readings as dominant, negotiated, or oppositional, they assume a locus of power. Locating those holding power, and then imagining the interpretations they prefer, is often an ambiguous endeavor; it requires interpretation and assumptions about audiences' preferences.

Because of these subtleties, the "oppositional" reading of *Run the World (Girls)* is, in some ways, dominant. To criticize Beyoncé's right to sexual agency through the display of her body through costume, dance, and other movements can be considered a form of "slut shaming." Women are expected to fall within what is often called the "virgin/whore" dichotomy, where women are expected to be chaste, and any display of sexuality is considered "slutty." This consideration is further complicated because it cannot be separated from femininity's intersection with race. Woman of color are often hypersexualized, and interpretation of Beyoncé's sexuality may be influenced by an audience member's perceptions of her racial identity as well (Willis, 2010). The "oppositional reading" of her sexuality earlier described is, in its own way, both oppositional and dominant; it challenges a simplistic message of "female empowerment," but in order to perform this oppositional reading, it may simultaneously stigmatize sexual freedom through the virgin/whore dichotomy and slut shaming. This "oppositional reading" simultaneously supports and challenges hegemony.

Similarly, the dominant reading can in certain respects be seen as subversive. There is reason to believe that Beyoncé and her collaborators play upon norms of women's sexuality. While many of the women in the video wear lingerie, they also wear army boots. This juxtaposition of sexualized clothes with the boots might arguably be a way to recontextualize lingerie, to make it unsexy, thus robbing it of the power to objectify female bodies. Another analysis might conclude that, although the women wear overtly sexual costumes and objectify their bodies, their ability to consciously "tempt" overly libidinous men who are powerless to do anything in response is a real and productive form of agency. These additional analyses suggest that the oppositional reading does not necessarily challenge patriarchy, but instead reinforces it, just as, conversely, the dominant reading has oppositional elements. As a result, the binary of dominant and oppositional flattens the ambiguous meanings of a work, missing the complicated nuances in which listeners understand the music.

This blurring of the lines suggests that interpretations do not fit into a neat binary between "duped" dominant and "enlightened" oppositional readings. Rather, audiences' relationships with music are ambiguous, often overlapping, and sometimes contradictory. This ambiguity reveals the educational merits of negotiated readings. As noted with respect to Hall's (1980) framework, negotiated readings are a sort of pseudo-consciousness; they are a half-realization of a full-fledged opposition to the hegemony supposedly embedded within a text. As Morley (2006) suggests, "[i]t may well be that the original model, in its search for overtly political forms of opposition to the culturally dominant order, overvalues 'oppositional' rather than 'negotiated' decodings" (p. 110). This perhaps comes from Halls's Marxist commitment to create an emancipated class that becomes conscious of how hegemonic influences have "duped" them. But, a different understanding of negotiated readings may aid education that values diversity and pluralism over leading students to the "right" answer of becoming "class conscious." Rather than foster a pseudo-consciousness that fails to gather the "true" oppressive meaning of a text, a negotiated reading can be conceived as a mindset that seeks to discover the ambiguities of texts and to understand how and why others interpret those ambiguities. Educators can encourage negotiated readings and value a diversity of perspectives so that they may open up meanings instead of leading to predetermined answers.

These ambiguities suggest that there is truth in both dominant and negotiated readings. Meaning is derived from continual question and examination of Hall's (2005) "dialectic of cultural struggle" (p. 67) between containment and resistance. For example, as already explained, there are aspects of Beyoncé's video that are "oppressive" and aspects that challenge patriarchy. Educators might want their students to gain the ability to understand both opposition and dominance, to interrogate how they are dialectically related, and to question how one's position in society shapes interpretation and experience. This ability to see and accept polysemy is what a thoughtful negotiated reading entails. A negotiated reading of Beyoncé's video, for example, would require students to consider and debate the merits of the dominant and oppositional readings in order to come to their own conclusions. But it also requires students to realize that their interpretation is not a matter of individual choice. Rather, choice is made within a nexus of power that is influenced by their experiences and interests. From this standpoint, educators should privilege negotiated readings because they help students develop an understanding of the polysemy of texts and to see multiple perspectives.

While privileging polysemy and pluralism allows educators to help students explore a variety of interpretations, it does not absolve them of ethical responsibilities. There are times when media and popular culture clearly exploit students by promulgating racist, sexist, homophobic, able-bodied, and classist lyrics and images in ways that are often unrecognized. There is a danger that educators may employ a falsely pluralistic approach that reduces all positions to matters of opinion to circumvent, consciously or unconsciously, the difficult but necessary ethical obligation to confront these socially unjust issues in popular music. This well-intentioned, but misguided, engagement with polysemy counteracts the educational aims of using texts to challenge students to question political and societal aspects of popular music. As in all pedagogy, educators should continually reflect upon any unintended motivations and honestly evaluate any hidden curriculum that may subvert their aims of creating a socially just music education.

These limits complicating Hall's encoding/decoding theory do not render the framework ineffective; they make it more valuable to educators in that this approach can prompt extended inquiry into the meanings of texts and the contexts in which they function, thereby undermining what are thought to be infallible conclusions about texts. Negotiated readings open up possibilities, rather than didactically telling or indirectly leading students to a teacher's predetermined meaning of the work.

CONCERNS OF THE EDUCATOR

The encoding/decoding framework, along with the thought-provoking types of interpretation it makes available, provides a means for educators to address issues of social justice in popular music, including issues associated with gender and sexuality. However, because contemporary popular music rapidly changes, educators must remain open to finding and replacing the material used in their classrooms. Beyoncé's video, for example, will fade from the popular imagination, and educators will probably need to replace it with similar material. Luckily, popular music is replete with interesting texts to analyze. In the months during the preparation of this chapter, several videos became possible texts to discuss with students. Educators could, for example, examine the viral video of the "Drumming Grandma," in which a seemingly feeble septuagenarian from Wisconsin surprised people with her virtuosic drum performance. A dominant reading might focus on this woman's personal fulfillment and the cliché of "you're only as old as you act." An oppositional reading, however, might question why an elderly woman playing the drums should surprise viewers, revealing that sexism and ageism might influence the interpretation of the video. Miley Cyrus's performance at the 2013 MTV Video Music Awards similarly leads to questions about sexuality and race. Was Miley's appropriation of "twerking," a dance associated with female African American urban culture, where dancers shake their hips, a celebration of diversity, or another iteration in the trope of hypersexualized Black female bodies becoming the loci of exoticism and slut shaming for White audiences? Similarly, educators can analyze the lyrics of sexual domination in Robin Thicke's *Blurred Lines*. Are the song and video overtly about misogyny and dominance, or is it a parody of those issues? Do the lyrics in the song "Royals" by the artist Lorde question the excessive materialism of contemporary popular music or merely celebrate commercialism? Popular music seemingly serves as an inexhaustible source for asking these and other questions.

Since these examples will probably appear passé even by the time of this chapter's publication, educators need to continually replace the material they use in class with equally interesting texts. The educators' goal, then, is to continually engage with popular culture, looking for new educational material. This process of exploration is, in some ways, familiar to music educators. Ensemble directors regularly seek out new repertoire, carefully considering the works' educational and artistic merits as well as the strengths and needs of their students. A teacher who uses popular music for issues of social justice makes similar considerations, albeit with different criteria. Teachers will need to assess students' maturity, ability, and needs, while simultaneously considering their own educational objectives when selecting appropriate videos and songs. Elementary students could not perform a symphony by Gustav Mahler because of its technical difficulties and should not read James Joyce's *Ulysses* because of the sophisticated language and sexual content, but these works are appropriate for collegiate study. Similarly, different popular culture texts are for students of different ages and abilities. Whenever teachers select educational materials they believe are best for their students and their communities, they carefully weigh both the constraints and the opportunities.

Ultimately, some works are more conducive to multiple readings than others. But this is necessarily true of all analyses. As useful as traditional Roman numeral analysis is in helping students gain a better understanding of the music in question, it is only one tool of inquiry and is accordingly narrow and limited. Other systems of analysis can also provide insight into the harmonies and tonalities in Wagner operas. Indeed, it is impossible and would be comical to attempt to analyze music by Milton Babbitt or the electronic artist Skrillex using traditional music theory based on Roman numerals. Like all analytical systems, the encoding/decoding framework is appropriate for some contexts, but not others. It provides an approach to popular music reception that complements the well-established pedagogies of popular music performance and composition. It serves as a starting point to engage students in interpretation, to examine social justice's relationship with music, and to approach popular music not simply as fluff or vapid, but as cultural texts that are replete with meaning and opportunities for educational inquiry. This neither unduly celebrates nor criticizes popular music, but holds each in tension as students reflect upon their lived musical worlds and become conscious consumers of popular music. Through this process, students and teachers openly engage the "dialectic of cultural struggle" through popular music in the aims of a socially just music education.

NOTES

1. This shift has encompassed many fields, and its demonstration can only be cursorily described. In philosophy and literacy criticism, Derrida's (1974) *différance,* Deleuze and Guattari's (1987) "rhizomes," and Nancy's (2006) "resonance" and "referral" all signal a shift from singular, monolithic meanings to the possibility of varying and diffuse interpretations of any phenomenon or object. In social science, researchers have shifted from quantitative and purely empiricist methodologies based on non-phenomenological metaphysics to qualitative and interpretive frameworks (see Denzin, 1997). In music, the so-called "new musicology" explores not the inter-sonic meanings of musical works derived from their elements, but how interpretations of musical works change throughout time and the sociopolitical meanings and historical conditions that gave rise to musical practices (for example, McClary, 1991). Hall's (1980) encoding/decoding framework, to be discussed shortly, investigates the effects of society's power structures upon various

interpretations of popular culture. These references stand in a much larger body of writings that signal this shift.

2. When this essay was reprinted in *Feminine Endings* (McClary, 1991), McClary took out the reference to rape, while still referring to it as violent.

REFERENCES

Abramo, J. (2010). Popular music and the guitar classroom. In A. Clements (Ed.), *Alternative approaches in music education: Case studies from the field.* (pp. 15–28). Reston, VA: MENC (National Association for Music Education).

Apple, M. (2000). *Official knowledge: Democratic education in a conservative age* (2nd ed.). New York: Routledge.

Butler, J. (1993). *Bodies that matter.* New York: Routledge.

Butler, J. (1999). *Gender trouble: Feminism and the subversion of identity* (10th ed.). New York: Routledge.

Crenshaw, K. (2003). Mapping the margins: Intersectionality, identity politics, and violence against women of color. In L. M. Alcoff & E. Mendieta (Eds.), *Identities: Race, class, gender, and nationality* (pp. 175–200). Malden, MA: Blackwell.

Daspit, T., & Weaver, J. A. (Eds.). (2000). *Popular culture and critical pedagogy: Reading, constructing, connecting.* New York: Garland Press.

Deleuze, G., & Guattari, F. (1987). *A thousand plateaus: On capitalism and schizophrenia* (B. Massumi, Trans.). Minneapolis: University of Minnesota Press.

Denzin, N. K. (1997). *Interpretive ethnography: Ethnographic practices for the twenty-first century.* New York: Sage.

Derrida, J. (1974). *Of grammatology* (G. C. Spivak, Trans.). Baltimore, MD: Johns Hopkins University Press.

Dewey, J. (1922/1957). *Human nature and conduct: An introduction to social psychology.* New York: The Modern Library.

Foucault, M. (1977). *Discipline and punish* (A. Sheridan, Trans.). New York: Vintage Books.

Foucault, M. (1980). *Power/knowledge: Selected interviews and other writings 1972–1977.* New York: Pantheon Books.

Giroux, H. A. (1994). *Disturbing pleasures: Learning popular culture.* New York: Routledge.

Green, L. (2008). *Music, informal learning, and the school: A new classroom pedagogy.* Aldershot, UK: Ashgate.

Grout, D. J. (1960). *A history of Western music.* New York: W. W. Norton.

Hall, S. (1980). Encoding/decoding. In S. Hall, D. Hobson, A. Lowe, & P. Willis (Eds.), *Culture, media, language* (pp. 128–138). New York: Routledge.

Hall, S. (2005). Notes on deconstructing "the popular." In R. Guins & O. Z. Cruz (Eds.), *Popular culture: A reader* (pp. 64–71). Thousand Oaks, CA: SAGE.

Kratus, J. (2007). Music education at the tipping point. *Music Educators Journal, 94*(2), 42–48.

McClary, S. (1987, January). Getting down off the beanstalk. *Minnesota Composers Forum Newsletter,* 4–7. Retrieved from http://composersforum.org/sites/composersforum.org/files/jan_1987.pdf.

McClary, S. (1991). *Feminine endings.* Minneapolis: Minnesota University Press.

Nancy, J. L. (2006). *Listening* (C. Mandell, Trans.). New York: Fordham University Press.

Rosen C. (2000). *Critical entertainments.* Cambridge, MA: Harvard University Press.

Tobias, E. S. (2012). Hybrid spaces and hyphenated musicians: Secondary students' musical engagement in a songwriting and technology course. *Music Education Research, 14,* 329–346. doi: 10.1080/14613808.2012.685459.

Van den Toorn, P. C. (1995). *Music, politics, and the academy.* Berkeley: University of California Press.

Weedon, C. (1997). *Feminist practice and poststructuralist theory* (2nd ed.). New York: Blackwell.

Willis, D. (Ed.). (2010). *Black Venus 2010: They called her "Hottentot."* Philadelphia, PA: Temple University Press.

CHAPTER 38

MUSIC EDUCATION AND THE INVISIBLE YOUTH

A Summary of Research and Practices of Music Education for Youth in Detention Centers

MAUD HICKEY

I feel like we should come together and make something good. So like the world can hear why we in here.

(Quote from a young man involved in a music program in a youth detention center)

Ralph Ellison, in the book *Invisible Man* (1952), eloquently reflects on 20 years of life living as a Black man in New York City and the subsequent struggle to be recognized as an individual: "To whom can I be responsible, and why should I be, when you refuse to see me?" (p. 14). The youth described in this chapter, already 60 years after the publication of Ellison's book, are also invisible: they are the incarcerated youth in cities across the globe, whom music educators often fail to think about when considering "standards," or best practices for learning and teaching.

The number of incarcerated youth around the world is not only high, but has grown at an unprecedented rate, especially in the United States (Hazel, 2008). In addition, the majority of incarcerated youth in the United States are disproportionately poor and from minority cultures when compared to the general population (Alexander, 2010). These youth are rarely considered from the perspective of those involved in public education—they are virtually invisible. And for the teachers and policymakers who focus on music education specifically, detained youth are not part of discussions concerning music education policy and practices.

Arts and music opportunities in juvenile facilities are a recent and growing trend (as is documented later in this chapter); however, the groups responsible for providing these services are either privately funded organizations or outreach arms of large cultural arts organizations, such as the Chicago Symphony Orchestra and Carnegie Hall (both which have recently provided programming in centers for incarcerated youth). And music has been used for many years as a therapeutic tool for "at-risk" juveniles, including those in detention settings (Crump, 2010; Gardstrom, 2013; McIntyre, 2007).

Yet, despite their seeming inactivity in detention centers, music educators are positioned to make a positive impact for detained youth, now more than ever, as the philosophy of these settings is evolving from a punitive approach toward a more rehabilitative one (Brown, 2008). The "Positive Youth Development" (PYD) model looks at the strengths, rather than deficits, of adolescents, and especially those considered "at-risk." PYD has been used in community organizations as well as educational settings (Lerner, Almerigi, Theokas, & Lerner, 2005), and is beginning to enter the dialogue of approaches toward greater juvenile justice (Butts, Bazemore, & Meroe, 2010; Cope, 2011). What seems to be missing from the current arts activity in juvenile detention centers are advocacy and educational and policy efforts from the K–12 school music education community.

There are many questions left unanswered when it comes to music education and incarcerated youth. Who is teaching the music to the youth in these settings? What is being taught and for what purposes? And how might music educators' understandings of these programs illuminate the need to extend music teacher education and policy discourse beyond the traditional boundaries of K–12 school institutions? And to examine the flip side of this question, what might the music education community learn from the efforts of other organizations teaching music in juvenile detention centers?

This chapter provides a summary and analysis of the research and pedagogical practices of music education of incarcerated youth. It concludes with a discussion of some inherent issues connected with the research and practice and suggests that music educators consider joining other communities to work together within a framework of social justice education.

SETTING THE SCENE

The United States has an infamous reputation for mass incarceration of both adults and youth. A 2011 census shows that there were 61,423 youth (ages 10–18) detained in detention facilities around the United States (National Center for Juvenile Justice, 2013). This number is considerably higher in the United States than in other countries, even though juvenile violent crime rates are only "marginally higher" in the United States than in other nations (Mendel, 2011, p. 2). Mendel reports that in 2007 only 37 percent of detained youth were non-Hispanic White compared to 60 percent of the youth population overall, highlighting the disproportionate number of minority youth in detention.[1] While education is mandatory in juvenile facilities, by law, as it is for all children in the United States, it differs in length of time in school and services offered for those in detention facilities (Sedlak & McPherson, 2010). There are no reports that detail the specifics of education in these settings, as rules differ state by state as well as institution by institution. Perhaps the *only* consistent finding about formal schooling in juvenile detention facilities in this country is that they are perilous: "America's juvenile corrections institutions subject confined youth to intolerable levels of violence, abuse, and other forms of maltreatment" (Mendel, 2011, p. 5).

The Status of Music and Arts Programming in Correctional Facilities

One would hope that within the education programs in detention centers, youth are provided with arts education, just as in regular K–12 schooling. However, as already suggested, there is little known about music and arts education in juvenile detention facilities. Williams (2008) sent a survey to 478 public residential juvenile correctional facilities (those listed in the American Correctional Association directory) with the purpose of determining the status of arts education in these facilities. Of the 175 institutions that replied, 100 (57.4 percent) of them reported that their institution had an arts program. Fifty percent of these described their programs as "educational" while 33 percent described theirs as "recreational" (16 percent replied both educational and recreational). Of the programs offered, visual arts was the most common (73 percent), musical/theater was next (9 percent), a combination of music and visual arts or musical theater and dance comprised 11 percent, and music alone comprised only 1 percent of the programs.

Cohen, Duncan, and Anderson (2012) attempted to document the number of *music* programs operating in US juvenile facilities but faced "numerous hurdles" (p. 76) when trying to gather information. They found 34 "structured music programs" in place out of the 265 juvenile facilities that they had contacted. Nearly half (16) of those programs were provided internally (as opposed to an outside agency). Though it is difficult to know exactly how many facilities exist, the number that offer music education, as found by Cohen et al. (2012), parallels the low number found by Williams (2008) and is, frankly, depressing.

In the following sections I share recent research studies and evaluation reports of music programs in juvenile detention facilities. The first section reports on research studies, and the second on practices of music education in youth detention facilities. These studies and reports point to an active community of artists who provide the music services, with the majority of the activties taking place in countries outside the United States.

RESEARCH

There is no doubt that providing arts access and education to at-risk youth has great potential for transforming the lives of those youth, and in fact studies show that arts activities are linked to achievement and productivity of at-risk adolescents (see Heath,

Soep, & Roach, 1998, and Catterall, Dumais, & Hampden-Thompson, 2012, for reviews of this literature). However, due to a lack of music activity in youth detention facilities, there are few studies that document the impact of *music* on youth in detention. Those that do exist are recent, as it seems to be a trend in this new millennium. While bands and choirs were prevalent in "reform schools" and juvenile detention centers around the turn of the twentieth century, music activity vanished from these facilities in the 1960s until a resurgence of music and arts programs in detention settings in the past two decades (Lee, 2010).

Music Therapy

There are many studies that examine the use of music therapy with delinquent or at-risk adolescents, and a small portion of these takes place in detention facilities. Gardstrom (2013) provides a review of music therapy studies with detained youth and details the types of music therapy procedures used (i.e., Receptive, Improvisational, Re-creative, and Compositional). Gold, Voracek, and Wigram (2004) provide a meta-analysis of the effects of music therapy for youth with psychopathology. Hip-hop therapy (HTT) and RAP therapy have also recently been cited as effective methods for helping youth with behavioral problems (e.g., DeCarlo & Hockman, 2003; Gann, 2010; Gonzalez & Hayes, 2009; Olson-McBride & Page, 2012; Tyson, 2002). Palidofsky's work using musical theater with incarcerated girls has shown to be a useful intervention for trauma issues (Palidofsky, 2010; Palidofsky & Stolbach, 2012).

What Gardstrom (2013) makes clear is that the adolescents held in detention facilities are far more likely to have special needs than non-detained youth. She reminds us that many detained juveniles have witnessed or have been victims of abuse and violence; many have been neglected, have psychiatric or substance abuse disorders; and most have some sort of learning disability. It requires specialized expertise when dealing with these issues through music therapy in juvenile detention facilities. These studies, however, are outside the scope of this chapter.

For the purposes of this chapter, I searched the research literature to find studies of music activities that were not for therapeutic purposes with youth in detention settings. I used the following criteria to select the studies that are presented here: the studies took place within a detention facility that served youth (ages 10–19); music was the main art form; and juveniles (not adults) were the main subjects/participants of the study.

Studies by Daykin, de Viggiani, Pilkington, and Moriarty (2012) and Daykin, Moriarty, de Viggiani, and Pilkington (2011) provide comprehensive reviews of the literature on music with juvenile offenders. In addition, a new "Arts Evidence Library" provides a database of evidence-based research on arts programs and intervention for incarcerated youth (www.artsevidence.org.uk). Because the studies that I present here, for the most part, overlap with the reviews of Daykin et al. (2011, 2012), rather than reiterate what those report, I synthesize them in Table 38.1 to highlight the salient

Table 38.1 Research Studies of Music with Incarcerated Youth

Study	Methodology	Participants	Activity or Intervention Description	Length of Time	Conclusions/Outcome
Kennedy (1998)	Quantitative; pre-post test experimental design.	45 males assigned to 5 experimental groups of 9 each. Ages 12–19	Guitar lessons and then various treatments: performance only (perform for peers and staff); performance and cognitive strategy (lectures to deal with performance anxiety along with performances); cognitive strategy only; vicarious experience (observed peers perform); no intervention.	3 months, 1 time per week	Musical performance and musical performance combined with cognitive strategies conditions scored significantly higher than the vicarious experience and cognitive strategies only conditions on musical self-efficacy. Vicarious experience and cognitive strategies only condition scored lower than the control condition on musical self-efficacy. Self-esteem scores for musical performance with cognitive strategies conditions significantly improved from pre- to post-test.
Tyson (2002)	Quantitative; pre-post test experimental design.	11 (males ages 15 and 16)	"Hip Hop Therapy"—a combination of bibliotherapy and music therapy with rap music.	3 weeks/4 sessions per week.	Inconclusive quantitative analysis. Qualitative outcomes pointed to enjoyment of being able to use rap music.
Ezell & Levy (2003)	3-year; mixed methods	41–86 youth male detainees	Multiple arts workshops (not detailed)	20–55 days	- No significant changes in self-esteem or peer-relations - All learning goals met - Majority of youth felt they learned skills - 70% of youth reported positive feelings - Of 24 follow-up youth, 16.7% recidivated compared to a benchmark of 32.9%.
Baker & Homan (2007)	Ethnography	Unable to interview students.	Piano, guitar, rap, and computer sequencing with an emphasis on positive lyrical expression. (Genuine Voices Program; see Table 38.2)	Twice weekly (for term of detainment)	Discussion of using rap in positive way to alter youth behavior

Study	Methods	Participants	Intervention	Duration	Outcomes
Woodward, Sloth-Nielsen, & Mathiti (2008)	Qualitative and quantitative		"Diversion into Music Education" (DIME). Music improvisation and composition through collaborative work on African marimbas and djembes.		Musical development; improved dispositions (e.g. happiness, excitement, sense of purpose); better behavior; less recidivism; better self-esteem.
Bittman, Dickson, & Coddington (2009)	Quantitative; randomized controlled crossover	52 (ages 12–18); 30 males, 22 females.	"Recreational Music Making" protocol (a drumming curriculum called "Adolescent Healtrhrhythms") included improvisation and "jam" sessions as well as call-response activities)	6 weeks. 1 hour per week.	Statistically significant improvements for experimental group in multiple measures: school/work role performance, total depression, negative self-evaluation, and anger. Also found improvements 6 weeks after completion.
Anderson & Overy (2010)	Mixed methods; pre–post test experimental design. Post-project interviews.	14 (male ages 17–21)	Guitar performance; writing and recording of lyrics in Garageband.	8 weeks. 3.5 hour sessions per week	Enthusiasm for program (interviews); behavior incidents decreased for music group; quantitative: experimental group engaged in more classes compared to control group; increase in self-esteem and self-control measures.
Barrett & Baker (2012)	Case study	17 male; 4 interviewed 3 times	Wide variety of skills including performing (playing drums and guitar), as well as reading and song writing.	5 months	Music learning outcomes; increased positive social behaviors, self-esteem, capacity to engage in and persist with learning tasks
Tett et al. (2012)	Case study; pre- and post-intervention focus groups.	3 Cases	Participants worked alongside the "Scottish Ensemble" in learning to play and record music in small rock groups (guitar, keyboard, percussion and Garageband). Performance at end.	4 months	• More positive attitudes toward learning (numeracy, writing, talking, listening); increased confidence and self-esteem; development of collaborative and responsible group work skills
Wolf & Holochwost (2014)	Mixed-methods; non-randomized pre–post test design. Participant reflections	54 (20 female, 34 male) at 2 facilities	Choir, songwriting workshops	2 weeks, 2.5 hours daily	• Levels of effort and engagement increased, formation of social networks grew, • Incidence of poor behavior decreased • Greater sense of self as a result of the program

information. My summary of these studies follows. What I believe to be of specific interest to music educators are the types of activities used and the proposed (or found) outcomes.

Research Summary

The outcomes from the studies presented in Table 38.1 fall into four categories: musical, psychological, learning non-musical skills, and altering behavior. The programs that produced greater musical skills or enhanced musical self-efficacy were reported in studies by Kennedy (1998), Barrett and Baker (2012), and Woodward et al. (2008). The majority of studies, however, examined and found positive *extra*-musical psychological outcomes, such as improved confidence and self-esteem (Anderson & Overy, 2010; Bittman, et al., 2009; Ezell & Levy, 2003; Tett, et al., 2012; Tyson, 2002; Wolf & Holochwost, 2014; Woodward, et al., 2008). Bittman et al. (2009), Anderson and Overy (2010) and Tett et al. (2012) also found music to improve other learning skills, and two studies (Anderson & Overy, 2010; Tett et al., 2012) found that the musical intervention improved behavior and reduced recidivism. (A report by Hillman, 2004, of six multi-arts programs in youth detention centers also cites lowered recidivism by youth who participated; *however*, the methodology and evaluative details in that study are lacking, and hence are not included in Table 38.1). Wolf and Holochwost (2014) were able to document improved behavior, but this was modified by the facility (one facility had greater behavior issues than the other).

It is clear that there is a need for more studies, including more rigorous quantitative studies, before any solid conclusions can be reached about the effects of music programs in juvenile detention settings. There also is a need for studying the long-term impact of these programs for youth.

MUSIC PROGRAMS FOR YOUTH IN DETENTION CENTERS

As indicated previously, there are a growing number of music programs in juvenile facilities that are funded and operated by independent arts organizations. The instructors for these programs are often teaching artists, independent musicians who are hired by the arts organizations to provide the instruction. In order to document and provide a summary of these programs, I searched various resources, including the "Arts Evidence Library" (www.artsevidence.org.uk) and others from the database provided on the Prison Arts Coalition website (http://theprisonartscoalition.com/). The criteria for including them here are that they are not one-shot programs, but have been active for more than a year, are relatively current, and work with youth in juvenile detention centers. Summaries of these programs are shown in Table 38.2 and are presented in alphabetical order. Most of the programs have been evaluated by their funding agencies and so the citations (listed in the outcomes column) refer to those documents.

The projects presented in Table 38.2 show similar profiles to the studies presented in Table 38.1. That is, most of the objectives are related to extra-musical outcomes and behaviors. And similar to the studies shown in Table 38.1, the types of music activity are mostly related to popular genres such as rock band and rap. The DIME (Woodward et al., 2008) and *Good Vibrations* (Henley, 2012) projects are unique in that they use instruments from non-Western traditions such as African marimbas and djembes, and the Javanese Gamelan, respectively. Only the Carnegie Hall project (Wolf & Holochwost, 2014) and *Storycatchers* (Palidofsky, 2010; Palidofsky & Stolbach, 2012) programs utilized anything resembling a "classical" music approach, in those cases involving choir and musical theater.

Bridging the Gap Between Detention Center and Community

Many of the program evaluations cited in Table 38.2 call for the need to work with juveniles once they leave their detention settings. Participants who have positive experiences with these music programs within the detention walls, when they leave, often go back to neighborhoods or schools where the luxury of such artistic engagement has all but vanished. The youth leave these programs and become invisible once again. *NeON* of Carnegie Hall (http://www.carnegiehall.org/NeONArts/) and *Sounding Out* (see Cartwright, 2013), of the Irene Taylor Trust "Music in Prisons" project, are two examples of extending the impact beyond the short (often just two weeks) music activities provided in the juvenile facilities. This is an area of opportunity in which music educators in schools might be active in recruiting or connecting *with* youth who have been released from detention and who would benefit from continued musical activities in their schools.

So What? And Why?

One probably *does not* need to conduct a study to show that music activities in juvenile detention settings have at least some positive impact on the lives of those youths. The findings summarized in the previous section are not surprising. Rather, deeper and more philosophical questions need to be answered and examined from the perspectives of the music education community and those working in the detention settings.

Table 38.2 Music Programs in Youth Detention Centers

Program	Objectives	Activities	Outcomes (Based on Reports)
Australian Children's Music Foundation, http://acmf.com.au/programs/youth-at-risk/	Mental health benefits; reduce recidivism; engagement with learning; improve literacy and numeracy; incentive for good behavior	Songwriting, performance, and recording of original songs	Barrett & Baker (2008)—Music learning outcomes (performance skills, expanded repertoire). Extra-music learning outcomes: a developing capacity to work with others; increased confidence and self-esteem; increased capacity to persist at a task; increased skills of self-expression; the development of music as a positive leisure activity; an increased interest in learning how to learn; and motivation to share new music skills.
Genuine Voice (Boston), http://www.genuinevoices.com	To prevent youth violence and crime; assist youths in making positive life decisions; teach planning and creating finished music productions; participation in cultural events (from their website)	Original musical composition, and computer-based music "sequencing"	Baker & Homan (2007) (see Table 38.1)
Good Vibrations (England), http://www.good-vibrations.org.uk	To develop team working, communications, and other important life skills through participating in Gamelan (Indonesian percussion) workshops. (from their website)	One-week workshops in Javanese Gamelan improvisation, composition and performance.	Henley (2012)[a]—Musical development (ensemble skills, melody, dynamics, composing and improvising). Individual agency; positive social interactions with facilitator, staff, and peers
Irene Taylor Trust Music in Prisons (England), http://www.musicinprisons.org.uk	To provide "positive learning experiences that can act as a vital catalyst in the process of rehabilitation and the development of the life skills needed for prisoners to become valuable members of their communities." (From their website)	One-week workshops developing rock bands, culminating in a performance of original music.	Cox & Gelsthorpe (2008) (report on this project in 8 male *adult* prisons)—Improved well-being (autonomy, humanity, self-confidence, self-efficacy). Improved positive relationships (with peers and staff). Improved learning (literacy and communication, workplace management skills and behaviors)
Irene Taylor Trust Music in Prisons (England), http://www.musicinprisons.org.uk	See above	"Fair"—3-week workshop toward the production of an original musical theatre show.	Goddard (2006)—Learned a new skill; made new friends; had a positive first performance experience

Program	Purpose	Activities	Reports
Lost Voices (Michigan), http://lostvoices.org	To empower at-risk youth to find their creative voices. (from their website)	Create original "roots music," and then perform in front of peers in a "professional concert situation."	No report
Music in Detention (England), http://www.musicindetention.org.uk	1. To promote and ensure delivery of music as a creative vehicle for self-expression by immigration detainees 2. To improve detainees' quality of life through independently delivered music activities 3. Using music, to create channels of communication between detainees, places of detention, local communities, and the wider public.	A wide variety of cultural and non-Western music activities including music, dance, and performance workshops	(van Mannen, 2009, 2010)—Expressed themselves through the music activities; quality of life within the facilities improved; communication enhanced (Note: Music in Detention stopped working with youth in 2010 "owing to changes in government policy" [from http://www.musicindetention.org.uk/where/bedford-yarls-wood-irc/])
Musical Connections (New York), http://www.carnegiehall.org/aboutmusicalconnections/	"The purpose is not only to teach music or the possibility of ensemble work—it is to jump-start the sense of being a person with potential" (Wolf & Wolf, 2012, p. 6). Musical Connections introduces "positive communication techniques and strengthening links to family and community for inmates in correctional facilities." (from their website)	Two-week residences engaging juveniles in songwriting, instrumental playing, producing, and then performing (rock band ensembles; choir).	Wolf & Wolf (2012) Wolf & Holochwost (2014)
Storycatchers Theatre (Chicago), http://www.storycatcherstheatre.org	"[P]articipants learn writing and performance skills, achieve personal development goals, improve peer and family relationships, and acquire practical knowledge that can promote success in school, at home and, in their communities." (from their website)	Write, produce and perform original musical theater inspired by true personal stories.	Palidofsky (2010); Palidofsky & Stolbach (2012) Reduced trauma

[a] The *Good Vibrations* project takes place in several adult and youth prisons across England and has been studied by a number of researchers (e.g., Eastburn, 2003; Henley, Caulfield, Wilson, & Wilkinson, 2012; Mendonça, 2010; Wilson, Caulfield, & Atherton, 2009). It is an excellent model of a program that has been studied and documented extensively; however, only the Henley (2012) study is cited in the table because it is the only one that specifically includes the part of the project that works in youth centers.

For one, why do (or should) we use music in detention settings with juveniles: for recreational, rehabilitative, or educational purposes? Clements (2004) reminds us of the punitive aspects of prison, and the time where arts were not thought of as rehabilitative, but simply recreational. As Clements points out, that has changed because the arts "naturally encourage spontaneous and participatory learning, enabling a more liberating and self-directed rehabilitative process" (p. 169). The study by Wolf and Holochwost (2014) points extensively to the potential for an ensemble music experience (choir) to help juvenile facilities move toward a more strengths-based approach in their work with youth.

Most of the objectives for the programs outlined in Table 38.2 are extra-musical. The majority of these good-hearted "interventions" are put in place to fix the child, to hope for less crime, or to make "better." Few of the studies or programs examine the use of the arts, specifically music, as a way to simply enhance the quality of life for the young participants, much less empower them to see the injustices done to them. According to Wolf and Holochwost (2014), "We have fewer tools to capture the presence, onset, or development of youth assets. Yet these types of measurement—both quantitative and qualitative—are necessary for feedback to youth and families, for charting the success of services and facilities, and for capturing the effects of programs such as Musical Connections" (p. 30). Music education in youth detention centers could lead the way in creating models that highlight positive youth development.

From a music educator's perspective, it is interesting to note that the majority of the programs use participatory music activities such as composition and improvisation and through genres such as rap or rock music. Why are not (or should) these programs teaching the "classical canon" or music notation? Or, examining it from another angle, one might consider the popular music activities as furthering the divide between the "cultured" and the "at-risk." De Roeper and Savelsberg (2009) make this point about the binary divide between the uses of music to "fix" versus music as cultural capital for those in the "right" group.

> For instance, young people on the margins are often targeted for remedial intervention focused on addressing risk behaviours and basic needs, while other young people deemed to be 'high functioning' are able to access richer cultural opportunities through academic curricula and high-culture engagement with the arts. (de Roeper & Savelsberg, 2009, p. 212)

This "divide" relates directly to the potential danger of viewing musical activities as having a "civilizing" power. Both Shieh (2010) and Cahill (2010) point out tensions between agency and objectification that are so often overlooked when entering settings where the learner is at the tutor's mercy. "The answer," Shieh proposes, "rests in the interaction of the outsiders and to what degree they join the group and act in solidarity, as musical partners rather than as teachers and experts" (2010, p. 28). Cahill warns that the elements we define as risk factors may be "the very experience which helped to generate compassion, a sense of social justice, and the capacity to endure, persist and strive for goals" (2010, p. 19). So if, and when, music educators consider education for youth in detention settings, they must carefully consider the reasons for offering such, as well as the "what" that is taught. The Carnegie Hall *Musical Connections* project (Wolf & Holochwost, 2014) provides a model in which the project and research were done in collaboration with the juvenile justice agencies for the purpose of examining strength and asset development of youth. Unexpected findings pointed to how the differences in philosophy toward youth empowerment between the facilities can temper the positive outcomes.

There is also a danger in using the projects to glorify the institution's image. Harbert makes this evident in a story about using music as a manipulative tool in order to make Angola prison look good. "For the administration, music is part of a system of carceral techniques that regulates inmate behavior and, in the case of Angola, also expresses an image of reform to the public" (Harbert, 2010, p. 75). And it not just the incarceration setting that gains a positive image because of arts activities, but the institutions that deliver these "goods." This issue crosses my mind when I read front-page headlines of a famous symphony orchestra conductor working his classical music magic in a local youth detention facility.[2] In such cases, there is an inherent danger of manipulation and glorification (or the perceived image of such) that must be carefully considered when giving reasons that music educators should get involved with youth in detention centers.

CONCLUSIONS AND IMPLICATIONS

I have been asked on occasion what my own work at a local juvenile detention facility has to do with music education. I answer this question with a question: "What *doesn't* it have to do with music education?" We (meaning the traditional K–12 music educators) have so much to learn from work in the communities *outside* the traditional boundaries of schools, especially in the United States, where there is such a strong demarcation between the music experienced in school and elsewhere. The tension between in-school music education versus the music learning encountered in community music and other programs seems to be music educators' quagmire at this point. But Cohen et al. (2012) wisely remind us that

> rather than looking at who is providing the music programming to determine whether the music activity is 'community-based' or not, we need to examine the content, pedagogy, and functions of the music activities. . . . How do these comparisons impact our practice as music educators and community musicians? (p. 77)

The line should be blurred and we must all learn from each other. Concerns about social justice in music education are meaningless without breaking down walls and boundaries between the institutions and groups whom we perceive to be "Other."

So how do we bring the areas of music education, juveniles in detention, and social justice together in the end? As mentioned at the outset of this chapter, there is no doubt that juveniles in detention are currently "invisible" to school music teachers, while at the same time there is a burgeoning growth in the numbers of community artists and arts organizations who are actively bringing music to youth in detention centers. This current upsurge in arts- and music-based programming in youth detention centers makes this an opportune time for K–12 music educators and collegiate music teacher educators to look for collaboration and engagements with these communities. It is a chance for music educators to learn from the invisible youth.

An immediate and most positive impact for K–12 educators would be on the students in university music education programs. Imagine the lessons our future teachers could learn about inequality and injustice in education by working with youth in detention facilities?[3] Future teachers' perceptions about the purposes and power of music for *all* youth would dramatically change with such opportunities.

In order to successfully move social justice forward in music teacher education, however, culturallly relevant pedagogy has to be at the forefront, and the youth that we prepare our music education students to teach must include *all* members of our communities, including those "invisible youth" within and outside schools. The focus of lessons in music teacher education must be about social change through contemporary, creative, and participatory music making. As Quinn, Ploof, and Hochtritt (2012) suggest, art education needs to be "engaged with context (the teacher and students' surroundings), contemporary art (current forms and perspectives) and critical social issues (the 'going' world and abiding justice-related concerns)" (p. xx).

Probably few of the programs presented in this chapter have gone as far as Quinn et al. (2012) suggest, but they at least have acted to engage in music with the youth who have been socially ostracized. It is hoped that this chapter will open up dialogue in traditional music education settings about the needs and lessons we might learn from the "invisible youth," and bring them, as social justice proponents would suggest, into the conversation.

Notes

1. This disparity is annotated for both imprisoned youths and adults in the United States (see Alexander, 2010).
2. See http://articles.chicagotribune.com/2013-10-07/news/ct-tl-warrenville-cso-20131001_1_storycatchers-theatre-muti-cso as an example; this is cited here with no intention to criticize the efforts of Maestro Muti, nor to single out the Chicago Symphony Orchestra for their efforts. It is a phenomenon repeated around the globe.
3. Two models of pairing college student mentors with juveniles in detention settings are the AMPED program at Northwestern University (http://www.engage.northwestern.edu/AMPED/) and the "Champaign County Juvenile Detention Center Arts Project" (http://ccjdcartsproject.weebly.com).

REFERENCES

Alexander, M. (2010). *The new Jim Crow: Mass incarceration in the age of colorblindness.* New York: The New Press.

Anderson, K., & Overy, K. (2010). Engaging Scottish young offenders in education through music and art. *International Journal of Community Music, 3*(1), 47–64. doi: 10.1386/ijcm.3.1.47/1.

Baker, S., & Homan, S. (2007). Rap, recidivism and the creative self: A popular music programme for young offenders in detention. *Journal of Youth Studies, 10*(4), 459–476.

Barrett, M. S., & Baker, J. (2008). *Developing song-makers: A case study of music learning and teach.* Executive Summary Report to the Australian Children's Music Foundation. Brisbane, Queensland: University of Queensland.

Barrett, M. S., & Baker, J. S. (2012). Developing learning identities in and through music: A case study of the outcomes of a music programme in an Australian juvenile detention centre. *International Journal of Music Education, 30*(3), 244–259. doi: 10.1177/0255761411433721.

Bittman, B., Dickson, L., & Coddington, K. (2009). Creative musical expression as a catalyst for quality-of-life improvement in inner-city adolescents placed in a court-referred residential treatment program. *ADVANCES, 24*(1), 8–19.

Brown, M. (2008). The road less traveled: Arts-based programs in youth corrections. In A. O'Brien & K. Donelan (Eds.), *The arts and youth at risk: Global and local challenges* (pp. 51–69). Newcastle, UK: Cambridge Scholars Publishing.

Butts, J. A., Bazemore, G., & Meroe, A. S. (2010). *Positive youth justice. Framing justice interventions using the concepts of positive youth development.* Washington, DC: Coalition for Juvenile Justice.

Cahill, H. (2010). Resisting risk and rescue as the *raison d'être* for arts interventions. In A. O'Brien & K. Donelan (Eds.), *The arts and youth at risk: Global and local challenges* (pp. 13–31). Newcastle, UK: Cambridge Scholars Publishing.

Cartwright, J. (2013). *An evaluation of the Irene Taylor Trust's Sounding Out programme.* London: The Irene Taylor Trust "Music in Prisons."

Catterall, J. S., Dumais, S. A., & Hampden-Thompson, G. (2012). *The arts and achievement in at-risk youth: Findings from four longitudinal studies.* Washington, DC: National Endowment for the Arts.

Clements, P. (2004). The rehabilitative role of arts education in prison: Accommodation or enlightenment? *International Journal of Art & Design Education, 23*(2), 169–178.

Cohen, M. L., Duncan, S., & Anderson, K. (2012). Who needs music? Toward an overview of music programs in U.S. juvenile facilities. In D. Coffman (Ed.), *Proceedings from the International Society of Music Education* (pp. 73–79). International Society for Music Education. Retrieved from http://issuu.com/official_isme/docs/2012_cma_proceedings?viewMode=magazine&mode=embed.

Cope, E. A. (2011). *Rebuilding character: The practices of Positive Youth Development teachers in a correctional setting.* Unpublished doctoral dissertation, University of Denver.

Cox, A., & Gelsthorpe, L. (2008). *Beats and bars, music in prisons: An evaluation.* Cambridge, UK: Institute of Criminology, University of Cambridge.

Crump, J. (2010). *An examination of therapeutic approaches employed by music therapists servicing children and teens with behavior disorders.* Unpublished master's thesis, The Florida State University, Tallahassee.

Daykin, N., de Viggiani, N., Pilkington, P., & Moriarty, Y. (2012). Music making for health, well-being and behaviour change in youth justice settings: A systematic review. *Health Promotion International, 28*(2), 197–210. doi: 10.1093/heapro/das005.

Daykin, N., Moriarty, Y., de Viggiani, N., & Pilkington, P. (2011). *Evidence review: Music making with young offenders and young people at risk of offending.* Bristol: Youth Music.

de Roeper, J., & Savelsberg, H. J. (2009). Challenging the youth policy imperative: Engaging young people through the arts. *Journal of Youth Studies, 12*(2), 209–225.

DeCarlo, A., & Hockman, E. (2003). Rap Therapy: A group work intervention method for urban adolescents. *Social Work with Groups, 26*(3), 45–59.

Eastburn, C. (2003). *Gongs behind bars: Evaluation report of the Good Vibrations Gamelan in Prisons pilot project.* Lincoln, UK: Firebird Trust.

Ellison, R. (1952). *Invisible man.* New York: Random House.

Ezell, M., & Levy, M. (2003). An evaluaton of an arts program for incarcerated juvenile offenders. *Journal of Correctional Education, 54*(3), 108–114.

Gann, E. (2010). *The effects of therapeutic hip-hop activity groups on perception of self and social support in at-risk urban adolescents,* Unpublished doctoral dissertation, The Wright Institute Graduate School of Psychology, Berkeley, CA.

Gardstrom, S. (2013). Adjudicated adolescents. In L. Eyre (Ed.), *Guidelines for music therapy practice in mental health* (pp. 622–657). Gilsum, NH: Barcelona Publishers.

Goddard, G. (2006). *The Irene Taylor Trust in partnership with National Youth Theatre at HMP YOI Bullwood Hall "Fair."* Final Evaluation Report. London: Irene Taylor Trust.

Gold, C., Voracek, M., & Wigram, T. (2004). Effects of music therapy for children and adolescents with psychopathology: A meta-analysis. *Journal of Child Psychology and Psychiatry, 45*(6), 1054–1063.

Gonzalez, T., & Hayes, B. G. (2009). Rap music in school counseling based on Don Elligan's Rap Therapy. *Journal of Creativity in Mental Health, 4*(2), 161–172.

Harbert, B. J. (2010). I'll keep on living after I die: Musical manipulation and transcendence at Louisiana State Penitentiary. *International Journal of Community Music, 3*(1), 65–76. doi: 10.1386/ijcm.3.1.65/1.

Hazel, N. (2008). Cross-national comparison of youth justice. London: Youth Justice Board.

Heath, S. B., Soep, E., & Roach, A. (1998). *Living the arts through language+learning: A report on community-based youth organizations.* New York: Americans for the Arts.

Henley, J. (2012). *Good Vibrations: Music and social education for young offenders. An evaluation of the musical and social learning processes that young offenders engage in during a Good Vibrations Javanese Gamelan Project and its potential for inspiring desistance from crime.* London: Institute of Education, University of London.

Henley, J., Caulfield, L. S., Wilson, D., & Wilkinson, D. J. (2012). Good Vibrations: positive change through social music-making. *Music Education Research, 14*(4), 499–520. doi: 10.1080/14613808.2012.714765.

Hillman, G. (2004). Arts programs for juvenile offenders in detention and corrections: A *guide to promising practices.* Washington, DC: National Endowment for the Arts.

Kennedy, J. R. (1998). The effects of musical performance, rational emotive therapy and vicarious experience on the self-efficacy and self-esteem of juvenile delinquents and disadvantaged children. Unpublished doctoral dissertation, University of Kansas, Lawrence.

Lee, R. (2010). Music education in prisons: A historical overview. *International Journal of Community Music, 3*(1), 7–17.

Lerner, R. M., Almerigi, J. B., Theokas, C., & Lerner, J. V. (2005). Positive youth development: A veiw of the issues. *The Journal of Early Adolescence, 25*(10), 10–16. doi: 10.1177/0272431604273211.

McIntyre, J. (2007). Creating order out of chaos: Music therapy with adolescent boys diagnosed with a behaviour disorder and/or emotional disorder. *Music Therapy Today, 8*(1), 56–79.

Mendel, R. A. (2011). *No place for kids: The case for reducing juvenile incarceration.* Baltimore, MD: The Annie E. Casey Foundation.

Mendonça, M. (2010). Prison, music and the "rehabilitation revolution": The case of Good Vibrations. *Journal of Applied Arts and Health, 1*(3), 295–307.

National Center for Juvenile Justice (2013). *Easy access to the census of juveniles in residential placement 1997–2011* (online tool). Retrieved from http://www.ojjdp.gov/ojstatbb/ezacjrp/asp/selection.asp.

Olson-McBride, L., & Page, T. (2012). Song to self: Promoting a therapeutic dialogue with high-risk youths through poetry and popular music. *Social Work with Groups, 35*(2), 124–137.

Palidofsky, M. (2010). If I cry for you. . . . Turning unspoken trauma into song and musical theatre. *International Journal of Community Music, 3*(1), 121–128. doi: 10.1386/ijcm.3.1.121/7.

Palidofsky, M., & Stolbach, B. C. (2012). Dramatic healing: The evolution of a trauma-informed musical theatre program for incacerated girls. *Journal of Child & Adolescent Trauma, 5*(3), 239–256. doi: 10.1080/19361521.2012.697102.

Quinn, T., Ploof, J., & Hochtritt, L. (Eds.) (2012). *Art and social justice education: Culture as commons.* New York: Routledge.

Sedlak, A. J., & McPherson, K. S. (2010). Youth's needs and services: Findings from the survey of youth in residential placement. *Juvenile Justice Bulletin*: US Department of Justice.

Shieh, E. (2010). On punishment and music education: Towards a practice for prisons and schools. *International Journal of Community Music, 3*(1), 19–32. doi: 10.1386/ijcm.3.1.19/1.

Tett, L., Anderson, K., McNeill, F., Overy, K., & Sparks, R. (2012). Learning, rehabilitation and the arts in prisons: A Scottish case study. *Studies in the Education of Adults, 44*(2), 171–185.

Tyson, E. H. (2002). Hip hop therapy: An exploratory study of a rap music intervention with at-risk and delinquent youth. *Journal of Poetry Therapy, 15*(3), 131–144.

van Maanen, K. (2009). *Interim evaluation report: Overview and impact of delivery work in year 2. April 2008–March 2009.* London: Kings Place Music Base.

van Maanen, K. (2010). *Evaluation report. 1st April 2007–31st March 2010.* London: Kings Place Music Base.

Williams, R. M. (2008). The status and praxis of arts education and juvenile offenders in correctional facilities in the United States. *Journal of Correctional Education, 59*(2), 107–126.

Wilson, D., Caulfield, L. S., & Atherton, S. (2009). Good Vibrations: The long-term impact of a prison based music project. *Prison Service Journal, 182,* 27–32.

Wolf, D. P., & Holochwost, S. (2014). *Building strengths: Examining the place for music in juvenile justice reform.* Unpublished report submitted to the National Endowment for the Arts.

Wolf, L., & Wolf, D. P. (2012). *May the songs I have written speak for me: An exploration of the potential of music in juvenile justice.* New York: Weill Music Institute, Carnegie Hall.

Woodward, S. C., Sloth-Nielsen, J., & Mathiti, V. (2008). South Africa, the arts and youth in conflict with the law. *International Journal of Community Music, 1*(1), 69–88.

CHAPTER 39

MUSIC

An Alternative Education in the South African Freedom Struggle

SHEILA C. WOODWARD

MY own perspectives on the South African struggle against apartheid, presented here through an academic lens, were initially informed by a series of events in my youth. While my stories are in no way representative of the totality of South African experience, I begin this chapter by sharing some personal accounts in order to paint a visual backdrop against which readers might see some of the directions that music took during the freedom struggle.

PERSONAL NARRATIVE

An ominous rumble distracts me from a chilly winter lunch-time stroll beneath the tall protective oaks in the magnificently manicured grounds of a high school for privileged White girls. Army helicopters barrel through the skies toward the "townships" for Blacks, where my friends have been facing police resistance to their street marches. I rush to find a teacher and ask if she has heard any radio news about what is happening. She wants to know why I am asking. "I'm worried about my friends who are protesting," I splutter, frustrated by the very question. With every ounce of concern for their safety, she implores, "You must tell them to stop so they don't get hurt!" I am jolted by her reaction. This is a tidal wave surging forward, slamming against decades of oppression. Why doesn't she know that nothing is going to stop this?

It is 1976 and South African youth are spilling out of their schools in defiance, undulating waves of chants and rhythms flowing through the city streets. Still clad in their uniforms, teenagers my own age are turning their backs on school. With their united voices chanting promises of freedom, they form human walls of courage that escort them into the face of army tanks, rifles, and tear gas. They protest with homemade placards, thumping their heavy feet into the red dust of the earth, forging toward the black pavements of the city, pounding the ears of their oppressors with relentless rhythms. Children are being shot, like 12-year-old Hector Pieterson, immortalized in a chilling photograph. Others are bundled into the back of police vans. The lucky ones scatter into hiding while a nation of parents is reeling in shock. Hounded by police with dogs, those who are identified as ringleaders are being smuggled out to countries in the North to train as freedom fighters on the borders. There is no going back. Schools are being burned in anger, as symbols of oppression. But the education of children is not ending: it is finding a new home in the songs of the people.

As White children, we are being guarded carefully in our homes, away from the violent streets. At night, our fathers take shifts, patrolling outside White schools, imagining they might become a target of attack, along with the Black schools being burned. After two days, I am feeling increasingly worried about the children protesting. I can bear staying at home no longer and board a train under the ruse of going to practice the pipe organ in a city church. I do not ask my parents for permission: I simply state a fact that any musician understands, "I cannot go one more day without practicing." Once on the train, I am separated from passengers who travel in the compartments for Non-Whites, as they are prominently labeled. I hurry onto the city streets, lined with elegant department store windows and a portentous police presence. A terrified child bolts across the pavement, fleeing from a uniformed policeman cracking his whip. That cruel image haunts me.

Just six months earlier, I had been dressed all in white, singing Christmas Carols, under the stars on a hot Southern Hemisphere night. Our school tradition of massed outdoor choirs folded the last days of the academic year neatly away. The purity of those soaring girls' voices belied the passions that were bursting to escape into holiday freedom. I had no idea my life would be changed forever after the holiday break that preceded my senior year of high school. During that vacation period, I attended a Scripture Union youth camp on a private campground and found myself meeting young Black people my own age for the first time. Sharing dormitories and singing choruses together seemed effortlessly natural, and I wondered how laws on housing, schools, and every imaginable activity had kept us separated during all these years of growing up. Firm friends were made, phone numbers exchanged, and promises of visits assured. Being only 17 years of age, I was not yet driving, but these new friends had an older member in their group who volunteered to fetch me. Sunday arrived and I watched at the upstairs window for their car to pull up outside my house. Not knowing how my parents would react, I told my mother I was going to church with some new friends of other races that I had made at camp. "As long as there isn't a romantic relationship involved," she warned, "you can go." Of course, I'd already fallen in love with a handsome young artist in the group, but that needed to remain a tight secret. I think my parents nearly had a heart attack when I climbed into a car full of "colored" people.

I was surrounded by thick, rich voices as we lustily sang hymns in the church, later walking arm in arm back to their family home. I felt comforted by the confident physical contact that cemented our friendships, noticing how different this was from the more aloof British cultural heritage to which I was accustomed. Their warmth flooded my being. Everyone piled onto the parents' double bed. I was introduced to Uncle Bertie, who was leaning against the headboard, strumming a banjo. Auntie Winnie was lying across the duvet cover. She smiled and patted her stomach, motioning me to join them and rest my head on her body, while we sang "Kaapse Klopse liedjies" to the banjo. I pondered how they lived a mere 15 minutes' drive from my house, but I had been sheltered in my cocooned White neighborhood. All these years, they might as well have been in a world apart. Yet, in one meeting, they treated me like family.

That radical change in my life had started six months earlier. Now, I was at school, hearing the menacing rumble of helicopters. The school bell rang and I ran home to phone my friends. The phone rang unanswered until the evening, "We were protesting and the police stormed our school grounds, throwing tear gas, then whipping us as we ran out, girls too!" I was shocked. I told my friends at school the next day, and one contested, "I don't believe you, police are good people." Newspapers reported the nationwide protests spreading from Soweto, like a fire across the country. Details were scant. I wrote a letter to the editor, asking why specific incidences of police violence against children were not being reported. But when I saw it published, I realized that all the details had been censored and only the philosophical comments remained. Television being a new phenomenon in South African homes, we were glued to the screen in the evenings, gleaning whatever scant news we could.

Two years later, as a young university student secretly engaged to the same young artist with whom I had fallen in love at that life-changing summer camp, I saw a large advertisement in the daily newspaper calling for women of all races to congregate at the City Hall. I thought about all my years growing up, when this splendid hall with its glorious pipe organ hosted twice weekly symphony concerts with Whites only on the stage and in the audience. Both university students at this time, I had defiantly taken my fiancé there for his first experience of the city orchestra, to hear Rodrigo's *Guitar Concierto de Aranjuez*, a composition that represented the passions I felt in our forbidden relationship. Thankfully, no one refused him entry. Answering the newspaper call, I joined the growing crowd of excited women, and the Women's Movement for Peace was founded. I volunteered to be an area chairwoman, and began a powerful collaboration with women of all races visiting each others' homes and writing declarations demanding freedom of the people, which were presented to the Ministers of Parliament. My mother was afraid I would be arrested for going into squatter camps, but I told her, "If the police want to arrest me for handing out blankets to the poor on cold winter nights, then they can go ahead, it won't stop me." I was impressed at how a home constructed with corrugated iron could be made relatively comfortable, lined with cardboard and wallpaper made from the wrappers of tin cans and equipped with a rug, a bed, and a paraffin stove. I hid down low as the car went through a police blockade. Des and Dawn Lindberg staged a run of multiracial performances of *Godspell* at the Quibell Three Arts Theatre, where musicians and audiences of all races celebrated a new freedom the people demanded in defiance of apartheid laws. Obviously a biracial couple, my fiancé and I attracted astonished stares.

As a young adult, I lived through another two decades of civil unrest, characterized by chanting, freedom songs, and protest music, creating a backdrop of theme music for a country apparently lurching headlong toward civil war. Incalculable loss was suffered, but the determined efforts of countless citizens and global supporters averted total catastrophe. Eventually, Mandela was released from prison and a pathway was paved toward peaceful elections that heralded in a new era in which my own children grew up in a multiracial neighborhood, surrounded by children of diverse cultures in their schools. The journey that South Africans had taken in achieving freedom was chronicled, supported, and inspired through music of all genres. While many students had been too angry to return to school, music provided a means to communicate, educate, and share outside the classroom, droning their pain, chanting their protest, intoning narratives of events, and humming dreams of freedom.

THEORETICAL BACKGROUND TO THE SCHOLARLY INVESTIGATION OF MUSIC, STRUGGLE, AND EDUCATION

My stories are the narrow personal lenses through which I saw those times of change. Later, as a music scholar, I began to theoretically investigate music's role in South Africa's "transition from apartheid to democracy" and, in the words of Ingrid Byerly (1998), to learn how music was able to "mirror while mediating; and mediate while prophetizing" (p. 37). Of course, the communicative functions of music had always been a natural part of indigenous cultural heritages. Long before Europeans had colonized the land, tribes were using music for storytelling, motivating, recording, and transmitting history, celebrating and mourning life's milestones, healing, teaching values and customs, and conveying messages. This period in South African history was no different. But with many schools ravaged by stones and fire, music took on an increasingly important role in both educating the youth and providing them with a public voice.

As literature pertaining to music in the South African struggle is presented here for review, a disclaimer is offered that my approach is as an educator, not as an ethnomusicologist. I aim to share a few humble perspectives and examples, rather than a comprehensive investigation. The reader should also take cognizance of the fact that no song can be adequately portrayed by a reading of its text in isolation from the performance of that song in the context in which it was sung. Additionally, myriad performance occasions and contexts would have rendered the song and its meanings overtly or subtly different in every instance. Inevitably, by pulling lyrics into an article such as this, the action "misplaces its concreteness in a Western format and establishes the song as a cultural object" (Coplan & Jules-Rosette, 2005, p. 286).

In exploring the music of the freedom struggle, particularly considering school-children marching through the city streets in protest, it is impossible to avoid issues of identity. The racial classification of children from birth determined virtually every facet of their daily existence, dictated by laws aimed at perpetuating White domination and Black oppression. For example, in the 1960s, Prime Minister Verwoerd declared, "When I have control over native education, I will reform it so natives will be taught from child-hood that equality with Europeans is not for them" (Abdi, 2002, p. 43). As Allen (2010) explains,

> The issue is that identity is not just a soft, 'belonging' thing, although it is also that. In many instances, a particular identity imparts or removes access to basic attributes of a decent life: access to safety, security, general well-being, economic opportunity, and in some cases, even to life itself. In other words, all too often identity, as the theoretical mechanism to categorize humans as different from each other is used to perpetuate unequal access to resources, power and privilege; to obtain and retain advantage for those humans considered like oneself, the 'us', and to block access to advantage for those considered 'them' or 'other.' (p. 3)

Collective identities are the motivating force for the establishment of social movements (McAdam, 2004), and culture is suggested to play different roles in what have been referred to as "settled" and "unsettled" times (Swinder, 1986). Culture is never static: it is always evolving. However, it is during the unsettled times that "we are more apt to experience culture as a tool kit" (McAdam, 2004, p. 226). The collective identity of an oppressed majority population of South Africa constituted a cultural motivation for the spearheading of country-wide movements such as the African National Congress (ANC), the Pan African Congress (PAC), and the South African Communist Party (SACP). As Gilbert (2007) explains, "Cultural traditions are mobilized and reformulated in social movements, and this mobilization and reconstruction of tradition is central to what social movements are, and to what they signify for social and cultural change." Against the backdrop of the notorious, borrowed understatement, "the natives are restless," we see the surge of political resistance as an unstoppable tide, with music being mobilized to play a "deliberate and focused" role in the anti-apartheid struggle (p. 423). Theories that have been applied to music in the American Civil Rights movement can be applied to what was happening in South Africa: "The music continued to serve as a means of identification, but added other communicative functions. . . . Music served as a source and sign of strength, solidarity, and commitment" (Eyerman & Jamison, 1998, p. 98).

As Perry (2014) explains, "Good music often has a beauty identifiable across the boundaries of nation and culture. And yet a musical composition, and music forms in general, have identities rooted in community. The community might be as small as an artistic collective or as vast as a continent" (p. 9). This analysis spans not just the Black community of South Africa, but a national population, rich in all its diversity, that was engaged in the struggle for liberty in South Africa. Multiple movements mobilized the people; however, this chapter does not allow space to even begin to identify them all.

There are arguments about whether music can actually cause social change or "be the inspiration that ultimately leads to such changes" (Weissman, 2010, p. 321). Where there is consensus, however, is that music "intersects with social movements in a wide variety of ways" (Rosenthal & Flacks, 2012, p. 9), and this investigation seeks to find evidence of it being a powerful voice in the South African freedom struggle—one that educated, shared, collaborated, and gave direction.

Culture was firmly identified as "a weapon of struggle" in South Africa's powerful anti-apartheid organization, the ANC. In this context, the term "culture" referred to artistic and intellectual works and activities and included a wide range of arts and crafts, practiced not only by recognized artists but by ordinary people (Gilbert, 2007, p. 421). Of course, culture (defined in a much broader sense) operates "within political institutions as well as outside of them" and plays an important role in "creating political opportunities" (Polletta 2004, p. 108). Looking back, Baleka Mbete, Speaker of Parliament in post-apartheid South Africa said, "Music has played such a role that I just don't see how one would have pulled through the many years of struggle at home, in exile, in camps, all over the world, without being sustained by song (Understanding apartheid, 2008, p. 59).

MUSIC AS RESISTANCE TO OPPRESSION

Decades prior to the swell of youth protests in 1976, hybrid popular music forms had developed in South Africa's urban townships, voicing protest against the rapid implementation and enforcement of apartheid laws by the ruling Nationalist government from 1948. While protest music appeared in a diverse range of traditional and contemporary ethnic and Western styles, these hybrid styles emerged as South Africa's unique forms of popular music. Tendencies from the 1920s to imitate church hymnody and American vaudeville/minstrel styles were followed in the mid-1930s by increasing political consciousness that resulted in determined integration of African elements into popular music (Ballantine, 1991). *Mbaqanga* (stiff maize-based porridge) was a name given to a popular style that many musicians reluctantly performed to earn "bread" money (Allen, 2003, p. 240). It was one of many styles, like *marabi* and *kwela*, that had been developed by the Black working class that "became symbols of what Black people could achieve in a White-dominated world" (Ballantine, 2012, p. 7). As the government increasingly enforced its restrictive apartheid laws toward the late 1950s, we see the music correspondingly reflecting the people's mounting anger and protest. Popular music consciously offered what Loots (1997) described as "a narrative of society intricately interwoven in ideology" (p. 176). The rise of the recording industry promulgated those voices, with protest songs sometimes receiving considerable radio airtime prior to their inevitable banning, such as the Troubadour studio's "uDr. Malan Unomthetho Onzima (Dr. Malan's government is harsh)" (Allen, 2003, p. 236). The purchasing power of the Black working class meant that music was well distributed, despite the monopolization of radio services by the South African Broadcast Corporation, which included

Bantu Radio, a service designed to mold the people's "intellect" and "way of life," while "promoting the mythology of Separate Development" (Hamm, 1991, p. 169). Vuyisile Mini, composer of the freedom song "Ndodemnyama" (1965, track 6) that warned Prime Minister Verwoerd to watch out, "here come the Black people (Nantsi ndodemnyama, Verwoerd pasopa)," was sentenced to death by hanging (Simpson, Markgraaff, & Hirsch, 2002). During the imprisonment of Albert Luthuli (the 1952 president of the ANC and the first South African to be awarded the Nobel Peace Prize), the people sang the song "Somlandela Luthuli, Lelijele licwele uyalandelwa [We shall follow Luthuli, the jails are full, they show that we struggle for our freedom]" (Understanding apartheid, 2008, p. 58).

Music as an Expression of Pain

Individual stories were told in songs that represented much larger political realities. Allen (2003) provides the example of Masuka's song "Mhlaba," which translates, "In the world we are having problems, Black people are sorrowful. Black people are having problems / Black people are sorrowful" (p. 235). The CD notes from a later digital rendition of the recording explain that Masuka wrote these lyrics after being prohibited from entering a restaurant and being with a certain person, due to her race (Allingham, 1991, p. 6). According to Allen (2003), summarizing the theories of Blacking (1995) and Erlmann (1996), "the lyricist's skill lies in the ability to imply layers of significance, leaving audiences the challenge of deciphering deeper meanings—a poetic strategy typical of South African hybrid musical styles" (p. 235). Women played a powerful role in the struggle, including through their capacity as artists. As Chief Luthili stated, "When the women begin to take an active part in the struggle, no power on earth can stop us from achieving freedom in our lifetime" (quoted in Mandela, 1995, p. 257). In the 2002 film documentary, *Amandla! A Revolution in Four Part Harmony*, Sophie Mcinga sings "Madam Please," the heart-wrenching song of a domestic "maid" working in the home of a White employee: "Madam please, before you shout about your broken plate, ask about the meal my family ate." The agony of a mother far from her children is felt: "Madam please, before you ask me if your children are fine, ask me when I last saw mine." Employers would question the many requests to miss work to attend a funeral, dismissing them as lies. Mcinga cries out: "Madam please, before you call today's funeral a lie, ask me why my people die" (Simpson, Markgraaff, & Hirsch, 2002).

Dorothy Masuka's "Ei Yow (Phata phata)," made internationally famous by Miriam Makeba (as "Pata Pata"), has been claimed in the media to have originated in prisons, including dance movements similar to prisoners shuffling forward in a line for food and being patted down in a body search, hence the lyrics "phata, phata," translated as "touch, touch" (Allen, 2003, p. 236).

Soon after adopting the 1950 *Group Areas Act*, and the 1954 *Natives Resettlement Act*, the Nationalist party began decades of forced removals of populations from one area to another, partly as a means of enforcing their policy of separate development. In 1955, 4,000 police and army surrounded Sophiatown, with residents refusing to leave. Homes were bulldozed and residents relocated to Meadowlands. A landmark song by Strike Vilakazi in 1956 epitomized the epic relocations, stating, "U tla a utlwa makgowa a re a re yeng eMeadowlands Meadowlands, Meadowlands, ons duck ni ons pola hi [You will hear the Whites saying let's go to Meadowlands, Meadowlands, Meadowlands, we are not leaving, we are staying here]" (Groenewald, 2005, p. 124). According to Allen (2003), government forces understood the song to be supportive of their program when it was, in fact, an iconic symbol of protest. This presents an example of Blacking's (1995) idea that music can "express values that transcend and inform the passing scene of social events" (p. 150). The lyrics of a much later song reflection, "Sophiatown," by Steff Boss and Tandie Klaasen (no date, track 5) describe how, as a 16-year-old singer in the jazz clubs of Sophiatown, Tandie lost her dreams along with her home: "I can see police on a winter night, breaking down the place where I was born." In the lyrics, Tandie laments that she "had no chance to say goodbye to romance." She describes Sophiatown as a place where her "dreams came true, until they broke it down" (Boss & Klaasen, n.d.).

At the 1955 *National Convention of the Congress of the People*, the historic *Freedom Charter* was written, stating that

> [w]e, the people of South Africa, declare for all our country and the world to know . . . that South Africa belongs to all who live in it, Black and White . . . and that no government can justly claim authority unless it is based on the will of the people. (quoted in Mandela, 1995, p. 203)

This declaration encouraged the people toward mass action. On March 21, 1960, Sharpeville was the site of a public protest against pass laws that required Blacks to carry identity documents restricting their geographical movements. Police opened fire on unarmed men, women, and children. Sixty-nine people were killed and hundreds wounded. The people lamented in repetitive stanzas, "Senzenina [What have we done?]" and "Sohlangana ezulwini [We'll meet in heaven]" (Simpson, Markgraaff, & Hirsch, 2002).

Winston Mankunku wrote his "Yakhal'Inkomo [The bellowing bull]" with a sound that "echoed and amplified the wail of the Black people" (Martin, 2013, p. 230). He had been a young 22-year-old, agonizing over repeated police arrests for not having his identity pass, a document required to be carried by Blacks at all times (Ansell, 2004). Famous early protagonists in the public burning of passes were Mahatma Gandhi and Nelson Mandela. After the Sharpeville massacres, the ANC Youth league increased its promotion of violence in resistance. In his first television interview, which was conducted by Britain's ITN reporter, Brian Widlake, Mandela expressed the ANC's changing stance: "There are many people who feel that it is useless and futile for us to continue talking peace and nonviolence against a government whose reply is only savage attacks on an unarmed and defenseless people." Having spent time out of the country in military training and fundraising, Mandela returned and was soon arrested. While in prison, he was issued an additional charge of sabotage. He defended himself in court prior to receiving a life sentence with these iconic words:

> I have cherished the ideal of a democratic and free society in which all persons live together in harmony and with equal opportunities. It is an ideal for which I hope to live and to achieve, but, if needs be, it is an ideal for which I am prepared to die. (Mandela, 1995, p. 438)

In the haunting song, "Nongqongqo" (1965, track 4), the people call out to their leaders in the Nonqgongqo prison, "Bahleli bonke kwa Nongqongqo [they are all together at Nongqongqo], nanko uMandela [there is Mandela], nanko, nanko etilongweni [there he is, there he is in prison]."

According to Ballantine (2012), "One of the reasons jazz was suppressed was that it aspired to (among other things) musical and social equality: it was precisely the musical idiom in and through which urban Black people were proving to themselves and to the world that they were the equals of Whites" (p. 10). The 1960s wave of police violence, bannings, and imprisonments led to many well-known jazz musicians fleeing into exile, including Hugh Masekela, Miriam Makeba, and Dollar Brand (who changed his name to Abdullah Ibrahim). A major benefit of their time in exile was the development of substantial international performing careers and recording opportunities (Allen, 2008; Ballantine, 1989). In 1974, a collaboration between well-known jazz musicians Abdullah Ibrahim, Robbie Jansen, Basil Coetzee, Paul Michaels, Monty Weber, and Morris Goldberg in Cape Town led to the release of the album *Mannenberg: Is Where It's Happening.* Essentially having a jazz aesthetic, it included delightful elements of *marabi, ticky-draai, ghoema*, and *langarm* styles and has been referred to as "the most iconic of all South African jazz tunes" (Ansell, 2004, p.153). Martin (2013) described it as a "landmark in the history of South African jazz" that "rapidly became an emblem not only of the Cape Town coloured communities, but of all the victims of apartheid who, having heard the message of the Black Consciousness Movement, looked for creations that could make them proud" (p. 231).

Music as Empowerment

On June 16, 1976, when the youth took their songs to the streets in protest against requirements to write exams in the Afrikaans language, no doubt the rhythmic chanting gave the youth a sense of identity and belonging to the group, but it would also have given them courage, empowering them to keep marching in the face of guns and army tanks. This concept is no different from views on the role that music played in the American Civil Rights movement: "You know you are going to get beaten, you know you might even get killed, but the sound, the power of the community, was watching over you and keeping you safe (Reagon, interviewed in Seeger & Reiser, 1989, p. 77). The youth marched through city streets shouting chants of "Amandla" (power), accompanied by the raising of a clenched fist and the singing of freedom songs. They sang the hymn "Nkosi Sikelel' i'Afrika [God bless Africa]," composed in 1897 by a 24-year-old teacher named Santonga for the students to sing at his mission school, which came "to symbolize more than any other piece of expressive culture the struggle for African unity and liberation in South Africa" (Coplan, 1985, p. 46). Freedom songs have been referred to as "probably the dominant musical medium of popular political expression" (Gilbert, 2007, p. 423), evidenced by their omnipresence at political marches, rallies, and meetings of every kind, religious ceremonies, and funerals. We see a parallel in Reed's (2005) theory about music in the American Civil Rights movement, according to which

> [m]usic becomes more deeply ingrained in memory than mere talk, and this quality made it a powerful organizing tool.... In singing you take on a deeper level of commitment to an idea than if you only hear it spoken of. The movement was all about commitment and singing was often a halfway house to commitment. (p. 28)

MUSIC AS STORYTELLING

Protest in popular music exploded on a larger scale than ever seen before, playing a transformative role as a "power of utterance: the voice of a culture—the narrative of its poetry, ideologies, beliefs and lifestyles" (Loots, 1997, p. 279). Miriam Makeba argued this narrative role of music in a CD flier in 1998:

> In our struggles, songs are not simply entertainment for us. They are the way we communicate. The press, radio and TV are all censored by the government. We cannot believe what they say. So we make up songs to tell us about events. Let something happen and the next day a song will be written about it. (*Sangoma* CD flier, 1998)

Makeba's landmark song, "Soweto Blues," written by Stanley Kwesi Todd and Hugh Masekela (Todd & Masekela, 1989, track 5), is a prime example of this, telling the tale of the 1976 youth uprising. It describes the demands passed down to the schools that final exams be written in the language of the White man: "The children got a letter from the Master. It said: 'No more Xhosa, Sotho, no more Zulu.'" Makeba sings of how the children stormed out into the streets, "refusing to comply," and of the fierce brutality of the police: "the children were dying, bullets flying, All the mothers screaming and a-crying." The lyrics describe how the police rounded up the ringleaders and how some escaped imprisonment by fleeing north: "The Border is ... waiting for the children, frightened and running."

MUSIC AS IDENTITY

There is a traditional saying in South Africa that "[i]f you strike a woman, you strike a rock." The attacks on and imprisonment of the children struck a massive blow to the mothers. Interviewed in the aforementioned and illuminating film documentary *Amandla, a Revolution in Four Part Harmony*, Sophie Mgcina, a mother and singer, recounts how the "children were killed because of a language, Afrikaans. We wrote the songs to tell the children: You are strong, you are beautiful, you are Black, you belong!" (Simpson, Markgraaff, & Hirsch, 2002). An example of a song exhorting children to be proud of their identity was written by Mthunzi Namba and Sibongile Khumalo (1996, track 3): "Little girl, when it seems you're all alone in the dream, believe in life.... Your arms are like the waves of the ocean.... Let your dream carry you." One of the young girls suffering in the struggle was singer Lorraine Klaasen, daughter of Thandi Klaasen, who many years later realized her dream of taking the music and its messages from South Africa to a global audience (Klaasen, 2008). In another interview on the same film documentary, Thandi Modise recounts her experience of 1976:

> One morning I woke up and was told I was a ring leader. I was being hunted down. I think I was just an average kid, a bit of a loud mouth. But I had also lost friends and the children were being arrested all over, children were being shot down. I thought, in 1977, I would be going to medical school... saw myself as a little country doctor somewhere and all that was, you know, just blowing in my face. So I was angry and I didn't believe I wanted to go back to school. I was too angry to be a student. (Simpson, Markgraaff, & Hirsch, 2002)

She described further in the interview how, after the events of 1976, the songs "became more militant and angry." "Shona Malanga" had been a celebratory song for domestic workers on their weekly day off. After 1976, the words were changed, signifying changes in political thinking, and suggesting meeting "in the African bushveld with our bazookas" to promote the struggle (Shona Malanga, 2009, track 5). The mournful but defiant "Thina Sizwe" was frequently sung at funerals in the 1970s, supporting the empowerment of the dark people who were crying for their land, which was taken by the White people, and directing the intruders to leave: "Thina Sizwe esimnyama Sikhalela izwe lethu, Elathathwa ngabamhlope, Sithi, mabayek' umhlaba wethu" (Thina Sizwe, 2009, track 1).

The songs echoed Steve Biko's exhortations for people to be proud of being Black, to teach their own history and culture, and to build a sense of their own humanity. As Biko (1978) told them, "Merely by describing yourself as Black you have started on a road towards emancipation, you have committed yourself to fight against all forces that seek to use your blackness as a stamp that marks you out as a subservient being" (p. 48).

Music as a Tool for Advancing the Struggle

There were messages to young people to be part of the struggle, providing reference to historical events. A young White father, stage-named Roger Lucey, wrote the "Thabane" ballad to his son, urging him to fight for justice as he grows up, telling him the story of Stephen Biko who "has been taken, but you know he's just one in many" (Drewett, 2005, p. 54). Protest theater, often including songs, was making its mark, such as *Pula*, which included the song of Tshaka, who became "a symbol of Black militancy" (Wakashe 1986, p. 46), with the lyrics "Uyababona bepheth'isibham? [Do you see them carrying guns?] ... Bayete, Zulu, bayete! [Hail, Zulu nation, hail!], Bayete, Tshaka, bayete! [Hail, Tshaka, hail!]."

In the 1980s, a style of rhythmic dance characterized street protests, called *toyi-toyi*. Twala and Koetaan (2006) describe it as "a medium to arouse the emotions of the oppressed and unify them in their quest for equality and justice" (p. 169). They provide examples of *toyi toyi* chants that called for the release of leaders, for example, "Oliver Tambo, thetha noBotha. Akhulel' uMandela [Oliver Tambo, speak to Botha to release Mandela]." Some song lyrics were derogatory about the rulers, for example, "Uyabalek' uBotha, nezinja zakhe [Botha is fleeing together with his dogs]" (p. 170). Others promoted violence "Leth' umshin' wam' umshin'wami [Bring that machine gun]" (p. 173). The plight of students rings clear in these refrains: "Bayakhala abafundi bathi Tambo [Tambo students are crying]," "Sithwele kanzima [They say, they are having it tough]," and "Bayakhalel' imfundo yabo [They are crying for their education]" (p. 177).

The song "Sabela," by Motsumi Makhene and Sibongile Khumalo (1996, track 7), prophesied the freedom of which they dreamed: "This is the time for rejoicing. The sun is shining bright." It motivated the people to think in new directions: "We are building a new nation" and called for immediate action: "The time is now, time to focus, to stop the abuse." The song exhorted the Black people to respond to the call ("Wemnt'omnyama Sabel'uyabizwa") and warned White people that change was calling them ("Wemnt'omhlophe Iyakubiza inguquko").

Outside the country, The Mayibuye Cultural Ensemble was an ANC organization established in 1975 in London, England, serving the purpose of educating the international public about resistance to South Africa's apartheid system. It "achieved considerable success in Europe with its agitprop performances incorporating narrative, poetry and song" while "simultaneously raising consciousness within the movement about the practical ways in which cultural activity could further the project of national liberation" (Gilbert, 2007, p. 422). The Amandla Cultural Ensemble emerged from the training camps in Southern Angola and surrounds, populated by the militant ANC Youth League exiles. Musicians among the groups, led mostly by trombonist Jonas Gwangwa, integrated choral singing, jazz, theater, and dance. The performances "were intended not only to raise awareness about apartheid, but also to present an alternative vision of moving towards a more dynamic, inclusive South African culture" (p. 422).

MUSIC AS INNOVATION, CREATION, AND COLLABORATION

One of the major messages from musicians of the 1980s was the power of intercultural collaborations that were taking place on a scale beyond anything seen previously. Examples included Johnny Clegg and Savuka, Jennifer Ferguson, P. J. Powers, and Mango Groove. Clegg's and Savuka's "One (hu)man, one vote" implores, "Don't let us slip back into the dark.... A new image of man, the shape of his own future now in his hands—he says: One 'man, one vote—step into the future" (Clegg & Summerfield, 1989, track 1). A group of brass players from the Cape Town Philharmonic Orchestra teamed up with Amampondo, a marimba ensemble from Langa, to produce the unique sounds of the album *Intsholo* (Haubrich, 1995). The historic international collaboration between Paul Simon and Ladysmith Black Mambazo launched the *iscathamiya* musicians into a global career that still thrives today. As Coplan (2005) says, "They served to humanize oppressed black South Africans to a mass audience overseas" (p. 13).

Young White Afrikaans musicians innovatively used *volksliedjies* (a style of Afrikaans folk music) to join the protests as "[s]ung verses and poetry in the vernacular became the center of a new cultural resistance for the Afrikaner, where English pop had previously been the fashionable cultural form" (Byerly, 1998, p. 17). South Africans were increasingly able to laugh at themselves, and satirical songs became more common, with favorite singers in the field such as David Kramer (Drewett, 2002). Kramer's 1993 song, "777 Heaven," satirizes a right-winger "searching for a heaven, where God wears a triple seven ... a place where there's no Bantus, no Muslims, no Hindus, none of the other people God made" (Drewett, 2002, p. 92). Major orchestral, choral, and opera compositions emerged as political and social statements, including works by Pieter Luis Van Dijk. His *Horizons* is based on a sixteenth-century San cave painting of a European ship bringing strange men, seen as gods, who would ultimately cause their extinction.

New choral sounds blending traditional, church hymnody, and jazz styles were brought to the stage by director, composer, and arranger Lungile Jacobs Ka Nyamezele, such as the Jabex Foley composition "Ekhaya Madoda [Feel at home, everyone]," which tells of the miners working in the bowels of the earth and, having completed their task, are going back home (Foley, 2005, track 4). According to Mojapelo and Galane (2008), the late 1980s brought "a new regiment of young musicians who blended traditional South African rhythms with elements of traditional jazz to create a uniquely South African sound" (p. 223). These included Selaelo Selota, who shared sounds and stories from his childhood through his guitar, Vusi Mahlasela, and Jimmy Dludlu.

Popular music was aptly described by the South African scholar Ansie Loots (1997) as a network of ideological expression, protest emancipation, and empowerment. She described the creative blending of rock songs with influences from the West, and infusions of African musical traditions. Sello Chicco Twala and Brenda Fassie's (1990, track 6) historic "Black President" offers a striking example of this in lamenting and celebrating the powerful story of Mandela's journey from prison to presidency (Coplan, 2005). The song describes Mandela being "sentenced to isolation," with "many painful years of hard labour." The powerful rhythmic energy in the djembe drumming reinforces that Mandela's "spirit was never broken." The song thrusts us finally toward the celebration of Mandela's release from prison in 1990, when "he walked the long road back to freedom." As he raised up his hand in the symbolic gesture of Black power, Mandela exclaimed "*Viva, viva my people.*" The song thanks God for hearing the people's prayers "night and day."

After Mandela's negotiated release in 1990, an interim constitution was written that would allow for the implementation of "one man . . . one vote," with South Africa holding its first democratic elections inclusive of all races in 1994. The new President Mandela celebrated the victory of his people in public rallies, dancing with the singing crowds to the triumphant song, which translates, "You've been fighting for freedom for a long time, now we've got it. No one can change that. You brought us peace, Nelson Mandela" (Simpson, Markgraaff, & Hirsch, 2002).

MUSIC AS VOICE FOR SOCIAL CHANGE

South Africans managed to avoid a full-scale civil war and achieve a democracy in a country that now boasts one of the most liberal human rights constitutions in the world. Understandably, the county continues to face daunting problems of poverty, crime, unemployment, illegal immigration, gangsterism, corruption, and more. These issues were boldly grasped in "a new subgenre of popular musical culture called *Kwaito*" that "gripped the imagination of black youths" (Kahn, 2010, p. 151). With a uniquely African hip-hop sound, musicians such as Skwatta Kamp continue to sing of the ongoing struggle against poverty, lamenting "a sense of disempowerment amongst the youth who expected more tangible results from the high table of freedom" (Kahn, 2010, p. 151). Despite all the challenges the country faces, South Africa stands as an icon of the power of perseverance and reconciliation. All through the turbulent years of struggle, voices rang out in song, carrying messages between the people. In the words of Thabo Mbeki, who followed Mandela as president of South Africa,

> At no time has the liberation movement not been singing. At no time has the liberation movement not been dancing. Everywhere, culture becomes a very central and a very important element in this act of rebellion, in this act of assertion that we are human. (Understanding apartheid, 2008, p. 59)

For music educators across the globe, perhaps our unifying mission is to challenge students with the vision that "[m]usic . . . can do more than mirror society, it can be a participating force in change" (Woodward, 1994, p. 198). What injustices do they see? What voices might be heard through their music? What part will they play, as musicians, in impacting change in the world? In the words of Eyerman and Jamison (1998) "in social movements, musical and other kinds of cultural tradition are made and remade; and after the movements fade away as political forces, the music remains as a memory and as a potential way to inspire new waves of mobilization" (p. 2).

REFERENCES

Abdi, A. A. (2002). *Culture, education, and development in South Africa: Historical and contemporary perspectives*. Westport, CT: Bergin & Garvey.

Allen, L. (2003). Commerce, politics, and musical hybridity: Vocalizing urban black South African identity during the 1950s. *Ethnomusicology, 47*(2), 228–249.

Allen, L. (2008). Remembering Miriam Makeba (4 March 1932–10 November 2008). *Journal of the Musical Arts in Africa, 5*, 89–90.

Allen, L. (2010). Cosmopolitan freedoms. *The Salon, 2*, 1–4. Retrieved from http://jwtc.org.za/the_salon/volume_2.htm.

Allingham, R. (1991). Hamba Notsokolo and other original hits. CD notes, Gallo Music Productions CD ZAK 60.

Ansell, G. (2004). *Soweto blues: Jazz, popular music and politics in South Africa*. New York: Continuum.

Ballantine, C. (1989). A brief history of South African popular music. *Popular Music, 8*(3), 305–310.

Ballantine, C. (1991). Music and emancipation: The social role of Black jazz and vaudeville in South Africa between the 1920s and the early 1940s. *Journal of Southern African Studies, 17*(1), 129–152.

Ballantine, C. (2012). *Marabi nights: Jazz, "race" and society in early apartheid South Africa*. Scotsville: University of KwaZulu–Natal Press.

Biko, N. M. (1978). The definition of Black consciousness. In *I write what I like: Selected readings* (pp. 48–53). Chicago: University of Chicago Press.

Blacking, J. (1995). The music of politics. In R. Byron (Ed.), *Music, culture and experience: Selected papers of John Blacking* (pp. 198–222). Chicago: University of Chicago Press.

Boss, S., & Klaasen, T. (n.d.). Sophiatown. Recorded by Tandie Klaasen. On *Together as one* (CD). Montreal: Magra Multi Media.

Byerly, I. B. (1998). Mirror, mediator, and prophet: The music indaba of late-apartheid South Africa. *Ethnomusicology: Journal of the Society for Ethnomusicology, 42*(1), 1–44.

Clegg, J., & Summerfield, B. (1989). One (hu)man one vote. Recorded by Johnny Clegg and Savuka. On *Cruel, crazy, beautiful world* (CD). Johannesburg: EMI.

Coplan, D. B. (1985). *In township tonight!: South Africa's black city music and theatre*. London: Longman.

Coplan, D. B. (2005). God rock Africa: Thoughts on politics in popular black performance in South Africa. *African Studies, 64*(1), 9–27.

Coplan, D. B., & Jules-Rosette, B. (2005). Nkosi Sikelel' iAfrika and the liberation of the spirit in South Africa. *African Studies, 64*(2), 285–308.

Drewett, M. (2002). Satirical opposition in popular music within apartheid and post-apartheid South Africa. *Society in Transition, 33*(1), 80–95.

Drewett, M. (2005). "Stop this filth": The censorship of Roger Lucey's music in apartheid South Africa. *South African Journal of Musicology, Samus, 25*, 53–70.

Erlmann, V. (1996). *Nightsong: Performance, power and practice in South Africa.* Chicago: Chicago University Press.

Eyerman, R., & Jamison, A. (1998). *Music and social movements: Mobilizing traditions in the twentieth century.* Cambridge, UK: Cambridge University Press.

Foley, J. (2005). Ekhaya Madoda. Recorded by Voices of Cape Town. On *Live @Artscape 2005.* Cape Town: Lungile Jabobs Ka Nyamazele.

Gilbert, S. (2007). Singing against apartheid: The ANC cultural groups and the international anti-apartheid struggle. *Journal of Southern African Studies, 33*(2), 421–441.

Groenewald, H. C. (2005). The role of political songs in the realization of democracy in South Africa. *Liberator, 26*(2), 121–136.

Hamm, C. (1991). The constant companion of man: Separate development, Radio Bantu and music. *Popular Music, 10*(2), 147–173.

Kahn, K. (2010). Re-locating South African hip hop into global intercultural communication. *Muziki, 7*(1), 148–160.

Klaasen, L. (2008). *Africa calling* (CD). Montreal: Justin Time Records.

Loots, A. (1997). *A critical approach to rock music from a cultural, historical, and theoretical perspective.* Doctoral dissertation, University of Port Elizabeth, South Africa.

Makeba, M. (1988). *Sangoma.* Warner Bros. Records. CD Flier.

Makhene, M., & Khumalo, S. (1996). Sabela. Recorded by Sibongile Khumalo. On *Ancient evenings.* (CD). Johannesburg: Sony Music Entertainment.

Mandela, N. (1995). *Long walk to freedom.* London: Abacus.

Martin, D. C. (2013). *Sounding the Cape: Music, identity and politics in South Africa.* Somerset West, SA: African Minds.

McAdam, D. (2004). Revisiting the US Civil Rights movement. In J. Goodwin & J. Jasper (Eds.), *Rethinking social movement: Structure meaning and emotion* (pp. 201–232). Oxford: Rowman and Littlefield Publishers.

Mojapelo, M., & Galane, S. (2008). *Beyond memory: Recording the history, moments and memories of South African music.* Somerset West, SA: African Minds.

Namba, M., & Khumalo, S. (1996). Little girl. Recorded by Sibongile Khumalo. On *Ancient evenings* (CD). South Africa: Sony Music Entertainment.

Ndodemnyama. ([1965]1990). Recorded by Miriam Makeba. On *An evening with Belafonte/Makeba* (LP). New York: RCA Victor Studio A.

Nongqongqo. ([1965]1990). Recorded by Miriam Makeba. On *An evening with Belafonte/Makeba* (CD). New York: RCA Victor Studio A.

Perry, I. (2004). *Prophets of the hood: Politics and poetics in hip-hop.* Durham, NC: Duke University Press.

Polletta, F. (2004). Culture is not just in your head. In J. Goodwin & J. Jasper (Eds.), *Rethinking social movement: Structure meaning and emotion* (pp. 97–110). Oxford: Rowman & Littlefield Publishers.

Reed, T. V. (2005). *The art of protest: Culture and activism from the civil rights movement to the street of Seattle.* Minneapolis: University of Minnesota Press.

Rosenthal, R., & Flacks, R. (2012). *Playing for change: Music and musicians in the service of social movements.* Boulder, CO: Paradigm Publishers.

Seeger, P., & Reiser B. (1989). *Everybody says freedom: The story of the Civil Rights movement in songs and pictures.* New York: W. W. Norton.

Shona Malanga. (2009). Recorded by African Cream Freedom Choir. On *Freedom songs* (CD). Parkwood: African Cream Music.

Simpson, S. (Producer), Markgraaff, D. (Producer), & Hirsch, L. (Director). (2002). *Amandla: A revolution in four part harmony.* Santa Monica: Artisan Entertainment.

Swinder, A. (1986). Culture in action: Symbols and strategies. *American Sociological Review, 51,* 273–286.

Thina Sizwe. (2009). Recorded by African Cream Freedom Choir. On *Freedom songs* (CD). Parkwood: African Cream Music.

Todd, S., & Masekela H. ([1989]1997). Soweto blues (Recorded by Miriam Makeba). On *Welela* (CD). Amsterdam: Philips.

Twala S. C., & Fassie, B. (1990) Black president. Recorded by Brenda Fassie. On *South Africa various artists* (CD). Johannesburg: EMI Music South Africa.

Twala, C., & Koetaan, Q. (2006). The toyi-toyi protest culture in the 1908s: An investigation into its liberating and unifying powers. *SA Journal of Cultural History, 10*(1), 163–179.

Understanding apartheid. (2008). *Apartheid Museum.* Cape Town: Oxford University Press. Retrieved from http://www.apartheidmuseum.org/resources.

Wakashe, T. P. (1986). "Pula": An example of Black protest theatre in South Africa. *The Drama Review, 30*(4), 36–47.

Weissman, D. (2010). *Talkin' 'bout a revolution: Music and social change in America.* Milwaukee: Backbeat Books.

Woodward, S. C. (1994). The impact of current functions of music in children's lives on music education philosophies. In H. Lees (Ed.), *Musical connections: Tradition and change.* (pp. 194–200). International Society for Music Education.

....

CHAPTER 40

NEW FACES IN OLD SPACES

Mexican American Musical Expressions and Music Equity within the Music Curriculum

....

AMANDA SOTO

CONJUNTO music is a traditional folk music that originated in the borderlands of South Texas with roots from Mexico. It has become a symbol of pride and cultural identity for many Mexican Americans. As conjunto music spreads across the United States, it mirrors the migration of Mexican Americans, their assimilation into American society, and their acknowledgment and preservation of their cultural roots. This music is woven into the cultural fabric of Mexican American children and youth, with many of them singing along, dancing to, and performing conjunto music.

Mexican American children and youth have been challenged in their education and schooling owing to the gap between classroom instruction and the cultural and language complexities inherent in being Mexican American. Music is a space that is used to create and confirm one's cultural identity in ways that are strongly intertwined with language. As explained in this chapter, educating a child without reference to his or her culture and identity within the curriculum can have potential negative effects on minority students' learning, thus widening the gap between the identities of minority children and those of the dominant culture, which are portrayed in the curriculum and presented within the classroom. However, US schools often fail to acknowledge, let alone include, conjunto music in music instruction.

This chapter describes conjunto music as a vital part of Mexican American students' musical and cultural identities, reveals the various ways in which youth are interacting with this musical genre in their everyday lives, and offers suggestions for its inclusion in the music education curriculum. If structured more equitably with respect to the diversity of music found in the curriculum and classroom, music programs can attract more Mexican American or other children while also contributing to their overall academic success relative to their peers by strengthening their self-esteem and sense of personal and cultural identity.

Who Am I? The Confluence of Two Musical Cultures

As I flipped through old childhood pictures with my mother, I came across myself as a second grade child performing in a school program, dressed in a ballet folklorico dress with multicolored ribbons woven through my hair. My mother and I recounted musical experiences of my childhood while in school. During the time when my grandmother would take care of me, I enjoyed listening to her sing in Spanish many Mexican children's folk songs. Throughout elementary school, I was a ballet folklorico dancer during our annual Cinco de Mayo celebrations in the school district. My mother laughed as she pointed to another photo of me singing a Juan Gabriel song with a microphone in my hand. Juan Gabriel is a famous, internationally known Mexican composer and singer even to this day. I remember the cool breeze as I was about to fall asleep while standing outside my grandmother's window with my uncles and extended family preparing to serenade my grandmother with *Las Mañanitas* at midnight on her birthday. Throughout my childhood, I heard my mother singing along with the radio to many of her favorite Spanish pop tunes while she cleaned the house.

As I entered the sixth grade, the silver flute was calling my name. I enrolled in my middle school band and with much dedication and practice rose to the position of first chair flute player. After starting to listen and play Western concert band music, however, I could not quite make the connection between this new music that I was learning in school and the conjunto, *Tejano* (a modernized version of conjunto music), and mariachi music I listened to at home and at community events. As I continued my formal study of music at school, my home-and-family music began to feel less interesting to sing, listen, and dance to. Although sometimes confused about the musical connections in my life, I stayed in band through high school and rose to the position of drum major during my last years of school. Leadership experiences in the school music program confirmed my decision to become a band director. During those four years of high school, I *really* learned how to dance to conjunto and Tejano music. I had always known the basic moves and could manage a dance with my father or brother, but after many weekends filled with dancing I became quite good at it. My friends and I would often show up at a wedding in the local town hall just so we could dance to the great conjunto and Tejano groups that were hired to play.

After graduation, I left for college to pursue a music education degree and delved deeper into the Western music paradigm through my studies. I also experienced Ghanaian drumming through participation in an ensemble and traveled to Ghana after graduation. These few experiences stirred my desire to explore musical experiences outside the Western art music culture, leading eventually to graduate studies in ethnomusicology. This distanced me somewhat from my home culture and its music. As I shifted my doctoral studies to music education with an emphasis on the study of world music pedagogy, I had to confront and reconcile the complexities of my musical identity and my long-held beliefs about music, especially "my" cultural music. I discovered that I was not alone either, in situating myself at the overlap of multiple musical identities.

Although I had grown up dancing and listening to many of the conjunto, Tejano, and mariachi songs, I still did not fully appreciate the music that surrounded me, the reason being that I was holding tightly to the American band culture into which I had been inducted in middle school. Graduate school, however, allowed the study of my musical culture, conjunto and Tejano music, and I was finally able to reconcile and reconnect my musical beliefs and sense of identity with my own cultural heritage.

While in graduate school in Washington, I was fortunate to have been able to participate in the Seattle Fandango Project, where I was able to play, sing, and dance to *son jarocho* (music from Veracruz, Mexico). Starting out as a university-community partnership with the University of Washington, this community music group brought in guest musicians to teach this music and tradition to university faculty, students, and members of the local community. Even though it was not the music that I had grown up with, it was similar in language and the use of various instruments and thus was familiar to me. There were moments at these rehearsals and music lessons when I felt more in tune with the music (and the essence of being a musician) than I had ever felt sitting in a concert band rehearsal or concert. I was able to witness young children discovering their own heritage, who could out-dance and out-play some of the adults in the group, thus developing their musical skills in this genre.

These musical experiences and conversations in Spanish would transport me back home and would bring tears to my eyes. I had initially left the Rio Grande Valley, trying to escape my Mexican heritage on a quest to become assimilated and educated, and to feel superior to my community. I had always felt that the music of my culture was not important—not good enough. It was I, however, who was misinformed. How ironic that the farther away I got from my culture, the more I longed for and appreciated it.

New Faces in Old Spaces: Changing School Populations

Mexican Americans are the largest group within the US Hispanic population classification, and many school populations (especially in California, Texas, New Mexico, and Arizona) consist of a Mexican American majority (Garcia, 2004; US Census Bureau, 2010). The school classroom demographics are changing rapidly in both urban and rural school districts. "More than half of the growth in the total population of the United States between 2000 and 2010 was due to the increase in the Hispanic population" (Ennis, Rios-Vargas, & Albert, 2011, p. 2). Hispanics of Mexican origin increased

54 percent from 20.6 million in 2000 to 31.8 million in 2010. Hispanics, as the largest student minority population, accounted for 22 percent of students who were enrolled in public school in the United States for the 2009–2010 school year. Mexican and Mexican American students are becoming a larger presence in our music classrooms, and therefore educators should understand and take into account in their curricular decisions the musical and ethnic complexities of these students.

Numerous educational models have been explored and implemented to allow for the success of bilingual Mexican American students, particularly those born in Mexico or into families who continue the language, customs, and values of Mexican cities and communities. However, in a review of Mexican American students' educational achievement scores, Garcia (2004) found that they are overrepresented among the nation's least successful students, scoring far lower on standardized tests and having higher dropout rates than other ethnic groups. In addition, they are underrepresented among students who are receiving bachelor, graduate, and professional degrees. Garcia also noted that the data from first grade are "a powerful reminder that the achievement patterns for all racial/ethnic groups are basically established in the early years of school," because the achievement levels did not undergo significant change between the early primary grades and grade 12 (p. 494).

Early goals of multicultural education were centered on the process of "Americanization," which was intended to assimilate small ethnic and linguistically diverse communities into a single dominant national institutional structure and culture. Valdés (1996) and Garcia (2001b) have argued that this is still the goal of many multicultural education programs aimed at Mexican American students (cited in Garcia, 2004, p. 498). Most often, bilingual programs use a student's native language as a bridge to learn the mainstream language and usually do not include content integration centered on promoting and respecting the historical and cultural contributions associated with the secondary language (Trueba, 1987). A significant part of the problem is that there is no single approach to the education of Mexican American students within multicultural and music education programs. Nevertheless, and despite the many challenges involved in accommodating their musical needs, Mexican American students deserve to have a school community that fosters, respects, and incorporates their personal and cultural values into the curriculum while receiving opportunities for success in those educational settings. As British sociologist of education Basil Bernstein (2000) cautions, in a democratic society, students in state schools have a right be included "socially, intellectually, culturally and personally" into the school community and curriculum, as when lacking that their education may suffer (p. xx). In the United States, a socially just music education curriculum needs to include a space in which Mexican American students' language, culture, and musical practices can be validated and held in the same regard as other musics. Yet, thus far, and despite the use of Spanish-language songs and attention to the mariachi genre in schools, conjunto music often remains ignored in music curricula, despite its popularity among many Mexican Americans.

SOUNDSCAPES OF MEXICAN AMERICAN STUDENTS

As Shelemay (2001) posited, soundscapes of a grand variety are found across the world, each a product of people's meaning-making within their environments. The multiple and overlapping soundscapes are sometimes found in children's lives, too, as they are exposed to musical expressions within their elementary schools, their home lives, and in the communities that enable them to construct or retain their musical and ethnic identities. Music serves as an important vehicle in the creation of one's identity because it is a means of communication that can unite people and can represent a significant part of their cultural legacy. Therefore, it is important to evaluate the curriculum content and methods of transmission in the music classroom, in this case as they relate to Mexican Americans.

There is a wealth of Spanish-language music available to American music teachers, much of it developed alongside the growth of the multicultural music education movement of the last quarter-century. The popular and most widely used American music textbooks for elementary and secondary music classes all have some component related to Spanish-language, Mexican, and Mexican American music traditions (Feay-Shaw, 2001).

Mariachi music has rapidly spread into schools, particularly at the secondary level, in the past 10 years. A mariachi music program would seem to be an important means of facilitating a bimusical identity among those students who may come to school with American mainstream musical experience but no experience in this Mexican and Mexican American genre (or vice versa), as well as supporting the presence of bicultural and bilingual education in schools. Mariachi affords a sense of cultural pride, self-esteem, and social acceptance for Mexican Americans in that it may be part of their personal or family cultural identity. For many students, mariachi is the music of their homeland, or of their parents' and grandparents' earlier experiences while growing up in Mexico. Many second- and third-generation Mexican American students may respond to the sound and social meaning of the genre, and therefore its inclusion in school programs may attract a student population that has often been ignored in the traditional school music program (Boss-Barba & Soto, 2008). School mariachi ensemble programs can thus be seen as a form of culturally responsive pedagogy because they are based on students' own cultural knowledge and their previous experiences while allowing their learning outcomes to be culturally, socially, and musically relevant and effective for them in and outside school (Gay, 2010).

Yet, despite a wealth of materials, including publications for teaching mariachi and Spanish-language songs of Mexican and Mexican American cultures, attention to the popular regional musical genre conjunto in schools is nearly nil. Nor is there literature that addresses the bicultural, bilingual, and bimusical realities of children of Mexican heritage in American school music programs. Music educators are instead teaching without reference to or knowledge of the musical, cultural, and linguistic experiences that Mexican American children bring to school.

CONJUNTO MUSIC

Conjunto was developed in the Rio Grande Valley and in various other cities in South Texas in the 1920s and 1930s. In Spanish, *conjunto* refers to a "group" or "ensemble." This ensemble centers on the music of the accordion; it came into its own recognizable form after World War II in 1935 (Pena, 1985, p. 2). Even though this folk music has musical roots from Mexico, it is one of the few musical genres that originated in the United States. As this author has recently explained elsewhere, "Today, conjunto music can be heard on car stereos, in concert and dance halls, weddings, quinceañeras, community festivals, Hispanic holiday celebrations, bars, music festivals, and community music schools. It has become a symbol of pride and cultural identity for *Tejanos,* which is Spanish for Texas Mexicans" (Soto, 2013, p. 282). The social nature of dancing, which is a key element of this musical genre, has been credited for keeping it alive today (Margolies, 2011).

The ensemble consists of four instruments: a diatonic button accordion, a *bajo sexto* (12-string guitar), guitar or bass guitar, and drums. Conjunto music combines a Mexican repertoire of *rancheras* (traditional folk songs performed by one singer with guitar), *cumbias* (based on a Columbian dance rhythm), *huqpangos* (based on the rhythmic style of the Son Huasteco genre), *danzones* (originating from Cuban dances), and *boleros* (a form of Spanish or Cuban slow dance) with polkas and waltzes borrowed from the Czech, Polish, and German immigrants that migrated to South Texas. Once hailed as the "music of the working class," conjunto music moved out of the fields and out of working-class neighborhoods and became part of the Mexican American sound-scape through the expansion of radio stations devoted to the genre, album sales, performance venues, and festivals that were created across South Texas and various parts of the country.

Conjunto music migrated out of South Texas by following Mexican American migrants who worked in various locations across the country and touring musicians who have spread this music to communities around the world. This music has also crossed musical genres with prominent musicians performing and recording albums with rock, pop, country, jazz, and R & B groups in the United States.

Student Interactions with Conjunto Music

Students are interacting with the conjunto music tradition in a variety of ways within and outside the traditional school music programs, both at the primary and secondary levels and in higher education. These interactions reveal the cultural connection and pride associated with a music genre that is an integral part of their cultural and family soundscape as they perform in public events, regional festivals, and paid private performances. Young children in the elementary school grades are participating in these ensembles by singing, dancing, and playing instruments like the accordion, drum set, or the *bajo sexto* (12-string guitar). Middle and high school students are participating in school-run ensembles or performing this music with their friends and family outside the school day. Tejanos are reclaiming the musical soundscape within the traditional music classroom and are following the inroads that were created through the mariachi music programs that were established long before.

Administrators, teachers, students, and community members are supporting the local music tradition and feel that it is important that this musical traditional continue through the next generation. Parents of the students who play in the San Benito School District's conjunto music program in South Texas, for example, formed a booster club to raise money for instruments, uniforms, and travel expenses for the school ensembles. Another parent whose daughter plays the *bajo sexto* emphasized the need for support: "If our kids like what they're doing, we want to support them. It's to bring tradition so they can have this in their future. These are our roots" (Del Valle, 2013, para. 11).

Participating in the Family Band

While teaching music in a bilingual elementary school in the Yakima Valley of Eastern Washington, I was able to get a sense of the musical soundscape with which the students were interacting outside the classroom. Students often spoke of family members who sang in a musical group, or played musical instruments like the guitar, accordion, and saxophone. One young student had much to say about her participation in her father's band, a conjunto group, proudly sharing her love of singing and of the frequency with which she and her siblings would sing ("almost every night"). I visited this student, named Linda, at her family home during one of her father's band practices, and was accompanied by my colleague, who later wrote of aspects of the experience (Lum & Campbell, 2009). Linda was singing while also playing on a miniature drum set complete with a small-sized snare drum, bass drum, and cymbals. Linda and her father learned together how to play the instruments and repertoire of the conjunto and other musical genres such as *banda* (a brass-based music that originated in Sinaloa, Mexico, that included elements of German and Polish polka music) informally, without private lessons, school instruction, or any other prior performance or formal instructional experience. According to Linda, her father's band members also learned how to play their instruments by listening to the radio or to the CD player and then imitating the music that they had internalized. Sometimes they could play through a song because of their familiarity with it well in advance of the rehearsal with the melody, its harmonies, rhythmic features, and sung texts, and at other times they would listen together to a piece, play and sing, listen again, check and correct themselves, and continue to "play it forward." Linda's father's band members consisted of cousins and work colleagues who rehearsed weekly, and even more frequently than that when preparing for performances at weddings, *quinceañeras* (a traditional Mexican celebration of the milestone coming-of-age fifteenth birthday), and various parties.

After a brief interaction in the living room of Linda's family home, we were invited to their makeshift band studio in the basement while the band warmed up and then played a few tunes. Linda played on the miniature drum set right alongside the adult band while her younger brother Alex, who was five years old, played a child-sized accordion (even though he could only figure out how to play a single drone). Alex was moving his hands and arms back and forth in imitation of the accordionist in his father's band. Linda was soon invited to join the band in singing "El Camaleon" (The Chameleon), a well-known banda piece by the group Los Diferentes de la Sierra. She sang with a light and tuneful voice, and she knew every word (even the fast rap-like sections). She did not shy away from the task but seemed completely in control in singing with the adult musicians. Linda's father wanted her to learn as many songs as she wished and to perform, singing with the group at various locations.

Performing in the School Conjunto Ensemble

For the past five years, the La Joya School District in South Texas has held an annual Conjunto Festival at the school's Performing Arts Center that allows each conjunto ensemble from the three high schools in the district to perform. This annual festival allows student groups to share the stage with well-known performers and local legends in the area who, between performances, share stories of their personal relationships with this musical genre. There are three student conjunto groups, Palmview High School's La Tradicion, Juarez-Lincoln High School's Sol, and La Joya High School's Los Diamantes, that have been showcased at the festival. The conjunto program began in 2000 and has about 75 students in the intermediate and varsity music programs (Conjunto Traditions, 2011). The ensembles were initially established as extracurricular activities or clubs, but have now become part of the school curriculum, with students receiving school credit. Mario Saenz, Jr., who has been playing conjunto music since he was 13 years old and has worked with the conjunto groups in the school district, observed, "It's been giving other kids a chance that aren't in mariachi or folklorico or football to do something" (Conjunto Traditions, 2011, para. 15). The student musicians gain recognition by performing with esteemed artists during the festival, as well as by performing original songs, recording their own records, and competing in statewide accordion competitions. Some of the student groups include siblings or cousins, as this music tradition is transmitted through extended families. Omar Garza, a conjunto student musician, obtained statewide recognition when he became a finalist for the Texas Big Squeeze competition and recorded an album, *Accordion Kings & Queens Live,* with great conjunto artists such as Flaco Jimenez, Los Texamaniacs, Dora & Her Zydeco Entourage, Ennis Czech Boys, three other contest finalists, and Big Squeeze champion Peter Anzaldúa. Peter was interviewed for an article in the local paper about his musical experiences at school and was quoted as saying, "It's cool because you get to hang out with your friends and play new music everyday, I love music. It's in my blood" (Conjunto Traditions, 2011, para. 25).

Conjunto in the Curriculum

Conjunto music can be incorporated into a music curriculum and/or music program through a variety of methods. Recordings, interviews with musicians, documentaries, and videos of performances can easily introduce the musical essence of conjunto, and allow students an in-depth look into the people and culture behind this music (Soto, 2008). Lesson plans, recordings, and videos can be accessed on the Smithsonian Folkways website (www.folkways.si.edu). Public Broadcasting Service television produced a documentary on the history of the conjunto, with a focus on the accordion, titled *Accordion Dreams* (Galán, 2001). *Tex Mex: Music of the Texas-Mexican Borderlands* (Marre, 1990) and *Songs of the Homeland* (Galán, 1995) videos also showcase the variety of musics in the borderlands of South Texas.

Reviewing a selection of earlier recordings by Narciso Martinez (the father of conjunto music) and making a place for an experience with the virtuosity of master accordionist Eva Ybarra are effective means for exploring the genre's stylistic and musical changes, while also coming to terms with the changes in social roles within conjunto, especially with regard to women performers. Listening to recordings can open the door to a whole host of classroom activities. Musical elements such as meter, key, tempo, harmony, syncopation, and vocal timbres can all be explored through repeated listenings. Students can learn to sing the chorus or sing along to an entire conjunto song in Spanish. Song forms such as the cumbia, ranchera, or polka can be analyzed and compared to other Latino musical genres that utilize them. Instrumentation and stylistic features of playing can also be examined through recordings. For example, the role of the 12-stringed *bajo sexto* today has changed from that of early performances, as have performance practices and types of accordions utilized. The use of accordion in conjunto and other musical genres can also be investigated, as can the influences of other genres such as the German, Czech, and Polish waltzes, polkas, and cumbia. Students can study how conjunto evolved into the more contemporary genre Tejano and explore the differences in performance practices and instrumentation. Information about immigration, acculturation, the challenges of straddling two cultures and countries, racism, working in the fields picking crops, family concerns or memories, and important historical events can be found within the thousands of conjunto songs that can be obtained and translated on sites such as Smithsonian Folkways, and connected with interdisciplinary lessons that expand a traditional music lesson (Soto, 2008).

With a bit of research, teachers and students can investigate methods of transmission among conjunto artists. An assessment of students' musical abilities and musicians in the community may reveal artists who may conduct interviews, lecture demonstrations, or offer to assist in instructing a student ensemble. Students can learn how to dance the basic cumbia dance steps. This popular driving dance rhythm originated in Columbia with influences from Africa, and is heard in duple meter. Students can also learn to dance the simple two-step movements (similar to country dancing) coupled with turns that accompany the music. Allowing time and resources for a student ensemble within the music program provides opportunities for students to fully interact with the music so that they may come to know their own musical culture that surrounds them, or to learn of a musical culture that may be far from their own. A conjunto ensemble in the music program should share time, resources, recognition, and performance opportunities equally among the other established ensembles in the music program.

NEW SPACES: SOCIAL EQUITY IN THE MUSIC EDUCATION CLASSROOM

Anderson and Campbell (2011) state that in order for us to carry out the National Association of Music Educators (NAfME) slogan that music is for every child, "school curriculum must be more broadly defined to encompass the ethnic diversity of American schools and society" (p. vii). Just as multicultural education reconceptualizes the curriculum to include diverse ethnic and cultural perspectives, music curriculum should incorporate a diversity of musics and musical practices in all grade levels and categories of music education (Abril, 2009). Teachers should also diversify their methods of delivery and curriculum, which can reflect the variety of music and modes of transmission that children encounter every day through the media, technology, and their home cultures. Calderón (2009) helps to explain this point with the admonishment to teachers that it is essential that marginalized students learn the knowledge and skills that will allow students to be successful both within and outside their home cultures. Similarly, Ladson-Billings (2009) states that African Americans should be able to choose academic excellence while still identifying with their African American culture. This notion should be applied to the music curriculum so that Mexican American and other minority students are able to develop relevant academic and musical excellence while identifying with their home cultures.

It is evident that Mexican American communities are encouraging children to develop their ethnic identities through knowledge of their heritage, language, and culture, including musical practices (Soto, 2012). The research suggests that these children are entering the music classroom with musical skills and knowledge that may not be acknowledged or valued within the mainstream culture, or that may not be related to the music that is taught in the common curriculum for general music, concert band, choir, and/or orchestra (Soto, 2012; Teicher, 1995). The danger in ignoring or overlooking this important aspect of children's ethnic and cultural identity is that it might be perceived as akin to what Anzaldúa (2007) describes as a form of "linguistic terrorism" that may make children feel ashamed because their language is not validated. As Anzaldúa continues,

So if you want to really hurt me, talk badly about my language. Ethnic identity is twin skin to linguistic identity—I am my language. Until I can take pride in my language, I cannot take pride in myself. Until I can accept as legitimate Chicano Texas Spanish, Tex-Mex and all the other languages I speak, I cannot accept the legitimacy of myself. Until I am free to write bilingually and to switch codes without having always to translate, while I still have to speak English or Spanish when I would rather speak Spanglish, and as long as I have to accommodate the English speakers rather than having them accommodate me, my tongue will be illegitimate. I will no longer be made to feel ashamed of existing. (p. 81)

Anzaldúa's comment about language and ethnic identity applies equally to music, which is also a form of communication and thus also a twin skin to both linguistic and ethnic identity. Thus, if teachers are not validating children's musical identities in the music classroom or music education program, are they sending negative messages to their students, causing them to feel ashamed of their bimusical (or multimusical) skill sets, or making them feel that music associated with their ethnic identities is illegitimate? Would the exclusion of their favored music make them feel or believe that they are less musical, or not legitimate musicians, because they are not valued within the school system and larger community? If children cannot take pride in the music that surrounds them in their everyday lives, can they take pride in being called "real" musicians?

This chapter has presented various ways in which Mexican American music and culture could be reflected in the music curriculum to create a more socially just classroom. As also suggested, similar ideas and strategies, however, could be applied to the music of other marginalized groups and cultures that are present in the school and surrounding community. Younker and Hickey (2007) advocate that teachers conceive of the pursuit of social justice "as arising from a community of learners, [as] a participatory democratic community in which opportunties for opinions, informed decisions, and justifications are understood and experienced," and in which students learn that traditions "preserve what is, and do not necessarily call for critical examination, nor demand progressive thinking" (p. 226). It is with this undertanding that music educators and researchers should go forth to evaluate the curriculum and content delivery of music in classrooms if they are to strive for a socially just classroom.

OLD FACES IN OLD SPACES: BACK TO WHERE IT ALL BEGAN

As I come full circle in my journey as a person and music educator, I am now guiding teachers in the incorporation of conjunto, Tejano, mariachi, son jarocho, and the music of other cultures into their music classrooms, even as I gain a better understanding and respect for the music of my own culture.

Children who are of a different generation of Mexican Americans are trying to understand their own cultural identity and to assimilate within mainstream American culture. This can be done in many ways, but it is always done with music. People have the music of "home" and of "family," which represents their personal and ethnic identities. I have held close to my own musical identity throughout my research. I do not want Mexican American children to struggle with their identity the way I did while in school. My desire is for the culturally relevant music (and language and culture) to be validated in the music classroom and surrounding communities. Music teachers must be guided to identify and understand how integral music is in the lives of students so they can learn to appreciate their heritage music alongside the music of the world's many cultures. Like my own adult reckoning with the music of my home and my formal training, Mexican American children can be knowledgeable and skillful with their first home or cultural music as well as the music they come to learn in school.

References

Abril, C. R. (2009). Responding to culture in the instrumental music programme: A teacher's journey. *Music Education Research*, 11(1), 77–91.

Anderson, W. M., & Campbell, P. S. (2011). *Multicultural perspectives in music education*. Lanham, MD: Rowman & Littlefield Education.

Anzaldúa, G. (2007). *Borderlands: The new mestiza = la frontera*. San Francisco, CA: Aunt Lute Books.

Bernstein, B. (2000). *Pedagogy, symbolic control and identity: Theory, research, critique* (rev. ed.). Lanham, MD: Rowman & Littlefield.

Boss-Barba, M., & Soto. A. (2008). Enriching or endangering: Exploring the positive and negative effects of recontextualising mariachi. *International Journal of Ethnomusicological Studies*, 3, 55–64.

Calderón, H. (2009). Response to Part 9, classrooms, pedagogy, and practicing justice. In W. Ayers, T. Quinn, & D. Stovall (Eds.), *Handbook of social justice in education* (pp. 722–724). New York: Routledge.

Conjunto Traditions: "It's Life." (2011, November 18). *Progress Times*. http://www.progress-times.net/news/local-news/1325-conjunto-traditions-its-life.html.

Del Valle, F. (2013, October 18). Locals and former locals turn out for regional dance, music. *Valley Morning Star*. Retrieved from http://www.valleymorningstar.com/news/local_news/article_564f426c-3870-11e3-acab-001a4bcf6878.html.

Ennis, S. R., Rios-Vargas, M., & Albert, N. G. (2011). The Hispanic population: 2010. http://www.census.gov/prod/cen2010/briefs/c2010br-04.pdf.

Feay-Shaw, S. (2001). The music of Mexican-Americans: A historical perspective of a forgotten culture in American music education. *Journal of Historical Research in Music Education*, 24(1), 83–102.

Galán, H. (2001). *Accordion dreams* [DVD]. Austin, TX: Galán Productions, Latino Public Broadcasting.

Galán, H. (1995). *Songs of the homeland* [VHS]. Austin, TX: Galán Productions.

Garcia, E. E. (2004). Educating Mexican American students: Past treatment and recent developments in theory, research, policy, and practice. In J. A. Banks & C. A. M. Banks (Eds.),

Handbook of research on multicultural education (2nd ed., pp. 753–769). San Francisco, CA: Jossey-Bass.

Gay, G. (2010). *Culturally responsive teaching: Theory, research, and practice.* New York: Teachers College.

Ladson-Billings, G. (2009). *The dreamkeepers: Successful teachers of African American children.* San Francisco, CA: Jossey- Bass Publishers.

Lum, C. H., & Campbell, P. S. (2009). "El Camaleon": The musical secrets of Mirella Valdez. In J. L. Kerchner & C. R. Abril (2009). *Musical experience in our lives: Things we learn and meanings we make.* (pp. 113–125). Lanham, MD: Rowman & Littlefield Education.

Margolies, D. S. (2011). Voz de Pueblo Chicano: Sustainability, teaching, and intangible cultural transfer in conjunto music. *The Journal of American Culture, 34*, 1.

Marre, J. (1990). *Tex-Mex: Music of the Texas Mexican borderlands* [DVD]. Newton, NJ: Shanachie.

Pena, M. H. (1985). *The Texas-Mexican conjunto: History of a working class music.* Austin: University of Texas Press.

Shelemay, K. K. (2001). *Soundscapes: Exploring music in a changing world.* New York: Norton.

Soto, A. C. (2008). Conjunto in the classroom. *Music Educators Journal, 95*(1), 54–59.

Soto, A. C. (2012). *Bimusical identity of children in a Mexican American school* (Unpublished doctoral dissertation). University of Washington, Seattle.

Soto, A. C. (2013). Conjunto. In *Music in American life: An encyclopedia of the songs, styles, stars, and stories that shaped our culture.* Santa Barbara, CA: ABC-CLIO.

Teicher, J. M. (1995). The children of the Thyagaraja festival: A study in bimusicality and cultural identity. *Quarterly Journal of Music Teaching and Learning, 6*(3), 76–88.

Trueba, E. T. (1987). *Success or failure? Learning and the language minority student.* Cambridge, MA: Newbury House.

US Census Bureau. (2010). Summary Tape Files 1 and 3. Retrieved from www.census.gov.

Valdés, G. (1996). *Con respeto: Bridging the distances between culturally diverse families and schools: An ethnographic portrait.* New York: Teachers College Press.

Younker, B. A., & Hickey, M. (2007). Examining the profession through the lens of social justice: Two music educators' stories and their stark realizations. *Music Education Research, 9*(2), 215–227.

CHAPTER 41

THE INTERSECTION OF MUSIC TEACHER EDUCATION AND SOCIAL JUSTICE

Where Are We Now?

JULIE BALLANTYNE AND CARMEN MILLS

"Social justice" is an issue that has recently moved from the periphery toward the center of research in music education (Bowman, 2007). In teacher education generally, it has certainly been an issue that has attracted much interest and research over the last 10 years (Cochran-Smith et al., 2009; Darling-Hammond, 2006; Zeichner, 2006). Why, then, should we explore social justice in music teacher education separately from either music education or teacher education? The answer lies with the ways that music teacher education students seem to view the topic: they see becoming a teacher, and becoming a teacher of *music*, as inextricably intertwined. The subject matter—music—is perceived to be central to all areas of music teacher education, including in establishing dispositions toward social justice in the music classroom (Ballantyne & Mills, 2008). The emphasis that developing teachers place on the importance of the subject matter can be at odds with the attitudes, beliefs, values, and virtues that are consistent with a "socially just" approach to the profession.

Research in the area of music teacher education and social justice often remains a theoretical discussion of possibilities and suggestions for future practice. This chapter provides evidence of where the field has been, and where we have yet to go in addressing the concerns of social justice in music teacher education. It argues for the importance of further research at the intersection of these areas, and does so by providing a thorough and systematic review of previous work in the field. This review seeks to uncover empirical research that can illuminate evidence *of* practice and *for* practice in the future. The guiding research questions are the following:

1. What are the research questions that are being answered in the literature?
2. What does this reveal about the development of socially just approaches to music teacher education?
3. What are the research questions that remain unanswered?
4. What are the implications for future research?

Method: Systematic Literature Review

Search One

We wanted to uncover all articles published in English over the past 10 years in peer-reviewed journals that had, as their central focus, music teacher education and social justice or diversity. Therefore, in October 2013, databases, including RILM Abstracts of Music Literature, Australian Education Index (AEI), Proquest, and ERIC, were searched using the Boolean search *teach* AND "social justice" AND (pre-service OR pre-service) AND educ* AND ab(music) AND (schol(yes) AND peer(yes))*. This search yielded 21 articles.

We also searched Music Index Online. The same Boolean operators yielded only two articles, and so we expanded the search criteria in this database to "social justice" and educ*, given that all the articles in Music Index Online should relate to music at some level. This search revealed 43 articles. All articles uncovered by the searches were entered into a spreadsheet, where they were individually assessed against the criteria for inclusion.

Results

Excluding those articles that were repeated (two), a total of 60 articles met our initial search criteria. We then applied exclusion criteria to all 60 articles. Articles were excluded if (a) social justice or diversity was not a central focus, (b) teacher education was not the focus of the study, (c) music education was not a central focus, (d) the article did not report on empirical research, (e) the article was not published in a peer-reviewed journal, (f) the study was published in a language other than English, or (g) the paper was unable to be sourced. In total, 54 articles were excluded because they did not meet the inclusion criteria (see Table 41.1).

A total of six articles were deemed to fit the criteria for inclusion. This was seen to be insufficient to capture the current state of research in the field of social justice and music teacher education. Accordingly, a further search was conducted (Search Two), in which the search terms were extended to include "diversity" in place of "social justice." "Diversity" was included as a search term owing to the prevalence of literature, both theoretical and empirical, that continues to be published on preparing teachers for diverse student populations. While these papers address how teachers might be prepared to

Table 41.1 Major Reasons Studies Were Excluded*

Reason for Exclusion	Number of Studies Excluded
Social justice/diversity was not a central focus	1
Teacher education was not the primary focus of the study	26
Music education was not a central focus	5
Did not report on empirical research	32
Not published in a peer-reviewed journal	0
Published in language other than English	0
Unable to be sourced	0

*Note: some papers were excluded on the basis of multiple categories.

deal with student diversity in socially just ways, some would not be identified by a search only capturing the terms "social justice" or "socially just."

Search Two

Databases, including RILM Abstracts of Music Literature, Australian Education Index (AEI), Proquest, and ERIC, were searched using the Boolean search *teach* AND (pre-service OR pre-service) AND educ* AND ab(music)) AND diversity AND schol(yes) AND peer(yes)*. This search yielded 53 articles. The same search in AEI revealed 21 results. Seven of these were repetitions from previous searches, and four were repeated articles from this search. Five were more than 10 years old and therefore were excluded.

In Music Index Online, the same search yielded no results. An advanced search using the BOOLEAN operators *educ* AND diversity AND teacher education AND schol(yes) AND peer(yes),* resulted in 14 articles published after 2003. Four of these were repetitions from previous searches. All found articles were entered into a spreadsheet where they were individually assessed against the criteria for inclusion.

Results

After removing repetition across searches, and articles published prior to 2003, there were 68 articles that fit the search criteria for Search Two. We then applied exclusion criteria to all 68 articles. As before, articles were excluded if (a) social justice or diversity was not a central focus, (b) teacher education was not the focus of the study, (c) music education was not a central focus, (d) the article did not report on empirical research, (e) the article was not published in a peer-reviewed journal, (f) the study was published in a language other than English, or (g) the paper was unable to be sourced. In total, 62 articles were excluded because they did not meet the inclusion criteria (see Table 41.2). Following this search, a further five articles were deemed to fit the search criteria for the systematic review.

Table 41.2 Major Reasons Studies Were Excluded*

Reason for Exclusion	Number of Studies Excluded
Social justice/diversity was not a central focus	19
Teacher education was not the focus of the study	16
Music education was not a central focus	1
Did not report on empirical research	15
Not published in a peer-reviewed journal	10
Published in language other than English	2
Unable to be sourced	1

*Note: some papers were excluded on the basis of multiple categories.

INCLUDED STUDIES

The 11 included studies are presented in detail in Table 41.3. They represent the empirical research that could be found (through standard database searches) that related to the intersection of music teacher education, social justice, or diversity.

As can be seen in the exclusions tables (Tables 41.1 and 41.2), many of the publications found relating to music teacher education and social justice did not move beyond theoretical discussions of possible approaches, or descriptions of approaches employed in teacher education. These typically were excluded because they did not present empirical data (qualitative or quantitative), or analysis of data. These papers, while extremely useful to the field in framing appropriate approaches and underlying theories for practice, were not the intended focus of this chapter, and therefore are not discussed. It should also be noted that some interesting articles were excluded on the basis that either the research methods could not be clearly identified, the research aims/questions were not clear, or the process leading to the presentation of findings, or of analyzing the data, was not clear. All such articles were excluded under the category of "did not report on empirical research."

Some articles were written with implications for teacher education, but the research data gathered were based in schools with teachers, rather than with teacher education students, or did not refer to teacher education explicitly. All such articles were excluded under category of "teacher education was not the primary focus of the study."

All of the research found was undertaken in either Australia or the United States. Most of the papers involved small-scale, qualitative, in-depth studies utilizing interviews, observations, personal reflective journals, and student work samples or assessment pieces as primary data sources. Three of the 11 articles also utilized survey responses and simple statistical analysis, predominantly for the purpose of describing participants' perceptions (see Table 41.3).

Table 41.3 Included Studies

Authors	Focus	Participants	Research Methods	Findings
Abrahams, Rowland, & Kohler (2012)	Explores the effectiveness of a music education immersion experience where two preservice music education majors conduct a choir of inmates.	Two music education majors (and coauthors on the paper); prison inmates. Study based in the United States.	Personal reflective journals completed by the preservice teachers after every rehearsal; quotes from the inmates.	The preservice music teachers came to view music as a powerful agent of change and gained confidence and the feeling that they were making a difference. They grew to see learning as a two-way process.
Ballantyne & Mills (2008)	Explores early-career teachers' perceptions of socially just and inclusive practices in the music classroom, while also providing insight into the ways that teacher education programs might inspire such practices in more effective ways.	The study followed six music teachers six months after graduation from one of three preservice education programs in Queensland, Australia.	Semi-structured interviews with six preservice teachers before graduating, and then again six months into their first year of teaching. The interviewees reflected on their understandings of what constitutes being inclusive in the music classroom and how these understandings have been influenced by their perceptions of both university and school experiences.	Some of the teachers interviewed appeared to have narrow understandings of what constitutes inclusive practice. They tended to see relevance only in courses that specifically dealt with "how to teach music." In order for them to see the relevance of courses on inclusion, these courses need to explicitly refer to music.
Baxter (2007)	Evaluates a class collaborative project exploring music instruction as catalyst for social consciousness and transformation. Within a multicultural music education model, participants attempted to move from theory to practice by authoring music curricula fostering principles of equity and social justice.	Thirteen music education majors from the Crane School of Music, State University of New York at Potsdam (US).	Thirteen students, enrolled in *Multiculturalism in the Classroom*, a music education elective course, participated in the four-week project. Data included questionnaires, participants' group curricular units, and videotaped interviews with the participants on conclusion of the project.	Ideals of equity and social justice became central to the students' understandings of their role as music teachers.

Bradley, Golner, & Hanson (2007)	Explores graduate students' and teachers' responses to a 15-week course on race issues in music teaching.	Two students and one instructor. The first author identifies as an anti-racism educator, and the two other authors are the two students who were enrolled in the course at the University of Wisconsin–Madison (US).	Data formatted as dialogues constructed from over 100 pages of reflective journals and feedback on said journals. Reflected the style and nature of the course.	Undergraduate training did not prepare these teachers to teach music from a critical multicultural perspective. Evidence that change occurred over the 15 weeks in the approaches of the students.
Emmanuel (2005)	Explores whether immersion experiences in an inner-city school (supported by guided reflection and reading) moved music teacher education students toward cultural competence.	Five students participated in the immersion experience. Three cases are presented. Project undertaken at the University of North Texas (US).	Multiple case studies. Data from the coursework: inventories, detailed autobiographies, interviews with family members, responses to readings, answers to questions about beliefs and transcriptions of classroom discussions. Data from the immersion experience: field notes, videotaped lessons, audiotaped conversations, focus group discussions, daily journals. Follow-up interviews 9 and 11 months later.	Evidence that the immersion experience changed the perceptions/dispositions of music education students, during, and after the experience. Leads the author to argue for possible evidence of permanent belief change.
Joseph & Southcott (2009)	Reports on a research project that explores final year preservice music education students' understandings of multicultural music and music education.	Four tertiary preservice teacher education students undertaking classes in music teaching methods (primary and secondary) from Deakin University and Monash University, Australia.	Two phases of research. Phase 1: online survey with final-year teacher education students undertaking music methodologies at two institutions in Australia. Probed past experiences and present understandings of cultural diversity in music education. Survey data informed the interview questions for Phase 2. The article reports on four of the semi-structured interviews (Phase 2).	Student teachers do not always have the opportunity to experience "multicultural music" in practice during practicum. Unless students see teachers modeling effective multicultural music education. they are initially constrained in their ability to teach cultural diversity, even if they have been exhorted to do so by their tertiary music educators.

(continued)

Table 41.3 (Continued)

Authors	Focus	Participants	Research Methods	Findings
Joseph & Southcott (2010)	Explores the perceptions of multiculturalism held by preservice music education students, and their understanding of teaching and learning of multicultural music in schools.	30 fourth-year music students from Deakin and Monash Universities in Victoria, Australia.	30 semi-structured interviews. The interviews explored fourth-year music students' understandings and experiences in multicultural music, in their personal backgrounds, their university courses, and during their school teaching placements.	Students appear to be well aware that multiculturalism should be an integral part of schools, but this was not apparently enacted in school music classrooms they observed. They had varying understandings of multiculturalism.
Kelly (2003)	Investigates the preferences of undergraduate music education majors in relation to where they would like to work, and what circumstances/topics they were most eager to employ in their chosen workplaces.	$N = 406$ undergraduate music education majors across four large universities located in different states in the United States. All participants were required to take a course in cultural diversity. This included a field experience component. 75% of respondents had already undertaken this course.	21-item survey. Closed response options detailing gender, race, college status, performance area, parental economic status, types of teaching positions desired, types of primary and secondary schools attended, perceptions regarding quality of music programs at their own schools. Simple descriptive statistics used in analysis.	Most came from large high school music programs, and most wanted to teach in these same types of schools. They also would accept a position at a private or church-related school. They would mostly prefer to teach in culturally similar circumstances to their own experiences.
Marsh (2007)	An inquiry-based fieldwork project undertaken by students majoring in music education at the Sydney Conservatorium of Music, University of Sydney. Discusses issues associated with teaching multicultural music education to music teacher education students in Sydney and investigates the effectiveness	10 students (approximately one-third of the cohort) selected on the basis of thoughtful remarks relating to changed understandings or attitudes (described in students' presentations or written reflections). Study conducted at the University of Sydney, Australia.	In the project, students recorded, transcribed, and researched the background of a song found in the non-Anglo-Australian community. They used their research around this song to conceptualize and develop a school music program, and shared this with their teacher education student colleagues. Reflection was a key part of their assessment	There was a shift in many of the students' dispositions, with the fieldwork project promoting a greater commitment to a more pluralistic approach to music programming in their future teaching. For some students, the fieldwork project created an awareness of the previous narrowness of their musical and

				social experience.
	of an inquiry-based fieldwork project in changing preservice teacher education students' attitudes.		Data: observations of student presentations, students' written reflections in assignments, and semi-structured interviews with students. Email and telephone correspondence with former students has also been included in the data for analysis.	
Power & Horsley (2010)	Explores the disciplinary knowledges and dispositions that preservice teachers bring to enable them to construct their understandings of global education.	*N* = 17 graduate music teacher education students from the University of Western Sydney. These students represented heritage from around the world, but all identified as being Australian. All had undergraduate degrees in music (14/17 students studied contemporary and popular music; 3/17 students studied "classical" Western art music).	Survey (subset of a larger survey with all students in an undergraduate education degree). Content analysis of responses compared to key global education concept codes in the global education survey instrument.	Among this small cohort, students come into courses with an understanding of global education, mostly gleaned from their broad musical experiences in their undergraduate degrees. Particular mention was made of the impact of particular types of ensemble work in this area. These teachers' knowledge of global education originates in their discipline (music) and is shaped by the musical experiences that they had as students.
Riley (2009)	This article aims to determine what preservice music teachers think about social justice and/or social consciousness as it relates to music education.	40 preservice music teacher education students in an introduction to music education course.	Open-ended survey given to students.	The majority of students surveyed showed a positive orientation toward merging social justice issues with their practice as music teachers. Their understandings of what this meant differed.

FINDINGS

Upon analyzing the included sample of research papers, it became clear that research questions in the field included those around student teachers' perceptions/understandings of social justice. In particular, most of the studies investigated the beliefs and attitudes that preservice music teachers hold in relation to socially just and inclusive classroom practices (Ballantyne & Mills, 2008; Emmanuel, 2005; Joseph & Southcott, 2010; Marsh, 2007; Power & Horsley, 2010; Riley, 2009).

The articles and chapters revealed a consistently positive orientation among preservice teachers to the idea of socially just and inclusive practices. The research of Joseph and Southcott (2010), for example, revealed consistent and positive acknowledgment among preservice teachers of the value of the inclusion of "multicultural music" in contemporary Australian classrooms, although the strength of this conviction varied. Similarly, the majority of students surveyed by Riley (2009) showed a positive orientation toward merging social justice issues with their practice as music teachers, although their understandings of what this meant differed. The Ballantyne and Mills (2008) study revealed that while preservice and early-career music teachers were positively oriented toward teaching for inclusion, they appeared to have narrow understandings of what inclusive practice meant. Interestingly, graduate music teacher education students compared favorably against visual arts and health and physical education teachers in the research of Power and Horsley (2010). The music education students seemed to have had more experience, knowledge, and a predisposition toward global education, evident through their emphasis on the importance of interacting with society and valuing and appreciating difference in the classroom.

Immersion experiences were central to two of the articles and their discussions of preservice music teachers' beliefs about socially just practices. While Marsh's (2007) article did not document the beliefs held by preservice teachers, it noted that after undertaking an inquiry-based fieldwork project, many students completely changed their approach to the teaching of music from one of monoculturalism to pluralism. There was also evidence that the immersion experience changed the perceptions/dispositions of music education students, during and after the immersion experience described in the research of Emmanuel (2005).

Kelly (2003), Power and Horsley (2010), and Baxter (2007) addressed the predispositions and experiences that influence preservice music education students' approaches to diversity/social justice. Although each of these research projects addressed this issue from a different perspective, the findings were revealing in terms of the impact that teacher educators can expect to have with students who experience diversity courses as part of large general education cohorts. Both Kelly (2003) and Power and Horsley (2010) found that, consistent with many other studies from outside music teacher education (e.g., Banks, 2001; Mills, 2008; Mills & Ballantyne, 2010), it is difficult to influence long-held beliefs and attitudes in the space of one stand-alone diversity course. That is, the background experiences of teacher education students are typically far more power-ful in determining dispositions and attitudes toward social justice than any coursework undertaken.

Kelly's (2003) innovative approach to this issue (finding out where teachers would like to teach) revealed that despite students undertaking diversity courses with practicum experiences designed to challenge dispositions toward social justice, most music teacher education students would prefer to teach in culturally similar circumstances to those experienced when they themselves were students. This research may be more reveal-ing than other similar pieces where students are asked (by their lecturers) to reflect on their likelihood of incorporating socially just principles and approaches in their teach-ing lives. Such studies may produce socially desirable responses from students who may feel the pressure to provide the "correct" responses in those contexts.

Power and Horsley (2010) explored the disciplinary knowledge and predispositions that preservice teachers hold, enabling the construction of their own understandings of global education. As a subset of the survey respondents, the 17 graduate music teacher education students were found to have come into diversity courses with an understand-ing of global education, mostly gleaned from their broad musical experiences in their undergraduate degrees. Special mention was made of the impact of particular types of ensemble work in this area.

While Power and Horsley (2010) looked at a large cohort of education students, of which music education students were a part, Baxter's (2007) research evaluated a small music curriculum class collaborative project exploring music instruction as a catalyst for social consciousness and transformation. Participants applied their understand-ings of theory in the area by authoring music curricula fostering principles of equity and social justice. Through this experience, Baxter (2007) witnessed ideals of equity and social justice, themes that had once seemed tangential to music teaching and learn-ing, gradually shifting to the center in her students' curricular frameworks—"teaching music through the lens of social justice had become teaching social justice through the lens of music" (p. 278).

A third key research question answered by the published papers focused on how music teacher education programs might inspire socially just and inclusive practices in their graduates (Ballantyne & Mills, 2008; Joseph & Southcott, 2009, 2010; Marsh, 2007). A core message from research in this area is the need for the field of teacher edu-cation generally, and music teacher education specifically, to move beyond fragmented and superficial treatment of diversity (Ballantyne & Mills, 2008; Joseph & Southcott, 2009; 2010). As the research of Ballantyne and Mills (2008) highlights, core courses need to embrace diversity in an authentic way, so that students can clearly see the value of such an approach, within the context of the courses they view as most relevant. In the case of music teacher education students, the courses that they see as most relevant are those that explicitly address music teaching. Joseph and Southcott (2009) support this view, arguing that "a day here or there, no matter how good that day is, is never enough to transform teacher understanding of inclusivity" (p. 469).

Along similar lines, meaningful, rather than tokenistic inclusion of diverse musics, is seen as key to promoting culturally inclusive music education (Joseph & Southcott, 2010). The goal here is to move from a mono-cultural and somewhat insular perspective to a broader, more inclusive position. As a first step, tertiary music educators need to encourage student teachers to examine their own experiences and understandings in "multicultural music" (Joseph & Southcott, 2010).

Inquiry-based fieldwork projects were also suggested as effective ways that music teacher education programs might change preservice teachers' attitudes and inspire socially just and inclusive practices in their graduates. Marsh's (2007) research documented a shift in disposition of many of the students who undertook such a project, with a greater commitment to a more pluralistic approach to music programming in their future teaching a result.

Joseph and Southcott (2009, 2010) argue that limited time in teacher education means that while the process of teaching multiculturalism should begin in teacher education, this should be supported through ongoing professional development and collaboration between community groups, governmental agencies, music education organizations, and individuals. That is, they argue for a reliance on other educational settings in the wider community, to provide opportunities for engagement with musical and cultural diversity.

The research presented by Abrahams, Rowland, and Kohler (2012), Emmanuel (2005), Kelly (2003), and Marsh (2007) provide an insight into how real-life experiences (musical and otherwise) deepen an understanding and valuing of social justice. All four of these papers provide examples of real-life experiences (or "immersion experiences," as described by Emmanuel, 2005), which were designed to disrupt and challenge students' understandings of social justice work, and its role in the music classroom. In Abrahams, Rowland, and Kohler (2012), the authors write of the experiences of two students (Rowland and Kohler) who weekly conducted a choir of inmates at a prison. These students' reflections and those of the inmates are presented as evidence of the impact of this experience in terms of increased confidence and change in the view of the power of music to effect change and to make a difference in people's lives. The repositioning of their role as teacher-as-collaborator was seen to be a key impact of the experience on their practice as future music educators. The research conducted by Emmanuel (2005) and Marsh (2007) similarly sought to evaluate the impact of deep community music experiences on understandings of social justice.

Somewhat similarly, in Marsh (2007), students were engaged in finding songs from the community, exploring the stories that surround those songs, and then using this knowledge to inspire curricular planning, which was then trialed and shared with student-colleagues in the university context (for assessment). The personal reflections of these students revealed a shift in students' dispositions toward the role of diverse community musics in broadening their own and others' musical and cultural understandings. This study also highlighted the "centrality of interpersonal contact between members of different cultures to the development of intercultural understanding" (p. 55). Students became more aware of their previous dispositions toward narrow and singular musical and social experiences, and reported a greater understanding of the challenges (personal, economic, and political) facing those in the broader Australian community.

Emmanuel's (2005) study similarly had students going out into the community, resulting in changed perceptions/dispositions of music education students. The inclusion of interviews 11 months after the immersion experience provides depth of evidence not seen in any of the other papers. In addition, the voices of the students are very clear in articulating real change in beliefs and the impact of the experience across all areas of their lives. As argued in the paper: "The results of this study have shown that immersion experiences combined with coursework with opportunities for guided reflection would likely have dramatic effects on the attitudes and beliefs of pre-service music teachers" (p. 59).

Kelly's (2003) method of addressing how real-life experiences (musical and otherwise) deepen an understanding and valuing of social justice took an unusual research approach. As this study focused on students articulating their preferences in terms of type of school, it is an example of a summative evaluation of dispositions separate from any real-life experiences offered by the students' coursework. In responding to this research aim, however, Kelly's article provides authentic indicators of change. These students had mostly (75 percent) undertaken real-world diversity courses that included placements, yet they showed a clear preference for teaching cohorts of students in contexts that were very similar to their own upbringings.

In Bradley, Golner, and Hansons's (2007) article, students personally confronted their own predispositions, but the catalysts for this self-reflection were in-depth explorations of the literature and small group discussions. Their journals and conversations over the course of a semester revealed the success of this approach in aligning students with socially just dispositions and practices.

Summary

This systematic literature review provided evidence of successful approaches to diversity and social justice teacher education for music teachers. Several key findings can be drawn for future practice. First, immersion or "real-life" experiences of diversity challenges or social justice issues, combined with guided reflection, enable preservice teachers to confront their own predispositions, which can provide the impetus for changing dispositions. This can result in ongoing change, particularly if the students are interested in this area prior to the coursework. Second, students who take diversity courses are not necessarily challenged to change their dispositions. It seems crucial for social justice to be addressed in terms of an "authentic" context where music takes place, particularly for music students. Those programs, which included involvement in music making, either as student or teacher, seemed to report greater impact in terms of changing student-teacher approaches (see Abrahams, Rowland, & Kohler, 2012; Joseph

& Southcott, 2009, 2010; Marsh, 2007; Power & Horsley, 2010). The exception to this was the Bradley, Golner, and Hanson (2007) study, which approached social justice first from the literature, successfully using a critical inquiry approach. And, finally, consideration and addressing of social justice issues needs to begin in university, but also should be continued through ongoing professional development, particularly contextualized to the music classroom.

Upon concluding this systematic literature review, it is apparent that there are research questions which remain, as yet, unanswered. The unanswered questions often reveal inherent weaknesses in the methodologies selected for individual research papers, but can also reveal underlying prejudices toward particular ways of looking at issues of social justice within music teacher education. As most of the research involved small-scale, qualitative studies, often with small numbers of highly motivated students, questions unanswered in these papers are related to the applicability of particular approaches to larger groups of students who may not be as highly motivated to challenge themselves and their dispositions toward social justice. In addition, mention was made in quite a few articles about the necessity for diversity and social justice to be addressed in a musical context, but details about what this might look like in a variety of contexts could be further explored. Along the lines of Power and Horsley (2010), further comparative research with preservice teachers in other curriculum areas could be revealing in terms of the specificity of music education students' perceptions of social justice and diversity. Finally, research around the ongoing, long-term effects of the courses and/or immersion/fieldwork experiences where dispositional change transpired would also be of immense value to the field.

This systematic literature review has highlighted areas within the field where research needs to be conducted in the future. In particular, research should broadly address (a) how predispositions translate into teaching practice in the music classroom, (b) how to access preservice music teacher identities and effect change beyond "tolerance," (c) the impact of prior experiences and dispositions, and the impact of these on developing professional identities, and (d) large-scale, comparative research in order to explore the specificity of music education students' perceptions.

References

Abrahams, F., Rowland, M., & Kohler, K. (2012). Music education behind bars: Giving voice to the inmates and the students who teach them. *Music Educators Journal, 98*(4), 67–73. doi: 10.1177/0027432112443711.

Ballantyne, J., & Mills, C. (2008). Promoting socially just and inclusive music teacher education: Exploring perceptions of early-career teachers. *Research Studies in Music Education, 30*(1), 77–91.

Banks, J. (2001). *Cultural diversity and education: Foundations, curriculum, and teaching* (4th ed.). Boston, MA: Allyn & Bacon.

Baxter, M. (2007). Global music making a difference: Themes of exploration, action and justice. *Music Education Research, 9*(2), 267–279. doi: 10.1080/14613800701384425.

Bowman, W. (2007). Who's asking? (who's answering?) Theorizing social justice in music education. *Action, Criticism & Theory for Music Education, 6*(4), 1–20.

Bradley, D., Golner, R., & Hanson, S. (2007). Unlearning Whiteness: Rethinking race issues in graduate music education. *Music Education Research, 9*(2), 293–304. doi: 10.1080/14613800701384516.

Cochran-Smith, M., Shakman, K., Jong, C., Terrell, D., Barnatt, J., & McQuillan, P. (2009). Good and just teaching: The case for social justice in teacher education. *American Journal of Education, 115*(3), 347–377.

Darling-Hammond, L. (2006). Assessing teacher education: The usefulness of multiple measures for assessing program outcomes. *Journal of Teacher Education, 57*(2), 120–138.

Emmanuel, D. (2005). The effects of a music education immersion internship in a culturally diverse setting on the beliefs and attitudes of pre-service music teachers. *International Journal of Music Education, 23*(1), 49–62.

Joseph, D., & Southcott, J. (2009). Opening the doors to multiculturalism: Australian pre-service music teacher education students' understandings of cultural diversity. *Music Education Research, 11*(4), 457–472.

Joseph, D., & Southcott, J. (2010). Experiences and understandings: Student teachers' beliefs about multicultural practice in music education. *Australian Journal of Music Education, 2*, 66–75.

Kelly, S. (2003). The influence of selected cultural factors on the environmental teaching preference of undergraduate music education majors. *Journal of Music Teacher Education, 12*(2), 40–50.

Marsh, K. (2007). Here, alive and accessible: The role of an inquiry-based fieldwork project in changing students' attitudes to cultural diversity in music education. In A. Brew & J. Sachs (Eds.), *Transforming a university: The scholarship of teaching and learning in practice* (pp. 47–55). Sydney: Sydney University Press.

Mills, C. (2008). "I don't have much of an ethnic background": Exploring changes in dispositions towards diversity in pre-service teachers. *International Journal of Pedagogies and Learning, 4*(3), 49–58.

Mills, C., & Ballantyne, J. (2010). Pre-service teachers' dispositions towards diversity: Arguing for a developmental hierarchy of change. *Teaching and Teacher Education, 26*(3), 447–454.

Power, A., & Horsley, M. (2010). Pathways from global education understandings to teaching music. *British Journal of Music Education, 27*(2), 141–150. doi: 10.1017/S0265051710000057.

Riley, P. (2009). Pre-service music teachers' perceptions of social justice and/or social consciousness as it relates to music education. *College Music Symposium, 49–50*, 83–92.

Zeichner, K. (2006). Reflections of a university-based teacher educator on the future of college- and university-based teacher education. *Journal of Teacher Education, 57*(3), 326–340.

CHAPTER 42

STRIVING FOR JUSTICE WITH DETERMINATION AND HOPE

An Epilogue

JANET R. BARRETT

SOCIAL justice is an intellectual ideal and an educational movement, as well as a fervent desire held by individuals committed to respecting the worth of persons. The authors in this collection have cast social justice as the calling of our time. In this epilogue, I step back from a close reading of the chapters to situate music educators within this broad landscape of theories, perspectives, and practices. For the field to embrace socially just practices as commonplace—answering the call with determination—good work must be initiated on many fronts. Music educators can draw on the clear and persuasive arguments offered here for expanding visions of music teaching and learning, while grappling with multidimensional challenges that attend social justice. This professional transformation will depend upon imaginative thinking and critical awakening, especially in contradistinction to the pervasive neoliberal milieu of the times. As music educators ask what social justice has to do with music learning and teaching, the contexts, pedagogies, and projects described by the authors can inspire and inform future action. Music teacher education holds special promise for developing and strengthening teachers' commitments to equitable, culturally responsive, and liberatory practices, especially when focused on dispositions that cultivate music teachers' sense of agency and caring. Striving together toward socially just music education will depend upon collective action, civil discourse, and hope.

This volume has been written by educators for educators. The potential beneficiaries of this work are students, teachers, and scholars whose lives can be uplifted by more equitable principles and practices integrated into musical encounters in schools, universities, and communities. The Handbook will be consulted by teachers and scholars seeking guidance in sorting through the multiple and sometimes conflicting discussions of the dimensions and scope of social justice. In its far-ranging breadth and depth, readers will be looking for shape and definition, for particular contours that make subtle abstractions more tangible. It will be consulted by those who yearn for models, who will find inspiration among numerous examples, instances, and narratives of music education already embodying the ideals of social justice. It will be examined by those who wish to critique its premises, entering into arguments that extend and complexify our understanding. One hopes that readers will come to this volume with an openness to a wider range of possibilities for music education, and a willingness to advocate for change.

An epilogue in a film often pulls us out of our moviegoer's reverie into the present, filling in gaps and details of the main characters' lives that fall outside the frame of the narrative. In some cases, the epilogue offers a sense of resolution for the powerful questions the film has posed. As viewers, this cinematic device compels us to stay in our seats until the loose threads are knotted. For this project, I was asked to provide an epilogue of sorts, although it would indeed be an act of hubris to claim synthesis or satisfying closure. I will not claim to be comprehensive or synoptic, for the landscape of ideas is far too panoramic for that. Instead, it is my intention that this epilogue will draw readers to think across the chapters to invite critical reflection and productive action. I was given the privilege of reading the chapters in their final draft form in order to identify interrelated connections that would link powerful ideas in a "balanced, complex, and synergistic" structure, an intention that was key to the editors' genesis of the book. In doing so, I kept a digest of powerful and provocative passages, grouped these into clusters, and then widened the aperture to glimpse patterns and pathways for action. Reading the chapters in sequence was a daunting task, the magnitude and gravity of the challenges nearly overwhelming. Again and again, the shortcomings of our field were apparent. Redemptively, the weight of the reading was also shored up by the appearance of hope, tempered by the spirit of determination, and expanded through imaginative openings that lead to change.

The overarching questions appear to include the following: What conceptions of social justice are held by the field, and is there consensus around its central aims? Why is music education particularly implicated in realizing these aims? How might the realizations of these aims—through projects, initiatives, narratives of experience—be widely disseminated in order to build greater support within the profession? What dispositions can move us toward hopeful realization of the goals of social justice?

CONCEPTIONS AND CONSENSUS

To strive toward social justice turns attention to shared meanings, as much as common understanding can be achieved, as well as particular translations of its principles into initiatives, plans, programs, and actions befitting our own spheres of influence. The authors have taken great care in framing the concepts and problems that are associated with social justice. They bring to the surface what has been submerged, seeking clarity and coherence within the expansive territory of concerns and critiques. To promote the cause of social justice, advocates must be able to convey its meaning in compelling ways, persuasively forwarding the superordinate ideals of justice writ large. Speaking in general terms requires that we avoid comfortable truisms, platitudes, and slogans that trivialize its enormous consequence. Several authors cite the clarion call of Ayers, Quinn, and Stovall, who affix the purpose of education as integrally entwined with social justice, in which schooling attends to creating "societies in which people can learn, love, and imagine more and suffer less" (2009, p. i), through the three principles of social justice education that serve as pillars: equity, activism, and social literacy, "nourishing awareness of our own identities and our connections with others" (p. xiv). Jorgensen in Chapter 1 of this Handbook contributes a highly dimensionalized view of justice that permits us to recognize its roots in many epistemic traditions, as distributive, commutative, restorative, poetic, and other forms. Transcending all, Jorgensen locates justice in the affirmative, generative interactions of teaching and learning, those moments in which, as Higgins echoes in Chapter 27, "justice is . . . ignited through the encounter and as such lies at the heart of an educative experience."

It does not take long, however, to realize how difficult it is to speak from any common stance about justice once we move away from positive commitments to equity, democratic practice, voice, empowerment, civility, and caring. Consensus is challenging when we begin to confront representations of difference, the Other, the kaleidoscopic permutations of selfhood and group membership diffracted through race, ethnicity, linguistic difference, gender, sexual identity, class, religion, and disability. Each of these dimensions of difference, and concomitant uses of difference to divide, oppress, and minoritize individuals and groups warrants relentless attention. Seen against multiple critiques of music education ably described by Gaztambide-Fernández and Stewart Rose in Chapter 28, the historical tracings of "ruling relations" characterized by Lamb and Dhokai in Chapter 8, and the oppressive legacies of schooling described by Bradley in Chapter 12, it becomes clear that music education is neither solely culpable nor immune in perpetuating social ills and disfigurements. As readers, we undergo numerous epistemic shifts in confronting naïve worldviews or in turning our assumptions inside out. One of these moments for me was in response to Darrow's Chapter 13 on disability, in which she spoke of viewing disability as a "natural form of human variation," rather than a deficit.

The call to justice is amplified when set against the sociopolitical milieu of the times. As a child of the 1960s, my life course has been intertwined with the reforms of the Civil Rights era, cycles of resistance to numerous wars, the social redefinition of women's lives, legislation that has made a substantive difference in educational opportunities for students with disabilities, and increasing public support for gay rights. Many incremental steps, bold acts of courage, and hard-earned sacrifices have contributed to a more humane society. Yet, we cannot be lulled into thinking of these gains as steady trajectories of progress. Substantial evidence tells a different story. Authors juxtapose the ideals of social justice in education with currents and counterforces. For example, they are set into sharp relief in the neoliberal and neo-conservative reforms in Europe (Rusinek & Aróstegui, Chapter 5), the conception of negative rights that privileges economic gains of the individual against more democratic ideals (Horsley, Chapter 4), and the appropriation of creativity for competitive market-driven ends (Kanellopoulos, Chapter 20). Wright in Chapter 21 reminds us that some of these assumptions are so deeply ingrained and embedded in curricula, standards, and pedagogical frameworks as to become nearly invisible to teachers. Conversations with teachers confirm how autonomy, praise for inventiveness, and trust in teachers' expertise are in short supply in schools. Spruce in Chapter 18 highlights the insidious way that rhetoric about student voice, when co-opted by technicist and managerial agendas, effectively mutes students' authentic voices within the "acoustic of the school." As we decide and debate for ourselves which practices to cast off as no longer fitting, humane, and worthy of our efforts, we must soberly acknowledge these entrenched and widespread ideological castings that compromise just intentions and outcomes.

The polyphonic texture of these perspectives astonishes and overwhelms. As Gaztambide-Fernández and Stewart Rose suggest in Chapter 28, the gravity of educational critiques could effectively paralyze us, if we are not vigilant. The critiques bring to light pernicious outcomes of discriminatory practices. They provide frameworks for recognizing and naming inequity. They reveal important alliances and affinities with related disciplines of sociology, art, media, cultural studies, and educational policy that seem particularly congruent with music education. Taken together, the dynamic interplay of perspectives on social justice provide an increasingly sophisticated understanding while opening up even vaster territories for action.

WHY MUSIC EDUCATION AND MUSIC EDUCATORS?

The central question of this Handbook is "why music education for social justice?" McCarthy in Chapter 2 reminds us of the historical aims of public education in cultivating and transmitting societal values, a function well suited to long-standing practices of music education. At the same time, this transmission, if unquestioned and habitual, simultaneously reinforces and reinscribes injustice as well. In Chapter 12, Bradley draws attention to the way that schools legitimize difference. Wide-awake teachers excavate ingrained patterns of injustice in the hope that they can be ferreted out, confronted, dismantled, and replaced by liberatory alternatives. Although we recognize that they are not solely responsible or free to shape their own priorities, music teachers, always straddling preservative and progressive forces, decide daily how students' identities, opportunities, and strengths will be affirmed or curtailed. In his call for self-examination in Chapter 3, Schmidt charges teaches to "amplify [their] critique of policies that generate misguided authority or power," especially in regard to the ways that students are labeled, categorized, sorted, sifted, and set apart as different.

Jorgensen in Chapter 1 discusses four main reasons that music teachers should take up the causes associated with social justice, among them its integral correspondence with visions of humane and civil society, its alignment with public policy, and its capacity for embracing relevant repertoires and dynamic musical practices. I believe that many teachers will find a deep affinity with the cause of social justice in Jorgensen's emphasis on the "worth, dignity, and preciousness of human beings." In its most altruistic sense, music's generous reach and the passion it engenders in young persons offer remarkable capacity to uphold these ideals. Teachers oriented toward justice view diversity as strength, aligned closely with personal and group expression through the creation, performance, and fulfilling pursuits of music.

As a field, music education has long struggled for legitimacy and recognition, a yearning to be viewed as central to the values of schools and communities as literacy, numeracy, science, or even athletic programs. The struggle has led to defensiveness and isolation, in which music educators become more sequestered, cloistered, and removed from the life of the school and community in order to protect instructional time in the curriculum, and to preserve diminishing resources. Understandably, the subsequent narrowing of the music curriculum can be explained, as music teachers focus on traditional expectations of high-quality performance with ever more select groups of students who elect specialized study. The field is especially adept in sorting students by audition into ensembles and honors groups leveled by skill and repertoire. Reconfiguring these robust expectations is difficult. Constant pressure to justify music's position results in holding tight to traditions that have served the field well in the past, hoping that if these traditions have "worked," they will continue to do so, even in the face of rapidly changing social conditions and student needs.

Entrenchment can be witnessed on national levels, as well, as high-profile initiatives have yoked music education to uncomfortable alliances with neoliberal campaigns. Consider, for example, the alignment of advocacy campaigns in the United States and elsewhere with the push toward STEM education (science, technology, engineering, and math), seeking the alchemy of the arts by adding an A for STEAM. The rhetoric of these agendas, with their emphasis on academic achievement, workforce development, and creativity for economic competitiveness, has little to do with social justice. Compound these supposed reforms with systems for teacher evaluation that lack a moral or ethical center, while rewarding conformity, and the potential for disenchantment widens. Benedict warns of the insidious and ubiquitous presence of the habits of compliance and control that undergird schooling, "that this discourse is so pervasive, insidious, and menacing that its rhetoric maneuvers its way in and shapes the very words that come out of our mouths even in our most aware moments."

For years, music education has struggled within itself to clarify its aims and to broadcast these aims to its constituents and supporters. Implicit in the social justice effort is the principle that music is and can be used instrumentally to achieve social ends. This notion has frequently been met with resistance, as potentially denigrating aesthetic ends, for instance. If we are to remain responsive and relevant, our aims must allow for elasticity and accommodation—inviting teachers' curricular experimentation in rapidly changing contexts. Traditional commitments of educating for citizenship are reconfigured in new guises when placed in classrooms where "motility, non-rootedness and global availability/accessibility" (Baumann, 1999, cited in Karlsen & Westerlund, Chapter 23) put any sort of assumed common knowledge or experience in peril. Indeed, Karlsen and Westerlund recommend replacing the familiar metaphor of "roots" as supporting musical identities, suggesting that contemporary students will find multiple styles, genres, and practices as "anchors" instead, enabling a lifetime of sailing through and around multiple types of musical expression. Astute teachers can look to students' polyglot, multinational, cosmopolitan lives as avenues for enrichment, invitations for dialogue and creativity, and opportunities for establishing empathic bridges through music.

Another forefront for music education may be to serve as a liminal haven in instances of "social uncertainty" (Marsh, Chapter 11), such as when students who because of refugee or immigrant status, cultural dislocation, or personal hardship find themselves in need of the communal interaction and psychological safety of music classrooms. In spite of the co-optation of creativity by neoliberal schemes, we can hold fast to generative and democratic images of music classrooms as sites for critical and creative thought, in turn prompting musical invention and new pedagogical approaches.

The purposes of scholarly engagement are implicated here as well. A small but growing body of research justifiably aligned with the ideals of social justice is emerging within music education. These studies yield remarkable insights into the lived experience of those at the margin, as well as into obstacles to student access to music learning. Those of us who are privileged to work in higher education, with liberal access to resources and support for research efforts, must take stock of the questions we ask, the projects we undertake, and the alliances we form in expending intellectual and institutional resources. It is clear in this scholarly quest that we look to relevant initiatives and voices in the arts, education, and social sciences for guidance. From my reading of these chapters, I noted authors' citations of Gert Biesta, Zygmunt Bauman, Stuart Hall, Hannah Arendt, and Basil Bernstein added to the roster of more frequently cited luminaries, including Paulo Freire, James Banks, bell hooks, Maxine Greene, Nel Noddings, and John Dewey. The scholars in these essays create bridges to key streams of thought that broaden our field of vision and ward against parochialism. Drawing from an eclectic range of scholarship can engender more collaborative exchanges across permeable boundaries of disciplines, institutions, and settings.

REPRESENTING SITES OF SOCIAL JUSTICE

Our moral imagination is stirred by the models of programs and practices represented here, those who are caught in the acts of justice. In translating the principles of social justice into practice, we have need for tangible examples and manifestations to fire the imagination, to agitate the spirit. In the grounded cases, narratives, performances, and programs, more abstract principles take on a human face. I am reminded of Yvonna Lincoln's observation that advances in interpretive research have revealed the "clandestine disfigurements and outrages of racism, sexism, homophobia, and class injuries" (2010, p. 4). Such accounts arouse empathy while also evoking indignation. They shake us out of complacency and self-congratulatory haze.

Throughout this volume, border-crossing is a clear theme in bringing together persons whose life circumstances rarely align and for whom music is the social glue. Here I think of the DubDubDub project (Savage, Chapter 30), the "inside/outside" prison choir (Cohen & Duncan, Chapter 35), cosmopolitan students in a Helsinki classroom (Karlsen & Westerlund, Chapter 23), and students from diverse religious traditions engaged in musical inquiry together (Spruce, Chapter 18). The cases described here also open doors so that we can view musical expression in juvenile detention centers and prisons (Hickey, Chapter 38; de Quadros, Chapter 31), in the nucleos of El Sistema (Shieh, Chapter 36), in an Arab town in Galilee (de Quadros), in firsthand accounts from Musicians without Borders (Burnard, Hassler, Murphy, & de Jong, Chapter 22) and in locations on the border (Soto, Chapter 40). We witness musical empowerment in elementary and secondary classrooms in Western Ontario (Wright, Chapter 21), as well as in college classrooms as preservice teachers analyze the polysemic texts of popular music to trouble questions of gender (Abramo, Chapter 37). These initiatives bring together musical genres not typically encountered, individuals not typically aligned, and settings not usually witnessed. Occasionally, the distinctive voices of students are heard, such as Marsh's moving account of Sia in Chapter 11, holding to music as a lifeline while navigating her own displacement from her Sierra Leonian homeland.

Well-meaning individuals often try to replicate forward-thinking initiatives (the many variants of El Sistema come to mind here). As these situated stories prompt response, difficulties in transferring specific forms of socially just projects arise. Rusinek and Aróstegui in Chapter 5 warn that patterns of injustice may be woven into the warp and woof of particular contexts, thus making generalized appropriations of programs possibly inappropriate and ill-advised. These projects also teach us valuable lessons about long-term and tireless commitments to meaningful professional change. Nowhere did I feel this as keenly as in reading Campbell and Roberts's observation in Chapter 17 on 50 years of work in multicultural music education, taking seriously their realization that for many music educators, more capacious views of music making are still off the radar and out of reach.

With the exception of a few high-profile ventures such as El Sistema and Musical Futures, I have the sense that many music educators in school and university settings are unfamiliar with promising programs. The profession may turn its attention to ways that justice-affirming projects can be disseminated through publication, presentation, social media, networks, and professional associations. The potential of these examples to provoke, inspire, challenge, and expand our vision is uplifting.

MUSIC TEACHER EDUCATION AS A CRUCIBLE
FOR SOCIAL JUSTICE

Music teacher education is often seen as the nexus of transformation in the field. We place enormous responsibility on music teacher educators to prepare young persons as capable and versatile musicians, knowledgeable and skillful teachers, and progressive and humane citizens. The kinds of transformation toward justice imagined here will require critical awakening and shared effort across elementary and secondary levels, preservice and in-service teacher education, and community venues. If we desire classrooms that are more equitable, culturally responsive, and liberatory, then our approaches to teacher education must be similarly equitable, culturally responsive, and liberatory. I am still surprised at the pervasive stranglehold of *training*, with its concomitant trappings of control, prediction, and regulation, as the default term when individuals refer to teacher education. Music teacher education for social justice requires curricular imagination, professional discernment, and trust in teachers' expertise. It requires us to grapple with the moral and ethical dimensions of teaching, in seeing teachers as public intellectuals, as viewing them in relation to the children and the communities they serve.

Teachers in these challenging times are beset by struggles and expectations of nearly superhuman proportions. If the kind of critical reflection advocated here is to take hold in our programs, institutions will need to provide more spaces for reflection in and on action, most crucially for the recognition of inequities to surface. I think of Arendt's notion of "stop and think," a call for deliberation in the midst of relentless and frenetic activity. It takes courage to relax tightly coiled schedules, to linger in dialogue with students, to be present to their concerns. Music teachers in particular seem to live in fealty to the clock. Putting efficiency aside for a moment to notice expectant faces and honor bright potentials may be among the most important dispositions teachers need to cultivate.

Music teacher education as social justice, most viscerally, necessitates conceptual integration throughout a program and beyond. McDonald and Zeichner (2009), in studying how teacher education programs influence the hearts, minds, and beliefs of preservice teachers, state that they are "more powerful when there is a unified vision of teaching and learning that permeates a program than when attention to a goal exists in only some program components" (p. 605). Ballantyne and Mills in Chapter 41 draw attention to a limited set of research studies that lean toward these aims. They provide glimpses of the potent mix of preservice teachers' beliefs, program components, and possible settings that set the stage for growth. Potentially transformative encounters with the complex and potentially contestable notions that attend social justice cannot be packaged into discrete units, courses, standards, or graduation requirements. If music teacher preparation programs choose to ascribe to these ideals (and one would question why they would not), collegial conversation must rise above state mandates and prescriptions for licensure to address teachers' agency, caring, and professional judgment. For example, Cochran-Smith (2010) advocates faculty deliberation on a theory of justice that allows for greater program coherence, a theory of practice that reflects the realities of teachers' lives in classrooms, and a theory of teacher preparation that articulates how learning to teach for justice can be realized. Our hopes for instilling culturally responsive practice and more widespread equity depend upon the integration of these animating ideas in higher education and across educational settings.

A paradoxical aspect of music teacher education is to accommodate preparation for specialization through comprehensive orientations toward musicianship, while at the same time avoiding a defensive and isolated view of music teaching. Wright, for example, cites Biesta's notion that students are inducted into disciplinary societies of thought via subject-matter studies, but with little direct engagement in shaping disciplinary involvements. So stands this criticism for teachers as well. Disciplinary specialization is a strength; it can also be a weakness if it fosters balkanization and insulation from larger goals and aims. A particularly telling instance of the infusion of sensibilities not normally found within a music teacher's purview comes from Ladson-Billings's description in Chapter 25 of hip-hop as a way of acting in the world, a potentially fruitful means for achieving greater relevance in the contemporary milieu by adopting its forms and styles—contemporaneousness, hybridity, representation, and ingenuity.

Striving Toward Justice and Critical Awakening

By this point, few readers need convincing of the enormity, gravity, and imminence of the challenges that music educators face in provoking change. Action begins with personal commitment. Working toward the realization of more equitable forms and settings through music will require dispositions of determination, empathy, caring, and criticality. We must believe in the power of groups to amplify these efforts. Whether these groups form within institutions, across professional specializations, or broadly within the field, sustaining energy requires that we hold one another up.

Gaps have opened up throughout this volume—gaps of awareness, gaps of ideology, and gaps of misplaced priorities. I became acutely aware of the gap in particular between music education in schools and music education scholars in higher education. Leaders in multiple realms of action must take on the challenge of working across these apparent divides to develop wider consensus and commitment to the aims of social justice. Each person must decide whether to place faith in professional associations, for example, as forums for dialogue, debate, and collaborative work. At their most useful, professional associations can serve as meeting grounds for addressing persistent, complex, and dynamic challenges, for enlisting broader engagement and awareness, for illuminating dark corners in our own institutions. Collaborative work is messy, complicated, time-consuming, and difficult to bring to fruition (much like editing a Handbook of this scope, I would imagine). Yet we cannot retreat from the difficult choices that are necessary if we wish to claim professional influence. When we speak with a collective voice, we stretch beyond self-interest toward more altruistic aims. We need, however, to develop greater professional discernment in wisely choosing research efforts, publication venues, and points of contact that will close these gaps. We need not be reminded that rhetoric is rendered impotent without action, and theory inert.

Not all are convinced that social justice is a responsibility that music educators should take up. As we stand up to convince and persuade, the ways that we enlist others telegraphs more than just the message. Jane Addams, the noted social reformer, understood this congruity of means and ends in remarking, "social advance depends as much upon the process through which it is secured as upon the result itself" (1922, p. 133). The ways that individuals coalesce into groups, deliberate, forge plans, implement and revise initiatives to raise the profile and visibility of socially just causes matters considerably. It is arduous and unsettling to work in the realm of entrenched beliefs with the intent of examining, dislodging, and confronting small-mindedness and narrowness of thought. Contentious rifts are unavoidable. Unmasking deeply rooted prejudices strikes close to the heart. Defensiveness is nearly inevitable. But to exercise civility in the pursuit of difficult subjects is to indeed practice what is preached.

Hope surfaced briefly in these chapters: in Higgins's desire (Chapter 27) that we claim "a heart toward justice," in Narita and Greens's belief (Chapter 19) that we hold the "potential to free ourselves from unjust and oppressive relations," in Karlsen and Westerlunds's sense (Chapter 23) that we can learn "the art of living with difference." Even when it is not sounded explicitly, hope can still be heard in the precepts and premises of social justice. The Sisyphean task of striving toward justice would be impossible without ascribing to the belief that individual and collective efforts will make a difference. The pivotal impact of social justice in music education rests on our capacities for hope, our images of the possible, and our robust desires for a wider embrace of students' and teachers' lives through music.

References

Addams, J. (1922). *Peace and bread in time of war.* New York: Macmillan.

Ayers, W., Quinn, T., & Stovall, D. (2009). Preface. In W. Ayers, T. Quinn, & D. Stovall (Eds.), *Handbook of social justice in education* (pp. xiii–xv). New York: Routledge.

Cochran-Smith, M. (2010). Toward a theory of teacher education for social justice. In A. Hargreaves (Ed.), *Second international handbook of educational* change (pp. 445–467). Dordrecht, The Netherlands: Springer.

Lincoln, Y. S. (2010). "What a long strange trip it's been . . .": Twenty-five years of qualitative and new paradigm research. *Qualitative Inquiry, 16*(1), 3–9.

McDonald, M., & Zeichner, K. M. (2009). Social justice teacher education. In W. Ayers, T. Quinn & D. Stovall (Eds.), *Handbook of social justice in education* (pp. 595–610). New York: Routledge.

INDEX